The Adams Papers

C. JAMES TAYLOR, EDITOR IN CHIEF

SERIES II

Adams Family Correspondence

Adams Family Correspondence

MARGARET A. HOGAN, C. JAMES TAYLOR,
HOBSON WOODWARD, JESSIE MAY RODRIQUE,
GREGG L. LINT, MARY T. CLAFFEY

EDITORS

Volume 8 • *March 1787 – December 1789*

THE BELKNAP PRESS
OF HARVARD UNIVERSITY PRESS
CAMBRIDGE, MASSACHUSETTS
AND LONDON, ENGLAND
2007

Funds for editing *The Adams Papers* were originally furnished by Time, Inc., on behalf of *Life*, to the Massachusetts Historical Society, under whose supervision the editorial work is being done. Further funds were provided by a grant from the Ford Foundation to the National Archives Trust Fund Board in support of this and four other major documentary publications. In common with these and many other enterprises like them, *The Adams Papers* has continued to benefit from the guidance and cooperation of the National Historical Publications and Records Commission, chaired by the Archivist of the United States, which from 1975 to the present has provided this enterprise with major financial support. Important additional funds were supplied from 1980 to 1993 by The Andrew W. Mellon Foundation, The J. Howard Pew Freedom Trust, and The Charles E. Culpeper Foundation through the Founding Fathers Papers, Inc. Since 1993, *The Adams Papers* has received major support from the National Endowment for the Humanities, and matching support from The Packard Humanities Institute, through the Founding Fathers Papers, Inc., and from The Charles Francis Adams Charitable Trust, The Florence J. Gould Foundation, The Lyn and Norman Lear Fund, and an anonymous donor. Any views, findings, conclusions, or recommendations expressed in this publication do not necessarily reflect those of the National Endowment for the Humanities.

∞ This volume meets all ANSI/NISO Z39.48-1992 standards for permanence.

Library of Congress Cataloging in Publication Data (Revised for vols. 5–8)

Adams family correspondence.
    (The Adams papers: Series II, Adams family correspondence)
    Vols. 3–4 edited by L. H. Butterfield and Marc Friedlaender.
    Vols. 5–6 edited by Richard Alan Ryerson et al.
    Vols. 7–8 edited by Margaret A. Hogan et al.
    Includes bibliographical references and index.
    Contents: v. 1. December 1761 – May 1776—v. 2. June 1776 – March 1778—[etc.]—
v. 8. March 1787 – December 1789.
    I. Butterfield, L. H. (Lyman Henry), 1909–1982. II. Friedlaender, Marc, 1905–1992.
III. Ryerson, Richard Alan, 1942– . IV. Hogan, Margaret A., 1970– . V. Series: Adams papers: Series II, Adams family correspondence.

E322.1.A27   929'.2   63–14964

ISBN 0–674–00400–0 (v. 1–2)   ISBN 0–674–01574–6 (v. 7)
ISBN 0–674–00405–1 (v. 3–4)   ISBN-13 978-0-674-02278-2 (v. 8)
ISBN 0–674–00406–X (v. 5–6)   ISBN-10 0-674-02278-5 (v. 8)

This edition of *The Adams Papers*

is sponsored by the MASSACHUSETTS HISTORICAL SOCIETY

to which the ADAMS MANUSCRIPT TRUST

by a deed of gift dated 4 April 1956

gave ultimate custody of the personal and public papers

written, accumulated, and preserved over a span of three centuries

by the Adams family of Massachusetts

The Adams Papers

The acorn and oakleaf device on the preceding page is redrawn from a seal cut for John Quincy Adams after 1830. The motto is from Cæcilius Statius as quoted by Cicero in the First Tusculan Disputation: *Serit arbores quæ alteri seculo prosint* ("He plants trees for the benefit of later generations").

Contents

Descriptive List of Illustrations

Mary Rutledge (1747–1832), the younger daughter of Dr. John Rutledge and Sarah Hext, married Charleston merchant Roger Moore Smith (1745–1805) in 1768. Mary's brothers John and Edward represented South Carolina in the Continental Congress and both later served as governor of that state. Roger, himself from a prominent mercantile family, made his early fortune in the slave trade. Their marriage produced thirteen children, only seven of whom survived infancy (*South Carolina Genealogies: Articles from the South Carolina Historical (and Genealogical) Magazine*, 5 vols., Spartanburg, S.C., 1983, 4:10–11, 132; *DAB*; N. Louise Bailey and others, eds., *Biographical Directory of the South Carolina Senate, 1776–1985*, 3 vols., Columbia, S.C., 1986, 3:1507–1508).

Mary traveled to London in 1785 so her children could receive the benefits of an English education. In 1786, she posed for a full-length portrait with her infant son Edward Nutt Smith (1785–1786) at the London studio of George Romney (1734–1802), a renowned English portrait painter. Members of elite society sought after Romney's refined and elegant artistic style, and at twenty guineas for a three-quarter length portrait, he charged considerably less than other well-known portrait artists. Romney became known for his portraits of families and children, and the depiction of Mary and her son captures the maternal bond as well as Mary's noted beauty. The artist also exhibits his technical skill in the rendering of varied surface textures, including the satin of Mary's dress, her elegantly coiffed hair, and the fine detail of the lace. The baby is posed with a piece of fruit, typically a symbol of life and vitality; sadly, he died not long after the completion of the painting (Maurie D. McInnis, ed., *In Pursuit of Refinement: Charlestonians Abroad, 1740–1860*, Columbia, S.C., 1999, p. 132; Grove *Dicy. of Art*).

Courtesy of the Historic Charleston Foundation.

"We have come into a house not half repaired, and I own myself most sadly disappointed," Abigail Adams wrote to her daughter in July 1788. "In height and breadth, it feels like a wren's house. Ever since I came, we have had such a swarm of carpenters, masons, farmers, as have almost distracted me—every thing all at once, with miserable assistance" (to AA2, 7 July 1788, below).

The house that would become John and Abigail's permanent residence was built about 1731 by Maj. Leonard Vassall (1678–1737), a West Indies sugar planter, who willed the property to his daughter

Anna Vassall Borland and her husband John Borland (1728–1775). After her husband's death, the loyalist Anna Borland fled to England, but her family reclaimed the house following the war. Royall Tyler then bought the property, perhaps with plans to make it a home for himself and Abigail Adams 2d, but he defaulted when Nabby broke off their engagement and his relationship with the Adamses soured. In September 1787, Cotton Tufts negotiated the purchase of the house and 83 acres for John and Abigail (vol. 3:264–266; Charles E. Peterson, *The Adams Mansion, Quincy, Massachusetts*, Philadelphia, 1963, p. 9–20).

Despite Abigail's initial disappointment about the state of the property, she and John grew to love the house. John wrote in his Diary on 8 September 1796: "I think to christen my Place by the Name of Peace field, in commemoration of the Peace which I assisted in making in 1783, of the thirteen Years Peace and Neutrality which I have contributed to preserve, and of the constant Peace and Tranquility which I have enjoyed in this Residence." The name would be supplanted later by "Montezillo," or "Little Hill," a self-deprecating allusion to Jefferson's Monticello. The most enduring name for the Adams family residence has simply been "the Old House" (JA, *D&A*, 1:74–75, 3:247–248).

The earliest known depiction of the house is this 1798 wash drawing by E. Malcom of New York. Nothing more is known of the artist. The building shown to the rear is an older farmhouse fitted out as a wood house with three arched doorways, a structure that no longer exists. The property is now owned by the U.S. National Park Service, which has operated the Adams National Historical Park as a museum since 1946 (Wilhelmina S. Harris, *Furnishings Report of the Old House, The Adams National Historic Site, Quincy, Massachusetts*, 10 vols., Quincy, 1966–1974, 2:177, 9:822–823).

Courtesy of the Adams National Historical Park.

3. QUINCY COAT OF ARMS, BY ELIZA SUSAN QUINCY, 1822   154

A visit to Winchester, England, in the summer of 1787 prompted Abigail Adams to contemplate her Quincy roots in a letter home to her sister. Abigail reported that a Saer de Quincy, 1st Earl of Winchester (d. 1219), was one of the Magna Carta barons and might be a forebear: "They bear the same Arms with those of our Ancesters except that ours Substituded an animal for the crest in lieu, of an Earls coronet. . . . You will Smile at my Zeal, perhaps on this occasion, but can it be wonderd at, that I should wish to Trace an Ancesstor amongst the Signers of Magna Carta" (to Mary Smith Cranch, 15 Sept. [1787], below; *DNB*).

Abigail's hope proved unfounded; rather, the American Quincy family probably descends from William Quincy of Aldwynkle, Northampton (ca. 1485–1550). Nonetheless, Abigail's American ancestors did use the Earl of Winchester's coat of arms. In the eighteenth century, Judge Edmund Quincy (1681–1738) installed an engraved stone on the family plot in the Braintree burial ground that bore the coat of arms of Saer de Quincy's son. The memorial was broken during the Revolution and removed entirely in 1812 (George Bellew, "English Ancestry of the Quincy Family," *NEHGR*, 92:30–31 [Jan. 1938]).

In 1822, the stone was reassembled and sketched by descendant Eliza Susan Quincy (1798–1884), a fourth cousin of John Quincy Adams and his siblings. Quincy was an historian, artist, and ardent protector of the family name. An obituary lauded "her intense interest in the historical past of her native New England, and of the family of which she was a member, her wonderfully retentive memory, her thorough knowledge of facts and dates, her indomitable perseverance and self-renouncing devotion" (*NEHGR*, 38:145–146 [April 1884]; MHi:Quincy Family Papers).

Courtesy of the Massachusetts Historical Society.

4. ADVERTISEMENT FOR SAYER'S BATHING MACHINE, 1791   157

The burgeoning eighteenth-century trend in therapeutic and recreational sea bathing required a bathing machine—a small, horse-drawn vehicle with two doors. The bather would enter at one end, change into bathing clothes, and be carried down to the sea to step out into the water through the other door. Benjamin Beale, a Quaker, was credited with inventing the bathing machine at Margate in 1750. By 1780, twenty bathing machines were registered at Margate with double that number by 1800. The use of bathing machines persisted at some English resorts into the early twentieth century with very little change to the original design.

The 1791 trade card for the Sayer bathing machines and seaside lodgings advertises, "For Bathing in the Sea at Margate, John & Mercy Sayer late Partners with M^r. Beale have good accommodations for Bathing, Where Favours confer'd on them will be gratefully acknowledg'd M^r. Sayer will attend ye Gentlemen & M^{rs}. Sayer ye Ladies as usual NB: By ye Favour of a Letter Lodgings & Stabling will be Provided." Like John and Mercy Sayer, local families offered lodgings for rent and advertised their services as bathing "guides."

The bathing machine depicted in Sayer's advertisement returning to the bathing house could transport five to six people and a guide. Decency required that the bathers be submerged in a proper depth of water and shielded from public view by a tent on the back of each machine. Strictly enforced rules for the use of bathing machines separated male and female swimmers from each other by at least 60 feet, and all were expected to dress in heavy cloaks.

Abigail "tried the experiment" of sea bathing while in Southampton, England, and reported to her sister, "the places are under cover, you have a woman for a Guide, a small dressing room to yourself an oil cloth cap, a flannel Gown and socks for the feet." Quite taken with the experience, Abigail lamented that "such conveniencys" were not available in Massachusetts' coastal towns (to Mary Smith Cranch, 15 Sept. [1787], below). Many years later, John Quincy Adams also developed a fondness for the water, but foregoing such modesty, he sometimes swam in the nude (Martin

Stanton, "Sea Bathing at Margate," *History Today*, 33:21–23 [July 1983]; John K. Walton, *The English Seaside Resort: A Social History 1750–1914*, N.Y., 1983, p. 159, 182; Lynn Hudson Parsons, *John Quincy Adams*, Madison, Wis., 1998, p. 154, 177, 266).

Courtesy of the Balnea Museum, Rimini, Italy.

5. "A NORTH VIEW OF BLENHEIM HOUSE AND PARK IN THE COUNTY OF

OXFORD," BY JOHN BOYDELL, 1752   181

When Abigail Adams visited Blenheim Castle in Oxford County, England, in the summer of 1787, she wrote six pages of superlatives about it to her niece Lucy Cranch: "This Castle is upon the Grandest scale of any thing I have ever yet seen. We enter the park through a spacious and elegant portal of the Corinthian order, from whence a Noble prospect is opend to the palace, the Bridge the Lake, with its valley, and other beautifull Scenes." She could not say enough about its decorations and furnishings, paintings and sculpture, vistas and gardens—and its romantic history (3 Oct. 1787, below). Built over two decades beginning in 1705 on land gifted to John Churchill, 1st Duke of Marlborough, by the British government, Blenheim was in the eighteenth century and is still today one of the most spectacular estates in England.

In the foreground of this illustration is the Doric "Column of Victory," which Henry Herbert, 9th Earl of Pembroke, and Roger Morris designed and built between 1727 and 1730. Standing 130 feet tall, the column is crowned by a statue of the Duke of Marlborough done by Robert Pit. Henry St. John, 1st Viscount Bolingbroke, wrote the inscription on the base (after Alexander Pope refused the work), which tells of the duke's victory at the Battle of Blenheim.

John Boydell (1719–1804) began his career as an engraver of landscapes, of which this image is a typical example. He also worked as a printer and publisher, through which he amassed a considerable fortune. His most noteworthy undertaking was the publication of a series of prints illustrating Shakespeare's plays, based on original pieces by English artists, a project designed to promote British art abroad (Christopher Hibbert, *The Marlboroughs: John and Sarah Churchill, 1650–1744*, N.Y., 2001, p. 162, 170–171, 340–341; *DNB*).

Courtesy of the British Library.

6. "A VIEW OF THE TRYAL OF WARREN HASTINGS ESQR.," BY ROBERT

POLLARD AND FRANCIS JUKES, 1789   237

The corruption trial of Warren Hastings, the first governor-general of India, began on 13 February 1788 and was the subject of intense interest in London. Multitudes attended the hearings in Westminster Hall, including Abigail Adams. "There is at present sitting here one of the most august Assemblies that this country can convene," she wrote to Cotton Tufts on 20 February. "The House of commons the House of Lord's the Bishops the judges &C all convened in westmister Hall for the Trial of Warren Hastings. about Two thousand persons half of whom are Ladies, attend this trial every day. it is opened with the utmost order & continued with the greatest regularity, & no person admitted to it, but with Tickets which are not very easily procured. as a Foreign ministers Lady I have had a Seat in the Box appropriated for them, and have had the pleasure of hearing mr Burk speak 3 hours" (below).

The London *Times* of the same day confirmed that tickets were highly prized. "Before eleven, not a seat was to be obtained," the newspaper reported. "The box allotted for the Royal Family, and the Prince of Wales's Box, were both full at a very early hour,— each, from the first Peeress in the realm, to the lowest rank of individuals, equally anxious to hear the oratory of the Speaker, and the fate of the decision."

Warren Hastings (1732–1818) went to India as a merchant in 1750. Working his way through the ranks of the colonial government, he was appointed its first governor-general. After twelve years of service, he left the post in 1785 and retired to England, but he soon faced corruption and bribery charges initiated by a bitter political rival, Philip Francis, whom Hastings had wounded in a duel in 1780. Francis' cause was championed by Edmund Burke and Charles James Fox and resulted in Hastings' impeachment. Although Abigail judged Hastings guilty, after a protracted trial of seven years' duration, he was acquitted of all charges on 23 April 1795 (*DNB*; Jeremy Bernstein, *Dawning of the Raj: The Life and Trials of Warren Hastings*, Chicago, 2000, p. 39, 82, 158–161, 165, 177, 263–264).

This engraving by Robert Pollard (ca. 1755–1838) depicts the trial in session on 13 February 1788 but was issued a year later. Pollard had been engraving since 1771 and often employed Francis Jukes (1745–1812) to aquatint his prints. The Hastings trial print is based on a drawing by Edward Dayes (1763–1804), a Royal Academy artist who favored classical and Biblical scenes but also created topographical and scenic work for the London market (Grove *Dicy. of Art*).

Courtesy of the British Library.

7. MRS. HENRY KNOX, CA. 1790   264

Lucy Flucker (1756–1824), daughter of Thomas Flucker, royal secretary of Massachusetts, first encountered the future general Henry Knox when she frequented his Boston bookstore prior to the Revolution. "A young lady of high intellectual endowments, very fond of books, and especially the books sold by Knox," Lucy fell in love. She and Henry married in 1774 against her family's wishes; Thomas Flucker, a tory, disapproved of his son-in-law's patriot leanings. By all accounts, the Knoxes had a happy marriage, despite hardships and lengthy separations during the Revolutionary War. Later, they were considered one of the leading couples in the new government and their home a social center. Together, they had twelve children, though only three survived to adulthood.

This amateur painted silhouette is attributed to one of the sons of Robert Morris, the financier, and was done in Philadelphia around 1790—at the same time Henry Knox was serving as secretary of war. While obviously a caricature, this illustration does demonstrate two of Lucy Knox's most commonly noted features: her girth and her hair. Abigail Adams Smith remarked to her mother in mid-1788 that "Mrs. Knox is much altered from the character she used to have. She is neat in her dress, attentive to her family, and very fond of her children. But her size is enormous; I am frightened when I look at her; I verily believe that her waist is as large as three of yours, at least" (15 June 1788, below). Likewise, Manasseh Cutler commented in his journal: "Mrs. Knox is very gross, but her manners are easy and agreeable. She is sociable, and would be agreeable, were it not for her affected singularity in dressing her hair. She seems to mimic the military style, which to me is very disgusting in a female. Her hair in front is craped at least a foot high, much in the form of a churn bottom upward, and topped off with a wire skeleton in the same form, covered with black gauze, which hangs in streamers down to her back." Nonetheless, given her genial nature, Lucy Knox probably enjoyed this gently mocking representation (Francis S. Drake, *Life and Correspondence of Henry Knox*, Boston, 1873, p. 16–17, 63, 66, 101–102, 111, 118, 125–126).

Courtesy of the Massachusetts Historical Society.

8. THE NEEDLES, ISLE OF WIGHT, BY WILLIAM WESTALL, CA. 1835   268

The Needles, located on the far western tip of the Isle of Wight, are a geological formation of three 100-foot tall white pointed rocks. An awe-inspiring sight, the Needles mark a notoriously hazardous passage of choppy seas and jagged rocks. The American minister plenipotentiary Richard Rush marveled at the spectacle during his passage in 1817 and noted, "the most exact steering seemed necessary to save the ship from the sharp rocks that compress the waters into the narrow strait below" (Richard Rush, *Memoranda of a Residence at the Court of London*, Phila., 1833, p. 27–28). A lighthouse, constructed high on a rocky bluff, guided the passage of John and Abigail Adams around the Needles in 1788 on their journey home to Massachusetts.

This watercolor by William Westall (1781–1850), dated around 1835, captures the sublime rocky coastline, with crashing waves in the foreground and a horizon dominated by the Needles' craggy chalk stacks. Westall's interest in topographical views inspired the subject matter of most of his works, and the Needles provided the artist with a unique opportunity to capture an evolving landscape. A solitary pillar of rock, known as Lot's Wife, once dominated the center of the formation but tumbled down in 1764; further erosion reduced a stratified archway to the small column and first rock on the left of the painting (William Henry Davenport Adams, *The Isle of Wight: Its History, Topography, and Antiquities*, London, 1882, p. 232–234).

Benjamin West recommended the eighteen-year-old Westall to serve as the landscape artist for an expedition to Australia commanded by Matthew Flinders, thus launching Westall's art career. His drawings from this voyage and subsequent trips to China and India were exhibited in England, and in 1812, Westall was inducted as an associate of the Royal Academy (*DNB*).

Courtesy of a private collection.

9. "FEDERAL HALL, THE SEAT OF CONGRESS," BY AMOS DOOLITTLE, 1790   342

On 30 April 1789, "the Great and illustrious Washington, the favourite son of liberty, and deliverer of his country, entered upon the execution of the office of First Magistrate of the United States of America." This first presidential inauguration marked the formal beginning of the U.S. government under the new Constitution. In a carefully staged ceremony, George Washington, accompanied by John Adams and numerous senators and representatives, stood on the balcony of Federal Hall in New York City to take the oath of office as given by Robert R. Livingston, chancellor of the State of New York. The decision was made to have the ceremony on the balcony "to the end that the oath of office may be administered to the President in the most public manner, and that the greatest number of the people of the United States, and without distinction, may be witnesses to the solemnity." After the ceremony and a speech by Washington, the entire party adjourned to St. Paul's Chapel for a service conducted by the chaplain of Congress (*New York Daily Gazette*, 1 May 1789).

This printed engraving by Amos Doolittle, issued in 1790 after a painting by Peter Lacour, is the only known contemporary rendering of this momentous occasion. Doolittle (1754–1832) was a self-taught engraver from New Haven, Connecticut, who produced portraits, maps, book illustrations, and, most notably, a collection of four pieces on the Battles of Lexington and Concord. Lacour was probably Pierre Lacour (1745–1814), a French painter and director of the Academy of Bordeaux who was best known for his historical and religious works. His original sketch or painting is apparently not extant (*DAB*; Stokes, *Iconography of Manhattan*, 3:537–539; Hoefer, *Nouv. biog. générale*).

Courtesy of the I. N. Phelps Stokes Collection, Miriam and Ira D. Wallach Division of Art, Prints and Photographs, The New York Public Library.

10. RICHMOND HILL, BY CORNELIUS TIEBOUT, 1790   352

In May 1789, John Adams rented the house known as Richmond Hill to serve as his residence in New York City while vice president. Located on the west side of New York facing the Hudson River in what is now Greenwich Village, it had previously been used as George Washington's headquarters early in the Revolutionary War. In later years, Aaron Burr and John Jacob Astor both owned the home for a time. After being moved, then converted to a theater, it was demolished in 1849 (Stokes, *Iconography of Manhattan*, 1:416–417).

As soon as John moved in, he encouraged Abigail to come along with their son Charles, and also invited Abigail 2d, William Stephens Smith, and their two children—William Steuben and John Adams Smith—to join them. Niece Louisa Smith arrived with Abigail in late June.

Abigail was enamored of the home as soon as she saw it, particularly loving its rural setting. She wrote to her sister Mary Cranch, "The House is situated upon a high Hill which commands a most extensive prospect, on one side we have a view of the city & of Long Island, the River in Front, Jersy and the adjasant Country on the other side, you Turn a litle from the Road and enter a Gate a winding Road with trees in clumps leads you to the House, and all round the House, it looks wild and Rural as uncultivated Nature" (12 July 1789, below). A contemporary account agreed with her assessment: "It is beautifully situated, near the city of New-York, on the Banks of the Hudson. . . . The venerable oaks, and broken ground, covered with wild shrubs, give it a very romantic air" (*New York Magazine*, June 1790, p. 317).

This illustration by Cornelius Tiebout (1777–1832), a young New York engraver, was originally published in the *New York Magazine* in June 1790. Abigail was not entirely pleased with the rendering, believing that "the great Beauty could not be taken upon so small a scale. . . . How I regret the thoughts of quitting it" (AA to Mary Smith Cranch, 4 July 1790, AA, *New Letters*, p. 54; *DAB*).

Courtesy of the New-York Historical Society.

11. "THE WASHINGTON FAMILY," BY EDWARD SAVAGE, 1789–1796   381

In 1789, two of Martha Washington's grandchildren accompanied her to New York: Eleanor "Nelly" Parke Custis (1779–1852) and George Washington Parke Custis (1781–1857). Her two other grandchildren, Elizabeth and Martha Custis, remained in Virginia. All four were the children of Martha Washington's son by her first marriage, John Parke Custis, and his wife Eleanor Calvert Custis (Washington, *Papers, Presidential Series*, 1:4–5).

The Washington Family, by Edward Savage, depicts a life-sized George and Martha Washington, along with their two grandchildren, Nelly and George Washington Parke, and a family slave, Billy Lee. Savage (1761–1817) was a respected engraver, painter, and museum proprietor. He initially composed individual portraits of the children in New York in 1789, then combined them with bust portraits of George and Martha Washington to create the family composition in Philadelphia in 1796. The face of each figure is carefully detailed, but the composite nature of the painting results in the family's lack of eye contact. Savage's technical skills as an engraver were superior to his brushwork as a painter; consequently, his figures appear slightly wooden.

Abigail Adams noted that "mrs Washington is a most frindly good Lady, always pleasent and easy doatingly fond of her Grandchildren to whom she is quite the Grandmamma" (to Mary Smith Cranch, 11 Oct. 1789, below). While the inclusion of the children in the portrait certainly suggests the closeness of the family that Abigail observed, only minimal interaction takes place between the figures. Martha Washington holds a corner of a plan for the new capital city while her granddaughter unrolls the opposite edge. George Washington sits across from her with his sword and hat close by; his grandson rests his hand atop a globe. In this way, the Washingtons play the dual role of devoted parents to their adopted children and their country.

Although Savage completed other portraits of George Washington, this family painting is his best-known work and was widely distributed as an engraving. A 17 March 1798 advertisement in the *Gazette of the United States* offered "an elegant Engraving" depicting "General Washington and his Lady (two capital likenesses) sitting at a table on which lies a plan of the Federal City" (Edward Savage, *Exhibition of the Important Oil Painting, Washington and His Family*, N.Y., 1892, p. 24–27; Grove *Dicy. of Art*; MHS, *Procs.*, 14:9–11 [Jan. 1905]).

Courtesy of Andrew W. Mellon Collection, National Gallery of Art, Washington, D.C.

12. "THE REPUBLICAN COURT (LADY WASHINGTON'S RECEPTION DAY)," BY DANIEL HUNTINGTON, 1861–1865   398

Throughout her husband's presidency, Martha Washington opened her home to polite society for Friday evening levees. While primarily a gathering for ladies, the president frequently appeared at these events and conversed freely with the women in attendance. Abigail Adams characterized the nature of the receptions in a 1791 letter to Cotton Tufts: "On fryday Evenings mrs washington has a drawing Room which is usually very full of the *well Born and well Bred*. Some times it is as full as her Britanick majesties Room, & with quite as Handsome Ladies, and as polite courtiers" (6 Feb. [1791], Adams Papers). Abigail hosted levees of her own once a week, and while an invitation was not required to attend, it was understood that only members of the social elite were welcome (AA to Mary Smith Cranch, 9 Aug. 1789, below).

Created during a four-year period between 1861 and 1865 in the midst of the Civil War, *The Republican Court (Lady Washington's Reception Day)* celebrated an earlier period of American unity. Daniel Huntington (1816–1906), an internationally known artist, had exhibited at major art institutions in the United States and at the Royal Academy in London and made a lasting contribution to the art world as a founder and vice president of the Metropolitan Museum of Art. For *The Republican Court*, he combined his interests in portraiture and history painting; the image includes 64 individual portraits of Revolutionary era political figures and their

wives. As a tribute to early national high society, the belles of the republican court—including the alluring Anne Bingham and Sarah Livingston Jay, both friends of Abigail's—occupy the very center of the painting, while other politically influential figures from this era are relegated to the outer edges of the crowd. All are present to pay their regards to Martha Washington on her raised dais, including Abigail Adams on the far left and John Adams shown fourth from the left. Given Huntington's desire to pay tribute to an era, rather than a specific event, some of his guests at the reception are anachronistic, including Nathanael Greene and Arthur Middleton, both of whom died before Washington took office (Karal Ann Marling, *George Washington Slept Here: Colonial Revivals and American Culture, 1876–1986*, Cambridge, 1988, p. 47, 49; Grove *Dicy. of Art*; *Description of Mr. Huntington's Picture of Lady Washington's Reception Day*, N.Y., n.d., p. 2).
Courtesy of the Brooklyn Museum.

13. PARK ROW AND ST. PAUL'S CHAPEL, NEW YORK, BY CHARLES MILBOURNE, 1798   415

"I have sometimes gone to St Pauls," Abigail Adams wrote to Mary Cranch in October 1789, three months after moving to New York. "There I find much more liberal discourses, but bred a desenter and approveing that mode of worship, I feel a reluctance at changing." She attended the Episcopal St. Paul's Chapel after tiring of the sermons of substitute preachers at the Presbyterian Church of New York. "They address their Audience with so much self importance, and Priestly despotisim, that I am really surprizd at their having any men of sense and abilities for their hearers" (4 Oct. 1789, below).

At St. Paul's, Abigail likely heard the sermons of Bishop Samuel Provoost (1742–1815). Provoost was appointed assistant minister of New York's Trinity Church in 1766, but he resigned in 1771 when his patriotic sermons raised the ire of loyalist members. After the evacuation of the British from New York, he returned to the city and his former parish. Trinity Church had burned in 1776, so Provoost was appointed to officiate at its ancillary St. Paul's and St. George's chapels. In 1786, he was elected the first Episcopal bishop of New York. On 30 April 1789, Provoost conducted services at St. Paul's in celebration of George Washington's inauguration (*DAB*).

Local stone was used to construct St. Paul's Chapel between 1764 and 1766. Manhattan's third Episcopal church building is traditionally attributed to Scottish architect Thomas McBean and resembles St. Martin-in-the-Fields in London's Trafalgar Square, the masterpiece of McBean's mentor James Gibbs. St. Paul's tower was designed by James C. Lawrence and added in 1794, and so was not present when Abigail Adams attended. Today St. Paul's is Manhattan's oldest surviving church (having narrowly escaped destruction on 11 September 2001 when the neighboring World Trade Center collapsed around it) and is considered one of the nation's finest examples of Georgian architecture (Morgan Dix, *Historical Recol-*

lections of S. Paul's Chapel, New York, N.Y., 1867, p. 25–26; Andrew S. Dolkart and Matthew A. Postal, *Guide to New York City Landmarks*, 3d rev. edn., Hoboken, N.J., 2004, p. 23–24).

Charles Milbourne painted this watercolor of St. Paul's in 1798. He emigrated from London in 1792 and worked as a theater-scene painter and landscape artist in Philadelphia and New York until 1816. In April 1794 *New York Magazine* lauded Milbourne's work: "The paintings and scenery are equal to the generality of the European, and do the greatest credit to the pencil and genius of Mr. Milbourne" (Martin P. Snyder, *City of Independence: Views of Philadelphia before 1800*, N.Y., 1975, p. 194–196; William Young, ed. and comp., *A Dictionary of American Artists, Sculptors and Engravers*, Cambridge, 1968).

Courtesy of the New-York Historical Society.

Introduction

The years from March 1787 to December 1789 covered by volume 8 of the *Adams Family Correspondence* represent an important transitional period for the Adams family. These letters chronicle John and Abigail Adams' final year in London and the beginning of their time as central actors in the United States government under the new Constitution. They also describe important changes in the lives of the Adams children, especially Abigail 2d's new experiences as a wife and mother, and John Quincy's graduation from college and the beginning of his legal training.

Because of these changes, the correspondence printed here provides a particularly rich view of this complex period in American history. It offers perspectives on the debates over the new Constitution from both Europe and America, from those directly involved in the ratification process and those observing from the sidelines. But as always with the family correspondence, these letters also comment on more intimate social and domestic issues, dealing with such diverse topics as education, travel, household management, matchmaking, and childbirth.

Once again, as in previous volumes in the *Adams Family Correspondence* series, fully 80 percent of the letters are written to or by Abigail Adams; roughly a quarter of those are letters to or from her sisters, Mary Smith Cranch and Elizabeth Smith Shaw. Their correspondence is especially vivid during Abigail's final year in London, but it also resumed in full force in mid-1789 when Abigail relocated to New York City. Mary and Elizabeth continued to be her eyes and ears in Massachusetts, reporting on the family's well-being, other household concerns, and local and national political news. They rejoiced with Abigail in the Adams children's successes and took on the difficult task of conveying the news of loved ones lost. Abigail in turn shared her private hopes and fears with her sisters and entrusted them with the responsibility of caring for her family in her absence.

The other major letter writers include John Adams, John Quincy Adams, and Abigail Adams Smith, though all three found their time for correspondence curtailed by other responsibilities: John's writing *A Defence of the Constitutions*, John Quincy's schooling, and Nabby's new role as mother. In particular, John Quincy and Nabby discontinued the lengthy journal-letters by which they had maintained their transatlantic communication. Now both in America, they continued to write to one another, albeit more sporadically, thus providing some perspective from the younger members of the family. And as they came into their own as adults within the family, their insights into national affairs matured accordingly.

1. RETURNING TO AMERICA

By early 1787, John and Abigail Adams had begun to make plans to move back to America. While Abigail had generally enjoyed her years abroad, the European lifestyle had lost its appeal. This, combined with the ongoing difficulties of serving as the wife of the first United States minister to Great Britain and increasing concern for the political turmoil within the United States, made her ready to go home. On 24 January 1787, John tendered his resignation to Congress, and by early March, Abigail wrote to her sister Elizabeth, "I hope to see you in the course of an other Year, as we are *determined* to return to America and share the fate of our Country whether she stand firm like mount Atlass—or make it treason to harbour an Idea that she will fall."[1]

Of course, such a departure could not be effected immediately. John had been in Europe for eight years and Abigail for three; it would be another year—and an active one for the family—before the Adamses finally set sail for Massachusetts. In April, they welcomed their first grandchild when William Steuben Smith was born to Nabby and William Stephens Smith. Abigail was quite giddy with delight over this event, gushing to her niece, "I am a *Grandmamma*! my Grandson be sure is a fine Boy, & I already feel as fond of him as if he was my own son, nay I can hardly persuade myself that he is not." Nabby came through the birth relatively well and was able to "dine below" three weeks later. With the aid of an especially attentive nurse—"the best Nurses I ever saw," according to Abigail, one of the rare situations in which she found the British way better than

---

[1] JA to John Jay, 24 Jan. 1787, PCC, No. 84, VI, f. 392–395; AA to Elizabeth Smith Shaw, 10 March, below. See also AA to Mary Smith Cranch, 8 March, and to Isaac Smith Sr., 12 March, both below.

the American—Nabby took to raising her son with her usual quiet enthusiasm.[2]

The family continued to socialize in London, albeit somewhat curtailed by Nabby's lying-in period and Abigail's recurring ill health. Nonetheless, Abigail found time to attend a series of scientific lectures, as always embracing an opportunity for the more formal education she had been denied earlier in life.[3] In June, Mary Jefferson, Thomas Jefferson's younger daughter, paid the Adamses a visit while en route to Paris to join her father and sister. This gave Abigail an opportunity to mother another young girl—a project she embraced with great zeal, perhaps recognizing and mourning somewhat the fact that her own daughter had moved on to another stage of life—and also introduced her to a young woman destined to play an important role in Jefferson lore, Sally Hemings. The teenage Hemings was chosen to escort Mary Jefferson from Virginia to Europe after an older slave was unable to make the voyage. Abigail did not think much of Hemings, complaining that she "wants more care than the child, and is wholy incapable of looking properly after her." Unstated but doubtless present was also Abigail's continuing skepticism over slavery in general, as either a moral or effective labor system.[4]

The Adamses found time to travel as well, taking an extended holiday along the west coast of England, visiting Axminster, Exeter, and Plymouth. The primary reason for the trip was Abigail's ill health. "I have been very frequently ill through the Spring & Summer," she complained to her sister Elizabeth, "and am advised to this journey as a restoritive." The family toured southwestern England for a month, covering over 600 miles and visiting such noteworthy sights as Blenheim Palace and Winchester Cathedral. As Abigail always did when she traveled, she kept a type of travel diary through her letters to her sisters and nieces, tartly observing and commenting not merely on the usual tourist sights but also on the people, customs, economy, and social practices of the areas she visited.[5]

John's public work led him on other excursions, to the Netherlands to negotiate two additional loans from the Dutch to keep the

[2] AA to Lucy Cranch, 26 April 1787, and to Mary Smith Cranch, 28 April, both below. For AA2's comments on her son, see, for instance, AA2 to Elizabeth Cranch, 19 July, below.

[3] See AA to Lucy Cranch, 26 April 1787, below.

[4] See AA's letters to Thomas Jefferson of 26 and 27 June 1787, and 6 and 10 July, and Jefferson's to AA of 1, 10, and 16 July, all below.

[5] AA to Elizabeth Smith Shaw, [19] July 1787; to Mary Smith Cranch, 15 Sept.; to Elizabeth Cranch, 1 Oct.; and to Lucy Cranch, 3 Oct., all below.

American government afloat, and to Portsmouth to chase down counterfeiters of American currency.[6] He also made further progress during this time on his *A Defence of the Constitutions of Government of the United States of America*, the first volume of which received favorable reviews in Europe and America in the spring of 1787. Richard Cranch, Abigail's brother-in-law, informed John that his book "is eagarly read by Gentlemen of all the learned Professions here. It came to America at a very critical Moment just before the Meeting of the grand Convention at Philadelphia for revising and amending the Confederation. . . . I have my self conversed with many Gentlemen here of the first Rank for Learning and Abilities, who, after reading your Book with great attention, gave it as their Opinion that you have supported your System of the Ballance in a most masterly manner."[7] John completed the second volume in September and a third in February 1788. While the work distracted John from other letter writing, he considered the topic too important to let go: "I cannot get mr Adams to write half the Letters I want him to," Abigail complained to her sister Mary, "He is so buisily employd about his Books, I tell him he will ruin himself in Publishing his Books, he says they are for the Benefit of his Country, and he allways expected to be ruind in her service."[8] While still in England, John was clearly already focused on the situation back in the United States and anticipating the political battles that would ensue over the creation of a new government.

Returning to America required dealing with a number of practical considerations. At the advice of Mary Cranch, who wisely realized that their old home would never adequately accommodate them, the Adamses assigned Cotton Tufts, their agent, the task of locating a new house for them in Braintree. Mary had watched over the Adamses' home while they had been away in Europe but warned them, "you can never live in that house when you return it is not large enough. you cannot crowd your Sons into a little bed by the side of yours now, & you will never inlarg it." She suggested that Abigail instruct Tufts to acquire the Vassall-Borland estate to serve as their new home, and in fact mentioned it to him before writing to the

---

[6] For the loans, see AA to WSS, [30] May 1787; JA to AA, 1 June; JA to AA, 11 March 1788; JA to AA, 14 March, all below, and Winter, *Amer. Finance and Dutch Investment*, 1:273–319. For the counterfeiting, see John Brown Cutting to AA, 25 April 1787, and AA to Cotton Tufts, 29 April, both below.

[7] Richard Cranch to JA, 24 May 1787, below.

[8] AA to Mary Smith Cranch, 8 Oct. 1787, 2d letter, below. See also vol. 7:365–366 for a fuller discussion of JA's *Defence of the Const.*

Adamses on the subject. With John and Abigail's approval, Tufts purchased the house in September 1787.[9] Ironically, the previous owner had been none other than Royall Tyler, Nabby's estranged former fiancé, who defaulted on the purchase of the house shortly after the couple broke off their engagement. This home, named Peacefield by Abigail and John, and commonly called the Old House by later generations of Adamses, remained the family's estate into the twentieth century.

While Tufts served as their agent on the ground, Abigail played an active role from afar in preparing the house, issuing specific instructions on its furnishings and decoration. "The east lower room to be painted what is calld a French Grey," Abigail ordered, "and as the furniture is red, a paper conformable, will look best. the Chamber over it will have Green furniture, and may be in the same manner, made uniform by a paper Green & white." Not even the style of locks and chimney backs were details too minor for Abigail's keen eye and exacting standards. She also saw to the concerns of the broader household, assigning long-time servant (and former slave) Phoebe Abdee to take charge of the dairy, making recommendations to Tufts for tenants and farmhands, and determining specific plantings for the gardens.[10]

After considerable planning, formal leave-taking from the Court of St. James, and good-byes to friends in England and to the Smiths, who were themselves leaving for New York, the Adamses finally began their voyage home in spring of 1788. It was not without its starts and stops. They were delayed first at Portsmouth and then again at Cowes, waiting for their ship to arrive, their baggage to be loaded, and for favorable winds to sail. The crossing itself was tumultuous. Their ship, the *Lucretia*, had barely gone beyond Weymouth when it was forced back to port by high winds; after a week there, Abigail reported to Nabby, "the wind changed, and we sailed with a northeaster; this lasted us just long enough to carry us out of the channel, when the west wind set in, and alternately we have had a violent blow, squalls, and then calms, from that day to the present." On 17 June, two and a half months after departing from London, the Adamses finally reached Boston, where Gov. John Hancock

[9] Mary Smith Cranch to AA, 22 April 1787, below. See also Cotton Tufts to JA, 13 June, and AA to Cotton Tufts, 1 July, both below. For a full discussion of the history of the Old House and its purchase by the Adamses, see vol. 3:264–266, and Descriptive List of Illustrations, No. 2, above.
[10] AA to Cotton Tufts, 6 Nov. 1787, 5 Oct., and 1 Jan. 1788, all below.

and many others formally welcomed them home to their native land.[11]

Despite this warm reception, the transition back to American life was not always easy for Abigail. The Vassall-Borland estate, while spacious by Braintree's standards, seemed to Abigail a mere "wren's house" compared with the Adamses' mansion at Auteuil, France, and their gracious home at Grosvenor Square in London. Abigail warned her daughter Nabby that if she and William Stephens Smith were to visit from Long Island, New York, where they had settled, "be sure you wear no feathers, and let Col. Smith come without heels to his shoes, or he will not be able to walk upright."[12]

But while the physical surroundings in Braintree did not always suit her, the opportunity to be back home, amidst her extended family, certainly did. Abigail expressed no regrets for making her European tour, but she also did not hesitate to state her preference: "I have never spent half so many pleasent hours in Europe, in the same space of time, as I have known at the foot of pens Hill."[13] If the house was too small and the travel inconvenient, John's uncertain political future frustrating and their finances worrying, the blessing of family and friends so nearby, the sheer familiarity of her dear Massachusetts, more than made up for it.

2. BECOMING ADULTS

While John and Abigail wrestled with all the implications of their return to America, the Adams children, too, were facing new challenges in their lives. The Puritan tradition in New England deemed that a son had not reached full adulthood until he had both a calling and a wife. By the late eighteenth century, however, the path to reaching that point had become increasingly complex. Consequently, the line between child and adult had begun to blur—and John Quincy, Charles, and shortly Thomas Boylston found themselves moving into that fuzzy in-between: no longer children but not self-supporting and fully adult either.[14]

---

[11] AA to AA2, 29 May 1788, and 7 July, both below.
[12] To AA2, 7 July 1788, below.
[13] AA to Mary Smith Cranch, 11 May 1787, below.
[14] For a full discussion of eighteenth-century attitudes toward the transition from childhood to adulthood, see Harvey J. Graff, *Conflicting Paths: Growing Up in America*, Cambridge, 1995, ch. 2.

John Quincy remains the most prominent brother in the *Adams Family Correspondence*. While Charles and Thomas Boylston are largely known from the words of others (no letters of theirs have been found for this time period), John Quincy appears in his own voice, as well as through the writings of other family members. As the eldest son, he faced the highest expectations—and in general succeeded in living up to them. Ironically, however, trying to be the best and the brightest sometimes left him single-mindedly focused on his schooling to the exclusion of a more rounded life, which in turn became a cause for some concern within his family. If anything, Abigail worried that he would become too obsessed with his studies, to his own detriment: "I fear a little that my Eldest son will be so much of a Book worm & Scholar that he will grow too neglegent of those attentions which are due to the World, & which tho they may appear little, & trifling, much of our happiness is found by experience to depend upon them."[15]

But his hard work paid off. Despite John Quincy's anxieties prior to the day itself—"oh Lord! oh Lord," he prayed, "I hope it will rain hard that all their white wigs may be wet who would not let us have a private commencment"—he performed admirably at his Harvard graduation exercises in July 1787. Elizabeth Shaw recognized that he might not have been the best speaker of the day (that honor went to one Nathaniel Freeman) but still believed that "the admirers of dignity of Sentiment, & Composition would at *least* have debated upon the Preference— I am sure no one could be a Judge of Mr Adam's Eloquence unless they kept their Eye fixed upon his Face, & saw each Passion, & each Feeling called up, & most strikingly, & happily delineated there."[16] After graduation, he took only a brief vacation before moving to Newburyport to begin his legal training with the noted attorney Theophilus Parsons.

John Quincy found life in Newburyport and the study of law more congenial than he had expected. "The study itself," he noted to his mother, "is far from being so destitute of entertainment, as I

---

[15] AA to Mary Smith Cranch, 28 April 1787, below. To date, no letters written by CA or TBA prior to 1790 and 1791, respectively, have been located.

[16] Mary Smith Cranch to AA, 16 July [1787], and Elizabeth Smith Shaw to AA, 22 July, both below. The *Massachusetts Centinel*, 21 July, reported that "the two principal performances were the Orations by Mr. *Adams* and Mr. *Freeman*. The first of these certainly declaimed upon a well chosen subject, in a manly, sensible and nervous style of eloquence. The publick expectations from this gentleman, being the son of an Ambassador, the favourite of the officers of the College, and having enjoyed the highest advantages of European instruction, were greatly inflated. This performance justified the preconceived partiality." For additional comment on the newspaper reports of the commencement, see JQA, *Diary*, 2:265–266.

had been led to expect." But prone to anxiety, John Quincy could not stop himself from fretting over the state of the legal profession and his own financial difficulties. His repeated need to request money from Cotton Tufts (acting as agent for John Quincy's parents) clearly mortified and frustrated him—he yearned to be independent and self-sufficient. On more than one occasion, his sister Nabby had to chide him out of his depression: "It gives me uneasiness my Dear Brother to observe from the tenor of your letter that you permit the Cross accidents of Life to affect your spirits too much, true Philosophy does not Consist in being insensible to them, but in supporting ourselvs above them with becomeing dignity, and in acquiessing with chearfullness to those events which are irremidable, and by striving to attain such a Station in Life as we may not be subjected to their influence."[17] His self-pity and occasional difficulties aside, by 1789, John Quincy was well on his way to a successful legal career.

Not everything went so smoothly for the younger sons. Charles found himself embroiled in a Thanksgiving day riot at Harvard in the fall of 1787, although it is not clear if he was an active participant or merely an unwitting witness (from his post as a dining-hall waiter) who took the blame rather than betray his friends by testifying against them. Either way, there were other indications of troubles. Cotton Tufts found that "some Imprudencies (at least) had given Countenance to Suspicion" about Charles' character and behavior. A year later, John Quincy felt the need to give Charles a serious talking to upon some unnamed misconduct: "I wrote him a very serious Letter three weeks ago and conversed with him at Haverhill upon the subject in such a manner as must I think lead him to be more cautious." Hints to the problem exist in letters from Abigail and Mary Cranch, both of whom expressed concern over the company Charles had been keeping.[18]

The family made the decision in May 1789 to bring Charles to New York even before his formal graduation from Harvard later that year, and to situate him in a law office—first that of Alexander Hamilton and later, once Hamilton became secretary of the treasury, that of John Laurance—right away. There he seemed to settle down and

[17] JQA to AA, 23 Dec. 1787; AA2 to JQA, 10 Feb. 1788; JQA to Cotton Tufts, 16 Feb.; and AA2 to JQA, 20 Aug., all below.

[18] Cotton Tufts to JQA, 5 March 1788; JQA to William Cranch, 27 May 1789; AA to JQA, 30 May; and Mary Smith Cranch to AA, 21 June, all below. For the Thanksgiving riot, see JQA to Cotton Tufts, 16 Feb. 1788, below, and JQA, *Diary*, 2:355–356, and note 1.

worked hard; his mother noted that he "will not go into any company but such as his Father or col Smith introduces him to. he appears steady and sedate & I hope will continue so." Abigail seemed anxious to reassure the family back in Massachusetts that he was once again behaving appropriately.[19]

The extant correspondence offers no direct explanation for the family's concerns about Charles beyond worry for the people with whom he associated. One possible explanation, however, is that he had begun to frequent taverns and drink excessively. Alcoholism plays a recurring role within the Adams family, and the family may have been especially sensitive to Charles' nascent problems in the wake of another family tragedy—the death of Abigail's brother, William Smith. A long-time alcoholic who had repeatedly deserted his wife, Smith died of jaundice in September 1787. At the time, he was estranged from all of his sisters, none of whom learned of his fatal illness until it was too late. His death provided the three sisters with an opportunity to contemplate both William's failings and how such a troubled man could have been raised in the same household with them. As Elizabeth Shaw put it, "The same air, *we* breathed—the same cradle rocked us to rest—& the same Parental Arms folded us to their fond Bosoms—& who can refrain full many a Tear at such a Death!"[20]

Thomas Boylston Adams remains in this volume the least noticed of the three sons. Also a student at Harvard (he would not graduate until 1790), he was apparently much beloved by his aunt Elizabeth Shaw and the other residents of Haverhill, who raised him while his parents lived overseas in Europe. By all accounts he was a respectable, well-behaved student, but references to him are unfortunately relatively rare, leaving a less clear picture of his character than exists for his other siblings.

The first extant letter from Abigail to her youngest son was written in March 1787 and reflects a typical parent's concern for her child's moral development: "Nature has implanted in the humane

[19] AA to Mary Smith Cranch, 12 July 1789, below. JQA firmly supported the plan to place CA more closely under his parents' supervision, arguing "that if any thing can keep him within the limits of regularity, it will be his knowlege of my fathers being [near him and the?] fear of being discovered by him" (to William Cranch, 27 May, below).

[20] Elizabeth Smith Shaw to AA, 17 Nov. 1787, below. See also Mary Smith Cranch to AA, 21 Oct.; AA to Cotton Tufts, 1 Jan. 1788; and AA to Mary Smith Cranch, 10 Feb., all below. Several decades later, CFA observed in his Diary that "the Smith blood seems to have had the scourge of intemperance dreadfully applied to it." Besides William Smith Jr., CA and TBA both suffered from alcoholism, as did JQA's children, JA2 and GWA (CFA, *Diary*, 5:143–144).

mind nice sensibilities of moral rectitude and a natural love of excellent & given to it powers capable of infinate improvement and the state of things is so constituted that Labour well bestowed & properly directed always produces valuable Effects. the resolution you have taken of persueing such a conduct as shall redound to your own honour & that of your family is truly commendable." But Abigail also did not hesitate to recommend more prosaic and practical skills for her son, including that he improve his handwriting and "learn the use of arms." Clearly still a child in his family's eyes, Thomas Boylston was the furthest away from achieving full independence.[21]

All three boys benefited from the care and concern of their aunts, Mary Cranch and Elizabeth Shaw. In Abigail's absence, they provided John Quincy, Charles, and Thomas Boylston with clothing, places to stay during the school vacancies, and much love and affection. Both sisters fretted over the boys' health and well-being, particularly that of John Quincy, who was prone to overwork and neglect himself if no one intervened. Mary wrote to Abigail of one such bout: "His staying at cambridge during the winter vacancy was of no service to his Health whatever it may have been to his mind. He look'd so pale & wan when he came home this spring that I was not a little alarm'd about him. . . . His complants are wholly oweing to want of air & exercise & too great an attention to his studys."[22]

Abigail's sisters similarly watched over the romantic lives of the Adams brothers, concerned lest the boys marry in haste and repent at leisure. Elizabeth Shaw especially was attuned to the boys' changing interests, which she dutifully reported to Abigail. Elizabeth confessed that she had been "very anxious for *your young* Hercules, lest his Heart might be subdued by *One* whom I knew his riper Judgment, could never approve." Fortunately, John Quincy himself was able to reassure her: "Indeed my Aunt (said he) I know you have been concerned for me, but you need not have the least fearful Apprehensions with regard to this Lady, for though I was exceedingly pleased at first, yet I have lived long enough with her to know her Principles, & see into the motives of her Conduct, & the Lord knows, *she* is not the Person who would engage my Affections."[23]

[21] AA to TBA, 15 March 1787, below. See also JQA to TBA, 3 May 1788, below, in which JQA lectures TBA on appropriate conduct as a college student. TBA's reaction to this letter is unknown, but CA was apparently frustrated enough by JQA's "*Mentorial* airs," as JQA recounted the situation, that he threatened to break off all correspondence with JQA.
[22] Mary Smith Cranch to AA, 22 April 1787, below.
[23] Elizabeth Smith Shaw to AA, 20 May 1787, below.

Introduction

Charles, too, had his interests, to judge by the number of hair rings Mary Cranch found in his pockets. "But my dear," she reported her conversation with Charles to Abigail, "have you left her any hair upon her head if all the rings you have are made of her hair you must have thin'd it a little at least." The middle brother also had noteworthy good looks: "The Misses think Charles a mere Adonis—a perfect Beauty," his aunt Elizabeth shared with Abigail. She added—then crossed out—the additional hope that "Minerva with her broad Sheild, preserve the dear Youth, from every Guile." Fortunately, Charles was apparently too busy flirting with various girls for the aunts to worry that he might settle down with just one. Thomas Boylston, by contrast, wanted no part of this nonsense. Mary observed that "honest Tom he does not think that the Ladys need so much attention—'is sure that they have Legs as well as he & may walk without leaning upon his arm.'"[24] Regardless of how quickly the boys matured, they remained fortunate to have a caring extended family to watch over them.

The situation for Abigail 2d was somewhat different. As a married woman and a mother, she was unquestionably an adult, even as she continued at times to live in her parents' homes, first in London and later in New York.[25] This new stage of life still certainly contained its challenges. Like her mother, Nabby was quickly confronted with one familiar difficulty of marriage to a diplomat: long separations. Mere weeks after the birth of their first child, Nabby's husband William Stephens Smith departed for a four-month trip to Portugal to deliver a message to the queen from the United States government. As Abigail noted to her sister, "it is the first seperation even of a day since he was married. Mrs Smith thought it a Sad affliction. She has not been innured like her mamma, and I hope she never may to such long dangerous & painfull seperations. she however behaved well when it came really to the trial."[26]

Also, Nabby's allegiances had to change, a process she (and the Adamses) sometimes found difficult. While Abigail was overseeing

[24] Mary Smith Cranch to AA, 19 Aug. 1787, and Elizabeth Smith Shaw to AA, 22 July, both below. See also Elizabeth Cranch to AA, 23 Sept., below.
[25] The transition to adulthood for women centered on marriage, the establishment of an independent household, and the rearing of children (see Graff, *Conflicting Paths*, p. 51–53). AA2 and WSS had initially established their own household following their marriage in June 1786 but returned to the Adamses' home in Grosvenor Square for the birth of their first child and WSS's subsequent departure for Portugal. Over the next several years, the Smiths would continue to alternate between living on their own and living with their respective families.
[26] AA to Mary Smith Cranch, 28 April 1787, below. For WSS's mission, see AA to JQA, 20 March, note 5, below.

xxxi

her and John's relocation to Massachusetts, Nabby was navigating a similar transition for her young family to New York, William's home state. They left England in the spring of 1788, arriving in New York City in late May. They settled into a home on Long Island, near the Smith family, and quickly found themselves immersed in the New York social scene. But Nabby's separation from her parents and siblings was not easy for any of them. She repeatedly encouraged them to come and visit her, bemoaning to John Quincy that "this seperation of families which prevents us from paying to each other those attentions which our affection would dictate is to me the most painfull circumstance in Life."[27] Still, Nabby had other activities to keep her occupied: she built close relationships with her new Smith relatives and, in November 1788, gave birth to her second child, John Adams Smith.

Some early concerns also arose around William Stephens Smith, whose disinclination to settle into a profession in New York worried his ever-ambitious in-laws. Smith had already had a distinguished career, first in the military and then in the American diplomatic corps, but his seeming contentedness to rest on his laurels did not sit well with John and Abigail. John felt strongly that William should pursue a career in law—like his father-in-law—and did not hesitate to make this recommendation to Nabby. William was less in a hurry to settle on a profession and felt to some extent entitled to a public office, given his earlier service to the nation.[28] This conflict would continue to fester for many years and lead to tensions between the Smiths and Adamses. For the moment, however, both families were content to wait and see what new circumstances New York and the new government there would bring.

3. THE NEW GOVERNMENT

In the wake of Shays' Rebellion and other signs of dysfunction within the Articles of Confederation, Americans began during this time to move toward restructuring the federal system to create a stronger central government. As keen observers of the troubles in Massachusetts, the Adamses supported this action, though John's distance from Philadelphia, where the Constitutional Convention

[27] AA2 to JQA, 28 Sept. 1788, below. For other letters from AA2 encouraging her family to come visit, see AA2 to JQA, 8 June; to AA, 15 June; to JQA, 20 Aug.; and to AA, 7 Sept., all below.

[28] JA to AA2, 16 July 1788, and AA2 to JA, 27 July, both below.

met, reduced substantially his influence on the process. Still, they followed events as closely as they could with a mixture of hope and anxiety. Abigail, writing to John Quincy, mused: "I wish most sincerely that the meeting of our Convention which is to take place this month, may reform abuses, Reconcile parties, give energy to Government & stability to the States, but I sometimes fear we Must experience new Revollutions, before we shall set under our vines in peace."[29]

News from the family back home significantly shaped the Adamses' perspective on circumstances in America. Mary and Richard Cranch, Cotton Tufts, and John Quincy faithfully reported on the aftermath of Shays' Rebellion in Massachusetts, commenting especially on the spring 1787 elections to the General Court, which repudiated many of the actions the Massachusetts government had previously taken to suppress the rebellion. As Cotton Tufts noted, "The Spirit of the Day has brought into public Life Characters that in sober Times would have been hissed off the Stage and been expelled as Members unfit to grace the Seats of Legislaters." Tufts reported derisively the election not only of some who had supported Shays' Rebellion but also, going further back in time, of loyalists who had opposed the Revolution altogether.[30]

The results of the Constitutional Convention, announced in September 1787, created an entirely new political firestorm as Federalists and Antifederalists vied for support during the ratification process. Again, Cotton Tufts weighed in to Abigail: "The System of Government reported by the late Continental Convention has afforded much Matter for Pens and Tongues. . . . which of the Parties will carry their Point, is difficult to say— Many of the Advocates for the Constitution are enthusiastic open & severe in their Attacks upon all that oppose it, those on the other Side act more secretly, but with great Success." John disliked some aspects of the new Constitution but argued strongly "for accepting the present Plan as it is and trying the Experiment. at a future Time Amendments may be made."[31] He had seen firsthand in Europe the difficulties created by a weak central government in America and longed for some improvement, even if the new system was not perfect.

[29] AA to JQA, 6 May 1787, below.
[30] Cotton Tufts to JA, 30 June 1787, below. See also Mary Smith Cranch to AA, 22 April; Elizabeth Smith Shaw to AA, 20 May; Richard Cranch to JA, 24 May; and JQA to JA, 30 June, all below.
[31] Cotton Tufts to AA, 18 Dec. 1787, and JA to Cotton Tufts, 23 Jan. 1788, both below.

John initially rejected the idea that he would take any new public position once he had resigned as minister to Great Britain: "It is mr A's intention to retire to Braintree as a private man," Abigail informed Cotton Tufts, somewhat disingenuously, "nor need any one fear that he will become a competitor with them for offices. he has always dealt too openly & candedly with his Countrymen to be popular." But even before he left Europe, his name had been raised as a possible vice president, and his daughter Nabby wisely recognized that "he would not I am well Convinced be Happy in Private Life."[32] While he succeeded in generally retaining a low profile initially after his return to the States, there was little doubt that his so-called retirement would be of brief duration.

Once the states' ratification of the Constitution advanced far enough to ensure its implementation, politicking for positions in the new government began. While everyone accepted that George Washington would be elected the first president, John Adams was one of a number considered for vice president. When the new Senate finally achieved a quorum in early April 1789, they proceeded immediately to counting votes from the electoral college and determined that John would indeed become the first vice president under the new Constitution. By mid-April, John was en route to New York amid much fanfare to take up his new office. Abigail followed a few months later, after she had made arrangements for the care of their home in Braintree and John had rented a suitable residence for them, an estate called Richmond Hill, located just outside of the city.

In New York both John and Abigail had to adapt to a very different lifestyle from that to which they had become accustomed either in London or in Braintree. John quickly discovered that his new position restrained and limited him. His only real work—serving as president of the Senate—was curtailed early on by the decision to disallow him to speak on any substantive issues other than procedural motions. He could cast his vote to break ties but nothing more. Needless to say, John found this incredibly irksome. Predictably, he launched into his usual litany of complaints to Abigail: "I have as many difficulties here, as you can have; public and private. but my Life from my Cradle has been a Series of difficulties and that Series will continue to the Grave."[33] Never lacking for an opin-

---

[32] AA to Cotton Tufts, 6 Nov. 1787, and AA2 to JQA, 10 Feb. 1788, both below.
[33] JA to AA, 14 May 1789, below.

ion on any subject, John—even as he dutifully attended every session—chafed at his inability to influence the critical decisions being made by Congress.

Abigail adjusted more successfully to her new life. She loved Richmond Hill, repeatedly singing the praises of this stately home to her sisters: "We are most delightfully situated, the prospect all around is Beautifull in the highest degree, it is a mixture of the sublime & Beautifull." She also enjoyed the company of the Washingtons—whom she particularly admired and felt compared favorably with the king and queen of England—and other old friends such as Sarah and John Jay. She did, however, find the pace of visits wearing. "I have never before been in a situation," she complained to her sister Mary, "in which morning noon & afternoon I have been half as much exposed to company." She was expected to hold regular levees herself and entertain all members of the Senate, as well as attend other ladies' gatherings on occasion. It made for a social whirlwind. But overall she was pleased with her newfound circumstances: "I fear they will Remove from this place I am too happy in the situation of it, I fear to have it lasting I am every day more & more pleased with it."[34] Abigail referred, of course, to the possible relocation of Congress to a permanent home—one of many contentious issues still to be settled as the president, vice president, senators, congressmen, and other interested parties sought to build the new federal government.

4. NOTES ON EDITORIAL METHOD

This volume marks the first Adams Papers publication using a substantially revised policy concerning the presentation of documents, as well as an adjustment of the selection policy for the *Adams Family Correspondence* series. Accordingly, it seems an appropriate opportunity to offer a full overview of the project's editorial method. Readers may still wish to reference the statements of editorial policy in previous volumes, most notably the *Diary and Autobiography of John Adams*, 1:lii–lxii, and the *Adams Family Correspondence*, 1:xli–xlviii, as they document the original conception of the Adams Papers project, but some aspects of those statements have now been superseded.

[34] AA to Mary Smith Cranch, 28 June 1789, 12 July, 9 Aug., and 1 Sept., all below. For more on Richmond Hill, see Descriptive List of Illustrations, No. 10, above.

Materials Included

The *Adams Family Correspondence* series continues to draw its material from the wealth of extant letters written between various members of the presidential line of the Adams family, whether related by blood or marriage. The editors also consider for inclusion in this series any letters from Adams women to non-family members, such as Abigail Adams' extensive correspondence with Thomas Jefferson and Mercy Otis Warren. Similarly, correspondence from Thomas Boylston or Charles Adams to non-family members may be included (as there is no plan to publish their papers separately), but only if such a letter speaks directly to issues related to the Adams family. Finally, in rare instances, the editors have printed letters between two non-Adams family members (usually letters between Abigail's two sisters or between a sister and a cousin) if they provide extended commentary or particularly rich insight into the Adamses themselves. However, only omitted letters to or from an Adams family member are included in the List of Omitted Documents found at the end of each *Family Correspondence* volume.

The bulk of this correspondence comes from the Adams Family Papers manuscript collection at the Massachusetts Historical Society, with important additional materials owned by other manuscript repositories and private individuals throughout the country. The series also occasionally reprints letters from nineteenth-century sources that are no longer available in manuscript form if those items are particularly important to complete the documentary record. The descriptive note at the end of each letter identifies the location of the original or the printed source, as appropriate.

As the Adams family has expanded over the project's chronological period, the editors have been and will continue to be increasingly selective about which letters to print in these volumes. The focus remains on John and Abigail Adams, with the correspondence between them and their children and siblings at the core, though as the children themselves have become more active correspondents, their letters appear with greater frequency. Increased selectivity in future volumes will especially extend to correspondence among more distant relations. For instance, letters between two siblings will receive priority over letters between first cousins, who in turn will receive priority over letters between second cousins.

The series is rapidly reaching the point where John Quincy Adams has matured to adulthood and begun to assume a public role.

Consequently, the editors intend to reserve more of his letters for printing in the series of volumes that will be devoted to his public papers, the *Papers of John Quincy Adams*. While any of his letters to family members are and will be considered for the *Family Correspondence* series, those that focus purely on public matters will be published in the *Papers* series instead. Such omissions will not be included in the List of Omitted Documents at the end of each *Family Correspondence* volume as they will be considered as part of the *Papers* series and dealt with there.

Within these basic guidelines, however, the editors continue to emphasize the quality and significance of each individual letter and judge each letter on its merits.

Treatment of the Texts

The editors have adopted a new textual policy. Beginning with the current volume, the texts are and will be rendered as literally as possible given the limitations of modern typography and the ability to translate handwritten manuscripts into printed documents. While some important but less extensive changes have been introduced to the edition (see *Adams Family Correspondence*, vol. 7, and *Papers of John Adams*, vols. 12 and 13), the publication of this volume marks the most important change from the earlier volumes in which the editors substantially intervened to regularize the presentation of the texts. The implementation of this policy to present a more literal interpretation preserves more of the original document and allows the reader to determine the significance of the authors' spelling, grammar, capitalization, and other mechanical aspects of their writing. In that spirit, the following is a summary of the specifics of the project's new policy.

Spelling is preserved as found in the manuscripts. Irregular spellings and spelling mistakes, even when they are obviously simple slips of the pen, are retained. The index will continue to offer corrected spellings of proper names and places, but no such corrections are made in the text itself. If a proper name is otherwise unidentifiable without some clarification, that explanation is provided in a text note.

Grammar and syntax are preserved as found in the manuscripts. Ambiguous statements resulting from grammatical errors may be explained in text notes. Inadvertent repetition of words, however, is silently corrected, and all new paragraphs receive a standardized indent, whether such paragraphs are indicated in the original manuscript by indents, extra space, hanging indents, extended dashes, or other conventions.

Capitalization is preserved as found in the manuscripts, even when it violates conventional standards, such as lowercase letters used for proper nouns or at the beginnings of sentences. In indeterminate cases, where the editors cannot be certain whether the writer intended for a letter to be capital or lowercase, the editors will follow modern usage.

Punctuation is preserved as found in the manuscripts. Occasionally, punctuation marks need to be supplied by the editors to preserve (or create) readability. In those instances, the punctuation is enclosed in brackets and rendered in italics to indicate that it has been editorially supplied. Additionally, as both John and Abigail Adams used periods and commas relatively interchangeably, the editors have retained some license to interpret those marks as makes sense grammatically, relying less on the structure of the character (both Adamses tended to use a single mark that might be either an elongated period or an abbreviated comma) than on the context of the sentence. Finally, the punctuation around abbreviations and contractions has been standardized in a limited fashion: (1) Underlining below a superscript is rendered as a period following the superscript. Similarly, two periods or commas under a superscript is rendered as a colon following the superscript. (2) Marks over letters used to indicate contractions or abbreviations have all been rendered as tildes. If such a mark appears over multiple letters within a word, the tilde is placed over the first letter.

Abbreviations and contractions, in general, are preserved as found in the manuscript. Ampersands are now retained in all instances, as are superscripts. Thorns, however, will be rendered as "th" and per symbols will be spelled out as "per."

Missing and illegible matter is indicated by square brackets enclosing the editors' conjectural readings (with a question mark appended if the reading is uncertain) or suspension points if no reading can be given. Three points are used to indicate a single missing word and four to indicate two missing words. When more than two words are missing, a footnote is provided indicating an estimate of the total amount of missing material. If a single letter of a word is missing, the editors may silently supply it.

Canceled matter in the manuscript (whether scored out or erased) is disregarded unless the editors deem it to be of some significance. In those instances, the text is included but crossed out typographically (e.g., "the further Reduction of public Securities ~~is unnecessary~~ will not be attempted this Session"[35]). The editors will no longer use angle brackets and italicized text to indicate canceled matter as was done in earlier volumes.

Variant readings (variations in text between two or more versions of the same letter) are ordinarily indicated only when they are significant enough to warrant recording, and then always in notes keyed to the basic text that is printed in full.

Interlineations are silently included within the body of the text unless the editors deem the placement of the interlineated material worthy of mention, most commonly when it is written at the bottom or along the margin of a page and marked for insertion. Such explanations are provided by text notes.

Editorial insertions are now relatively rare and used largely to indicate errors in dating or to supply necessary punctuation. The vast majority of editorial comment can be found in the annotation, rather than interpolated into the text. Editorial insertions are still rendered in italicized text in brackets.

As has been the policy from the beginning of this editorial project—and one of the few requirements of the Adams Manuscript Trust, which donated the papers to the Massachusetts Historical Society and created the Adams Papers project—all letters that appear in the Adams Papers volumes are printed in full.[36] The editors, however, reserve the right to omit publishing enclosures to letters. If multiple versions of a letter are available, the recipient's copy—the copy intended for the recipient, whether received or not—is favored over all others. Differences between that version and any other available versions of a letter (such as a letterbook copy or a draft) are explained in textual notes. In general, only significant differences (rather than mere stylistic changes) are so described, and no comment is made of material included in the recipient's copy but excluded from a letterbook copy or draft.

The formal parts of each document are organized as follows:

The *place- and dateline* is printed as literally as possible using the same standards outlined above. It is always placed at the head of the letter, even if it appears elsewhere in the manuscript (for in-

---

[35] Cotton Tufts to JA, 30 June 1787, below.
[36] Remarks of Thomas B. Adams, then president of the Massachusetts Historical Society and trustee of the Adams Manuscript Trust, in *The Adams Papers: A Ceremony . . . Marking the Publication of the* Diary and Autobiography of John Adams, 22 Sept. 1961, p. 5.

stance, at the foot of the text). Undated and misdated letters have their dates editorially supplied or corrected using italicized text inside square brackets.

The *salutation* is also printed as literally as possible on the left-hand side of the same line as the place- and dateline (space permitting). All punctuation is as it appears in the original except when a line is used to separate the saluation from the text. Such lines are silently omitted.

The *complimentary close* is printed literally but, in the interests of saving space, run together in paragraph style. Virgules are used to indicate line breaks within the complimentary close.

The *signature* is printed literally. If a letter was unsigned, it is printed as such without comment unless special circumstances require some explanation.

Enclosures are always acknowledged editorially but only printed selectively. If they belong in the sequence of family correspondence, they appear in their proper chronological places; if not, and they warrant printing, they are attached to the letter that originally covered them.

Annotation and Index

While the most important function of these volumes is to provide accurate and authoritative texts, the editors also strive to offer additional information to help readers fully understand the nature of the documents and the historical context in which they were written.

Following each letter is a *descriptive note* that indicates the physical nature of the document printed and the manuscript repository where the original is located. If the document is no longer available in manuscript form, the source from which it is reprinted is provided. The note also contains any markings on the original manuscript, including addresses (both cover and internal), endorsements (made by the recipient or on his or her behalf at the time of receipt), and docketings (made by the recipient or third parties at a later date). Additional notes on the manuscript may be recorded if the editors deem them of value. Any relevant comment on handwriting is also provided. Archivists' markings and postmarks/stamps are not recorded. As with the complimentary close, multiline text is run together with virgules used to indicate line breaks.

In addition, the descriptive note also now lists all variant versions of the document contained within the Adams Family Papers manuscript collection. Variant texts owned by other respositories are not listed unless those variants are referenced in the annotation of the document. Enclosures to the main document are listed here even if they are not reprinted in full.

The editors do not supply information on previous printings of letters published in the *Adams Family Correspondence* unless there are special reasons for doing so, such as the disappearance of the manuscript or earlier printing in an unexpected place or unusual form.

All other matters annotated—textual, biographical, bibliographical, and so on—are dealt with in a single series of numbered notes for each letter. In general, the editors hope that the letters in large part annotate themselves, that together they provide an overarching sense of the activities of the Adams family and of the events in which they were immersed. Still, certain categories of material require some additional explanation, and the editors attempt to supply that through brief factual notes. Among the types of information covered in the notes, the following are the most common:

1. *Persons and personal names.* The single largest category of notes are identifications of individuals, whether family members, friends, political colleagues, or acquaintances. While certainly not all of the people mentioned within the letters can be meaningfully identified, short biographies are provided for as many as possible at their first significant mention within one of the project's series. When an identification is tentative, the caveats "possibly" or "probably" are used to indicate the editors' level of uncertainty. Text notes are also used to clarify spellings of names when the variations are substantial enough to make locating them in the index difficult (in most cases, names are "corrected" or regularized only in the index) and to provide cross-references to identifications available in volumes in other Adams Papers series.

2. *Books and other publications.* The editors attempt to supply full bibliographical information on the books and publications mentioned in the letters, especially those being read by members of the Adams family. Information on whether the family owned the item in question—either in John Adams' library, now held at the Boston Public Library,[37] or in John Quincy Adams' library, now located at the Stone Library of the Adams National Historical Park—is also included when available.

---

[37] The Boston Public Library has recently completed a major effort to create an online catalog of the library of John Adams, including a record of the extensive marginalia John Adams generated in his books. See www.johnadamslibrary.org for more information.

3. *Correspondence among family members.* Demonstrating the network of correspondence among the Adams family members as well as with their other correspondents has long been of great interest to the editors of this project. Consequently, specific letters mentioned but not printed within the volume are explicitly located if the editors have any record of them, while those mentioned of which no record exists are designated in the notes as "not found." When precise identification of letters is not possible—most commonly due to faulty dating or vague references—the editors may offer likely suggestions.

4. *Other subjects* are annotated on an ad hoc basis, primarily in order to clarify the text, either by providing some historical context or to explain topics that the editors believe would be unfamiliar to modern readers.

After the documents, each volume contains an appended List of Omitted Documents. This includes all Adams materials eligible for inclusion in a particular volume but not printed in that volume, with information on the location of the manuscript, any additional copies contained in the Adams Family Papers manuscript collection, and any modern printed versions thereof. The selection principles for the *Adams Family Correspondence* are provided above. The principles for selection in the *Papers of John Adams* series will be provided in the introduction to volume 14 of that series, forthcoming.

In the *Family Correspondence* series, as in the *Diaries*, a chronology for each volume follows the appendix, providing a brief overview of the activities of the various members of the Adams family during the period covered by that volume.

An index now appears as the final section of each volume, no longer in every other volume, as was the practice through volume 6. The index, besides serving as a guide to locating people, places, and subjects covered in the book, also provides a wealth of additional information. Most notably, each individual's full name is provided (wherever possible), whether it was used in full in the text or not, along with a brief description of that individual, such as his or her profession, place of residence, connection to the Adams family, and so forth. Birth and death dates are additionally supplied for all members of the Adams family, including more distant relatives. These index entries also supply corrected spellings of names or spelling alternatives, as appropriate.

Main entries of any length are subdivided into subentries to offer easier access and more specific searching within the text. Initially, those subentries were provided in page number order, but in recent volumes (*Adams Family Correspondence*, vol. 7, and *Papers of John Adams*, vol. 13), the editors have begun to supply them alphabetically, to aid in their use.

5. RELATED DIGITAL RESOURCES

Beyond their continuing support of the Adams Papers editorial project, the Massachusetts Historical Society has also committed itself to making Adams resources available online. Two digital resources in particular supplement the *Adams Family Correspondence* volumes and will be of great interest to all Adams scholars and readers—the Adams Family Papers: An Electronic Archive and The Diaries of John Quincy Adams: A Digital Collection. Both collections are available through the Massachusetts Historical Society's website at www.masshist.org/adams.

The Adams Family Papers Electronic Archive offers images and text files of the complete correspondence between John and Abigail Adams owned by the Massachusetts Historical Society, all of John Adams' diaries, and his autobiography. The files are fully textsearchable and can also be browsed by date.

The digital collection of the Diaries of John Quincy Adams provides digital images of all pages of John Quincy Adams' enormous 51-volume diary, kept by him for nearly seventy years. The images can be searched by date or browsed by diary volume.

Finally, the editors are pleased to announce the forthcoming launch of a major new digital initiative to make all of the previously published Adams Papers volumes available online. Thanks to the generosity of the National Endowment for the Humanities, Harvard University Press, and the Massachusetts Historical Society, the Founding Families Digital Edition is scheduled to become available on the Historical Society's website in 2008. This project will provide fully searchable text files of 38 *Adams Papers* volumes (all except the *Portraits* volumes), as well as 7 volumes of the *Winthrop Family Papers*, published by the Historical Society in the early twentieth century. While the editors intend to continue making the Adams Papers available in letterpress editions, a complementary digital edition will greatly enhance the accessibility and utility of these volumes.

The 246 letters contained in volume 8 of the *Adams Family Correspondence* are best read in conjunction with the other published materials of the Adams Papers for this period, notably John Adams' *Diary and Autobiography*, 3:203–223, and John Quincy Adams' *Diary*, 2:167–465. Future volumes of the *Papers of John Adams* will further extend the story of John Adams' public life as he moved from his role as an American diplomat abroad back to his political roots in the United States as the first vice president.

Chronicling an important period of transition for the Adamses—from Europe to America, from adolescence to adulthood—and for the United States—from Confederation to Constitution—the correspondence in this volume provides the unique perspective of this preeminent family during a crucial time in American history.

Margaret A. Hogan
September 2006

Acknowledgments

As with all volumes of the Adams Papers, this book received assistance from many quarters without which it would never have come to fruition.

We are particularly grateful for the work of three new members of the Adams Papers staff—Founding Fathers Papers Fellow Karen Northrop Barzilay, and editorial assistants Sara B. Sikes and Judith S. Graham—each of whom made important contributions, providing invaluable help with annotation, verification, illustrations, and the entire production process. They have graciously pitched in on innumerable tasks, both large and small, always with great skill and good humor. Similarly, Paul Fótis Tsimahides, a former member of the Adams Papers staff now working on the Founding Families Digital Project, ably assisted with the early stages of the book.

Our copyeditor Ann-Marie Imbornoni once again saved us from many unfortunate errors, reviewing the entire manuscript with care and precision.

Many people contributed to the research behind this book. We particularly wish to thank Edward B. Doctoroff, Head of the Administrative Services Division at Harvard's Widener Library; and the reference staffs at Harvard University's Houghton and Lamont libraries, Radcliffe's Schlesinger Library, the Rare Books and Manuscripts Department at the Boston Public Library, and the New England Historic Genealogical Society.

As with previous volumes, Kevin and Kenneth Krugh of Technologies 'N Typography in Merrimac, Massachusetts, did an admirable job typesetting the volume. At Harvard University Press, we thank John Walsh, Assistant Director for Design and Production; Lisa Roberts, Paperback Manager; and Kathleen McDermott, Editor, History and Social Sciences, for all of their assistance with the publication and marketing of the book.

The Massachusetts Historical Society continues to provide this project with the use of its unrivaled collections and the support of its knowledgeable staff. In particular, we thank Dennis A. Fiori, Director; Peter Drummey, Stephen T. Riley Librarian; Conrad E.

Wright, Worthington C. Ford Editor; Brenda M. Lawson, Director of Collections Services; Mary E. Fabiszewski, Senior Cataloger; Kimberly Nusco, Reference Librarian; Rakashi Chand and Carrie Supple, Assistant Reference Librarians; Nancy Heywood, Digital Projects Coordinator; and Anne E. Bentley, Curator of Art. Finally, we also greatly appreciate the contributions made by the Adams Papers Administrative Committee to the success of this project.

Guide to Editorial Apparatus

The first three sections (1–3) of this Guide list, respectively, the arbitrary devices used for clarifying the text, the code names for prominent members of the Adams family, and the symbols for the various kinds of manuscript originals used or referred to, which are employed throughout *The Adams Papers* in all its series and parts. The final three sections (4–6) list, respectively, the symbols for institutions holding original materials, the various abbreviations and conventional terms, and the short titles of books and other works that occur in volume 8 of the *Adams Family Correspondence*.

1. TEXTUAL DEVICES

The following devices will be used throughout *The Adams Papers* to clarify the presentation of the text.

[. . .]	One word missing or illegible.
[. . . .]	Two words missing or illegible.
[. . . .]¹	More than two words missing or illegible; subjoined footnote estimates amount of missing matter.
[ ]	Number or part of a number missing or illegible. Amount of blank space inside brackets approximates the number of missing or illegible digits.
[roman]	Conjectural reading for missing or illegible matter. A question mark is inserted before the closing bracket if the conjectural reading is seriously doubtful.
~~roman~~	Canceled matter.
[*italic*]	Editorial insertion.
{roman}	Text editorially decoded.

2. ADAMS FAMILY CODE NAMES

First Generation

JA	John Adams (1735–1826)
AA	Abigail Adams (1744–1818), *m.* JA 1764

Second Generation

AA2	Abigail Adams (1765–1813), daughter of JA and AA, *m.* WSS 1786
WSS	William Stephens Smith (1755–1816), brother of SSA
JQA	John Quincy Adams (1767–1848), son of JA and AA
LCA	Louisa Catherine Johnson (1775–1852), *m.* JQA 1797
CA	Charles Adams (1770–1800), son of JA and AA
SSA	Sarah Smith (1769–1828), sister of WSS, *m.* CA 1795
TBA	Thomas Boylston Adams (1772–1832), son of JA and AA
AHA	Ann Harrod (1774?–1845), *m.* TBA 1805

Adams Family Correspondence

Third Generation

GWA	George Washington Adams (1801–1829), son of JQA and LCA
JA2	John Adams (1803–1834), son of JQA and LCA
MCHA	Mary Catherine Hellen (1806–1870), *m.* JA2 1828
CFA	Charles Francis Adams (1807–1886), son of JQA and LCA
ABA	Abigail Brown Brooks (1808–1889), *m.* CFA 1829
ECA	Elizabeth Coombs Adams (1808–1903), daughter of TBA and AHA

Fourth Generation

LCA2	Louisa Catherine Adams (1831–1870), daughter of CFA and ABA, *m.* Charles Kuhn 1854
JQA2	John Quincy Adams (1833–1894), son of CFA and ABA
CFA2	Charles Francis Adams (1835–1915), son of CFA and ABA
HA	Henry Adams (1838–1918), son of CFA and ABA
MHA	Marian Hooper (1842–1885), *m.* HA 1872
MA	Mary Adams (1845–1928), daughter of CFA and ABA, *m.* Henry Parker Quincy 1877
BA	Brooks Adams (1848–1927), son of CFA and ABA

Fifth Generation

CFA3	Charles Francis Adams (1866–1954), son of JQA2
HA2	Henry Adams (1875–1951), son of CFA2
JA3	John Adams (1875–1964), son of CFA2

3. DESCRIPTIVE SYMBOLS

The following symbols are employed throughout *The Adams Papers* to describe or identify the various kinds of manuscript originals.

D	Diary (Used only to designate a diary written by a member of the Adams family and always in combination with the short form of the writer's name and a serial number, as follows: D/JA/23, i.e., the twenty-third fascicle or volume of John Adams' manuscript Diary.)
Dft	draft
Dupl	duplicate
FC	file copy (Ordinarily a copy of a letter retained by a correspondent *other than an Adams,* for example, Jefferson's press copies and polygraph copies, since all three of the Adams statesmen systematically entered copies of their outgoing letters in letterbooks.)
Lb	Letterbook (Used only to designate Adams letterbooks and always in combination with the short form of the writer's name and a serial number, as follows: Lb/JQA/29, i.e., the twenty-ninth volume of John Quincy Adams' Letterbooks.)
LbC	letterbook copy (Letterbook copies are normally unsigned, but any such copy is assumed to be in the hand of the person responsible for the text unless it is otherwise described.)

M	Miscellany (Used only to designate materials in the section of the Adams Papers known as the "Miscellany" and always in combination with the short form of the writer's name and a serial number, as follows: M/CFA/32, i.e., the thirty-second volume of the Charles Francis Adams Miscellany—a ledger volume mainly containing transcripts made by CFA in 1833 of selections from the family papers.)
MS, MSS	manuscript, manuscripts
RC	recipient's copy (A recipient's copy is assumed to be in the hand of the signer unless it is otherwise described.)
Tr	transcript (A copy, handwritten or typewritten, made substantially later than the original or other copies such as duplicates, file copies, or letterbook copies that were made contemporaneously.)
Tripl	triplicate

4. LOCATION SYMBOLS

DLC	Library of Congress
DSI	Smithsonian Institution
MeHi	Maine Historical Society
MB	Boston Public Library
MH-Ar	Harvard University Archives
MHi	Massachusetts Historical Society
MU	University of Massachusetts, Amherst
MWA	American Antiquarian Society
NjMoHP	Morristown National Historical Park
NAll	Albany Institute of History of Art
NHi	New-York Historical Society
NN	New York Public Library
NNC	Columbia University
ViMtvL	Mount Vernon Ladies' Association

5. OTHER ABBREVIATIONS AND CONVENTIONAL TERMS

Adams Papers

Manuscripts and other materials, 1639–1889, in the Adams Manuscript Trust collection given to the Massachusetts Historical Society in 1956 and enlarged by a few additions of family papers since then. Citations in the present edition are simply by date of the original document if the original is in the main chronological series of the Papers and therefore readily found in the microfilm edition of the Adams Papers (see below).

The Adams Papers

The present edition in letterpress, published by The Belknap Press of Harvard University Press. References to earlier volumes of any given unit take this form: vol. 2:146. Since there is no overall volume numbering for the edition, references from one series, or unit of a series, to another are by title, volume, and page, for example, JA, *D&A*, 4:205.

xlix

Adams Papers, Adams Office Manuscripts
> The portion of the Adams manuscripts given to the Massachusetts Historical Society by Thomas Boylston Adams in 1973.

APM
> Formerly, Adams Papers, Microfilms. The corpus of the Adams Papers, 1639–1889, as published on microfilm by the Massachusetts Historical Society, 1954–1959, in 608 reels. Cited in the present work, when necessary, by reel number. Available in research libraries throughout the United States and in a few libraries in Canada, Europe, and New Zealand.

Thwing Catalogue, MHi
> Annie Haven Thwing, comp., Inhabitants and Estates of the Town of Boston, 1630–1800; typed card catalogue, with supplementary bound typescripts, in the Massachusetts Historical Society. Published on CD-ROM with Annie Haven Thwing, *The Crooked and Narrow Streets of the Town of Boston, 1630–1822*, Massachusetts Historical Society and New England Historical and Genealogical Society, 2001.

6. SHORT TITLES OF WORKS FREQUENTLY CITED

AA, *New Letters*
> *New Letters of Abigail Adams, 1788–1801*, ed. Stewart Mitchell, Boston, 1947.

AA2, *Jour. and Corr.*
> *Journal and Correspondence of Miss Adams, Daughter of John Adams, . . . Edited by Her Daughter* [Caroline Amelia (Smith) de Windt], New York and London, 1841–[1849]; 3 vols.
>   Note: Vol. [1], unnumbered, has title and date: *Journal and Correspondence of Miss Adams*, 1841; vol. 2 has title, volume number, and date: *Correspondence of Miss Adams . . . Vol. II*, 1842; vol. [3] has title, volume number, and date: *Correspondence of Miss Adams . . . Vol. II*, 1842, i.e., same as vol. 2, but preface is signed "April 3d, 1849," and the volume contains as "Part II" a complete reprinting, from same type and with same pagination, of vol. 2, above, originally issued in 1842.

AFC
> *Adams Family Correspondence*, ed. L. H. Butterfield, Marc Friedlaender, Richard Alan Ryerson, Margaret A. Hogan, and others, Cambridge, 1963– .

ANB
> John A. Garraty, Mark C. Carnes, and Paul Betz, eds., *American National Biography*, New York, 1999–2002; 24 vols. plus supplement.

Ann. Register
> *The Annual Register; or, A View of the History, Politics, and Literature for the Year*, ed. Edmund Burke and others, London, 1758– .

Appletons' Cyclo. Amer. Biog.
> James Grant Wilson and John Fiske, eds., *Appletons' Cyclopædia of American Biography*, New York, 1887–1889; 6 vols.

Biog. Dir. Cong.
> *Biographical Directory of the United States Congress, 1774–1989*, Washington, 1989.

1

Guide to Editorial Apparatus

Boston Directory, [year]
Boston Directory, issued annually with varying imprints.

Boston, [vol. no.] Reports
City of Boston, Record Commissioners, *Reports*, Boston, 1876–1909; 39 vols.

Braintree Town Records
Records of the Town of Braintree, 1640 to 1793, ed. Samuel A. Bates, Randolph, Mass., 1886.

Brewer, Reader's Handbook
E. Cobham Brewer, *The Reader's Handbook of Famous Names in Fiction, Allusions, References, Proverbs, Plots, Stories, and Poems*, rev. edn., London, 1902.

Catalogue of JA's Library
Catalogue of the John Adams Library in the Public Library of the City of Boston, Boston, 1917.

CFA, Diary
Diary of Charles Francis Adams, ed. Aïda DiPace Donald, David Donald, Marc Friedlaender, L. H. Butterfield, and others, Cambridge, 1964– .

Colonial Collegians
Colonial Collegians: Biographies of Those Who Attended American Colleges before the War of Independence, CD-ROM, ed. Conrad E. Wright, Robert J. Dunkle, and others, Boston, 2005.

DAB
Allen Johnson, Dumas Malone, and others, eds., *Dictionary of American Biography*, New York, 1928–1936; repr. New York, 1955–1980; 10 vols. plus index and supplements.

Dexter, Yale Graduates
Franklin Bowditch Dexter, *Biographical Sketches of the Graduates of Yale College with Annals of the College History*, New York and New Haven, 1885–1912; 6 vols.

Dipl. Corr., 1783–1789
The Diplomatic Correspondence of the United States of America, from . . . 1783, to . . . 1789, [ed. William A. Weaver], repr. edn., Washington, 1837 [actually 1855]; 3 vols.

DNB
Leslie Stephen and Sidney Lee, eds., *The Dictionary of National Biography*, New York and London, 1885–1901; repr. Oxford, 1959–1960; 21 vols. plus supplements.

Doc. Hist. Ratif. Const.
The Documentary History of the Ratification of the Constitution, ed. Merrill Jensen, John P. Kaminski, Gaspare J. Saladino, and others, Madison, Wis., 1976– .

Doc. Hist. Supreme Court
The Documentary History of the Supreme Court of the United States, 1789–1800, ed. Maeva Marcus, James R. Perry, and others, New York, 1985– .

Evans
Charles Evans and others, *American Bibliography: A Chronological Dictionary of All Books, Pamphlets and Periodical Publications Printed in the United States of America [1639–1800]*, Chicago and Worcester, 1903–1959; 14 vols.

First Fed. Cong.
Documentary History of the First Federal Congress of the United States of America, March 4, 1789 – March 3, 1791, ed. Linda Grant De Pauw, Charlene Bangs Bickford,

Helen E. Veit, William C. diGiacomantonio, and Kenneth R. Bowling, Baltimore, 1972– .

First Fed. Elections
The Documentary History of the First Federal Elections, 1788–1790, ed. Merrill Jensen, Robert A. Becker, Gordon DenBoer, and others, Madison, Wis., 1976–1989; 4 vols.

Fleet's Pocket Almanack, [year]
Fleet's Register, and Pocket Almanack, Boston, 1779–1800; 22 vols.

Fowler, Baron of Beacon Hill
William M. Fowler Jr., The Baron of Beacon Hill: A Biography of John Hancock, Boston, 1980.

Grandmother Tyler's Book
Grandmother Tyler's Book: The Recollections of Mary Palmer Tyler (Mrs. Royall Tyler), 1775–1866, ed. Frederick Tupper and Helen Tyler Brown, New York and London, 1925.

Greenleaf, Greenleaf Family
James Edward Greenleaf, comp., Genealogy of the Greenleaf Family, Boston, 1896.

Grove Dicy. of Art
Jane Turner, ed., The Dictionary of Art, New York, 1996; 34 vols.

Hamilton, Papers
The Papers of Alexander Hamilton, ed. Harold C. Syrett, Jacob E. Cooke, and others, New York, 1961–1987; 27 vols.

Haraszti, Prophets
Zoltán Haraszti, John Adams and the Prophets of Progress, Cambridge, 1952.

Harvard Quinquennial Cat.
Harvard University, Quinquennial Catalogue of the Officers and Graduates, 1636–1930, Cambridge, 1930.

History of Hingham
History of the Town of Hingham, Massachusetts, Hingham, 1893; 3 vols. in 4.

History of Weymouth
History of Weymouth Massachusetts, Weymouth, 1923; 4 vols.

Hoefer, Nouv. biog. générale
J. C. F. Hoefer, ed., Nouvelle biographie générale depuis les temps les plus reculés jusqu'à nos jours, Paris, 1852–1866; 46 vols.

JA, D&A
Diary and Autobiography of John Adams, ed. L. H. Butterfield and others, Cambridge, 1961; 4 vols.

JA, Defence of the Const.
John Adams, A Defence of the Constitutions of Government of the United States of America, London, 1787–1788; repr. New York, 1971; 3 vols.

JA, Earliest Diary
The Earliest Diary of John Adams, ed. L. H. Butterfield and others, Cambridge, 1966.

JA, Legal Papers
Legal Papers of John Adams, ed. L. Kinvin Wroth and Hiller B. Zobel, Cambridge, 1965; 3 vols.

JA, *Papers*
　　Papers of John Adams, ed. Robert J. Taylor, Gregg L. Lint, and others, Cambridge, 1977– .

JA, *Works*
　　The Works of John Adams, Second President of the United States: with a Life of the Author, ed. Charles Francis Adams, Boston, 1850–1856; 10 vols.

JAH
　　Journal of American History.

JCC
　　Journals of the Continental Congress, 1774–1789, ed. Worthington Chauncey Ford, Gaillard Hunt, John C. Fitzpatrick, Roscoe R. Hill, and others, Washington, 1904–1937; 34 vols.

Jefferson, *Papers*
　　The Papers of Thomas Jefferson, ed. Julian P. Boyd, Charles T. Cullen, John Catanzariti, Barbara B. Oberg, and others, Princeton, 1950– .

JQA, *Diary*
　　Diary of John Quincy Adams, ed. David Grayson Allen, Robert J. Taylor, and others, Cambridge, 1981– .

Laurens, *Papers*
　　The Papers of Henry Laurens, ed. Philip M. Hamer, George C. Rogers Jr., David R. Chesnutt, C. James Taylor, and others, Columbia, S.C., 1968–2003; 16 vols.

Malone, *Jefferson*
　　Dumas Malone, *Jefferson and His Time*, Boston, 1948–1981; 6 vols.

Mass., *Acts and Laws*
　　Acts and Laws of the Commonwealth of Massachusetts [1780–1805], Boston, 1890–1898; 13 vols.

Mass., *House Jour.*
　　Journals of the House of Representatives of Massachusetts [1715–1779], Boston, 1919–1990; 55 vols.

MHS, *Colls., Procs.*
　　Massachusetts Historical Society, *Collections* and *Proceedings.*

Morison, *Three Centuries of Harvard*
　　Samuel Eliot Morison, *Three Centuries of Harvard, 1636–1936*, Cambridge, 1936.

MVHR
　　Mississippi Valley Historical Review.

Namier and Brooke, *House of Commons*
　　Sir Lewis Namier and John Brooke, eds., *The House of Commons, 1754–1790*, London, 1964; 3 vols.

NEHGR
　　New England Historical and Genealogical Register.

Nieuw Ned. Biog. Woordenboek
　　P. C. Molhuysen and others, eds., *Nieuw Nederlandsch Biografisch Woordenboek*, Leyden, 1911–1937; 10 vols.

Notable Amer. Women
　　Edward T. James and others, eds., *Notable American Women, 1607–1950: A Biographical Dictionary*, Cambridge, 1971; 3 vols.

NYGBR
> New York Genealogical and Biographical Record.

OED
> The Oxford English Dictionary, 2d edn., Oxford, 1989; 20 vols.

Oxford Classical Dicy.
> Simon Hornblower and Antony Spawforth, eds., *The Oxford Classical Dictionary*, 3d edn., New York, 1996.

Parliamentary Hist.
> The Parliamentary History of England, from the Earliest Period to the Year 1803, London, 1806–1820; 36 vols.

Pattee, *Old Braintree*
> William S. Pattee, *A History of Old Braintree and Quincy, with a Sketch of Randolph and Holbrook*, Quincy, 1878.

PMHB
> Pennsylvania Magazine of History and Biography.

Princetonians
> James McLachlan, Richard A. Harrison, Ruth L. Woodward, Wesley Frank Craven, and J. Jefferson Looney, *Princetonians: A Biographical Dictionary*, Princeton, 1976–1991; 5 vols.

Repertorium
> Ludwig Bittner and others, eds., *Repertorium der diplomatischen Vertreter aller Länder seit dem Westfälischen Frieden (1648)*, Oldenburg, &c., 1936–1965; 3 vols.

Roof, *Smith and Lady*
> Katharine Metcalf Roof, *Colonel William Smith and Lady: The Romance of Washington's Aide and Young Abigail Adams*, Boston, 1929.

Sabine, *Loyalists*
> Lorenzo Sabine, *Biographical Sketches of Loyalists of the American Revolution*, rev. edn. by Gregory Palmer, Westport, Conn., 1984.

Schama, *Citizens*
> Simon Schama, *Citizens: A Chronicle of the French Revolution*, New York, 1989.

Schama, *Patriots and Liberators*
> Simon Schama, *Patriots and Liberators: Revolution in the Netherlands 1780–1813*, New York, 1977.

SCHGM
> South Carolina Historical and Genealogical Magazine.

Sibley's Harvard Graduates
> John Langdon Sibley, Clifford K. Shipton, Conrad Edick Wright, Edward W. Hanson, and others, *Biographical Sketches of Graduates of Harvard University, in Cambridge, Massachusetts*, Cambridge and Boston, 1873– .

Smith, *Letters of Delegates*
> Letters of Delegates to Congress, 1774–1789, ed. Paul H. Smith and others, Washington, 1976–2000; 26 vols.

Sprague, *Annals Amer. Pulpit*
> William B. Sprague, *Annals of the American Pulpit; or, Commemorative Notices of Distinguished American Clergymen of Various Denominations*, New York, 1857–1869; 9 vols.

Sprague, *Braintree Families*
> Waldo Chamberlain Sprague, comp., *Genealogies of the Families of Braintree, Mass., 1640–1850*, Boston, 1983; repr. CD-ROM, Boston, 2001.

Stokes, *Iconography of Manhattan*
> I. N. Phelps Stokes, *The Iconography of Manhattan Island, 1498–1909*, New York, 1915–1928; 6 vols.

Suffolk County Deeds
> Registry of Deeds for Suffolk County, Boston, Massachusetts, 1639– .

Trumbull, *Autobiography*
> *The Autobiography of Colonel John Trumbull, Patriot-Artist, 1756–1843*, ed. Theodore Sizer, New Haven, 1953.

U.S. Census, 1790
> *Heads of Families at the First Census of the United States Taken in the Year 1790*, Washington, 1907–1908; 12 vols.

U.S. *Statutes at Large*
> *The Public Statutes at Large of the United States of America, 1789– *, Boston and Washington, 1845– .

VMHB
> *Virginia Magazine of History and Biography.*

Warren-Adams Letters
> *Warren-Adams Letters: Being Chiefly a Correspondence among John Adams, Samuel Adams, and James Warren* (Massachusetts Historical Society, *Collections*, vol. 72–73), Boston, 1917–1925; 2 vols.

Washington, *Diaries*
> *The Diaries of George Washington*, ed. Donald Jackson and Dorothy Twohig, Charlottesville, 1976–1979; 6 vols.

Washington, *Papers, Confederation Series*
> *The Papers of George Washington: Confederation Series*, ed. W. W. Abbot and others, Charlottesville, 1992–1997; 6 vols.

Washington, *Papers, Presidential Series*
> *The Papers of George Washington: Presidential Series*, ed. Dorothy Twohig, Mark A. Mastromarino, Jack D. Warren, Robert F. Haggard, Christine S. Patrick, John C. Pinheiro, and others, Charlottesville, 1987– .

Weis, *Colonial Clergy of N.E.*
> Frederick Lewis Weis, *The Colonial Clergy and the Colonial Churches of New England*, Lancaster, Mass., 1936.

Winter, *Amer. Finance and Dutch Investment*
> Pieter J. van Winter and James C. Riley, *American Finance and Dutch Investment, 1780–1805*, New York, 1977; 2 vols.

Young, *Night Thoughts*
> Edward Young, *The Complaint; or, Night Thoughts on Life, Death, and Immortality: In Nine Nights.*

VOLUME 8

Family Correspondence

March 1787 – December 1789

Adams Family Correspondence

Abigail Adams to John Cranch

Dear sir;   London, March 7. 1787:[1]

your obliging Letter of November 7[th.] came safe to hand, as well
as a couple of Hares since Received, for which accept my acknowledgments:[2]

I was happy to find that the Books I sent were acceptable to you,
tho they painted some of your Countrymen in very black coulours;
and one cannot refrain from being affected by the disgraces brought
upon their Country from the evil conduct of it's Members, tho they
abhor the measures & detest the Authors[.][3]

I wish I could say that a Change of Administration since the
peace, had effected a change of sentiment with respect to America,
but this Nation, sir, is still persueing measures which daily, more &
more, alienate America from her; & force her into a closer connection with France:[4] how much this will benefit England, time will
discover:

I take the Liberty of sending you a late publication stiled the defence of the American Constitutions,[5] which have been attacked, as
you will see, by great Men: how ably they are defended the publick
will judge; but something appeard necessary at this time to settle
the minds of the Americans, who appear to feel inconveniencies
without tracing them to their true source: it will perhaps afford you
some amusement, not only as a Friend to America, but to the Liberties of mankind[6]

By the latest accounts from America (the 10 of Febry)[7] general
Lincoln had marched against the insurgents dispersed and quelld
them; so that I hope they will no longer impede the course of Justice, or disturb the good order of society. Ebullitions of this kind will
break out in all free governments, like humours in a Healthy Body;
but I presume they cannot proceed to any dangerous height—

1

Mr and Mrs Smith present their compliments and thanks for your kind congratulations. Mr Adams joins me in ye sentiments of Esteem and / Regard with which I am / Dear sir your Humble Servant

A Adams

RC (MB:Dept. of Rare Books and Manuscripts); addressed by AA2: "John Cranch. Esqr. / Axminster."; endorsed: "7. March 1787– / From the lady Ambass: / Adams." Dft (Adams Papers), filmed at 5 March.

¹ "March 5th" in Dft.

² Vol. 7:389–390.

³ See AA to John Cranch, 21 Oct. 1786, and note 3, vol. 7:378–379.

⁴ At this point in the Dft, the following passage was struck out: "they will not enter into a treaty with America nor have they deignd to send a minister in return for the one sent to this court. the concequence will be a recall of the American minister and I can truly say the sooner that event takes place the more agreeable it will be to me, tho there are individuals in this Nation for whom

I Shall ever entertain the highest respect & esteem."

⁵ For JA's *Defence of the Const.*, see AA to Cotton Tufts, 10 Oct., note 14, vol. 7:365–366.

⁶ In the Dft the first sentence of the following paragraph reads, "by my last Letters from America our friends were well, tho some what troubled by a number of insurgents who had molested the peace & good order of society by unlawfully assembling & stopping the courts of justice."

⁷ See AA to Mary Smith Cranch, 8 March 1787, note 2, below.

Abigail Adams to Mary Smith Cranch

My dear sister   London March 8. 1787

It was not untill yesterday that captain Callihan brought us the bundle containing Newspapers and some Letters, one from my Neice, but none from you tho you refer to a former one in that which I acknowledg'd the recept of by captain Barnard,¹ the New york packet arrived in 18 days passage & mr Adams received Letters to the 10 of Feb^ry & a Boston paper of the 5th by which we have an account of general Lincolns success.² I lament that so atrocious an offender as shays should escape least he should in future create more disturbances; the measures which government appear now to persue will give a permanancy to it, and I hope suppress every tendency to future Rebellion, at the same time that every rational & reasonable redress of grievences will be granted, that the community in general are suffering from a want of confidence in the publick Faith is a Sorrowfull Truth, and this distrust creates an artificial scarcity of a circulating medium, could confidence be restored, you would soon find this evil diminished;

I have written you so lately that I have little to add. The Winter here has been remarkably mild & the verdure upon the ground is equal to what we have in May. I wish you would get somebody to take the dimensions & shape of a floor Cloth for our little parlour at Braintree, and the room next to it, they are so much better prepaird here painted years before they are worn that they wear forever tho dear— so you see that I am thinking Seriously of returning to you & trimming my little cottage once more. Should I ever have a better I will rejoice if I cannot I will be content, the Education of my children is more at my Heart than any other object.

I have Sent by captain Scot a couple of small Chamber Lamps which I have found very usefull, & two Boxes of wicks, one be so good as to send to sister shaw, the other is for your self & if your oil is good it will burn 3 Nights with the same wick. I have also sent you Lutestring for a gown. I deliberated some time whether to send you that or a peice of Linnen upon the whole I concluded to send the silk as it was an article I knew you would not purchase tho you might want it ever so much. The green is for you & the Blew for sister Shaw. You will use your prudence either to make it up, or let it lie by till more favourable times. I do not expect to have it in my power to shew you in future how gratefull I feel towards you for all your motherly kindness to my dear Boys, in any thing more than words but you know my Heart.— You will trouble me exceedingly if you express any anxiety on account of Charging the Board of the Children—³ do I not know my sister? do I not know the difficulty of the times I do know very well your prudence your oeconomy & that of my dear Neices, and at the same time I am sensible of your generous disposition and of that care and attention to me and mine which cannot be estimated by pounds & shillings.

I will write to my Neices if I have time before Scot sails adieu my dear / Sister, most affectionatly / yours   A A

March 10th

I send some old stockings to you for mrs Payne—

RC (MWA:Abigail Adams Letters); addressed by WSS: "Mʳˢ: Mary Cranch / Braintree."

¹AA had not yet received Mary Smith Cranch's letter of 31 Dec. 1786, one of at least two Cranch sent to AA by Callahan; see Cranch to AA, 31 Dec. 1786, 10 Jan. 1787, and [*post* 10 *Jan.*], vol. 7:420–423, 430–433.

²For the newspapers the Adamses had received regarding Shays' Rebellion, see Cotton Tufts to AA, 6 Feb., and note 3, vol. 7:458–459. The letters conveyed to JA from the New York packet probably included ones of 9 and 10 Feb. from Rufus King, the former of which contained various enclosures on the rebellion, including copies of Thomas Dwight to Rufus King, 1 Feb.; Luke Day to Gen. William Shepard, 25 Jan.; and Luke Day to Daniel Shays, 25 Jan. (all Adams Papers).

³For discussion of board for the Adams boys, see vol. 7:433, 473.

Abigail Adams to Elizabeth Smith Shaw

My dear Sister   London March 10 1787

Tho I have already acknowledged all your Letters, I will not let captain Scoet sail without a few lines from me, I had not time to write you by Barnard, but Cushing had Letters for you

I write now to inform you, that the more quarrelsome and turbulent you grow, the more anxious I am to be with you, not that I think it pleasent fishing in troubled waters, but because immaginacion paints higher than reality, and the danger apprehended is always worse than that which is experienced, in short I have seen my Countrymen armed one against the other, and the divided house falling to the ground.

Blessed are the peacemakers said a great Authority, for they restore harmony in which all nature delights, order is heavens first Law. if there was not a much greater proportion of good than evil predominating in the World, who could suffer being here below? if as a good divine observed those objects which administer to our delight and comfort, had been created merely to anoy & harrass us, then we might have had some reason to complain that the evils we sufferd were not oweing to our blindness and folly; if that had been the design of providence, the Bee would have been without her Honey & the rose devoid of its fragrance, the feilds would have been destitute of their Chearfull green & gay flowers the Fire would have scorched instead of warming us, and the Light of day dazzeld without cheering us. every Breath of air would have cut us like the point of a sword, every taste would have been a bitter & every sound a Scream, every sense would have been a torment instead of a pleasure, but the real state of things is totally different, & the Benificent Creater made all things good. Tis man alone who perverts his Laws & creates the evils which he justly suffers.

but whither am I running? I took my pen to tell you, that God willing, I hope to see you in the course of an other Year, as we are *determined* to return to America and share the fate of our Country whether she stand firm like mount Atlass—or make it treason to harbour an Idea that she will fall—trip & stumble, I fear, but as uncle Toby said on an other occasion—She Shall not fall.[1]

pray how does my worthy good Friend mr Thaxter do? I am very much in his debt, I know he is a good patriot in these times, be-

4

cause he is an honest Man. my Love to him, and to my old friend mrs Allen. tell her I hope one Day to see her in her own habitation, and upon the first intimation of an heir, I will send her the Christning cap. I am rejoiced to find by your account that she is so happily situated.

I have sent you by captain Scot a little chamber Lamp, which with a small quantity of oil; burns the whole night. I found them very usefull to me, & thought they would prove so to my sisters. I have also sent you a peice of silk, I was deliberating some time whether it should be virgin white; or sky blew, upon the whole I concluded that you had more pretentions to the Skys; than to the Appellation annexed to the White, so I bought the blew, which is *vastly the* present taste. I hope it will meet your approbation, as I have already fancied how well it will become you, & how pretty you will look in it, no trimming is used at all, unless a narrow white ribbon down the Sides. The Aprons are made very *dressy* of gauze with a lace round them & white ribbon crimped in pleats, an other row a quarter from the bottom & little flowers stuck between— black lace is much worn both on handkerchiefs & Aprons. handkerchiefs very bustly no great change since last year; caps as many forms as fancy can devize; so you have a subject for your Haverhill Bells, I believe the silk is a prohibited article, so you must keep the secret;[2] I hope my little nephew has got his Books, & my Neice her skirt,[3] perhaps the Next time I write you I may be turnd into a *grandame*[4] as it is now a fine sunshine day, and my spirits tolerably, good; I do not feel so ancient as that event will make me,[5] Mrs Smith is now sitting by the table trimming with lace a white muslin slip, round the neck; & sleaves; & looking as sober as a Deaconess; she would grumble a little if she knew I had been writing of her.— she is very well and sends her duty to you; Mr. Adams is still buisy in writing, whether for the publick; will depend upon the reception his Book already gone into the World; meets with[6]

adieu my dear Sister— remember me kindly to all your Haverhill Friends judge Sergants family in a particular manner & to mrs White and believe me with the sincerest affection / yours

A Adams

N.B

all the cocks tails round London for 50 miles have been robbed to decorate the Ladies Caps. The long feathers amounting to 6 or 8 are tied in a bunch & worn at the side of the cap & are sold from half a Guiney to 18 shillings sterling a bunch, an excellent commodity for exportation, have you any old cocks?

RC (DLC:Shaw Family Papers). Dft (Adams Papers).

¹ Probably a paraphrase of Laurence Sterne's *The Life and Opinions of Tristram Shandy*, vol. 6, chap. 8, in which Uncle Toby vehemently responds, "He shall march. . . . He shall be supported. . . . He shall not drop. . . . He shall not die," when Trim suggests that Lt. LeFever will fall if he returns to his regiment.

² Silk was taxed but not prohibited (Mass., *Acts and Laws*, 1786–1787, p. 117).

³ See AA to Elizabeth Smith Shaw, 20 Jan., vol. 7:453.

⁴ AA became a grandmother for the first time on 2 April, when AA2 gave birth to a son, William Steuben Smith, at Grosvenor Square.

⁵ The Dft concludes with the following: "Mr & Mrs Smith join me in Love affection & esteem for you & family. she is just gone out to ride & is now very well but I do not expect that she will keep about longer than April as the Book of futurity is closed from the Eyes of Mortals, let us thankfully enjoy the present & commit the future to the all wise arbiter of events fully satified with the wisdom of the government & the justice of its dispensations. This temper of mind I wish ever to possess— commend me to my good Brother Shaw & remember me kindly to all Who inquire after."

⁶ JA's second volume of the *Defence of the Const.* was published in August.

Abigail Adams to Cotton Tufts

Dear sir   London March 10ᵗʰ 1787

your Letters by Captain Callihan did not come to hand untill the 7ᵗʰ ult. and I embrace the earliest opportunity of writing you.¹ in yours you mention the account forwarded by you last fall, which was duly received, and I thought it had been acknowledged; I sometimes leave these matters in hopes mr Adams will notice them, but he is too much engaged in publick affairs, to attend at all, to his private buisness, by which means he is often a sufferer I believe History will scarcly find an instance of a person who have held the distinguishd offices that he has been employd in for ten years past, borrowed and transmitted such sums of money as he has, & received so little advantage from it, if he had received only one single pr cent, he would have been in possession of an handsome fortune,—but thus it is.— by captain Cushing I transmitted you the acct which I mentiond to you. it is hard to pay money here at a loss of a years interest, as well as the advance upon Bills for those who think no more of it. records & papers are not to be searched & procured here for any trifling sum; you will find by captain Barnard an accompt & Rect to the amount of 35 guineys advanced to mr Cutting on account of mr McKean chief Justice of the state of Deleware. this money is also advanced to search records at his request, &

promise to pay the Bill upon sight, I hope you meet with no further trouble than the distance of negotiating it.[2] there are fifty six guineys which I look upon wholy lost, which under various pretences & promises of immediate payment, upon the arrival of a mr Noyes, have been lent to col Norten, but really and in truth Swindled out of us. I was very loth he should have it, particularly the last but mr Adams believed him, till to his cost, he found himself deceived. he has made every American tributary to him, been once in Newgate, from whence he was relieved by their subscriptions, and is now shufling about living no one knows how. he has quite left our House mr A having dealt very freely with him, & represented the disgrace he was bringing upon his state & Country.[3] has he any property in America? I fear not, and that we shall lose the whole.

mr Elworthys Bill will be answerd immediatly, but mr Adams wishes you in future to make an even sum when you draw either for one or two hundred guineys, as that is our usual method of taking from the Banker, and do not let us be in debt, rather keep a sum before hand in your Hands— I am sorry for the Luck of our House, but suppose it is oweing to the Times— the paper of America will be redeemed I have no doubt, but one must wait for interest, & run risks, but at all events it will fetch what is given for it. I hope the affairs of our Country will wear a more favourable aspect. many of the difficulties you experience must arise from want of publick confidence. could that be restored, your paper would rise in value. I wonder land should sell so dear when specie is so scarce. by the New York packet we learn the dispersion of the insurgents. I wish there may be an end of the troubles—but has our government exerted itself with that vigor and dignity which it ought to have done? why has it addrest when it ought to have commanded. why has it submitted to insults which it ought to have punished. Honestus is realy become a partizan for government. he first kindled & fomented the storm, & to his publications may be in a great measure attributed, the very resistance against the courts of justice which has now risen to a Rebellion—[4]

But I quit a subject so unpleasent to assure you of my best and warmest Regard and / the affection with which / I am dear sir your / Neice   A Adams

RC (NjMoHP); addressed by WSS: "The / Honourable / Cotton Tufts Esquire / Boston"; endorsed: "M^rs: Adams Lett of / March 10. 1787— rc^d April 27—" and "rec^d. the 27 April."

[1] Cotton Tufts to AA, 14 Oct. 1786 and 2 Jan. 1787, vol. 7:370–372, 423–426.

[2] Thomas McKean (1734–1817) held multiple political positions and appointments throughout his life, some simultaneously in two states, notably in Delaware as a member of the Continental Congress from 1774 to 1783 and Pennsylvania as chief justice from 1777 to 1799. He never, however, served as chief justice of Delaware. Dr. John Brown Cutting, who had recently arrived in London to study law at the Inner Temple, was advanced money by JA for probate searches and traveling expenses necessary to recover the estate of William Atlee, father of William Augustus Atlee, senior justice of the Supreme Court of Pennsylvania and McKean's friend (*DAB*; vol. 7:122, note 8; Thomas McKean to JA, 1 July 1786, John Brown Cutting to JA, 13 Dec., and Thomas McKean to JA, 30 April 1787, all Adams Papers).

[3] Col. Beriah Norton of Martha's Vineyard was in London on behalf of the Vineyard's residents attempting to reclaim their property losses from the war. After several unsuc-

cessful years, the residents accused Norton of lavish spending and dereliction of duty. He wrote to JA in Nov. 1786 asking for a meeting to defend himself against claims of misconduct. Dr. Nathaniel Noyes, an apothecary from Boston, had previously accompanied Norton to visit the Adamses in July 1785, although their relationship is unclear. Noyes, too, was trying to recover property losses, but he appeared to be working on his own behalf (Charles Edward Banks, *The History of Martha's Vineyard*, 3 vols., Boston, 1911–1925; Samuel Adams to JA, 17 April 1784, Adams Papers; JA to Samuel Adams, 25 June, NN:George Bancroft Coll.; Beriah Norton to JA, 27 Nov. [1786?], Adams Papers; vol. 6:207, 7:9; *Sibley's Harvard Graduates*, 15:439–442).

[4] AA blamed Honestus' (Benjamin Austin Jr.) 1786 publication *Observations on the Pernicious Practice of the Law*, taken from a series of articles in the Boston *Independent Chronicle*, for Shays' Rebellion. He was elected to the state senate from Suffolk County in 1787 and again from 1789 to 1794 (*DAB*; vol. 7:168, 170).

Abigail Adams to Isaac Smith Sr.

My dear sir   London March 12th 1787

I have sent by Captain Scott the Books you wrote for,[1] and if there is any thing else in which I can serve either you or my cousins, I shall be happy to do it—

it is with much pleasure I learn that my cousin W.S. is like to be so pleasingly connected, and with a family to whom both you, & my Late parent, were much attached by a long accquaintance, and established Friendship.[2] Educated under virtuous parents, & possessing an amiable dispositions are pleasing presages, of a happy union: they have my best wishes for their prosperity. I thank you sir for extending to my Children, the same indulgence, you and my late dear Aunt confered upon me. your House was always the habitation of Hospitality; and ever seemed to me a Home. tho I doubt not of your continued kindness; it can never be to me what it once was; the loss we have both sustained, cannot be repaired.

By way of Newyork we have received accounts of General Lincolns success in dispercing the insurgents. I fear my Countrymen do not know, properly to estimate the blessings they enjoy. if they are harder-prest by publick burdens than formerly,[3] they should consider it as the price of their freedom. if Britain had succeeded against us, the same scenes would probably, have taken place, as have been acted in India, for we have no reason to doubt but that England could have produced more than one Hastings—[4]

Mr Adams is seriously determined to return Home, & has informd Congress of his design.[5] since England has wholy forgotten that Such a place as America ever existed, it is a pitty to take any pains to refresh their memory; every Member in the House of commons Majority and minority studiously avoid the subject, & when it was forced upon them by the publication of monssieur de callone Letter; they noticed it only, as a proof of the subtlety and duplicity as they termd it, of the Court of France, & gave America the go by[6]

By all accounts from America your winter has been terrible.[7] I hope you have had snow enough to suffice for several. I know not how I shall bear the Heats and colds, after an abscence of three years. the season has been uncommonly mild here, and the Trees have already budded & are bursting into Blosom. the verdure is equal to june with us.[8] this has commonly been called a foggy Island. it is true that the Smoke of the city creates a fog, but go only one mile into the Country, and you will have as fine weather, and clear a sky as we can boast in America nor do I think the climate more Subject to fogs, if the manners of the people, were as pure as their Air, no one would have reason to complain.

please to present my regards to mr & mrs otis to cousin Betsy & the mr Smiths. mr Vassel and family drank tea & spent the Evening, with us last week. they inquired very kindly after you, so did mr John Boylstone who was my Gallant during my stay at Bath. he bears his age surprizingly well. mr storers family I hope are well; I am indebted to Charles, will write him soon

I am dear sir with Sentiments of Esteem and affection—your Neice   A Adams

RC (MHi:Smith-Carter Family Papers); addressed by WSS: "To— / Isaac Smith Esquire / Boston—"; notation by WSS: "fav^d. by / Capt. Scott." Dft (Adams Papers), filmed at [1787].

¹ Not found.

² For the marriage of William Smith and Hannah Carter, see vol. 7:422–423, and note 4.

³ In the Dft, AA completed the paragraph with the following: "Still they have bread to eat & rayment to cloath them, provided they will labour—let only behold the poor of Europe, & they would have reason to be Silent."

⁴ For Warren Hastings, former governor-general of British India, and his trial for corruption, see Descriptive List of Illustrations, No. 6, above.

⁵ JA tendered his resignation to Congress on 24 Jan. 1787; see vol. 7:471, 474.

⁶ Charles Alexandre de Calonne, comptroller general of the finances of France, sent a letter on 22 Oct. 1786 to Thomas Jefferson detailing a plan for improved commercial relations between the United States and

France. The letter was published in the New York *Independent Journal*, 30 Dec., and read before the British House of Commons in late Feb. 1787, after which it was reprinted in the London newspapers (*Dipl. Corr., 1783–1789*, 1:827–829; London *Daily Universal Register*, 23 Feb.).

[7] The winter of 1786–1787 in the Northeast was notable for three early and very heavy snowstorms in December. Boston, Nan-

tucket, and Newport were badly damaged, and all of eastern Massachusetts experienced severe cold (David M. Ludlum, *Early American Winters, 1604–1820*, Boston, 1966, p. 68–72). See also vol. 7:400, 401–402, 421, 434, 458, 460; JQA, *Diary*, 2:136–139.

[8] At this point in the Dft, AA included the following: "but most people fear that the fruit will be cut of."

Abigail Adams to Thomas Boylston Adams

Dear Tommy London March 15th 1787

I would not omit writing you, because you seem to think you have been agrieved. I do not recollect what I wrote you, but I have Some Idea, that it was an enumeration of the various accidents you had met with, and advising you to more care and attention in future.[1] I had no occasion to chide you for want of application to your studies, because your uncles your Aunts & your Brothers had been witnesses for you, and all of them had Spoken well of you. it has indeed been a great and an abundant pleasure both to your Father & to me to hear the repeated & constant testimony of all our Friends with regard to the conduct of all our Sons, and I flatter myself that what ever else may be our lot & portion in Life, that of undutifull and vicious children will not be added to it.— Not only youth but maturer age is too often influenced by bad exampls, and it requires much reason much experience firmness & resolution to stem the torrent of fashion & to preserve the integrity which will bear the Scrutiny of our own Hearts. virtue like the stone of Sysiphus has a continual tendency to roll down Hill & requires to be forced up again by the never ceasing Efforts of succeeding moralists. if humane nature is thus infirm & liable to err as daily experience proves let every effort be made to acquire strength. nature has implanted in the humane mind nice sensibilities of moral rectitude and a natural love of excellence & given to it powers capable of infinate improvement and the state of things is so constituted that Labour well bestowed & properly directed always produces valuable Effects. the resolution you have taken of persueing such a conduct as shall redound to your own honour & that of your family is truly commendable. it is an old & just observation, that by aiming at perfection we may approach it much more nearly than if we sat down inactive through despair—

you will do well to join the military company as soon as you are qualified. every citizen should learn the use of arms & by being thus qualified he will be less likely to be calld to the use of them.[2] War cannot be ranked amongsts the liberal arts, and must ever be considerd as a scourge & a calamity, & should Humiliate the pride of man that he is thus capable of destroying his fellow creatures— I am glad to find you mending in your hand writing, during the vacancies you & your Brother Charles would do well to attend to that. it is of more importance than perhaps you are aware of, more for a Man than a Woman, but I have always to lament my own inattention in this matter. inclosed you will find a little matter which you will make a good use of. your sister sends her Love and will write you soon. I am my dear Son / most affectionately / Yours   A A

Dft (Adams Papers); docketed by AA: "Thomas Adams / March 15 1787."

[1] This is the earliest extant letter from AA to TBA and the only one from the 1780s. No letters from TBA to AA prior to 1792 have been found.

[2] AA probably refers to Harvard College's Marti-Mercurian Band, though her suggestion that TBA join this military company is unique in her extant letters to her sons. JQA mentions the company several times in his Diary during his Harvard years but always as an observer rather than as a member. The company never saw action, and though members wanted to march against the Shays insurgents, they were not permitted to do so (vol. 7:398, 401; JQA, *Diary*, 2:57, 58–59, 95, 103, 185, 190, 236).

Abigail Adams to John Quincy Adams

My dear Son   London March th 20th 1787

I have procured the Books for you, and Captain Folger not sailing quite so soon as I expected, I have sent them to mr Boylstones Store requesting him to send them for me.[1] I think it would be worth while to inquire at the post office in Boston with regard to the other Books which were put into the Bag with the Letters, & must have gone to the post office, or have been taking out, before they went from the NewEngland coffe House. I cannot think they were, because I allways carry or send what ever Letters or packages are going by any of the captains to that House; & leave them in the care of the Waiter, & I never lost any thing before. if you should find them give one Set to your cousin Cranch— your sister has not received any Letter from you, tho in yours to me, you mention writing her.[2] the Younger captain Folger is just arrived & with him mr Gill, whom I have not yet seen.[3] he was asked to dine with us yesterday, but being prengaged could not come. Cushing Barnard & Scot who have all sailed; had letters for you; I hope you got one which I wrote you by way of N^wyork during the winter.[4] Col Smith by order of congress is going to Pourtugal upon Buisness as soon as your sister gets to Bed which I expect she will the begining of April.[5]

Callihan will sail in April by whom I hope to write you agreeable intelligence with respect to her—

I have written to your Brothers by mr Martin who sails with captain Folger.[6] I quite long to return to America. pray how does my old friend mrs dana? give my Love to her when you see her & my respects to Madam Winthrope. I fear you will grew too Indolent. I very Seldom hear of you at Boston or any where out of colledge your Blood will grew thick & you will be sick. your Pappa is sure of it. he is always preaching up excercise to me and it would be a very usefull doctrine if I sufficiently attended to it. I was afflicted last fall with a slew nervous fever attended with Rhumatick complaints, and I am now labouring under the same disorder for several days past, except that it is not attended with the Rhumatism. as soon as I can get the better of it I am determined to be very punctual in daily walking— your pappa enjoys better Health than I believe he has for many years, reads & writes every Evening; which you know he could not do in France before this reaches you, his Book will have arrived. I should like to know its reception.[7] I tell him they will think in America that he is for sitting up a King. he says no, but he is for giving to the Governours of every state the same Authority which the British King has, under the true British constitution, balancing his power by the two other Branches—

I only intended you a line, but how I have spun—adieu

your affectionately   A A

RC (Adams Papers); addressed by AA2: "To / Mr John Quincy Adams / student at Cambridge / Near Boston"; endorsed: "My Mother 20. March 1787" and "M^{rs:} Adams March 20^{th:} 1787"; notation: "pr captain / Folger."

[1] Thomas Boylston, a merchant and sugar refiner, operated out of Paul's Wharf, 25 Upper Thames Street, London (MHi:Boylston Family Papers, Box 18, letters of 20, 27 March).

[2] In JQA's letter to AA of 30 Dec. 1786, he expressed an intention to write to AA2. He wrote the letter on 14 Jan. 1787, but AA2 did not acknowledge it until 10 June (vol. 7:417–420, 433–440; AA2 to JQA, 10 June, below).

[3] There were two Captain Folgers plying the waters between Boston and London in 1787, George Sr. of the brig *Diana* and George Jr. of the ship *Rebecca*. Possibly they were George Folger Sr. (1730–1813) and his son George Jr. (1756–1809) of Nantucket and

Dartmouth. George Sr. left Boston for London in the *Diana* on 10 Feb.; George Jr. returned to Boston from England in the *Rebecca* on 21 May (*Vital Records of Nantucket, Massachusetts, to the Year 1850*, 5 vols., Boston, 1925–1928, 1:480, 5:263; *Vital Records of Dartmouth, Massachusetts, to the Year 1850*, 3 vols., Boston, 1929–1930, 2:184–185; *Massachusetts Centinel*, 10 Feb.; *Boston Gazette*, 21 May).

Moses Gill (1762–1832), Harvard 1784, was a son of Boston printer John Gill. He had come to London to study law at the Middle Temple (vol. 7:459; AA2 to JQA, 10 June, below; Francis Everett Blake, *History of the Town of Princeton, Massachusetts*, 2 vols.,

Princeton, 1915, 1:272, 2:116; *Harvard Quinquennial Cat.*; *Mayflower Families through Five Generations*, 16 vols., Plymouth, 1975–2004, 16.3:39–41).

⁴ AA to JQA, 28 Nov. 1786, vol. 7:405–406.

⁵ The primary purpose of WSS's mission to Portugal was to deliver a letter from the Continental Congress to the queen of Portugal thanking her for her protection of American vessels in the Straits of Gibraltar against the Barbary pirates. Congress passed the resolution confirming his mission on 3 Feb. 1787, and he was formally notified of his diplomatic commission on 11 April (JA to WSS, 11 April, LbC, APM Reel 113; Rufus King to JA, 9 Feb., Smith, *Letters of Delegates*, 24:84–85). See also AA to Lucy Cranch, 26 April, and WSS to AA2, 26 April, both below.

⁶ Only AA to TBA, 15 March, above, has been found.

⁷ On 20 April the *Massachusetts Gazette* carried an advertisement for the sale of JA's *Defence of the Const*. The same issue carried the first of many positive reviews, calling the work "a very valuable book . . . well worthy the attention of every American at this important crisis of our publick affairs." The *Defence* also received negative press, beginning on 31 May when the *Gazette of the State of Georgia* reprinted a London review that attacked JA for advocating "any check upon the voice of the people." While the work was widely quoted in the press, it was never mentioned during the debates of the Constitutional Convention and ultimately had little effect on the framing of the U.S. Constitution (*Doc. Hist. Ratif. Const.*, 13:81–90; C. Bradley Thompson, "John Adams and the Science of Politics," *John Adams and the Founding of the Republic*, ed. Richard Alan Ryerson, Boston, 2001, p. 257–259).

Mary Rutledge Smith to Abigail Adams

My dear Madam   Charleston April the 12th. 87

I have the happiness to inform you that we are again settled, in Charleston, we had a Passage of seven weeks, it was as you may suppose, disagreeable, it blew a heavy gale for ten days, & the patience of every person on Board, was exhausted, except our little Boy, who is both, by Sea, & Land, an excellent traveller.¹ When we left London, you intended a visit to Bath, I hope nothing happened to prevent that agreeable excursion, there can be no doubt, of your admiring, that part of the World, as it affords a most pleasing variety— at present you are in a more desirable Country, than we are, Carolina wears a gloomy face, nothing looks as it did twelve years ago, our inhabitants, are much to be pitied, for they are in reality extremely poor, yet have an anxious desire, to appear other wise. My Brother is one of the Delegates (appointed by this State) for the Federal Convention,² many people are very sanguine, in their expectations, from that assemblage, of wise Men, for my part, I shall hold myself in readiness, to give them all that they may merit, but my hopes, have so frequently fallen to the ground, that I have learned from experience, to wait patiently for the event. If I am right in my conjecture, before this arrives, you will be a Grand-mother, if so, you have my warmest congratulation, on the occasion, & I will only say, that I most sincerely wish, that your amiable Daughter, may be as happy a Parent, as she deserves to be— Caroline intends writing

1. MARY RUTLEDGE SMITH, BY GEORGE ROMNEY, 1786
See page ix

to Col^l. Smith, as she promised, & she cannot suppose, that he has forgot so *important* a matter,[3] Be pleased to present our united respects, to M^r. Adams, My Compliments also, to those friends that we passed, many happy hours with under your *hospitable* Roof, where we received repeated acts of kindness—for which I shall ever think myself indebted, & only regret, my dear Madam, that, I can do no more than *feel* the obligation—but be assured, it will ever be kept in remembrance—

I am my dear Madam / with the utmost esteem / Your very sincere friend   Mary Smith

RC (Adams Papers).

[1] Seven children of Roger Moore Smith and Mary Rutledge Smith had accompanied their parents to Europe in 1785. The "little Boy" was likely their youngest son, ten-year-old Benjamin Burgh Smith (1776–1823) (vol. 6:385, 389; Maurie D. McInnis, ed., *In Pursuit of Refinement: Charlestonians Abroad, 1740–1860*, Columbia, 1999, p. 33; *South Carolina Genealogies: Articles from the South Carolina Historical (and Genealogical) Mag-* *azine*, 5 vols., Spartanburg, S.C., 1983, 4:5, 10–11, 20, 21, 132). See also Descriptive List of Illustrations, No. 1, above.

[2] John Rutledge, former governor of South Carolina and JA's colleague in Congress, 1774–1777 (*DAB*).

[3] No letter from Caroline Smith (1773–1862) to WSS or any other member of the Adams family has been found (*South Carolina Genealogies*, 4:11).

Mary Smith Cranch to Abigail Adams

My Dear Sister   Braintree April 22d 1787

Captain Cushing arriv'd last Monday after a tedious Passage It was so long since I receiv'd any Letters from you that I began to be very impatient. Cousin JQA had one in the winter but I have only heard of it.[1] he forgot that I should want to see it & so did not bring it with him this vacancy your sons are now all of them with me. cousin JQA return'd last evening from an excurtion. I perswaided him to make with a number of his class to Sandwich. Mr Burr one of the Tutors was ordain'd there last wednesday. The President & his Lady Mr Hilliard & Lady were also in his train[2] They have had fine weather only a little too cold. your son looks better for his journey. His staying at cambridge during the winter vacancy was of no service to his Health whatever it may have been to his mind. He look'd so pale & wan when he came home this spring that I was not a little alarm'd about him. He has lost so much Flesh within these nine months that I have been oblig'd to take in his wastcoats a full quarter of a yard. His complants are wholly oweing to want of air & exercise & too great an attention to his studys. His Food does not digest well— I am continually urging upon him the necessaty of more exercise. He always promises fair—but a favorite Author will soon make him forget it all. I have got Doctor Tufts to talk very plainly to him & tell him what his fate will be unless he pursues a different method. The Doc^r. says he does not need any medicine—air & exercise with a proper attention to his Diet is all he has to depend upon to restore him. His time at college will be soon up. He must then for a little while devote himself to riding about & visiting his Friends There is so little to be done at present in a Lawyers office that mr Cranch designs Billy shall study at home for a year at least under the direction of some Gentleman in Boston[3] he will attend the office the last weeks before the courts & can attend all the courts. we must take that method which will be least expencive if we can make it any way as advantagous. If we should pursue this plan we shall be greatly oblig'd if mr Adams will permit him the use of his Law Library He will take great care of the Books & I hope make a good use of them He is at present both steady and studious.

I am glad that so many of my Letters have reach'd you. those by Scott & Folger have done so too I hope before this time if they have you will know that your Trunk came safe & that you have my warmest gratitude for the things sent to me & the children. The Blue cloth is now making for your sons. The Buff will not be made till next winter as it will not be wanted & they grow so fast that it would be folly to make it till it will. as to cousin Tom I can keep nothing to fit him a month I believe he will be as tall as Billy. He is a fine shap'd youth & has more of your countenance than I ever expected he would have—but not so much as my dear cousin JQA. In his Face I can see every amiable Feature of my sister, but tis not in his Face alone that his mama is to be trac'd The perfections of both Parents are most happily blended in him. He has quallities which command the highest esteem & the tenderest affection of his Freinds & you may believe me when I tell you that he has found a way to acquire the affections of his class, & The admiration & approbation of his Teachers, although he possesses advantages at least if not abilities, superior to [most] of them & notwithstanding his most hearty contempt of —— that dignity which is acqur'd by Pomposity & self importance— your advice & his sisters has had its weight I dare say he has had the same from his Friends here. His Talant for satire was all that we had to give us any fears about him. The parts he has had given him in the publick exibitions is a proof of the character he sustains & do him Honour

27th

Our children are all return'd to college cousin JQA is much better, says he has nothing to do this Quarter but to ride about & take the air. In six weeks he will return here. He thinks he shall live a little while with mr Dana & study Law with him. His motive is truly Fraturnal. The care & attention of such a Brother will be of no small advantage to your younger sons Tom told me very gravely the other day that a young Fellow must be very steady & very resolute to pass thro college without being often led into some scrape & that if he had forty sons he should be affraid to send one of them to have their education there. "dear youth said I do you not know that temptations are stro'd thick in every Path. being sensible that the one before you is so full of them will make you careful how you walk I hope. Begin right & persevere, you will not find your difficulties so great as you think. after a few dinials to do wrong you will not be solisited again you must not set up to censure or reform, but by your example you will then acquire both the esteem & Love of your class." he is belov'd by the Family he is in, & he is so attach'd to them that he seems loth to leave it. he is affraid he shall be more in the way of company, & he complains of want of time for his studys now. this is no bad sign. He has his health very well excepting now & then a stif shoulder or knee. he had a complant of this kind when he was here last week, but a few drops of Guiacum[4] & sassafras Tea gave him the use of his Limbs again

I thank you my dear sister for the Porter, cheese, & the Peas— The two former are prohibited articles however as it could not be known, we shall meet with no difficulty about them. The Court have been call'd together unexpectedly to chuse another Treasurer the Death of mr Ivers rendering it necessary. mr Hodgden is chosen.[5] There were others who had Porter besides us on Board Cushing. they Petition'd the court & had leave to have all landed as the news of the prohibition was not known when he sail'd. The court will be up soon & our worthy Governor will resign his seal to a—not more worthy Man I am sure.[6] you will not form a very high Idea of the virtue of the People I believe when you have a list of the next General Court There are some very good men in the Senate, & some miserable ones it will be so I suppose in the house if so can you think we shall have any thing but quarreling & protesting all the next year—

17

Mr cranch is left out of the senate this year, because he is a Justice of the common Pleas, & it has just been found out that it is unconstitutional for any of them to be in the House or Senate— A gentleman of our acquaintance who thought he had no Political Friends in Braintree or weymouth[7] has said it & I believe made it his business to perswaid the People to think so— I hear this was the only reason why Mr Cranch was not voted for in his Town some of them have told me so— mr Morton asserted the same in Boston at their meeting. Why he should do it was a mistery to me for some time. Those who wish'd to annihilate the court of common Pleas have said that while so many of the Judges of it were in the Senate it could not or would not be done. as mr M. was not one of those, I could not concieve his motive untill I recollect'd that a son of the Gentleman before mention'd study'd in his office[8] could I suppose that either of them thought what they said I should think they did right. was it really so I do not believe mr Adams would have had any hand in obtaining his Friend the office & There is no one who assisted in framing the Constitution who understood it better than he—[9] you have been too long conversant with Courts to be astonish'd at any thing that belongs to them or you would be suppriz'd to see the coalitions which are taking place among some of our great Folks. The Bitterest & most inveterate Political ennemys are becoming Friends— He who would not allow a good quallity to be possess'd by a former G–v–n–r has I am told both by himself & children made all the interest he could to get him elected this year, & althou he would not accept the highest office he could have under him formerly, would now accept of a lower if offer'd him The good Lady is made to believe any thing or she would not have asserted the other day in company where she was complaining that her Freind was neglected by the People that mr W̶-̶r̶-̶n̶ never askd any Person for their vote or for their interest for himself. A Lady present said to another "she does not know then that he ask'd my Papa for his & that his son wrote to mr Thaxter for his & told him that his Papa would be oblig'd for it—" This gentleman has no longer to complain of having no Political Friends he has found many this year: He has so openly censur'd almost all the late measures of goverment especially those relating to the rebels that he has made himself extreemly Popolar.— "Nothing has gone right since I was in office, when I was there we did more business in a week than is done in a Session now" "I heard a gentleman say last night that the reason you was so neglected was because you was so honest that you would speak your mind let what would be the conseiquence"– "It is very true my dear, I *once* had the affections of this People so much & was so popolar, that I tremble'd for my self." "could you have trim'd like some others you might have retain'd them" A modest conversation between a Gentleman & his Lady at a Table full of company– do you not think?

And so my dear sister I suppose by this time you are a Grand-mama. I hope I may give you joy, but it is impossible not to feel anxious at this distance I long for the arrival of more vessels, & yet I cannot expect to hear till midsummer. I wish I could be with you for your sake not my own I am sure. You was never I think with a sister at such a time. what we suffer for our children is more distressing than what we feel for ourselves. dear Girl she has my sincere prayers for her safety–& could I be with her I would convinc her how tenderly I love her. I would if possible regain those affections which I lost by endeavouring to preserve her from being miserable. She did not Love me when she went away. I know she did not. I thought I did right she mistook my motive or she would have thought so too. I shall leave it to her reason & good sense to determine whether I do not desirve a higher place in her affections than what her civillity obliges her to give me as the sister of her dear Mama—[10]

your account of Bath has entertain'd us much & is Such as I had form'd an Idea of before & at least that part which regards it amusemints—[11]

May 20th

I have receev'd a charming Pacquit from you by Scot Barnard & Folger with fresch proofs of your affection & Beneficence.[12] The Lamp I find very useful & how long one of the wicks will last I cannot yet tell you. I have burnt one Ten nights & it does not appear to be half consum'd. The silk I shall not make up at present. notwithstanding we are to have a publick commencment, such it is at last determind to be. your Son has an English oration & ours an English conference with one of his class. these are to be their parts. now as it is to be an ecconimical plan that every one is desir'd to pursue in their entertainment no new cloath are to be made upon the occation.[13] I must therefore only thankfully acknoledge it with gratitude to my sister, & keep my Gown till better times—but I fear I have very far to look for those. such a motly assembly as we shall see this year was never before seen in america consisting of very good & very bad ones some are chosen who were commit'd to Jail by the last years Court.[14] general Warren is chosen to represent milton see now if he does not accept— Coll: Assa White for Weymouth & Coll. Thayer for this Town mr Boydoin for Dorchester & a very good man at Hingham.[15] all these will do right I dare say although one of them has talk'd very wrong—

I have had a Tailor at work with me for a month almost & have been so busy that I have not had time to reply to your Letters as I wish too. I shall send this to go by the first vesel & write more by the others. I have sent you some meal to scour your hands I would have sent more but I suppose the Freight would be more than the meal would be worth when you had got it & besides I hope you will come home before you want more. oh my Sister I hardly dare to look forward to that time. So many things may happen to sadden our hop'd for scenes of joy, but why should I anticipate evils which may not happen. That dissorder malignant almost as the Plague is raging in a number of Familys in Haverhill Where it has so often raged with unrelenting fury. I mean the Throat distemper in its worst kind. I have receivd a Letter from Sister Shaw which has distress'd me by the accounts of a number of Deaths. Both young & old are seiez'd one Family lost Four Children in one week & it was all they had. every other day they were call'd to close the eyes of a dear child some of them grown up There Grandmother now lays sick of the same dissorder. several of her nearest Neighbours have lost their children I do not wonder that our sister is in low Spirits— Heaven preserve her & hers—[16]

your Freinds & neighbours are well your Mother Hall & Brothers Family are all so—uncle Quincy not got of his Farm yet—Mrs Quincy & Miss Nancy send Love—Lucy came from Cambridge last evening she carried Betsy & left Her to make a visit among her cambridge Friends. She is now at Doctor William's.[17] our sons were all well Cousin JQA filling up his Wastcoats fast.

your Things at your Cottage as you call it are in as good a situation as I could expect, every thing has been done that we could to preserve every thing from the moths your Cloth & carpet were safe a few weeks since. both keep'd pind up in linnen & only took out to be examind, but about thise oil cloths, we will send you the dimentions of your rooms but my advice is not to get them cut to them. you can never live in that house when you return it is not large enough. you cannot crowd your Sons into a little bed by the side of yours now, & you will never inlarg it you had better buy mr Bow-lands or Build one. He has offer'd to sell it I hear. The present Posseser cannot possibly have any use for it at new york—but I forbear.[18] the newspapers will give a History the york ones especially of what will not greatly delight you.[19] I want to add one scene. It should be of a man writing comedys in one state while he is suffering his interest in another to be all taken by execution & sold at vendue, even to the Boards & lumber which he had got to repair his House & *Mill* with. The Boards you have, to fit up the house mr Belcher lives in— we have got nothing yet not even a note of hand & forty pounds is too much for us to lose. I hope his Genious for comedy will not fail him if it does not we may get it. mr Cranch said he would not distress him, but it was ungenerous to go off without settling. It was impossible to make him do it without forcing him. I have talk'd to the Doctor about Buying the House I have mention'd for you. I hope he will write about it. it has led me unawares to say more than I design'd about a person that I know you never wish'd to hear off again, but whatever you may wish it seems he has determind otherways. I want to see this extraordinary *effort* of Genious. It is said to be very pointed, & that he is affraid to have it printed. those who know him say it was written at least party before he went to york, but I can form no judgment till I see it, but hush, hush this is not keeping my promise forgive me— well but the carpit, had you not better have that on your office painted— I will write more soon Love to every one from your affectionate Sister   Mary Cranch

I shall be dreadfully mortified if this Letter does not get to town soon enough to be put on Board Barnard or Davis. what will my sister think to have two vesells arive Tuscorora rice & all without a Letter

RC (Adams Papers); docketed by AA2: "Mrs Cranch April 22^d 1787 / April 22^d 1787—"; notations by AA: "Mrs Cranch—" and "digest."

[1] Probably AA's letter of 27 Sept. 1786, which JQA acknowledged receiving on 11 Jan. 1787 (vol. 7:344–348, 419).

[2] JQA and a number of other Harvard students and faculty journeyed to Sandwich from 16 to 21 April for Jonathan Burr's ordination on the 18th. Burr (1757–1842), Harvard 1784, was a tutor at the college from 1786 to 1787. Those in attendance included President Joseph Willard and his wife, Mary Sheafe, and Rev. Timothy Hilliard and his wife, Mary Foster of Boston. Hilliard (1746/47–1790), Harvard 1764, was the minister at Barnstable, just east of Sandwich, from 1771 to 1783, and later pastor at Cambridge and for the college (Frederick Freeman, *The History of Cape Cod: The Annals of Barnstable County, Including the District of Mashpee*, 2 vols., Boston, 1860, 1:645; *Harvard Quinquennial Cat.*; *Sibley's Harvard Graduates*, 16:59–63, 253–265; JQA, *Diary*, 2:206–209; Boston, *30th Report*, p. 65; Charles Henry Pope, *Willard Genealogy*, Boston, 1915, p. 92).

[3] William Cranch read law with Thomas Dawes of Boston (JQA, *Diary*, 2:280).

[4] Both the sap and wood of the guaiacum tree, native to the warmer parts of the Americas and the West Indies, also known as *lignum vitæ*, were used in a variety of medicines (*OED*).

[5] Thomas Ivers (1730–1787) died on 11 April while serving as state treasurer. The legislature appointed Alexander Hodgdon (1741–1797) to replace him on 27 April (*Massachusetts Gazette*, 13 April; *American Herald*, 30 April).

[6] John Hancock defeated James Bowdoin in the 1787 spring elections. Hancock recorded a three-to-one margin in the contest, which drew a 40 percent increase in voter turnout (John L. Brooke, *The Heart of the Commonwealth: Society and Political Culture in Worcester County, Massachusetts, 1713–1861*, Cambridge, 1989, p. 225; Fowler, *Baron of Beacon Hill*, p. 265).

[7] Cranch quotes here from AA's description of James Warren in her letter of 25 May 1786 (vol. 7:197–202). For more on Warren's political career, and AA's views thereof, see that letter as well as AA to Mercy Otis Warren, 24 May, vol. 7:194–195.

[8] George Warren (1766–1800), the only one of James Warren's five sons to practice law, probably studied with Perez Morton. In Feb. 1788 Morton sponsored Warren to serve as an attorney of the Court of Common Pleas (D/JQA/31, 2 Feb. 1820, APM Reel 34; JQA, *Diary*, 2:427; Emily Warren Roebling, *Richard Warren of the Mayflower and Some of His Descendants*, Boston, 1901, p. 25–28; MHS, *Procs.*, 19:162 [Dec. 1881]).

[9] Cranch presumably refers here to Part 1, Art. 30 (Chap. 1, Art. 31, in JA's draft) of the Massachusetts Constitution, which reads: "In the government of this commonwealth, the legislative department shall never exercise the executive and judicial powers, or either of them: the executive shall never exercise the legislative and judicial powers, or either of them: the judicial shall never exercise the legislative and executive powers, or either of them: to the end it may be a government of laws and not of men" (www.mass.gov/legis/const.htm, 9 Feb. 2006; JA, *Papers*, 8:242, 264).

[10] AA2's frustration with Mary Smith Cranch was probably connected to Cranch's concern over AA2's relationship with Royall Tyler and her criticism of his behavior, which Cranch voiced repeatedly in her letters to AA; see, for example, Cranch to AA, 25 April,

19 July, and 8 Nov. 1785 (vol. 6:93–94, 236, 456).

[11] See AA to Cranch, 20 Jan. 1787, vol. 7:445–452.

[12] See AA to Cranch, 8 March, above.

[13] For the decision to hold a more economical commencement, see JQA, *Diary*, 2:136–137.

[14] Three of the legislators elected to the General Court were included on Massachusetts attorney general Robert Treat Paine's "Black List" of Shaysites who had allegedly committed crimes: Samuel Willard of Uxbridge, Josiah Whitney of Harvard, and Benjamin Josselyn of New Braintree. Another spent time in prison—Luke Drury of Grafton was jailed and released after a March appeal to the governor (*American Herald*, 4 June; Leonard L. Richards, *Shays's Rebellion: The American Revolution's Final Battle*, Phila., 2002, p. 145; MU:Luke Drury Papers). See also JQA to JA, 30 June, and note 4, below.

[15] Gen. Theophilus Cushing was selected to represent Hingham (*American Herald*, 4 June; *History of Hingham*, 2:161).

[16] A three-part article describing the symptoms of throat distemper (diphtheria) first appeared in the *New Hampshire Gazette*, 18 Nov. 1786. It noted that the disease had initially appeared in York County, Maine, in the autumn of 1784, and that it had rapidly spread through the back towns and more slowly toward the coast. Newspapers further reported two instances of a single family losing four children: the Durant family in Newton, Mass., and the Harris family of Gorham, Maine (*Massachusetts Centinel*, 11 Feb. 1786; *Massachusetts Spy*, 23 Feb., 30 March).

[17] Probably Dr. William Spooner, for whom see vol. 7:287, note 3.

[18] Royall Tyler had intended to purchase the Vassall-Borland estate, but the property reverted back to Leonard Borland after Tyler stopped his payments. For a full discussion of the history of the Borland estate and its purchase by the Adamses, see vol. 3:264–266; Cotton Tufts to AA, 21 May and 20 Sept. 1787; Tufts to JA, 13 June; and AA to Tufts, 1 July, all below.

[19] Royall Tyler's *The Contrast*, credited as the first comedy written by an American to be professionally produced, opened on 16 April at the John Street Theater in New York. The *New York Journal*, 19 April, reported that the play opened "amid continued roars of

applause" and succeeded in "holding high to view, in letters of the purest gold, all the virtues of the human heart." Tyler, reluctant to attach his name to a theatrical piece, published it as "A Citizen of the United States," but reviews immediately identified him as the author (G. Thomas Tanselle, *Royall Tyler,* Cambridge, 1967, p. 51–53).

John Brown Cutting to Abigail Adams

Wednesday Evening 25. April 1787.
Portsmouth

Dear Madam,

It may perhaps afford you satisfaction to learn that Mr Adams and his secretary pro tempore[1] arrived at the Crown Inn within the ramparts of this naval arsenal last evening before eight, after a journey as pleasant as coud be expected considering the unverdant aspect of far the greater portion of the country through which we travel'd. To speak candidly (excepting the farm at Cobham) I never beheld so complete a fulfilment of Churchills prophesy of famine as stares one in the face on each side of the hedge from Kingston to Portsmouth.[2] Mr Adams protests that he will never return by the same road: how chearfully do I acquiesce!

The culprit Muir was had before us this morning and underwent an examination. His answers were all contradictory inexplicit and evasive. He seems to be either a subtle and supereminent practitioner in dissimulation, or a vulgar villain without capability of mighty mischief or any ingenious system of enormity. I am rather inclin'd to the latter opinion at present. Perhaps he may be the agent of more crafty contrivers. He says he is a native of Scotland. I believe him. He has a hollow, hungry hanging look. The Court of Quarter Sessions, who have conducted with extreme propriety in this bussiness have just recommitted him for three months. This measure is pleasing to Mr Adams since it furnishes time to investigate & detect whatsoever may or can be investigated or detected in London or elswhere.[3]

Mr Wren guided us to view Fortune Prison this afternoon—and tomorrow if the weather shall be favourable Mr Adams is resolute to survey on horseback the rural felicity of the Isle of Wight. He has just gone to rest in high spirits at the prospect. I believe from circumstances we may condescend to revisit the smoak of the Metropolis within a fortnight.

Particular compliments to Mrs Smith and little Steuben. from, Dear Madam, Yours respectfully   John B Cutting

RC (Adams Papers).

[1] That is, Cutting himself.

[2] JA and Cutting traveled the seventy miles from London to Portsmouth on 24 April, passing through Kingston upon Thames and the village of Cobham in Surrey, site of the gardens at Painshill, which the Adamses had previously visited in June 1786. Charles Churchill's 1763 political satire *The Prophecy of Famine* predicted that a growing Scottish influence on English culture would result in a metaphorically barren England of the future: "Far as the eye could reach, no tree was seen, / Earth, clad in russet, scorn'd the lively green." In 1787, the Portsmouth Road was already known for passing through particularly barren country, "past ragged heaths, tumbled commons, and waste lands, chiefly unenclosed" (Karl Baedeker, *Great Britain: Handbook for Travellers*, 8th edn., N.Y., 1927, p. 55; AA to Mary Smith Cranch, 13 June 1786, note 9, vol. 7:221; Thomas Lockwood, *Post-Augustan Satire: Charles Churchill and Satirical Poetry, 1750–1800*, Seattle, 1979, p. 133–139; Charles Churchill, *The Prophecy of Famine*, London, 1763, p. 15; Charles G. Harper, *The Portsmouth Road and Its Tributaries: To-day and in Days of Old*, London, 1895, p. 194, 197).

[3] In March Robert Muir, a native of Scotland, arrived in London from Charleston, S.C., in the guise of "a common seaman." He soon began contacting engravers and printers in an attempt to counterfeit the paper currency of North and South Carolina. London metalworker William Caslon made plates of decorative elements on the currency at Muir's request in early April. When Muir approached London engraver Richard Carpenter and Portsmouth printer Walter Mowbray, however, they reported his plans to authorities, and Muir was arrested and imprisoned. Rev. Thomas Wren, who had assisted American prisoners of war in Forton Prison in the late 1770s, hosted JA when he visited Portsmouth to interrogate Muir. From April to July, Wren sent JA updates on the case, acted as a liaison between American and British officials, and advanced funds for Muir's board in jail. On 25 June, JA wrote to recommend that Muir be released for lack of evidence. Wren responded on 12 July to say that rather than be released as innocent, Muir would be tried later that month and acquitted for lack of evidence, an outcome that had been judged more likely to serve as a deterrent to further nefarious activity (Sheldon S. Cohen, "Thomas Wren: Portsmouth's Patron of American Liberty," *The Portsmouth Papers*, 57:11, 23, 28 [March 1991]; vol. 4:201; Thomas Wren to JA, 12 July, Adams Papers; JA to Wren, 21 April and 25 June, both LbC, APM Reel 113; *Dipl. Corr., 1783–1789*, 2:738–739, 741–744; Devon Libraries Local Studies Service, *The London Book Trades 1775–1800: A Checklist of Members*, www.devon.gov.uk/etched, 6 Feb. 2006).

Abigail Adams to Lucy Cranch

my dear Neice   London April 26 1787—

I write you a few lines my dear Lucy to thank you for your kind Letter, and to inform you that I am a *Grandmamma*! my Grandson be sure is a fine Boy, & I already feel as fond of him as if he was my own son, nay I can hardly persuade myself that he is not, especially as I have been sick for six weeks, I cannot however Nurse him so well as his mamma, who is already so fond of him, that I sometimes quote mrs Storer to her. who could have thought it?

He was Christened last thursday[1] by dr Price and called William after his pappa. in this Country Children are not carried to church, so we had the Christning in the House and about a dozen of our Friends together upon the occasion. we supped & drank the young Heroes Health, & that of our Country and Friends. Mrs Smith dinned below with us, the day 3 weeks frum her confinement, and I

have carried little master to ride 3 or four times already. he is very
quiet and good, but his pappa is already obliged to leave him, & yesterday morning very reluctantly set of on a journey to portugal, in
his way to which he takes France & Spain, & will be absent we expect near four Months, but thus it must be with those who are in
publick office. at the same time mr Adams set of for portsmouth in
order to hear the examination of a set of villians who have been
counterfeiting the paper money of the American States, and mr
Cutting accompanied him, so that we are quite alone. as soon as
mrs Smith is able we shall make a little excursion into the Country,
which I hope will reestablish my Health. My disorder has been long
accumulating, & arises from a Billious state of my Blood. it has afflicted me spring & fall for several years, and has at last produced a
slow intemitting fever. some days I am able to go out, others not,
but it has wholy prevented my attendance upon Routes dinners[2]
theatres &c and o Lamentable, I have not been able to go to saint
James for more than two months. all this I could have borne with
tolerable patience, but what has been really matter of regret to me,
is that I have been dissapointed of Seven Lectures out of 12 to
which I Subsribed, and which I fear I shall never have the opportunity of attending. they would have afforded me much matter for future recollection & amusement from a retrospect of the Beauties of
Nature, and her various opperations manifested in the Works of
creation, an assemblage of Ideas entirely new, is presented to the
mind. the five Lectures which I attended were experiments in Electricity, Magnetism Hydrostatics optics pemematicks, all of which are
connected with, and are subservient to the accommodation of
common Life.[3] it was like going into a Beautifull Country, which I
never saw before, a Country which our American Females are not
permitted to visit or inspect, untill dr Moyes visited America,[4] all
experimental Phylosophy was confined within the walls of our
Colledges— The Study of Household Good, as milton terms it, is no
doubt the peculiar province of the Female Character.[5] Yet surely as
rational Beings, our reason might with propriety receive the highest
possible cultivation. knowledge would teach our Sex candour, and
those who aim at the attainment of it, in order to render themselves
more amiable & usefull in the world would derive a double advantage from it, for in proportion as the mind is informed, the
countanance would be improved & the face ennobled as the Heart
is elevated,[6] for wisdom says Soloman maketh the face to shine.[7]
even the Luxurious Eastern Sage thought not of rouge or the milk

of roses—but that the virtuous wife should open her mouth with wisdom & the law of kindness dwell upon her Tongue,[8] nor did he think this inconsistant with looking well to the ways of her household, or suppose that she would be less inclined to superintend the domestick oeconomy of her family, for having gone beyond the limits of her dressing room & her kitchen I quote Soloman on this occasion, as we may naturally suppose the picture drawn of a virtuous wife to be the result of his experience & his wisdom, after ranging at large amongst the Eastern Beauties: he pronounces the price of a virtuous woman to be far above rubies & the only character on which the Heart of a Husband may safely rest—[9] the present mode of fashionable education is not calculated to form the rising generation upon the system of soloman. futile accomplishments are substituded in stead of rational improvements settled principals of Truth integrity & Honour are little attended to, Laudible motives of action & incentives to virtue, give place to the form of the Body, the Grace of motion, and a conscious air of superiority which knows neither the Blush of modesty, or diffidence. a Boarding school miss, that should discover either would be thought quite a novice—

But whither has my subject led me? I must return to the Female sphere & talk to you of fashions— the Sandals which I send, I fear will prove too large, but the shoe maker says they are according to the measure. the Novelty of taste has brought the immitation of the Scotch plad into vogue, Waistcoats Bonets & ribbons are all plad, sashes &c I send you a specimin of their Beauty and must quit my Pen to pay my devotions to the kind goddess of Health; whom I am to seek in the Park, or if warm enough in kensington gardens. Flora & Virtumnus[10] will meet me there. adieu my dear girl. may the best of Heavens blessings rest upon you

Your ever affectionate   Aunt A Adams

May 6th

from the Character of the reviewers I bought Louissa a novel[11] the story of which is very interesting I send it you for your amusement

RC (MWA:Abigail Adams Letters). Dft (Adams Papers), filmed at 25 April.

[1] 19 April.

[2] In the Dft AA adds "Card parties, &c." here.

[3] Robert Young taught a twelve-week lecture series discussing "the Mechanism and Motions of the Universe," which began on 30 January. The lectures were held at No. 43, Gerard Street, in Soho (London *Daily Universal Register*, 27 Jan. 1787).

[4] Dr. Henry Moyes, a blind "philosopher of Natural History" from Britain, had lectured in Boston in fall 1785 (vol. 6:419, 420, 501).

5 Milton, *Paradise Lost*, Book IX, line 233.

6 The Dft ends the paragraph on a more secular note: "& thus may she become a pleasing companion to the man of Science & of Sensibility, enabled to form the minds of her children to virtue & to knowledge & not less capable or willing to superintend the domestick oeconomy of her family for having wanderd beyond the limits of the dressing room & the kitchen, to which even some men of sense have been illiberal enough to wish us confined but as mankind appear in the present age to acquire more freedom of thought & action in politicks in Phylosophy & in religion, it is to be hoped that the liberality of their Sentiments with extend to the cultivation & improvement of the Femal mind which stands much in need of motives & incentives to draw it from the present pernicious modes of fashionable Levities & polite accomplishments—as they are termed to more rational & durable improvements, what is life, or its enjoyments without setled principals Laudable purposes & mental exertions, a mere vapour indeed & as pope expresses it

'Born to no end, they worse than useless grow
as waters poison when they cease to
  flow' "

The quotation is not from Pope but from William Whitehead, "On Ridicule," *Poems on Several Occasions*, London, 1754, lines 45–46.

7 Psalms, 104:15, and Ecclesiastes, 8:1.

8 Proverbs, 31:26.

9 Proverbs, 31:10–11.

10 Flora was the Roman goddess of flowering plants; Vertumnus was the Roman god of seasons and plant life, especially orchards (J. Lempriere, *A Classical Dictionary*, N.Y., 1816).

11 Elizabeth Helme, *Louisa; or, The Cottage on the Moor*, London, 1787. The *Critical Review* described *Louisa* as "a pleasing little artless tale, much superior, both in its plan and conduct, to the numerous productions of this class. Curiosity is skilfully excited, expectation kept momentarily alive, and, at last, the intricacies are unravelled very satisfactorily" (63:308 [April 1787]).

William Stephens Smith to Abigail Adams Smith

York House, Dover, April 26th, 1787.[1]

I dare say, my friend, when you receive this, you will think I have moved with great rapidity.

There have but two things occurred on the road which are worth mentioning; the one is my having met Mr. Rucker; we stopped, jumped out of our carriages, I into the dust, and he out of it; he had a great coat on, and his beard he brought from Paris with him; I wonder how it passed the custom-house officers at this place, for they are as sharp as need be. As to the other, it happened between this and Canterbury; but I must insist in the first place that you do not receive it as a Canterbury story. Well, silence gives, or at least in this instance must pass for, consent, which being granted, I proceed to this ignus fatuus, or Jack-o-lanthorn story.

Curioni was perched, bolt upright, in front of the postillions, who were lashing their nags and clattering away, as if ten thousand musquetoes were after them, when behold, we found ourselves upon an extended plain, and the sable curtains of the night falling apace: what was to be done in this case? Some would attempt an answer here, but I, like Will-o-the-Wisp, am above this, and proceed to tell you what I did—I took out my little tin case, and with a match lighted the lamps. The horses stopped, Curioni rose perpendicular and cried: "Sir, I begged them not to be alarmed, but the one to set down, and the other to drive on, that no one would hurt them." "Oh," said the postillion, "what's this?" "Phosphor," said I; crack went the whip, and they moved with such rapidity, it struck me they were anxious to arrive at some inhabited place, and wished themselves safe home again. I must not practise this in Spain or Portugal, or I may be detained.

Yours,   W. S. S.

MS not found. Printed from AA2, *Jour. and Corr.*, 1:125–126.

[1] Between late April and late August, while on a diplomatic journey to Portugal by way of France and Spain, WSS wrote at least 23 letters to AA2. They were dated 26 April, from Dover, England; 27 (2 letters) and 28 April, and 5, 10, 14, 19, and 20 May, from France; 25 and 31 May, 6, 10, 18, 21 [25], and 30 June, and 3 and 9 July, from Spain; 16 and 31 July, from Portugal; and 20, 22, and 27 Aug., from southwest England. All are printed in AA2, *Jour. and Corr.*, 1:125–202, which is their only extant source.

Three considerations have persuaded the editors to print only three of these letters (26 April, 6 June, and 22 Aug.) in *AFC*. First, no replies from AA2 have been found. Second, they give no information about the Adams family and its life in England. Finally, because no holographs have been located, the editors can add nothing textually to the printed source, beyond correcting a few obvious errors of date or fact that any perceptive reader can perform.

Abigail Adams to Mary Smith Cranch

My dear sister   London April 28th 1787

I have now to acknowledge your kind favour of April 7th[1] by Captain Folger— I have already written to my Neices[2] and informed them of the addition to my family— you will rejoice with me that an event which as a parent so nearly concernd me, is so happily over, and that the mother and Child are both finely. indeed I never saw a healthier Lad in my life. he has not even had those complaints incident to children, which I partly attribute to the care of the nurse who leaves all to Nature without even tea drink or doses of any kind. she has been a Nurse 21 years, & never had a child with a soar mouth. She washes little master with cold water from the day of his Birth, & is exceedingly attentive to Cleanliness. the Nurses here never think of going to Bed during the whole month, they lay themselves down on a settee, or sleep in an easy chair, & I do not see But what they are quite as contented & as Bright as ours, who go to bed & frequently let a pour woman suffer. tis true they do nothing else, but attend to the Lady and Child. the Cook of the family makes all the victuals, & the maid carries it up, and they are well pay'd for their trouble, but still they are the best Nurses I ever saw— how happy would it make me; could my dear sister look in upon us. I have been very unwell all this Spring. a slow intermitting fever, and Billious complaints have greatly afflicted me, I am better than I was a month ago, as the fever has lessend, but still the cause is not wholy removed, and the doctor tells me, it must be a work of time & care;[3] I had similar complaints the spring before I left America, only not to so great a degree. I have not escaped one spring or fall since. the dampness of this climate & the little tendency that there is to perspiration encreases this disorder greatly, I must try a journey soon—

we have accounts by way of New york to the 8th of march, which inform us that general Lincoln had met with more resistance from the insurgents, than we had reason to expect from former accounts, that an engagement had taken place, in which several persons on both sides fell, but we do not learn who, that Shayes had got off into vermont, where it was probable he would meet with protection. I hope these accounts are not well founded.[4] Let not the Patriots of our Country be discouraged or disheartned altho their affairs are much embarrassed. the Country is fruitfull in resources, patience perseverence industery and frugality will accomplish great things. our Countrymen create most of the misfortunes they feel, for want of a disinterested Spirit; a confidence in each other, & a union of the whole. it is a great misfortune when one state thawrts the measures of 11 or 12 and thus injures, the credit & reputation of the whole.[5] the situation of our Country greatly damps the pleasure I should feel in anticipating my return to it. you may well suppose that falshoods in abundance are circulated here, an attempt to pub-lish the Truth; or contradict them, would have no other affect than raising a Nest of wasps & Hornets, & would employ the whole time of one person. an extract of a Letter publishd from dr Rush to dr price, giving an account of the establishment of 2 or 3 new societies, drew upon the latter so much abuse & Scurility as would disgrace any people. the writer like an envenomed toad spit forth his poison.[6] there are a set of Refugees residing here, the enormity of whose of-fences forbids their ever returning again to America,[7] like Satan they look to the Heights from which they have fallen, with a malice and envy similar to that which the arch Fiend felt when he beheld the Glory of the new world, and like him they wish to destroy the happiness of its inhabitants.[8] such is Galloway, & Smith who is gone prime minister to Lord Dorchester, a few days before he left the

Country, he gave it as his solid opinion that, he did not doubt he should live to see America sue to Britain for protection & to be received again by it, he might have added; it should not be his fault if they did not.[9] I hope a watchfull Eye will be kept over Lord Dorchester & all his movements— This Government are as much disposed to sow seeds of dissention amongst us as ever, & build wholy upon our splitting to peices. But I will quit this subject[10] for our own Domestick concerns. you ask my opinion respecting the wives talkd of for our uncles. Second marriages at their age can be considerd only as affairs of convenience the heyday of the Blood is tame, and waits upon the judgment, as Hamlet expresses it.[11] the same ardor & passion so suitable in Youth would be ridiculous in age, nor is it improper to consult even Interest as well as convenience. Good dispositions fair Characters and a regard to the station which was formerly held by the parties, ought to be more maturely considerd than at an earlier period of Life. young people more easily accommodate themselves to each other, too great a disparity in years often makes second marriages not only Ridiculous but unhappy— I know not the person whom I should like so well or one who would do more credit to the Relation, or discharge the duties of her station with greater honour to herself than the Lady you have mentiond for our good uncle S——[12] She is the only one, which has occured to my mind, since the discease of our dear Aunt— as to the other Lady of the same Name, I can only say if I was in her situation I would not exchange it for a residence at Weymouth tho I have not a personal knowledge of mrs W.[13] from the Character which she sustaind in this Country, the visisitudes of fortune which she experienced with great equinimity, the many handsome things I have heard dr Jeffries say of her, who attended her through a most distressing sickness the perfect Harmony in which she is said to have lived with her former partner, all serves to hold her up to my view as a Lady highly deserving & well calculated for any situation in Life affliction is the best school for wisdom, and knowledge, but whereever my worthy Friends may fix; I most sincerely wish them happy and I am sure they will not give me a Relation whom I cannot respect.— I am very glad that Miss Mayhew has so pretty an addition to her fortune, she did not however stand in need of that recommendation in my Eye to qualify her for a good wife. I have no doubt she would have shone in that character, and I cannot help thinking that it argues cowardice in the gentlemen that she still remains single. she has a strength of mind, and an understanding, which will always ensure her respect, provided the heriditary talant which she has at Satire; is properly regulated. This I conceive has been the weapon that has terrified all the gentlemen, conscious perhaps how justly it may be levelld against them, but no woman of sense will ever make her Husband an object of Ridicule; for in proportion as she lowers him she lessens herself. neither the Character of Lady G. or miss How, are to be immitated by the Woman of true delicacy of sentiment,[14] but miss Mayhews talant has always been display'd with so much good humour when ever I have been witness to it that I think I could not have been angry, if I had been the subject of it, yet my dear sister I have ever observed that it is a most Dangerous thing for a Female to be distinguishd for any quallification beyond the rest of her sex. Whatever may be her Deportment, she is sure to draw upon herself the jealousy of the men and the envy of the women, nor do I see any way to remedy this evil but by increasing the number of accomplished women, a monopoly of any kind is always envidious

I have never received a Line from mr Hay since she left England, which I have wonderd at considering the intimacy which subsisted between us when here. I thought her reasons good for chusing to go to America. it was natural for her to wish to be with her relations during the long voyages of captain Hay, rather than to reside at Board abroad. I know she endeavourd to influence him to go with her, but he was in good buisness here, & saild with more safety in a British Ship, than he could in an American vessel subject to the capture of Algerines as he thought at that time. he was about taking a voyage when she left him, in which he expected to be absent 15 months I think I should have done as she did, if I had been in her place I know Captain Hay met with a dissapointment, by his owners loosing his Reason, by which means captain Hay was detaind here a long time—nor do I know how long he has saild when circumstances are known, it greatly alters appearences[15]

Mrs Elworthy I saw at her House not long ago. She was well then. they live in the city & have but very small appartments not calculated to see company. they are people of Buisness honest industerous & obliging but their whole House is very little larger than your office.[16] mr John Cranch and I have the honour to correspond sometimes, he frequently sends us game from the Country, I inclose a letter from him which I received a few days ago to cousin Betsy. I fear I must acknowledg myself a delinquint with respect to my dear Brother Cranch I received his excellent Letters, and one of them was answerd, but it was at a time when no vessel was going for a long time and I did not think it worth a postage from Newyork so it grew old & out of date—[17] mr Adams is frequently chargeable with omissions to his correspondents, but he has more to plead in his excuse than I have, as his time is occupied in investigating more important Subjects—but when a vessel is near sailing you can hardly form an Idea what a call there is upon my pen and yet I leave some of my much esteemed Friends without a Line. I hope the vessels by which I have written are all safely arrived, and the articles I sent by them. Captain Callihan is so kind as to take a peice of Linnen for Tommys use it is not fine but a good fabrick. Remember me to all our Friends I shall write to several of them if I am able, if not they must attribute it to indisposition, as I am seldom able to set up a whole day at a time; & I ride out when the weather permits

Col Smith set of this week to portugal. it is the first seperation even of a day since he was married. Mrs Smith thought it a Sad affliction. She has not been innured like her mamma, and I hope she never may to such long dangerous & painfull seperations. she however behaved well when it came really to the trial, and the little Boy is a great amusement to her. I send the Caps for my worthy parent to whom present my duty & that of her great grandson.

I fear a little that my Eldest son will be so much of a Book worm & Scholar that he will grow too neglegent of those attentions which are due to the World, & which tho they may appear little, & trifling, much of our happiness is found by experience to depend upon them. his cousins must gaurd him against this error— it was a maxim of Epictetus's that it was incumbent on every one to offer libations and sacrifices conformable to the customs of his Country, with purity, and not in a slovenly manner, nor negligently,[18] that is, the muses & graces should join Hands—

adieu my dear sister and believe me with the tenderest sentiments of affection / your   A Adams

Remember me affectionately to all my Friends & Neighbours

Esther is well & so is Brisler who is one of the best of of Servants; Indeed I know not how I should keep house in this Country without him, on both my Americans I can depend. I never knew them deceive me, but the very best English servants which I have had, & I have been very fortunate, think deception & fibing no harm.

RC (MWA:Abigail Adams Letters). Dft (Adams Papers), filmed at 27 April.

¹ The Dft has "Febry 9ᵗʰ," which is correct; see vol. 7:462–466. No Mary Smith Cranch letter of 7 April to AA has been found.

² See AA to Lucy Cranch, 26 April, above; no letter to Elizabeth Cranch of this period has been found.

³ In the Dft AA notes, "I am now fully Satisfied that what I thought Rhumatick complaint was Billious."

⁴ Both the *New York Journal* and the New York *Daily Advertiser* reported on Shays' Rebellion in their issues of 8 March. AA's account most closely resembles that of the *Daily Advertiser*, which reported that "Gen. Lincoln is not at present so secure as we wish him to be." When government forces met the insurgents in a battle at Sheffield at dawn on 27 Feb., the newspaper reported that three died and "many more much injured." The insurgents then headed north: "Many, too many, of the rebels have fled to Vermont, where their security is much too evident." The Adamses may have received the newspaper from either John Jay or Samuel Osgood and Walter Livingston (Jay to JA, 2 April, Osgood and Livingston to JA, 4 April, both Adams Papers).

⁵ At this point in the Dft, AA wrote and then struck out, "the treasury of France seems to be in as deranged a state as the finances of the united States—in short." After omitting the RC's next sentence, she resumed, "you may well suppose. . . ." The state that "thawrts the measures of 11 or 12" was New York; see AA to JQA, 13 June 1786, vol. 7:216–217.

⁶ At this point the Dft adds the sentence, "this is only one instance amongst many others which shew the good will of this Nation—but I trust I shall live to see them Humbled & if America was but wise the time would not be very distant—"

⁷ The Dft replaces the previous sentence with "there are a set of Refugees residing here the magnitude of whose crimes forbids them ever to return to America. whose whole study it is to injure & abuse the country."

⁸ On 23 April 1787 the *Morning Chronicle and London Advertiser* published a letter from Benjamin Rush to Richard Price announcing the formation of several Pennsylvania institutions: Franklin College (later Franklin and Marshall College) in Lancaster, Pittsburgh Academy (later the University of Pittsburgh), the College of Physicians of Philadelphia Medical Society, and the American Philosophical Society. On 26 April a writer calling himself "A Hater of Incendiaries" published a letter in the same newspaper that characterized Rush's vision of a prosperous America as an "Empty delusion." American independence was "a flame which has consumed the lives and properties of thousands," and America is in fact suffering empty shops, vacant ports, and idle shipyards: "Is it not a fact that loyal British songs are publickly sung in the streets, and in companies in the great towns in North America (New-York particularly) with great applause, and with repeated marks of lamentation for the boasted independency?"

⁹ Lord Dorchester (Sir Guy Carleton), former commander of the British troops in America, was re-appointed governor of Quebec on 11 April 1786. William Smith (1728–1793), former chief justice of New York, served as Carleton's chief justice of Quebec beginning in either 1785 or 1786. Smith left America for London after the evacuation of New York in 1783, and he and Carleton became close associates (A. G. Bradley, *Sir Guy Carleton*, Toronto, 1966, p. 224; Sabine, *Loyalists*; *DAB*; *DNB*).

¹⁰ The Dft has "but to quit this Banditti. . . ."

¹¹ "The heyday in the blood is tame, it's humble, / And waits upon the judgment; and what judgment / Would step from this to this?" (Act III, scene iv, lines 68–70).

¹² Cranch recommended Ann Marsh Quincy, widow of Josiah Quincy, who had died in March 1784 (vol. 5:388, note 2; 7:463).

¹³ Elizabeth Rogers Willard, a loyalist who returned to Boston after her husband Abel's death in 1781 (vol. 7:465, note 3).

¹⁴ Charlotte Grandison and Anna Howe are the witty correspondents in Samuel Richardson's *The History of Sir Charles Grandison* (1765) and *Clarissa* (1747) (Albert J. Rivero, ed., *New Essays on Samuel Richardson*, Basingstoke, 1996, p. 8–9, 185–186).

¹⁵ The Dft notes that AA had seen Capt. John Hay twice since Katherine Hay had left England.

¹⁶ Here the Dft continues, "mr Elworthy came on some buisness here one day not long after we came & said it was the first time in his life that he was ever in this

square, tho it is Esteemed the first in London—"

[17] The Dft confirms that AA's "old & out of date" reply was never sent. Her next ex-tant letter to Richard Cranch is 10 May, below.

[18] Epictetus, *The Enchiridion,* ch. 31.

Abigail Adams to Cotton Tufts

my dear sir.   April 29 1787 London

yours of Febry 6th did not reach me untill Folger had saild.[1] I take the first opportunity to write you respecting the vermont land. I thought I had conversd with you upon it before I left America and related all the circumstances relative to it, you know I suppose that no person could hold more than one Right in their own Name. mr Adams's Name stands upon the Grant as an original proprieter of one Lot, & that is the Lot which remain unsetled. you will find four deed taken in the Names of other persons & transferd to 3 of the Children. mr davis forgot the Name of Tommy, & one of the deeds was transferd to mr Adams. these four I pay'd for at the time, & told mr Davis that the deeds unrecorded did not appear to me a sufficient security. before the other was setled, I wisht to have them renderd more valid. he replied that it would be done as soon as the affairs of vermont became more stable, that no taxes would be calld for till 3 years after the peace, & that it would be best before that time, for some person to attend the division of the Lots, & to make exchanges if necessary; that each persons property might lye compact. it was also Left at the option of each owner; to clear five acres of Land, or build a house & settle a family. there was no promise of interest, nor any fixed time for the payment of the money for the remaining lot: mr Cranch who owns there, can tell you perhaps more than I am able to recollect & of some person in Boston I forget who, that has a copy of the original Grant, by which mr davis himself owns the Township— I wish however if you could make it convenient, that you would take a ride there with one of my sons who may be glad to settle there for ought I know. I wish Congress had made them a 14 state. the British would have been less inclined to have tamperd with them. it is whisperd here as if Lord Dorchester was in treaty with them, and was engaging all their produce, & perhaps their aid to blow up future dissentions. how happend it that the delligates of Massachusetts should vote against them when on all former occasions they had been for receiving them into the union?[2]

If our state want any thing to make them Sick of the Idea of a paper currency, please to inform them that there is a combination here a set of scotch raskals who are procuring plates to counterfeit the money of the different States. about a month ago an engraver from the city, Carpenter by Name, was applied to for plates & to engrave a large sum of the money of carolina. he took a memorandam of the Bills, (the Signers name was torn from it,) gave the man encouragement that he would do them, but in the mean time came & gave information of the intended forgery, & said that he thought the man ought to be immediately detected, for tho he would not do the dirty Buisness, the man would find others who would. Col Smith applied to a justice in the city, but he said it was no offence against the Laws of this Country & he could do nothing in the matter an advertizement was inserted in the publick papers describing the Man & his designs & information sent to Carolina which was all that could be done as no proof could be had; that any of the Bills had been utterd here.[3] last week an express was sent from portsmouth to mr Adams informing him that a man was taken up there; who had applied to a printer having every thing ready to strike of his money & that he wanted a thousand Bills immediately. the Name of the printer who was applied to was mowbray, a very honest man as appears by his Letter and his conduct.[4] mr Wren the Worthy Clergyman of portsmouth who was the Father & friend of all the American prisoners who were confined in Forten prison during the war, interested himself in the detention of the man, & wrote also to mr Adams,[5] who upon recept of the Letters applied to Lord Carmarthen & from him to Sir Sampson Wright, who behaved with great honour in the affair & seemd disposed to do every thing in his power to prevent the Villiny, wrote to the Mayor of portsmouth to imprison the man as a suspicious person & to take away all his tools & impliments.[6] mr Adams thought it best to go to portsmouth and hear the man examined & find his accomplices if possible. he is a mean looking fellow in the habit of a sailor, tho it is thought he is in disguise says he is a Native of Scotland and that his Name is muir that he came from carolina in March last, but his answers were evasive & contradictory, sometimes saying that he came in one ship & sometimes in an other. his tools were all put into the custody of the majistrate & he recommitted to prison untill the next term he would not name any accomplices & was very shy in his answers only observing that he knew not what the magistracy of this country had to do with his proceedings, as it affected only the Country beyond the atlantick. he does not appear to be the same person who applied to mr Carpenter, & there is reason to believe that there are others engaged with him here; & not improbable that he was Sent from Carolina for this purpose. the Money that Carpenter was applied to for, was North Carolina this is for South—[7]

I think it would be well to put every State possesst of paper money upon their Gaurd

as to the politicks of this Country with respect to Ameria, they are neither wiser or better than they were, and it lies wholy with America to say what their future conduct shall be towards us. when ever congress possess powers sufficent to draw the resources of the Country into action Britain will look about her, at present they despise us and our Governments—

Mr Adams is advanced in his second vol[m] & says his Friends must not expect any Letters but printed ones from him. we have a young soldier, added to our family, if he possesses the Spirit of his Father, he may make a general on some future day

I think sir you must find Weymouth Dull; without a companion, it is not good for man to be alone. I dare say you have already experienced, but your son sir is a great delinquint, pray tell him that a man gets no good living single after his years. it is surely an unsatisfactory Idea to live and die without persueing any other purpose, than mere personal gratification, if we have received pleasures & advantages from the efforts of others, it is also incumbent upon us to do Something for the benifit of those who are to follow us, and where can a young Man begin this good work so well as by properly connecting himself & rearing a family? but I must leave this subject to his future consideration, and subscribe myself Dear sir your / ever affectionate / Neice   A Adams

P S inclosed you will find a curious act drawn up by Galloway as I am informed, but dismisd by the House of Lords. it is said on a petion of some British merchants, not withstanding it was moved by one chancellor & Seconded by an other. it will serve to shew the politicks of many in power.[8]

RC (Adams Papers); endorsed: "M[rs.] Adamss Lett[r.] April 29. 87 / Rec[d] July. 17. / *Vermont Lands.*"

[1] Vol. 7:457–459.
[2] Lord Dorchester had made recent attempts to entice Vermonters to ship their produce through Canada to the British West Indies. Those contacts were one of the results of Congress' vote on 3 June 1784 to deny Vermont statehood because of continuing questions about boundaries with New York, New Hampshire, and Massachusetts. Two of the three Massachusetts delegates had sided with the majority in refusing to consider statehood (JA to John Jay, 19 April 1787, *Dipl. Corr., 1783–1789,* 2:739–740; JCC, 27:529–536; Edward Brynn, "Vermont and the British Emporium," *Vermont History,* 45:21 [Winter 1977]).

[3] For Robert Muir's counterfeiting scheme and Richard Carpenter's role therein, see John Brown Cutting to AA, 25 April, note 3, above. Various American newspapers, including the Philadelphia *Independent Gazetteer*, 26 July, and the *Boston Gazette*, 6 Aug., reported on the story.

[4] Walter Mowbray informed JA that he had been approached "to print off a considerable number of notes of different Provinces," and that he sought "to destroy in embryo a scheme artfully calculated to invade private property, and materially injure the credit of a commercial nation" (Mowbray to JA, [20 April 1787], Adams Papers).

[5] Thomas Wren to JA, 20 April (Adams Papers), in which Mowbray's letter was enclosed.

[6] Sir Sampson Wright had been chief magistrate of London's Bow Street Magistrates Court since 1782. The mayor of Portsmouth was Sir John Carter. In JA's report to Jay on the situation, dated 30 April, he noted that the magistrates in both London and Portsmouth believed that the crime was "an offence against the law of nations, against commerce, against private and public property, against the whole world" (Sir Basil Thomson, *The Story of Scotland Yard*, rpt. edn., Whitefish, Mont., 2005, p. 39; Sheldon S. Cohen, "Thomas Wren: Portsmouth's Patron of American Liberty," *The Portsmouth Papers*, 57:23 [March

1991]; *Dipl. Corr., 1783–1789*, 2:740–741).

[7] JA did not share AA's skepticism that Muir was the man who had approached Carpenter. The press, likewise, unambiguously identified Muir as the culprit (JA to Jay, 30 April, *Dipl. Corr., 1783–1789*, 2:740–741; *Boston Gazette*, 6 Aug.).

[8] On 4 April the *Morning Chronicle and London Advertiser* carried a report on a proposed bill in the House of Lords entitled "An Act for Better Preventing Vexatious Suits Being Brought for the Recovery of Debts Contracted in America Previous to the Treaty of Peace with the United States." The act would have allowed British courts to expunge prewar debts contracted in America by loyalists whose property had been confiscated. A letter signed "Plain Truth" appeared in the *Morning Chronicle* on 28 April castigating "The Committee of Merchants Trading to America" for opposing the bill on "the flimsy pretext" that it was a violation of the peace treaty. The writer claimed that the merchants had another motivation for their opposition, "which you conceal, because it will not bear the test of humanity or justice": the fact that much of the debt due from loyalists was owed to English merchants. JA reported to John Jay on 19 April that the bill had been defeated, but that it nevertheless "shows the spirit of the present Ministry" (*Dipl. Corr., 1783–1789*, 2:739–740).

Abigail Adams to Elizabeth Smith Shaw

my dear sister   May 2d 1787 London

mr Blodget is going passenger in Captain Callihan and has offerd to take a Letter to you, who are his great favorite. he will be able to tell you that he has seen my little Grandson who was, not the first, but the 2d of April Born. we had him brought down on purpose that mr Blodget might report to you, that he is a fine Boy. His Mamma is as well as persons usually are she dinned below the day 3 weeks from her confinement, rather for the pleasure of dinning with mr Smith, who was to set of for portugal the next day, than because she was more than usually robust, for I think that she is so good a Nurse, that it keeps her rather feeble than otherways. She sends her duty to you, and little master would send his to his *great Aunt* if he knew her. you may put up with the term, since your sister is obliged to; with that of *Gandmamma* I have spirits my dear sister, but my

37

Health is very feeble. I have been labouring with Billious disorders, and a slow intermitting fever near two months. I hope however that it is leaving me

your kind Letter of Febry 8th came safe to hand.[1] As to our publick affairs, they make me sick, having weatherd the storms of War, I had hoped peace would have confirmed to us the Blessings we had dearly Earned, but this rather proves the wish of Benevolence, than an investigation into the Character of Humane Nature—an unprincipald mob is the worst of all Tyrannies. Wisdom to our Rulers and uninimity to our patriots, and virtue to all our fellow citizens, will remedy the present Tumults, and to their Honour, no small share of these qualities have already shewn themselves most sincerely can I join in the prayer of the Churchmen. Give us peace in our day good Lord. I shall form my judgment of the sentiments of the people by their Elections. one of the best symptoms will be the Reelection of the Governour, and such senators, and members as have taken the most open and decided part in favour of government, and the quelling that spirit of sedition against the Bar & Bench, which first fomented, and Countananced this Rebellion. Shays has not been a greater incendary than Honestus. Shame to our citizens that they should wish to curtail the sallery of their Governour. do they want to make him a man of straw?[2] it is impossible whilst humane Nature is such as we find it that the people should venerate a man unless he is supported according to his Rank and station. they are the first to despise & laugh at him and to contemn his power and Authority—

You will see by the Defence of the American Constitutions, what the Sentiments of my Friend are. the Book has met with a favourable reception here, and the critical Reviewers of last month, who are mostly Scotchmen, and concequently unfriendly to America, have treated it with great civility, nay they have said as many Handsome things of it, as could have been expected.[3]

it was really the work of 3 months only. the subject is still persueing with more leisure in a 2d volm

I am very glad to find my Friend Mrs Allen like to increase her family. I have kept my word & send the Christning suit by mr Blodget to your care, pray deliver it with my Love to her and best wishes for her safety. the suit cost one pound sixteen & six pence sterling. I mention this only to you that in case any Bodys curiosity should be excited, they might be satisfied and not to enhance the value of my present. in the same Box you will find a sash for my little Neice, sent not for the Beauty of it in my Eye, but to shew you how various a dame Fashion is, wastcoats Bonnets ribbons, all in the plad figure & coulours. I expect we shall have silks & calicoes in the same manner.

I hope my Neice received the Books I sent her & my dear sister the silk.[4] it is a great pleasure to me to find Tommy so well situated. it would be strange indeed if a visit to your House, was not like going Home. can there be a more agreeable sensation than that of being joyfully received by Friends who Love us? a pleasure of which I have been deprived for near 3 years, but which in the course of an other, I hope to experience. adieu my dear sister. The sun breaks out, and I must go and ride in quest of Health. present me affectionately to mr Shaw mr Thaxter & all inquiring Friends and believe me / your ever affectionate / Sister   A Adams

May 6th

PS—mrs Smith has had a large Boil gather upon one of her Breast which tho not so bad as a broken Breast, has made her very sick & brought her quite low it broke to day, & she is much better— accept my dear sister a bit of muslin for a slip for my Neice I think if you make the skirt a yd long & wealt it, there will be enough for 2 waists—

RC (DLC:Shaw Family Papers); addressed by John Brown Cutting: "Mrs Elisabeth Shaw / Haverhill"; endorsed: "May 2d 1787"; notation by AA: "favourd pr mr / Blodget." Dft (Adams Papers), filmed at 29 April.

[1] Vol. 7:459–462.
[2] On 10 March, Gov. James Bowdoin vetoed the General Court's attempt to reduce the governor's salary from £1100 to £800. The veto added to Bowdoin's growing unpopularity and contributed to John Hancock's victory in the spring elections (*DAB*; Mass., *Acts and Laws*, 1786–1787, p. 976–978).
[3] The April issue of the London *Critical Review* praised JA's *Defence of the Const.*, saying, "Dr. Adams examines different plans with care; objects to those parts which are deficient; supports his objections, and defends the American constitutions with sound argument. . . . We need not repeat our commendations of this work; or seek for little faults, when the whole is, in general, so well executed" (63:248–253). For more on reviews of the *Defence*, see vol. 7:365–366, note 14, and C. Bradley Thompson, "John Adams and the Science of Politics," *John Adams and the Founding of the Republic*, ed. Richard Alan Ryerson, Boston, 2001, p. 258–259.
[4] On 20 Jan., AA had sent books to her nephew William and silk to her niece Elizabeth Quincy Shaw (vol. 7:453). More recently, on 10 March, above, AA had sent silk to Elizabeth Smith Shaw but made no mention of books for Betsy Quincy.

Abigail Adams to John Quincy Adams

My dear son   London May 6 1787

I would not omit writing you by captain Callihan, as your sister is unable to perform that office herself.

I know you will be anxious to hear from us, and in particular from her. Learn then my dear son that you became an uncle on the 2d day of April & that your Nephew is as fine a Boy for a month old as ever I saw. he has the Brow of his Grandpappa & the Shape & form of his Father. This will be no bad assemblage when Years mature the one & time strengthings & enlarges the other.

your sister has been very well, till within a few days, when from the badness of the weather she took cold and is again confined to her Chamber by a feverish disposition, but I hope it will prove only slight, and leave her in a few days

I have been sick myself with an intermitting fever, which has been an irregular companion for two months, by a proper Regimin and excercise I hope to rid myself of it, I am much better than I was.

Col Smith set of for Lisbon as I wrote you he would; as soon as he thought it safe to leave your sister, after her confinement, but we feel his absence not a little. he was not only the sensible rational companion, but the enlivener of all our scenes; & the soul of our little parties. mr Shipping & cutting are our *domesticated* acquaintance.— Mr & Mrs de Valney are here from France & have spent sometime in England;[1] What think you of French politicks? The Death of Count de Vergennes the Disgrace of de Callone, & the meeting of the Notables, together with the objects presented to their discussion, will form a grand Epocha in the Reign of Louis the 16th[2] it is said that the King of Spain is going to call an assembly of the Nobles of his kingdom.[3] in Holland, Amsterdam & Roterdam have had a singular triumph lately, over the orange party, but of this the paper inclosed will inform you.[4] in short there seems to be a universal commotion in the political World.

I wish most sincerely that the meeting of our Convention which is to take place this month, may reform abuses, Reconcile parties, give energy to Government & stability to the States, but I sometimes fear we Must experience new Revollutions, before we shall set under our vines in peace.

I hope you have received all my Letters & particularly, that by way of Newyork

I send you a performance of Your Friend murrys[5] I have also sent to mr Cranch, the critical Review, in which the defence of the American Constitutions are Spoken as highly of as so hasty a performance as it really was could expect to be treated, but you know the subject has been long contemplated, and was in that respect no sudden work—the 2d Volm is in no small readiness—

adieu I shall write your Brothers if I have time, if I have not give my Love to them and be / assured of the affectionate / tenderness of your Mother   A A

RC (Adams Papers).

¹ For Eunice Quincy and Joseph de Valnais, the former French consul in Boston, see vol. 5:430.

² The Assembly of the Notables began on 22 Feb. at Versailles. Charles Alexandre de Calonne, the comptroller general of finances, addressed France's financial crisis, blaming it on the fiscal policy of the former French minister of finance, Jacques Necker, while justifying his own. Calonne's speech was published as a pamphlet, and Necker refuted Calonne's charges with a pamphlet of his own. Calonne was soon implicated in suspect real estate transactions and other financial scandals involving public monies and was dismissed on 8 April. The Comte de Vergennes had died on 13 Feb., depriving Louis XVI of a crucial advisor and Calonne of an influential defender at a key point in the political crisis (Schama, *Citizens*, p. 227–247). See also *Objets proposés a l'Assemblée des notables*, Paris, 1787; *The Speech of Mr. de Calonne, Comptroller-General of the Finances, Delivered by the Order and in the Presence of the King*, London, 1787; and *Mr. Necker's Answer to Mr. de Calonne's Charge against Him in the Assembly of Notables*, London, 1787. For a newspaper report of the pamphlet war, see London *Gazetteer and New Daily Advertiser*, 25 April.

³ Although the *Morning Chronicle and London Advertiser* reported on 30 April that Charles III of Spain had called for a *cortes*, or national assembly, to meet in Madrid in the summer, no assembly was held until after his death in 1788. While the cortes was a powerful branch of the Spanish government in the seventeenth century, the Bourbon kings had vastly reduced its role, and it met only three times during the eighteenth century (John Lynch, *Bourbon Spain 1700–1808*, Cambridge, 1989, p. 106–107, 298; W. N. Hargreaves-Mawdsley, *Eighteenth-Century Spain 1700–1788: A Political, Diplomatic and Institutional History*, London, 1979, p. 11–12).

⁴ Dutch society in the 1780s was rife with revolutionary political struggle. In April 1787, the Council of the Regency in Amsterdam and Rotterdam voted to dismiss members who were not adherents to the Patriot party cause. The Patriots' political attacks on the pro-British Orange party turned to armed conflict in May 1787 when rioting broke out on the streets. News of the unrest received extensive coverage in the London press throughout the conflict and, in the early stages of the fighting, the Patriot party gained considerable ground (Schama, *Citizens*, p. 248–252). For press coverage see, for example, *Morning Chronicle and London Advertiser*, 3 May; London *Daily Universal Register*, 17 April and 17 May; and London *Gazetteer and New Daily Advertiser*, 30 May. See also JA to AA, 1, 2, June, both below.

⁵ William Vans Murray, *Political Sketches, Inscribed to His Excellency John Adams, Minister Plenipotentiary from the United States to the Court of Great Britain*, London, 1787. Murray (1760–1803) was a friend of JQA and an ardent political disciple of JA. In *Political Sketches*, Murray responds to Abbé de Mably's *Remarks Concerning the Government and the Laws of the United States of America: In Four Letters, Addressed to Mr. Adams*, London, 1784. Mably's belief in state control of the press and church, his contention that luxury was incompatible with democracy, and his belief that the American system of government was doomed to failure all came under vigorous attack in Murray's work (Alexander DeConde, "William Vans Murray's *Political Sketches*: A Defense of the American Experiment," *MVHR*, 41:631–634 [March 1955]).

Abigail Adams to Richard Cranch

Dear sir   London May 10th 1787

Inclosed Sir I send you the Review of the defence of the American constitution, which if you please you may have published in the Boston papers,[1] and an other pamphlet is inclosed; calld political Sketches, written by a mr Murry a young Gentleman from Maryland who is a student in the Temple. you will see that he has parts, and Genious, tho I think he has sometimes renderd his meaning obscure by too many words.

I acknowledge myself much indebted to you for two excellent Letters,[2] and mr Adams is your debtor also, but he says his Friends must not expect any but printed Letters from him. he is persueing the same subject through an other volm in which he is considering the Ialian Republicks through the middle age a work of no small labour—as well as expensive in the article of Books.[3]

The Royall family appear at present a House divided against themselves— mr Fox has been authorized by the Prince to declare in the House, that no ceremony like a marriage had ever taken place between him & mrs Fitzherbert— those believe it who can, but with what Face then has the Prince introduced her into all companies, amongst those who certainly would not have received her as his xxxxx—it is still a mistery. I have sent my son a pamphlet calld anticipation of speaches upon Alderman Newnhams motion for Relieving the Prince from his debts & increasing his Revenue[4] the writers have not spaired his Character, nor yet exagerated his faults, he will lend it you— you will see by the papers the account of things in France. Holland appears determined upon a through Revolution in favour of the people. I inclose you a little publication of mr Neckers,[5] and some French papers which Mr Adams takes, may afford you some amusement

By the latest accounts which we have received from your side the Water, it appears that the Rebellion is pretty well quelld. I wish most sincerely that all your other difficulties were in as fair a train, but I fear they will be increased by an event which has spread an amazing allarm here within a few Days. I mean the protesting to the amount of Forty thousands pounds worth of mr Morris & co Bills Some make the sum much larger, but I speak only from the [au]thority of the House who was to answer them, whether the deficiency is in America, or in France time must determine, but it is a terrible stab to what little remaind, of credit to America. What renders this event more terrible at this Time, is that the Board of Treasury had sold to mr morris tobaco & taken his Bills for the payment of the interest in Holland, which is due in june transmitted here to Mr Adams, to be tenderd by him to the House of Rucker but mr Rucker & family had left the Kingdom and the Bills are protested, and mr Adams is in anxiety enough to know what can be done.[6] this last matter you will keep private. as to his other Bills being protested, the whole city rings with it, and I suppose in concequence of it every House with which he is concernd will push him at once. What the concequence will be no one can Say. will newyork still persist in refusing the impost? what [is to] become of us?[7]

RC (NAII:Cranch-Greenleaf Papers); endorsed: "Letter from M[s.] / Adams, Lady of / his Ex[cy.] / May. 10[th.] 1787." Some loss of text due to a torn manuscript.

[1] The review of JA's *Defence of the Const.* from the April 1787 *Critical Review* was reprinted in the *Massachusetts Centinel*, 22, 26 September.

[2] Richard Cranch's last two extant letters to AA were dated 13 April and 5 July 1786 (vol. 7:138–140, 242–244).

[3] JA retained in his library, now at MB, a number of books on Italian history, including Domenico Buoninsegni, *Historia fiorentina*, Florence, 1581; Gasparo Bombaci, *Historie memorabili della città di Bologna*, Bologna, 1666; Cherubino Ghirardacci, *Della historia di Bologna [parte prima]*, Bologna, 1605; Pietro Giannone, *Istoria civile del regno di Napoli*, 5th edn., Naples, 1770; Francesco Guicciardini, *The History of Italy*, 3d edn., transl. Austin Parke Goddard, London, 1763; Niccolò Machiavelli, *Works*, 2d edn., transl. Ellis Farneworth, London, 1775; Lodovico Antonio Muratori, *Annali d'Italia dal principio dell' era volgare, sino all' anno 1750*, 12 vols. in 6, Naples, 1773; and Muratori, *Dissertazioni sopra le antichità italiane*, Milan, 1751 (*Catalogue of JA's Library*; Haraszti, *Prophets*, p. 47).

[4] *Anticipation of the Speeches Intended to Be Spoken in the House of Commons, on Friday, May 4: Upon the Motion of Alderman Newnham, Relative to the Affairs of the Prince of Wales*, London, 1787.

[5] Probably *Mr. Necker's Answer to Mr. de Calonne's Charge against Him in the Assembly of Notables*, for which see AA to JQA, 6 May, note 2, above.

[6] In March 1787, Robert Morris had given bills of exchange worth 75,000 florins to the U.S. Board of Treasury for the sale of his tobacco in France. The bills, however, were protested for nonpayment. John Rucker, who served as Morris' financial agent in London, was discredited by this nonpayment, which also served to undermine the United States' ability to pay the interest on its Dutch loan. Rucker and his family left England as a result of the scandal (*Dipl. Corr., 1783–1789*, 2:751–754; JA, *Works*, 8:444–445; JA to Samuel Osgood, Walter Livingston, and Arthur Lee, 8 March [May], LbC, APM Reel 112). See also AA2 to JQA, 10 June, below.

[7] At this point in the manuscript the remainder of the page was cut off.

Abigail Adams to Mary Smith Cranch

My dear sister   May 11. 1787 London

Captain Callihans delay gives me an other opportunity of writing you, tho I have nothing material to add, but that I have pleasd my fancy in a peice of chintz which I have sent to my Neices. when I first came to this country near 3 years ago I bought one for mrs smith & an other for myself like it. it wore so well, washt so nice, & lookd so pretty; that I have been frequently seeking the same pattern: but as there is but one man in England who printed the pattern I never could find but one peice of it; which I bought for mr Jefferson last spring. the other day in comeing up the Strand I cast my Eye upon this very peice, and I did not let the opportunity slip of buying it for my dear Neices I hope it may please them as much as it has done me, and be received by them as a token of my affection. their Books are put up in the Same bundle with some pamphlets I have sent their Father. I bought 2 waistcoat patterns one for J Q A & the other I ask your sons acceptance of. he may take his choice. you will find in the same Bundle some dimity for draws, for my son that stands most in need. I have divided my parcels between captain Callihan & mr Blodget, that I may not over load either. if they were not so good as to put them in their Trunks for me, many of the articles would be obliged to pay a duty— mrs Smith is yet confined, not with a real broken Breast, but with a succession of Boils which tho a little more than Skin deep, have been very troublesome. She has had half a dozen of them for myself I have been better for a week past than, for two months.

I have not heard from you for a long time, at least it seems so to me. The terrible event which has happend to our American affairs & which mr Cranch can explain to you, has obliged the only American family who resided here to quit the Kingdom; even without taking leave, mr Ruckers family whom I have frequently mentiond to you: both she & her sister were in habits of intimacy here. mr Rucker personally I suppose is not concernd any otherways than as an agent for mr Morris—but he is the last American House there is to run away (I except those who have taken up their final residence here)— indeed I know not but it will come to our turn, sooner rather than we intended; for if we cannot get even our sallery, we must quit too, at present the allarm is so great that I know not the concequence. mr Adams is in great perplexity for the credit of the united states, but he must Suffer in silence, & devize means & Rack his Brain for some expedient to save it.

I wish I was safe in America, but that will be a little like; getting out of the frying pan into the Fire—and I do not foresee what is to become of us there. We shall have corn & Beans I hope, & that will be a luxery after having lived without so long— I am not apt to distress myself. I can ride in a one horse chaise the rest of my Life without being at all mortified, and very happy if I can get that, and I can do many other things, which I do not now. I have never spent half so many pleasent hours in Europe, in the same space of time, as I have known at the foot of pens Hill, and there I hope to be blessed again in the Society of my Sisters and Friends. I look forward to the day with pleasure and / am most tenderly yours

A Adams

RC (MWA:Abigail Adams Letters); addressed: "To / Mrs Mary Cranch / Braintree"; notation: "favourd pr mr / Blodget."

Abigail Adams to Mercy Otis Warren

my dear Madam[1]   London May 14 1787

I have lately been reading Mrs Montague's essays upon the Genious and writings of shakspear, and I am so well pleased with them; that I take the Liberty of presenting them to you.[2] The Lady is still living, a widow, and possessd of an ample fortune, without any children, she has a Nephew who bears the same name and has lately been returnd a member to parliament.[3] I should have wished to have formed an acquaintance with her,[4] if I had not learnt that she was a voilent Anti American, tho a sister of a mr Roberson who has written some things in favour of our Country, and who has always been Friendly to our cause.[5]

I have resided in this Country near two years and in that time, I have made some few acquaintance whom I esteem and shall leave with regreet, but the customs and manners of a Metropolis are unfriendly to that Social intercourse which I have ever been accustomed to. Amusement and diversion may always be purchased at the Theatres & places of publick resort, so that little pains is taken to cultivate that benevolence & interchange of kindness which sweetens life, in lieu of which mere visits of form are substitued to keep up the union; not only the wrinkeled brow of age is grasping at the card table & even tricking with mean avarice, but the virgin bloom of innocence and beauty is withered at the same vigils. I do not think I should draw a false picture of the Nobility and Gentry of this Metropolis, if I was to assert, that Money and pleasure are the sole objects of their ardent persuit, publick virtue, & indeed all virtue is exposed to Sale,[6] and as to principle, where is it to be found, either in the present administration, or opposition? Luxery dissapation and vice, have a natural tendency to extirpate every generous principle, and leave the Heart susceptable of the most malignant vices. to the total absence of principle must be ascribed the conduct of the Heir apparant to the British Throne, which is the subject of much speculation at this moment. The World have Supposed that a marriage had taken place between the prince, and a Lady known by the Name of Fitzherbert, whom for 3 years he persued driving her for more than half that time out of her country to avoid him. as she was in independant circumstances, of an ancient & respectable family; of a Fair Character and honorable connections every person presumed her married to him, Tho contrary to the establishd Laws of the Land, & this not only by a Catholick priest, but a protestant one too, every step for more than a year has confirmed this Idea, as the Lady has attended him; not only to the Watering places, but into all publick, and private parties, and at the princs request has been countananced by the first persons in the Kingdom, and the publick papers have announced the report & given credit to it uncontradicted throughout all Europe, but now at a Time when he wishes to be relieved from the load of debt he has contracted, and finds that this affair is like to become a subject of parlimentary discussion, he authorizes Charles Fox (A Man as unprincipald as the prince) to declare the whole story a malicious falsehood, and in the most explicit terms to deny even the shadow of a marriage.[7] yet not a person whom I have heard mention the subject since believes; a syllable of mr Fox's assertion thus does this young man set both Law & Decency at defience; his Friends are even so barefaced as to pretend that no connexion but of the platonick kind has ever subsisted between them, he a mere Scipio, & she a vestal. What a prospect for this Country? What a prostration of Honour & virtue! the Heir Apparant, frequenting the Haunts of intemperance and vice, his greatest intimates Sycophants and Knaves, appearing in company so disguised as to lose himself, and commit the greatest rudeness, which was the case not a month Since— Yet when sober really possessing the outward appearence of a well bred gentleman, by Some he is held up as a man of Learning and abilities, but of this I cannot learn any Specimins; not even a refinement in his vices, since he is branded with a taste, for the lowest & most vulgar—but I will quit him, Since I shall never owe him; either honour or Allegence, and will turn my attention to my own Country, which tho not terrified with the prospect of a proffligate prince to govern it appears to be in an untranquilized state, embarrassed in its Finances, distresst in its commerce and unbalanced in its Governments, but I have Faith that will remove mountains, and as distress and difficulties in private life, are frequently Spurs to dilligence, so have we seen publick industery excited in the same manner, during the late War. Success crowned our efforts and gave us Independance, our misfortune is that then we became indolent and intoxicated; Luxery with ten thousand evils in her train, exiled the humble virtues. Industery & frugality, were swallowd up in dissipation.

"but it is not upon Record, says a late writer that any state was ever yet so exhausted, but that whilst it enjoyed Liberty it might draw new resources from its own vitals. Though the tree is lopped, yet so long as the root remains unhurt, it will through out a greater Luxuriancy of Branches, produce fruits of better flavour and derive fresh vigor from the ax—"[8]

Why my Dear Madam, may we not console ourselves with Ideas of this kind, instead of giving way to despondency? I was very happy to learn that my young Friend Harry distinguishd himself with the ardour of a patriot, and the zeal of a Good Citizen in accompanying General Lincoln in his late expedition.[9] had Pericles lived in the present day, he could not have made the boast, which he does in his funeral oration over the Athenians, Saying that they were the *only people*, who thought those who did not lend their assistance in State affairs—not indolent—but good for Nothing.[10] it is indeed a pleasing presage of future good, when the most promising Youth, shrink not from danger, through a fondness for those delights, which a peacefull affluent Life bestows "but bare their bold Breast, & pour their generous Blood"[11] esteeming it a dishonour that their Country should stand in need of any thing which their valour can acchive.[12]

I Long my dear madam to return to my native land. my little Cottage encompassed with my Friends has more charms for me than the drawing Room of St James,[13] where Studied civility, and disguised coldness, cover malignant Hearts.

I will not close this letter without informing you that I am—a Grand—o no! That would be confesing myself old, which would be quite unfashionable and vulgar—but true it is. I have a fine grandson. I regreet a little that it was not a daughter, for then I would have claimd the little one for the great one. Mrs Smith desires me to present her respectfull compliments to you, with thanks for your kind and Friendly Letter, which she will notice as soon as she is able.[14] be so good as to present my Regards to the Genll, and all your Worthy family. I must acquit myself of a promise made to a young Gentleman, who requested me when I wrote to you, to lay him respectfully at your feet, by which I presume he meant that I should express, the high esteem and profound veneration, which he always professes towards You, and I knew not how to do it better: than by giving you his own words. I dare say you will be at no loss to recollect this Gentleman by the Name of Shipping; who is as Geenteel well Bred a youth as any one from our Country, and who is quite at home with us as well as his companion mr Cutting, who I think will make a figure in Life, as he has both abilities and application.

I know not what to say for my companion that he has not written a single Letter by this opportunity, but that he is so much engaged in travelling through the Itallian Republicks that I cannot draw of his attention, except only to official Letters. he says his Friends must accept his printed letters. I will not apoligize for the length of my Letter, concious as I am of all my Sins of omission, but be assured dear Madam, That neither a want of affection or Regard are in the number, for those my Heart shall not reproach

Your assured Friend   Abigail Adams

RC (MHi:Warren-Adams Coll.); docketed by James Warren: "Mrs Abigail Adams / May 14th 1787"; notation: "No 17." Dft (Adams Papers).

[1] AA initially started the Dft with the following paragraph: "my dear Madam Tis a long time since I had the pleasure of receiving a line from you. I have written you twice to which I have never had any replice, if mrs Warrens pen was not more interestingly employd I should find it in my Heart to complain, yet so much time as she employs in that way, an old Friend might at least claim a small portion— if there has been any delinquincy in that way let it not be imputed to any failure in Friendship but merely." She then abandoned that attempt, turned the paper over, and began again.
Warren had last written to AA on 18 Sept. 1785 (Adams Papers).

[2] Elizabeth Robinson Montagu, *An Essay on the Writings and Genius of Shakespear*, London, 1769. Montagu (1720–1800) was a renowned British author and London hostess whose assemblies inspired the term "bluestocking," possibly a reference to the color of stockings worn by the women who attended these gatherings (*DNB*).

[3] Matthew Robinson (1762–1831) took his aunt's name of Montagu in 1776 and inherited her estate after her death in 1800. He

was elected as a member of Parliament beginning in 1786 and served intermittently through 1812 (Namier and Brooke, *House of Commons*, 3:157).

[4] Instead of the previous phrase, the Dft has the following: "I should have taken some steps to have got introduced to her by dr Shippis who is acquainted with her."

[5] For examples of Matthew Robinson-Morris' pro-American writing, see vol. 1:202–204, and note 11; 7:87–88, and note 5.

[6] At this point in the Dft, AA included the following: "dr price was mentioning a saying of his Friend mr Robinson whom I mentiond in the former part of this Letter, 'we have says he an Ignorant administration and a wicked opposition mr Fox mr Sheridan & Burke are all men of desperate fortunes[']."
The sentiments attributed to Robinson-Morris are in line with those he expressed in his 1786 tract *The Dangerous Situation of England*, in which he described the interaction of British political parties: "Administration produces and imposes taxes: Opposition echoes back and calls for taxes; for numerous, extensive and effective taxes." He also decried the influence of merchant compa-

nies on public officials: "What are such institutions other than the contrivances of greedy
and selfish men to engross into a few hands
the general rights of all and perhaps the
unjust indulgence of administrations arising
from partiality or a desire of corruption?"
(Matthew Robinson-Morris, *The Dangerous
Situation of England*, 2d edn., London, 1786,
p. 2–3, 57).

[7] AA was prompted to revisit the affair of
the Prince of Wales' secret marriage to Maria
Anne Fitzherbert by Fox's false declaration in
the House of Commons in April that the
marriage had never occurred. In May the
affair was again in the news when Fitzherbert was subpoenaed to testify in a case in
which Lord George Gordon was charged
with libeling the queen of France (vol. 7:xi–
xii; London *Daily Universal Register*, 1 May;
Percy Fitzgerald, *The Life of George the
Fourth*, N.Y., 1881, p. 110).

[8] Vicesimus Knox, *Essays Moral and Literary*, 6th edn., 2 vols., London, 1785, 2:180.

[9] Henry Warren served as Gen. Benjamin
Lincoln's aide during the campaign to suppress Shays' Rebellion (vol. 7:464).

[10] In "Pericles' Funeral Oration" in Book
II of *The History of the Peloponnesian War*,
Thucydides quotes Pericles as saying, "Our
public men have, besides politics, their private affairs to attend to, and our ordinary
citizens, though occupied with the pursuits
of industry, are still fair judges of public

matters; for, unlike any other nation, regarding him who takes no part in these duties not
as unambitious but as useless, we Athenians
are able to judge at all events if we cannot
originate, and, instead of looking on discussion as a stumbling-block in the way of action, we think it an indispensable prelimi-
nary to any wise action at all."

[11] Prodicus of Ceos, *The Judgment of Hercules, A Poem*, transl. Robert Lowth, Glas-
gow, 1743, line 130. See also vol. 3:23; 7:13,
25, 78, 80.

[12] The Dft includes the following paragraph: "I should however esteem it a blessing
that the valour of our youth might never
again be called forth but to quell a foreign
foe whilst on the one hand we have reason to
lament the fatal delusion which armed the
Rebel hand against Law & Government. we
can pleasingly reflect upon the spirt that has
crushd the Serpent before its venoum
Spread further & wider–"

[13] The Dft initially included the following:
"the cordiallity of a Benevolent Smile would
warm my Heart from the most unpolishd
Neighbour would warm my Heart, more
than the studiest civility the disguised coldness which covers the malignant Hearts of
George & charlott," but AA crossed it out,
leaving only the paragraph as it stands in
the RC.

[14] Not found.

Elizabeth Smith Shaw to Abigail Adams

My Dear Sister—   Haverhill May 20th. 1787—

Yours of July 19th which either did, or was to have come in Callihan last Fall, I did not receive 'till the 6th of March[1]—where it had
lain, or where Peabody got it from I cannot tell—but this I know, I
am glad I have it, for it is a valuable acquisition to me, as rich, &
precious Treasure, as all my dear Sisters Letters are—

Your eldest Son made us a Visit of a few Days in March— He says
he enjoys fine Health— He is much thiner than he was in Europe—
But what he loses in Flesh, he gains in Beauty— He looks more, &
more like his Mother— Upon my word, I know not a likelier Youth—
He behaved in so modest, agreeable, & pleasing a manner, as if he
wished to convince us that the *only* Error which we ever suggested
to him, was intirly removed; as I presumed it would be, after a few
more years had ripened his Judgment, & Experience had shewn that

the wisest, & best of Men differed greatly in their Opinions, & Ideas of Things, & that it was no easy matter to fix the exact point, where

> "Error ended, or the Truth begun—"[2]

I had much rather see a youth tenacious of his own Sentiments, & Opinion, than appear as though he had none— The latter implies a stupid, dissolute, dissapated state of Mind, while the former indicates Thought, & Reflection— In the one, the Soil appears either weak, or polluted—while the other wants nothing but Time, & the gentle hand of Affection to prune the excresent Branches, to make it yield Fruit in abundance fair to the Eye, & rich to the Taste—

Your Son is possessed of one quality, which must forever endear him to his Friends—& that is a communicative, facetious Disposition— He appears to have nothing which he need *wish* to secrete, & therefore feels happy in communicating his Pleasures, & Amusements— How calm, how serene, must *his* retired Moments be— How very different when compared with the dark, artful, intriguing Youth, whose versatility, & duplicity, whose Artifice, & Flattery, simulation & disimulation render him the most fearful, suspicious, as well as the most uneasy Thing in Nature—

There was a *Time*, when I was very anxious for *your young* Hercules, lest his Heart might be subdued by *One* whom I knew his riper Judgment, could never approve—[3] I knew she had the most brilliant Talents, & could assume the most enchanting manners, whenever she pleased for the purpose of Conquest— She often made me think of those Lines of Young—

> "O how she rolls her *charming Eyes* in spite!
> And looks *delightfully* with *all her might*—

but too vain, & too volatile to fix with Choice,

> "She conquers for the *Triumph*, not the Prize."[4]

We were conversing together one Day, when he was boasting rather too much I thought of his own *Security*, against every female Charm, when I took occasion to tell him, I feared, *that* was a Rock which would endanger him— For when Persons thought the outworks *safe* it had not been an unusual thing for the Citidal to be conquered— This brought on a very confidential & interesting Conversation— He told me that while he was in Europe, he became acquainted with a young Lady of great delicacy, & merit—a Person

whose Character, & Manners nearly resembled his Cousin E——
C——s, & that his heart *almost* became a Vassal to her many Virtues–that this early attachment had secured him against the Snares,
& inroads of a less worthy Object– And though it was left to his
Choice to return, or to pursue his Studies with *her* Father, yet he
prefered the former, as the most compatible with his Plans, & future Prospects–[5] I could not help looking upon the amiable Youth
before me, with additional love, & respect– Sure (thought I) "Wisdom hath entered into thine Heart– Knowledge is pleasant unto thy
Soul– Discretion hath preserved thee– & may Understanding still
keep thee–"[6]

"Indeed my Aunt (said he) I know you have been concerned for
me, but you need not have the least fearful Apprehension with regard to this Lady, for though I was exceedingly pleased at first, yet I
have lived long enough with her to know her Principles, & see into
the motives of her Conduct, & the Lord knows, *she* is not the Person who would engage my Affections–" So true it is, that

> "Arts on the Mind, like paint upon the Face
> Fright him that's worth your Love, from your
>   embrace."[7]

I assure you this tete a tete gave me great releif, for I had seen a
Peice inscribed to *Delia*,[8] & had critically observed each movement– But there appeared so much openness in his Countenance,
& manner, as left me no room to doubt his Sincerity–

When he was here last he seemed to be very anxious & thought-
ful what he should do with himself, & who he should Study with
after Commencement– He seemed inclined to go to Worcester–
But I told him that was because his *Father* had acquired his knowledge of the Law there– Times were altered– The Gentleman his
Father had lived with, was not now there–& if he was, perhaps he
would not prefer his living with *him*–[9] There were several Gentlemen he mentioned that we did not know– Judge Lincoln,[10] & Mr
Parsons of Newbury, Mr Shaw is personally acquainted with–&
upon many accounts gave the preference to the latter–though they
are both great Practitioners, & eminent in their Proffession–

The time will soon arrive when he will commence– He will not
like many of his fellow students have his Proffession to chuse, for in
that he has been determined for these many Years– And if application can make a Man distinguished, I presume, he will shine with

no inferior Lustre— The President has not grieved, nor vexed him with a Syllogism—but has conffered upon the honour of an English Oration—

Mr Shaw has three Pupils, who will take there Degrees this year— If my Health, & the health of my Family will permit, I am determined to go—And then the Sky-born Silk, which you kindly fancy I have some pretensions to, will be made up, & worn—

It is thought most for the honour of the Colledge to have a publick Commencement, though a very *Economical One*—

I believe the Idea of performing before so crowded an Auditory, must have a very great Influence upon the Mind of an ambitious Youth—And it must be a mean spirited Fellow who does not feel its force, & double his Diligence—

If I had written half so much about any-other Person, but your own Son, I should feel ashamed to send it— But what Subject can be more pleasing to a Parent, than the Concerns of her dear Children—

I was greatly affected (as I presume you will be) at hearing of the Death of that Man God, the Rev^d Dr Gay—[11]

The very particular, & great Friendship which subsisted between him, & my Father, made him doubly dear to me— I was taught to love, & respect him from my earliest Infancy— I can remmember when I have stood by him, & sought to be noticed, as if I had believed a stroke over my Head, a Pat upon my Shoulder, & a Squeze of his hand would infuse some heavenly Virtue—

Never shall I forget his Visiting my Father in his last Sickness— when with Eyes full of Compassion, & tender Sympathy—with faultering Steps, & trembling accents, he approached the Bed, & said, "my Brother I did not expect *you* would get to heaven before me."

Pity for the extreme Distress of our dear Parent, called up every tender emotion of his benevolent Soul, & stopped the Utterance—

He was not *himself* called to pass through such dire Conflicts— He had his wish, that he might wear, & not rust out—For he was preparing for the duties of the Day, & looking over his Notes, when he was called to go a Sabbath Days Journey—& I presume sweet was the Journey to the Sky, which this wondering Prophet took—for—

> "Sweetly he lay his fainting head,
> Upon his Maker's Breast,
> His Maker kissed his Soul away
> And laid his Flesh to rest—"[12]

I have received yours of Jan. 20th, & March 10th—[13]

O my Sister! what shall I say to you for your repeated acts of kindness— what return can I make— It is written that it is more blessed to give, than to receive— I believe you think it is or you would not be so continually pouring your Favours upon us—

Betsey Quincy sends her Duty, & thinks the Silk you sent her will make her a nice sam,[14] & afterwards do for a Skirt— As to poor WSS he almost fainted away, he was so elated with the Sight of his Books— He did not sleep till late, & was awake at break of Day— They are excellent Books & well calculated to pour the fresh Instruction over the Mind—

Mr Shaw is very much dissappointed at not receiving his from Mr Adams—Since by what you wrote, there was one intended for him— & the Subject upon which it treats, never could have been published at a Time, when there appeared a greater necessity for something of the kind—[15]

I never knew greater Electioneering than has been this year—A new Governor—a new Senate—new Representatives— Mr Osgood is chosen to represent H——ll—in the room of Capt Marsh—[16]

The way to creep into Office at this day is to declaim loudly against a Republican Government—against Salaries—Inferior Courts— Lawyers—& to extoll a paper Currency— This will gain them whole Sheets of Votes—Yes! & in Letters of Gold too—

When I consider of the Motives which have procured many the Suffrages of their Constitutents, & see them taken from among the lowest of the People—I blush, & am ashamed for my Countrymen— The reins of Government must e'er long be drawn closer, & they are preparing for themselves Whips, & Scorpions—

Mr Sparhawk (I believe) must be disconcerted at the Interview you mentioned— Truth may do good, though it is unpleasing to the Ear— It was most certainly a Bow, shot at a Venture—[17]

I find you entertain the same opinion which we do of Mr Blodget, that is, that he is a queer Creature—I miss him—for he used to be very good to us—

He is a sensible Man, of an Inquisitive turn, & has benevolence enough to wish to apply, & improve his knowledge, for the benefit of Mankind— You may tell him his family are all well if you please, & that his Wife is as well as she was when she lived at Andover but very gloomy—[18]

So then my dear Neice is like to make me a great Aunt— I have written to her twice since I have had a line from her—[19] she is cumbered about many things, I suppose— But what a young, blooming Grandmamma you will be— I shall want to look in upon you now more than ever—

My Prayer is, that all may be well—that Peace—Health—& Plenty may ever smile arround, & lighten your Habitation—

I shall not make my usual Visit this Spring— There has been a Disorder among us for these two months past which has struck a dread upon me little less than the Plague—I mean the Throat Distemper— At first it proved very mortal among us, baffling all the Skill of the Phisician—but for this fortnight, there has not any died in the Parish—

It is a most distressing Disorder— Betsy Quincy has been sick with it— But Providence has dealt very favourably with her— She looks finely within a Week—& I cannot but hope that mercy's healing balm is sent down, & that "his rough wind is staid—"[20]

We have all had something of it, but are better now— Mr Shaw has had a great Task lately—enough upon his head—heart—& hands— for you must think, it must be very grievous to him, to see the Lambs of his Flock cut down—

This Sickness has prevented my writing, & I fear I shall not have an Oppertunity to send this Letter 'till Mr Shaw goes to Election— I shall not dare to leave home, while this Distemper is among us—

And 'till you My dear Sister return more than half the pleasure of my Visit there, will be wanting, to / Your truly Affectionate Sister

Eliza Shaw—

PS Mr Allen, & Mrs Allen are well—for pities sake, hasten the Christening Cap as soon as possible—

W S Shaw desires I would tell you, that he is very sorry he cannot send you a Cocks Tail— He had a very beautiful white One—but having a dispute with a Neigbours They concluded to decide the matter with the point of the Bill, & Spur— The Contest was long, & furious—& returned crowing with Pride—but vexed to see another Competior in his own yard—fell with redoubled fury upon him— His strength was almost exhausted in the former Combat, having lost an Eye, & his Tail, he fell now a Victim to his insolence, & Pride—

Mr Shaw begs your acceptance of his respectful Love, & a Sermon of Mr Shutes upon the Death of Dr Gay—[21]

RC (Adams Papers); docketed by AA2: "M^rs. Eliza Shaw May 20th / 1787."

¹ Vol. 7:263–266.

² Perhaps a paraphrase of *The Intriguing Coxcomb; or, The Secret History of Sir Edmund Godfrey*, 2 vols., London, 1759, 1:26: "Where experience begins there error ends."

³ Shaw here refers to Anna (Nancy) Hazen who had boarded with the Shaw family for one year. For JQA's relationship with her, see vol. 7:165, note 4, and JQA, *Diary*, vols. 1 and 2, *passim*.

⁴ "O how she rolls her charming eyes in spite! / And looks delightfully with all her might! / But, like our heroes, much more brave than wise, / She conquers for the triumph, not the prize" (Edward Young, *Love of Fame, the Universal Passion. Satire V. On Women,* lines 39–42).

⁵ For Anna (Nancy) Dumas, daughter of C. W. F. Dumas, see vol. 4:356, note 2; 7:155, note 4.

⁶ Proverbs, 2:10–11.

⁷ Young, *Love of Fame, the Universal Passion. Satire V. On Women,* lines 559–560.

⁸ In Haverhill on 12 Dec. 1785, JQA wrote the 52-line "An Epistle to Delia" as he struggled to accept that he would not have a romantic relationship with Nancy Hazen: "Let Poets boast in smooth and labor'd strains / Of unfelt Passions and pretended pains / To my rude numbers, Delia now attend, / Nor view me, as a Lover, but a Friend" (M/JQA/28, APM Reel 223, p. 3–5, lines 1–4; JQA, *Diary*, 2:96).

⁹ JA read law with James Putnam of Worcester, Mass., from Aug. 1756 to Oct. 1758. Putnam, a loyalist, left for England in 1779 and in 1784 moved to New Brunswick where he was appointed senior judge and member of the Council. He died at St. John in 1789. JA wrote in his Autobiography that Putnam "treated me with Civility and Kindness," though in his Diary he wrote that his teacher "thought me incapable of Gallantry and Intrigue." Putnam neglected to present JA to the bar before JA departed Worcester, an apparent oversight that embarrassed the young lawyer when he attempted to begin work in Boston without proper credentials (JA, *Earliest Diary*, p. 10, 92, note 5; JA, *D&A*, 1:56, 58–59, 88, 3:270; *Sibley's Harvard Graduates*, 12:57–64).

¹⁰ Levi Lincoln (1749–1820) of Worcester was an attorney and probate judge from 1777 to 1781. In 1781, along with other members of the Massachusetts bar, he argued three

landmark cases that abolished slavery in the state (*DAB*).

¹¹ Rev. Ebenezer Gay died at Hingham on 18 March (*Sibley's Harvard Graduates*, 6:64).

¹² Isaac Watts, "The Presence of God Worth Dying for; or, The Death of Moses," lines 25–28.

¹³ Vol. 7:452–454 and 10 March, above.

¹⁴ Possibly a sham, a false outer garment of fine quality to be worn over a plain one (*OED*).

¹⁵ AA's letter to Shaw of 20 Jan. notes that JA had sent John Shaw a copy of the *Defence of the Const.* (vol. 7:453).

¹⁶ Isaac Osgood (1724–1791), a Haverhill merchant and distiller with investments in Penobscot lands, was chosen as representative from Haverhill in the 1787 May elections. He replaced Capt. Nathaniel Marsh (1739–1815), a veteran of the Revolution whose company had escorted Gen. John Burgoyne and the Convention Army from Saratoga to Cambridge (Boston *American Herald*, 4 June; Mass., *Acts and Laws*, 1786–1787, p. 267; *Sibley's Harvard Graduates*, 11:472–473; *Genealogy of the Family of George Marsh*, Leominster, Mass., 1887, p. 27).

¹⁷ See AA to Elizabeth Smith Shaw, 21 Nov. 1786, vol. 7:391–392, 393, note 1, for Nathaniel Sparhawk's meeting with JA and his business dealings. The quote here paraphrases 1 Kings, 22:34, and 2 Chronicles, 18:33: "And a certain man drew a bow at a venture, and smote the king of Israel between the joints of the harness."

¹⁸ Hannah White (b. 1726) of Haverhill married the merchant Samuel Blodget in 1748 (*Vital Records of Haverhill Massachusetts to the End of the Year 1849*, 2 vols., Topsfield, Mass., 1911, 1:34, 2:310). See also vol. 7:392–393.

¹⁹ 4 June and 27 Nov. 1786 (vol. 7:213–216, 402–405).

²⁰ Isaiah, 27:8.

²¹ Rev. Daniel Shute (1722–1802) of Malden, Harvard 1743, was minister to the Second Congregational Church of Hingham. His sermon, entitled *A Sermon, Delivered at the Meeting-House in the First Parish in Hingham, March 23, 1787 at the Interment of the Rev. Ebenezer Gay,* Salem, 1787, was published at the request of the First Congregational Church of Hingham, Gay's former parish (*Sibley's Harvard Graduates*, 11:304–309).

Cotton Tufts to Abigail Adams

Dear Con.   Weymouth May. the 21. 1787.

I rec^{d.} your several Letters of Jany. 24. Feby. 8^t & March the 10th. by Cushing, Barnard & Scott who all arrived in the latter End of April.[1] Before the Receipt of Mr. Adams Letter I had purchased the Half of the House & Land occupied by Belcher at £70— although it appeared to me to be dear— yet as it stood connected with your Land and the other half of y^{r.} Building would go to Ruin unless something was speedily done to prevent it by Repairs to the other and further if you should hereafter be disposed to divide the Farm and lease it out to Two Tenants, as well the having a Place under your Command so near you, which if People disagreable to you should live therein, would be very troublesome, were preponderate^{g.} motives to purchase it even at a high Price—[2] Belcher remains in one half for which he gives with a small Garden Spot 11 Doll^{rs.}/Year Turner in the other half of the House with the like Pervilege gives 11 Dol^{rs.} also—[3] 5 acres remain to be imporoved in Common with the Farm so that after the Expence of some Repairs which I am now making, & are indispensably necessary, it will yield a Profit little short of £6 per C^t if not exceed it— Mr. Willm. Vesey the other Day offered me his House & Land adjoyning y^{r.} Farm—said that Mr. Adams engaged him to give him the Refusal of it, that as he was determined to sell he accordingly had applied to me on y^r Behalf— he said he could have had formerly £300— but his present Price I could not obtain, but seemed to be desirous that I should write to you on the Subject and I assured him I would— You will therefore return me an Answer— As you have as much Land as can be managed with Advantage unless of a better Quality—I was doubtful whether you would wish to purchase it—more especially if you should have in Contemplation Borlands House & Farm— I believe it is now at your Service if you incline to purchase, as the late occupants Time & Attention is so fully taken up at New York in writing Comedies for which he is become *famous*, that whether Creditors or Collectors attach his Windmill, make distreint on the Stock of the Farm or the materials provided for Repairs of the Fences & Buildings or who purchases the Farm out of his Hands, cannot be an object of equal Importance as that of acquiring the Fame of a Writer of Comedies and the receiving the Claps of Applause & Acclamations of a crowded Stage—

The Buildings on this Place are much out of Repair— it will not probably fetch so much by several Hundreds, partly for that Reason and partly on Acc$^{tt.}$ of the Scarcity of Specie as it would have done several years past—

I have purchased between 3 & 4000 Doll$^{r.}$ of Appletons Loan Office Notes and shall as Opportunity presents, proceed further— these stand in about 2^s/5^d per £ Consolidated Notes of this State are sold @ 4^s/ per £ the Interest upon their nominal Sum has generally realized about 10^s/ in the Pound that is to say a Note of £100— which you buy for £20— produces an Interest of £6— this paid in orders, those sold will at present average 10^s/ per £ w$^{ch.}$ makes £3— for the £6—[4]

I am not surprized at y^r Loss of 50 or 60 Guineas by a certain Cape Gentleman, whose Character ever appeared to me problematical you may recollect, in some former Letter— my Queries respecting him I wish you may not suffer similar Losses by your Advancements for particular Persons and for public Uses—That for public Papers which you refer to will not probably be paid by the L$^t.$ G—r till you return— I shall however drive the Matter— Believe me I cannot write on these matters without feeling an Indignation at my Countrymen— But to proceed— M$^r.$ Adams order is sent forward to The Hon^l M$^r.$ M$^{c.}$Kean and will I trust be duly honoured— this I committed to Stephen Gorham Esq. who is gone to Philadelphia; to him also I committed an Acc$^{tt.}$ against Will$^{m.}$ Barrells Estate together with Stephen Collins Adm$^r.$ on Barrells Estate Acc$^{tt.}$ against Mr Adams which was transmitted by Collins to Un. Smith—who will adjust the same and pay a small Ballance due to Barrells Estate—[5] The Goods you sent by Cushing—were prohibited Articles I.E. the Porter & Cheese, the former might be drank here, as we do not make Beer sufficient, but *the latter* we must consider as not eatable here without some little Degree of remorse— we had much trouble to prevent these being sent back to England— However we finally got them landed, paying former Duties— The Cheese will make but an awkward appearance at Commencement— probably your Friends will do your Farm the Honour of gracing the Board—with some of its last years Production, which I hope will vie with any made in Europe— Since the last Impost Act, All Articles brought in the Captains Chests or otherwise must be entered and they are inspected—[6] if you have any Articles to send, other than some small Book, Pamphlet or Packet—they had better be put up in a Box & consigned as it makes great Difficulty in entring at the Impost office— The Officers permitted the Volumes sent by Mr Adams to be received Duty free— these have a very considerable Run—& are spoke off with great Praise & will I hope be a Word in Season to our Countrymen— in them they may read their own Fate— I wish you to send y^r Bro^{r.} Shaw one of those Publications— as I percieve it was y^{r.} Intention, altho omitted in Mr. Adams List, of Distribution—and I have so disposed of the whole of them—as not to leave One for him— in my Letter to Mr. Adams I have given him an Acc^{tt.} of my Procceedings with respect to them— the 80— Vol^{s.} disposed of will neat 10^s/ Lawfmoney per Vol—

Our public affairs remain yet critical, although the Rebels in Arms, have in great Numbers been taken, their Forces broke to Pieces and their Leaders driven out of the State, yet they have found an Asylum in the out Skirts of New York, Vermont & Connecticut— Shays, Days & other their principal officers fled to Canada, they are said to have returned— 700 or 800 are mustering from their lurking Places & will probably make some onset— their Object We are informed is to rescue those who are condemned— Great Numbers have been tried 12 or 15 in Worcester Hampshire & Berkshire have been convicted of capital Crimes 4 or 5 only are under Sentence of Death, the Rest are pardoned. We have had for some Time past 1000 Men in Service stationed in those Counties, their Enlistments will expire in Six Weeks or two Months[7] Much depends on the next General Court I might have said—every Thing— The People have in great Number of Towns given unequivocal Proof of their Disapprobation of the late Measures of Government— They have elected More late County Conventioners—fomentors of the late Rebellion—others Advocates for Tender Acts & Paper Money & for paying off public Securities at the going Price (, which is a very popular Matter) others declaimers against Lawyers, against Government and every thing that is good & great— There are however a Number of very respectable Characters chosen from diverse Towns— If Time permits I will write further a few Days hence [In] the mean Time Am with Affection Y^{rs.}   C Tufts

RC (Adams Papers); addressed: "Madam Abigail Adams / Grovesnor Square / London—"; internal address: "Mrs. Abig. Ad[ams]"; endorsed: "Dr Tufts 21 May / 1787." Some loss of text where the seal was removed.

[1] For AA's letter to Cotton Tufts of 24 Jan., see vol. 7:454–455. The 10 March letter is above, but the 8 Feb. letter has not been found.

[2] JA, in a 15 Jan. letter, instructed Tufts not to pay more than fifty pounds sterling for the Belcher property (Adams Papers).

[3] John Turner served JA as a servant in 1777 and later advertised as a stocking weaver. Turner had resided in the Belcher

house since 1785 (vol. 2:304, 341, 6:87). See also vol. 7:144, note 1.

[4] From 1777 to 1787, AA and JA purchased steeply discounted state bonds in several lots with a total face value of $8,000. JA opposed bond speculation on principle because he believed that it deflected capital from agriculture, manufacturing, and trade, but he acquiesced to AA's desire to enter the market. The investment paid off handsomely, yielding a profit of more than 400 percent when Congress funded state and federal debts in 1790 (Woody Holton, "Did Democracy Cause the Recession That Led to the Constitution?" *JAH*, 92:457–460 [Sept. 2005]).

[5] William Barrell was a New England merchant who operated a store in Philadelphia from 1774 until his death in 1776. JA's debt probably dated to 1774 and 1775 when he charged goods in Barrell's store during

his service in the Continental Congress. The administration of the Barrell estate by Stephen Collins, a Quaker merchant of Philadelphia, was much complicated by the war and took more than a decade to complete (JA, *D&A*, 2:121, 170, 171; Winthrop Sargent, "Letters of John Andrews, Esq., of Boston," MHS, *Procs.*, 8:318–319 [1864–1865]; vol. 1:238).

[6] "An Act to Raise a Public Revenue by Impost" required that captains and commanders report the contents of their vessels immediately upon arriving at their ports of destination. The act, which went into effect on 1 Jan. 1787, also provided for the search of vessels thought to contain contraband or smuggled goods (Mass., *Acts and Laws*, 1786–1787, p. 117–130).

[7] The previous sentence was written in the margin and marked for insertion here.

Richard Cranch to John Adams

My dear Bro[r.]   Braintree May 24[th.] 1787

I herewith send you the News-Papers by which you will see the state of our publick proceedings.[1] Our most excellent Governor M[r.] Bowdoin is to be left out this Year—M[r] Hancock will doubtless succeed him. Strenuous efforts have been made at the present Election to get a Gen[l.] Court that will suit the minds of the Insurgents and their Friends—Many good Men, however, will be chosen into both Branches, who will, I hope, stem the Current in some degree and support in some measure the Dignity of Government. Our excellent Friend Doct[r.] Tufts is one of them. I am left out—the ostensible reason is my belonging to the Court of Com: Pleas, which Court the Populace want to have abolished, and many People now pretend that it is inconsistant with the spirit of the Constitution that any Justice of that Court should have a Seat in the Legislative Body or Council, and they are generally left out this year. The following Gentlemen who are Justices of that Court and were of the Senate and Council last year are not chosen this year. Viz[t:] Spooner & Durfee from Bristol County; Gill, Ward & Baker from Worcester; Prescot and Fuller from Middlesex; Holton and S: Philips jun[r.] (the late President of Senate) from Essex; Freeman from Barnstable; Wells from York; Cranch &c.[2]

Your most excellent Book (for one of which I thank you) is eagerly read by Gentlemen of all the learned Professions here. It came to America at a very critical Moment just before the Meeting of the grand Convention at Philadelphia for revising and amending the Confederation, when the Subject matter of your Book will naturally be much talked of, and attended to by many of the greatest States-men from all parts of the United States. I have my self conversed with many Gentlemen here of the first Rank for Learning and Abilities, who, after reading your Book with great attention, gave it as their Opinion that you have supported your System of the Ballance in a most masterly manner. I find that the Litterati themselves are amazed at the vastness of your Reading on the Subject of Legislation and Government, from which you have been enabled so fully to bring your Theory to the Test of historical Facts, and to shew that the Continuance and Steadiness of every free Government, of any large extent, has been and must be in a just Proportion to the Perfection or Imperfection of that Ballance between the Powers of Government which you have so clearly and fully pointed out.

The Young Gentlemen of the Class who are to take their Degree next Commencement have petitioned for a private Commencement on account of the present Difficulty of raising money enough to defray the necessary charges of their Education, but their Petition was rejected so far as respected a private Commencement. The Corporation and Overseers Ordered, however, that the greatest œconomy should be observed, so as to save all needless Expences on that Occasion. It was Ordered that no [families] should give any Entertainment out of Colledge un[less the] Parents lived in Cambridge—that a cold Collation in a frugal Stile at their Chambers should be all that should be provided on that Occasion—That no new Suits of Clothes should be procured for that Day, but that the Schollars should all appear in their Black Gowns—That three Dollars of the Sum formerly paid towards the publick Dinner by each Schollar who took his Degree, should be remitted this Year &c. I suppose the Class will be satisfied with those Regulations. I hear that your very worthy and amiable Son is to deliver an English Oration on that Day; And my Son is to bear a part in a publick Conference *on the necessity of having three independant Powers in Government, each having a negative on the others.*— Please to present my best Regards to your most amiable Friend, and to Col: Smith and his Lady. I am with Sentiments of the highest Esteem your obliged and affectionate Brother—   Richard Cranch

We are all well in the several connected Families, and earnestly wish to see you safely returned to Braintree again, of which your late Letters give us the pleasing Prospect.

M^rs. Cranch wrote to Sister Adams by Capt. Barnard who sailed on Monday [last].³

P:S. Since writing the [above] I find M^rs. Cranch's Letter, (which was given to the Pilot by Uncle Smith after the Ship was gone down) came back again rumpled and dirty as you will see, and I have now enclosed it in the Pacquet.

RC (Adams Papers); addressed: "To His Excellency / John Adams Esqr. / Grosvenor Square / Westminster."; endorsed: "Mr Cranch. 24 / may. 1787—" Some loss of text where the seal was removed.

¹ The results of the statewide election were not official until 30 May and not published in complete form until they appeared in the *Massachusetts Gazette*, 1 June. The Boston *American Herald*, 9 and 16 April, and *Worcester Magazine*, 24 May, however, reported scattered results that showed John Hancock far ahead of James Bowdoin in the race for governor.

² Walter Spooner (1720–1803) of Dartmouth, Thomas Durfee (1721–1796) of Freetown, Moses Gill (1734–1800) of Princeton, Artemas Ward (1727–1800) of Shrewsbury, Samuel Baker (1722–1795) of Bolton, James Prescott (1721–1800) of Groton, Abraham Fuller (1720–1794) of Newton, Samuel Holton (1738–1816) of Danvers, Samuel Phillips Jr. (1752–1802) of Andover, Solomon Freeman (1733–1808) of Harwich, Nathaniel Wells (1740–1816) of Wells (now Maine), and Cranch served their respective counties as senators in the 1786–1787 session but were not put forward in the 30 May elections (*Massachusetts Spy*, 1 June 1786; Charlestown, Mass., *American Recorder*, 2 June; *Massachusetts Gazette*, 1 June 1787; John A. Schutz, *Legislators of the Massachusetts General Court, 1691–1780: A Biographical Dictionary*, Boston, 1997).

³ Mary Smith Cranch to AA, April 22, above, which Cranch did not complete until 20 May, but see also Cranch to AA, 27 May, below.

Mary Smith Cranch to Abigail Adams

My dear Sister · · · · · · · · · · · · Braintree May 27th 1787

I went to Boston yesterday & had the mortification to find my Letters did not go by Barnard or Davis although they had been on Board each of them. they got to town just as the vessels were sailing. Knox the Pilot took them as he was going on Board, & promiss'd to deliver them to the captain, but forgot it So after wearing them in His Pockit four or five days he return'd them as dirty as I suppose you will recieve them.¹ captain Scot Who now has them, is to sail this day & although a week after the others he may arrive first— I had been uncommonly busy about the time I wrote my Letters or I Should not have been so late with them: I wanted to write much more & keept them back hopeing to have done it. I will not be so foolish again

I have receiv'd the shirts for your eldest son, & the Linnen & cambrick for the others. the latter came as snug as could be nobody was the wiser for it. I Thank you my dear sister for your Present to my son. He sends his Duty & his thanks also— I saw cousin Charles yesterday in Boston he was well, & said his Brothers were too. There was a Publick exhibition at the end of the last term, the day before the spring vacation. your son JQA had a conference with two others upon this Question: which was the most benificial to mankind Law, Physic or Divinity? JQA mantaind the usefulness of Law. they all did well. your son was greatly applauded, both for the manner & matter, as also for the composition[2] There were a number who presented Pieces to the gentlemen who were met that Day to inquire into the state of the college— Billy present'd a calculation of a Transit of Venus which is to take place some years hence & was so happy as to find that it agree'd within a few seconds with the calculations of some celebrated Astronomers.[3] It was a labourious work for the Head—but he got himself honour by it.

June 10th.

We have had a great bustle in Braintree about our Representitive The two upper Parishs are Plague'd with a number of People unfriendly to goverment. Steven Penneman & captain Vintin set up in opposition to Coll. Thayer who appear'd firm last year in supporting it for which reason he had the vote of every Friend of it, & got his Election by a majoraty of 12 this so nettle'd & dissapointe'd that party that they got the select men who by the way are every one of their side, to call a Town meeting, which they did in so private a way warning the People of a Sunday for the next day, & warning only such as they knew would answer their purpose that the meeting was over several days before the greatest part of the Town knew there had been one. In this meeting they agree'd to Petition the court to exclude coll Thayer from a seat in the House for the reasons set forth in the Petition some of which were, That many voted who were not qualified, some put in more votes than one & some whole handfulls. The great schoolar Faxen drew this wonderfull Instrument which for spelling grammer & composision was just what we could have expected from such a profound genious It was sign'd by a hundred & Two persons old capt Beals & his wise son Natt, were

all who sign'd in this Parish— They got mr Morton to support their
cause before a committee of the court which was chosen to consider
of it— As soon as this was known our Party sent in a Petition also
sign'd by a much greather number, of People all of them Men of
property & respectability uncle Quincy & mr Cranch at their Head,
declaring that they knew of no such transactions that most of them
were present at the choise & did not hear of, or see any such things
done. They beg that the matter may be examin'd into & if it should
be found that they had no foundation for their charges they pray
that their Petition may be dismiss'd as "The Brat of a Party who are
endeavouring to raise sedition & tumults in the commonwealth."
Last Friday they had a hearing, all Braintree were there almost they
were not able to support one charge & look'd very silly. They beg'd
for another hearing which they are to have, but they will make nothing of it.[4] Coll[n.] Thayer had no reason to expect the support mr
cranch has given him when he consider'd how ill he had formerly
treated him: Coll Bass's son told him he would not have him too
proud upon the occation That it was not him but the cause we were
supporting. This son of coll. Bass is a very worthy sensible man—one
of the last acts of mr cranchs Political Life was to get mr Thaxter &
him made a Justice of the Peace

The governor has got such a counsel as I should think would
mortify him at least some of them. The Friends of goverment chose
such of the Senate as they knew would refuse in order to get a
chance to chuse out of the People at large some good men but they
missd their aim by seting up men which the others hated. General
Warren is Speaker of the House, & nobody now is so proper for the
chair as mr Hancock— He is more Learn'd more wise, more every
thing, than mr Bowdoin

> "get Place & Wealth, if possible with grace.
> If not, by any means get wealth & Place"

well apply now to some characters as well in those days when Pope
writ these lines[5]

June 13th

Cushing is to sail in a few days I hear I hope I shall not be too
late for him. I wish I had any thing to send you that would be acceptable—but why should I be proud? no— I will rejoice that Providence has set you above the want of any thing I can do for you— I

was in Boston yesterday & found all uncle Smiths Family with Doc^r. Welsh & Lady seting off for Newbury to the wedding of our cousin William— he is to be married this day. May they be as happy as virtue & good dispositions can make them— mrs otis & her Brother went yesterday morning earley. I should have lik'd to have seen him— I wonder when he will leave Blushing. we could not speak to him about miss Hannah without fetching up his colour— Mrs Otis & Welch are increasing in size fast—[6]

Your Son JQA & mine were in Boston yesterday[7] They were well your other sons were so also. I told you in my last Letters that cousin would remain in Cambridge. he tells me he has alter'd his mind & thinks he shall live with mr Parsons— We are making some little preparation for commencment. I have sent my most *respecfull* complements to mr Tufts & Family at Newbury with an invitation to commencment—

There are to be three english orations Bridge who was to have held a conference with Billy has obtain'd leave not to be present at commencment, so that instead of a conference, he is to have an oration upon Goverment He has been studying his uncle Adams late publication with care. I hope he will perform well He will not excell as a speaker till he has several more years over his head—but he will have no conceit'd airs—

I drank Tea at mrs Quncys as I return'd from Boston yesterday. mrs Hall & miss Polly were there, they were dress'd in their new gowns & look'd very well. The thought of seeing her dear children return seems to give her new spirits she desires that I would give her kind & affectional Love to you all. Mrs Quincy & Nancy express their Joy at the prospect of your return as extatically as usual— our good uncle Quincy is as well as usual but cannot yet be perswaid'd out—

Before this time you are I hope dandling your little Grandchild upon your knee—does it not make you feel old? or do you fancy it is your own & so feel your youth renew'd? as these relations increase you will find your unwillingness to have them settled at any great distance will not diminish—

Betsy & Lucy are making up the linnen you sent your sons. We make cousin Tom no more than just sufficcent for present use he grows so fast it is imposible to keep any thing to fit him three months. JQA has two dozen which he has never yet had on. I often tell the girls they mend more than you would. your eldest son will want some more cotton stockings soon those he brought with him are so fine that I have been oblig'd to put new feet to them several times. those you sent will do much more service, & are cheaper than I can get them made here—

We have been much affraid that mrs Russel was in a consumtion & are not yet without our fears although she appears to be much better She is with her Parents. She has a fine Baby but has been oblig'd to wean it, or rather to get a nurse for it. she carrys them about with her wherever she goes. I hope she will recover. She was always lovely, but appears more amiable now than ever— Her gentle spirit seems fitted for a better World, but we cannot help wishing to detain her a little longer with us—

Remember me affectionatly to mr Adams to mr & Mrs Smith, to mrs Elworthy & Family also whenever you see them. tell her I mean to write when I can get time & believe me my dear sister yours affectionatly

Mary Cranch

RC (Adams Papers); endorsed: "Mrs Cranch / May 27 1787"; docketed by AA2: "Mᵣˢ Cranch."

[1] Cranch to AA, 22 April, above. Thomas Knox served as the first appointed Boston Harbor pilot from 1783 to 1790 (Ralph M. Eastman, *Pilots and Pilot Boats of Boston Harbor*, Boston, 1956, p. 3, 24-25).

[2] For the text of JQA's composition, see his *Diary*, 2:199–204. JQA also noted that he did not particularly like the subject and had difficulty writing on it (*Diary*, 2:175, 176, 177).

[3] The next transit of Venus would not occur until 1874. The transit prior to this, in 1769, was promoted, calculated, and recorded by the American Philosophical Society and, especially, Harvard's John Winthrop, America's first astronomer. Europeans noticed the accuracy of their predictions, resulting in prestige and future funding for the American scientific community (Brooke Hindle, *The Pursuit of Science in Revolutionary America, 1735–1789*, Chapel Hill, N.C., 1956, p. 146-165; *Sibley's Harvard Graduates*, 9:240-264).

[4] On 17 May 1787 the Braintree town meeting elected Ebenezer Thayer Jr. as representative by a margin of twelve votes over Stephen Penniman (1743-1827) and John Vinton (1735-1803). The election was protested on 4 June when a second town meeting appointed Azariah Faxon (1731-1802), Eliphalet Sawin (1722-1801), and Vinton to "take cair of and surport Petition of a num-ber of the Inhabitants of this town to the General Court objecting to the choice of our Representative, being legal." Benjamin Beale (1702-1793) and his son Nathaniel (1753-1832) are the men Cranch reports as favoring the petition. The action went no further than the hearing before the legislative committee sponsored by Perez Morton. Thayer, who had been the subject of an unsuccessful recall effort in January as well, was re-elected in 1788 (*Braintree Town Records*, p. 574-581; Sprague, *Braintree Families*, p. 493-494, 3767R; John Adams Vinton, *The Vinton Memorial*, Boston, 1858, p. 57-61; George L. Faxon, *The History of the Faxon Family*, Springfield, Mass., 1880, p. 71-72; Thomas E. Sawin, *Sawin: Summary Notes Concerning John Sawin, and His Posterity*, Athol, Mass., 1867, p. 9; vol. 7:463, 465).

[5] Pope, *Satires, Epistles, and Odes of Horace*, Epistle I, Book I, lines 103-104.

[6] Mary Smith Gray Otis, wife of Samuel A. Otis, gave birth to a daughter, Harriet, in Dec. 1787. At about the same time, Abigail Kent Welsh, wife of Dr. Thomas Welsh, gave birth to a son, Henry. See Cotton Tufts to AA, 18 Dec., and Mary Smith Cranch to AA, 22 Dec., both below.

[7] JQA and William Cranch went to Boston to hear the debates in the legislature (JQA, *Diary*, 2:239).

John Brown Cutting to Abigail Adams

Dear Madam   Hague Monday Even^g May 28. 1787.

Agreably to the intimation in the note I had the pleasure to address you from the Inn[1]—we reached Harwich the next morning by eight, where Capt Flynn soon recognized his Excellency and congratulated himself on the prospect of once more conveying him to Holland. Yet he did not forget politely to regret that Mrs Adams was now absent and cou'd not therefore join in "his triumph nor partake the gale":[2]—a finer western one never fill'd a mainsail. For which reason I suppose as we shou'd not want any earthly eatable, the kind Landlord at Harwich put up provisions and refreshments sufficient for a transatlantic voyage It was in vain to remonstrate—he propounded and Mr Adams concluded—Thus amply victual'd, water'd, brandied, pepper'd and chocolated, we were boated on board the Packet, and hoisted anchor at 1/2 past three—The breeze fair and full as it cou'd untempestuously blow.

Our female fellow passengers permit me first to introduce to you. Imprimis two dutch matrons with one goodly child and two fine bundles of fresh asparagus. Item a dutch virgin—reputed tutress to the infants of the house of orange. A trig decent person laced in a tight boddice in a cloth riding dress—a cap with a cambrick border—filleted close to her temples with a yellow ribband—cotton hose and white slippers. A german woman of uncommon corpulency and scarlet features—mincing like a new made Countess, breathing like a porpoise and prating like a magpie—An inoffensive and well-behaving maid servant. An impertinent and saucy english woman, of age and occupation dubious—but acting on board, as the guide and guardian of a pretty affable, entertaining demi- (perhaps emaculately) virtuous maiden, with pearly teeth, dark eyes, auburn ringlets, clear complexion tho' a little redden'd by art, who is full of american french, and english anecdote, and delineates characters both public and private with equal justness and facility.

Beside Mr Adams and myself, there were only a german merchant and a well-temper'd Hollander of the masculine gender. They seemed, civil, decent painstaking sort of animals—distinguished by no striking excellence or obvious absurdity.

Precisely at five o clock I began to diminish in fluency of dialogue and to feel as if I cou'd not help it. I was much obliged to Mr Adams and took it very kindly that he condescended to sympathise with me from the very bottom of his heart. It is a happy thing to have a friend in our distresses who can feel for us. Our efforts were truly social and reciprocal for many hours. They were not at the time joyous but very grievous—and continued so until sunday morning—with a few intervals of slumber. About eight we were landed pale and puny as the flitting ghosts of departed plumpness.

Having quietly permitted six impositions ere we had proceeded as many paces—we hasten'd to a seventh—in hiring horses and a carriage. To the commissary we hasten'd and intreated for the same. The Commissary knew our wants better than we did. Two carriages were he thought few enough in all conscience. Thro' our wan visages he beheld a dignity that no sea sickness nor rueful length of beard cou'd conceal. Two carriages and six cattle (the postilions included) were slowly paraded, accepted, occupied and paid for on the spot. Rotterdam was the City toward which our stomachs and wishes equally yearned. Our twin vehicles attracted the croud. They gazed with admiration at two entire carriages. Had the Commissary proposed four additional ones I do think Mr Adams might possibly have objected. In an open car painted with all the colours of the rainbow—built in the *age* and moulded after the *manner* of the *Goths*—the three coffers of baggage William our loyal domestic, a low dutch domini in the habit of his order and as doughty a driver as any in Batavia led the Van of the cavalcade. But the antiquity and barbaric grandeur of that nameless structure in which the philosophic minister and his renowned secretary were wafted over the muddy marle, beggars all description. Conceive of a vehicle neither resembling chaise, waggon cart chariot or wheelbarrow yet partaking the ugliness and all the ill qualities of each—distressing to the eye of taste, incommodious to the traveller, wearisome even to Elephants on a turnpike—with cushions and lining of crimson damask—broken windows, warped sides, cracked leather, hideous images, wooden springs, rope tackling, and no harness—conceive in short all the misshapen forms into which a cargo of timber can be hewn, be carved, be gilded, be twisted and bedevil'd—and when you have mingled these ideas, the result will only be a type of that machine in which after uncounted jolts and bruizes, horse baitings & bear baitings, perils by ferriage, and dangers by dykes, twinges of hunger extortion for poached eggs, beside an unenumerated catalogue of minor distresses, we arrived at seven in the famous City of Roterdam.

Having sip'd a corroborating cup of tea at the Marschall Turenne Hotel, we encompass'd the City round about—saw the Mynheers and the maidens—their short bodies and long feet—clear complex-ions and clean hose—Beheld *in* a church a decent display of bata-vian pulpit oratory and *out of it* gazed at the grandeur of gigantic windmills. Paid homage at the statue of Erasmus—and after survey-ing, prim hedges, neat parterres, lofty tulips, trim trees and capital canals, return'd facetious, and retir'd fatigued.[3]

This morning renovated and refreshed, having breakfasted and discharged every extravagant item in the bill we embarked at eight on the canal for the Hague. Disappointed in not engaging the state room—M[r] Adams and myself are crouded by six fat redoubtable dutchmen who after fumigating us with tobacco for two hours without pity, at length expel us from [th]e hive half-suffocated. To escape the smoak we flee into an unmerciful shower, with which we are genially moisten'd during the residue of the voyage. I fret, M[r] Adams laughs—the Hollanders smoke—until we arrive at a comfort-able Inn, where Mons[r.] Dumas having paid his respects to M[r] Ad-ams and made many, many enquiries after the Ladies in Grosvenor Square, M[r] A. and this narrator, dine sumptuously drink strong cof-fee redundantly, and beg leave to superscribe this scrawl for you be-fore the post goes off for England.

Therefore / Dear Madam / Your Most Obed[t] & very Humb[l] Serv[t]

John Brown Cutting

Particular compliments to M[rs] Smith and Steuben, the precious Steuben.

RC (Adams Papers); addressed: "M[rs] Adams / At the house of the / American Minister / Grosvenor Square / London"; internal address: "M[rs] Adams."; endorsed: "M[r Cutting] / May 2[8 1787]." Some loss of text where the seal was removed.

[1] Cutting wrote to AA on 25 May (Adams Papers) letting her know that he and JA had arrived at the "Inn near Mr Rigby's Farm," where they stayed the night before crossing the Channel to Holland.
[2] "Say, shall my little bark attendant sail, / Pursue the triumph, and partake the gale?" (Pope, *An Essay on Man*, Epistle IV, lines 385–386).
[3] The Erasmus statue, by Hendrik de Keyser, was the fifth and last sculpture of Erasmus, erected in Rotterdam in 1622 (JA, *D&A*, 2:445; vol. 7:316; Nicolaas Van Der Blom, "The Erasmus Statues in Rotterdam," *Erasmus in English*, 6:5–9 [June 1973]).

Abigail Adams to John Adams

my dearest Friend   London may 29 1787

I received mr Cuttings Letter on Monday morning, and was glad to find you had stoped Short of Hardwick. I prognosticated from the wind on saturday that you made your passage by nine or ten on sunday morning. I commisirated your sickness, and that I might feelingly sympathize with you, used mr Hollis's prescription yesterday morning, finding a return of some of my former complaints. the effect proved the necessity of the application. I hope you will be benifited by your journey, but the weather here is not favourable, cold & sour. I fancy it is not mended [by] passing over Stagnant waters & meddows— your companion [ho]wever, will I hope exhilarate your spirits by the brilliancy of his fancy. Neptune & the Naides cannot be invoked in vain in their own particular element.

inclosed you will find a Letter which came last evening. I do not Suppose you can do any thing yet it may be proper you should know the unfortunate Situation of the gentleman.[1] Nothing new has transpired since you left us except the Bill which has past making four free ports in the west Indies, Kingstone in Jamaica, St Georges in Grenada, Rosea in Dominica, Nassau in New providence, but till we see the Bill it will be uncertain what benefit America can derive from it.[2]

The prince of Wales is seazid with a voilent fever occasiond by over heating himself in dancing at the Dutchess of Gordons Ball on fryday evening last.[3]

Mrs Smith & I are quite solitary and should be more so, if it was not for the young one. to day we shall have company.

Mrs Smith Sends Duty to you & compliments to mr Cutting. the little fellow smiles assent.

Let me hear from you by the next post. I shall be anxious to know how you got over, as well as the state of your Health, in which no one can be equally interested with your ever affectionate

A Adams

compliments to mr Cutting & thanks for his Letter—
Since writing the above the inclosed Letter has come in[4]

RC (Adams Papers); addressed by AA2: "His Excellency / John Adams Esquire / Minister Plenipotentiary &cᵃ / To the care of Messʳˢ˙ Willinks / Amsterdam"; endorsed: "mrs A May 29ᵗʰ / 1787." Some loss of text where the seal was removed.

[1] Probably Richard Swanwick to JA, 17 May (Adams Papers), who wrote regarding the imprisonment of Thomas Barclay at Bordeaux for the personal debt he had incurred while acting as U.S. consul to France. Swanwick was a native of Great Britain who came to Pennsylvania with his family in the early 1770s. His son John became a Pennsylvania congressman and successful merchant as a partner in the firm of Willing, Morris & Swanwick of Philadelphia, while his father held a minor office for the British. Richard later returned to Great Britain seeking compensation for his property losses (*ANB*; John Swanwick to JA, 18 July 1786, Adams Papers). See also JA, *D&A*, 3:120; AA to JA, 7 June, below.

[2] "An Act for Allowing the Importation

and Exportation of Certain Goods, Wares and Merchandize . . . under Certain Regulations and Restrictions" was passed by the House of Lords on 28 May. The act expanded the original free port act of 1766 that had opened a limited number of British West Indies ports to foreign vessels for the purpose of importing raw materials not produced in Britain and providing markets for British manufactures. The 1787 act addressed the United States' transformation from British colony to foreign power by excluding American vessels from trading in free ports (*London Gazette*, 26–29 May; Frances Armytage, *The Free Port System in the British West Indies: A Study in Commercial Policy, 1766–1822*, N.Y., 1953, p. 53–60).

[3] The prince's illness, the result of vigorous dancing at a ball hosted by Jane Gordon, Dutchess of Gordon (1749?–1812), was widely reported in the London press (*DNB*; *Morning Chronicle and London Advertiser,* 28 May).

[4] WSS to JA, 19 May (Adams Papers), which also deals with the Barclay situation.

Abigail Adams to William Stephens Smith

My Dear Sir: London, [30] May, 1787.[1]

I have written you only a few lines since your absence; and those conveyed to you rather an unpleasing account, but you will find my letter attended with so many others of a different complexion, that I hope it will not give you a moment's uneasiness. Mrs. Smith is now very well, and sitting here at the table, making herself a mourning bonnet, for the Princess Carolina Wilhelmina, whom neither she or I care a farthing for.[2] What a farce this court-mourning is; and indeed most other European mournings out of the numerous tribe who wear the garb, how few sorrowful hearts does it cover.

Mrs. Smith has given you the history of the bills, drawn by a certain house, which have been noted for non-payment, and the consequent flight of a gentleman and family to America. The amount of bills noted, Mr. Parker tells me, is a hundred thousand pounds; seventy-five thousand guilders for the payment of the June interest is a part. When this took place Mr. A. wrote to his friends, requesting their advice what step could be taken. In reply, they informed him that, in consequence of delaying only two days, the advertising the payment of the June interest, the obligations had fallen two per cent., and would continue to depreciate, unless a new loan was opened. That money there was scarce, and could not be obtained at less than eight per cent.; that they had called the brokers together, stated the matter to them, and that his presence was necessary immediately to save the honour and credit of the United States, as they must advance on their own account, until he could attend to sign the obligations. No time was to be lost, and at two day's notice the journey commenced. Mr. Cutting has gone as companion and secretary. On the 25th they sat out; and I have not yet heard of their arrival.[3] This is a sad stroke, but there is less commotion here in consequence of it than could have been expected. The general idea is that the house will stand it, but I fear the contrary; and what Congress will say to the step taken I know not; yet what else could be done? Mr. B. has drawn a bill for three hundred and fifty pounds since you left us, or rather I believe it has been accepted since you left us.[4] Mr. A. must protest any farther drafts, should they come. Nothing certainly can be done for him with regard to his private affairs, how muchsoever we may feel for his situation. I shall forward your letter last night received, by this day's post, as well as one received from Mr. Swanwich upon the same subject.[5] So here we go up, and there we go down, as I sing to your boy every day, who grows so fat we can scarcely toss him.

As to news here, I know of nothing worth communicating, except a bill which has passed, making four free ports in the West Indies; Kingston in Jamaica, St. George in Grenada, Mosea[6] in Dominica, and Nassau in New Providence. I have not seen the bill, so cannot say whether America is the most unfavoured nation in it. I dare say they will find a way of being benefited by it.

All is love and harmony here. The Royal Father and Son, are perfectly reconciled—the one to give, the other to receive. The household is again established, the jeweller in a hopeful way of receiving his thirty thousand debt, the confectioner his seven, and even the spur maker his hundreds.[7] Mr. Hartley has just made me a morning visit. He has had a return of his disorder, though not so bad as before.[8] He is going to write to you, therefore it is needless to say more about him, for if his pen is half as prolific as his tongue, he will not need an assistant.

We are to have a large party to dine with us to-day, invited previous to Mr. A.'s excursion; I have engaged Mr. Shippen as an assistant. Of the number is Sir George Stanton and Mr. Hollis.[9] I cannot tell how much we miss you; in short if it was not for the boy, it would be *dummy* all.

We begin to dine abroad again, and I hope to prevail with Mrs. Smith to go into the country for a little excursion, when Sir returns; but she is rather averse to the idea, and says without she had some one to go and see, she cannot find a pleasure in it.

Remember me to Mr. Harrison when you meet. I have a most sincere esteem for him, and frequently drink his health in the good wine which he procured for us. If any vessel should be bound for Boston, request the favour of him to ship two such casks of wine for that port, as he imported here for us, addressed to Isaac Smith, merchant, Boston, and draw his bill here for the payment of it. The sooner he does it the more agreeable to us.

It is scarcely worth while to say a word about return, till at least you reach the place for which you sat out. So I waive that subject, only observing that the sooner it is, the more agreeable it will be to your affectionate friend,   A. A.

RC not found. Printed from AA2, *Jour. and Corr.*, 1:121–125. Dft (Adams Papers), filmed at [*May 1787?*].

[1] The dating of this letter is based on AA's statement that she had received WSS's letter to JA of 19 May "last night." In her letter to JA of 29 May, above, she indicated that WSS's letter had come in on the 29th.

[2] Princess Carolina Wilhelmina (b. 1743), the sister of Dutch stadholder William V, died on 6 May. AA2's preparation of a bonnet was part of the court's prescribed mourning dress. Its requirements were widely reported in the press. See, for example, London *Gazetteer and New Daily Advertiser*, 28 May.

[3] As a result of the nonacceptance of Robert Morris' bills of exchange, JA was obliged to go to Amsterdam to secure a new loan to pay the interest on an earlier Dutch loan (*Dipl. Corr., 1783–1789*, 2:751–753; AA2 to JQA, 10 June, below).

[4] That is, Thomas Barclay.

[5] In the Dft the second paragraph to this point reads as follows: "but to the Subject I meant to write you upon the intelligence I mean to communicate is no secreet therefore no cypher is needed. Soon after your absence the N. Y—k packet arrived & brought a letter from the Board of Treasury containing Bills to the amount of 75 thousand Guilders for the payment of the june Interest the morning after their arrival *Sir*—I will add, J. That it may look more respectfull, Sir J. went to mr R—r to offer them for acceptance, but found the family gone into the Country, & no Clerk. the next day he repeated his visit. When the clerk unfolded the mistery, the Bill were then noted for non payment, & mr R & family had embarked for A— What was then to be done? Sir J— wrote to H—d the circumstances & requested to know whether a loan could be obtain sufficient for the purpose, in replie they wrote it was indispensable, for in concequence of the advertizing the payment of the june interest being delayed only two

days, the obligations had fallen 2 pr cent, but that the Brokers had refused to proceed in the Buisness untill Sir J. came upon the spot to sign the obligations. two days only were given to prepair for the journey and on fryday last Sir J Sat out accompanied by Secretary C—g What will be the concequence of a hundred thousand pounds worth of Bills going back for nonpayment to the House by which they were drawn. time will determine. Money is said to be very scarce in H—d & not to be had but at the monstrus premium of 8 pr cent. What C—ss will say I know not. yet nothing else could be done to save their affairs from total destruction. the Letter this Evening received from you shall forward by tomorrows post, but know not what can be done."

[6] "Rosea" in the Dft copy. AA's capital "R" can easily be misread for an "M." Roseau is now the capital of Dominica.

[7] The Dft adds the following at this point: "Mrs F—t has been the Sacrifice. mr Fox declaring in the House of commons by authority as he said, that not the least foundation was ever given for the reports which had gone forth to the world, who well knew that it was impossible any such thing could legally take place, but not only so, but that it had never taken place in any way whatever— he should have gone still further & have said that the prince was as chast as Scipio—& that mrs F. was a vestal, that there was no distinction between virtue & vice but in our Ideas & that no moral obligation was binding upon a prince."

The Prince of Wales had spent £54,000 on Maria Anne Fitzherbert and owed creditors £270,000 when in May he convinced friends to ask Parliament to pay his debts. An angry George III ordered a full accounting and a repayment schedule before increasing the prince's £50,000 annual allowance by £10,000. Parliament voted an outlay of £160,000 to pay the creditors, and the prince agreed to close his London residence, sell his horses and carriages, and move to a more modest abode in Brighton (James Munson, *Maria Fitzherbert: The Secret Wife of George IV*, London, 2001, p. 172–173; Valerie Irvine, *The King's Wife: George IV and Mrs. Fitzherbert*, N.Y., 2004, p. 51, 54).

⁸Former British envoy David Hartley (1731–1813) may have suffered a relapse of an unidentified illness that struck him in France in the spring and summer of 1784 just after he and the American commissioners exchanged the ratified Treaty of Paris (George Herbert Guttridge, *David Hartley, M.P., An Advocate of Conciliation, 1774–1783*, Berkeley, Calif., 1926, p. 319).

⁹Sir George Staunton (1737–1801), born in Galway, Ireland, was a physician, medical writer, and diplomat who served the British in a public capacity in a number of positions, especially in India and the West Indies. He married Jane Collins in July 1771 (*DNB*; AA to Mary Smith Cranch, 16 July, below).

John Adams to Abigail Adams

My dearest Friend   Amsterdam June 1. 1787

We are lodged in our old Chamber at Amsterdam, and Sleep as soundly as if there were not a dozen houses plundered every night. The two nights before the last were very Seditious. last night was quiet, and the Precautions which Secured the Peace then, will be continued, so t[hat] all will be still.— dont be anxious for Us, nor believe half the Reports that will be circulated. Such Events are often exaggerated at first. Mʳ Cutting and myself are very Safe. The Party for the Prince, appears to be so feeble in Amsterdam, that every thing will be quieted, very soon.¹

I cannot Say when We shall return, but I believe We Shall recross from Helvoet to Harwick, by next Wednesdays Packet, so that you may expect Us by Friday or Saturday. Yet We may be detained a Week longer.

I have accomplished the Business I came upon, and have this Day signed the Contract for a Million of Guilders at five Per Cent. so that Congress will be at ease for another year.² My Love to Mʳˢ Smith, and a Kiss for my Grand Boy.

My Libel is much applauded here. They call it "The Breviary of Liberty, Safety and good order" a Compliment more flattering to me, than all the Ingenuity of my own Self Love & Vanity, could have invented. I am forever yours   John Adams

RC (Adams Papers); addressed: "England / Madame / Madame Adams / chez Le Ministre des / Etats Unis De L'Amerique / Grosvenor Square / London"; internal address: "Portia."; endorsed: "Mr Adams june / 1 1787–"; docketed by WSS: "JA— to Mʳˢ· A / June 1ˢᵗ 1787." Some loss of text where the seal was removed.

¹On 21 April throngs of Patriots occupied Amsterdam's Dam Square and ousted re- gents who supported Stadholder William V. After supporters of the expelled officials

challenged the validity of these actions, Patriots rampaged on the night of 29 May. The deliberate destruction of bridges to the center of the city made it difficult for troops loyal to the stadholder to reach the affected area, leaving Patriots free to ransack the homes and businesses of their opponents over several days. When a semblance of order was restored through military force, many of Amsterdam's wealthy families fled the city (Schama, *Patriots and Liberators*, p. 115–117).

[2] JA signed a contract with the Amsterdam banking firms of Nicolaas & Jacob van Staphorst and Wilhem & Jan Willink for a loan to the United States of one million guilders, to be paid back over fifteen years at 5 percent interest. This was the third loan JA negotiated on behalf of the United States, the first two of which included the firm of De la Lande & Fynje along with the Staphorsts and Willinks. An initial borrowing of five million guilders was made in 1782, and a second loan of two million guilders was taken out in 1784. JA would negotiate a fourth loan in March 1788, on the eve of the Adamses' departure from Europe, of one million guilders, also with the Staphorsts and Willinks (Winter, *Amer. Finance and Dutch Investment*, 2:1086–1089; JA to AA, 14 March 1788, below). For more on JA's first loan from the Dutch, see JA, *Papers*, 13:*passim*.

John Adams to Abigail Adams

My dearest Friend   Amsterdam Saturday June 2. 1787

I wrote you Yesterday, that I had executed the Contract and should return to England by the Packet of Wednesday the Sixth of June. But as the Money Lenders, whether to make a mere Compliment to me, whether to shew their Patriotism, or whether from simple Caprice, made it an original Condition that my Name should be Subscribed to all the obligations, as it was in the first loan, instead of being Signed only once before the Notary Public, as it was in the last, I shall be detained till tuesday in amsterdam. Two thousand Signatures will take me two Days, for altho I once wrote my name 2500 times in one day, I would not do it again, for more Money than I ever got by all my Loans, that is to say for nothing.—[1] I shall not now be able to embark at Helvoet, before Saturday or the following Wednesday.

I am grieved for M[r] Barclay and his amiable Family but can give them no relief.

The two last nights have been quiet: but I am told that near thirty houses have been rifled.— Some Persons of note have decamped, and discoveries are Said to have been made, but I give little Credit to what I hear, because Reports at such times are given out, with design: and I am not in any Secret, because I will not be. I am but a Passenger.— it is given out that there will be Seven Executions this Morning. a Scene that my Nerves are not in tune to see.[2]

one Truth is now manifest to all, namely that the Patriotick Party, is all powerful at Amsterdam, and consequently the Prince must comply, or do worse.

My Love to Mrs Smith and her dear Boy.— I am very glad You again complyed with Mr Brand Hollis's advice for your health is ever dear to your ever affectionate   John Adams.

RC (Adams Papers); addressed: "England / Mrs Adams / at the American Ministers / Grosvenor Square / London"; internal address: "Portia."; endorsed: "Mr Adams june / 2d 1787."

[1] JA probably refers to the bonds he was obligated to sign for his 1782 loan; see JA, *Papers*, 13:172, 517, 528, 529.

[2] Newspapers reported hangings occurring during and after the riots, both as atrocities in the heat of battle and punishments in its aftermath. The London *Gazetteer* reported "fourteen of the Stadtholder's adherents were seized in the streets on the second day of the rioting, and hanged by the mob of the opposite party." Punishments were meted out to rioters beginning on 2 June 1787 as JA anticipated, but the early reports were exaggerated. Rather than seven hangings, "one of the rioters, who was caught pillaging, was hung up with very little ceremony" (London *Gazetteer and New Daily Advertiser*, 8, 11 June).

William Stephens Smith to Abigail Adams

My dear Madam—   Aranjuez June 4th. 1787.

I have recived your agreable Letter of the 5th. of may[1] and am much obliged for it, at the same time I had the happiness of getting one from my dear Abby[2] I ask your pardon Nabby you like best and when I am acquainted with what will give my friends pleasure— I shall alway's attend even to the minutest particle—therefore to you Nabby is the word—Amelia to herself—my daughter for Sir—& for myself I know no single term in the English Language which can properly convey the tender & interesting Idea which my mind is filled with relative to her— your immagination therefore is left free— permit it to expand and embrace every thing that my soul holds dear, connect it with *Nabby* and as I am concerned most intimately in every thing which relates to & may possibly contribute to the happiness of her friends & herself, I shall heartily subscribe to it— I wrote her from Madrid, on the 31st. ul^to. 1. & 2^d. in^st. which as it goes by the same post with this, you may if you can agree on the subject exchange Letters, but I immagine you will have done reading first— my Letters to her from Paris, Bourdeaux Bayonne & old Castile will fully inform you of my Movements—[3] I flatter myself M^r. A. will think the time spent at Paris Versailles and the disagreable check which I met with at Bourdeaux in consequence of M^r. Barclay's imprisonment—were necessary—and that my progress thus far to carry into execution the orders of Congress—has been effected with as much rapidity as possible— I am one of those animals who are ever anxious & pressing forward to the Compleation of some point or other and when entrusted with the Business of my Country never at rest untill I have fully done my part to put it in the most eligable train of operation in my power— I shall be necessarily detained here a few day's—to pay the attentions expected at Court— I waited yesterday on His Excellency The Comte D^e· Florida Blanca, and delivered the Letter which the Chevalier D^e Campo gave me, & was recieved with great civility—[4] I dined in company with M^r· Carmichael at the Swedish Ministers & passed the day very agreably—[5] I find M^r· Carmichael perfectly well received & much respected here—but he is so cramped in his salery as really to be obliged as to content himself without making those returns to the Civilities of his friends & the Hospitality of the Corps-diplomatic, which he would be happy in doing if the salery from his Country would admit of it— but I tell him he must keep himself cool it is the same in England & in France— I have no doubt but every care will be taken of my Little friends while I am away— I flatter myself that the one has recovered from her cold and that the other encreases in pleasantry & good humour— I am rather anxious to be with them—& I am apprehensive when I return you may all be in the Country—is it possible for you my d^r· Mama—to give me some information relative to your movements that I may know when I land in that Isle of Beef & Pudding where to find you all— Thus far I had got in the morning it is now 8 o:Clock in the evening & the post is on the point of departure— I have been to Court & made my bow to His Most Catholic Majesty—& dined agreably with the English Minister—[6] every one here appears disposed to be polite, & hitherto my jaunt has been as agreable as the rapidity of my motion and the roughness of the roads in spain could in any degree admit of— Inclosed I send you the writ of the Parliament of Bourdeaux for the liberation of M^r· Barclay— I have bit a week on the lines—"Mais une Nation nouvelle, qui doit son existence à la protection de sa Majesty & au puissance secours des Armes francaises."[7]

I will not say what others ought to do—but for myself I think I would consent to remain in a dungeon for Life rather than be liberated by an order which containd such a Line— I deny it in toto as a Soldier & as a Citizen—we were of ourselves competent to the task I acknowledge they contributed to hasten its period—

I am glad D.H. & your have been so successful in your negotiations—[8] present me to your lesser half shake *Nabby* by the hand for me, Kiss the Boy & be assured of the regard & affection with Which I am / Dʳ· Madam— / Your obliged & dutifull / Son—

W.— S.— S.—

RC (Adams Papers); internal address: "Mʳˢ· Adams—"

¹ Not found.

² This letter has not been found, but WSS received it on the evening of 1 June and replied to it the next day (AA2, *Jour. and Corr.*, 1:162–164).

³ WSS wrote letters to AA2 datelined Paris, 28 April and 5 May; Blois, 10 May; Bordeaux, 14 and 19 May; Bayonne, 20–21 May; Old Castile, Spain, 25 May; and Madrid, 31 May – 2 June (AA2, *Jour. and Corr.*, 1:131–164).

⁴ José de Moñino y Redondo, Conde de Floridablanca (1728–1808), was Spanish foreign minister under Charles III; Bernardo del Campo had been his secretary and was now Spanish minister plenipotentiary to the Court of St. James (JA, *Papers*, 9:134, 12:143;

vol. 7:36, 45).

⁵ William Carmichael served as the acting American chargé d'affaires at the court of Spain from 1782 until 1790 and then as the officially commissioned chargé d'affaires from 1790 to 1794. Carl August, Baron von Ehrensvärd, was the Swedish minister to Spain, 1784–1799 (*DAB*; *Repertorium*, 3:416).

⁶ Sir Robert Liston (1742–1836) was the British minister to Spain from 1783 to 1788. He served as the minister to the United States during JA's presidency (*Repertorium*, 3:177; *DNB*).

⁷ But a young nation, which owes its existence to his Majesty's protection and the potent help of the French army.

⁸ Probably David Hartley.

William Stephens Smith to Abigail Adams Smith

My Dear Friend: Aranjuez, June 6th, 1787.

I was much pleased this morning by the receipt of yours of May 19th.¹ Look at the dates—May 5th, Paris, and Blois, May 11th—the places are very distant, and it is impossible to write in a chariot going post. I have answered your mamma's letter from this place; I have not gone through the necessary visits to the royal family, but they are nearly finished. I find everything here much more agreeable than I expected; the corps diplomatic, are very different gentlemen at this court, from those at the court of London; here friendship, hospitality, and good humour, sweeten society, and sweeten the political career. I have been here four days, and have dined very agreeably three of them, with the English, Swedish, and the Dutch Ministers;² I am engaged to dine with the Comte de Florida Blanca on Saturday, and shall begin to think of proceeding to Lisbon; but I am rather uneasy about Curio; the fatigues of the journey have proved too great for him, and he is now sick and a-bed; he is well attended, and I hope will recover in a few days; if he does not, I shall with very great reluctance be obliged to proceed without him; he has conducted himself so well, that I shall miss him much—and at Bayone took him in the carriage with me, so that all through

Spain he has fared in every respect equal with myself. But notwith-standing that, he is sick and I am as usual, in greater health for the active life I have passed.[3] It is my element; sloth and inactivity will sicken me; but the other will ensure me health and spirits.

June 7th.

The grand procession of the court this day, has engaged the atten-tion of every one in and about this place; the palace was thronged with "reverend r——s in robes," adorned with all the insignia of their respective stations, and cutting no despicable figure; on the con-trary, the whole was solemnly magnificent, and worthy the attention of a stranger. After the solemn march was over, all parties perambu-lated the gardens, where taste and elegance, accompanied with all the graces of the Spanish court, were laid open to view. I was enter-tained and shall spend this afternoon at a bull feat; but I am told it will not be equal to what I shall see in the course of a day or two; but you shall have more of this in detail, my friend, when I shall again seat myself contented by your side. I thank you for the infor-mation you give me in cypher; there is great pleasure in having my companion a little of a politician. The news came agreeable and ap-ropos. Yours,   W. S. S.

MS not found. Printed from AA2, *Jour. and Corr.*, 1:164–166.

[1] Not found.
[2] The Dutch minister to Spain was Jacob Godefroy, Graf van Rechteren, who served from 1773 to 1793 (*Repertorium*, 3:269).

[3] Curioni's ill health continued until at least 18 June. It contributed to the delays that kept WSS at Madrid until 3 July (AA2, *Jour. and Corr.*, 1:172–173, 183).

Abigail Adams to John Adams

My Dearest Friend   London june 7th 1787

I expected to have heard from you by the last post, but was diss-apointed, only a few lines from Mr Cutting have come to hand since you left me. I wrote you on the 29th of May, and inclosed two Let-ters respecting mr Barclay. Since that time a Letter from the Frenchs, has arrived, in which they inform you that Mr Barclay was liberated by applying to the Parliament of Bordeaux in virtue of his commission to moroco, but they make most heavy complaints stat-ing their case to you, and conceiving it in your power to relieve them.[1] I do not think it prudent to commit the Letter to the post. mrs Smith has a Letter from mr Smith dated at Bayonne the 26 of may. he had received a Letter from his Friend mr Harrison informing him that mr Charmical had procured him Letters & a passport from the King of Spain, which might facilitate his progress and serve him on his journey.[2]

The News here is that stocks have fallen 5 prcent in concequence of a paragraph in his Majestys Speach respecting Holland.[3] the News papers tell us of terible Roits committed by the patriotick party and make one almost anxious for their Friends there.[4]

The prince of Wales has been most dangerously sick, has been Bled Six times, his disorder a voilent fever which fixd upon his Lungs. the papers tell us that his Royall highness bore his disorder with *Christian fortitude*; he is better to day—[5]

The monthly Reviewers have made open war upon the Defence of the American constitutions, and torn it all to peices, "ostentatious display of learning, an embarrassed affectation of Elocution— The balances the balances are perpetually rung in our ears like Lord Chesterfields graces, but in all the constitutions here passed in Review before the reader, those of America and England not excepted, there is not given a distinct account of the real balancing powers of any State, or the particulars in which the balance consisted had the Book been written by a youth with a view to obtain some academical prize we should have said, that it afforded indications of an active mind that gave hope of future acquirements, but that the young man too eager to discover the extent of his reading, had carelessly adopted some confused notions of government and hastily skimmed the surface of the subject without having taken time to investigate particulars and sift the matter to the bottom, but we cannot bring ourselves to think that a man of dr Adams's known abilities could possibly be in the same prediciment, for which reason we conclude that he must have some point to carry, some object in view beyond the atlantick with which we are not acquainted. the Book may indeed amuse the ignorant it may mislead the unwary, but neither can inform nor entertain the phylosopher nor the man of Letters."[6] In various parts I thought I discoverd Satans cloven foot, but did not know that any individual was permitted to send in his comments upon a work untill I heard this peice ascribed to that poor envy ridden, contemptable, Ignorant self conceited wretch Silas dean.[7] This at once disarmed me of my resentment, (for I own it fretted me for one Night so that I did not sleep quietly) and I felt in perfect good humour. I have only given you a small portion of the compliments of which he has been very profuse, & having got his lesson by Heart has retaild it in all companies, mr Shippen is my Author.

79

I am very anxious to hear from you, and to know when I may expect your return. The Weather remains very cold here. I hope you find it warmer in Holland compliments to mr Cutting, from your affectionate   A A

                                                                    thursday P M.

just after writing this Letter, yours & mr. Cuttings was brought me by the post. I was very glad to hear you were well and safe. mr cuttings Letter carried me to Holland made me Sick on board the packet jostled me in the Waggon, in short so pictureish were his descriptions that I realized them all. The little Boy is well and perks up his Head like a Robbin. his Mamma has had a little of the Holland disorder[8] bordering upon an ague. my Ladyship is better. I send this to Harwick with order to forward it if you do not come in Wednesdays packet, adieu—

RC (Adams Papers); addressed: "His Excellency john Adams / Minister plenipotentiary from the / united States of America to His / Britanic Majesty / Harwick"; endorsed: "Mrs A june 7 / 1787."

[1] V. & P. French & Nephew wrote to JA on 26 May to recount Thomas Barclay's "disgrace brot. on himself by his unwarrantable Conduct" four years earlier when he diverted a shipment of goods contracted to them to another port and "Sold the Cargo applying it to Some other purpose." Barclay had been released from prison by order of the Parliament of Bordeaux, the Frenches reported, leaving them no choice but to write to JA "hoping for Justice thro' your Excellency, the protector of the oppressed" (Adams Papers).

[2] Not found. On 31 May WSS reported to AA2 that he had received a letter from Richard Harrison assuring him that a passport would be waiting for him in Bordeaux. In fact no travel document was left for him, and he was forced to pay 27 Spanish dollars to border officials to cross into Spain (AA2, *Jour. and Corr.*, 1:157).

[3] In his closing speech to Parliament on 30 May, George III noted that dissension within the Netherlands posed a "real concern." At least one London newspaper later reported that the king's speech had negatively affected the price of stocks in England (*Parliamentary Hist.*, 26:1123; London *Daily Universal Register*, 9 June).

[4] The *Morning Chronicle and London Advertiser* reported on 6 June of the "sad doings in Amsterdam," saying that Patriots had plundered homes and businesses and

that supporters of the stadholder had carried out attacks on Patriot homes in reprisal. "Commerce is at a stand in that once opulent city. The principal houses have shut their counting-houses, and are removing their effects to their country seats."

[5] The prince's illness was reportedly severe; a rumor of his death on 4 June occasioned St. George's Church to fly its flag at half-mast. By 7 June his condition had greatly improved (*Morning Chronicle and London Advertiser*, 7 June; London *Daily Universal Register*, 8 June).

[6] AA is quoting from the review of JA's *Defence of the Const.* in the *Monthly Review*, May 1787, 76:394–399.

[7] JA blamed Silas Deane for the negative review the *Defence of the Const.* received in the *Monthly Review*. In reality, James Anderson (1739–1808), an economist, was the author; Deane was never a contributor to that periodical. The enmity between the Adamses and Silas Deane began when Deane was accused of financial impropriety while serving as commissioner to France and recalled in Nov. 1777. Congress chose Adams as his replacement leading to rumors that Adams had conspired in his downfall. Deane attempted to defend his actions by publishing an address "To the Free and Virtuous Citizens of America," which JA believed caused divisions in Congress. JA continued to question

Deane's moral character—which was further damaged by the publication in 1781 of some of Deane's private letters advocating reconciliation with Britain—and considered him a traitor to the American cause (Benjamin Nangle, *The Monthly Review, First Series 1749–1789: Indexes of Contributors and Articles*, Oxford, 1934, p. x, 1, 14, 49; John Ferling, *John Adams: A Life*, Knoxville, Tenn., 1992, p. 187–188, 207–208; JA, *D&A*, 2:345–346; *DAB*).

[8] A colloquial term for a strain of malaria that was usually not fatal but that resulted in persistent fevers and shaking. The amount of water in and around the Netherlands made the country susceptible to malaria, which is carried by mosquitoes (Alan Macfarlane, *The Savage Wars of Peace: England, Japan and the Malthusian Trap*, Cambridge, 1997, p. 195).

Abigail Adams Smith to John Quincy Adams

London june 10th 1787–

my Conscience really reprimands me for having so long omitted writing my Dear Brother, for several months past I must plead in excuse the want of Health, in December last we made an excursion to Bath and by going to Balls or Concerts every night for One week I cought such a Cold—as Confined me for a long time, and indeed I did not wholy recover till April. Mamma has already informed you[1] of the new relationship which commenced on the Second of April—and I have now the pleasure to assure you that your Nephew is a fine Boy and grows Surprisingly— But I allmost fear too fast for his Mamma to retain her strength— I have been troubled for this Month past with tooth ack ague—and fever—and a long ectaera of ills too tedious to particularize I only mention them as an appology for my too long Silence— I am at present I hope recovering—from them all—and shall not fail of writing as often as opportunities may present—

I have the pleasure to acknowledge the receipt of yours of Jany and Febuary.[2] I cannot but regret that you so very decidedly judge that whatever you write must be uninteresting—from that want of variety which you Suppose essentialy necessary to render a detail interesting however as I have been so very deficient myself I cannot in reason—Complain of you— I do not doubt of your disposition to perform all the Duties which you consider yourself called upon to act in and I have had too many and pleasing proofs of your attention—to doubt of your disposition to Confer favours upon your friends, when they may not be incompatiable with your Studies or more important avocations

the reasons you have given for passing the vacation at Cambridge are Sufficient in my mind— I had no doubt but your motives were good—before I knew them so particularly, I am very much in favour of peoples parsueing those plans which appear to themselvs the most advantageous or as the most probable means of promoting their own pleasure, but you will very rarely find those, who consider themselvs entitled to judge of our actions—disposed to be pleased with our Conduct unless—it exactly coincides with their wishes— and they will stigmatize with the Character of eccentricity—those who from the best motives dissent from them in jugement opinion or Conduct—

from the Characters you have drawn of the Two Ladies I can easily discern which is the most amiable, and which is the greatest favourite—with you—however we may be amused and entertained with that satirical tallent which you represent the former to possess. we are all of us I beleive too Conscious of some imperfections—in ourselvs—not to fear the Lash of satire— I have often admired this tallent—but have allways feard it and you know—Love casteth out fear—[3] I am rather inclined to beleive that most People are inspired with fear for such a character more than Love—

Mamma and myself have been quite alone for this forght night past Pappa was obliged to make a journey to Holland upon Business—and M[r] Smith has been absent six weeks on his journey to Lisbon. I heard from him on the 22[d] of May att Bayonne rapidly advanceing on his Tour.[4] I suppose he will be absent two or three Months Longer— Congress acted with their *Usual* Wisdom in Commanding M[r] S. to undertake this journey—attended with such an expence as it necessarily must be—only to deliver a Letter—of acknowledgements to the Queen of Portugall—for her having ordered her fleet to protect American Ships—and to inquire after the Treaty— it appears to me that this *respectable Body* are deficient in Common Sence—in judgment they most assureedly are— when there are two ways of doing things—they seem invariably to take the wrong— I think they want some Wise Heads to direct their Counsells—

there has lately taken place an Event here which has made some Noise. M[r] Rucker was you know an agent from M[r] Morris's house appointed to reside here to answer M[r] Morris's Bills. M[r] M— sent His tobacco to France where it was sold, and *le Couton* was his Banker there,[5] by the last Ships and the April packett there came Bills drawn by M[r] Morris to the Amount of 98 thousand pounds which have been noted for non payment. M[r] Rucker received to the amount of £15 thousand which he had not the means to answer and early in the Month of May took himself off— where he is gone is yet uncertain—some suppose to America—others to Germany—there to

Continue till the affairs blows over— the Board of Treasury had bought Mr Morris's Bills to pay the june Interest in Holland and when they arrived here they could not be paid— the time was too short to send to America and had the Interest failed of Being paid in Holland the Credit of the U States must have fallen. from matters standing thus your father was obliged to Open a new loan in Holland and the money Lenders insisted upon his going over to sign the Bonds—which obliged him to sett of at two days Notice he took Mr Cutting with him as a Companion—and last Evening they returnd the disturbences which exist at present in that Country, render it not a very pleasant residence, at this time

You have doubtless heard much of the Coldness that has subsisted for the last year between the King and the Prince of Wales— you are also I suppose acquainted with the Measures taken by the Prince this time last year—such I mean as giving up his Household appropriating a Certain sum to the payment of his Debts—and Living upon 10 thousand a year quite in the Stile of a private Gentleman, the last Sessions Alderman Newnham was going to bring forward a Motion to Sollicit an addition to the Prince's income—but this was much objected to and by some means or other it brought on a reconciliation between the Sovereign and the Heir appearant, the former Calls upon his *faithfull Commons* to pay his debts and Grants him ten thousand in addition to his former Income.[6] all this has made much Subject for Conversation of Late, and great rejoiceings were *anticipated* upon the Birth day— But the week before last the Prince was seized with a violent fever—for which on the Last Sunday he was let Blood for the Seventh time—and has been extreemely ill— on Thursday last his Phisicien pronounced him out of danger—but he Continues very Low—

Horn Took has Published a Letter to a friend—in which he asserts that the Prince is Married to Mrs Fitzherbert—that although it is Contrary to some acts of Parliament yet it is not Contrary to Law— that he had a right to Marry a Subject and that it must be Considered a happy Marriage and a fortunate one for the Country—that Mrs F. can be considered in no other light than as her Royall Highness the Princess of Wales—[7]

Madam de Poligniac you know I suppose—has been dismissed from the Government of the Royall offspring—the Cause Why; is Said to be from a difference in opinion to the Queen who ordered to the Duke of Normandy a portion of physic which had not been prescribed by his Physicien, and Madame de P—— refused to administer it upon which a dispute arrose—the King Comeing into the room when the Subject was in debate decided upon it against the Queen—but Madam de P—— was dismissed— She has lately arrived in this Country and is now att Bath accompanied by her favourite the Count D'—— who still Continues at this Court— thus you see, that from *trivial causes great Events arrise*[8]

Mamma has sent you by Callihan—your friend Murrys Publication—addressed to your father, he called upon us yesterday and looks in Better Health than I have seen him for a long time I think he neglects his own advantage by staying from America— in Short there appears to me some facinating power which holds some of our Young Men here—they had rather Live in Europe *unknowing* and *unknown* than to return to their own Country where they might be Loved and respected, to me it appears astenishingly Strange— they are not of the ambitious Mind of *him* who prefered being the first Man in the Village to the Second at Rome—[9]

I suppose Mamma has informed you of Pappas having written to Congress requesting his recall— he is Now I beleive in earnest—and wishes to return, although I beleive he will do more good in America than he can possibly do here—yet I Confess the Idea of his returning gives me pain— you my Brother know, from what Cause it arrises—and will feel it with me—it springs from a scource which *we* know aught not to exist—

july 16th 1787—

Barnard Davis and Scot have arrived and not a Singe line from either of my Brothers we have been a little anxious upon the Subject Aunt Cranch in her Letter to Mamma mentions my Brother Thomas as being Well and of yourself that your Health was suffering from your neglect of exercise[10] Why my Brother will you trifle with this inestimable blessing—your Health! when once you are deprived of it—it is not easily regained and without it you Can enjoy no other,—but no body mentioned our Brother Charles—which has made us fear that he was sick—or that this silence respecting him was to Conceal some misfortune or other, the imagination ever fertile in invention has furnished us with this supposition—but *I* will Still hope that it was otherwise

Your Father and Mother propose setting out this week upon an excursion into the County of Devonshire—and propose being absent three weeks or a Month—and they have persuaded me to Accompany them during the Absence of Mr Smith I hope we shall have an agreeable Tour but I shall not be disappointed if we do not—[11]

Barnard and Scot are to Sail before our proposed return—so that my time is now wholy employed in writting my friends who have been too long unattended to—

I Suppose that at this time you are very busy in prepareing for Commencement—which if I am not mistaken takes place within a few days— Mr Cranch informd Your father that you were to Speak the English Oration, I hope you will Send it to me by the first opportunity—do not forget how interested we feel in every thing that respects your rising fame. before Mamma received her own Letters by the late Ship—she received a Letter from Mr John Cranch Containing a very agreeable Account of M^r JQA's—quarterly performance which had been sent to him by Miss Betsy Palmer of which, no mention was made in any Letters to this family from Boston—[12] indeed I must tax you with being very negligent— Our Father however says you are perfectly right, but he is I think too favourable to you in this decission—

Mr Morris's Bill which I mentioned in the former part of this Letter are like to be paid regularly as they become due— those for May and june are already paid—and M^r R— is sensured by *some persons* for going away— he was either deceived by the *then* appearances—or he formed his resolutions too hastily I hope that the issue will not prove injurious to him as I beleive him to be a Worthy Man and I esteem Mrs Rucker very much—

We have another American family arrived here since their departure a Genral Stewart who is a Native of Ireland—and served in the American Army—the last War—Married a Lady in Philadelphia—and intends to settle in that Country they have been two Years in Ireland upon a visit to his relations— they spend a few Months more in England and then return to America—[13] M^rs S— is an intimate friend of Mrs Bingham—and in *some* respects a Simular Character— there are not at present many Americans here—and I do not recollect any from Boston—except J— Appleton— it is a matter of surprise to know what has brought him here again— he knows his own affairs best I presume— he told me that he called upon you at Cambridge a few days before his departure from *Boston*— Mr Barret has lost his Wife in France, She has been extremely discontented ever since her arrival there—as I am informed— Mr Jeffersons other Daughter arrived here from Virginia about three weeks ago—and on Wedensday last set out (with Petit whom Mr Jefferson sent for her) for Paris.

Poor little Girl almost broke her Heart at Leaving us—and a more amiable Child I never saw—intelligence and sensibility sparkle in her eyes, She is only eight years old. She is quite as amiable as her Sister and much handsomer[14]

We have since our residence here made Several very agreeable acquaintances—in families where we are treated with friendship without Ceremony;— we are to spend this Evening at Sir George Stountons, he has uniformly been in favour of Our Country—An Irish Man by Birth and Created a knight after his return from India with Lord Mackartney[15]—for his Services Whilst their, there are a few of such Liberal Minded People—but it is supprising that there are not more this Man seeks an Acquaintance with every American of whom he Can get any knowledge—goes to the American Coffe Houses—after an Arrival and reads the News Papers—and makes inquiries respecting that Country of every one he can find—and when he meets such a *Simple One* as a Mr *Moses Gill* who has come here to Study in the Temple—he does not receive a very favourable account of us—

Mr Barclay has been imprisoned at Bordeaux upon account of goods—sent to America by the House of Barclay Moilon &c—but the parliament of Bordeaux released him upon account of his being in Commission as a Minister Plenipo—to Morroco— he is certainly a most dilatory Man he left Madrid last December and arrived at Bordeaux in April—the same distance Mr Smith went lately in *Eleven days* Poor M^rs B—— is at St Germains as unhappy as a Person Can be— I Grieve for her Situation it is the most deplorable that I can have an idea of— adieu my Dear Brother write often to your affect. Sister   A— Smith

Pappa & Mamma desire to be remembered to you— I dont know whethey they will write by this opportunity— My Son desires his respects to his Uncle—[16]

RC (Adams Papers); endorsed: "My Sister—10. June 1787." and "My Sister. June 10. 1787."

[1] See AA to JQA, 6 May, above.
[2] JQA to AA2, 14 Jan. – 9 Feb., vol. 7:433–440.
[3] 1 John, 4:18.
[4] WSS to AA2, 20–21 May, which is WSS's only letter from Bayonne (AA2, *Jour. and Corr.*, 1:150–152).
[5] Morris' banker in Paris was Le Couteulx & Co.

[6] Nathaniel Newnham (ca. 1741–1809) had proposed a motion requesting that the king allow an examination of the Prince of Wales' debt. At least one London paper reported that the Prince's "distressed" financial state would bring "disgrace" to England. On 4 May, however, Newnham announced to the House that his motion was no longer necessary as the king had already appointed a

commission to study the issue (Namier and Brooke, *House of Commons*; London *Gazetteer and New Daily Advertiser*, 30 April; *Morning Chronicle and London Advertiser*, 21 April; *Ann. Register*, 1787, 29:129).

[7] John Horne Tooke (1736–1812), a British politician, published a pamphlet in London in 1787 entitled *Letter on the Reported Marriage of . . . the Prince of Wales*, which questioned the legitimacy of the Marriage Act (*DNB*). The pamphlet excited much discussion in the press. See, for example, London *Daily Universal Register*, 2, 11, and 12 June; and *Monthly Review*, June. For more on the purported marriage of the Prince of Wales and Maria Anne Fitzherbert, see AA to Mercy Otis Warren, 14 May, and note 7, and AA to WSS, [30] May, and note 7, both above; and vol. 7:xi–xii.

[8] In February the London press reported that Yolande Martine Gabrielle de Polastron, Duchesse de Polignac (1749–1793), had been dismissed by Marie Antoinette from her position as governess to the queen's children. The dutchess' sister-in-law, Diane de Polignac, Comtesse de Polastron, was having an affair with a political foe of the queen, the Comte D'Artois, who would later become Charles X of France (1757–1836). The cause of the Duchesse de Polignac's dismissal, however, was apparently neither her sister-in-law's affair nor a dispute over the administering of medicine to the future Louis XVII (then known as the Duke of Normandy). Rather it was an illness that caused the dutchess to abandon her duties and retire to Bath, England, for a period of two months (London *Gazetteer and New Daily Advertiser*, 7 Feb.; W. R. H. Trowbridge, *Seven Splendid Sinners*, London, 1924, p. 249, 254, 263, 267, 271–272; Hoefer, *Nouv. biog. générale*).

[9] "I had rather be first in a village than second at Rome," attributed to Julius Caesar.

[10] See Mary Smith Cranch to AA, 22 April, above.

[11] For AA2's journal of her trip to Devonshire with her parents, see AA2, *Jour. and Corr.*, 1:85–94.

[12] [*Ca. 23 June*], below.

[13] Gen. Walter Stewart (1756–1796) was a native of Londonderry, Ireland, and a partner in the Philadelphia firm of Stewart & Nesbitt. During the war he had served as aide-de-camp to Horatio Gates and was a close associate of George Washington. On 6 July Stewart's wife, Deborah McClenachan Stewart (b. 1763), delivered the couple's fourth child, Walter Jr., in London (Washington, *Papers, Presidential Series*, 3:470; *PMHB*, 22:381–382 [1898]).

[14] See AA to Thomas Jefferson, 26 June, below.

[15] Lord George Macartney (1737–1806), Irish diplomat and politician, was appointed colonial governor of Madras in June 1781. He returned to England in Jan. 1786 (*DNB*).

[16] This final paragraph was written sideways in the margin on the final page of the letter.

John Cranch to Abigail Adams

Madam; Axminster, 13. June, 1787:

I should have addressed your excellency sooner, but that my mind, which is *the weakest*—(or, as I had rather settle your excellency's idea of it, *the most delicate*)—thing in the world, has been for sometime suspended between the contrary fears—of trespassing upon your more important attentions, on the one hand, or against the obligations of gratitude & decorum, on the other: The last has, finally, prevailed; and I will now submit to be thought as "impertinent" as your excellency pleases, provided I may be acquitted of the "ingratitude":

But, in presenting me with the "Defence of the political constitutions of America," what did you, my dear madam, but make me your debtor for one of the greatest pleasures of my life? Should I

⟨then⟩ withhold acknowledgements which it is even *duty* to make; or should I dare apprehend, from a noble American Matron, such *coquetry of benevolence*, as first to excite the sensibilities of a gratefull heart, and then either to refuse, or contemn, it's humble *returns?*

This delightfull season being so far advanced, I begin to fear that I may not enjoy the promised pleasure of attending your excursions into this part of England: May I presume to intimate, that the accomodations of my cottage, though humble, and ⟨what is worse⟩ not yet hallowed by the arrangements of a prudent "Goody Baucis,"[1] are not despicable; and that it's deficiencies can be supplied by very excellent inns: The expectation of entertaining ⟨though but for an hour⟩ the father of American Liberty, will *stimulate* my endeavours to make that entertainment agreeable;— The remembrance of such an honor will amply *reward* them: I would by way of inducement, add, but that his excellency already knows it ⟨perhaps better than myself⟩ that, to say nothing of the amusing varieties of Devonshire in *general*, we have in this town in which I live, some capital peculiar manufactories; and that those of wool, and thin cloths, about Exeter, are also of great consideration:[2] But one hint more will I dare give— "You shall be as *public*, or as *private* as you please."

I shall be highly obliged to you, madam, or to mrs. Smith, for any information relative to our friends at home—I mean *America*. Be persuaded, nothing can be trivial, to me, that comes from those friends, & that country.

Pray accept my respectfull compliments of thanks & good wishes, for yourself & for doctor Adams and mr. and mrs. Smith; and permit me, madam, to have the honor of confessing, and on every occasion demonstrating, myself to be / Your Excellency's / obliged, faithfull / humble servant   J. Cranch.

RC (Adams Papers); addressed: "for Mrs Adams."; endorsed: "J Cranch june 13 / 1787."

[1] In classical mythology Baucis and Philemon were an elderly couple who offered hospitality to the gods Jupiter and Mercury when others refused to do so. They were rewarded by having their cottage transformed into a temple (Brewer, *Reader's Handbook*). Jonathan Swift celebrated "Goody Baucis" in his poem, "Baucis and Philemon."

[2] Textile making was the dominant industry of southwestern England. Axminster and Exeter were known especially for their cloth finishing. By the end of the eighteenth century, Axminster had achieved a worldwide reputation for its carpets though the cloth-finishing industry itself was in decline (W. G. Hoskins, *Industry, Trade and People in Exeter, 1688–1800*, Manchester, 1935, p. 37; Geoffrey Chapman, *A History of Axminster to 1910*, Wilmington, 1998, p. 108–109).

Cotton Tufts to John Adams

S^{r.}   Boston June 13. 1787—

In my Letter to Mrs. Adams Pr. Capt. Scott, I mentioned to her, That Mr. S. Q. was negociating for Borlands Place— it was then my Opinion that He would purchase it— Yesterday Mr. Cranch informed me that he had learnt from Mr. Borland that Mr. S. Q. had given up the Matter—and that Mr. B. is determined to make Sale of it as soon as he has settled with M^{r.} T——r. I conclude therefore that it will be very soon open for any Purchaser—[1]

We have a new General Court, the House of Repres^{ves.} made up of new Members chiefly, not more than 50 or 60 Old Members, a majority of the new in favour of the late opposition to Government— A general Indemnity, the withdrawing of the Troops, Removal of the Court from Boston—a liberal Tender Act—Abolition of the Court of common Pleas—payment of public Securities at the going Price &c &c are with them favorite objects

I suspect there is a Majority in the House sufficient to carry some of these if not all—Notwithstanding the late succesful Efforts of Government—I think there is the highest Probability,—that a Revolution is not far distant. some of our Politicians—friends to a stable Goverment, say it is no matter, how soon— By Capt. Cushing who will sail in a Fortnight or Three Weeks shall write further In the mean Time Am Yours—

RC (Adams Papers); docketed by AA: "Dr Tufts / june 13. 1787."

[1] On 26 May, Cotton Tufts wrote to AA informing her that Leonard Borland had offered Samuel Quincy the Vassall-Borland estate, which Royall Tyler had previously attempted to buy, for £600 (Adams Papers). Quincy declined, and the Adamses finally purchased the property on 26 Sept. (Adams Papers, Adams Office Manuscripts, Box 2, folder 16). For a full discussion of the history of this estate, which became the Old House and then the Adams National Historical Park, see vol. 3:264–266, and Descriptive List of Illustrations, No. 2, above.

John Cranch to Abigail Adams

For Mrs. Adams: [*ca.* 23 *June* 1787]

Substance of miss Palmer's account of the University exhibition at Cambridge, the 10th. of April: To J.C.

"—— preceded by a band of Music, consisting of such of the pupils as had a taste for Music—among whom were John and Charles Adams and William Cranch: When the president and governors arrived, the exercises began in the following order:

2. PEACEFIELD, BY E. MALCOM, 1798

See page ix

1[st.] Forensic dispute in english:—subject—'whether Man has a natural right to destroy the inferior animals'—Peter Eaton & T. Harris:[1]

2d—Syllogistic dispute in latin by John Treadwell —— Underwood and William Hill:[2]

3d. Hebrew oration by James Prescott:[3]

4th. Greek oration by John Phillips:[4]

5th—Dialogue from the tragedy of Tamerlane: Oliver Baron and Benjamin Abbott:[5]

6th. Conference upon divinity—physic & law—Nathaniel Freeman—Moses Little—& J. Q. Adams:[6]

7[th.] English oration by Bossenger Foster:[7]

A grand Musical Symphony & chorus, concluded:

The gentlemen all performed to acceptation: Those who held the 'conference' were loudly applauded: M[r.] Adams, in the excellent composition, sound sense & unusual candour, of his argument, happily united the scholar, the man of sense and the gentleman: He spoke well, and his action was easy:— In every sentiment he beathed the spirit of his father: M[r.] Freeman's beautifull face, elegant person and gracefull manner were captivating: He spoke well—and what he said was good—Yet M[r.] Adams had greatly the advantage, as a gentleman, by the delicacy with which he avoided drawing a paralel between the three professions—allowing them to be *equally* necessary in a well-ordered community, while the others contended for a *partial* superiority:

Afterward the lads assembled in military form &c— &c."

Madam;   Midsummer eve, 1787—

Among other agreeable informations from America I have just received the above: It reads so interesting, that I really cannot in conscience keep it to myself; and I flatter myself with your pardon for the liberty I take, by supposing, that though you should already be in possession of the circumstances of fact, it may be only from those whom Modesty and decorum will not permit to do *themselves* justice in their descriptions of this important and pleasing entertainment.

I intreat my respectfull compliments to m[r.] Adams, and to Mr & Mrs Smith; and have the honor to be, / Madam, / Your Excellency's / very faithfull / Humble servant   J. Cranch.

RC (Adams Papers); addressed: "For / His Excellency John Adams Esq / Grosvenor square, / London."; endorsed: "J Cranch june— / 1787."

¹ For Peter Eaton and Thaddeus Mason Harris, see JQA, *Diary*, 2:184–185, 198–199.

² John Dexter Treadwell (1768–1833) became a physician in Marblehead and Salem, Mass. Nathan Underwood (1753–1841) became a Lincoln clergyman. William Hill died in 1790. All three graduated from Harvard in 1788 (*NEHGR*, 60:194 [April 1906]; 38:402 [Oct. 1884]; *Harvard Quinquennial Cat.*).

³ James Prescott (1766–1829), Harvard 1788, of Groton, Mass., became a lawyer and chief justice of the Middlesex County Court of Common Pleas (William Prescott, *The Prescott Memorial*, Boston, 1870, p. 75).

⁴ John Phillips (1770–1823), Harvard 1788, became the first mayor of Boston and the father of abolitionist Wendell Phillips (*NEHGR*, 20:297–299 [Oct. 1866]).

⁵ Oliver Barron Jr. (1766–1809), Harvard 1788, was the son of Chelmsford legislator Oliver Barron Sr. Benjamin Abbot (1762–1849), Harvard 1788, would serve as headmaster of Phillips Academy in Andover for fifty years. Their recitation was from Nicholas Rowe, *Tamerlane: A Tragedy*, 1702 (*Vital Records of Chelmsford, Massachusetts, to the End of the Year 1849*, Salem, 1914, p. 21; *Harvard Quinquennial Cat.*; John A. Schutz, *Legislators of the Massachusetts General Court, 1691–1780: A Biographical Dictionary*, Boston, 1997; *NEHGR*, 4:99 [Jan. 1850]).

⁶ For Nathaniel Freeman and Moses Little, see JQA, *Diary*, 2:190, 218. See also JQA to JA, 30 June, below.

⁷ For Bossenger Foster, see JQA, *Diary*, 2:188.

Abigail Adams to Thomas Jefferson

my dear sir   London june 26 1787

I have to congratulate you upon the safe arrival of your Little daughter, whom I have only a few moments ago received.¹ She is in fine Health and a Lovely little girl I am sure from her countanance, but at present every thing is strange to her, & She was very loth to try New Friends for old. She was so much attachd to the Captain & he to her, that it was with no Small regreet that I Seperated her from him, but I dare say I shall reconcile her in a day or two.² I tell her that I did not see her sister cry once.³ she replies that her sister was older & ought to do better, besides she had her pappa with her. I Shew her your picture.⁴ She says she cannot know it, how should she when she should not know you. a few hours acquaintance and we shall be quite Friends I dare say. I hope we may expect the pleasure of an other visit from you now I have so strong an inducement to tempt you. if you could bring miss Jefferson with you, it would reconcile her little Sister to the thoughts of taking a journey. it would be proper that some person should be accustomed to her. the old Nurse whom you expected to have attended her, was sick & unable to come⁵ She has a Girl of about 15 or 16 with her, the sister of the servant you have with you—⁶ as I presume you have but just returnd from your late excursion, you will not put yourself to any inconvenience or Hurry in comeing or Sending for her:⁷ you may rely upon every attention towards her & every care in my power. I have just endeavourd to amuse her by telling her that I would carry her to sadlers wells, after describing the amusement to her with an honest simplicity. I had rather Says She See captain Ramsey one moment, than all the fun in the world.

I have only time before the post goes, to present my compliments to mr Short. mr Adams & Mrs Smith desire to be rememberd to you. Captain Ramsey has brought a Number of Letters. as they may be of importance to you to receive them we have forwarded them by the post— miss Polly sends her duty to you & Love to her Sister & says she will try to be good & not cry. so she has wiped her Eyes & layd down to sleep—

believe me dear sir / affectionately yours &c &c   A Adams

RC (DLC:Jefferson Papers); endorsed: "Adams mrs̃."

[1] Thomas Jefferson's youngest surviving daughter Mary (Maria) "Polly" Jefferson (1778–1804) had remained in Virginia when her father sailed for Europe. After receiving a convent education in France, she returned to Virginia in late 1789 with her father. Mary's death at the age of 25 prompted AA to write a letter of condolence to Jefferson, a gesture that temporarily ended the rift between the families caused by growing political differences in the early republic. While only a brief exchange of letters followed, it presaged the eventual resumption of correspondence between JA and Jefferson beginning in 1812 (Gordon Langley Hall, *Mr. Jefferson's Ladies*, Boston, 1966, p. 61; *DAB*; Edith B. Gelles, *Portia: The World of Abigail Adams*, Bloomington, Ind., 1992, p. 86).

[2] Mary Jefferson sailed to London aboard the ship *Arundel* under the care of the vessel's captain, Andrew Ramsay (Hall, *Jefferson's Ladies*, p. 82; Jefferson, *Papers*, 11:351, 524, 556).

[3] AA and AA2 had spent time with Mary's sister Martha in 1784 and 1785 during the Adamses' stay in Auteuil, France (vol. 6:75; Hall, *Jefferson's Ladies*, p. 65–66, 73–77).

[4] A Mather Brown portrait of Jefferson, for which see vol. 7:287, 288–289.

[5] Jefferson had asked that "A careful negro woman" slave named Isabel be sent to accompany Mary to Europe, but Isabel had given birth in April and thus could not make the trip (Jefferson, *Papers*, 8:451; Byron W. Woodson Sr., *A President in the Family: Thomas Jefferson, Sally Hemings, and Thomas Woodson*, Westport, Conn., 2001, p. 9).

[6] Sally Hemings, Jefferson's fourteen-year-old slave, accompanied his daughter on this voyage. In 1784 Sally's brother James had come with Jefferson to Paris, where he was trained as his cook (Jefferson, *Papers*, 7:364, 10:296, 11:502).

[7] Thomas Jefferson had just returned to Paris on 10 June after a fifteen-week tour of southern France and northern Italy. The purpose of Jefferson's trip was to seek out the curative properties of the mineral water at Aix-en-Provence as a remedy for his crippled wrist, but he also used it as an opportunity to tour the ports of France where the United States traded and, more importantly, to document the canal system at Languedoc (Noble E. Cunningham Jr., *In Pursuit of Reason: The Life of Thomas Jefferson*, Baton Rouge, La., 1987, p. 107–108; Jefferson, *Papers*, 11:96).

Abigail Adams to Thomas Jefferson

dear sir   London june 27 1787

I had the Honour of addressing you yesterday and informing you of the safe arrival of your daughter. She was but just come when I sent of my Letter by the post, & the poor little Girl was very unhappy being wholy left to strangers this however lasted only a few Hours, & miss is as contented to day as she was misirable yesterday. She is indeed a fine child. I have taken her out to day and purchased her a few articles which she could not well do without & I hope they will meet your approbation. The Girl who is with her is quite a child, and captain Ramsey is of opinion will be of so little service that he had better carry her back with him, but of this you will be a judge. she seems fond of the child and appears good Naturd.

I sent by yesterdays post a Number of Letters which captain Ramsey brought with him not knowing of any private hand, but mr Trumble has just calld to let me know that a Gentleman sets off for Paris tomorrow morning. I have deliverd him two Letters this afternoon received, and requested him to wait that I might inform you how successfull a Rival I have been to captain Ramsey, & you will find it I imagine as difficult to Seperate miss Polly from me as I did to get her from the Captain. She stands by me while I write & asks if I write every day to her pappa? but as I have never had so interesting a subject to him to write upon [. . . .] hope he will excuse the hasty scrips for the [. . .] intelligence they contain, and be assured dear Sir / that I am with Sentiments / of sincere esteem your / Humble Servant

A Adams

RC (DLC:Jefferson Papers); endorsed: "Adams mrš." Some loss of text due to a torn manuscript.

Mary Smith Cranch to Abigail Adams

My dear Sister   Braintree June 29th 1787

I have sent one Letter on Board capt Cushing[1] but it is so long since that unless I Write again you will not feel as if you had heard from me for a long time— Cousin JQA & Billy have been at home above a week. Cousin charles was here yesterday. he came to wait upon mrs Hilliard & Daughter—[2] your Sons are all well

We are busy prepairing for commencment for although we do so little by way of entertainment yet their is many things wanted & much to be done. Betsy is very unwell this Summer. a dissagreable complaint in the back of her head gives her not a little trouble. she is going to try a cold bath for it—& ride a singlle Horse. She is grown very thin—

Miss Nancy Quincy has been here a week upon a visit. She is as chearful as ever & as fond of musick. She plays upon the Harpsicord too, so that we have musick of some kind or other in some of the rooms from morning to night. She is a good girl. What a Pity that she should be older than any of our young Gentlemen— Madam Quincy is well & desires to be remember'd in the kindest manner to you—

We have taken the dimentions of your little room & the other, but I cannot think you will cut a cloth to them Mr Adams Will be imploy'd in publick business when he returns. that house will not be large enough for you—

Cousin JQA will want some more cotton stockings soon those he brought with him were thin & fine & will not hold on much longer. I have put three or four pair of new feet to many of them already

Callahan is not yet arriv'd. I am all impatience to hear from you. Mr & Mrs Smith are rejoicing I hope over their little one, but my dear Sister does it not make you feel old or does it give you new Spirits?

The news papers will give you Politicks enough but I know you want to step behind the scene & see some of the springs which gives such strange motions to the Political Machine— I have been lately viewing some of its parts— I have been visiting where I have heard every transaction of administration for two years past represented as the result of Passion. The insurgents declar'd to be a people oppress'd to death by goverment Who ought to have a pardon offer'd unask'd, without any conditions Whatever, that the late offers of pardon shakel'd as they were—were an insult to them— "Have you read mr A——s defence of the American Constitutions" "yes—mr —— had one sent him—& I like it, & so does mr —— upon the whole— he thinks in many things as mr A. does—["] pretty cool however thought I—[3]

Does mr A. [talk?] of returning soon "yes madam you shall hear what he & mrs —— says about it & their opinion of the measures of goverment if you please—" I never read any thing will a better will in my Life

"I am sorry mr —— thinks of returning, because I think he will be happier where he is—"

This is but a part a very small part of the conversation, but I have not now time to give you more of it— M[rs. Q?] was with me & we had a warm afternoon of it

I wish you would be so good as to send two yards of silk like the patterns I send if you can pattern them two yds of each, & send the price— I have sent the Pattern of your Gowns— your Friends are all well—sister Shaw has been poorly but was better when she wrote me—

you will always remember me affectionately to mr Adams I hope & accept of the warmest affection / of your Sister   M Cranch

RC (Adams Papers); addressed by JQA: "Mrs Abigail Adams / Grosvenor Square / Westminster."; endorsed: "Mrs Cranch june— / 29. 1787"; docketed by AA2: "Mrs Cranch june—1787." Some loss of text where the seal was removed.

[1] Mary Smith Cranch to AA, 22 April, above.

[2] Mary Hilliard (1772–1847), the eldest daughter of Rev. Timothy and Mary Foster Hilliard, would marry Francis Sales of Cambridge in 1796 (*Sibley's Harvard Graduates*, 16:62; *Vital Records of Cambridge, Massachusetts, to the Year 1850*, 2 vols., Boston, 1915, 2:726).

[3] James Warren wrote to JA on 18 May 1787 to say that he had read the *Defence of the Const.* "with great pleasure. . . . I do not recollect a single Sentiment different from my own, except we might differ a little with respect to the first Magistrate, and perhaps not very essentially" (*Warren-Adams Letters*, 2:291). For previous discussions between Mary Smith Cranch and AA regarding the Warrens, see vol. 7:199, 249.

John Quincy Adams to John Adams

Dear Sir   Braintree June 30th: 1787.

I am at length released from the multiplicity of business which has employ'd so much of my time, for the last eighteen months: during that period I had scarcely a leisure moment, and was forced to a degree of application, which has been injurious to my health. but as I am left at present free from every employment, I shall have time to recruit; and I shall also be able to give more frequent testimonies of the attachment to my friends in Europe, who perhaps have just grounds to complain of my neglecting to write, notwithstanding all that I have offer'd for my justification.— On the 20th: of the present month, I concluded my collegiate course, and return'd here; as the senior Class are always dismissed four weeks before Commencement.— At an exhibition which took place in the beginning of April, I delivered the enclosed piece upon the profession of the Law.[1] Two of my classmates, perform'd at the same time; one of which spoke upon physic and the other upon Divinity: the comparative utility of these professions was the topic, and the performance was honour'd with the approbation of the audience: it may favour perhaps of vanity in me to mention this Circumstance; & I should have said nothing of it, was it not from the hope, that it would afford satisfaction to the best of parents.— I have allotted to me, for Commencement an English Oration, upon the importance, and necessity of public faith to the well-being of a Community:[2] the subject is noble, and of the greatest consequence; it deserves a more able defender and indeed requires it; for our public faith at present is in a sad condition.— I am led unawares into political ground, and now I am there I must indulge myself— M^(r:) Hancock, was again elected governour, this year, and out of 18000 votes he had more than 13000; this plainly shows, that the people in general, are displeased with some part of M^(r:) Bowdoin's conduct: but it is the caprice of an ungrateful populace, for which it must ever be impossible to account. M^(r:) Hancock is very much involved in debt, if common report be true: it is even confidently asserted that his present estate would not by any means do justice to his creditors.[3] it is therefore concluded that he would favour tender acts, paper currencies, and all those measures, which would give the sanction of the law to private fraud and villainy. it was supposed that a Senate and an house of representatives would be chosen, perfectly willing to abolish all contracts public and private, ready in short to redress the people's grievances, that is, to gratify their passions and justify their crimes. but these fears were not entirely well grounded; there are indeed several Senators and many representatives, who would stick at nothing: A Willard, a Drury, A Whitney, and many others, who have openly espoused the cause of treason and rebellion, are now among the legislators of the country;[4] intestinam aliquam quotidie perniciem reipublicae molientes.[5] there is however in both branches of the legislature a majority of well meaning men; who will support the dignity of the government, and who will not prostitute the honour of their Country. A motion was made a few days since, that a committee should be appointed to examine the merits of a paper currency, and to report upon the expediency of an emission at present; but there was a majority of more than 60, even against the committing it. It has been resolved that the Court should move out of the town of Boston, and the committee have finally recommended Concord, as the most proper place to which it may be removed.[6] The people in the country are very earnest in this point; and as usual, without knowing why.— The salaries of all civil Officers, which are now too small will infallibly be reduced still lower. M^(r:) Hancock, who has a peculiar talent of pleasing the multitude, has compounded this matter by offering to make a present to the public of 300£. but I consider this as a pernicious precedent; a palliative, worse, than it would have been, had the legislature curtailed the Salary. for if one man gives up 300£, another, fishing equally for popularity, may give more, and the chair of government, may finally be offered to the lowest bidder.— It is impossible for a free nation to subsist without parties, and unfortunately our parties are not yet form'd. The democratical branch of our government is at present quite unrival'd; and we severely feel the want of sufficient strength in the other branches: the Senate indeed has several times within these 18 months saved the commonwealth from complete anarchy, and perhaps from destruction: but its hands are tied; and the people are too generally disposed to abolish the senate, as an useless body. I have indeed great hopes that the defence of the constitutions, will produce an alteration, in their sentiments; it will certainly have great weight: one printer in Boston is employ'd in printing a new edition of this book, and another is retailing it twice a week, in a newspaper; so that I hope, it will be sufficiently spread throughout the Commonwealth.[7] As to the monarchical power, it appears to be entirely out of the question, and unless by a revolution it be established upon the ruin of the two others, it will never possess influence sufficient to hold the balance, between them.

There was this year no choice of a lieutenant governor by the people. M[r.] Cushing and general Lincoln, were the primary candidates, M[r.] Gorham and gen[l.] Heath had likewise some hundreds of votes.[8] the house sent up M[r.] Cushing & M[r.] Gorham to the Senate, because gen[l.] Lincoln was a military character. The Senate were unanimous in favour of M[r.] Cushing, who will probably drop, at the next election.— M[r.] Adams, has been much opposed to gen[l.] Lincoln, and had sufficient influence to prevent his being chosen even as a councillor, because he is a member of the Society of Cincinnati: it is strange, that no one dares attack this institution openly: it is daily acquiring strength, and will infallibly become, a body dangerous, if not fatal to the Constitution.[9] Immediately after the death of gen[l.] Greene, it was voted by one of the state Societies that his eldest son, at the age of 18, should take his seat as a member. I was perfectly astonished to see no notice taken of this measure, by the public. by dropping the hereditary part of the institution, they will after some time reduce themselves to a small number; and by admitting the sons of the most distinguished characters, they obtain their end, as completely as if it were professedly hereditary. but as they are not immediately dangerous, and there are so many other difficulties that engage the attention of the public; nothing is said, or done upon the subject, and they are suffered to take their own course: a free people always were & always will be ready to strain at a gnat, and swallow a camel.

But I find, I have run out my paper, and must therefore omit several circumstances at present, & shall mention them to Mamma, to whom I will write by the present opportunity if I can have time to prepare a letter.

Your dutiful Son, J. Q. Adams.

RC and enclosure (Adams Papers); endorsed: "J. Q. Adams."; enclosure endorsed: "John Quincy Adams / june 30 1787." For the text of the enclosure, see note 1, below.

[1] For the text of JQA's oration, entitled "A Conference Upon the comparative utility of *Law*, *Physic*, and *Divinity*," and his comments on the exhibition, see *Diary*, 2:199–204.

[2] For the text of JQA's commencement oration, entitled "An Oration. Upon the importance and necessity of public faith, to the well-being of a Community," his comments on it, and its publication history, see same, 2:255–266.

[3] In 1781 John Hancock and his business partners had lost 20,000 acres of northern New England land due to a failure to pay property taxes. At the time, Hancock was in arrears for other taxes but also was owed substantial sums by associates on both sides of the Atlantic. To alleviate his situation, Hancock employed debt collector William Hoskins, whose heavy-handed methods in 1782 and 1783 alienated many and prompted gossip about Hancock's financial woes. Hancock's hope of renewing his import business after the war did not come to fruition. Despite his difficulties, Hancock continued to indulge his expensive tastes in goods and household furnishings (Fowler, *Baron of Beacon Hill*, p. 251–253).

[4] Shaysites Samuel Willard of Uxbridge, Luke Drury of Grafton, and Josiah Whitney of Harvard all had been elected to the General Court in May 1787 (David P. Szatmary, *Shays' Rebellion: The Making of an Agrarian Insurrection*, Amherst, 1980, p. 114). See also Mary Smith Cranch to AA, 22 April, and note 14, above.

[5] Plotting daily from within the city the destruction of the state ("Intestinam aliquam cotidie perniciem rei publicae molientem") (Cicero, "Oratio in Catilinam Prima,"

in Louis E. Lord, *The Loeb Classical Library: Cicero, The Speeches with an English Translation*, Cambridge, 1953, p. 18, 19).

[6] On 2 May, the General Court passed a resolution allowing the Supreme Judicial Court to sit at Concord. From 9 to 23 May the court tried the cases of men from Middlesex County who had allegedly participated in Shays' Rebellion (Mass., *Acts and Laws, 1786–1787*, p. 539–540; Robert A. Feer, *Shay's Rebellion*, N.Y., 1988, p. 410).

[7] The *Massachusetts Gazette* published portions of the *Defence of the Const.* twice weekly beginning on 22 June and continuing through 7 September. As early as 20 April, the paper also advertised copies for sale at the Boston Bookstore. Meanwhile, the printer Edmund Freeman was preparing a Boston printing of the volume, which appeared in 1788.

[8] Gen. William Heath (1737–1814) had retired from military service in 1783 but with little experience in politics, he garnered only 1,200 votes for lieutenant governor in May 1787 (*ANB*; *American Herald*, 28 May).

[9] The Society of the Cincinnati, a national organization of former Revolutionary officers, had come under scrutiny as a hereditary aristocracy and was perceived as a threat to republican government. The opposition to the society in Massachusetts was formidable; in 1784 the legislature ordered a formal investigation, which led to its condemnation. JA was among the Cincinnati's many critics, a view shared by JQA (Minor Myers Jr., *Liberty without Anarchy: A History of the Society of the Cincinnati*, Charlottesville, Va., 1983, p. 26, 51; *Massachusetts Spy*, 1 April 1784; Lafayette to JA, 8 March 1784, Adams Papers; JQA, *Diary*, 2:249).

Cotton Tufts to Abigail Adams

Dear M^rs· Adams—   Boston June 30, 1787—

I beg you to inform M^rs· Smith, that I have forwarded to M^r M^c·Connell enclosed in a Letter to Miss Margaret Smith the Picture she requested me to send and have rece^d Information f^m· D^r· Crosby of M^r· M^c·Connell's having rec^d· my Letter—[1] By M^r· Gorham who lately went to Philadelphia I sent M^r· Adams's order on Hoñ Thos· M^c·Kean Esq, M^r M^c·Kean was gone on the Circuits— and Mr Gorham failing of seeing him brought it back— it lays on Hand for another Opportunity M^r· Ty——r is somewhere I dont know where—whether at Braintree Boston, or Virginia where it has been said some days since that He intended to settle—But I cant obtain any Settlement from Him— M^r· Doane has repeatedly promised to pay the Debt from his Fathers Estate—but neglects— Lamberts Debt is not yet paid I have ordered the High Sheriff of the County of Lincoln to be sued in Case that Debt is not immediately paid— Our Tender Act operates disagreably with respect to the recovery of Debts—But we must have Patience—it is continued to Jan^y· next— Great Complaints are made of the Want of Circulation of money & of Inability to pay Taxes, yet our Stile of Living is not reduced to a State that will justify the Complaint. New Houses, new & Large Bridges among which is Penney Ferry are dayly encreasing, one also over Beverly Ferry is petitioned for—[2] New Manufactures, revivals of old and New Improvements in Agriculture & the Spirit of Husbandry encreasing these last are the only remaining Symptoms (I had almost said) of Recovery that are to be seen amonst us— I wrote to M^r· Adams by a Vessell that saild a few Days agone for Bristol— acquainting him that Mr Cranch had been informed by M^r· Borland that Mr Quincy had given up the Thoughts of purchasing his Place and having agreed with Tyler to relinquish his Claims he should wish to sell it— I took the earliest opportunity to give this Information as I suspected from some Enquiries in your former Letters, that you had in Contemplation the purchasing it should an Opportunity present— It is greatly out of Repair—and been much abused by bad Tenants— it may however be purchased at a tolerable good buy—by any Person that stands in Need of it—

I have executed Your order in Part respecting the purchase of public Securities, have expended £100 sterling & upwards in several purchases of them—and shall proceed as favorable Opportunities present but apprehend that Delay in this Business can be no Detriment as the Prospect here is against their rising and greatly in favour of sinking still lower– There is a Tract of Land adjoyning to yours, owned lately by one Haden dec^d· laying upon the Hill in the Commons not far distant from John Fields the Tanners—about 56 Acres which may be purchased @ 25s/ per Ac^re· Mr Cranch has mentioned it to me several Times and wishes to take a part of it—but whether Your Interest will be advanced by further Purchases of Land You are best able to judge, knowing your own future views & Designs &c[3]

It being Saturday & just proceeding for Weymouth, least Cushing should Sail before my Return, have wrote in Haste omitting sundry Matters which should have mentioned had Time permitted and Am / Your Affectionate Friend & H Ser   Cotton Tufts

RC (Adams Papers); internal address: "Mrs Abigail Adams."

[1] "The Picture" was a miniature of AA2 that Tufts had retrieved from Royall Tyler. In January AA2 had asked Tufts to send it to her sister-in-law, Margaret Smith, by way of New York merchant Daniel McCormick (not McConnell). Columbia College professor Ebenezer Crosby was an Adams family friend from Braintree (vol. 7:441–442; vol. 6:231, note 18).

[2] On 1 March the legislature approved plans for a bridge over the Mystic River to connect Malden and Charlestown. The 2,420-foot Malden Bridge opened later in the year and replaced a "penny ferry." Likewise, on 17 Nov. a bridge was approved to connect Beverly and Salem. That 1,484-foot span opened to travelers in Sept. 1788 (Mass., *Acts and Laws*, 1786–1787, p. 216–219, 582–

586; John Hayward, *A Gazetteer of Massachusetts*, Boston, 1849, p. 192–193; James R. Newhall, *The Essex Memorial for 1836: Embracing a Register of the County*, Salem, 1836, p. 257).

[3] Neither JA nor Richard Cranch purchased the 56 acres offered by the estate of Braintree housewright Henry Hayden (1750–1786). The estate sold the entire lot for £70 on 2 July to Braintree cordwainer John Cleverly. John Field (1752-1826) had removed from Braintree to New Hampshire in 1786 (Suffolk County Deeds, 164:26–27; Sprague, *Braintree Families*, p. 1669R, 2242, 2242R; John Resch, *Suffering Soldiers: Revolutionary War Veterans, Moral Sentiment, and Political Culture in the Early Republic*, Amherst, Mass., 1999, p. 54–55).

Cotton Tufts to John Adams

Dear S^r·   Boston June 30. 1787

On conversing with M^r· Parsons relative to Your Sons entring into the Study of the Law, I found him disposed to take him under his Instruction, and it being the Wish of your Son to live with him, I accordingly agreed with M^r· Parsons on the Subject— After Commencement Vacation Mr John will repair to Newbury Port— M^r· Parsons's Terms are £100— for Thrree Years exclusive of Board, the money to be paid at the End of the Term As he does not incline to board his Pupils, I shall procure a Place at my Brothers or some other good Family—

Mr Johns continued & persevering Application to his Studies must in Time injure his Health unless he carefully attends to Exercise, a Doctrine I have frequently inculcated upon Him and shall urge, previous to his going to Newbury Port, a few Weeks of Relaxation—

What shall I say to you My Friend with Respect to the State of my Country, with Respect to the Complexion of our new Court and the Measures pursuing & pursued by it. The Spirit of the Day has brought into public Life Characters that in sober Times would have been hissed off the Stage and been expelled as Members unfit to grace the Seats of Legislaters. Fomentors of the late Rebellion are found in Council, Senate and in the House of Representatives. In the House are some who from the Beginning were Enemies to the late Revolution, secret in Opposition when it could best serve their Purposes and open when Prospects of Success presented, avowed Friends to Monarchy and to Despotism—that have taken every Advantage of Discontents and encouraged every Kind of Faction— Disappointed Whigs, Convention Men & Debtors not a few— The object of the first is to throw all into Confusion and introduce a new Form of Government— the Disappointed Whigs & Convention Men are most of them Mushrooms that have sprung up on a sudden are tools of the Former but in Principle Levellers— The Debtors join their Force hoping for an Annihilation of public & private Debts, among these are some whose Characters once shone with Lustre— But are now meanly courting the Populace and practising the Arts of Corruption— These Characters came to Court with a Determination, and from many Towns with Instructions, if possible to undo the Measures of the late Administration to remove the Troops stationed for the Suppression of the Rebellion and the Protection of the Western Counties—to remove all Disqualifications, to obtain a general Goal Delivery of all State Prisoners and a general Indemnity & Pardon as well to those condemned to Death as those that have not come in and accepted former Terms of Mercy & Pardon— although the latter have been and are dayly making Depredations— The Removal of the Court from the Town of Boston—as more *liberal* Tender Act—or a Continuation of the Former—with some an Emission of Paper of Money—with others a Discharge of public Securities at the going Price—are favourite Objects— It is doubtful whether, the Court will be removed from Boston— The Tender Act

so called will be continued till January next— Paper Money is repro-
bated—and the further Reduction of public Securities ~~is unneces-
sary~~ will not be attempted this Session—

Among the high handed Offenders that have been capitally convicted and sentenced to Death, not one as yet has been executed—
Pardon was granted for all in Berkshire & Hampshire County except
Four— These were reprieved for a Month, now again for Six Weeks—
one in the County of Worcester was also marked out for the Hal-
ter—but is pardoned— the most criminal of the whole a Shattuck by
name—of the County of Middlesex convicted several Times during
the War of raising Mobs to oppose the Payment of Taxes & the Execution of Laws, was sentencd to have been executed on Thursday
last—but is reprieved for a Month— It seems to be the Opinion
of most that all these Gallows deserving Fellows will be set at Liberty—[1] Resolves have passed this Session, for a new Pardon to all
except Nine—and a Removal of all Disqualefications— it was with
great Difficulty that a Vote could be obtained to replace the Troops
stationed in the Western Counties, whose Time of Enlistment is just
expiring—[2] Very little Business of Importance to the Public has been
transacted although the we are got in to the 5$^{th.}$ Week of the Session—Nearly Three fourths of the House and a considerable Number of the Senate being new Members— I fear that the Benefits arising from this Session will hardly compensate for the expences— This
Court is I believe larger in Numbers than any former by One
fourth—[3] But I must break off Politics & conclude by informing You;
that You have the Thanks of the best Judges & Patriots among us for
y$^r.$ Judicious & timely Publication, it has already passed through one
Impression at New York and is now reprint^g at Boston—

Yrs—

I wrote [some time?] since by the Way of Bristol, informed You,
that Bor[lan]ds Place may be purchased, if you like—[4]

By Capt Cushing who will sail in a Day or two, I shall draw in
Favour of Mr Elworthy for £100— Folger & Callihan have been expected for some Days but have not as yet arrived—

RC (Adams Papers); addressed: "His Excellency John Adams Esq— / Minister
Plenip$^y.$ from the / United States of America / to the Court of London / Grovesnor
Square / London"; endorsed: "Dr Tufts, June. 30, / ans$^d.$ Oct. 15. 1787"; notation on
the first page: "not answerd." Some loss of text where the seal was removed.

[1] By 30 April, six men were condemned to
death for treason, two each from Berkshire
and Hampshire Counties, one from Worcester County, and Job Shattuck from Middlesex County. Several reprieves were granted
over the next several months until all were

pardoned by Gov. John Hancock on 13 Sept. (Robert A. Feer, *Shay's Rebellion*, N.Y., 1988, p. 416; Mass., *Acts and Laws*, 1786–1787, p. 994; Cotton Tufts to AA, 20 Sept., below).

[2] On 15 June the General Court passed a resolve that allowed for the re-enlistment of 500 to 800 troops in western Massachusetts. The same resolution also pardoned all citizens who had participated in Shays' Rebellion, with the exception of nine, and restored all rights and privileges to citizens, thus repealing the Disqualification Act of 16 Feb.

(Mass., *Acts and Laws*, 1786–1787, p. 176–180, 677–679).

[3] The May election increased the number of House members from 190 to 266. The number of Senate members increased from 31 to 36. Nineteen of the Senate members were new (Leonard L. Richards, *Shays's Rebellion: The American Revolution's Final Battle*, Phila., 2002, p. 144; Mass., *Acts and Laws*, 1786–1787, p. 265–266, 663–667).

[4] See Cotton Tufts to AA, 21 May, above.

Abigail Adams to Cotton Tufts

my dear sir   London july 1 1757 [1787]

your two Letters of May 21 & 26 were yesterday deliverd.[1] captain Scot has not yet got up. I hope by him to receive Letters from my other Friends. I have been not a little anxious that Barnard and Davis should arrive without a Letter either from Braintree or weymouth as this is to go by the packet, I will confine myself wholy to buisness and as mr Adams has written you respecting mr Borlands place, I have only to second his request that you would purchase it without Delay.[2] perhaps he may be induced to take less for the money in hand, but what can be done respecting the wood Land sold by mr Tyler to mr Webb & an other piece of Land to Deacon Bass, for which I presume he received the Money tho I do not imagine their deeds can be valid.[3] Yet one would not like to get into a squable with ones Neighbours if mr Borland gives a deed he must warrentee us. Mr Tyler always told me that his agreement with mr Borland was, in case he could not give him a Title to the Estate. The money he had paid, was to be considerd as borrowed & he was to be allowed interest for it, if so I should presume the matter might be setled with him. I should be glad to be informd whether the frame he put up was ever coverd & whether he made any repairs upon the House, his creditors I presume cannot take off the frame. Who is now the Tennant & what repairs are necessary? if you purchase it as I hope you will, I should like to know the heights of the rooms & the paper they will take to paper them as well as the bigness of them, painting will be a necessary buisness both without and within. I fancy mr Tyler owes money to mr Cranch would it not be best for him to secure himself if he can by attaching the material for repairs? mr Adams will not hesitate even at the 600. What shall I say to you respecting veseys place? counteract my dears Frinds plan, by no means—it has always been his wish to Buy that place, and he would have done it long ago if I had not persuaded him to the contrary. 300 is certainly 50 pounds too much as money is so scarce & the place so poor. it will not neat 4 prcent do you think it worth more? Suppose you make him that offer but you see mr Adams is disposed to have it, even at the very high price, but I think more of the other place. an other House we must have if it was only to hold our Books. I should speak within Bounds if I was to say that the Books which mr Adams has purchased in order to qualify himself for a through investigation of the subjects he is persueing, cost him within these six months a hundred & fifty Guineys. Many of the Italian Works were very high priced & very scarce, he reads Italian as easily as French, and applies so constantly both to writing & reading that I fear he will injure his Health. Yet it is vastly mended since his residence in England, when I first came abroad he could not write even a single Letter without suffering. now he writes six or eight hours in a day—

With regard to my own Health I cannot say much in favour of it, a little fever still Lurks in my veins & I cannot get rid of it. perhaps a sea voyage may serve it, but I dread the ocean and yet more the turbulent spirit of my Countrymen. it is a damp to all the pleasureable Ideas of a return to it— God save the people is a prayer in which I can most sincerely join—but I said I would write only on Buisness—yet out of the abundanc of the Heart &c I will send by the first opportunity the Reviews you desire my trangression with respect to porter & cheese were those of Ignoranc I Submit to the chastisement & pray the cheese may be only used as a foil. I will remember in future & put all I send in a trunk with the articles enumerated & the price.—

Mrs Smith desires to be rememberd to you & all her Friend. Col Smith is not yet returnd from portugal I presume I must have Letters by Scot. as you have not mentiond my Friends I hope they are all well— a Letter came to hand by the penny post soon after Barnards arrival in which you mention Bills drawn in favour of mr Hill,[4] but no such Bill has been yet presented— adieu my dear sir. I will not despair of the commonwealth whilst their is good sense enough to Elect my good Friend into the Senate. The Single virtue of Cato did much towards the preservation of Rome. may your Success be equal to your virtuous Efforts is the ardent wish / of your sincere Friend   A A

RC (Adams Papers); endorsed: "M^rs· Adams July 1 1787 / rec^d· Sept· 7^t:— relative to / Purchase of / Borlands Place."

[1] For Cotton Tufts' letter to AA of 26 May, see Tufts to JA, 13 June, note 1, above.

[2] Letter not found.

[3] Mr. Webb is probably Jonathan Webb, son of Deacon Jonathan Webb and later called deacon himself after his father's death. Webb the younger held a number of posts in Braintree, including surveyor and town assessor (*Braintree Town Records*, p. 585, 760).

Deacon Benjamin Bass (b. 1719) had served the town of Braintree in various capacities, including constable, surveyor of highways, and warden (same, p. 355, 371, 394, 706).

[4] Probably Alexander Hill, a Boston merchant whose son Edward had studied law with JA (vol. 6:427).

Thomas Jefferson to Abigail Adams

Paris July 1. 1787.

A thousand thanks to you, my dear Madam, for your kind attention to my little daughter. her distresses I am sure must have been troublesome to you: but I know your goodness will forgive her, & forgive me too for having brought them on you. Petit now comes for her. by this time she will have learned again to love the hand that feeds & comforts her, and have formed an attachment to you. she will think I am made only to tear her from all her affections. I wish I could have come myself. the pleasure of a visit to yourself & m͂r Adams would have been a great additional inducement. but, just returned from my journey, I have the arrearages of 3. or 4. months all crouded on me at once. I do not presume to write you news from America, because you have it so much fresher & frequenter than I have. I hope all the disturbances of your country are quieted & with little bloodshed. what think you of present appearances in Europe? the Emperor & his subjects? the Dutch & their half king, who would be a whole one? in fine the French & the English? these new friends & allies have hardly had time to sign that treaty which was to cement their love & union like man & wife, before they are shewing their teeth at each other. we are told a fleet of 6. or 12 ships is arming on your side the channel; here they talk of 12 or 20, and a camp of 15,000 men. but I do not think either party in earnest. both are more laudably intent on arranging their affairs.—[1] should you have incurred any little expences on account of my daughter or her maid, Petit will be in a condition to repay them. if considerable, he will probably be obliged to refer you to me, and I shall make it my duty to send you a bill immediately for the money.— Count Sarsfeild sets out for London four days hence. at dinner the other day at M. de Malesherbe's he was sadly abusing an English dish called Gooseberry tart.[2] I asked him if he had ever tasted the cranberry. he said, no. so I invited him to go & eat cranberries with you. he said that on his arrival in London he would send to you & demander á diner. I hope mrs̃ Smith and the little grandson are well. be so good as to present me respectfully to her. I have desired Colo. Smith to take a bed here on his return. I will take good care of him for her, & keep him out of all harm. I have the honour to be with sentiments of sincere esteem & respect Dear Madam / Your most obedient & / most humble servᵗ   Th: Jefferson

RC (Adams Papers); internal address: "Mʳˢ· Adams"; endorsed: "Mr Jefferson july 1 / 1787."

[1] The French criticized the Anglo-French Commercial Treaty of 1786 as unfair to their manufacturing interests, leading them to believe that the trade agreement had worsened their fiscal crisis. As a result, reports that the French and British were preparing for war were widespread by mid-July 1787 (*Morning Chronicle and London Advertiser*, 23 May, 4 June, 16, 18 July; London *Daily Universal Register*, 11 July).
[2] For Chrétien Guillaume de Lamoignon de Malesherbes, see JA, *Papers*, 9:229; JA, *D&A*, 2:387.

Abigail Adams to Thomas Jefferson

my dear sir   London july 6 1787

If I had thought you would so soon have Sent for your dear little Girl, I should have been tempted to have kept her arrival here, from you a secret. I am really loth to part with her, and she last evening upon petit's arrival, was thrown into all her former distresses, and bursting into Tears, told me it would be as hard to leave me, as it was her Aunt Epps.[1] She has been so often deceived that she will not quit me a moment least She should be carried away, nor can I scarcly prevail upon her to see petit. Tho she says she does not remember you, yet she has been taught to consider you with affection and fondness, and depended upon your comeing for her. she told me this morning, that as she had left all her Friends in virgina to come over the ocean to see you, she did think you would have taken the pains to have come here for her, & not have sent a man whom she cannot understand. I express her own words. I expostulated with her[2] upon the long journey you had been; & the difficulty you had to come and upon the care kindness & attention of petit, whom I so well knew, but she cannot yet hear me. she is a child of the quickest Sensibility, and the maturest understanding, that I have ever met with for her Years. she had been 5 weeks at sea, and with men only, so that on the first day of her arrival, She was as rough as a little Sailor, and then she been decoyed from the Ship, which made her very angry, and no one having any Authority over her; I was apprehensive I should meet with some trouble, but where there are such materials to work upon as I have found in her, there is no danger. she listened to my admonitions, and attended to me advice, and in two days, was restored to the amiable lovely Child which her Aunt had formed her. in short she is the favorite of every Creature in the House, and I cannot but feel Sir, how many pleasures you must lose; by committing her to a convent, yet situated as you are, you cannot keep her with you. The Girl she has with her, wants more care than the child, and is wholy incapable of looking properly after her, without Some Superiour to direct her.

As both miss Jefferson & the maid had cloaths only proper for the Sea, I have purchased & m up for them; Such things as I should have done had they been my own; to the amount of about Eleven or 12 Guineys. the particulars I will send by petit.[3]

Captain Ramsey has Said that he would accompany your daughter to paris provided she would not go without him, but this would be putting you to an expence that may perhaps be avoided by petits staying a few days longer. the greatest difficulty in familiarizing her to him, is on account of the language. I have not the Heart to force her into a Carriage against her Will and send her from me, almost in a Frenzy; as I know will be the case,[4] unless I can reconcile her to the thoughts of going and I have given her my word that petit shall stay untill I can hear again from you.[5] Books are her delight, and I have furnishd her out a little library, and She reads to me by the hour with great distinctness, & comments on what she reads with much propriety.

mrs Smith desires to be rememberd to you, and the little Boy his Grandmamma thinks is as fine a Boy as any in the Kingdom—[6] I am my dear sir with Sentiments of Esteem Your Friend and Humble / Servant

A Adams

RC (DLC:Jefferson Papers); addressed by JA: "his Excellency / Thomas Jefferson / Ambassadour from the United / States of America, at the Court / of Versailles / Paris"; endorsed: "Adams mrs"; notation: "France." Dft (Adams Papers).

[1] Jefferson's younger daughter Mary had lived with her aunt, Elizabeth Wayles Eppes (b. 1752), for four years in Virginia prior to joining her father in France. Elizabeth was Martha Wayles Jefferson's half-sister and was married to Francis Eppes. Their son, John Wayles Eppes, would eventually marry his cousin Mary Jefferson in 1797 (Noble E. Cunningham Jr., *In Pursuit of Reason: The Life of Thomas Jefferson*, Baton Rouge, La., 1987, p. 82; Malone, *Jefferson*, 1:432; *DAB*).

[2] In the Dft AA also wrote, "my little girl for so She chuses I Should call her."

[3] At this point in the Dft AA wrote: "I

should have done something more for the maid with regard to the article of Linnen which She wants, to have Saved you trouble, but we hear that English goods are cheeper in Paris than here, so that for her I have only purchased cloth for 2 Aprons & calico for 2 Jackets & coats which my maid made up for her and amounted to one pound forteen & four pence I have still to add Some stockings & a few articles more."

⁴ In the Dft AA also included, "indeed I have not the Heart to do it, & her Girl has no more influence over her than a straw."

⁵ AA wrote here in the Dft, "unless she is willing to go with him before. I Shall write again by miss Jefferson and answer some queries which you put in your Letter."

⁶ In the Dft AA included the following: "duty to my pappa miss adds, & kindest Love to sister Patsey but do pray write him how I want to stay here."

Abigail Adams to Thomas Jefferson with a Memorandum of Purchases

Dear sir   London july 10ᵗʰ 1787

When I wrote you last I did not know that petit had taken places in the Stage & paid for them. this being the case I have represented it to your little daughter & endeavourd to prevail with her to consent to going at the time appointed; She says if I must go I will, but I cannot help crying, so pray dont ask me too. I should have taken great pleasure in presenting her to you here, as you would then have seen her with her most engageing countana[nce.] some lines of an old song frequently occur to me as different objects affect her.

> What she thinks in her Heart
> You may read in her Eyes
> For knowing no art
> She needs no disguise

I never saw so intelligent a countanance in a child before, and the pleasure she has given me is an ample compensation for any little services I have been able to render her. I can easily conceive the earnest desire you must have to embrace so lovely a child after so long a Seperation from her. that motive, & my own intention of setting out next week upon a journey into the County of Devonshire, has prevaild with me to consent to parting with her so soon, but most reluctantly I assure you. her temper, her dispositition, her Sensibility are all formed to delight, yet perhaps at your first interview you may find a little roughness but it all subsides in a very little time, and she is soon attached by kindness. I inclose a memorandum of the articles purchased [I have be]en a little particular, that you might know how I [. . .]d of the money. if at any time I can be of service in this [wa]y [i]t will give me pleasure. I have desired petit to Buy me 12 Ells of black lace at 8 Livres pr Ell & 1 dozen of white & one of coulourd Gloves. you will be so good as to place them to my account & Col Smith will take them when he returns.

As to politicks, to avoid touching so dissagreeable a subject, I send you the Boston News papers received by the last vessels.

Mrs Paridise has just left me and desires to be rememberd to you. She is just upon the eve of departure for Virginia. Whether he can be prevaild upon to go on Board altho their passage is taken, & every thing in readiness, is very uncertain. She is determined at all Hazards, he most assuredly will get a seat in Kings Bench if he stays behind. his affairs are daily worse & worse.[1] mr Adams will write you— he has not a portrait that he likes to send you. mr Trumble talks of taking one.[2] if he Succeeds better than his Brethren, mr Adams will ask your acceptance of it. you will be so good as to let me hear from my dear little Girl by the first post after her arrival. my Love to her Sister whom I congratulate upon Such an acquisition.

I have not been able to find Mrs Kinlock yet, but hope two, if I Should not, mr Heyward is going to carolina in a few days and I will send the package by him. all your other Letters were deliverd as directed.[3]

With Sentiments of the highest Esteem I am dear Sir Your Humble Servant   A Adams

I have received of Petit Six Louis d'ors [. . . .] What the exchange is, but the remainder you w[ill?] [. . .] as to let him purchase, me some lace & Gloves with the remainder.

ENCLOSURE

Memorandum of articles by mrs Adams
for miss Jefferson & Maid

	£	s	d
paid for bringing the Trunks from Tower Hill		5.	6.
four fine Irish Holland frocks[4]	3.	10.	
5 yd white Dimity for Skirts		15	
4 yd checkd Muslin for a frock	1.	10	
3 yd lace Edging to trim it		6.	6
To making the frock		5.	
3 yd flannel for under Coats		7.	6
A Brown Bever Hat & feathers		13.	
2 pr leather Gloves		2.	4

5 yd diaper for arm Cloths	5.	10
6 pr cotton Stockings	13.	6
3 yd blew sash Ribbon	3.	
To diaper for pockets linning tape		
cloth for night caps &c	5	6
To a comb & case, comb Brush, tooth Brush	1.	6

For the Maid Servant

12 yds calico for 2 short Gowns & coats	1.	5.	6
4 yd half Irish linen for Aprons		7	4
3 pr Stockings		6.	
2 yd linning		2.	
1 Shawl handkerchief		4	6
paid for washing		6	8

Sterling 10 15. 8

11. 16. 2 should be[5]

Received Six Louis d'ors, of petit.   A Adams

RC and enclosure (DLC:Jefferson Papers); addressed by AA2: "His Excellency Thomas Jefferson / Minister Plenipotentiary from the United / States of America / residing / att / Paris—"; endorsed: "Adams mr̃s"; notation by Jefferson on the enclosure:

"Mrs. Adams's expenditures for me as on the other side	£10–15–8
error of addition to her prejudice	1–0–6
	11–16–2
Cash pd her by Petit 6 Louis @ 19/6 the Louis	5–17–0
pd by do for black lace 75tt	3–1–[ ]
2 doz. pr̃ gloves 27tt–12	1–10–6
balance due to mrs̃ Adams	1–7–8
	11–16–2."

Some loss of text due to a torn manuscript.

[1] The Paradises' growing financial problems forced them to leave London for Lucy Ludwell Paradise's Virginia estate. They arrived in late September over £2,000 in debt, which Lucy blamed on her husband's mismanagement. In Feb. 1788, the Paradises learned that their younger daughter Philippa had died in England, forcing them to return to Britain without having put their finances in order. Thomas Jefferson came to their aid by appointing a supervisor to manage their Virginia estate and arranging a repayment schedule for their many creditors (Archibald Bolling Shepperson, *John Paradise and Lucy Ludwell of London and Williamsburg*, Richmond, Va., 1942, p. 207–211, 273–274, 293–295; Jefferson, *Papers*, 10:69, 255–256; 13:457, 472, 537, 543–545).

[2] In London, in the summer of 1787, John Trumbull added JA to the canvas of his famous painting, *Declaration of Independence*. At that time the group portrait was incomplete; Trumbull continued to add to it as he met with the men who had signed the Declaration (Trumbull, *Autobiography*, p. 146–147).

[3] Anne Cleland Kinloch (d. 1802) was the widow of Francis Kinloch (1720–1767) of South Carolina. Jefferson hoped that Kinloch could be located in London and that she would deliver a package of rice to William Drayton, also of South Carolina. Jeffer-

son's letter to Kinloch of 1 July remains in the Adams Papers, confirming AA's inability to find her (H. D. Bull, "Kinloch of South Carolina," *SCHGM*, 46:64–65 [April 1945]; Jefferson, *Papers*, 11:520–521).

⁴ "Holland" refers to a fine white linen

originally imported from Holland but later manufactured in Ireland. The fabric was often used for children's clothing (Mairead Dunlevy, *Dress in Ireland*, N.Y., 1989, p. 188).

⁵ This recalculated amount is in Jefferson's hand.

Thomas Jefferson to Abigail Adams

Dear Madam   Paris July 10. 1787.

This being the day on which, according to my calculation, my daughter would be crossing the channel, I had calculated the course from Dover to Calais and was watching the wind when your favour of the 6th. was put into my hands. that of June 27. had been received four days ago. I perceived that that had happened which I had apprehended, that your goodness had so attached her to you that her separation would become difficult. I had been in hopes that Petit would find means to rival you, and I still hope he will have done it so as that they may be on their way here at present. if she were to stay till she should be willing to come, she would stay till you cease to be kind to her, and that, Madam, is a term for which I cannot wait. her distress will be in the moment of parting & I am in hopes Petit will soon be able to lessen it.— we are impatient to hear what our federal convention are doing. I have no news from America later than the 27th. of April. nor is there any thing here worth mentioning. the death of mr̄ Saint James & flight of M. de Calonnes are perhaps known to you.¹ a letter of M. de Mirabeau to the K. of Prussia is handed about by the Colporteurs.² I will endeavor to find an opportunity of sending it to mr̄ Adams.— your kind advances for my daughter shall be remitted you by Colo. Smith when he returns or some other good opportunity. I have the honor to be with sentiments of gratitude for your goodness and with those of perfect esteem Dr. Madam your most obedt. humble sert   Th Jefferson

RC (Adams Papers); addressed: "Mrs. Adams / London"; internal address: "Mrs. Adams."; endorsed: "mr Jefferson july 10 / 1787."

¹ Claude Baudard, Baron de St. James (1738–1787), was the treasurer general of the French Navy and a wealthy businessman with vast interests in banking, shipping, mining, and manufacturing. By January, however, he was bankrupt, which, in turn, contributed to the country's growing fiscal crisis. He was investigated by a royal commission on suspicion of impropriety in his role as

treasurer general, but the charges were later dropped. He died on 3 July, leading one London newspaper to speculate that his death was accelerated by his financial ruin (J. F. Bosher, *French Finances 1770-1795: From Business to Bureaucracy*, Cambridge, Eng., 1970, p. 96, 185-186; *Morning Chronicle and London Advertiser*, 16 July).

Charles Alexandre de Calonne's dismissal

as minister of finance on 8 April led to criminal charges, causing him to flee to The Hague and later to England (Schama, *Citizens,* p. 245–246; J. F. Bosher, *The French Revolution,* N.Y., 1988, p. 110; Jefferson to AA, 16 July, below).

² Honoré Gabriel Riquetti, Comte de Mirabeau (1749–1791), a French statesman and writer, went on a secret diplomatic mission to the Prussian court in 1786. There he met with various advisers to first Frederick the Great and later Frederick William II but ultimately failed to gain their assistance in

effecting a Franco-Prussian alliance. Mirabeau's *Lettre remise a Frédéric-Guillaume II, roi régnant de Prusse, le jour de son avénement au trône* (Letter presented to Frederick William II, King of Prussia, on the day of his accession to the throne), a lengthy piece on the obligations of the new monarch to his subjects, was first published in Berlin in 1787 (Barbara Luttrell, *Mirabeau,* N.Y., 1990, p. 80–83; Honoré Gabriel Riqueti, Comte de Mirabeau, *Secret Memoirs of the Court of Berlin,* rpt. edn., Washington, D.C., 1901, p. ix–xiii, 349).

Abigail Adams to Mary Rutledge Smith

My Dear Madam   London july 14th 1787

I received your agreeable Letter with much pleasure: having only before heard of the arrival of the vessel in which you embarked. I can my dear Madam most Sincerely rejoice with you on the happiness of meeting kind Friends, and endearing Relatives, after the Seperation you experienced. I fancy my Lovely Carolina Eyes Sparking with a joy which adds fluency to her Tongue, whilst her more reserved, but not less amiable sister, feels more than she can express. These Social ties, these family endearments give a zest to all the other enjoyments of Life. "poor is the Friendless master of a World" as the poet expressess it,¹ ours is the Country for a union of Hearts, and conubial felicity. Europe, "for the rich mountains of Peru, who drawn by kindred charms of Gold,["] look not for any other pleasures than what their wealth can bestow, hence arises that infidelity so common in Europe.²

I hope you find your Health much benifitted by your late voyage. should you relapse, will you permit me to recommend my Native state as a much more salubrious climate than that which you inhabit, and there I should rejoice to find you on my return, which I hope will be the next Spring You gave me some reason to hope that you would visit the Northern States. I think you would be pleasd with the Tour. the dissagreeable Situation of the Massachusetts for some months past is changed I presume for the better, and I would hope the Rebellion quite Surpressd. The discontents of the people cannot be grounded in reason, for there is no Country in the world where the liberties and properties of the subject are more sacredly preserved, nor are there any subjects who pay less for the ease and security which they enjoy, but the Idea of these insurgents is that they ought to pay nothing nor be at any trouble for preserving to themselves the Blessings of Peace & security. to please Such persons is impossible, and the dissagreeable alternative of reduceing them to obedience by force was the only resource this has Stained our annals with a civil war, and gratified the benevolence of our Good Friends on this Side of the water. I hope with you that the united Efforts of our wisest & ablest Countrymen who are now convened, may prove Succesfull in extricating us from our present embarresments, but they cannot work miracles, & unless a Spirit of Eoconomy industery & frugality, can be diffused through the people they will find their labours a mere Penelopean web.[3]

you Guesd very right with regard to my venerable title. on the 2d of April I was vested with it, & have now a fine Grandson 3 months old Mrs smith is very well & Nurses her little Boy. Col Smith is absent in Spain upon bublick buisness which must apoligize to mrs caroline, for not hearing from him by this opportunity mr Adams joins me in compliments to mr Smith & to your Brother who was your fellow passenger, and to his old associates in congress, whom I have not the pleasure of knowing—

our Friend mrs Channing continues in poor Health but good spirits.[4] many American have left London Since the spring and we are now going to lose mr Gibbs & mr Heyward. The latter is kind enough to be the bearer of this Letter to you. I propose Setting out on a journey to plimouth next week for the benifit of my Health, having been a great part of the Spring confined by sickness. I hope you will continue to write me during my residence here be assured dear madam that I shall always take great pleasure in hearing of the Health & happiness of yourself & family by a Gentleman lately from France who lodged in the Same House with your Son I had the pleasure of learning that his Health was perfectly restored.[5] be so good as to present me affectionately to the young Ladies & believe / me most sincerely your / Friend & Humble Servant   A A

Dft (Adams Papers); notation by AA: "To Mrs / Smith of / Carolina july 14 / 1787."

[1] Young, *Night Thoughts*, Night II, line 571.

[2] "Not sordid souls of earthly mould / Who drawn by kindred charms of gold / To dull embraces move: / So two rich mountains of Peru / May rush to wealthy marriage too, / And make a world of love" (Isaac Watts, "Few Happy Matches," lines 13–18).

[3] AA alludes to Penelope, the wife of Odysseus, who put off various unwanted suitors by promising to select one as soon as she finished weaving a shroud. She would weave all day and then undo her work each night, leading to the adage of Penelope's web—labor that is unproductive and unending (*Oxford Classical Dicy.*).

[4] Joanna Gibbes Izard Channing, formerly of South Carolina, had moved to London in 1769 with her husband John Channing. She stayed in Britain when he returned to the United States in 1782 (Laurens, *Papers*, 16:26–27, note 1).

[5] Thomas Rhett Smith (1768–1829), the Smiths' eldest child, had been ill in Paris in 1786. He recovered and eventually returned to South Carolina where he served in the state's general assembly from 1792 to 1801 (N. Louise Bailey, *Biographical Directory of the South Carolina House of Representatives, vol. 4, 1791–1815*, Columbia, S.C., 1984; Jefferson, *Papers*, 10:524).

Abigail Adams Smith to Lucy Cranch

London july 14th 1787—

most readily my Dear Lucy do I acknowledge the tittle of friend with which you address me—and am very happy to have preserved your esteem thus far in Life— I wish it had been my fate to have enjoyed the Society of my friends more than it has,— three years have now elapsed since I parted with every *female* friend that I had acquired from my earliest infancy to the age of Nineteen; and I have not been so fortunate as to have acquired any in Europe to Supply their Loss— in America I have gained a Whole family of friends and Sisters My Best friend—has Six sisters—whose friendship I Consider a great acquisition—and promise myself great sattisfaction from a Personall knowledge of them—[1] we already Correspond—and by their Letters and from the affection expressed for their Brother I know them to be very amiable and agreeable— from the manner of their Sollicitude to possess the friendship of their Brother you would imagine them rival favourites Contending by every assiduity and attention, to gain an assendance over each other in his affection—

You ask me my Dear a very queer question (whether my Husband possesses my whole Heart) but I can answer without hesitation that he does—nor would I have given my hand to any One who did not possess it— but my Dear it does not exclude any other friend who had a prior claim upon it, but has strengthened every other friendly attachment.

You are I suppose informed that my Parents intend returning to America the ensueing Spring and I dare say will rejoice at an event which must Contribute so much to your happiness, I hope the Period is not far distant when your Cousin will also have the pleasure of paying you a visit and of Presenting to you her friend—and a young Stranger who made his appearance a few Weeks since— he is a fine Boy—and the play thing throughout the House

my father and Mother intend makeing an excursion the next week into Devonshire and they have persuaded me to accompany them during the absence of Mr Smith who is gone to Portugoll upon some Publick business—and Cannot return before the beginning of September. they intend going as far as Plymouth and I think it is there that some of Your friends reside if we should see them I will give you some account of our visit upon my return, and write you a longer Letter than it is in my Power att Present. Barnard is to sail in a few days and I have many other Letters to write before we set out

Let me hear from you frequently and beleive me your friend

A Smith

RC (MWA:Abigail Adams Letters); addressed: "Miss Lucy Cranch / Braintree / Massachusetts"; internal address: "Miss Lucy Cranch—"

[1] WSS's six sisters were Margaret (Peggy), Belinda, Charity, Sarah (Sally), Elizabeth (Betsy), and Ann (Nancy) Smith. For more on WSS's siblings, including AA's observations about them, see AA to Mary Smith Cranch, 15 Dec. 1788, below.

Abigail Adams to Mary Smith Cranch

my dear sister   London july 16 1787

If as the poet says, expectation makes the blessing sweet,[1] your last Letter was peculiarly so, as you conjectured I was not a little anxious that neither Captain Barnard or Davis brought me a line. I was apprehensive that Something was the matter some imminent danger threatning some Friend, of which my Friends chose not to inform me untill thir fate was decided. I sent on board the Ship, the Solitary Box of meal was searchd throughout. What not one line, from my dear sister Cranch, she who has never before faild me, can it be possible, uncle Smith did not as usual say in his Letter that all Friends were well. Dr Tufts for the first time omitted mentioning my children, that might be because they thought that they had written, thus was my mind agitated untill Captain Scotts arrival who brought me your kind Letter of May the 20th,[2] but none from either of my Neices or Children those dear Lads do not write so often as I wish them to, because they have nothing more to say than that they are well, not considering how important that intelligence is to an affectionate parent. mr J Cranch wrote me soon after Barnards arrival and sent me an extract of a Letter from miss B Palmer with a particular account of the performances in April at Cambridge, in which your son & mine bore a part. These Young Gentlemen are much indebted to her for her partiality, and the very flattering manner in which she describes them. I hope they will continue to de-

serve the esteem of all good judges and do honour to themselves
and their Country. the account you give me of the Health of JQA, is
no more than I expected to hear. I warnd him frequently before he
left me, and have been writing him ever since. I hope he will take
warning before it is too late. it gives me great satisfaction to learn
that he has past through the university with so much reputation,
and that his fellow Students are attached to him. I have never once
regreeted the resolution he took of quitting Europe, and placing
himself upon the Theatre of his own Country, where if his Life is
spaired, I presume he will neither be an Idle or a useless Spectator.
Heaven grant that he may not have more distressing scenes before
him, and a Gloomier stage to tread than those on which his Father
has acted for 12 years past, but the curtain rises before him, and
instead of peace waving her olive branch, or Liberty seated in a triumphal car or commerce Agriculture and plenty pouring forth their
Stores, Sedition hisses Treason roars, Rebellion Nashes his Teeth.
Mercy Suspends the justly merited blow, but justice Striks the
Guilty victim. here may the Scene close and brighter prospects open
before us in future. I hope the political machine will move with
more safety and security this year than the last, and that the New
Head may be endowed with wisdom sufficient to direct it. there are
Some good Spokes in the Wheels, tho the Master workmen have
been unskilfull in discarding some of the best, and chusing others
not sufficiently Seasond, but the crooked & cross graind will soon
break to peices, tho this may do much mischief in the midst of a
jouney, and shatter the vehicle, yet an other year may repair the
Damages, but to quit Allegory, or you will think I have been reading
Johnny Bunyan. The conduct of a certain Gentleman is rather curious.[3] I really think him an honest Man, but ambition is a very wild
passion, and there are some Characters that never can be pleasd
unless they have the intire direction of all publick affairs, and when
they are unemployd, they are continually blaming those in office,
and accusing them of Ignorance or incapacity, and Spreading
allarms that the Country is ruined and undone, but put them into
office, and it is more than probable they will persue the same conduct, which they had before condemned, but no Man is fit to be
trusted who is not diffident of himself Such is the frailty of humane
Nature, & so great a flatterer is Self Love, that it presents false appearences, & deceives it votaries.

The comedy writer has been drawing his own Character and an
other Gentlemans I fancy. strange Man, would he act as well as he

can write, he might have been an ornament to Society, but what signifies a Head, without a Heart, what is knowledge but an extensive power to do evil, without principal to direct and govern it? "unstable as water, thou shalt not excell" I have often quoted to him.[4] I look upon him as a lost Man. I pity his folly, and am sorry he is making himself so conspicuous. I think Sir John Temple was the writer of the Letter from Newyork giving an account of the Play, Birds of a Feather—[5] The House at Braintree which you mention I would not fail of having, & am sorry the dr did not bargan for it without waiting to hear from us. We have written him twice upon the subject, as to building we shall never be able to do that, if the dr should purchase it. I wish you would look it over and let us know what repairs are necessary. I shall not be able to write much by Captain Barnard, as we are prepairing for a long jouney. I have been so very unwell through the Spring and winter that the dr Says a jouney and change of air is absolutely necessary for me our intention is to visit Devenshire & to go as far as plimouth which is about 200 & 30 miles. as we take the Baby and a Nursery maid, Esther a footman & coachman we shall make a large calvacade and be absent a month or 5 weeks. Col Smith we do not expect back till September. we hear from him by every post. I am distrest for Sister Shaw & her children the disorder is of the most infectious Nature, and a House, linen, & every thing & person requires as much cleansing as with the Small pox, of which I fear people are not sufficently aware. When Mr Copley about a year & half ago lost two fine children with it, the doctors advised to these precautions, & gave large doses of the bark to the attendance. I think Sister Shaw would have done well to have sent both her children out of Haverhill. I pray Heaven preserve them— I did not get a line from her by either of the vessels. I have had with me for a fortnight a little daughter of mr Jeffersons, who arrived here with a young Negro Girl her Servant from Virginia. mr Jefferson wrote me some months ago that he expected them & desired me to receive them. I did so and was amply repaid for my trouble a finer child of her age I never saw, so mature an understanding, so womanly a behaviour and so much sensibility united is rarely to be met with. I grew so fond of her, & she was so attached to me, that when mr Jefferson sent for her, they were obliged to force the little creature away. She is but 8 years old. She would Set some times and discribe to me the parting with her Aunt who brought her up, the obligations she was under to her & the Love she had for her little cousins, till the Tears would stream down her cheeks, and now I had been her Friend and she loved me, her pappa would break her Heart by making her go again. she clung round me so that I could not help sheding a tear at parting with her. she was the favorite of every one in the House. I regreet that Such fine spirits must be spent in the walls of a convent. She is a beautifull Girl too, my little Boy grows finely and is as playfull as a Lamb, is the Healthest child I ever saw, and pretty enough. his Mamma I think looks the better for being a Nurse. he is very content with being twice a day supplied by her, feeds the rest, and never misses being twice a day carried out to walk in the air when it is fair weather You see what a mere Grandmama I am that can fill up half a page in writing of the child. this I presume is commencment week. I dare say the young folks feel anxious. I dont know whether I should venture to be a hearer if I was in America I should have as many pertubations as the Speakers. I hope they will acquit themselves with honour. mr Adams desires me to tell cousin Cranch that any of his Books are at his service I believe we must send some of these Young Men to settle at Vermont. can they get their Bread in Massachussets? but the World is all before them, may providence be their Guide.

I send my dear sisters each a tea urn, which must prove comfortable in a hot summers day I have orderd them put up in a Box together and addrest to uncle Smith. the Heater, & the Iron which you put it in with, is to be packed in the Box by the Side of them. whilst your water is boiling, you heat the Iron & put it in to the little tin inclosure always minding that the water is first put in. this keeps it hot as long as you want to use it.— how are English Goods now? cheeper I suppose than I can buy them here, and India much lower, in the article of Spice could you credit it if I was to tell you that I give 2 pound Eleaven Shillings sterling pr pound for Nutmegs—and other Spice in proportion yet tis really so— I cannot write my Neices now, but hope my journey will furnish materials—my Love to them. who owns Germantown now, is mr Palmers family in any way of Buisness? how is miss payne, & where is she?— Mrs Parkers arrival will be an acquisitions to our American acquaintance. she appears an agreeable woman we have a General Stuart & Lady here Philadelphians, lately from Ireland. I knew him when I first came here. he went to Ireland and has been there with her two years, they spend the winter here. Mrs Gardner has never visited me untill yesterday, tho she has been here a Year concequently I have never Seen her, for it is an invariable rule with me to receive the first visit. I

have formed a very agreeable acquaintance with a Sir George
Stanton & Lady. I know not a warmer American. he cultivats their
acquaintance, and is a very sensible learned Man. Lady Staunton is
an amiable woman and we visit upon very social and Friendly terms.
I must however add that Sir George is an Irishman by birth & I have
invariably found in every Irish Gentleman, a Friend to America. it is
an old observation that mutual Sufferings begets Friendships. Lady
Effingham is just returnd to Town after an absence of a 12 Month.[6]
her Ladyship drank tea with me on Sunday, & I Supd & spent the
Evening with her the week after. She has traveld much in Russia Sweeden Denmark Holland France Ireland, and has a most
Sprightly lively fancy: joind to a volubility of Tongue which united
with good sense & a knowledge of the World renders her a pleasing
companion, but She like all the rest of the English Ladies, with
whom I have any acquaintance is destitute of that Softness & those
feminine graces which appear so lovely in the females of America. I
attribute this in a great measure to their constant intercourse at
publick places. I will see how they are in the Country. I have been
gratified however in finding that all Foreigners who have any acquaintance with American Ladies give the preference to them, but
john Bull thinks nothing equal to himself and his Country; you
would be Surprizd to see & hear the uncivil things Said against
France, and all its productions I have never found so much illiberal-
ity in any Nation as this, but there are many Worthy & amiable
Characters here whom I shall ever respect, and for whose Sakes this
Country is preserved from total Ruin & destruction. but I am running on at a Strange rate. adieu my dear sister, remember me to my
Worthy Mother Brothers & all my Nephews Neices & Neighbours,
and believe me at all times your affectionate / Sister

Abigail Adams.

PS having sent you a Lamp I now Send you something to Light it
with the directions are with it. I have given these into the care of a
mrs Wentworth who came here last Spring in persuit of an estate
which I have no doubt belongs to her, but for want of Money She
cannot come at it.[7] She is a virtuous well behaved deserving woman.
she has been I believe as much as a month at different times in my
family, and can tell you more about us than perhaps 20 Letters. Dr
Bulfinch recommended her to us, when she came.[8] I tried to get her
some employ but could not succeed, and she is now obliged to return much poorer than when she came, and without any prospect of

Success. when you go to Town, if you send for her to uncle Smiths, She will come and see you as I have desired her.— Inclosed you find a Louis d'or⁹

RC (private owner, 1957).

¹ " 'Tis expectation makes a blessing dear" (Sir John Suckling, "Against Fruition," line 23).

² 27 May, above.

³ James Warren.

⁴ Genesis, 49:4.

⁵ Royall Tyler's *The Contrast* was reviewed in the New York *Independent Journal*, 5 May. The author, "Philo. Dramaticus," described the play as "an extraordinary effort of genius. . . . America may one day rank a *Tyler* in the Dramatic Line as she already does a *Franklin* and a *West* in those of Philosophy and the Fine Arts." Temple was in New York at the time serving as British consul general to the United States (vol. 5:272).

⁶ For Catherine Howard, Countess of Ef-

fingham, see vol. 6:188, 193.

⁷ Mary Wentworth wrote to AA on 13 Aug., just prior to sailing for the United States, to thank her "for all your Favours. Words Cannot Express the Sense I have of your Goodness to me: What an unhapy Destitute Creature I Should have bene, in my Disapointᵈ, Preplexing Situation Without your Kind assistance: it is to you: By Gods premision I Shall owe, the Blessing of Seeing my Belovedᵈ Husband and Family again" (Adams Papers).

⁸ For Dr. Thomas Bulfinch of Boston, see vol. 2:16.

⁹ AA may have intended to scratch out this final sentence. See also the postscript to AA to JQA, 18 July, below.

Mary Smith Cranch to Abigail Adams

Braintree July 16th 1778 [1787]

My dear sister will I am sure excuse me if I send her now but a short Letter—when she is inform'd that there is but one day between this & commencment & that I have but just hear'd that capt. Folger will sail this week

It is true we are doing but little but it makes us more work than Ten such entertainments at home. every thing is dress'd here, & to be cut cold at cambridge except Green Peas. we are allamoding *Two* rounds of Beef, Boiling four Hams of Bacon & six Tongues. They smell finely I assure you. this will be all our meat—cider Punch wine & Porter our drink: we have had our Tables & seats made here, nothing but Boards plain'd, making them hear will save us five or six-dollars we have Milk Bisket & plumb Cake to be eat with our Tea. Betsy Smith from Haverhill has been here some time. She & Lucy are gone to day mr JQ.A. & Billy also. tomorrow mr Cranch & I go. Betsy is not well enough to be in such a Bustle so she will stay at home & take care of the House— her nerves are so weak that she cannot bear to be in the company of strangers without being distress'd she has lost her Flesh surprizingly within two months I feel very anxious about her. was it Lucy I should certainly in a consumtion, but this poor Girl is so subject to dissorders & so apt to recover them that I cannot but hope she will be again restor'd Cousin JQA has lost as much Flesh as she has but he looks much better than he did in the spring he is going a journey to Haverhill after commencment

I heard the other day by a Letter Mr Gill writ his uncle that mrs Smith was safe a Bed with a son nam'd after the Baron Stubend.[1] I most sincerely congratilate you all upon this event but the same Letter inform'd us you was confin'd to your chamber by sickness— Joy & sorrow follow each other in swift succession in this imperfect state— I fear you do not use exercise enough any more than your eldest son— He will take a journey after the Bustle of commencment is over to Falmouth & then sit down to the study of the Law will mr Parsons. There will be a hard parting on Billys side at least. He wishes to study with his cousin but we cannot pay his Board & the demands of a Teacher also at least for a year or two the expence of the last year has been very great & yet Billy has been as prudent as a child could be, but I hope we shall get through it without injuring any one & that it will not be lost upon him. He has behav'd well & pass'd thro college without a censure Tomorrow he will compleat his eighteenth year— There is no time of Life exemted from temtations, but I have thought that there was none more critical for a Gentleman than from eithteen to twenty two. Passion is then the strongest & is too apt to prove an over match for Reason. we have some melancholy instances of it in our young Freinds upon Milton Hill you will drop a tear when you know what characters they have acquir'd in the world.[2] The Parents have taken it amiss that our sons do not visit them more & that there is not a greater intimacy with their Children—but my dear sister—I have beg'd them if they value their reputations not to have the least appearenc of any with them— I expect to have a complaint enter'd against me before your Ladyship upon the account of it, but sure I am that was you here you would do the same I am greev'd for their Parents— Let us teach our children humility—& not to think more highly of themselves than they ought. Let us teach them that no rank of their ancestors be if ever so high will secure them the approbation esteem & respect of the world without the strictest attention to the rules of honour morality, & Religion

our sons look a little anxous as the Day approaches—I wish it was over. Billy is too busy assisting us too think much but my Nephew walks about with his hands hung down crying "oh Lord! oh Lord—I hope it will rain hard that all their white wigs may be wet who would not let us have a private commencment—" be compos'd said I, perform your Parts well & you will find that the Honour you will gain & the pleasure you will give your Freinds will over ballance all the anxietys you have experienc'd—

adieu for the present I must go & pack to send another cart to-morrow one is gone to day. I am almost sick with a cold & cough— I have been pouring down medicene for two days hoping to remove it—but it sticks fast & is obstinate— If callahan should get in & I should hear good tydings from my dear Friends it may do much to help me—

RC (Adams Papers).

[1] William Steuben Smith's father had served with Friedrich Wilhelm Ludolf Gerhard Augustin, Baron von Steuben (1730–1794), a veteran of the Prussian Army who joined the Continental Army in 1778 (DAB; Roof, *Smith and Lady*, p. 141).

[2] For Winslow Warren's financial and legal troubles, see vol. 7:104, 111. Many years later, on 2 Feb. 1820, JQA would write a scathing analysis of the entire Warren family in his Diary. He recalled that James and Mercy Otis Warren "during my earliest infancy were the dearest and most intimate friends of my father and Mother. They had then five sons— James, Charles, Winslow, Henry and George, of whom the two youngest were very nearly of my age— They were five as handsome, well-bred and promising boys as ever kindled the hopes of a parent; and among the earliest and profoundest of my recollections are the constant and urgent admonitions of my dear mother to look to those children as my model and to imitate their deportment and manners— Yet eve'ry one of them has turned out unfortunately—" JQA went on to elaborate on their misfortunes, including James' injury during the Revolution, which left him a "helpless cripple"; Charles' early death from consumption; George's "intemperance"; and Winslow's "licentious and adventurous life . . . the plaything of practised harlots." Only Henry received some praise for achieving "a more respectable standing in Society" though he too had to be "removed from a public office for malversation" (D/JQA/31, APM Reel 34).

Thomas Jefferson to Abigail Adams

Dear Madam   Paris July 16. 1787.

I had the happiness of receiving yesterday my daughter in perfect health. among the first things she informed me of was her promise to you, that after she should have been here a little while she would go back to pay you a visit of four or five days. she had taken nothing into her calculation but the feelings of her own heart which beat warmly with gratitude to you. she had fared very well on the road, having got into favor with gentlemen & ladies so as to be sometimes on the knee of one sometimes of another. she had totally forgotten her sister, but thought, on seeing me, that she recollected something of me. I am glad to hear that m͞r & mr͠s Paradise are gone or going to America. I should have written to them, but supposed them actually gone. I imagined m̃r Hayward gone long ago. he will be a very excellent opportunity for sending the packet to m̃r Drayton.[1] Petit will execute your commissions this morning, and I will get m̃r Appleton to take charge of them. he sets out for London the day after tomorrow. the king & parliament are at extremities about the stamp act, the latter refusing to register it without seeing accounts &c.[2] M. de Calonne has fled to the Hague. I had a letter from Colo. Smith dated Madrid June 30. he had been detaind by the illness of his servant. but he was about setting out for Lisbon. my respects attend his lady & m̃r Adams, and eternal thanks yourself with every sentiment of esteem & regard from Dear Madam / Your most obedient / & most humble serv^t   Th: Jefferson

RC (Adams Papers); addressed: "A Madame / Madame Adams / Grosvenor square / á Londres."; internal address: "M^rs. Adams"; docketed by AA2: "Mr Jefferson july 16 1787–"

[1] William Drayton (1732–1790), a lawyer and former chief justice of East Florida, was the chairman of the South Carolina Society for Promoting and Improving Agriculture to whom Jefferson was sending a sample of Italian rice (*DAB*; Jefferson, *Papers,* 11:520–521; AA to Thomas Jefferson, 10 July, above).

[2] The Parliament of Paris was steadfast in its refusal to register the new stamp and land taxes proposed at the Assembly of Notables the preceeding February. Finally, on 20 Sept., Louis XVI relented and agreed to drop them (J. F. Bosher, *The French Revolution,* N.Y., 1988, p. 111).

Abigail Adams to John Quincy Adams

my Dear Son   London july 18 1787

I give you joy of the day, as I presume it is commencment with you at Cambridge, and as it is about 4 oclock in the afternoon, I imagine you have past through your performance, I hope with approbation of the hearers, and reputation to yourself, pray favour me with a sight of it by the next opportunity and now I Suppose you will be deliberating with yourself what is next to be done? but why have you never told me whether you got my Letter from Newyork,[1] and you proposed, should we return next Spring, perhaps you might chuse to persue your Studies with your Father, that we shall return then if our Lives are Spaired I have no doubt, but till that time you would not chuse to be Idle your Aunt mentiond that you had thoughts of going to mr Dana your pappa would leave you intirly to your own choice, & to mr Dana he can have no objection, and I do not wonder that you should give him the preference on many accounts. it is a very agreeable family if you could get to Board in it. I have a sincere Friendship for Mrs Dana. be sure you give my Love to her; & tell her I hope to Spend many more Sociable Evenings with her, when I return to America. I have been sorry to think that her reason for not writing me was oweing to my being in a different station of Life from what I formerly was. I should despice myself if I thought it made any alteration in my sentiments towards my Friends. I had much rather attribute it to her indolence, & love of ease, that she did not chuse the trouble of it. now this I can forgive, and knowing her so well that I am determined, to believe the other a mere flight, tell her I shall have it to settle with her when I return—

your Aunt Cranch wrote me that you had been unwell, and I heard from others that you had lost your Flesh.[2] the latter I should not regreet, if ill Health and too close application did not occasion it. I have so frequently admonished you that I would not tire you by a repetition. light food is necessary for a student. if as usual your Stomack abounds with acid, Lime water mixd with milk, which takes away the dissagreeable taste you would find the best antidote, one pound of stone Lime, upon which pour a Gallon of Boiling water Let it stand till clear then pour it of & bottle it, take it twice a day, a large tea cup full mixd with milk— now you need not laugh, for if your food sours, it is impossible it should digest, & from thence arise your complaints—

I have been in such poor Health through the winter and spring, that the Dr advises to my going a long jouney— tomorrow we set of for Plimouth & expect to be absent a Month,— I have sent you by Captain Barnard Cloth for a coat, it is a fashionable coulour, & the buttons very tasty. you will find a waistcoat pattern with it, and I have given to mrs Wentworth a Boston woman who is a passenger Sattin for a pr of Breeches, which she will leave at uncle Smiths for you; she has been a good deal in the family with me, and I have every reason to believe her a trust worthy woman you have not acknowledg the receipt of your shirts, or told me if they fitted you.[3] Mr Hollis was in Town to day from the Hide, and dined with us. he has left in my care the works of Dr Jebb, to be sent to Harvard college.[4] I will Send you a Set as soon as I can get them bound. he was one of the choise ones of the Earth.— I shall direct them to be left at uncle Smiths— our Good Friends the Dutch are in a dissagreeable situation, as you will see by the publick papers. England and France are arming at all points, what will be the result, time only can devellope— your sister writes so much by this opportunity that I hope I may be excused, [as I] am prepairing for so long a journey, &

am obliged to go [in] such a calvacade. your sister & Nephew accompanies us Remember me to your Brothers. I will write them by the next opportunity— adieu most affectionately yours—

Abigail Adams

inclosed you find a Louis d'or

RC (Adams Papers); addressed by AA2: "Mʳ John Quincy Adams / Boston / Massachusetts"; endorsed: "My Mother. 18. July 1787." and "Mʳˢ: Adams. July 18. 1787." Some loss of text where the seal was removed.

¹ AA to JQA, 28 Nov. 1786, vol. 7:405–406.
² See Mary Smith Cranch to AA, 22 April 1787, and Elizabeth Smith Shaw to AA, 20 May, both above.
³ AA to JQA, 17 Jan., vol. 7:442–443.

⁴ John Disney, *The Works, Theological, Medical, Political, and Miscellaneous, of John Jebb: With Memoirs of the Life of the Author,* London, 1787.

Abigail Adams to Elizabeth Smith Shaw

my dear sister   London july 20 [*19*] 1787—¹

I will not plead in excuse that I have not by any of the late vessels received a Line from my Sister, and on that account omit writing to her. I know she would have written to me if she had known early enough of the opportunity I hope she has before this time received all the Letters I have written to her, & the little matters I have sent her— Mrs Cranch wrote me that the Thoat distemper had broken out, with great voilence in Haverhill it is a terrible disease & frequently Baffles the Skill of the Physician. it is so infectious as to expose every person who attends the sick to it, and therefore taking large doses of the Bark in powder is considerd as a good antidote & preservative, but smoking airing washing & cleansing ever article as after the Small Pox in the natural way, is considerd here as absolutely necessary. it has been known to break out in families after the disease had quitted it, only from some infectious garment. I should have advised my sister to have Sent her children immediately out of Town. as she would from the Small Pox in the natural way burning pitch & Tar, Hot viniger, are all good purifiers of the air; I pray Heaven preserve you & yours— I want, yet feel affraid to hear, from you. I hope the warm weather will be the means of abating and removeing the disease. I am something relieved by a Letter from Dr Tufts of the 15 of june² if any of my Friends had been sick, he would have mentiond it.

I am going tomorrow to set out in a journey of between 2 & 3 hundred miles in hopes that it will essentially serve my Health. I have been very frequently ill through the Spring & Summer, and am advised to this journey as a restoritive. we shall be absent about a month. we mean to visit Devonshire & to see the place of our dear Brother Cranchs nativity. it is said to be one of the finest counties in England Mrs Smith & the little Boy accompanies us, Col Smith we do not expect back till Sep^{br}. I have by Captain Barnard Sent you a Tea urn, it is packd in a Box with one for Sister Cranch. you will find an Iron calld a heater. This when the water is boild, you heat red hot & put in the tin middle peice which keeps the water hot during the whole process of tea making. I have also sent you a little contrivence for lighting a candle when your fire is out, the directions for useing are round the case— The Box is addrest to uncle smiths care. I think you will find the urn of great service in Hot weather.

I have only to add my regards to Brother Shaw & a Book which was forgotten by the last opportunity Mr Adams joins me in affectionate Regards to you and yours Mr Sparhawk was so good as to call & offer to take a Letter I am Sensible of his civility, but as I Shall be absent when he Sails. I think it best to commit all my Letters to captain Barnard. I am my dear Sister with Sincere wishes for / your Health & happiness / your ever affectionate / Sister

A Adams

RC (DLC:Shaw Family Papers); addressed by AA2: "M^{rs:} Elizabeth Shaw / Haverhill / Massachusetts"; endorsed: "July 20th 1787"; notations: "Sh: 2." and "Pr. Poste."

[1] The corrected date is based on the fact that the Adamses set off on their trip to Devonshire on 20 July; see JA to Richard Cranch, 20 July, below.
[2] Possibly Cotton Tufts to JA, 13 June, above. A letter by Tufts of 15 June has not been found.

Abigail Adams Smith to Elizabeth Cranch

London july 19th 1787—

to what Cause my Dear Eliza am I to attribute that Air of Mistery which reigns throughout your last Letter to me,—[1] you ever Possessed my friendship Esteem and affection, nor do I know that you have ever intentionally forfeited either, why then my Dear Girl do you imagine them estranged from you,— there is one Epoch of our Lives which I Consider as the Ordeal of friendship, if we are so fortunate as to Pass this Period and retain the friends of our Youth I think we may flatter ourselves that the attachment will withstand the future vicissitudes of time, Happily my friend has your Cousin passed and She hopes in Possession of your affections, and those of her other Partial friends, and She can form no wish that can more promote your happiness than that She may soon have the pleasure of returning your Congratulations so Kindly expressed in yours of November the 18th which Letter should have been long ere this acknowledged had not indisposition the Last Winter prevented me from returning those attentions to my friends which their Letters really demanded from me—

Should you not be amused my Dear Eliza to see your Cousin performing her part in the Character She has lately become an Actress in I wish it was in my Power to Present my Son to you—for he is a cleaver Boy—and I think resembles my Brother Charles—*but a quiet Soul just like his Mamma*—he is not however wanting in sprightliness—

It would greatly Contribute to my happiness were it in my Power to partake of some of those Cares and attentions which you are so kind during our absence to undertake for my Dear Brothers their judicious and manly Conduct would I am sure be a full recompence for any little trouble they might occasion, the Worthy and amiable Characters which they Sustain is a scource of great Sattisfaction to us—

I dare say the parting of the Happy friends which will I suppose take place within a few days from this time will be with mutual regret— if the day for Commencement was yesterday and we may form any idea of your season by this you were very fortunate—for it was very Cool and pleasant here—we thought of it much—and wished to be transported to the scene—

tomorrow we set out upon an excurssion into the West of England— we propose setting our faces towards Plymouth—to traverse the County of Devonshire and to take up our quarters for some time at Exeter, Plymouth, and wherever elce we may find it inviting the season is fine—and the weather not so *Cold* as Usual—which reminds me more of my own Country than any season I have ever passed here—& this is no small inducement to render it agreeable—

Whilst on our Tour or after our return I will indeavour to give you some idea of it— I should anticipate more Plasure if *my friend* was to accompany us—but he is absent upon Public Business in Portugal—and cannot return these six weeks— there are always upon Such excursions *little* if not *great* difficulties to encounter and he Possesses the Happy faculty of removeing them and rendering every thing easy to those who accompany him—

Barnard is expected to Sail before our return which makes me sollicitous to write to as many of my friends before we set out as I can and will I hope be a sufficient appology to my Cousin for the Haste of this—

be so good as to Present my Duty and respects to my Grand Mamma—and add those of her Great Grandson my Compliments and regards as they are due—to Nancy Quincy I ought to write and did intend it but have not time left by this opportunity—remember me to her and beleive me / yours sincerely   A Smith

RC (MHi:Christopher P. Cranch Papers); addressed: "Miss Eliza Cranch / Braintree / near Boston / Massachusetts—"; internal address: "Eliza Cranch—"; endorsed: "Mrs A Smith / 1787."

[1] No letters from Elizabeth Cranch to AA2 have been found.

Abigail Adams' Diary of a Tour from London to Plymouth, 20–28 July 1787

MS (M/AA/1, APM Reel 197). PRINTED: JA, *D&A*, 3:203–208. AA's Diary of the family's trip through west England describes only the first nine days of their month-long excursion. For the period it covers, the Diary provides considerable detail on the family's activities. AA notes all of their stops, where they lodged (and the quality of those lodgings), and who they met, as well as historical facts about some of the sites. Not surprisingly, she also takes the opportunity to comment on the impoverished state of English society: "Through a Country as fertile as Eden and cultivated like a Garden you see nothing but misirable low thatchd Huts moulderd by time with a small old fashiond glass window perhaps two in the whole House. . . . On some lone Heath a Shepeards Cottage strikes your Eye, who with his trusty dog is the keeper of a vast flock owned by some Lord, or Duke. If poverty, hunger and want should tempt him to slay the poorest Lamb of the flock, the penal Laws of this Land of freedom would take his Life." The journal breaks off abruptly, mid-sentence, in the midst of AA's description of their visit to Exeter, where they met with members of Richard Cranch's family.

JA and AA2 also kept journals of their travels. JA's notes (printed at *D&A*, 3:208–212) contain only one lengthy entry and are otherwise fragmentary. AA2's comments (printed in AA2, *Jour. and Corr.*, 1:84–94) are more extensive, but no manuscript copy is extant, and the printed version is somewhat unreliable, therefore it has not been reprinted here. Still, both supplement AA's Diary, as well as the correspondence printed below, in recording the family's tour.

John Adams to John Quincy Adams

My dear Son,   London July 20. 1787

We Suppose, that you had your Degree last Wednesday, and upon that Supposition, I congratulate you upon it. it is hinted that you think of studying Law with Judge Dana till next Spring. if you can have the Honour and the Priviledge of studying under, two such great Masters as Judge Trowbridge and Judge Dana, I approve very much of the design.[1] You cannot be in so good hands. but will the Gentlemen of the Bar, be willing that you should enter, under the Judge and compute your three Years from the time you begin?— You should be frugal of that Article of time.— if you like it, I will take you into my own office, next June, by which Time I expect to be at Braintree, and to undertake the Pleasing Office of Preceptor to my own Sons, and perhaps you will find upon the whole as many Advantages in this as in any other Plan.— I do not however mean, to divert you from your own Choice.— At all Events I think you ought to be entered on the Books of the Bar, as a student as early as possible.—[2] My love to your Brothers.   John Adams

RC (Adams Papers); internal address: "Mr J. Q. Adams."

[1] Edmund Trowbridge (1709–1793) of Cambridge, Harvard 1728, held a number of prominent positions including that of Massachusetts attorney general and judge of the Superior Court (*DAB*; *Sibley's Harvard Graduates*, 8:507–520).

[2] Lawyers were required to petition the bar for permission allowing a student to study with them. Law students were required to have a college education, or education that the bar deemed equivalent, and the petitioning attorney was required to ask for consent at a general meeting of the bar. The student then had to complete a three-year apprenticeship with a barrister before he could practice law independently. JQA had been admitted as a student in the Essex County bar association by 27 Sept. (Hollis R. Bailey, *Attorneys and Their Admission to the Bar in Massachusetts*, Boston, 1907, p. 21–22; JQA, *Diary*, 2:296).

John Adams to Richard Cranch

My dear Brother   London July 20. 1787

I have only the time to inform you, that this morning I am to Sett out, with My Wife and Daughter, with her little Son, to See your Country of Devonshire.— The air of London like that of Paris and Amsterdam, is in Summer, tainted to Such a degree, that all who can possibly get out of it; fly it, like a Pestilence. Mrs Adams, has for the last nine months been affected by this Climate, with Complaints that are common in it, and is advised by her Physician and by all her Friends, to make a Tour. it is not less necessary for Mrs Smith. Nor should I dare venture to Stay in London thro the Summer. We propose to see Plymouth, Exeter Axminster &c— This will probably be the last Excursion, We Shall make, till We bend our Course, to Braintree. I hope Dr Tufts will buy me, Mr Tylers House: if not We shall return to the old Place.— The Voyages that have been commenced in February have been so long and distressing, that I shall not dare to expose my Family in their tender health, to embark before the Spring Equinox.— We shall take our Passage in the first ship that Sails in the latter End of March or beginning of April.

The Accounts We have of the Uneasy State of the Minds of our Countrymen: their innumerable Projects, and fluctuating Politicks are perhaps more distressing to Us, than they are to you who are on the Spot.— Are We all to become Champions and soldiers for a Bowdoin or a Hancock, a Livingston or a Clinton, a Morris or a Franklin &c &c &c. Is every State to have two or three families Scrambling for the first Place, and the disposal of the Loaves and Fishes, and is every Body to be obliged to take his side, and Scramble for one or the other.? Let Solon who compelled every citizen to take a Side say what he will, I cant see the moral Obligation on any one to take a side in Such Squabbles. if our Constitutions are Such as produce necessarily Such Contests, Let Us correct and amend them. and if the People will not consent to such Amendments: but are so in love with Blood and Carnage that they will have it, What shall We Say? It is no new fault in the World. Most Nations have been infected with it, and have suffered accordingly.— I Shall soon Send you a Volume of Romances, for Such you will think them, tho they are true History, which Will show our People what they are about and what they may expect.—[1] if they are determined to go down the Precipice, it is fit they should see it, before they take the Leap and prepare for Death.— For my own Part I am too old and feeble, to fight.— They must put me to death for my Neutrality: for I will not be a Party Man. The Laws and their Defence, must have my Wishes and all the little Efforts I can make in my own Way. But I will neither be a Game Cock for Bowdoin nor Hancock, Lincoln nor Cushing. My Duties and Affections where they are due   John Adams.

RC (MeHi:Presidents File); addressed: "The Honourable / Richard Cranch / Boston"; internal address: "The Hon. Richard Cranch."; notation: "P^r. Captain / Barnard."

[1] That is, the second volume of JA's *Defence of the Const.*

Mary Smith Cranch to Abigail Adams

My Dear Sister   Boston July 21^d 1778 [1787]

The Day—the mighty Day is over, & our Sons have perform'd their Parts—& receiv'd the Honour of the college in a manner which will do them credit while they Live— never did you see two Happier Faces than theirs when they return'd from meeting— I do not believe they will ever feel so happy again— If to excell where all did well—can give pleasure your Son must feel a peculiar one. He has a faculty of throughing expresson into his countinance beyond any person I ever met with— I was not in the meeting house, but I am told that he excell'd in his manner every one who ever Spoke in it— The performences of the Day are said by every one to have been the best composition, & the best spoken of any since the universitys were created—

Every thing was conducted in our Chambers with the greatest order & regularity— Mr Beals who lives on our place at Weymouth had the whole care of delivering out drink & we had uncle Smiths Primus—& a Black Servant of cousin Willm. Smiths & our Pheby to attend the Tables—[1] she was exceeding useful to me after dinner in washing up the Dishes & clearing the Tables we had two chambers one for the Tables & the other for our company to Sit in. We made no Tea but had cake & wine carried about in stead of it which sav'd us a great deal of trouble

We din'd above a hundred People & treated with cake & wine above four hundred I am very certain we were honour'd after Dinner with the company of His excellency the Governer & L—— Govr. & a number of the Senate—The Resident Professor & Tutors, who all came to congratulate us— In short I had enough to do to set & receive the congratulations of our Friends & acquaintance I most sincerely wish'd you with me to have taken your share— We were not only congratulated that we had a son & Nephew who had done themselves such Honour, that day but that they had sustain'd such amiable good characters during their residence at college— I had as much small Talk to do as their Majestys upon a presentation day— but they never felt half as much pleasure your sons all felt like my own & I presented them as my adopted ones till your return & proud enough I am of them—

Although we had so much company we had enough & to spair of every thing we made 28^{lb} of Flower into cake & fine Plumb cake it was. I sent mrs Hall a nice one & several of our common Frinds a slice who could not attend. I hope I have given general satisfaction to all our Freinds we ask'd general Palmers Family two days before commencment they took it into their Heads to be mift because they were not invited sooner & would not come, but if they knew how little I car'd & how little notice I should take of such unreasonable affronts they would keep them to themselves. Cousin Polly poor girl is not long for this world I believe. she fails very fast—² The rest of the Family are well. The general is very busy erecting large salt Works upon the neck— I hope they will answer his expectations.—

To add to my happiness callahan arriv'd two days before Commencment & brought me an account of your being better than my imagination represented you. I long more than ever for your return— You must take more care of your health these complaints of yours are hard to be cur'd— I have suffer'd much in the same way for the two last years but have injoyd. my health finely sinc last summer till this ugly cold I have now got I was sick enough to have been upon the Bed on Wednesday but I got thro better than I expected too, & am going home this afternoon to be nurs'd up & to rest a little.—

I rejoice to hear of the Safety of my Niece & her little one. I hope her health is perfectly restor'd by this time. pray give my Love to her & to little master & tell him to grow firm enough to receive a hearty Squeeze from his great Aunt when she sees him— If Coll^n Smith is returnd tell him I had the pleasure of Coll^n. Humphrys company at our chamber on Wednesday last. That he talk'd of his Friend & that we both wish'd him & indeed all of you with us. The Coll. has promis'd to make us a visit at Braintree with Coll. Hull, Who is a great favourite of mine & Elizas. mrs Hull has just got to Bed with her fourth child³ I have lately been to see them

I have again to thank you for your kind presents to our children They have not time to write by this conveyence, but will soon but my sister why did you procure such costly Scandles. I fear it will not be in character for them to wear them. The maker has mortified them in the length of them for they cannot possible wear them. I wonder what kind of Feet he thought we had in america. I have not seen the chintz but dare say it is pretty. I believe we should have made up our silks if it had not have been for the peculiarty of the times but we did not think it prudent to do it— To say I thank you for all your goodness to us will not express half what I feel— I have receev'd the wastcoats & the linnen for cousin Tom we have not yet made up the fine Piece you sent him before, but are making some for him of the coarser Piece you sent by Scot. he will want them for winter & we thought if best to make it of this because the frost would not cut it as if it was finer, & we can only make him just enough for present wear he grows so fast— I shall fix cousin JQ.A well with every thing to last him till the spring. he will lay by his shirts & other matters that will require much mending till he makes us a visit— I wish to have it all done here but some little matters must be done there

Sister Shaw & Sister Smith have both been with us but are re-turn'd without going to Braintree. Sister Shaw looks very well for her—her children are well—but the Sickness prevails yet but it is not so mortal as it has been—

I was call'd off just now to your Friend mrs Rogers for the first time since she return'd. her health is poor. she rejoices to hear from you & mrs Smith hop'd for a Letter sends her Love—

I must leave a thoussand things to say for the next vessel as mr cranch is waiting to put a Packet a Board Folger mr cranch is much gratified with his Letter, thanks you will write as soon as he has time

tell Coll^n Smith he must not live in new york. we cannot spare my Niece & her little Family—& Grandmamma will not be able to do it I am sure

My Love to mr. Adams—as to you my sister I know not how to bid you adieu— may God preserve you & bring you once more safe to my arms— This is the constant Petition of you / affectionate Sister

M Cranch

RC (Adams Papers); endorsed: "Mrs Cranch july / 21 1787"; docketed by AA2: "Mrs Cranch july 21st 1787."

[1] "Primus" was likely Primas Cooley of Weymouth, who had married Rachel, "a Ne-gro Woman," in 1775 (*Vital Records of Weymouth Massachusetts to the Year 1850*, 2 vols., Boston, 1910, 2:225).

[2] Despite her ill health, Mary (Polly) Palmer survived until Nov. 1791 (MHi:Peabody Family Papers, Mary Palmer Letters, 1790–1791). See vol. 7:201–202, note 5, for an account of the accident that caused her illness.

[3] William and Sarah Hull's fourth child, Nancey, was born on 19 June 1787 (*Vital Records of Newton, Massachusetts, to the Year 1850*, Boston, 1905, p. 104).

Elizabeth Smith Shaw to Abigail Adams

My Dear Sister—   Haverhill July 22^d 1787

The last Week has indeed been a Week of Joy to me— We have "eat our Bread with gladness, & drank our Wine with merry Hearts—"[1]

My dear Nephews have done themselves, & their Friends honour by their publick Performances— And Mr Shaw, & myself shared in a very particular manner, the general satisfaction, & Festivity of the Day—

William Cranch had a Dissertation shewing the Utillity, & necessity of three Branches in the Legislature.—

Your Son spoke an English Oration upon the importance of preserving publick Faith, &ce—

Leonard White had a Conference with Loyd, & Amory upon the Question, which had the greatest Influence upon Mankind, Wealth—Power—or Fame—[2]

Freeman from Sanwich spoke a most excellent Oration, both as to matter, & manner, & I should be too partial, if I had not preserved a Wreath, to bind around *his* Head—

I think both the Orators (for I cannot now recollect, & separate each part) represented to us the honourable, happy state we were in, at the close of the last War—marked out in very striking coulours, each footstep by which we had fallen into our present state, & shewed that Idleness, & Luxery ever did, & ever would bring on loss of Credit—Scorn, & Derission—Civil Wars—Anarchy, & all its dreadful Consequences—

J,Q,A, & Freeman were the Competiors of the Day, & seemed to vie with each other who should excell the most— The young Ladies charmed with the gracefullness of Freeman, would no doubt have presented him with the Palm—But more accurate Judges, & the admirers of dignity of Sentiment, & Composition would at *least* have debated upon the Preference—

I am sure no one could be a Judge of Mr Adam's Eloquence unless they kept their Eye fixed upon his Face, & saw each Passion, & each Feeling called up, & most strikingly, & happily delineated there—

It is 17 years since I have attended a Commencement before this— They speak now, there Performances cheifly in English, & of late years have greatly improved in the Art of Speaking—[3] I have thought Oratory was too little attended too by this University—& many of our most sensible Youths have suffered sadly by the neglect— I wish they may not now run into the oposite extreme— For whoever expects *now* to be noticed, & wishes to make a Figure, reads Sheridan, & Blair with the greatest avidity, to the too great neglect (I fear) of Classickcal Authors, & more substantial knowledge— For after all, it must be considered only, as an exterior ac-

135

complishment as an elegant Dress to a fine Woman, rendering her more conspicuous, & strikingly lovely—

The Centinel I see, has conveyed to the World with its *usual good-humour* some strictures upon Commencement Performances— But malevolence shall not cast a shade nor Scurility pluck the Laurel from their Brow—[4]

The Young Gentlemen may well content themselves, with the ample applause of the Day—

The Monday before Commencement we had a very fine rain, & the weather was uncommonly pleasant the whole of the week, I believe there never was so cool a Commencment known— Mr Shaw, & I, lodged at Professor William's— He rose early in the morning to take a walk anew over the classick ground, & found People who were making Booths upon the Common, thressing their Arms acros's their Breasts, to keep themselves warm—A curious sight this upon our Commencment Day—

Dr Tufts, & Mr Cranch had provided a very elegant, & genteel Entertainment— There was quite a large Company at the Chambers; but there was enough of every-thing, & to spare— There was not anything wanting but *you*, & *part of you*, to grace, & crown the whole—

It was exceeding pleasant for me, to see, & to recognize so many of my former Friends, & Acquaintance— I stood above an hour answering, & passing the usual Compliments of the Day— I thought of you at the Levee—Though there was this difference I suppose— Complacency & all the social affections of the Heart shone in their Countenances, which is never, or very seldom seen, in a Company of Strangers, wholly uninterested in each others welfare—

The Family Tenants were all there—Belcher—Beale & Pratt—who were very necessary, & useful— But as I returned from Meeting, passing the Colledge Entry, there sate in state our sable Domestic, accompanied by her solemn faced Partner, with his sabbath Day Coat, & tie Wig full powdered, looking like a piece of mock majesty— I could not but be diverted after Dinner to see him devouring the delicious Fragments—now mouthing a sweet crumb of Bread— now a fat slice of Bacon, & Tongue—now a rich piece of alamode Beef—& now a fine spoonful of green Peas—Lettice—Pickles &cc— clearing Plate by Plate & handing them, to his charming dewy, oderiferous Phebe, who was so kind as to wash them—

But what (my Dear Sister) gave a relish to every other enjoyment was the arrival of Callihan the Monday before, which brought us Letters announcing the welfare of your Family, & the Birth of your

Grandson– May you ever have Cause to rejoice in the Day– Kiss the sweet Fellow once–twice–three & tell the little Cherub his Aunt sent all she could–as a Token of her Love, & ardent Wishes, that his Life, & Health may be preserved– And in this Wish is included a sincere Petition, that its Parents may be surrounded with every Circumstance that can render Life delightful–smooth the Brow of Age–or sweeten the Bed of Death–

Your Letters gave me peculiar pleasure, for though they informed me of your poor Health, yet you was so much better than I feared, that I really felt releived–For my whimsical Brain had suggested to me that something was the matter– Last Fall, my Sisterly Spirit crossed the wide Ocean, & carefully attended you in your Illness–& early this Spring it went forth, & was siting by your side, nursing you night, after night, & kindly endeavouring to alleviate every Pain–

You may say, many wise Things upon this Subject–That I ought not to "believe in lying Vanities, & forsake real mercies–"[5] I feel its force–But had much rather *hear all were well*, than read whole Volumes, upon the Folly of Enthusiasm–[6]

Judge Blodget deliverd to me your Packet, filld with *every Expression* of kindness To say I thank you, does not convey half the gratitude I feel– Mrs Allen too sends her Love, looked quite pleased & gratified when I presented her with the Box– She has been a little unwell with Billious disorders–but expected every Day those little matters would come in use–

August 21st.

When I began this Letter I hoped to have sent it imediately, but could not get it into Town soon enough– Mr & Mrs Evans have spent a fortnight with us– He is a worthy, good, sensible man, though the People of Weymouth can hardly say as He passes, "the Lord bless & prosper you"– He was reading in the Book you sent me, (which is an excellent one) the Authors opinion of early marriage He dissaproved of it greatly– I did not think his reasons sufficient– I told him very few had, or could have those Opportunities for improving which Mrs Evans had been favoured with– I was pleased to see they were not lost upon her– She is really a fine woman– An equality of Age, I see is as nothing in the Eye of Affection, for I know of no persons who seem more delighted, & happy in each other company– He is now gone with her to Exeter, & is preaching there–

Your Sons have each of them favoured us with a visit— Thomas has grown so much; you would scarce believe it was the little Lad you left with us— He is as good as ever— The Misses think Charles a mere Adonis—a perfect Beauty— I said to him one Day "Charles the Girls fancy you are handsome"— ["]Do not forget it is a Gift of Nature, & as it is not your own acquisition, you can have no title to be vain— We would wish you to be esteemed (& I think we have Cause) & admired for the more lasting, & valuable Qualities of the Mind—" I hope I shall not make my sister anxious, she has no reason to be—but at a critical age— ~~May Minerva with her broad Sheild, preserve the dear Youth, from every Guile~~— They are happy in having one who knows the dangers, & Temptations

RC (Adams Papers); endorsed: "Mrs Shaw july 22 / 1787." Dft (DLC:Shaw Family Papers).

[1] Ecclesiastes, 9:7.

[2] For James Lloyd Jr. and Jonathan Amory, see JQA, *Diary*, 2:97, 218–219, 223, 224.

[3] Early Harvard commencement exercises were conducted nearly entirely in Latin. By the late eighteenth century, they had shifted to include more English, a trend that continued into the early nineteenth century by which time they were performed almost entirely in English (Morison, *Three Centuries of Harvard*, p. 33–34, 247).

[4] The review of the exercises of the graduating class in the *Massachusetts Centinel*, 21 July, was largely complimentary, though in part in a rather backhanded fashion. The piece commented, "We shall premise, that the whole tenor of the performances reflected the highest honour upon the Patrons of the University, as well as upon the gentlemen who exhibited. The tediousness of fulsome syllogism was considerably abridged of the length to which it is usually extended, and we are induced to hope, that this species of scholastic jargon, so unprofitable to the hearer, and so mortifying to the disputant, will soon become unfashionable upon this day— All sound argument is indeed grounded upon syllogism, but it would surely be more entertaining and instructive, to discover this mode of reasoning in conferences and orations, than to view it in the ungraceful garb in which the schools have clothed it."

[5] "They that observe lying vanities forsake their own mercy" (Jonah, 2:8).

[6] The RC ends here, presumably missing its final page. The last three paragraphs are reproduced from the Dft.

John Quincy Adams to Abigail Adams

Dear Madam. Braintree August 1st: 1787.

At length the scene of my collegiate life is closed, and about a fortnight ago I made a public exit from the university: by the public papers you will have some account of the performances of the day. In one of them (the centinel) you will see it very positively asserted that Freeman, who spoke the other oration is my indisputable superior in style, elegance and oratory. in another paper that account is said to be ridiculously partial;[1] those of the audience, who were friendly to Freeman, perhaps all thought like the writer in the centinel: my friends who were present, perhaps thought me worthy of the preference; but an observer perfectly impartial, might not be willing to give an opinion on the subject, but might say, like Sir Roger de Coverley that *"much might be said on both sides."*[2] The critic in the centinel, you will easily perceive is not entirely guided by the hand of candor; especially when speaking of me: he mentions my being the son of an Ambassador, & the favorite of the officers of college, as if those circumstances were any thing to the purpose at that time. You perhaps may think it much to my honor that I should be so much in favor with the College government; but it was in fact the most invidious circumstance that could have been mentioned: but the compliment or the accusation, whatever it be, is not true: I have it is true been distinguished twice by allotments for Exhibitions, and by that of an Oration at Commencement. but Freeman perform'd at the same exhibitions, and had likewise an Oration at Commencement. these are the only marks I ever had of their favor. In all other respects they have always treated me, as they do every student who behaves with propriety towards them; I have often laugh'd at the awful superiority, which most of them assume when in company with a student: and at other times I have expressed my opinion freely upon certain transactions, in which they were not wholly justifiable; and further, that opinion has been reported to them: so that abstracted from the characters of preceptor and student I know I am far from being the favorite of some of those officers.– I have a warm and sincere friendship for Freeman; his natural abilities are very good and his disposition is amiable. his oratorical talents are great; and I should never wish to be considered as his rival or competitor: if however we must be view'd in that light, I have not the most distant pretensions to superiority, nor am I conscious of a decided inferiority. our manner both of writing and speaking is very different, and– but I have already said too much on this subject, and hope you will forgive these effusions of vanity, and attribute them to the desire of convincing you that I have not entirely neglected to improve those advantages, which, by the kindness of my parents I have enjoy'd.

I consider as one of the most fortunate circumstances of my life, that I came from Europe, as I did. it has been of great and real service to me in many particulars. It has reduced my opinion of myself and of my future prospects to a nearer level with truth: so that making allowances for the general exaggerations of youth, I do not overrate myself more than people in general are apt to do. it has enabled me to form an intimate friendship, with a number of worthy characters of the same standing in life, with myself: and it has been the means of turning my attention to several important branches of study, which otherwise I must have neglected.— There are at the university two private Societies form'd upon a similar plan to that which you mention in one of your late letters. of these Societies, friendship is the soul, and literary improvement the object; and consequently neither of them is numerous. I was received as a member of both these Societies, very soon after my admission at the university; and I am certain that the institutions, are of great service to those who belong to them.[3] In short I am now so firmly persuaded of the superior advantages of a public education, that I only regret I did not enter the University a year and an half sooner than I did.

And now having closed with the University, you will naturally Enquire, what I am at present about;?— I have engaged to study with Mr Parsons at Newbury-port, and expect to fix myself down there in five or six weeks from this. I should wish to get upon the business sooner, but Doctor Tufts advises me, to ride about, and remain idle, for a month or two, in order to recover and establish firmly my health, which has suffered by my living so much retired, during the last eighteen months.

And now, my dear Madam, after having talked so long entirely about myself, I will acknowledge the receipt of several letters from you. I have received both sets of Blair's lectures, and according to your desire shall present one of them to my cousin. the vessel by which the first set was sent was driven from the coast in a storm, and was sometime, in one of the West India islands: so that I received it but a short time before the other set came—[4] I read with pleasure the pamphlets which came by Callahan, with your letter of May 6th: the name of the author of one of them is kept secret, but from the peculiarity of the stile, I strongly suspect they are both the productions of the same pen. Affairs seem to assume quite an extraordinary appearance in France. And I see by the papers that the Marquis de la Fayette, has got his finger in the pye; (to use a vulgar expression.)[5] it was well for de Vergennes that he died as he did; though probably had he lived, he would have prevented any assembly, which might take his conduct into consideration. The marquis appears to me, to be venturing "like little wanton boys who swim on bladders," and I shall be surprized, if he does not in the end, find himself "far beyond his depth."[6] It is dangerous to tread upon a snake, and if the marquis is influenced merely by disinterested patriotism, that circumstance, in a court, will only be the means of making his enemies the more numerous.

I wrote to my dear father about 3 weeks since; and will write soon to my Sister.[7] in the mean time, will you please to present to her my congratulations upon her new character, and tell her I hope she will fulfill the duties of it as well as she has those of all the characters in which he has appeared before. I would complain of her if I dared: I would remind her that seven months have elapsed since I received one line from her;[8] but as I fear she might in some measure retort the charge, I will e'en be silent and wait with patience.

But my paper stops me, and I can only add, that I am, your dutiful and / affectionate Son.   J. Q. Adams.—

RC (Adams Papers); endorsed: "J Q A– / august 1. 1787."

[1] For a discussion of the conflicting newspaper reports of JQA's oration, see JQA, *Diary*, 2:265–266.

[2] *The Spectator*, No. 122 (20 July 1711). Sir Roger de Coverley was a character Joseph Addison created and used in various issues of *The Spectator* (DNB).

[3] JQA was admitted to three societies shortly after he matriculated at Harvard in spring 1786: the Tea Club on 30 March, the A. B. Club on 29 May, and Phi Beta Kappa on 21 June. The Tea Club was formed for social pursuits, the others were primarily literary. Later in the year he also joined the Handel Society (*Diary*, 2:12, 14, 42–43, 52–53, 91, 103).

[4] See AA to JQA, 28 Feb. 1787, vol. 7:474, and 20 March, above.

[5] The Marquis de Lafayette led the criminal impeachment charges against Charles Alexandre de Calonne (*Morning Chronicle* and *London Advertiser*, 21 April; *Massachusetts Centinel*, 11 July).

[6] "Oh! I have ventured like little wanton boys who swim on bladders, these many summers on a sea of glory—but far beyond my depth" (*New-Haven Gazette*, 22 March). This quotation comes from *The Anarchiad*, a faux-epic poem by the so-called Connecticut Wits, David Humphreys, Joel Barlow, John Trumbull, and Lemuel Hopkins. The piece originally appeared over twelve issues in the *New-Haven Gazette* between Oct. 1786 and Sept. 1787 (David Humphreys et al., *The Anarchiad: A New England Poem* (1786–1787), repr. edn., Gainesville, Fla., 1967, p. vi, 39).

[7] AA2 acknowledged a 3 Aug. 1787 letter from JQA in hers of 10 Feb. 1788, below, but it has not been found.

[8] AA2 to JQA, 1 Sept. – 12 Oct. 1786, vol. 7:328–333.

Lucy Cranch to Abigail Adams

My dear Aunt—   Braintree August 18– —87

I wrote you a few hasty lines, from Boston the Monday before Commencement, inclosing two news-papers which Mr Jinks was to carry,[1] I went to Cambridge that afternoon: I heard in the evening that Calahan had arrived. I never hear of a ships arrival from London, but what I feel a mixture of pain with the pleasure, 'till we have got the Letters— I always tremble when they are opened. I never felt the sensation stronger than at that time, I had so many things to make me happy, that I trembled least I should hear something that would make me otherwise, the last we had heard from you was, that you was unwell.

Cousin Charles went to Boston Tuesday Morning. I watched his face when he returned before he was half over the Common. it wore the same pleasing smile it ever does. I never felt happier than when he gave me a letter from his Mama—²

I hope your health is perfectly restored, before this. your anxiety for Mrs Smith was too powerful for your Nerves, and made you worse. we all rejoice with you, that she is so well over her illness— and that you have so fine a grandson.

You will have so many accounts of Commencement that I shall have little left to say—but what others have said before me. it was impossible to have a finer day. it was so cold in the morning that the Men on the common were glad to clap there hands against their sides to warm them. the meeting House was not crowded so much as usial, it is said the assembly was the most respectable, that has been known for many years, every thing that belonged to our part went on with great regularity. we had a large company to dine yet we have had much more hurry with a small party. every thing was done at home, that could be— Tables and benches were made here, that there was nothing to be done at Cambridge but set the Tables which was done on Tuesday— what we had and all those matters Mama will inform you—

I went to meeting all day. I think that the performances in general were better than ever I knew them—

Your Son gained deservedly great applause—he spoke with great fire and energy, with a spirit that did honour to the Son of a Patriot and Statesman, had his Father heard him he would have felt young again.

Tho' Mr J.Q.A. resembles you more than either of your Children, yet I never saw the likeness so stricking as when he pronounced his oration. it was your mouth that smiled when he addressed the Ladies. it was your eyes that glistened when he bad his Classmates adieu—

My Brother spoke better than I expected—as he is not naturally fluent. you will know the subject of his dissertation by the Newspapers,—they say too, that it should be remembered as an *excuse* for his encomiums, of the Defence of the American Constitutions that the Auther of that was his Uncle—

142

No person presumes to say that Mr Freeman who also spoke an English Oration had an equal. perhaps it was because I felt more interested, and partial, that though Mr Freemans voice was more musical, and his action might, be more gracefull, yet his Oration did not give me so much pleasure, as Mr J.Q—A's—

Billy Smith is quite settled down in the family way Mrs Smith cannot boast of beauty— she has those more valuable qualifications of the heart which will be more lasting, and which enables her to make her husband happy and give pleasure to her friends—

They live in Mr Gores House, which makes it very agreable to both families especially to Betsey Smith, who is now quite alone[3] she is a fine Girl, and behaves with as much steadiness as possible she pays the greatest attention to her Father, and conforms in every thing to his wishes the family goes on with the same pleasing regularity it used to. Uncle has not recovered his spirits since my Aunts death. he is himself very unwell. he has a bad Leg—from scraping a peice of the skin off—

You my dear Aunt are so continually loading me with favours, that I fear it will never be in my power to return them half. the will shall not be wanting— the Chints I think extremly beautiful, the Sandals are much too large. if the ribband had not come from England, and the dispotic title of fashion—anexed to it, I should think it was very ugly, one would think we had been rumageing the trunks of Mr Wibirds Grand-mother, we had thoughts of making him a present of it to tye up his gown—

can you believe it Madam that this same good Gentleman, did not go to Commencement. you will not easily guess the reason, the very important reason—his Chaise was broke and he did not like to wear boots in warm weather:

You have given us hopes my dear Madam that you will return next Spring, do not disappoint us. your return will add happiness to many, many hearts, among which will be hers who is with every sentiments of respect and / esteem, your obliged and grateful / Neice.

Lucy, Cranch.

RC (Adams Papers); endorsed: "Lucy Cranch / August 19 1787."

[1] Not found.
[2] AA to Lucy Cranch, 26 April, above.
[3] Samuel Gore's house and business were located at 61 Court Street very near the Court Street home of Isaac Smith Sr. Gore ran the Painter's Arms, importing and selling paints and oils (*Boston Directory*, 1789; MHi:Samuel Clough Papers, [Atlas of Boston]; Boston *Continental Journal*, 11 July 1782).

Mary Smith Cranch to Abigail Adams

My Dear Sister   Braintree August 19th 1787

   The vacancys of our Sons always produces a hurry in our business & although we endeavour to keep every thing in good order for them from week to week—yet when they come home they have many wants which we could not foresee— we have sent your two youngest Sons in good health & good repair to college & are now fixing your eldest for Newbury & our own for Boston Cousin Tom has made a visit to Haverhill sir Charles *touch'd* there— A pair of *beautiful Eyes* & *heavenly* eye-Brows were too attracting to permit him to fix till he had reach'd newburry port— Why charles who is this divine creature who has made you look so languid—"oh aunt["]—"oh Cousin["]—"It is a Neice of mrs Williams mama She *is* a pretty Girl She was there when I was this spring—"¹ "well cousin Betsy did you ever see such *heavenly* Eye-brows—& she is as amiable as she is pretty" "but my dear have you left her any hair upon her head if all the rings you have are made of her hair you must have thin'd it a little at least" "but I observe a great variety of shades & colours in your Rings— I fancy you are a general admirer of the sex if so—your heart is in no danger at present" I am always a little affraid my dear Nephew when I find a schoolars Pockits so full of hair Rings that his head will not be as well Stor'd with Greek & Latten— "He will get it over soon said JQA— I was so two years but I would study out of spight—" I am mistaken my cousin if you are not a little poorly now although you will not own it— Lovely Nancy is oftener play'd upon the Flute than any other tune—² as to honest Tom he does not think that the Ladys need so much attention—"is sure that they have Legs as well as he & may walk without leaning upon his arm" If my own soon has had any twitches he takes care not to discover it— His attentions appear to be the result of Benevolence & politness only & such I hope they will continue untill he has acquir'd something to support a Family—

   Mr Wainwright a native of Liverpool who came here with capt Beals Family & who about a week since sail'd for England—desir'd to take a Letter for you he will spend the winter in London—³ I design'd to have given him one but I had not time to write. he will see you I suppose. if he should—I wish you would tell him why I did not. he was so kind as to offer to take Letters or any thing I had to send could I send you some corn & Beans I know I should give a Feast if you retain the same relish for them that you use'd to have— I wish I could send you any thing that would refresh you as much as the Porter you sent us has mr cranch this summer— He has apply'd himself to the cultivation of his little Farm & has work'd so hard himself that if he had not drank Porter & water freely I know not whither he would have had an ounce of flesh left— He can have work enough at the Treasurers office—but can get nothing but paultry orders for pay—which will not sell for more than eleven shillings upon the pound what is allow'd a day will not pay—at this rate— the man we hire to work upon the Farm I believe I told you that mr Belcher works for us this Summer—& an excellent hand he is I have Molly Burrel for a Dairy Maid sister Smith brought her up— she makes fine cheese & is a very neat good Girl— I have had very good health this season & have many very many blessings to be thankful for—

Betsy Smith is gone home Polly is now with me. She is a fine sensible sprightly child has quite done freting & is by much the smartest of sisters Daughters— Louisia is to make me a visit next—[4] Sister Smith is in poor health a pain in her side & a difficulty of breathing are her complaints I feel concern'd about her—she is too anxious about her children.

I know not what will become of uncle Quincy or his Estait. That vixen which he keeps for a house keeper does what she pleases—& to help his repose & to amuse him in his retirement from the world. Miss Sally Tailer is come to spend the Summer with him—& really if he had not the other she would be no bad companion if she would not talk quite so much.[5] It is not in our power to get uncle from home & miss Tailor says he is very dull—sometimes— How much happier would he be if he had such a sprightly wife as our good Grandmother was a man wants a wife for a companion more I think when he is far advanc'd in Life than when he is young nobody feels clever to look about them & not see a creature who cares whether they live or dye—

General Palmers salt works upon Boston neck are almost ready to work. I hear they are to live in one of the Houses upon the neck cousin Polly yet lives but is very low I really thought about a month since that she could not have surviv'd till this time— Cousin Betsy is to be married to cousin Jo Cranch as soon as he gets establish'd in business— Their education has been very different the superiority is on the wrong side— Her Papa has been *bitterly* against it his Pride is sadly hurt. you know his temper & can guess what she may have suffer'd— If he submits it will be because he knows she is determined— He is a good temper'd young Fellow I wish he had a better faculty to push himself into business— General Knox has a good opinion of his honesty & his abbilities as a good Gun Smith & will do every thing in his power to assist him—[6] I wish them both well

August 27th

I am just come from visiting our good uncle Smith. He is dangerously sick. He has had a swelling in one of his Legs for above two months, which has increas'd to such a degree that it has reach'd his body, His Leg & thigh are as hard as a stick & inflam'd to a purple colour, you know he never could bear confinement without being dull, His spirits are sunk to nothing. He has had a bad cough all summer. & Doctor Tufts has said that unless he would lay by & attend to his health—he would not live long. but he would not be perswaided while he could stand upon his Leg, he has lost his Flesh & his appetite & has some disorders besides which waste him fast. He lays upon the bed & groans & looks so much like our dear Father that I could not take my eyes from him; I sat by—& fan'd him the whole of last satturday afternoon. but it was a scene almost too much for me. His voice was so much like Fathers that it would sometimes make me Start— you know what a Family of Love they are & will not wonder that they are greatly distress'd Cousin Isaac & Betsy look as if their hearts would break, The Loss should it be the will of Heaven to take him from us, will be very great indeed to us all—not only to his Friends but to the community.—

I carried my son to Boston & left him with mr Dawes,[7] I have left him an innocent youth with a strong sense of Religion & Honour upon his mind— I hope he will never be drawn aside from the path of virtue. His cousin JQA & he will find it hard to part. they Love as Brothers & as Friends as well as classmates

September 1[d]

I went again yesterday to see uncle Smith & found him much better—tho far from being out of danger— your son JQA went with me & is on his way to newburry— He was more affected at leaving us than I could have imagin'd he would have been— Although he has been toss'd about the world in such a manner—he had dissagreable feelings at the thought of going to a place where he knew no one. & where he care'd for nobody, & nobody care'd for him. as he express'd himself to me as we were riding, dear youth he found it nec-

146

essary to draw the back of his Hand across his Eyes when he said it—& from sympathy or a tenderer Cause your sister did the same I told him he forgot that he would be within 14. miles of his aunt Shaw, who love'd him like a Parent—& to whom—he must go, if he was unwell at any time. He promiss'd to write to us & to visit us in the winter. We have fix'd him of so well that I think he cannot want much done for him till then—

your Neices have made the chintz you sent them & of all pritty things it is the [mos]t beautiful for Gowns I cannot sufficiently thank you [my] dear sister for your kindness to them

your present came in season [for] mrs Allen. She has a fine Daughter— Hannah Austin is [yet] living but is in the last stage of a consumption.[8] mrs Cutts has another son— mr cranch desires his Love to you all—will write as soon as he can but my sister when am I to see you. I hope I am not to be disappointed another year— I want to see my new relations & my dear Neice, & to see what a good Mamma she makes

I shall have this Letter put into the bag tomorrow least callahan should slip away without a Line, I shall write again before the vessel sails. if she does not go sooner than is talk'd off

I made your mother Hall a visit last week & found her very well—
yours affectionatly   M Cranch

The Girls beg you to send them some good Needles they cannot find any here

RC (Adams Papers); addressed by Richard Cranch: "To / Madam Abigail Adams / Grosvenor Square / Westminster"; endorsed: "Mrs Cranch / August 19. 1787." Some loss of text where the seal was removed.

[1] Possibly Anna Frazer (b. 1772) of Newbury, whose father, John Frazer, was the nephew by marriage of Jane Prime Frazer. Her daughter by a later marriage in turn married Samuel Williams, the Harvard professor (*Vital Records of Newbury Massachusetts to the End of the Year 1849*, 2 vols., Salem, 1911, 1:174, 2:183; *Vital Records of Rowley Massachusetts to the End of the Year 1849*, Salem, 1928, p. 79, 297; *Sibley's Harvard Graduates*, 15:134).

[2] "Lovely Nancy," written by Scottish composer and publisher James Oswald, first appeared ca. 1745 in his collection, *The Caledonian Pocket Companion*, vol. 2. Originally composed for the fife, the melody was popular and used at the time of the Revolution as a retreat signal ("The Birth of Liberty: Music

of the American Revolution," liner notes, p. 15, New World Records Album No. 80276, www.newworldrecords.org, 3 April 2006).

[3] Peter Wainwright was an English merchant who moved to Boston shortly after the American Revolution (*DAB*, entry on Jonathan Mayhew Wainwright).

[4] For Elizabeth (Betsy), Mary (Polly), and Louisa Smith, all daughters of William and Catharine Louisa Smith, see vol. 5:230, 231; 7:3, 112.

[5] Norton Quincy's housekeeper was probably Sarah Whiting Pope (1734–1800), the widow of Micajah Pope of Braintree. After Sarah Pope's death in 1800, AA commented to her sister Mary Smith Cranch in a letter of 15 Jan. 1801, "I feel most sensibly for our dear Respected and venerable uncle— I

know not, nor do I think it possible to supply to him the loss he has sustaind; tho mrs Popes temper was not pleasent, She was attentive towards him, knew all his wants and wishes— She was prudent and saveing of his interest—and had many excellent qualities" (Sprague, *Braintree Families*, p. 3853, 3855; MWA:Abigail Adams Letters).

Sarah (Sally) Tailer (Taylor) (b. 1720) was the daughter of former Lt. Gov. William Tailer. JQA described her in his Diary as "a genuine old maid" and "an incessant talker" (Boston, *21st Report*, p. 68; *Diary*, 2:269, 270).

[6] Joseph Cranch (1746–1806), a nephew of Richard Cranch, married his cousin Eliza-beth Palmer on 2 May 1790. He was trained as a gunsmith and served for a time as the superintendant of the U.S. armory at West Point, N.Y. (*Braintree Town Records*, p. 870; *Grandmother Tyler's Book*, p. 56, 109–110).

[7] William Cranch studied with Thomas Dawes (1757–1825), Harvard 1777, a Boston lawyer who later became associate justice of the Massachusetts Supreme Court. Dawes and Cranch married, respectively, sisters Margaret and Anna Greenleaf (*Sibley's Harvard Graduates*, 19:forthcoming).

[8] Hannah Austin of Charlestown, daughter of Nathaniel and Anna Kent Austin, died on 3 Sept. 1787 at age 24 (*Massachusetts Gazette*, 9 Sept.).

William Stephens Smith to Abigail Adams Smith

Falmouth, August 22d, 1787.

I wrote you, my love, the first thing I did after my landing here on the 20th;[1] I then proposed setting off from this, yesterday or this morning; but I am in *check*. I was yesterday at 4 o'clock, visited by an ague and fever, which shook and warmed me alternately pretty tolerably; this day I am free from it, and with the advice of a very good doctor who attends me, I hope soon to be allowed to put myself in motion towards one who possesses all my affections and merits all my love. The acquaintance which I formed in this place when I arrived from America,[2] and the letters of introduction which I brought from Lisbon, insure me every civility and respect I can wish. I am visited and attended in a very particular manner, and want for nothing but to be enabled to bid them farewell, and hasten to you. It is a painful detention to be so near, and upon the same island, and not be able to advance. You must not write, my friend, for I am in hopes before this reaches you to be on my way to you. I shall pass through Exeter, Taunton, Bath, Marlborough, &c., as being the best road—having the best horses and accommodations—for a few days longer, and this painful separation I hope will be at an end.

Yours, W. S. S.

MS not found. Printed from AA2, *Jour. and Corr.*, 1:200–201.

[1] See AA2, *Jour. and Corr.*, 1:199–200.

[2] WSS had traveled through Falmouth on his way to London to take up his appointment as secretary to the U.S. legation in May 1785 (Roof, *Smith and Lady*, p. 90).

John Adams to Cotton Tufts

Dear Sir   Grosvenor Square Aug. 27. 1787

You mention to Mrs Adams a Piece of Land adjoining to me, of 56 Acres at 25^s an Acre: but are at a Loss, whether it will be for my Interest to purchase it, as you are not informed of my Views, &c.— My View is to lay fast hold of the Town of Braintree and embrace it, with both my Arms and all my might. there to live—there to die— there to lay my Bones—and there to plant one of my Sons, in the Profession of the Law & the Practice of Agriculture, like his Father.— To this End I wish to purchase as much Land there, as my Utmost forces will allow, that I may have Farm enough to amuse me and employ me, as long as I live. that I may not rust, alive.— You will therefore oblige me very much if you will purchase that Piece of Land and every other, that adjoins upon me, which is offered to Sale, at what you shall judge an Advantagious Price, especially Salt Marsh & Wood land.[1] I know very well, that I could employ my little Modicum of Means more profitably—But in no Way so much to my Taste and humour—or so much for my Health and Happiness. To the Publik I have been long enough a Slave, and to little enough Profit. in other Words I have made more than my share of Sacrifices. Had I followed my own Business with as much Attention and Industry as I have those of the Publick, I could have owned, the whole Town of Braintree at this hour, or the Value of it, for what I know, without running one risque. Now I must be content to be poor, and my Children too, unless they Should have more Wisdom than I have had. If I Serve the Publick, in future, it must be in Retirement and in my own Way, with the feeble share of Forces that remain to me, and the short Period of time: for you will remember I am not a Child nor a Youth, nor a middle Aged Man, nor has my Carcass or my Spirit, been Spared, for old Age.

My dear Love to all our good Friends, and believe me ever yours.

                                                        John Adams.

RC (MHi:Misc. Bound Collection); addressed by WSS: "Honble· Cotton Tufts Esquire / Boston—"; internal address: "The Hon. Cotton Tufts Esq"; endorsed: "J. Adams Esq / Aug. 27. 1787."

[1] See Cotton Tufts to AA, 30 June, and note 3, above.

Thomas Jefferson to Abigail Adams

Dear Madam   Paris Aug. 30. 1787.

I have omitted writing sooner to you in expectation that Colõ Smith would have taken this in his route: but receiving now information from him that he embarks from Lisbon, I avail myself of the opportunity by mr̃ Payne of thanking you for the disbursements you were so kind as to make for my daughter in London, and of stating to you our accounts as follows.

	£	s	d
Disbursements of mrs̃ Adams as summed up in her state of them[1]	10	15	8
Error in addition to her prejudice	1	0	6
	11	16	2
Cash paid by Petit to mrs̃ Adams, viz. 6. Louis d'ors @ 19/6	5	17	-
paid by do· for black lace 75₶. which at the same exchange is	3	1	-
do· for 2. doz. pr̃ gloves 37₶–12ˢ	1	10	6
balance due to mrs̃ Adams	1	7	8
	11	16	2

which balance I will beg the favor of Colo· Smith to pay you and to debit me with.

I am afraid, by the American papers, that the disturbances in Massachusets are not yet at an end. mr̃ Rucker who is arrived here, gives me a terrible account of the luxury of our ladies in the article of dress. he sais that they begin to be sensible of the excess of it themselves, and to think a reformation necessary. that proposed is the adoption of a national dress. I fear however they have not resolution enough for this. I rejoice in the character of the lady who accompanies the Count de Moustier to America, and who is calculated to reform these excesses as far as her example can have weight. simple beyond example in her dress, tho neat, hating parade & etiquette, affable, engaging, placid, & withal beautiful, I cannot help hoping a good effect from her example. she is the Marquise de Brehan, sister in law to the Count de Moustier, who goes partly on account of a feeble health, but principally for the education of her son (of 17. years of age) which she hopes to find more masculine there & less exposed to seduction.[2] the Count de Moustier is of a character well assorted to this. nothing niggardly, yet orderly in his affairs, genteel but plain, loving society upon an easy not a splendid tone, unreserved, honest, & speaking our language like a native. he goes with excellent notions & dispositions, and is as likely to give satisfaction as any man that could have been chosen in France. he is much a whig in the politics of his own country. I understand there is a possibility that Congress will remove to Philadelphia.— my daughter talks of you often & much, still fancies she is to pay you the visit she promised. in the mean time she is very contented in the Convent with her sister.[3] both join me in compliments to mr͡s Smith and in assurances to yourself of the attachment & respect which I have the honour to proffer for them as well as for, dear Madam, your most obedient & most humble servant   Th: Jefferson

RC (Adams Papers); addressed: "M^rs· Adams / London"; internal address: "M^rs· Adams."; endorsed by AA2: "Mr Jefferson August 30th 1787."

[1] See AA to Thomas Jefferson, 10 July, above.

[2] Elénore François Elie, Comte de Moustier, France's minister to the United States, arrived in New York in Jan. 1788. Their official relationship notwithstanding, the Marquise de Bréhan, an artist, was widely believed to be the Comte de Moustier's mistress. Her son Armand Louis Fidèle de Bréhan (1770–1828) later served in the Royal Lorraine cavalry and became the Marquis de Bréhan (Jefferson, *Papers*, 12:66, 219; 14:291, 340–341; *Doc. Hist. Ratif. Const.*, 9:877–878; Washington, *Diaries*, 5:417). See also AA2 to AA, 18 May, below.

[3] Martha and Mary Jefferson were educated at the convent school of the Abbey of Pentemont in Paris. Both girls apparently enjoyed their school, and Martha even gave some consideration to becoming a nun, a vocation her father opposed (Jefferson, *Papers*, 14:xl–xli, 356–357).

Abigail Adams to Thomas Jefferson

Dear sir   London Sep^br 10th [1787]

your obliging favours of july and August came safe to Hand. the first was brought during my absence on an excursion into the Country. I was very happy to find by it, that you had received your daughter safe, and that the dear Girl was contented. I never felt so attached to a child in my Life on so short an acquaintance, tis rare to find one possessd of so strong & lively a sensibility. I hope she will not lose her fine spirits within the walls of a convent, to which I own I have many, perhaps false prejudices.

Mr Appleton delivererd my Lace & gloves Safe. be so good as to let Petit know that I am perfectly satisfied with them. Col smith has paid me the balan[ce whic]h you say was due to me, and I take your word for it, but [I do] not know how. the Bill which was accepted, by mr Ada[ms i]n the absence of col Smith, I knew would become due, in our absence, and before we could receive your orders. the money was left with Brisler our Servant, who paid it when it was presented. on our return we found the Bill which you had drawn on mr Tessier, but upon presenting it he refused to pay it, as he had not received any letter of advise tho it was then more than a month from its date, but he wrote immediatly to mr Grand, and by return of the next post, paid it.[1]

with regard to your Harpsicord, Col Smith who is now returnd, will take measures to have it Sent to you. I went once to mr Kirkmans to inquire if it was ready. his replie was, that it should be ready in a few days, but [. . . .][2] no orders further than to report when it was [. . . .][3] to write you, but he seemd to think that he had done all [that was] required of him.[4] The Canister addrest to mr Drayton deliverd to mr Hayward with Special directions, and he assured me he would not fail to deliver it.

The ferment and commotions in Massachusetts has brought upon the Surface abundance of Rubbish; but Still there is Some sterling metal in the political crusible. the vote which was carried against an emission of paper money by a large majority in the House, shews that they have a sense of justice: which I hope will prevail in every department of the State. I send a few of our News papers, some of which contain Sensible speculations.[5]

To what do all the political motions tend w[hic]h are agitating France Holland and Germany? will Liberty finally gain the assendency, or arbitrary power Strike her dead.

Is the report true that is circulated here, that mr Littlepage has a commission from the King of Poland to his most Christian Majesty?![6]

we have not any thing from mr Jay later than 4th of july. there was not any congress then, or expected to be any; untill the convention rises at Philadelphia[7]

Col Smith I presume will write you all the politiks of the Courts he has visited—and I will not detain you longer than to assure you that I am at all times / your Friend and Humble Servant   A A

RC (DLC:Jefferson Papers); endorsed: "Adams mrs." Some loss of text where the seal was removed and due to a torn manuscript.

[1] Louis Tessier had served as the Adamses' London banker since 1780. Ferdinand Grand had performed the same function in Paris since 1778 (JA, *Papers*, 9:140, 245, 393, 398, note 3; JA, *D&A*, 2:303; Jefferson, *Papers*, 12:194).

² Approximately three words missing.

³ Approximately three words missing.

⁴ The firm of Jacob Kirckman (1710–1792) and his nephew Abraham Kirckman (1737–1794) was one of London's leading harpsichord makers in the late eighteenth century. Jacob came to London from Alsace in the 1720s and began producing instruments in 1744. The firm shifted from harpsichord to piano construction after its founder's death and operated until the end of the nineteenth century. Thomas Jefferson purchased a Kirckman harpsichord in 1786 (Raymond Russell, *The Harpsichord and Clavichord: An Introductory Study*, N.Y., 1973, p. 79, 82, 90–91).

⁵ The *Massachusetts Gazette*, 26 June 1787, reported that on 23 June, the House of Representatives had rejected a motion to issue paper money by a majority of 56.

⁶ Lewis Littlepage (1762–1802), a native of Virginia, was appointed chamberlain by King Stanislaus II of Poland on 2 March 1786. He negotiated treaties for Poland with Russia and Spain and served as a secret commissioner to France and other European courts (*DAB*).

⁷ John Jay reported to JA on 4 July 1787 that the proceedings of the Constitutional Convention had brought the activities of Congress to a standstill; consequently, he had found no opportunity to present formally JA's resignation. If the secret proceedings of the convention were to fail, Jay wrote, "the Duration of the Union will become problematical. For my own Part I am convinced that a national Government as strong as may be compatible with Liberty is necessary to give us national Security and Respectability" (Adams Papers).

Abigail Adams to Mary Smith Cranch

my dear sister   Sepbr 15ᵗʰ [*1787*] Grosvenour Square

When I wrote you last, I was just going to Set out on a journey to the West of England. I promised you to visit mr Cranchs Friends and Relatives, this we did as I shall relate to you we were absent a month, and made a Tour of about six hundred Miles. the first place we made any stay at, was Winchester. There was formerly an Earl of Winchester, by the Name of Saar de Quincy. he was created Earl of Winchester by King john in 12.24. and Signed Magna Charta, which I have seen, the original being now in the British Museum with his Hand writing to it.¹

it is said that the year 1321 the Title became extinct, through failure of male Heirs, but I rather think through the poverty of some branch unable to contend for it. the family originally came from Normandy in the Time of William the Conquerer. they bear the same Arms with those of our Ancestors except that ours Substituded an animal for the crest in lieu, of an Earls coronet. I have a perfect remembrance of a parchment in our Grandmothers possession, which when quite a child I used to amuse myself with. this was a Geneological Table which gave the descent of the family from the Time of William the conquerer this parchment mr Edmund Quincy borrowed on some occasion, & I have often heard our Grandmother Say with some anger, that she could never recover it. as the old Gentleman is still living, I wish mr Cranch would question him

3. QUINCY COAT OF ARMS, BY ELIZA SUSAN QUINCY, 1822
See page x

about it, & know what Hands it went into, & whether there is a probability of its ever being recoverd, and be so good as to ask uncle Quincy how our Grandfather came by it, & from whence our Great Granfather came? where he first Settled? & take down in writing all you can learn from him, & mr Edmund Quincy respecting the family.[2] you will Smile at my Zeal, perhaps on this occasion, but can it be wonderd at, that I should wish to Trace an Ancesstor amongst the Signers of Magna Carta, amongst those who voted against receiving an explanatory Charter in the Massachusetts, Stands the Name of our venerable Grandfather, accompanied only with one other. this the journals of the House will shew to his immortal honour.[3] I do not expect either titles or estate from the Recovery of the Geneoligical Table, were there any probability of obtaining it, yet if I was in possession of it, money should not purchase it from me.

But to return to winchester, it is a very ancient place, and was formerly the residence of the Saxon and Norman Kings. there still remains a very famous Cathedral church, in the true Gothic Architecture, being partly built in the year 1079.[4] I attended divine service there, but was much more entertaind with the Venerable and Majestic appearence of the Ancient pile, than with the Modern flimsy discourse of the preacher, a meaner performance I do not recollect to have heard, but in a Church which would hold several thousands it might truly be said, two or three, were met together,[5] and those appeard to be the lower order of the people. from Winchester we proceeded to Southhampton, which is a very pretty sea port Town and much frequented during the summer months as a Bathing place, and here for the first time in my Life I tried the experiment. it would be delightfull in our warm weather as well as very salubrious if such conveniencys were Erected in Boston, Braintree, Weymouth, which they might be with little expence. the places are under cover, you have a woman for a Guide, a small dressing room to yourself an oil cloth cap, a flannel Gown and socks for the feet;[6] we tarried only two days at Southhampton, and went ten miles out of our way in order to visit Weymouth merely for its Name. this like my Native Town is a Hilly country a small sea port, with very little buisness, & wholy supported by the resort of company during the Summer Months, for those persons who have not Country Houses of their own, resort to the Watering places as they are call'd, during the summer months, it being too vulgar and unfashionable to remain in London, but where the object of one is Health, that of 50 is pleasure, however far they fall short of the object. this whole Town is the property of a widow Lady. Houses are built by the Tenants & taken at Life Rents, which upon the discease of the Leasors revert back again to the owner of the Soil; thus is the landed property of this Country vested in Lordships, and in the Hands of the Rich altogether. the pesantry are but slaves to the Lord, notwithstanding the mighty boast they make of Liberty, 6 pence & 7 pence pr day is the usual wages given to Labourers, who are to feed themselves out of the pittance. in travelling through a Country fertile as the Garden of Eden, loaded with a Golden harvest, plenty Smiling on every side, one would imagine the voice of poverty was rarely heard, and that she was seldom seen, but in the abodes of indolence and vice, but it is far otheways. the Money earned by the sweat of the Brow must go to feed the pamperd Lord & fatten the Greedy Bishop, whilst the misierble shatterd thatched roof cottage crumbles to the dust for the want of repair. to hundreds & hundreds of these abodes have I been a witness in my late journey. the cheering Rays of the Sun are totally excluded, unless they find admittance through the decayed roof equally exposed to cold & the inclemnant season, a few Rags for a Bed, a joint Stool, comprise the chief of their furniture, whilst their own appearence is more wretched, than one can well conceive. during the season of Hay and Harvest, Men women & children are to be seen labouring in the Fields, but as this is a very small part of the year, the little they acquire then is soon expended, and how they keep soul and Body together the remainder of the year; is very hard to tell. it must be oweing to this very unequal distribution of property that the poor rate, is become such an intollerable burden. the inhabitants are very thinly scatterd through the Country, though large Towns are well peopled. to reside in & near London, and to judge of the Country from what one sees here, would be forming a very eronious opinion. How little cause of complaint have the inhabitants of the united States, when they compare their Situation, not with despotic monarchies, but with this Land of Freedom? the ease with which honest industry may acquire property in America the equal distribution of justice, to the poor as well as the rich, and the personal Liberty they enjoy, all all call upon them to support their Governments and Laws, to respect their Rulers, and gratefully acknowledge their Superiour Blessings, least Heaven in wrath Should Send them a. . . .

From Weymouth our next excursion was to Axmister the first Town in the County of Devonshire. it is a small place, but has two manufactures of Note, one of Carpets & one of Tapes—both of

4. ADVERTISEMENT FOR SAYER'S BATHING MACHINE, 1791
See page xi

which we visited; the manufactory of the carpets is wholy performed by women and children. you would have been suprized to see, in how ordinary a Building this rich manufactory was carried on, a few glass windows in some of our Barns would be equal to it. they have but two prices for their carpets wove here, the one is Eighteen shilling, and the other 24, a square yard. they are wove of any dimensions you please, and without a seam, the coulours are most beautifull, and the carpets very durable here we found mr J Cranch, he dined with us, and we drank Tea with him; this is a curious Genious, he is a middle sizd man of a delicate countanance, but quite awkerd in his manners. he seldom looks one in the Face, and seems as if he had been crampd and cow'd in his youth; in company one is pained for him, yet is he a man of Reading and an accurate taste in the fine Arts, poetry, painting, musick, sculpture, Architecture; all of them have engaged his attention. his profession does not seem to be the object of his affections, and he has given up the practise, with an intention of persueing some other employment; he appears to me to be a man whose soul wants a wider expansion than his situation & circumstances allow. dejected spirits he is very liable to, I do not think him a happy man, his sentiments are by no means narrow or contracted; yet he is one by himself— he accompanied us in our journey to Exeter Plimouth and Kings-Bridge. at Exeter we tarried from Saturday till monday afternoon mr Bowering came to visit us. you know him by character, he appears a Friendly honest worthy man, active in buisness a warm and Zealous Friend to America, ready to serve his Friends, and never happier than when they will give him an opportunity of doing it his wife and daughter were on a visit to their Friends at Kings Bridge, so that we did not see them. he requested however that we would drink tea with him after meeting, and as our intention was to see mr Cranchs Brother Andrew, he engaged to get him to his House. the old Gentleman came, with some difficulty, for he is very lame and infirm; he seemd glad to see us, and asked many questions, respecting his Brother & sister in America. I think he must have had a paralityc stroke as his Speach is thick. he has not been able to do any buisness for a Number of years, and I believe is chiefly supported by his son, who is in the Clothiers buisness with mr Bowering. Mrs Cranch, tho near as old as her Husband, is a little smart, sprightly active woman, and is wilted just enough to last to perpetuity. She told me that her Husband took it very hard that his Brother had not written to him for a long time. I promised her that he should hear from him before long;

and I know he will not let me be surety for him; without fulfilling my engagement. mr Cranchs daughter married mr Bowerings Brother, they have three sons. she is a sprightly woman like her Mother, and mr Bowerings daughter married a son of mr Natll Cranchs, so that the family is doubly linked together, and what is more; they all seem united, by the strongest ties of family harmony and Love.[7] from Exeter we went to plimouth there we tarried Several days, and visited the fortifications, plimouth dock, & crossd over the water to mount Edgcume; a seat belonging to Lord Edgcume.[8]

the Natural advantages of this place are superiour to any I have before seen, commanding a wide and extensive view of the ocean, the whole Town of plimouth, and the adjacent Country with the Mountain of cornwall— I have not much to Say with respect to the improvements of art, there is a large park well stockd with Deer, and some shady walks, but there are no Grottos Statuary Sculpture or Temples.—

at Plimouth we were visited by a mr & mrs Sawry; with whom we drank Tea one afternoon; mr Sawry is well known to many Americans, who were prisoners in plimouth jail during the late war. the money which was raised for their relief, past through his Hands and he was very kind to them, assisting many in their escape.—[9] from plimouth we made an enterprize one day to Horsham and as we attempted it in a coach & four, we made a curious peice of work, taking by mistake a wrong road, but this part of my story I must reserve for my dear eliza.

our next Movement was a Kings Bridge, but before I relate this, I ought to inform you, that we made a stop at a place call Ivey Bridge where we dined, and mr Adams accompanied mr Cranch to Brook about 3 miles distant, to visit his uncle mr William Cranch, who has been for several years quite lost to himself and Friends. there is some little property in the hands of the family who take charge of him, sufficient to Support a person who has no more wants than he has. he appeard clean & comfortable, but took no notice either of the conversation, or persons. the only thing which in the least roused him, was the mention of his wife, he appeard to be wrestless when that Subject was touchd. The Character of this Man, as given by all his Friends and acquaintance, leads one to regreet in a particular manner the loss of his intellects, possesst of a Genious superiour to his station, a thirst for knowledge which his circumstances in Life permitted him not to persue, most amiable and engageing in his manners, formed to have adornd a superiour Rank in Life, fondly attachd to an amiable wife, whom he very soon lost, he fell a sacrifice to a too great Sensibility, unable to support the shock, he grew melancholy and was totally lost.—[10] But to return to Kings Bridge, the Chief resort of the Cranch family. we arrived at the Inn, about Six oclock a saturday Evening, about 8 we were saluted with a ringing of Bells—a circumstance we little expected. very soon we were visited by the various Branches of the Cranch family both male & female amounting to 15 persons, but as they made a strange jumble in my Head, I persuaded my fellow Traveller to make me out a Genealogical Table, which I send you.[11] mr & mrs Burnell mr & mrs Trathan, both offerd us beds and accommodations at their houses, but we were too numerous to accept their Kind invitation, tho we engaged ourselves to dine with mr Burnell, & to drink Tea with mr Trathan the next day. Mrs Burnell has a strong resemblance to mrs palmer she is a Geenteel woman, and easy & polite. we dinned at a very pretty dinner, and after meeting drank Tea at the other House mr Trathans. their Houses are very small, but every thing neat and comfortable, mr Burnel is a shoe maker worth 5000 pounds and mr Trathan a Grocier in good circumstances.[12] the rest of the families joind us at the two houses. they are all serious industerius good people amongst whom the greatest family harmony appears to Subsist. the people of this County appear more like our Newengland people than any I have met with in this Country before, but the distinction between Tradesmen & Gentry as they are termd is widely different from those distinctions in our Country. with us in point of Education and manners the Learned professions and many merchants Farmers & Tradesmen, are upon an equality with the Gentry of this Country. it would be degrading to compare them with many of the Nobility here. as to the Ladies of this Country their manners appear to be totally depraved, it is in the middle ranks of society, that virtue & morality are yet to be found. nothing does more injury to the Female Character, than frequenting publick places, and the rage which prevails now for the Watering places and the increased Number of them, is become a National evil as it promotes and encourages dissapation, mixes all characters promiscuously, is the resort of the most unprincipald female characters who are not ashamed to shew their faces wherever men dare to go modesty and diffidence, are calld ill Breeding, and Ignorance of the world. an impudent stare, is substituted in lieu of that modest deportment and that retireing Grace which aws, whilst it enchants. I have never seen a female Modle here, of such unaffected modest, & sweetly amiable manners, as mrs Guile mrs Russel, & many other American females exhibit.—

Having filld 8 pages I think it is near time to hasten to a close. Cushing and Folger are both arrived, by each I have received Letters from you. a new sheet of paper must contain a replie to them, this little Space Shall assure you of what is not confined to Time or place / the ardent affection of your / sister   A Adams.

RC (MWA:Abigail Adams Letters).

[1] Saer de Quincy (d. 1219) was created the 1st Earl of Winchester in 1207. He was one of the 25 barons who demanded that King John accept the provisions of the Magna Carta in 1215. Contrary to AA's comments, none of the barons signed the actual charter. AA may have seen instead a list of the barons, two of which were held by the British Museum (*DNB*; J. C. Holt, *Magna Carta*, 2d edn., Cambridge, Eng., 1992, p. 56–57, 478; Claire Breay, *Magna Carta: Manuscripts and Myths*, London, 2002, p. 38).

[2] AA's hope that she was descended from Saer de Quincy was apparently misplaced. AA's American ancestors, however, did use the coat of arms of one of his sons, for which see Descriptive List of Illustrations, No. 3, above. A twentieth-century study rejected the claim of descent from Saer de Quincy, instead documenting the American line to William Quincy of Aldwynkle, Northampton (ca. 1485–1550), and tentatively extending it to Geoffrey Quincy of Suffolk (b. ca. 1290). The fate of the parchment genealogy to which AA refers is unknown (*DNB*; MHi:Quincy Family Papers; George Bellew, "English Ancestry of the Quincy Family," *NEHGR*, 92:30–31 [Jan. 1938]).

[3] The original 1629 charter of Massachusetts was dissolved in 1684 and replaced by a second charter of 1691. While the original had assigned all governing powers to local officials, the second gave the king the power to appoint the governor and provincial council and to veto laws. The Explanatory Charter of 1725/26 amended that of 1691 and further reduced local control. Fearing that a refusal to accept the Explanatory Charter would result in additional curtailments, 48 members of the Massachusetts House of Representatives voted to accept it. AA's grandfather, John Quincy (1689–1767), was among the 32 members who voted against it (Rich-

ard L. Bushman, *King and People in Provincial Massachusetts*, Chapel Hill, 1985, p. 11–12, 31, 114; Mass., *House Jour.*, 1724–1726, 6:457–460).

[4] The building of Winchester Cathedral commenced around 1079. It was dedicated in 1093 although its construction is believed to have continued until ca. 1120. At the time of its building, it was the longest church in Britain and the second longest in Europe, measuring roughly 540 feet from end to end (Christopher Brooke, "Bishop Walkelin and His Inheritance," in John Crook, ed., *Winchester Cathedral: Nine Hundred Years, 1093–1993*, West Sussex, 1993, p. 3).

[5] "For where two or three are gathered together in my name, there am I in the midst of them" (Matthew, 18:20). The phrase appears in the Prayer of St. Chrysostom in the Anglican *Book of Common Prayer*, commonly used for Morning Prayer services.

[6] Sea bathing and English seaside resorts became popular in the mid-eighteenth century among the aristocracy and gentry who sought out new venues for holidays, entertainment, and the medical benefits of the sea. Resorts became places of social mingling as the habit of the seaside holiday quickly spread among the merchant, professional, and working classes, and rising income levels provided leisure time, opportunities for pleasure, and conspicuous displays of wealth. Bathing was segregated by gender and required a bathing machine, for which see Descriptive List of Illustrations, No. 4, above (John K. Walton, *The English Seaside Resort: A Social History 1750–1914*, New York, 1983, p. 5–13, 182).

[7] John Bowring was in the clothiers business with Christopher Cranch, whose mother, Sally Bowring, was married to Andrew Cranch (d. 1787), Richard Cranch's brother. Andrew and Sally also had three daughters:

Julia, Sally, and Mary Ann. Another of Richard's brothers, Nathaniel Cranch, had four sons: Nathaniel Jr., Jeremiah, Andrew, and Richard (JA, *D&A*, 3:207–210; MHi:Cranch-Bond Papers, Extract from a Register of the Bond and Cranch Families, 1852). See also AA to John Bowring, [*ante* 30 *March 1788*], below.

⁸ Mount Edgcumbe House was built in 1553 by Sir Richard Edgcumbe, sheriff of Devonshire (1499–1562). The current occupant of the estate was his descendant, George Edgcumbe, Viscount Mount-Edgcumbe and Valletort (1721–1795), a retired admiral of the Royal Navy (*DNB*).

⁹ Miles Saurey, a linen draper of Plymouth, England, assisted American prisoners at Mill Prison during the Revolution by providing them with food, clothing, newspapers, and cash (JA, *Papers*, 12:89, note 2; Laurens, *Papers*, 15:469).

¹⁰ William Cranch married Elizabeth Fairweather of Horsecombe, England. She died six weeks after the marriage; he died on 21 Feb. 1788 (Richard Cranch to William Bond, 19 May 1788, Extract from a Register of the Bond and Cranch Families, 1852, both MHi:Cranch-Bond Papers).

¹¹ Not found.

¹² On 10 March 1788 William Cranch of Kingsbridge reported that "Our old Neighbour Mʳ· Trathan died about a fortnight agone in a violent Fit of the Asthma" (Richard Cranch to William Bond, 19 May 1788, MHi:Cranch-Bond Papers).

Cotton Tufts to Abigail Adams

Dear Cousin   Weymouth Sepᵗ· 20. 1787

Yours & Mʳ· Adams of the 1ᵗ· & Yours of the 4ᵗʰ· of July I recᵈ· the 6ᵗʰ· Inst. the former by a British Vessell the latter by the Way of New York—¹ being then in Boston, I immediately applied to our Friend Dʳ· Wilch to prepare the Way for the Purchase of Borlands Farm thinking it best to conceal your Name, till we were sure of accomplishing the Business— The Dʳ· applied and found that Mʳ B. was then repairing the House, that his Mother was to remove into it shortly and that Mʳ· B. had given up the Thoughts of selling it, but upon the whole Mʳ B. said that he would sell it for £800 the Dʳ· offered him £550 & left him Mʳ· B. having so far receeded as to say that 700 was his Ultimatum— After some Days the Dʳ· saw him again, found him disposed to converse on the Subject & finally offered him £600 including the Repairs, which after a few Days Consideration he agreed to and as soon as I have raised the Money by Bills shall close the whole and make such Repairs as are of Necessity for securing the Buildig, I shall send you the Dimensions of the Floors—all paper Hangings are prohibited from Importation If I remember right—and the best & neatest are made here at a very reasonable Price— I wish for your particular Direction with respect to Paintings and the Color if you have any particular Choice The Repairs must be very considerable— Mʳ B——d compleated all matters with Mʳ· T——r. and is in full Possession of all the Lands, except those sold to Deac W[eb]b & Bass which Mʳ B. has given them a Deed of— Mʳ· T. is said to have expended £100 lawful money on the

Build^{g.} &c and in the Purchase of Materials, such as were not used on the Buildings were swept off by his Creditors—the Wind Mill gone also to them— I have repaired Belchers House at as little Expense as I could possibly and have made it, tenantable—have also made a New Fence between that Place & the Wid^w Veseys adjoining— There is wanting a great Quantity of manure for your Lands, I have made repeated Enquiries but cannot as yet obtain any—it is every where engaged— The Spirit of Husbandry rises fast— People are dayly improving the Mode of managing their Farms—the great Price which English Hay bore for many Years—has produced such an Increase as to reduce the Price as low or lower than it was before the Revolution— Salt Hay is less in Use & consequently Salt marsh less valuable— Grain is more cultivated than formerly— My Friend on revisiting his Farm will not find it in such a State as to meet his Wishes— Our Scituation has neither encouraged nor permitted any further Exertions than what present Necessity required—and I am pretty sure that the Picture of Barreness & Poverty exhibited I wish it may not be known to any Body, that I ever had Instructions for buying that Place—unless hereafter it should be purchased—[2] in Veseys Place will extinguish any Inclination for the Possession of it— And as M^{r.} A—— has not seen it for many Years—I know He will forgive me if I postpone the Purchase, till He can personally judge of the Quality of it &c

You have before this Time rec^{d.} Letters by Capt Cushing & others—from your Friends. My Letters have informed You of the Terms agreed upon with Mr. Parsons for the Instruction of Y^r Son—also of the Part assignd Him at Commencment—the applause he obtained and of his Design to enter on his Studies in Sept^{r.}— Last Week He went to Newbury for that purpose— By a Calculation we made His annual Expence including his Instruction will amount to £90 Pr. Ann^{m.} He boards @ 15/ per Week which was the lowest Price we could obtain— The Expence for the Children for the last Year youll be able to form some Judgment of by my Account enclosed,[3] tho not so fully as if it had been more particular but much writing I am both for want of Time & weakness of Eye Sight obliged to avoid— Mr John did not call upon me for Pocket Money while at College— He is prudent and knows how to use Money— In my Account you will form some Judgment of what has been delivered to Charles & Thos. If it exceeds your Expectations I wish for your Remarks— their Quarter Bills are delivered in to me and are in general personally discharged by me— Necessaries (if they are to be called such) Tea,

Sugar & Liquors have been generally procured for them, that Buttery Scores might be prevented—and as all Articles from the Buttery I find to be charged at a large Advance, I have advised them in future to have no Account at the Buttery— a very considerable Part of the money paid your Sister was for purchasing Cloathes for the Children, discharging Taylors Bills &c—

The Produce of your half of the Farm amounted to about £30 the last year, a considerable Part of this is absorbed in Taxes & Services done by Pratt and is accounted for in the Settlement of his Account and no more of it enters into my Account than you find Credited to you— I have vested about £200 sterlg in public Securities part of which is included in this Acctt. & the Remainder in the next. I think it must be for your Advantage to lay out as little as may be in Lands at present and to keep as much as you can in personal Property that will not be visible and at the same Time productive. whether this may be best effected by the purchase of public Notes is problematical the Interest from them is distant, the Continental are at 2/6 per £ State Notes @ 3/6— Bills of Exchange are fallen much— They have been purchased within a fortnight past from £5 pr. Ct. to Par at 30 Days. I have sold one Bill this Day dated the 15th. Inst. to Mr. John Osborn of £150 sterlg at 30 Days Sight 5 pr Ct above par of which I have given Mr. Adams Notice in a Letter by Capt Kettlewell bound to Liverpool but am doubtful, whether I shall get so much again[4]

We are, in the Massachusetts, at present *in a State of Peace* and *Quietness*, waiting for the Result of the federal Convention— Pardon has been granted to all those Traitors that were under Sentence of Death— The sudden Departure of a small French Fleet which came here about 5 or 6 Weeks past and which were expected to have lain here for some Time longer, has occasioned much Speculation—and leads many to fear that Storms are rising in Europe and will shortly overspread many Nations.[5]

Mr. Adams's Defence has gone through several Editions in America—it has met with great Applause there are a few however, that seem to be disgusted with his Encomiums on the British Constitution and the Spirit which the Defence discovers against pure Democracy There are some whom we may suppose to be fomentors of Faction under british Influence and perhaps employed to poison the Minds of People & sew Discord, who have endeavoured to insinuate into the Minds of some People, That Mr. A. was for Monarchy and his Plan to introduce one of the young Princes of England to take the Throne in America the Remarks of the London Monthly Reviews have been published here a few Days past and those of the critical Reviewers follow them as a contrast—[6] The Ill nature of Great Britain towards America—American Ministers & American Productions will continue untill we have a national efficient Government—

I forgot to mention, that M^r. Thos. Allen late of Braintree died in S^o Carolina the 25 of Augt. last; previous to closing with Mr Borland, I sounded M^r. Abel respecting the of his Farm. He wished to sell it—but his Price I found to be from 28 to 3000 £ a Price so high that he will not be able to sell it— His Fathers Death will probably occasion the Sale of it at what it will fetch be it more or less—[7]

At Weymouth We are far advanced towards the Settlement of a Minister (Who is not a *married Man*) by name Mr Jacob Norton, Son of our Cous. Sam Norton Esq. of Abington, He will probably be ordained in a fortnight or Three Weeks— He is young, possesses good Abilities, & a good Character—as yet but little acquainted with the World—[8]

Our good and worthy Uncle Smith has for some Months manifested a declining State of Health; for years past he has been affected with a scorbutic Humour in one of his Legs— Sometime in July upon the going of a severe Cough, it became very troublesome accompanied with a swelling & Inflammation of the Limb which rose to such a Degree as to threaten a Mortification and for some Days every Symptom indicated the Loss of Life—the Danger however from his Limb subsided— But the general State of his Health gives us no very flattering Expectations of his recovering his former State and for Ten Days past, I cannot find any material Amendment other than in the diseased Limb—

24^t.

To morrow a Committee of the Overseers will visit our University we shall then have Specimens of the Students Improvements and I hope to have the Pleasure of seeing Mas^r Charles acquit himself with Honor—a Part in the Exhibition (I am informed) is assigned Him—

Our Cousin Willm. Cranch is studying Law with Mr Dawes—

I have taken a View of the Buildings & Fences, at Borlands, and find much to do— The West Room which is finished with Mohogany—Would you have it painted?—if so inform me— It would perhaps be an Amendment, if one or two Windows were cut out at the West End of it and the Closets removed. The Front Rooms below &

Chambers above as well as the outside of the House require Painting— The Walls of the East Room & Chamber over it must be papered or painted—the Hangings are all removed—

The Floor of the East Room below is 17 by 15 1/2 Feet If you provide a Floor Cloth, the Hearth I suppose must be taken out, which is 5 Feet long—18 Inches wide (I. E. projecting out to the Floor)— the West Room 16 by 16 1/2 Hearth 5 1/2 F$^{tt.}$ long 2 F$^{tt.}$ 2 Inches Wide— I am repairing the Windows (which will require a 15$^{l.}$ of Glass) and what else that may be of immediate necessity & shall make preparations against the Spring for completing the whole before which Time I shall receive your Instructions[9] You will embrace the first opp$^{y.}$ to give such Directions relative to the Buildings &c that you may think necessary

Adieu Your Affect$^{e.}$ Friend   Cotton Tufts—

RC (Adams Papers); endorsed: "Dr Tufts Sepbr / 20th 1788" and "Dr. Tufts Sepbr / 20 1787." Some loss of text due to a torn manuscript.

[1] JA's letter to Tufts of 1 July has not been found. In AA's 4 July letter, she repeats her 1 July request, above, that Tufts purchase the Borland property and states that she would send the letter by a second ship to ensure the message reaches him as soon as possible (Adams Papers).

[2] The previous 25 words were written at the bottom of the page and marked for insertion here.

[3] Not found.

[4] Possibly John Osborn, a merchant who sold paints and gold leaf in Boston in the 1780s (*NEHGR*, 27:422 [Oct. 1873], 140:231 [July 1986]).

Capt. Ottiwell Kettlewell of the brig *Favourite* sailed for Liverpool from Boston in early September (*Massachusetts Gazette*, 28 Aug.).

[5] The *Massachusetts Centinel* reported on 12 Sept. that a French cutter had arrived in Boston Harbor the day before bearing orders from Paris that the French fleet quartered in Boston should sail immediately. Growing fears in Paris that the tumultuous developments of the Patriot Revolution in Holland would embroil France and the other powers of Europe in a wider war likely prompted the orders (Washington, *Papers, Confederation Series*, 5:348–349, 361–362).

[6] The review of JA's *Defence of the Const.* from the May issue of the London *Monthly Review* was reprinted in the *Massachusetts Centinel* on 12 September. See also AA to Elizabeth Smith Shaw, 2 May, and note 3; AA to Richard Cranch, 10 May, and note 1; and AA to JA, 7 June, and note 6, all above.

[7] Thomas Alleyne (d. 1787) owned the Braintree estate of immigrant Edmund Quincy (1602–1637), AA's great-great-great-grandfather. A Quincy descendant had sold the property in 1763, and AA had long hoped to reacquire it. Widow Mary Alleyne (d. 1781) purchased the property in 1769 and willed it to her son Thomas and his wife, Dorothy Harbin Alleyne. Their son Abel (d. 1807) sold the 258-acre property at auction in Jan. 1788 to Benjamin Beale of Dorchester for £981 (Sprague, *Braintree Families*, p. 176R, 178, 179, 3975R, 3983R; vol. 4:295–296; Suffolk County Deeds, 162:73–74).

[8] Jacob Norton (1764–1858), Harvard 1786, was ordained minister of the First Church in Weymouth on 10 Oct.; he would eventually marry Elizabeth Cranch on 11 Feb. 1789. The parish had been searching for a permanent replacement since the 1783 death of AA's father, Rev. William Smith, and Norton would remain in the Weymouth pulpit for 37 years. His father, Samuel (1721–1810), was a first cousin of both Cotton Tufts and AA's mother (*Harvard Quinquennial Cat.*, p. 201; *NEHGR*, 12:184 [April 1858]; vol. 7:111; *History of Weymouth*, 4:444–445; *History of Hingham*, 3:92–94).

[9] From this point on, the remainder of the letter was written sideways in the margin.

Mercy Otis Warren to Abigail Adams

Milton Sept 22 1787

I thank my dear Mrs Adams for Mrs Montagues observation, on the writings of shakespear which I received by Calihan.

though every part of your letters always Give me pleasure I found a Certain Satisfaction peculiar in that paragraph in your last which Gives an intimation that you mean to return to America in The Spring. uncertain as all human events are I cannot but look forward & in a degree anticipate the pleasure of haveing Friends I so highly esteem again in my Neighbourhood. & even if we should leave milton the distance to plimouth will appear very inconsiderable to so Great a traviller. But here reflection Gives a check to expectation— and when I survey the changes of time & the large portion I have already trodden over I Cannot have a right to Calculate for much: on this side the Grave. That silent asylum has my dear madam enwraped many you loved on this side the atlantic since you left us. You are doubtless prepared to see new tenants in the hospitable manssion of your uncle & aunt Smith.—

I Go this afternoon to Visit the Good M^rs allen who has lately recevied the sad tidings of the Death of her husband, who made his exit in the Carolinas where he was about to remove his Family.

Politics I shall leave till the next conveyance at least. as a dead Calm reigns among us that I fear will be suceeded by contrary appearances when the doings of The Convention are divulged or at least before we have a strong permanent a Wise tranquil & Free Goverment: many are dispossed to adapt the result of Their deliberations be they what they may: others are perversly bent on opposition though ever so well digested a Federal plan may appear: a third Class will as obstinatly oppose what appears to them wrong as they will decidedly support whatever they think right: or that tends to the General welfare.— well—half a page on a subject I just promised not to touch. *thus* the *Itch* of scribling often betrays us into inconsistancy & somtimes exposes to other inconveniencies—but silence is impossed on my pen with regard to one of my most Respecteed & most punctual Correspondents had Mr Adams Condesended even to *answer* it would not have been so severe as a total neglect. and was it not for one circumstance I should suppose by the uniform reserve of the whole Family that a packet sent by Calihan to the american minister never reached his hand.[1] if it did he will Gratify my curiosity by the monosyllable Yes & I will not wound his delacacy by urging him to say more—

I am very sorry to hear you do not enjoy perfect health. but hope if your excussions over the pleasant Island of Great Britain dos not restore. a Voyage to america will reestablish a Blessing so necessary for the enjoyment of all Others.

Mr Warrens most Friedly regards to You & Yours accompany the best wishes of one who is happy in subscribing / Mr Adams & Your ever / affectionate Friend   M Warren

RC (Adams Papers); endorsed: "Mrs Warren / Sepbr 22 1787."

[1] Mercy Otis Warren's last extant letter to JA was dated 7 Jan. (Adams Papers). He replied on 25 Dec. (*Warren-Adams Letters*, 2:300–301).

Elizabeth Cranch to Abigail Adams

Braintree Septr. 23d. 1787—

A Letter from my dear Aunt Adams recievd last July remains unanswered;[1] I am almost ashamed to reccollect it; but for a long time indisposition tottally prevented my using my pen at all: it was under absolute prohibition— within these few weeks my health seems mending—& possibly I may injoy a comfortable degree of it this winter: the pleasing hope of your return in the Spring, which I now permit myself to cherish will I am sure have a great influence upon my body & mind— it will sofiten the dreary storms of december & shorten the duration of the rigorous Season; I have not one object in view which appears to me of half the importance—or that promises half the pleasure which your safe return will afford; my heart bounds at the idea, & my fancy portrays innumerable scenes of happiness in which *I* may be a participater, they are not illuminated by one ray of *Splendour*, but appear only enlightened by the mild radience of pure affection & Friendship—shall we not in reallity enjoy them? I am sincerely afflicted at your indisposition: with what ready assiduity of affection would I have attended you could I have been with you: & only have felt as if discharging a part of a debt which I had long ago contracted; in kind:— You can *never* know my dear Aunt how severely *we* have felt your absence; not all our other friends could possibly supply your place: tho absent, you make us feel your goodness continually, & your kindness to myself in particular demands much more than bare acknowledgements; at present they are all I can return—some future time may perhaps give me oppertunity of making some more suitable—

168

Congratulations may seem almost unseasonable by the time you recieve this upon the birth of your grandson: but I do really rejoice with you all—at the event; My Cousins happiness has I dare say recievd a large augmentation, & the exercise of maternal affection under all its different modifications will prove to her a constant source of delight: now will she find her own improvements of most essential service, when she finds it necessary "to rear the tender thought & teach the young Idea how to shoot—"[2] her own plans of education used to be perfectly rational—& if she can practise as well as she used to theorise—she will make an excellent Mother— I find she follows the examples of most Matrons—in laying aside the pen as not a utensil pertaining to domestick Life: but from her good Mamas example she may surely learn that the use of it is not by any means incompatible with the full performance of every domestick duty— I shall certainly give her a hint of it soon— You do not even mention her return with you; I suppose we may surely expect her—& must *she* live at N—York? cannot Coll[n.] Smith make it as advantageous to take up his abode in N—England?— *You* cannot surely part with her—so far!

My Cousin John, Mama has I suppose informed you—has fixd down in Newbury—& my Brother at Boston. they have both conducted so well thus far as to recieve universal praise & esteem— To tell you the satisfaction we all feel in consequence of it—would be unnecessary— My younger Cousins I hope will merit equal applause: Charles is a very lovely youth—& if Minerva will spread her shield as a defence from Cupids arrow—he will be safe—but Charles says "O Cousin Betsey! such heavenly Eyes; such lovely Hair—such a beautiful mouth—& above all such goodness—so amiable— Miss F—— is a most charming Girl—["] Alas poor Charles! Cousin Betsey very gravely advises him to ward off the shafts of beauty at present—& only sollicit the smiles of the Muses—but this is the cold precept of 24— One thing however secures my lovely Cousin, the impressions are not so deep—but that Novelty can efface them—& another observation—I have lately met with—& believe it generally true—of Beauty—"that its Caprice is a natural antidote to its poison—"[3] & more especially—it may happen so of the Beauty of 14— My Cousin Thomas said to me the other day with his usual *plainess* of expression—speaking of the disadvantage of having too much society with young Ladies in the years devoted to study—"for my part I dont care a sixpence about them *all*—& dont think *I* shall *ever* be in *Love*—" I belive he spoke the truth entirely—& mereley as a matter of *amuse-*

ment, the Gun & Ball have infinitely greater charms for him than— the most finshd face & form—& after *qualifying* & *mollifying*, his protestation, a little, I told him it had my entire approbation—

I am particularly obliged to you for [the] Books upon gardning— but my poor Garden makes but a s[. . .] I am however pleas'd with each individual flower—& watch with unremmiting care its rinng- ing—budding, blowing & decline—taken all together—they boast not of any beauty in appearance or disposition— Our Garden *is* & *ought* to be for use—a few little beds & borders are all which I call mine— when you leave England—if you should bring some flowers seeds from your Garden there—they may perhaps produce you some flow- ers here— those you sent me from France—many of them would not grow here—some I have now—& they have encreasd abundantly— Tommorrow My Sister & myself intend to go to Cambridge—to at- tend an exhibition the next Day—in which my Cousin Charles has a part— he has had one public performance before in which tis said he display'd many *real graces* of Oratory— Adieu my dear Madam—& present my best regards to my Uncle—& M^r & Mrs Smith—& believe most affectionately / Your Neice   E. Cranch—

RC (Adams Papers); addressed: "Mrs Adams— / Grosvenor—square."; endorsed: "E Cranch— / Sep^tr. 25. 1787." Some loss of text where the seal was removed.

[1] AA to Elizabeth Cranch, 18 July 1786, vol. 7:256–259.
[2] James Thomson, *The Seasons: Spring*, lines 1152–1153.
[3] "An antidote in female caprice lies / (Kind Heaven!) against the poison of their eyes" (Edward Young, *Love of Fame, the Universal Passion. Satire V. On Women*, lines 448–449).

Mary Smith Cranch to Abigail Adams

My dear Sister   Braintree September 23^d. 1787

I wrote to you about three weeks since thinking clallahan would sail immediatly but he is not yet gone & I find Folger will go before him—but my Letters will be old unless I add a short one now— I was not a little dissapointed by not receiving a Line by the Last vessel which arriv'd Doctor Tufts receiv'd one from you & he got it before those you sent by the way of new york[1] He will tell you about the Purchase he has made of Mr Borlands Estate for you—we think you have an excellent bargain. I am rejoic'd that you will have a house big enough to hold your self & Friends when they visit you—you must make a square house of it— It will take one large room to hold Mr Adams Books If you make it with Alcoves like the college Library it will make a beautiful appearence— We are amuseing ourselves with the alterations which it is probable you will make. I have seen your Mother Hall this Day—she is well & looks I tell her several years younger for the prospect she has of having you so near her. She wishes you here now nine months are nine years to one at her time of Life— you will have very agreable neighbours in Mr Woodwards Family, Doctor chancys Daughter Mrs Adams is a pritty sociable woman.[2] she Boards with them—but you have met with a real Loss in the Death of Mr Alleyne—He possess'd a most benevolent heart, never meant to injure any one & always rejoice'd to do good & make his fellow creatures happy— He dy'd going from Wilmington to charlestown—was out but four days— we have not yet heard his dissorder you know what a Family of Love they were & will not wonder that they are greatly afflected Mr Abel tells me the House & Farm must be sold immediately. I wish you had it—& we that which you have bought. We should be just near enough together then— as to the Estate we live upon I know not whether it will ever be sold—it is going to ruin fast It is not yet determin'd yet who it belongs to

We have not heard one word from your son JQA since he went to Newbury— your other sons were well yesterday Lucy & Billy went to see them & carry them some clean Linnin There is to be a publick Exebition next Teusday cousin charles is to speak a Dialogue with a Mr Emmerson of concord—who looks much like him & is his bosom Friend—[3] My nephew was much affected yesterday by the rustication of one of his class Lucy said he look'd as if he had shed tears— & I suppose he had— He was his chum the Freshman year—& study'd with him at Mr Shaws— He is a youth of great spirits—& one would have suppos'd they would have preserv'd him from so mean an action as stealing from any one especially his classmates— What could tempt him to this vice I cannot conceive. His Father is the richest man in Bradford & he an only child—but the old man lives very mean & is very close The young man spoke very handsomely before the governer—of the college denys the fact although the goods were found lock'd up in his chest— I am griev'd for him. He is a fine genious & has naturally a good disposition[4]

uncle Smith remains much in the same state he was when I wrote before his Leg grows better—but his other complaints are not remov'd—

you have sent for the height of your Rooms but paper for rooms the Doctor says are so well made here that he thinks you will not attempt to bring any—

171

The report of Mr Adams returning soon has set the tools of the present administration spiting like so many Cats but I know he will not care for them

our Friend Mrs Russel remains very low & Nancy Sever is worse than her sister—[5]

I wish you would make a very particular inqueery how the gloscesshire [Che]ese is made—in what manner they prepair the Roun[ds—]how they give the yellow colour to the cheese you kn[ow ou]r procss in making cheese, discover if you can every var[iat]ion from our method— My cheeses look finely this summer & some of them want nothing but the colour inside to make them every way as good as English ones— I have not had more than four cows this summer & I think I have seven hundred weight of cheese—& I have made all the butter we have eat. We have had a large Family all summer—some of sister Smiths children have been with me ever since May Cousin Ebbit cranch & Eliza Bond have been with us six weeks— mr cranch has been at home all summer & is turnd quite a Farmer— by this account of our Family you will not suppos—we have been very Idle this season—

Doctor Tufts will transmit you our commencment accounts—I believe you will not think we were very extravagant—& yet I assure you we had enough of every thing & it was all very good—& every body seem'd pleas'd—

I have had no occation to advance any money for your sons Pockit expences. Doctor Tufts has given them quite as much as has been necessary for them— too much would be a great injury to their studys— The prudence of your eldest son might have been trusted with thousands—

When I think of your return I rejoice with trembling may god protect you & return you safe to your native country & to your affectionate sister

Mary Cranch

old Mrs Thayer is upon her annual visit to this Parish she is eighty nine years old she hopes "she shall live to see dear Madam Adams return["][6]

RC (Adams Papers); addressed by Elizabeth Cranch: "Mrs Adams— / Grosvener-square—"; endorsed: "Mrs Cranch / Septr. 23. 1787." Some loss of text where the seal was removed.

[1] AA to Cotton Tufts, 1 July, above.

[2] Likely the family of Joseph Woodward, for whom see vol. 7:397. Sarah Chauncy Adams (1733–1799), wife of Amos, was the daughter of Rev. Charles Chauncy of Boston (*Sibley's Harvard Graduates*, 6:441; 13:183, 185).

[3] William Emerson (1769–1811), Harvard

1789, father of transcendentalist Ralph Waldo Emerson, later served as pastor of the First Church of Boston (Lemuel Shattuck, *History of the Town of Concord: Earliest Settlement to 1832 and of Other Towns*, Boston, 1835, p. 250).

[4] Samuel Walker, Harvard 1790, eventually confessed to the theft and was allowed to return the following year (JQA, *Diary*, 2:294, note 3).

[5] Sarah Sever Russell (1757–1787) died in Boston on 24 November. Her sister Ann (Nancy) Warren Sever (1763–1788) died of consumption in Kingston in Jan. 1788 (*NEHGR*, 26:309, 311 [July 1872]; *Vital Records of Kingston, Massachusetts, to the Year 1850*, Boston, 1911, p. 379).

[6] Sarah Thayer lived to the age of 103, dying in Nov. 1800 (Boston *Columbian Centinel*, 22 Nov. 1800). See also Mary Smith Cranch to AA, 1 Nov. 1789, below.

Mary Smith Cranch to Abigail Adams

My dear Sister   Braintree Sep 30th 1787

I went to Boston last Monday & there found that Barnard had arriv'd & brought me Letters both from you & Mrs Smith—[1] I carre'd all mine for you & put them on board Folger—who said he should sail immediatly, but I hear he will not till next Teusday. I thought I had said every thing & told you all you would wish to know in my large Pacquet—but your Letter has given me new subjects—& first let me thank you for my urn & my Lamp lighter— I have not seen them yet but I know they will be very useful. I have found my Lamp very much so, one of those little wicks will burn six weeks if you do not pull them up & there is not the least necessaty of doing it— Betsy thinks she cannot sleep in the house without its being lighted. I wish my dear sister it was in my Power to return you some of those endearing proofs of your Love & esteem—you must accept a willing heart—

I had not time to see mrs wentworth when I was in Town— I design to go on purpose this week

I am very anxious for your Health. I hope it is mended—for by this time I suppose you are return'd from your excurtion into the West I wait with impatience for your account of it— The time till you return will seem longer to me than all that has past since you went away— I have not seen your new House yet but design to go over it & see what it will want. I should think it would not be best to make many alterations in it till you return. We will then consult together what will be best— I am sincerly glad you have it. Mr Fairweather & not mr Alleyne is the owner of the House & Farm which Mr Alleyne liv'd in— He has had a deed of it for a long time—[2] you may remember the Barn stands in a bad place— you will I think move it back, & will remove or pull down the Building erected by mr Tyler. It intirely takes off all & indeed the only extencive prospect you have— Mr Cranch will take a Plan of the House The measure of the rooms & every thing else which he thinks will gratify Mr Adams— your old House & ours will hold your Family till you can get your new one done mr Cranch cannot bear the thought of Mr Adams buying that place of Mr Veseys there will be so much better land to be sold joining upon that which you have lately purchas'd mr veseys is miserable poor.

Uncle Smith told me he had receiv'd a Letter from you—but said he should never write to you again—& indeed I believe he never will[3] He sinks fast— I think you will never see him more— He dyes of a broken Heart if ever Man did— with Tears & even with sobs he told me that he had been declining for more than a year "I have said but little but I have thought the more. I have had sleepless nights— without communicating the cause—" these were his words He will have but a few more I am perswaid'd before he meets his kindred soul. The saint he has been pining after—but what a loss shall we meet with—

Billy had a Letter from cousin Adams last week[4] he is will but studys too hard to retain his Health I fear— His Friend Ware is to be ordain'd in the october vacancy at Hingham—[5] I hope your son will come to it—

your sons at college were well this week I was not at the exebition but I hear that cousin charles perform'd well

I shall write to mrs Smith by Callahan he will sail in a few days thank her for her Letter if you please & tell her—that her cousins will write also—

Mrs Field has been here this day inquiring about Ester—she sends her Love & is well Betsy is very pale & thin—her heart has been wounded & you know how long it takes to heal it— It never more than skins over—a slight matter will again wound it. was you hear I would whisper something—but it will not do[6]—come home my dear sister & make us all happy sister shaw was well a few days since I had a Letter by mr *Moris* & Nancy Hayzen[7]

adieu   M—C

RC (Adams Papers); endorsed: "Sepbr [ ] [. . . .]." Some loss of text due to wear at the fold.

[1] See AA to Mary Smith Cranch, 16 July, and AA2 to Lucy Cranch, 14 July, both above.

[2] Thomas Fayerweather (1724–1805) of Cambridge had purchased a 400-acre Braintree estate from Thomas and Dorothy Harbin Alleyne for £1,600 on 18 April 1786 (*NEHGR*, 145:57–66 [Jan. 1991]; Suffolk County Deeds, 159:90–91). Cranch appears to be confusing the Fayerweather property with the Edmund Quincy estate, which would be auctioned by Abel Alleyne in Jan. 1788; see Cotton Tufts to AA, 20 Sept. 1787, and note 7, and Mary Smith Cranch to AA, 23 Sept., both above.

³ 12 March, above.

⁴ Not found.

⁵ Henry Ware, Harvard 1785, was ordained as minister of the First Church of Hingham on 24 October. For JQA's comments on Ware and his ordination, see *Diary*, 2:viii, 308–309.

⁶ This appears to be the first hint of the kindling of a romantic relationship between Mary Smith Cranch's daughter Elizabeth and newly ordained Weymouth pastor Jacob Norton.

⁷ Not found. Cranch was probably referring to Nancy Hazen's uncle, Haverhill tanner Benjamin Mooers (1725–1799), or one of his four living sons: Moses (1756–1813), Benjamin (1758–1838), John (1762–1803), or Jonathan (1764–1805) (Tracy Elliot Hazen, *The Hazen Family in America*, Thomaston, Conn., 1947, p. 88–90).

Abigail Adams to Elizabeth Cranch

my dear Eliza   october 1 1787

I am very sorry to find by your Mammas Letters that you are unwell. I wish you could have made an excursion with me to have visited your Relations in this country We often talkd of you, and I always told them how good you all were, at which they appeard to be much gratified. Your cousin J Cranch who travelld a great part of the way with us thinks he has a very accurate knowledge of you. I am not sure that if he was in America, he might put a pr of Buckles into his shoes & hold up his Head. he often brought young Hill who formerly studied with your uncle to my mind.¹ he is certainly a Man of talants, but he wants the manner of displaying them to advantage. whilst we were at plimouth we proposed a visit to Horsham about 8 miles distant, but a part of the road only was Turnpike. we inquired if we could go in a carriage, and we were told that we might, but the persons who gave us this advise did not attend to the difference between a coach & a post chaise. We set out in our own carriage & four, but not being a turnpike we took a wrong course and squezd through the narrowest way that a carriage ever past before the hedges on both sides meeting, I expected every moment when the coach man & postilion would have shared the fate of Absolom.² about 2 miles before we came to the House we were compleatly stoped a Good man seeing our difficulty advised to pass through two wheet feilds, but there we were obliged to dismount and leave the carriage for the Servants to get on as well as they could. the lane which led to the House was so wet and Springy that we could not walk it without being over our Shoes, & this as I had Silk on was not quite so convenient, & through the Fields the hedges which we had to climb over were so high that it was totally impracticable to attempt. mr J Cranch who had never been at the place before, Scrachd his head & Scolded his cousin for permitting the road to be so obstructed, but finding a Gate Sampson like he lifted it from the hinges & made it serve for a Ladder to pass over the hedges, but still we could not avoid near a mile of wet & mud. we were determined however not to give out, tho the weather was very Hot. Miss Palmer who by our long detention & struggl, had got intelligence of our comeing came out with Pattens for us & met us half way. She accosted us with affibilyty and welcomd us with politeness. her manners were easy and unaffected, her countanance full of sensibility, and Sprightliness her form Geenteel her face more pleasing than Beautifull. I could trace many Lines of her Brother, to whose memory she still paid a tributary Tear— the Brother with whom she lives I did not see, but all Relations & acquaintance alike represent him as the merest clown in nature.[3] I was sorry he was absent, as I could scarcly credit that such a Brother as you knew & such a sister as I saw, could be from the same stock with this cimon. the house is a ~~tidy~~ decent farm House retird from all the world beside & there is a good Farm, but it is a Life Rent. by the Time we had rested ourselves the carriage got up by taking out the horses & drawing the coach by hand. we could only stay an hour and we parted with mutual regreet I believe returning an other road we took a guide and were obliged to dismount only once, but steep precipices rocks Bogs & hedges put us every moment in Bodily fear, and we were the first coach & four that ever attempted Horsham House. we should all have mounted on Horse back & then we should have Succeeded to our wishes—

A Adams

Dft (Adams Papers); notation: "To Elizabeth Cranch / ocbr 1st 1787."

[1] Edward Hill (1755–1775), Harvard 1772, of Boston studied law with JA from 1772 until JA's departure for Philadelphia in 1774, though Hill continued to work in JA's law office. Hill died in 1775 of camp fever in occupied Boston (*Sibley's Harvard Graduates*, 18:100–102).

[2] Absalom, the son of David, was killed when his head was caught in the boughs of an oak tree as he rode under it (2 Samuel, 18:9–10).

[3] For John Palmer of Horsham, see vol. 6:61.

William Cranch to Abigail Adams

Madam,   Boston Oct[r.] 1st. 1787.

Not to acknowledge the many favours I have recieved from you, and the obligations they have laid me under, would be ingratitude in the greatest Degree. The only method now in my power of Cancelling those obligations is to acknowledge them & perhaps prevent your being dissapointed, should Callahan arrive before Folgier. For upon the supposition that Folgier would sail first, all the Letters for You were put on board him, but I have since heard that they will both sail tomorrow. I hear'd this morning that my Cousins at Cambridge were both well. I reciev'd a Letter from John Q. Last week, he likes his situation at Newbury-port very well. I hear'd from Braintree this morning, our friends were all well there.

With the greatest Respect believe me / Madam Your Afft. Nephew
WCranch.

RC (Adams Papers); addressed: "Mrs A. Adams / Grosvenor square / Westminster"; notation: "Capt. Callahan. / Hond. by Mr. Bromfield."

Abigail Adams to Lucy Cranch

London october 3 1787

I thank you my dear Lucy, for writing by mr Jenks tho only a few Lines, but that was very excusible considering how much she was engaged, both your mamma and you must have had your hand full. I hope the fatigue was not too much for her, the applause which all agree, your Brothers obtaind, must be to so benevolent a mind as my dear Neices, be some compensation for the fatigue an anxiety which she experienced. I thank you most sincerely for all your Labours of Love, and still solicit the continuance of them to those who yet call for your friendly assistance— you learnt by Captain Barnard that I was going a journey. I have given your mamma and sister some account of my late excursion to Devonshire. we returnd Home through Bristol and took oxford in our way, from Whence we went to Woodstock and visited Blenheim, the Seat of the Duke of Marlborough, which was built at the publick expence, and Granted by the crown to the Duke for the services he had renderd his Country.[1] this Castle is upon the Grandest scale of any thing I have ever yet seen. We enter the park through a spacious and elegant portal of the Corinthian order, from whence a Noble prospect is opend to the palace, the Bridge the Lake, with its valley, and other beautifull Scenes.[2] the Front of this Noble Ediface which is of Stone, is 348 feet from wing to wing. on the pediment of the South Front, towards the Garden is a Noble Busto of Louis the 14th, taken by the Duke from the Gates of Tournay.[3] this the Gardner told us, he never faild pointing out to all the French Gentlemen who visited the place and that, they shrugd their shoulders, & mon dieu'd.— but before I describe to you the Gardens, I will attempt to give you a short, tho imperfect account of the palace, it would require a week to view it, & a vol^m to describe it particularly; I will therefore only collect from my little journal, the most remarkable objects.– we enterd the palace through a magnificent Hall supported by Corinthian pillars, over the door going into the Salon, is a Bust of John Duke of Marlborough and two statues in Bronz, viz the venus of medicis & a Faun. the Ceiling is painted Allegorically, Representing victory crowning John Duke of Marlborough, and pointing to a plan of the Battle of Blenhiem. from the Salon we pass through a Suit of Rooms, all of them containing a most costly & Beautifull collection of paintings, many of them originals of the first masters. in the dining Room is a family peice, the present Duke & duchess and six of their Children by sir Joshua Reynolds.[4] the furniture of the rooms is different couloured damasks. the family being at the House, we saw only the lower appartments. the winter drawing Room is of Tapestry upon which is represented the Cardinal virtues, Chairs & curtains white damask. from a series of smaller tho Magnificent appartments, we were suddenly struck at entering the Library, which is 183 feet long, and the most costly as well as Beautifull place I ever saw. the Doric pilasters are of Marble, with compleat columns of the same, which support a rich entablature, window Frames the surrounding basement of black marble, and the Stuccoed compartments of the vaulted ceiling, are in the highest Taste both of design, and finishing: there is a person who always attends at these seats, who has by Heart the whole History of all that is to be seen, and they make very handsome sums of money by it. This Library was originally intended as a Gallery for paintings but the Late Duke of Marlborough, chose to have it furnishd with the Noble collection of Books made by Lord Sunderland, his Graces Father which amounts to 24.000 volums; and is said to be the best private collection in England: they are kept under Gilt wire lattices: and make a superb appearence.[5] at one end of the Room is a highly finishd Marble statue of Queen Ann, with this inscription, "To the memory of Queen Anne under whose Auspices John duke of Marlborough conquerd, And to whose Munificence, He, and his posterity, with Gratitude owe the possession of Blenheim in A D. 1746.["] There are Two marble Busts over the Chimny, one of Charles Earl of Sunderland, who collected the Books, and an other of Charles Spencer Duke of Marlborough and at the further End of the room, is a fine Greek Bust of Alexander the Great, and 14^teen full length family portraits.

from two Bow windows in this Noble Gallery, the Eye is delighted with a view of the declivity descending to the water, and the gradual assent of the venerable Grove which covers the opposite hill. in short whether we look within, or without, all is on the Scale of the sublime and the Beautifull. I must not overlook the Chaple which makes one of the wings of the House, and in which there is a proud monument of white marble to the memory, of the renoued Duke & dutchess of Marlborough. the Group of marble figures Large as Life upon this Monument, are the duke and dutchess with two of their Sons who died young, they Supported by two figures, Fame, and History.[6] the Alter peice is the best painting I ever saw, our Saviour taken down from the cross.—[7]

From the House we visited the Gardens and here I am lost, not in confusion, but amidst scenes of Grandeur magnificence, and Beauty. they are spacious and include a great variety of Ground. the plain, or as the artists term it, the Lawn before the palace is kept in the most perfect order, not a single spire of grass, rises above an other, it is mowed & swept every other day, and is as smooth as the surface of a looking Glass. The Gardner who has lived 25 years upon the place, told us that he employd about Sixty 3 Hands during the Summer in mowing Sweeping pruning loping, and in ornamenting the Grounds— from this Lawn is a gradual descent to the Water, and you pass through Spacious gravell walks not in strait lines, as Pope expresses it,

> "Where each Alley has a Brother
> and half the platform just reflects the other"[8]

but pleasing intracacies intervene, through the winding paths and every step opens new objects, of Beauty which diversified Nature affords, of Hill, Vallay, Water, and Woods, the Gardens finally are lost in the park amidst a profusions of venrable oaks some of which, are said, to have stood, nine hundred years. the Gardens are four miles round which I walkd, the park is Eleven. there is a magnificent Bridge consisting of 3 Arches the Water which it covers, is formd into a spacious Lake, which flows the whole extent of a capacious vallay. this was built at the expence of Sarah dutchess of Marlborough, as well as a column which I shall mention in Turn. The Gardner who was very Loquacious, and swelld with importance, told us that Since his residence there; the present duke had greatly enlarged and improved the Grounds; that he had Beautified them by the addition of some well placed ornaments; particularly the Temple of Diana; and a noble cascade, round which are the four River Gods, represented as the Gaurdian Genii of the water

This celebrated park was first inclosed in the reign of Henry the first, his successor Henry ye second resided at this Seat, and erected in this park a palace, and encompassed it with a Labyrinh which was Fair Rosamonds bower, celebrated by Addisson. there are now no remains of it except a spring at the foot of the hill, which still bears the Name of Rosamonds Well—[9] this palace, is celebrated as the Birth place of Edmund 2 son of Edmund the first, and of Edmund the black prince Elizabeth was kept a prisoner there, under the persecutions of Queen Mary, and it continued to be the Residence of Kings till the Reign of Charles the first, but it was demolished in succeeding times of confusion.[10] there are now two Sycamores planted as a memorial upon the Spot where the old palace stood. the column will close my narative. this is in Front of the palace of Blenheim at about half a miles distance & is 130 feet high, on the Top of which is John Duke of Marlborough on which is the following inscription, Supposed to be written by the Late Lord Bolingbroke

> The Castle of Blenheim was founded by Queen Anne
> In the fourth year of her Reign
> In the year of the Christian Æra 1705
> A Monument designed to perpetuate the Memory of
>   the Signal Victory
> obtained over the French and Bavarians
> on the Banks of the danube
> By John Duke of Marlborough
> The Hero not only of this Nation but of this Age
> whose Glory was equal, in the Council and in the
>   Field
> who, by wisdom, Justice, candour, and address
> Reconciled various, and even opposite, Interest
> Acquired an Influence
> which no Rank no Authority can Give
> Nor any Force, but that of superiour virtue
> Became the fixed important centre
> which united in one common cause
> The principal States of Europe
> Who by military knowledge, and Irresistible Valour
> In a long series of uninterrupted Triumphs

5. "A NORTH VIEW OF BLENHEIM HOUSE AND PARK IN THE COUNTY OF OXFORD," BY JOHN BOYDELL, 1752

See page xii

Broke the power of France
when raised the highest, and when exerted the most
Rescued the Empire from desolation
Asserted and confirmed the Liberties of Europe

Thus is the Gratitude of the Nation expresd, & thus do the Heirs of Marlborough Triumph.[11] the present Duke is a man of literary persuits domestick, and a great Astronomer he has a fine observatory & Apparatus, from this observatory he makes Signals to Herschal at Windsor; and they Study the Stars together.

I have made a very long Letter of it I hope it may prove an amusement to you;

Remember me kindly to all inquiring Friends and believe me my dear Neice / your ever affetionate   Aunt A. Adams

RC (MWA:Abigail Adams Letters); addressed by WSS: "Miss Lucy Cranch / Braintree"; notation by WSS: "To the care of / Isaac Smith / Esqr· Boston."

[1] The land on which Blenheim Palace sits and its original manor house, called Woodstock, were given by the English government to John Churchill, 1st Duke of Marlborough (1650–1722), in 1705 in recognition of his services at the Battle of Blenheim in Bavaria. Marlborough hired the architect John Vanbrugh to build the castle, which was started in 1705 but not completed until 1724 (Karl Baedeker, *Great Britain*, 8th edn., Leipzig, 1927, p. 222; *DNB*).

[2] The entrance to the home, called the Triumphal Arch, was designed by Nicholas Hawksmoor and built at the direction of Sarah Jennings Churchill, Duchess of Marlborough (1660–1744), John's wife, in tribute to her husband the year after his death. On the arch, she had inscribed, in part, "The services of this great man to his country the Pillar will tell which the Duchess has erected for a lasting monument of his glory and her affection for him" (Christopher Hibbert, *The Marlboroughs: John and Sarah Churchill 1650–1744*, N.Y., 2001, p. 341).

[3] This giant bust of Louis XIV, which weighs 30 tons, had originally stood on top of the fortress at Tournai, Belgium. Marlborough apparently admired it during the siege of Tournai in June 1709 and arranged to have it brought across the English Channel to Blenheim (Hibbert, *The Marlboroughs*, p. 239–240).

[4] In the fall of 1777, Sir Joshua Reynolds came to Blenheim to paint George Spencer,

4th Duke of Marlborough (1739–1817), his wife Lady Caroline Russell, and six of their children. Reynolds completed the portrait in 1778. The palace also contained paintings by numerous other important artists including da Vinci, Titian, Holbein, Rubens, and van Dyck (*DNB*; William Eccles, *A New Guide to Blenheim Palace*, 5th edn., Woodstock, Eng., 1852, p. 21–30).

[5] Charles Spencer, 3d Earl of Sunderland (1674–1722), a noted bibliophile, married Anne Churchill, Marlborough's daughter, in 1700. Blenheim Palace received in 1749 a portion of Sunderland's library, to which his son, Charles Spencer, 3d Duke of Marlborough and 5th Earl of Sunderland (1706–1758), subsequently made additions. The library was sold at auction by the 6th Duke of Marlborough for £30,000 (*DNB*; Hibbert, *The Marlboroughs*, p. 339). For a listing of titles in the library at the time of its sale, see *Bibliotheca Sunderlandiana: Sale Catalogue of the . . . Library of Printed Books Known as the Sunderland or Blenheim Library*, London, 1881–1883.

[6] The Marlboroughs had two sons, both of whom died young: John Churchill, Marquess of Blandford (1686–1703), and Charles Churchill (1690–1692). They also had four daughters—Anne, Elizabeth, Henrietta, and Mary (Hibbert, *The Marlboroughs*, p. 340; Virginia Cowles, *The Great Marlborough and His Duchess*, N.Y., 1983, p. 122, 133, 136).

[7] This piece, *Our Saviour Taken Down*

from the Cross, was by Jacob Jordaens (1594–1678), a Dutch painter from Antwerp (*A Description of Blenheim*, 12th edn., Oxford, n.d., p. 44; John Corner, *Portraits of Celebrated Painters*, London, 1825, n.p.).

[8] Pope, *Moral Essays*, Epistle IV, lines 117–118.

[9] A palace known as Woodstock existed in some form on this site as early as 866. Henry I was responsible for enclosing the park and establishing the town. Henry II was allegedly responsible for erecting the labyrinth to allow his mistress, "Fair Rosamond" (Rosamond Clifford, d. 1176?), to reach the palace secretly. Their relationship was celebrated in Joseph Addison's *Rosamond, an Opera, Humbly Inscrib'd to Her Grace the Dutchess of Marlborough*, London, 1707 (*Description of Blenheim*, p. 104–107; *DNB*).

[10] Edmund of Woodstock, youngest son of Edward I, was born here in 1301, as was Edward III's eldest son, Edward (1330–1376), known as the Black Prince. Others who spent time at Woodstock include Chaucer and the future queen Elizabeth, imprisoned there by her half-sister Queen Mary (*Description of Blenheim*, p. 111–117; *DNB*).

[11] For the "Column of Victory," see Descriptive List of Illustrations, No. 5, above. Henry St. John, 1st Viscount Bolingbroke, wrote the inscription but only after Alexander Pope refused the work. AA's transcription is missing a single line; she left out the words "Near the Village of Blenheim" after the phrase "obtained over the French and Bavarians" (Hibbert, *The Marlboroughs*, p. 341; Eccles, *Guide to Blenheim Palace*, p. 58–59).

Thomas Jefferson to Abigail Adams

Dear Madam   Paris Octob. 4. 1787.

By mr̃ Cutting I have an opportunity of acknoleging the receipt of your favor of Sep. 10[th.] inclosing one for my daughter Polly.[1] when she received it she flushed, she whitened, she flushed again, & in short was in such a flutter of joy that she could scarcely open it. this faithful history of her sensibility towards you must stand in lieu of her thanks which she has promised me she will write you herself: but at this moment she is in the convent where she is perfectly happy. by mr̃ Cutting you will also receive the 5. aunes of cambric which Col[o.] Smith desired me to have purchased for you at 12. livres the aune. I am sorry you were put to the trouble of advancing the money for mr̃ Sullivan's bill:[2] I thought myself sure that mr̃ Grand's bill would reach you in time, and did not know he had omitted to advise mr̃ Teissier of it. he is always afraid to give to any body a complete power to call on him for money. mr̃ Littlepage is here under a secret commission from the King of Poland. possibly it may become a permanent one. I thank you for the American newspapers, and am glad to find that good sense is still uppermost in our country. great events are I think preparing here: and a combination of force likely to take place which will change the face of Europe. mr̃ Grenville has been very illy received. the annunciation by mr̃ Eden that England was arming, was considered as an insult: after this & the King of Prussia's entrance on the territories of Holland, mr̃ Grenville's arrival with conciliatory propositions is qualified with the title of "une insulte tres gratuite." I am not certain that the final decision of this country is yet taken. perhaps the winter may be employed in previous arrangements unless any thing takes place at sea to bring on the rupture sooner. the Count de Gortz told me yesterday that the Prussian troops would retire from Holland the moment the states of Holland should make the expected reparation of the insult to the Princess. may not the scene which is preparing render it necessary for mr̃ Adams to defer the return to his own country?[3]

I have the honor to be with very sincere sentiments of esteem & respect Dear Madam—your most obedient & most humble servant

Th: Jefferson

RC (Adams Papers); internal address: "mrš Adams."; endorsed: "Mr Jefferson / ocbr 4th 1787."

[1] Not found.

[2] On 29 May, Gen. John Sullivan, president (governor) of New Hampshire, had written to Jefferson asking him to reimburse WSS for money Sullivan had drawn in the United States against WSS's account (Jefferson, *Papers*, 11:384).

[3] Prussia under its new king, Frederick William, had hesitated to become involved in the revolt in the Netherlands. But when the king's sister, Princess Wilhelmina, was arrested, confined, and apparently insulted while attempting to enter The Hague in late June, he finally resolved to invade in support of the Orangists, although it was more than two months before troops actually crossed the border. Some believed that France too would invade in support of the Patriots—which would have drawn Britain into the war as well—but a visit by William Grenville to the Netherlands convinced Frederick William, rightly, that France had no intention of becoming involved, and Britain accordingly also pulled back. By 10 Oct., the Prussians had conquered the last of the Patriot resistance and temporarily restored William V to power (Schama, *Patriots and Liberators*, p. 126–132).

Johann Eustach, Baron von Görtz, was the Prussian envoy extraordinary to the Netherlands (*Repertorium*, 3:333).

Abigail Adams to Cotton Tufts

Dear sir London october 5th 1787

Your obliging favour by captain Folger came safe to Hand, and brought me the agreeable intelligence of my Eldest sons having received His degree, and performed his part to the satisfaction of his Friends, and his own credit. you know Sir from experience, that there is no musick sweeter in the Ears of parents, than the well earned praises of their children.

I hope he will continue through Life to mantain the Character of an honest man; and a usefull citizen I am anxious for his Health, and hope you will advise him to pay more attention to it, than he is inclined too

I presume before this time mr Adams's & my letters must have reachd you, respecting the purchase of Borlands place. I hope to hear from you upon this subject by Callihan: Mr Adams has written to you concerning our Farm and thinks it best to take it into his own Hands, as it will want manure, and many other things done; which we cannot expect from a Tenant, but as some arrangements will be necessary before we shall be able to reach America, I have thought whether Pheby would not undertake the dairy, with an assistant, and whether the other buisness might not be performd by hireing a man & Boy & agreeing to pay him a certain Sum he finding himself—

I know it is much easier to propose these things than to do them, and that it is putting a great deal of trouble upon you. Belcher used to be a good Hand & knows the place perfectly well, if you should buy mr Borlands place, that also will require attention. I hope we may be able to get home in june at furthest.—

Every thing here looks Hostile, and England is arming with all expedition and seem fully bent upon war, without a single object of Benifit, or conquest. The Nation appear very well pleasd at the prospect. The Conduct of France towards Holland, betrays either weakness or Fear. She has by her late conduct faded the laurels which she won in America. She has left her Ally, in their greatest distress, a prey to the orange mob, & the prussian Army To the machinations of British politicks, & the Tyrranny of the Stadholder. The Country will in a manner, be depopulated, the wealth of it transferd to other Nations, and the Prince of orange the Monarck of Frogs, perhaps the insolence of this Nation may provoke France to strike some unexpected stroke, but it will be too late to save Holland. The Patriots have already experienced the most outrageous conduct, and wanton cruelty, in the destruction of their Houses, and the ravage of their property, every personal indignity, and a constant threatning of their lives.

Such is the Mobility of all countries when once let lose, another lesson for America. I hope She will be wise enough to keep clear of the Blaize which threatnes Europe. She may rise into power and concequence, even by the Calamities of other Nations if she improves their folly arright

Mr Adams has finishd his other volm and requests when they arrive you would distribute a 2d volm to all those Gentleman to whom he sent the first, as well as those you added to the List, not forgetting Brother Shaw—[1] The Reviewers to this month are sent you.

Remember me to your Son and believe me dear sir / most affectionately yours, A Adams

185

RC (Adams Papers); addressed by WSS: "The Honble. / Cotton Tufts Esqr. / Boston"; endorsed: "M^rs. Adams Octob. 5–/ 1787–" Dft (Adams Papers), dated and filmed at 4 October.

[1] The Dft also notes that "his 3d vol is just going to the press."

Abigail Adams to Mary Smith Cranch

Dear sister   october 8th 1787–

I inclose a pamphlet upon darying[1] which when you have read, be so good as to give to Pheby provided she becomes my dairy woman, and be so good as to procure me the following List of Herbs & send me in small Bags Catnip mint penny Royal & Hysop. You will laugh I suppose, but I want them for my Voyage, & what I get here are good for very little. Catnip is an herb I never could find here. I have sent to my Neices a small band Box with some Gauze for Bonets, and little modle. there ingenuity will put them together I doubt not, they are the newest fashion, & as the Bonets are not made, there is no prohibition upon them

I am obliged to make up what package I have least the vessel should sail, and must trust to getting what I shall write to sister shaw & my children on Board afterwards

Esther has been sick this fortnight, but is Some thing better. She is such a poor weakly creature that I fear sometims I shall never get her back alive, if she had not lived where the utmost care and attention has been paid to her, she would long ago have been dead.

pray remember me to Mrs Quincy & miss Nancy to mr Alleyne family, and to all inquiring Friends—and believe me always your affectionate / sister   A A

RC (MWA:Abigail Adams Letters); addressed: "To / Mrs Mary Cranch / Braintree."

[1] Probably Josiah Twamley, *Dairying Exemplified; or, The Business of Cheese-Making*, London, 1784.

Abigail Adams to Mary Smith Cranch

My dear sister   London october 8th 1787

I have just sent some Letters to go by Captain Folger, but find he does not sail so soon as captain Cushing. Should he arrive before Folger without a Line I know by experience how fruitfull your imaginition would be of conjectures, and tho I have said all that appeard to me of importance, & perhaps more than others will think of any, in my Letters on Board Folger, I forgot to inclose a paper which I promised, and which will require my other Letters to explain.

Pray is our Native Town yet destitute of a setled Pastor? What is become of mr & mrs Evans? and where is my old Friend Charles Storer, indeed I feel conscious that I have not used him well. I am indebted to him for Several Letters, but I really have so many to whom I am by duty as well as inclination obliged to write that, when a vessel is going to sail, my whole time is occupied—

I think of all my Friends with an unabated affection, & hope the period is not far distant when I shall meet them again. Some alass, I shall miss—but this is the portion of mortality.

Remember me affectionately to mr Cranch. I cannot get mr Adams to write half the Letters I want him to. he is so buisily employd about his Books, I tell him he will ruin himself in Publishing his Books, he says they are for the Benefit of his Country, and he allways expected to be ruind in her service, but I am really affraid he will kill himself in her service too, for his unwearied application has brought a nervious pain in his Head which allarms me at times.— he is not now a young man, and has Served the publick Years enough to have been at his ease the remainder of his Life, if half the assiduity had been employd in his own private affairs.

adieu my dear Sister Remember me to all Friends, for this is the only Letter which I shall write by Cushing— I have sent the Critical Reviews to dr Tufts by Cushing, the Letter to him Folger has—

ever yours   A Adams

RC (MWA:Abigail Adams Letters).

Abigail Adams to John Quincy Adams

My dear son   London october 12th 1787

I cannot begin my Letter by thanking you for yours. You write so seldom, that you, do not give me the opportunity, yet I think you would feel dissapointed if you did not get a few Lines from me. I congratulate you upon your Success at Commencment, and as you have acquired a reputation upon entering the stage of the World, you will be no less solicitious to preserve and increase it, through the whole drama. it is said of Hannibal that he wanted nothing to the compleation of His martial virtues, but that when he had gained a victory, he should know how to use it.[1] it is natural to the humane Heart to swell with presumption when conscious of superiour power, yet all humane excellence is comparative, and he who thinks he knows much to day, will find much more still unatained, provided he is still eager in persuit of knowledge. Your Friends are not anxious that you will be in any danger through want of significant application, but that a too ardent persuit of your studies will impair your Health, & injure those bodily powers and faculties upon which the vigor of the mind depends. Moderation in all things is condusive to human happiness, tho this is a maxim little heeded by Youth, whether their persuits are of a sensual, or a more refined and elevated kind

It is an old Adage, that a man at 30, must be either a fool or a Physician. tho you have not arrived to that age, you would do well to trust to the advise, and experience of those who have. our Bodies are framed of such materials as to require constant exercise to keep them in repair, to Brace the Nerves and give vigor to the Animal functions. thus do I give you Line upon Line, & precept upon precept.

By the Time this reaches you, you will have heard of the Humiliating condition of Holland. History does not furnish a more striking instance of abject Submission, and depression totally and almost unresistingly conquerd by a few prussian troops, a Nation, that formerly withstood the whole power & force of spain, and gave such proofs of Bravery and prowess as astonishd surrounding Nation, now Humbled to the dust, by an imperious & haughty woman, backed by the Troops of Prussia, for a mere trifling affront or rather this has been the speicious pretence for all the Horrors which are brought upon the patriots & Friends of Liberty in Holland. May her Name descend with eternall obloquy to future ages. Poor Dumas & family have lived in a state worse than death, since to exist in constant dread of being drag'd a victim to an enraged mob, who were constantly threatning him, & his family with destruction: is worse than death. his Friends all forsook him or dared not appear in his behalf. he wrote a most afflicting account to your pappa, & beg'd him to claim protection for him as acting for the united States, but as he never had any publick character, or rather never was commissond by Congress, it could not be done.[2] mr duma you know has been engaged in the Service of France, and has received a Sallery from that Government, besides his being opposed to the measures of the Stadtholder, all of which renders him particularly obnoxious to the princess, and her party

This Nation, piqued at the Treaty of alliance, which was last Winter, made between France & Holland have been ever since seeking

Revenge, by fomenting the troubles in Holland; and Seizd the first opportunity She had in her power to Bully France.[3] The Death of de Vergennes and the deranged State of the Finnances in France, the dispute between the King and his parliament, all, all have contributed to hasten the downfall of Liberty in Holland. England has held a very high Tone, & given it out, that if France marchd a single man to the assistance of Holland, it should be considerd as a commencment of Hostilities, and from the conduct of France, she appears to have been intimidated, and held in Awe by it. This is an other lesson to us, not to put our trust in princes. England not content with the Tame, & pacific conduct of France, is arming with a zeal, and Eagerness really astonishing, to every person of reflection, who can See no object which she can have in view, adequate to or as a compensation for the horrur and distress, she must bring upon her Subjects by the increase of expences and the accumulation of the National debt.

If I was not present to hear, and see it I could scarcely credit, that a whole people Should not only tamely Submit to the evils of war, but appear frantick with joy at the prospect, led away by false Glory, by their passions & their vices they do not reflect, upon past calamities, nor approaching destruction and few of them have better reasons to offer for their conduct than the Lady with whom I was in company the other day, who hoped their would be a war. pray said I how can you wish so much misiry to mankind? o said she, if there is a war, my Brother, & Several of my Friends will be promoted. In the general Flame which threatnes Europe, I hope & pray, our own Country may have wisdom sufficient, to keep herself out of the Fire. I am sure she has been a sufficiently burnt child.

Remember me to your Brothers, if I do not write to them. I have sent you some cotton stockings, and am / Your affectionate mother

A. Adams

RC (Adams Papers); endorsed: "My Mother. 12. Oct[r.] 1787." and "M[rs.] Adams. Oct[r.] 12 1787."

[1] AA is quoting directly from Samuel Johnson, *The Rambler*, No. 127.

[2] C. W. F. Dumas wrote to JA on 25 Sept. (Adams Papers) requesting his assistance. JA replied on 1 Oct. (LbC, APM Reel 113), offering to allow Dumas and his family to reside at the Hôtel des États-Unis in The Hague and arranging for money for its repair. JA had also previously made arrangements to ensure that Dumas continued to receive his salary as U.S. chargé d'affaires at The Hague until Congress formally determined Dumas' status (JA to Dumas, 5 Sept., LbC, APM Reel 113).

[3] The Dutch and French had signed a treaty of alliance and friendship in Oct. 1785. This represented a victory for the Patriot Party over the stadholder, whom the British supported (Schama, *Patriots and Liberators*, p. 106).

Abigail Adams to Elizabeth Smith Shaw

Dear Sister   London october 12 1787

Your obliging Letter was handed me, on my return from a journey into Devonshire. it was one of the most agreeable excursions I ever made. The Season was delightfull, and we performd our journey by easy Stages, always sure to find good accommodations at the Inn's. The whole country through which we travelled was like a Garden, and the cultivation Scarcly admits of an other improvement; I wish I could say as much in favour of the inhabitants, but whilst one part of the people, the Noble and the wealthy, fare sumptuously every day, poverty hunger and Nakedness is the Lot, and portion of the needy pesantry, who are the inhabitants of the County Towns and villages, by whom the Earth is manured, and the Harvest gatherd in, yet are the most industerous of them; stinted, to Six pence or seven pence a day from which pittance, they must not only feed them-selves, but perhaps a wife and family. Youth and age experience the extreems of misiry their mud cottages, and misirable Huts astonishd me, Starving in the midst of plenty, Tantulas like. The Sheepherd who with his faithfull Dog, is the Watchman of a thousand Sheep, must answer with his Life to his Lord, if the pressing hunger of his family should tempt him to purloin the meanest Lamb of the Flock, Nor is he permitted to Touch the winged passengers of the air, tho they no more belong to the owner of the Mansion, than the Sun Beam, which equally Shines, upon the Cottage and the palace, but he is a Lord, and claims as exclusive right to the commoners of Na-ture himself

Poor is the opulence, and little the Grandeur which would en-gross the very light of Heaven if it were possible, and the air in which we Breath. what I formerly read as Romance I have been an Eye witness too, in this Land of Feedom this boasted Island of Lib-erty. there is such an inequality of property, that the lower order of the people, are abject and servile, the higher insolent, and Tyranni-cal, yet are they, less wetched than the common people of most other Countries.

Can it be, that one part of the Humane Species, and those a small propoportion, were deignd to subjugate the rest of their fellow mortals, yet such is the use they make of their freedom, that one is led to the inquiry, Homer was however of a different opinion, when he said,

"Jove fix'd it certain, that whatever day
makes man a slave, takes half his Worth away"[1]

When I reflect upon the advantages which the people of America possess, over the most polished of other Nations, the ease with which property is obtain, the plenty which is so equally distributed, their personal Liberty, and Security of Life and property, I feel gratefull to Heaven, who marked out my Lot in that happy land, at the same time I deprecate that restless Spirit, and that banefull pride Ambition, and thirst for power which will finally make us as wretched as our Neighbors

"Aspiring to be Gods Angles fell,
Aspiring to be Angle man rebell'd"[2]

The account my dear Sister gave me of her Nephew, was peculiarly pleasing to me, it is no small proof of his merit, that he has obtain the Eulogyum of so amiable a Character,[3] and so benevolent a Friend, let me Solicit a continuence of Your Friendly advice. I am sure it will always have weight with him.

Let my little Nephew know, that I was highly gratified by his very pretty Letter, and as a reward for his attention to his Books I Send him two little volms for his Sundays amusement[4]

My Grandson grows a fine Boy, and will get too much of my Heart I fear.[5] he stood his journey very well, and was a great amusement to us. Mrs Smith is very [. . .] makes a very good Nurse. how is my old Friend mr Thaxter, tell him tho I have not wrote him a long time, it is not oweing to any abatement of Esteem or Regard.[6]

Remember me to all our Haverhill Friends.

The time is near approaching when I expect to quit this Country.[7] the ocean appears the only great obstical to me, but sufficent to the day, &c[8]

affectionate Regards to mr Shaw mr Adams has directed a 2d vol^m of the defence to be presented to him

I hope the disorder which distrest your Friends and parishoners has left the place. it is in [. . . .][9] this Country. with regard to my own Health, I have b[een?] [. . . .] a month past, than for six months before. my Love [. . . .][10] Neice. She is grown I dare say a fine girl by this Time

adieu my d[ear Sister] and believe me with the tenderest Sentiments / your affectionate   [A Adams]

RC (DLC:Shaw Family Papers); addressed by WSS: "To / M[rs. Eli]zabeth Shaw / at / Haverhill / near / Boston"; endorsed: "October 12 1787." Some loss of text where the signature was removed. Dft (Adams Papers), dated and filmed at 10 October.

¹ Homer, *The Odyssey*, transl. Alexander Pope, Book XVII, lines 392–393.

² Pope, *An Essay on Man*, Epistle I, lines 127–128.

³ At this point the Dft also says, "may he long deserve it, and may that attention be continued to him as he is like to be a resident near you."

⁴ Letter not found.

⁵ Here the Dft continues, "I hope to hear mrs Alleyne is happily a Bed, I feel anxious for her, tis hardly fit to begin a Buisness, at a time of Life when one should be leaving off." Elizabeth Kent Allen was forty years old when her daughter Betsey was born in Aug. (*Vital Records of Charlestown Massachusetts to the Year 1850*, 2 vols. in 3, Boston, 1984, 1:381).

⁶ At this point in the RC, AA heavily crossed out three lines of text.

⁷ At this point the Dft concludes: "I could wish I had not the ocean to encounter, but necessity has no law & I cannot See my country and Friends without Submitting to it, I Shall have few regrets, considering the political Situation of this country."

⁸ "Take therefore no thought for the morrow: for the morrow shall take thought for the things of itself. Sufficient unto the day is the evil thereof" (Matthew, 6:34).

⁹ Approximately three words missing.

¹⁰ Approximately three words missing.

Abigail Adams to Mary Smith Cranch

my dear sister   [*ante 18*] october London 1787¹

I have already written you a long letter giving you an account, of my journey, this must relate Chiefly to private affairs. your Letters by captain cushing and Folger came safe to hand.² I thank you for your pleasing account of commencment, as well as for your care and attention to my sons, which it is unnecessary to solicit a continuance off because I am perfectly sure of it. I am sorry a certain family took it into their heads to be affronted, but it is not the first instance in which they have held them too high. America is very apt to make Englishmen forget what they once were, or that they owe all their importance to her. I often think of an observation of our Grandmothers, who used to say, that it was a mercy to the World, some people were kept poor, since were they rich their haughtiness and insolence would be intollerable.

I feard the Sandles would prove too long. I sent them back once to the Shoemaker, thinking he must have made a mistake in the measure. I have endeavourd to pattern the Silk you sent, but the Shop where I purchased the other, upon the late rise in silks, sold of the whole stock. I pray these four yds may be considerd as a part of the other, and not as they say split an Acorn. a dozen pr of cotton stockings Captain Folger will take charge of for my son J Q A, and some blew broad cloth for my others, as they will want one coat a year I presume. I hope your Urn went safe by Barnard, as well as some articles I sent to JQA—

I begin to think seriously of arranging matters, for our return in April Next, and I wish for your advise relative to our affairs in America. mr Adams thinks it best that mr Pratt should go of in April as he means to take the management of the place into his own Hands and to endeavour to recover it from the poverty into which it has fallen through want of manure, &c there must be somebody to look after the dairy, and I think it may with safety be trusted to Pheby provided she will undertake it, but then she must have an assisstant The Question is, can she get one? or keep one after she has got her? There must also be some hands to look after the place, and to do the out door Labour. mr Adams will not have any corn raised upon it, so that the Labour will be much lessned, as things are so circumstanced. I think it would be best to Hire a man by the month & let him find himself. I hope we shall arrive in May or june, the Gardens we would wish cultivated, and such roots &c put in as we may stand in need of. If the doctor has purchased mr Borlands place for us, there will necessaryly be many things to do there I wish to have the Garden cultivated that we may at least have some vegetables to live upon when we return, but upon this subject I shall be better able to judge when I hear again from the Doctor. I hope you will get an opportunity to write to me what you think best to be done and consult with the Dr to whom I shall write, and agree with Pheby upon some terms, if the Dr and you should approve—I do not know a more trust worthy Hand.

every thing in this Country wears a Hostile appearence. France is said to be arming in concequence of it, and the Prussians have subjugated Holland—alass! poor Holland, like a sheep has it been deliverd to slaughter, panic struck she has submitted, discouraged and disheartned, unassisted by France her ally, who could not, or would not interfere, in season bullied by England. she seems now determined to resent it. Amsterdam still holds out, but tis Generally believed she will negotiate & make the best terms she can. The Patriots at the Hague & in delft, have been abused insulted & treated by the orange mob, with every species of indignity, unheard of wanton cruelties have been perpetrated, their Houses destroyed, their property laid waste, and every moment in jeopardy of their lives—in short the scene is too dismall to relate. read mr Adams's second volm his History of the Italian Republick, and you will find a History of what is now acting in Holland.[3] This Court have had the greatest Hand in bringing these calamities upon the Dutch, and are now going to War with all speed to continue them in it, & to support the stat-holder the whole Nation appeard engaged in it, and perfectly satisfied that it should be so. I hope & pray that our Country may be wise enough to keep out of it, and if they do they may milk the cow as it is termd, and it may prove benificial to their Trade, and commerce—

Col smith has returnd about a month since, but not without encountering a fit of sickness, in the Hot climates of Spain, & portugal, which like to to have cost him his Life. he got home looking like a shaddow, but has recruited finely since

My Grandson I cannot call him little for he is as fat as his Mamma was when she was a Baby. he is very well & sprightly. we talk of innoculating him for the small pox. I feel rather loth, but he is exposed to take it every time he goes out. he has cut two Teeth, there never was a healther child. we often tell him how Aunt Cranch would squeze him. I think my Journey was of service to my Health, I have been much better Since

Believe me my dear sister most affectionately / yours

A. Adams

RC (MWA:Abigail Adams Letters).

[1] The dating is based on AA's discussion of the plan to inoculate William Steuben Smith, which occurred on 18 Oct.; see AA to Mary Smith Cranch, 20 Oct., below.

[2] Mary Smith Cranch to AA, 27 May, 29 June, 16 July, and 21 July, all above.

[3] JA's 2d volume of the *Defence of the Const.* focuses on the Italian city-states, which JA used as examples of the necessity of balanced government: "If it appears, from the history of all the ancient republics of Greece, Italy, and Asia Minor, as well as from those that still remain in Switzerland, Italy, and elsewhere, that caprice, instability, turbulence, revolutions, and the alternative prevalence of those two plagues and scourges of mankind, tyranny and anarchy, were the effects of governments without three orders and a balance, the same important truth will appear, in a still clearer light, in the republics of Italy" (p. 1).

Abigail Adams to Mary Smith Cranch

Dear sister   London october 20th 1787

As captain Folger is not yet gone I write a few more lines by him, tho I have nothing new to acquaint you with, only that two days ago my little darling was inoculated for the Small pox. if whenever you come to have Grandchildren, you will scarcly know any difference between them & your own children, particularly if you should be under the same roof with them;

I have got mr Jenks to take the little Box & the Bonet wires for my Neices. they will observe in making them, to put the Gauze round the crown higher than the small pattern sent, which is only a minature I have sent by him addrest to you 3 yd of mock marcells which is a pattern for 4 waistcoats, 2 of which are designd for my Nephew, & the other two for my Eldest son. They are much in fashion just now, tho they may not be worn in winter with you, they will look well for summer, and I think we can manufacture winter Cloaths in America much better than summer. it may have been an Eoconomical plan to Some person, putting the Scholars into a uniform, but it is not so to me, because I could have made use of Cloaths that must now be useless to me, and when my sons are all grown up, a 2d hand coat will not be so acceptable to them.

Sister Smith has a large family of Boys[1]—would not some of the childrens Cloaths which they have out Grown be usefull to them. if so you will give them to her. where is our Brother? is he in any buisness I hope he does not suffer for want of the necessaries of Life, tho he has been so underserving.

pray who lives upon Germantown, I have never heard, and how does mr P——r family exist? where is Mrs Payne? What is become of mr T——r

I was much pleased with mr Daws's oration, and I sent it out to mr Hollis at the Hyde, together with the News paper which mentiond the Honorary degree of Dr of Laws conferd upon him.[2] inclosed is his answer[3] the portrait he mentions, was one of his present Majesty, a most ridiculous thing be sure, but a most striking likeness and I sent it to him to put with his curiosities. I mention this circumstance to explain a part of his Letter.

We have all been to the Hyde and spent a very pleasent week there. it is just 24 miles from Town. mr Hollis's American Friends as he calls them flourish finely, these are a number of American plants & Trees—which he has fancifully named after his Friends

adieu my dear sister excuse these hasty lines from your ever / affectionate

A A

RC (MWA:Abigail Adams Letters); addressed by AA2: "M$^{rs:}$ Mary Cranch / Braintree / near / Boston / Massachusetts."

[1] For William Smith Jr. and Catharine Louisa Smith's three boys and three girls, see vol. 5:230, 231.

[2] Thomas Dawes Jr. (1757-1825) had been appointed by the Boston Board of Selectmen to deliver a Fourth of July oration at the Stone Chapel following a military parade. Harvard College conveyed an honorary doctorate of law upon Thomas Brand Hollis in July, which was reported in the 23 July issue of the *Boston Gazette* (*Massachusetts Centinel*, 9 May, 4 July; Boston *American Herald*, 9 July).

[3] Not found.

Mary Smith Cranch to Abigail Adams

My dear Sister   Braintree october. 21ᵈ 1787

To hear that our dear good uncle Smith is added to the number of the Friends who have departed this Life since you left america will not greatly surprize you if you have receiv'd my Letters by the last ships which sail'd: yes my sister That good Man last monday morning about Two a clock clos'd his Eyes upon this vain world never more to open them till the last joyful Trump shall Wake to life all the nations of the earth— His disorder was something like coll. Quincys excepting that there was not a mortification— He did not suffer much Pain after the swelling abait'd in his Leg but he continu'd to sink a way & his life went out like the last snuff of a candle—without a sigh or groan. Five or six hours before he dy'd as he was laying upon the couch—he call'd Nabby & told her to send for all his Friends—His children & Brothers & sisters he meant Doctor & mrs Welch were of the number—"That he wish'd to see them once more"—"He was almost sure he should not live till the morning" They came—he gave them his blessing charg'd them to live in Love & harmony with each other & to take care of nabby & never to let her want any of the comforts of Life— He then desir'd that mr Clark might be sent for—¹ he had often visited him in his sickness— He Lov'd him he said & was comforted by his conversation— when he came—he told he that he had sent for him to pray with him once more— He sat up & said all this with as strong a voice as when he was well— The Docʳ did not think but he might have liv'd a week & told him so— no said he I shall dye this night— at ten the Doc found his Pulse alter'd— he went to sleep, but was restless & uneasey— nabby got up at one to give him some thing to take. he told her, that he could not help himself at all— she went to the Bed to assist him but found she had to close his Eyes— I went to town the next day to see him not knowing that he was dead— I had seen him almost every week since he was taken sick— He was most tenderly affected towards his Friends— the Letter he receiv'd from you by Barnard affected him so much that he shed Tears—² I went in just as he had done reading of it— "Thank her for me" said he to me "& tell her that I shall never write to her again— tell her also that I have notic'd one thing which I do not like— she often mentions going to meeting in the morning & having company to dine & spend the afternoon— I know she can not avoid it now—but I do not like it— I hope they will

196

not do it when they return—tell her I say so—" I promis'd him I would— you know the strict manner in which they use'd to keep the sabbath would ill agree with the loose manners of Europe—

He has left a most excellent character behind him many besides his children will rise up & call him blessed we my dear sister have lost in him another Parent— cousin Betsy bears the loss of Father much better than she did of her Mother. she has had time to prepair her mind for this. the other was sudden & it was the first real sorrow she ever knew— she looks calm & placed— cousin William sustains his loss with the most firmness— as to the amiable Preacher His Soul is bow'd down with sorrow He has no command of his tender Passions He is naturally low spirit'd—& he feels his loss more for not having a Family of his own & being in such an unsettled State—

uncle has left his Estate to be equally divided between his children only he has given cousin Betsy 150^{lb} more than the others to make her equal to mrs Otis to whom he has given firniture. Betsy will live with her Brother Will$^{m.}$ It is very happy for her that he has such a charming woman for his wife—you will admire her

uncle Smith is the seventh Person who has dy'd in our Familys since you left us—but my dear sister I have an eighth to add who tho he has long since been lost to us—yet while life remain'd I did hope would sooner or later return & be a comfort to us—

Sister last week receiv'd a Letter from a mr Barnard who says he was his Physician informing her that her Husband dy'd the 10th of september of the black jandice that the Family he was in took good care of him in his illness. That he was so well three days before his death as to be able to do considerable writing—but of what kind I do not know— He liv'd four miles from him & was not with him when he dy'd so cannot he says tell what the state of his mind was in that decicive moment— sister is going to answer his Letter— we shall know more I hope by his reply— your own mind will furnish you with the best Idea of what I feel upon this occation a meriful God will do right—[3]

When I was in town I heard of an English vesil just ready to sail— but I could not get a moment to write there— I had a great deal of business to do your sons from college are with me & I expect cousin JQA from Newburry with Mr Shaw & sister tomorrow— I must set my Tailors to work to fix them for winter— Miss Nancy Quincy Betsy Cranch & her Brother came from Haverhill last Friday & left all well Mr Thaxter is publish'd this day & is to be married next month—

I long & fear to have cushing arrive your account of your Health makes me very uneasey— I wish you was with me & under Doc[r.] Tufts care— I hope your journey has been of service to you— your sons Mother Hall & all your Braintree Friends are well— I have not time to say anything about your house now I shall write again soon— I have much to say— mr cranch & the children send Love to you & yours

accept it also from your sister

RC (Adams Papers).

[1] Presumably Rev. John Clarke of Boston's First Church, for whom see vol. 5:281.

[2] Probably AA to Isaac Smith Sr., 12 March, above. AA's letter was actually carried by Capt. James Scott, who arrived in Boston around the same time as Capt. Barnard (*Massachusetts Centinel*, 28 April 1787).

[3] William Smith Jr. (1746–1787), AA's brother, had long been estranged from his three sisters. Although he served as a militia captain at the Battles of Lexington and Concord, he soon became better known within his family for his intemperance, his debts, and his repeated desertions of his wife, Catharine Louisa Smith, and their six children. In 1785, Catharine wrote AA that Smith "has not been in this part of the Country for almost two years. I seldom hear from him and when I do the intelegence is not what I could wish. Poor unhappy man!" He was also at one point tried for counterfeiting notes in New York State, though ultimately acquitted. AA and her sisters frequently commented on their "poor unhappy connexion, whose Life has been one continued Error," and he was still estranged from his family at the time of his death (vol. 2:408; 5:230, 231; 6:357, 358–359, 447, 486, 487).

For AA's reaction to his death, see AA to Cotton Tufts, 1 Jan. 1788, and to Mary Smith Cranch, 10 Feb., both below.

Isaac Smith Jr. to Abigail Adams

my dear Mrs Adams   [*30 October 1787*]

The last year I acquainted you with the death of my mother, & I am sorry that I have now to inform you of that of my father, an event which has renewed my griefs, & will again excite your sympathetic feelings.

If any person bid fair for length of years, I thought this was the Case with my late valuable parent, but heaven it seems, to whose decisions it becomes us always humbly to submit, as wise & fit, had determined that he should not long survive my dear mother, sorrow for the loss of whom, accompanied with much inward anxiety for the welfare of his family, which he knew he should not leave in such easy & happy circumstances, as he wished to do, & as he once supposed it was in his power to have done, preyed upon his vitals & proved the means of bringing his days to a period, I ought not to say too soon, but sooner than I had flatter'd myself they would have ended, & sooner than the good wishes of his friends in general would have extended them. He had lived long enough to answer the great purposes of life; with the partner of his cares, with your own excellent & kind parents, whom I consider'd too in some sort as mine, & with other of our dear relatives & friends, who have been taken from us, in your absence, he is gone to rest, & may it be my concern to follow him.

I feel thankful, that I am not an infidel. When we once part with the Consolations of the Gospel, what support have we left, worthy to be mentioned, in such circumstances as those in which I am now placed? The idea of annihilation I Can never adopt. How pleasing the prospect of a revival, & how fond should we be of cherishing the thought of a reunion with our friends, with those among them more especially whom we have most highly esteemed, & of our being permitted to enjoy infinitely greater pleasure & satisfaction in the company of each other hereafter, than is possible here, where our happiness is so often liable to interruption, & is never free from some mixture of alloy. It was with the highest relish I read Dr Price's dissertation on this subject some years ago, & as you frequently see this goodman, if you think it worth while to do so, I beg you will give my respects to him.[1] With very different views of the probable Consequences of a revolution in America, from what he, & many others, whom I have known & respected, on both sides of the water, possest, I have yet at the same entertained the sincerest veneration for him. A vol. of his sermons has lately been received & read here with much approbation.[2] I have not myself as yet been gratified with the perusal of them.—

Of our political situation at present, you will hear eno' from other quarters, & will therefore not expect any thing from me[.] We are on the eve I hope of a change for the better, b[ut I] would not undertake to say what events, the jealousy [. . .] ignorance, ambition, or restless disposition of individual [. . .] may produce in the course of a few months, the evils arising from which it may not be in the power of the wisest counsels to prevent.—

If my father's affairs are settled in such a manner, as to prevent the loss of it to his family, my brother, who is connected in marriage with a partner that makes us all happy, will take the house, & my sister Betsey will live with him. As to me, the College to which I have returned the third time, will be my home.—[3] Mr Otis goes the next week to Congress, & leaves Mrs O. in a situation, in which she stands in need of comfort—[4] Mr & mrs Atkinson with their little family have gone to New York— Chas. Storer is a resident at Passamaquoddy, & his sister Polly is with him either there, or in Nova Scotia.— You will please to remember me to Mr Adams, & Mrs Smith. I am, my dear Mrs A., with the greatest affection, Yours,

I Smith

RC (Adams Papers); addressed: "Mrs A. Adams / Grosvenor Square / London"; endorsed: "Mr I Smith / 30 october 1787"; docketed by JQA: "Dated Octr. 30th. 1787." Some loss of text where the seal was removed.

[1] Richard Price, *Four Dissertations: III. On the Reasons for Expecting That Virtuous Men Shall Meet after Death in a State of Happiness*, London, 1767.

[2] Price, *Sermons on the Christian Doctrine as Received by the Different Denominations of Christians*, London, 1787.

[3] Prior to his appointment as Harvard's librarian in 1787, Smith had attended as a student, graduating in 1767, and served as a tutor from 1774 to 1775 (*Sibley's Harvard Graduates*, 16:523–525, 527).

[4] Samuel A. Otis served in Congress from 1787 to 1788 (*Biog. Dir. Cong.*).

Cotton Tufts to Abigail Adams

Dear Cous^n.   Boston Octob^r. 31. 1787

In my last Letter to M^r. Adams I inform'd Him of the Death of our beloved Uncle Smith—[1] had we enjoyed his Life much longer, it would have been greatly desireable—but Heaven was kind in continuing that rich Blessing for so long a Time we have the utmost Assurance that He is happy tho' We have lost one Source of our temporal Felicity— His Virtues may we imitate and with him share in a better World the Rewards of good & faithful Servants—

I am told Capt. Barnard is to sail to Day, which obliges me to omit many Things, not expecting his Departure for some Days—

as I take it for granted, that you will return in the Spring, it will be necessary to conduct your affairs upon that Expectation— I wish you therefore to give me as early and particular Information relative to the Repairs of Borlands Place & any other Matters as your Distance will permit and that you think necessary to be done—

M^r. Teal who is on your Farm at Medford is an excellent Tenant—[2] He informs me that the Farm House is scarcely tenantable, that it is the opinion of those who have viewed it, that it will be best to rebuild it.— I propose to examine it—but would wish for your Directions whether to rebuild in case it should be found necessary—the Cost will be from £120 to 130—

I expect to see & consult Mr Shaw this Week—he will exchange next Sabbath with Mr Norton our late ordaind Minister— Mr Shaw & his Wife attended the ordination of M^r. Ware at Hingham the Week past & are now on a Visit to his Father—

In one of your Letters, you enquire, whether it would not be best to dispose of your House in Bost^n I think not—as but very few Repairs will be required for a long Time to come—at present it yields a clearer Income than all your Lands & Estate in Braintree—

The Genl Court is now sitting— a Resolve has passed for calling a Convention in this Commonwealth to take into consideration the form of a Constitution of Government for the United States &C[3] I cannot make any Conjecture what will be the Issue It has warm Advocates for and warm Enemies against it— M^r. John spent the last Evening at my lodgings and is well— He will be at Cambridge to day & attend the Supreme Court some part of their Sitting— Charles & Thomas are well—return to Cambridge to Day from the fall Vacation— present my affectionate Regards to Mr Adams and accept of my best Wishes for your Health & Happiness.

Yours—   Cotton Tufts

RC (Adams Papers); internal address: "Mad^m. Abig^l Adams—"

[1] Cotton Tufts to JA, 18 Oct., Adams Papers.

[2] Benjamin Teal (b. 1763) of Medford had taken over the farm from his uncle, also Benjamin Teal, upon the latter's death in 1784 (vol. 5:472, 6:87; *Vital Records of Medford, Massachusetts, to the Year 1850*, Boston, 1907, p. 138).

[3] On 19 Oct. 1787, a joint committee of representatives from the House and the Senate of the Mass. General Court, including Cotton Tufts himself, met to discuss how to respond to the proposed Constitution. Their report recommended calling a state ratifying convention. After some debate, the General Court agreed on 25 Oct. and arranged for the convention to start on 9 Jan. 1788 (*Doc. Hist. Ratif. Const.*, 4:124–125). For the text of the resolution, see same, 4:143–146.

Abigail Adams to Cotton Tufts

Dear Sir   London Nov^{br} 6th 1787—

Last week Captains Folger & Callihan arrived by whom we received all your Letters & Bills.[1] the Bills were imediatly accepted, & will be paid when due. I feel under great obligations to you my dear sir, for all your kind care, & attention to our affairs. I am glad to find the buisness closed with mr Borland, and at a price which I think must be reasonable judging by what was formerly given for it, for I do not recollect how many acres of Land there are belonging to it. I know there is a wood lot containing 25 acres, & an other Lot of four, besides the Six which were sold to deacon Webb.— with regard to the repairs painting both without & within I should be glad to have compleated as soon as possible in the Spring, as the Smell is always pernicious to me. the east lower room to be painted what is calld a French Grey and as the furniture is red, a paper conformable, will look best. the Chamber over it will have Green furniture, and may be in the same manner, made uniform by a paper Green & white. the mahogany room, I know not what to say about it,[2] making the two windows into the Garden will dispell much of the Gloom, & if it is not much abused & injured, had it not better remain as it is? can there be a Closset contrived in the Room when the windows are made, I could wish to have one, to make a uniform appearence, must there not be windows in the Chamber above, in the east Room. I think there are two clossets by the side of the Chimney. what would be the expence of taking them away & making arches in the Room of them? Iron Backs to the Chimneys & Brass Locks upon the Doors of the two best rooms & Chambers are all the particular directions I think of at present with regard to the other part of the House I shall leave it wholy to your judgment to make such repairs as you deem necessary and consistant with œconomy. as to any aditional building we cannot at present afford any. in some future day perhaps we may think of making the House Square by adding a Library, which mr A will really want, but at present, some chamber must be a substitute. The Frame set up by mr T. you do not mention. it is best to let it remain in its present state untill we return. in the painting you will be so good as to employ a person who properly understands the Buisness. I mention this, because I once Sufferd & was obliged to have a room 3 times painted when one would have answerd—[3]

Mr Adams has written to you respecting our Farm, & mr Pratt. it has become so poor & misirable, that we must take some measures for making it better that we may be able to get our Bread from it. indeed I think I should enjoy better Health, to come Home & make butter & Cheese, raise poultry & look after my Garden, than by the inactive Life I am compelld to lead here.[4] it will require my strickest attention to oconomy to be able to live & compleat the Education of our children, but this does not terify me. I can conform to Whatever is necessary, with regard to the pocket expences of Charles & Tommy—you know sir, that on the one hand, we would not wish to have them too Spairingly Supplied, nor on the other permit them so much, as to lead them into Idleness & dissapation. if any thing of the kind appears you will check your Hand. Mrs Cranch knows what her son expended, and I do not see why mine Should require more. I shall write to them both, & exort them to prudence in their expences. I would venture Sir one hundred pounds more in the purchase of paper. I am fully of your mind with respect to Land and whatever purchases we may make in future, I could wish it might be better than what we already own—

it is mr A's intention to retire to Braintree as a private man, nor need any one fear that he will become a competitor with them for offices. he has always dealt too openly & candedly with his Countrymen to be popular, & whatever they[5] may assert with regard to his principals,[6] he says they may be assured that he will never conceal a Sentiment of his Heart, however unpopular it may be, which he considers for the interest of His Countrymen to know & consider, altho he should forfeit by it the highest offices in the united states. he was never yet the partizan of any Country,[7] nor will he ever become a Tool to any party, if fourteen years unremitted attention to the Service of his Country has not convinced them that he is their unshaken Friend, it would be in vain to attempt a conviction at this day. The English Review which you mention & which I see several of the states have carefully reprinted, was written by that Honour to his Country Silas Dean, who lives here as his appearence indicates, in real want & Horrour, and is Said to be a half crown Gazzet writer. I have only room to add that the Form of Government by the late Convention is esteemed here as a sublime work. they add that it is so good that they are perswaided the Americans will not accept it, it may admitt of some amendments but it is certainly a great Federal Structure. I shall write to all my Friends by Folger. my little Boy has got well through the small pox. adieu yours / &c &c

A A—

RC (Adams Papers); endorsed: "M^rs. Adams Lett^r of Nov. 6. / 1787 / rec^d. Feby 21. 1788." Dft (Adams Papers), dated and filmed at 5 November.

[1] Besides Cotton Tufts to AA, 20 Sept., above, Tufts also wrote to JA on 18 Sept. with additional information regarding the purchase of the Borland property (Adams Papers).

[2] In the Dft AA added, "I should like it half way up. I do not not know in what state it is if it is thought best to paint it I would have it done."

[3] The Dft concludes the paragraph, "as we shall take out a part of our furniture I could wish the House might be ready to put it in to save the expence & trouble of a second removal."

[4] In the Dft AA did not include the remainder of this paragraph but wrote instead, "and as to any examples of Luxery or extravagance, I promise my dear country women they shall have none from me, & it would be well for all of them, if they would make a virtue of necessity."

[5] The Dft identifies "they" as "democrats or Arostocrats."

[6] The Dft further describes them as "monarchacal principals."

[7] In the Dft AA specifies "France England or Holland."

Elizabeth Smith Shaw to Abigail Adams

My Dear Sister.—   Haverhill November 17.th 1787

Friend, after Friend is severed from my Heart—I have lost many near, & dear Relatives, as well as kind Benefactors, since you left America.

I know you will be much affected by hearing of the Death of our worthy & much lamented Uncle Smith.— You my Sister knew how bright the humane & christian Virtues shone in his Life, & cannot wonder if the Land mourns when the godly Man ceaseth, & so faithful a one fails[1]—for such are the Pillars of Society.—

I think he has been upon the decline, ever since the Death of our dear Aunt—the beloved Wife of his Youth.—

He was to see us in June, after his Sons Wedding— He said if he had consulted his own feelings he should have tarried at Home— that Life had lost its relish—& that everything in which he formerly took pleasure, seemed rather to renew, & to aggravate his Sorrow.

But he was not suffered to grieve long—for in sixteen Months he was permitted to join her gentle Spirit, with those of the "just made perfect—"[2] & (I presume) is triumphing in those happy Regions, where they are as the Angels—where love, & Bliss immortal reign—

We heard of his Death two Days before we sat out upon our Journey to Bridgwater—

You cannot think how my heart recoiled at the Idea of going into Boston, & seeing my second Fathers House desolate, & sit solotary, where so late its dear owners with sweet, & endearing hospitality smiled upon each Guest, & Peace, & Plenty, cheared the social Board—

Cousin Betsy behaves with great propriety. Her Mothers Death was the severest stroke she can ever feel. Her Spirit till then was unbroken— She had no cause before, ever to shed a Tear— She is now happy in having her Brother William married to so fine a Woman— The House is prized at twelve hundred—he will take it, & she will live with them—

My Uncle lost a vast deal in the War—at its commencement, he was worth 40000 sterling, but now there will be but little left for the Children—So precarious are Estates—For almost every Family shews me the necessity of Childrens being taught Oeconomy, & bred early to Buisiness— My Cousins have this to comfort them, that it was

not extravagance which reduced the Estate—but a train of unforeseen Events—

Mrs Otis is to be pitied— Mr Otis is gone to Congress, & must
leave her for the Winter.— You my Sister can feel for her—

But there is not one of the Family, who feel their loss so sensibly,
as our worthy Cousin Isaac He is almost overwhelmed with Grief—
he mourns indeed with great bitterness of Soul— He says he has *no
Home now*—no kind Parents House—

Just before his Fathers Death he accepted of the Office of Librarian— I rejoiced when he left the Castle, that Den of Theives, &
Miscreants, & was placed among the Literati, in a Circle much
more agreeable to his Worth, Taste, & Feelings—

They have at last got an exceeding agreeable Young Gentleman
settled at Weymouth— I dare say you will be pleased with him— He
supplied Mr Shaws Pulpit one Sabbath, & our young People all fell
in Love with him—

Hingham too have been wise in the choice of Mr Ware, a young
Gentleman whom your Son JQA lived with the first Six months of
his residence in the University—& of whom he speaks with great
affection, & respect—

They are all enthusiastically fond of him at Hingham— One Man
said, Father Gay had gone to the third heaven, & had sent an Angel
to take the charge of his Flock—[3]

Mr Shaw, & your Sister, Mr Thaxter, & Mr James, & Miss Betsy
Duncan, your Sons, & Neices were with a multitude of Others, at
this Ordination—where every thing was conducted with the greatest
Decency &cc—

Mr Thaxter upon the 13th of November between the Hours of six
& seven, resigned his seat in batchelors Hall, & commenced the
married Man—

Mrs Russel was alive when I was in Boston, but was growing
weaker every Day— She had thought of going to Carolina for the
sake of the warm Climate But I presume she will soon be in a Climate, much more agreeable to her exalted Mind— Mrs Hay has
been with her, for these two months— You know how tender she was
of her Sister Weld—[4] The Doctors are at a loss which will go first—
Nancy Sever, or Mrs Russel— The Scene is distressing—

Cousin Hannah Austin died the beginning of September— Mrs
Austins tender Heart was much affected by her Daughters Death—
Mrs Allen makes a fine Nurse, & little miss grows fast—

Our poor Brother—He is gone too—died with the black Jandice the 3ᵈ of September after a very short Illness—

Our feelings I suppose are similar upon this ocasion—

The same air, *we* breathed—the same cradle rocked us to rest—& the same Parental Arms folded us to their fond Bosoms—& who can refrain full many a Tear at such a Death!— It is some consolation to hear, he was well taken care of in his Sickness—but poor Creature he had not lived out half his Days—he was not I think quite forty years old—

By yours of the 20ᵗʰ of July you inform me of your poor health, though I cannot but flatter myself you are better, & that your Journey has removed every disorder— I want to have you come Home more than ever— I cannot bear to think of your being sick at such a Distance—

The throat Distemper has left the Town, & our Family has been so blessed as to escape this dreadful Disease—

I must thank my Sister for a thousand expressions of kindness— I believe you sit contriving what good you can do—& how much you can oblige your Friends— The Tea Urn has come safe, it is very useful, as well as ornamental but it would never have been in my power to purchased it— The little candle Case too is very curious— Mr Shaw desires his best respects may be accepted—& thinks himself highly favoured, & obligated by Dr Adam's kindness, & attention—

The Constitution you have before this, I suppose— Every body asks, what do you think Dr Adams will say & will he approve of it, or not— It is a matter of solemn importance— Mr Bayley Bartlett, & Capt Marsh are chosen by this Town to convene at Boston, upon this ocasion—⁵

Your Son J Q A kept Sabbath with us, & has promised to keep Thansgiving with your affectionate Sister   E Shaw—

Love in abundance awaits every Soul of my kindred—⁶

RC (Adams Papers); endorsed: "Mrs Shaw / Novᵇʳ 17. 1787."

¹ "Help, Lord; for the godly man ceaseth; for the faithful fail from among the children of men" (Psalms, 12:1).

² Hebrews, 12:23.

³ "I knew a man in Christ above fourteen years ago, (whether in the body, I cannot tell; or whether out of the body, I cannot tell: God knoweth;) such an one caught up to the third heaven" (2 Corinthians, 12:2).

⁴ Katherine Farnham Hay's sister, Hannah Farnham, was the second wife of Rev. Ezra Weld of Braintree before her death in 1778 at age 27 (*Colonial Collegians*; *Vital Records of Newbury Massachusetts to the End of the Year 1849*, 2 vols., Salem, 1911, 1:164).

⁵ The town of Haverhill formally voted on 19 Nov. to send Bailey Bartlett and Nathaniel Marsh as representatives to the Massachusetts state ratifying convention (*Doc. Hist. Ratif. Const.*, 5:893, 6:1154).

⁶ The final paragraph, signature, and postscript were written sideways in the margin.

Thomas Brand Hollis to Abigail Adams

my Dear madam   The Hide Decem 4th. 1787.

you put too much value on trifles which are only small marks of real regard & affection to you & yours.[1]

I have always conceived it to be more difficult to give than receive. as the sense of obligation sets heavy on minds inflated with riches or pride & not capable of enlarged ideas or of the pleasing sensations which arise from mutual gifts & good offices abstracted from their intrinsick value. as riches are only fortuitous, hard and deplorable indeed would be the fate of the possessors of them if they were only permitted to indulge their own personal gratification. but I am secure you will receive with the same sentiment with which things are presented and at the same time partake of & contribute to the pleasing sensations.

The pamphlets you will please to keep till I have the pleasure of seeing you in town.

The prospects are dismal but just & truly delineated I fear will now do us little good.— all parties were inclined for war for the reasons there assigned private interest.

not one patriot in the house or without, to justify the —— —— inteference in the Dutch government by proposing to give them a free & equal Commonwealth in which the people should have part. at present having no share & of course no Country. from such a government justly balanced no state in Europe would have had any apprenhension of them, nor would have dared the attempt to have subjugated them.

This would have returned the benefit they conferred upon us & have been worthy of England in her better days. but these are scenes too grand—

> and tho they shine in youth's ingenuous view,
> the sober gainful arts of modern days
> to such romantick thoughts have bid a long Adieu.[2]

I was with you in spirit on friday but could not personally attend.— my compliments of health & spirits to Mr Adam & Mr Smith & shall be exceeding glad to see them here & happy they think of it. I hope the Col's health will not prevent but I must beg two nights—that we may have one walk the next day— monday is the only day I am engaged from home. the beds well aired by Mrs Jebb & Dr Disney &

207

shall be repeated when known when they come. I wished to have been in town to attend upon our college this day to hear some orations but it was impossible. my compliment to Mrs Smith I am Dear Madam with great truth / your obliged & affect Friend

T. Brand Hollis.

RC (Adams Papers).

[1] On 4 Nov., Thomas Brand Hollis had written to AA sending her "a set of prints which are valuable for their rarity and the emminent persons they represent" (DSI:Hull Coll., on loan). AA's letter to Brand Hollis, presumably to thank him for this gift, has not been found.
[2] Mark Akenside, "Ode II: To Sleep," lines 38–40.

Abigail Adams to Thomas Jefferson

London Grosvenour square December 5th 1787—

Mrs Adams presents her respectfull compliments to Mr Jefferson and asks the favour of him to permit petit to purchase for her ten Ells of double Florence of any fashionable coulour, orange excepted which is in high vogue here. Mrs A excepts green also of which she has enough. Mr Rucker if in Paris will be so kind as to take Charge of it, & mrs Adams will send the money by mr Trumble who will be in Paris some time next week—

By Letters this day received from Boston, it appears that a convention was agreed too, by both Houses, & that it is to meet, the second wednesday in Jan^ary

Mr King writes that mr Jeffersons commission, is renewed at the court of France, & mr Adams's resignation accepted, so that we shall quit this country as soon in the Spring as we can go with Safety.[1]

Love to the Young Ladies & thank my dear Polly for her pretty Letter—[2]

RC (DLC:Jefferson Papers).

[1] Rufus King to JA, 27 Oct., Adams Papers.
[2] Not found.

John Quincy Adams to Cotton Tufts

Dear Sir.   Newbury-Port. December 9th: 1787.

If it should be convenient to you, I would be obliged to you for a supply of money. I endeavour to avoid all expences, but such as are really necessary; yet I am not only exhausted, but somewhat in debt.— I can scarcely tell how the money goes, but I have an account of all my expences, which assures me that none has been lost.

Your brother informs me that it will be more convenient for him to take an order for what I am indebted to him, and therefore I have not paid him. He has also some money for you, which he has offered me, and if I should take it the amount of the order will, I imagine be about £.7.

I am not in immediate want of a supply from you, especially if I should take the additional sum from your brother. but for the sake of having money at hand, I should be glad to receive it as soon as you can make it perfectly convenient to send.

Respectfully your's   J. Q. Adams.

RC (Adams Papers); addressed: "Honble: Cotton Tufts Esqr: / Weymouth."; endorsed: "John Adams Jun / Decr 9. 1787"; notation: "To be left with the / other letter."

Cotton Tufts to Abigail Adams

Dear Cousin   Weymouth Decr. 18. 1787.

The System of Government reported by the late Continental Convention has afforded much Matter for Pens and Tongues— The Friends & opposers of it are distinguished by the Party names of Federalists & Antifederalists— These Names I suspect will continue as long as Whig & Tory— which of the Parties will carry their Point, is difficult to say— Many of the Advocates for the Constitution are enthusiastic open & severe in their Attacks upon all that oppose it, those on the other Side act more secretly, but with great Success— A prevailing Sense of present Weakness & Danger for want of an efficient Government together with the Fear of having one that shall be the Result of Force, will probably reconcile many to this, who would otherwise be decidedly against it— The Choice of Delegates (for our State Convention) in the County of Suffolk & Essex so far as they have proceeded, has in general fallen on the most respectable Characters The Town of Braintree, has done itself Honour in the Choice of Bro^r Cranch & the Rev^d. Mr Wibirt— also there are some of the first Characters from other Parts of the Country— Newyork is said to be opposed to this Plan—and have not as yet called a Convention— Pensylvania is said to have met & adopted it—[1] The Determination of all the States will not probably be had in a less Term than a Year till which Time We must wait with Patience—

In a former Letter I informed You of the Death of our worthy Uncle— I am exceedingly grieved to find that his Estate is in Danger of being represented Insolvent, in Consequence of the Deprciation of our public Securities— To the House of Champion & Dickenson he was indebted & made Remittances during the War to the amount of £10 or 11000, (Scarce any other Merchant made Remittances during that Time) he sent to Europe Two Vessells, which had they not been taken, would have discharged his whole Debt now amounting to £6, or, 7000 Sterl^{g}— discouraged in his attempts he vested this Money in public Securities for the purpose of answering that Debt whenever Peace should arrive— Was that Debt to be paid in the public Notes left on Hand—at nominal Value—there would still remain on hand some Estate to be divided among the Children but if the Demand be made in Specie only—the whole real Estate must be sold— other Debts against the Estate are but small— Forty years Business he carried on with that House—and to such an Amount—as they must have made an Estate from it—and I hope they will have goodness enough to make a reasonable Composition, since like an honest Man He did the best that lay in his Power to secure their Interest—

The Town of Boston entertained an high Esteem of the deceased and as a Mark of their Respect, have chosen his Son William as his Successor in the office of Overseer of the Poor. for a Time before his Fathers Death, He married to a Daughter of Mr Nathl Carter. of Newbury Port, to the great Delight of his Connections— Our Cousin Isaac not long since was appointed Librarian to our University— M$^{r.}$ Otis is gone (a Member of Congress) to New York— His Wife last week brought him a Daughter—

At Weymouth We have ordained a Mr Norton and are I think happy in our Choice— Hingham has settled a M$^{r.}$ Ware. Scituate a M$^{r.}$ Dawes in the Parish formerly Rev$^{d.}$ Mr Grovernors, Pembroke M$^{r.}$ Whitman as a Colleague with Rev$^{d.}$ M$^{r.}$ Smith. Titicut (part of Bridgewater) M$^{r.}$ Gurney, in the Room of Rev$^{d.}$ Mr Reid dec$^{d.}$[2] all in the Space of Two Months— what Think you? Are't We growing Good Folks in this part of the Country?—

Your Children were all well, last Week & your other Connections Wishing you all Happiness & a safe return to America

I am yours respectfully C. Tufts

P.S. Would it not be best to send a Collection of Seeds for your Garden by some of the Spring Vessells, such as Peas—Beans—Cabbage &C— I wish to hear from you by the first Conveyance.[3]

Dec. 27

Delaware & Jersey States as well as Philadelphia have acceded to the proposed Plan of Government—[4] I should have been highly gratified to have received M[r.] Adams Sentiments upon it previous to our Deccision, but as our State Convention will meet on the Second Wednesday of January next, I must be deprived of that Happiness—till at a more distant Period— I confess I feel more than commonly anxious, for although I have seen my Country trampling down Law & Government & sporting with Right & Justice & have wished for a Government adequate to our Necessities. Yet I should be exceeding sorry to see any other than a Government of Laws— Is the present Plan well calculated to produce a Government of Laws? Does it not favour too much of Aristocracy for future Freedom Quiet & Duration? Does it provide for an adequate Representation? Is the Executive sufficiently independent? Are the Powers properly defined & sufficiently explicit? Are the Three Powers duly balanced? Where is the Bill of Rights or is it unnecessary? These are Questions which I hope My Friend will one Day do me the Pleasure to resolve, versed in the Knowledge & Study of Government— His Advice reasonings & Council would weigh to much— I Wish him to write me what the Situation of Europe is with Respect to War, for although we abound with News, yet We have but very little that can be relied on— Youll be pleased to inform M[r.] Adams, that I drew an order on him in favour of M[r.] Elworthy for £100 Sterl[g] dated the 26[th.] Inst—

RC (Adams Papers); addressed: "M[rs.] Abigail Adams / Grovesnor Square / London"; internal address: "M[rs.] Abigail Adams"; endorsed: "C. Tufts / December 18 1787."

[1] The Pennsylvania ratifying convention met from 20 Nov. to 15 December. On 12 Dec., it voted by a margin of 46 to 23 to ratify the Constitution (*Doc. Hist. Ratif. Const.*, 4:xxi).

[2] Rev. Ebenezer Grosvenor (1738/39–1788), Yale 1759, had been Scituate's minister from 1763 to 1780. After a period apparently without a settled minister, Scituate called Rev. Ebenezer Dawes (1756–1791), Harvard 1785, who was ordained there in Nov. 1787; he served until his death (Weis, *Colonial Clergy of N.E.*; *Church Manual . . . of the First (Trinitarian Congregational) Church of Christ in Scituate, Mass.*, Boston, 1844, p. 6; *Harvard Quinquennial Cat.*).

Rev. Thomas Smith (1706/7–1788), Har-

vard 1725, served as Pembroke's minister from 1754 until his death in July 1788. Rev. Kilborn Whitman (1765–1835) was ordained at Pembroke in Dec. 1787 and became Smith's successor (Weis, *Colonial Clergy of N.E.*; H. W. Litchfield, *The First Church in Pembroke 1708–1908*, Pembroke, Mass., 1908, n.p.).

Rev. Solomon Reed (1719–1785), Harvard 1739, served as the minister of the Titicut Separatist Parish, which lay part in Bridgewater and part in Middleborough, Mass., from 1756 until his death. Rev. David Gurney (1759–1815), Harvard 1785, succeeded him in Sept. 1787 (Weis, *Colonial Clergy of N.E.*; *Sibley's Harvard Graduates*, 10:400; *Harvard Quinquennial Cat.*; S. Hopkins Emery, *The*

History of the Church of North Middleborough, Middleborough, Mass., 1876, p. 35–36).
³ This paragraph was written sideways in the margin.
⁴ On 7 Dec., the Delaware ratifying convention approved the Constitution by a vote of 30 to 0 after meeting for only five days. The New Jersey convention convened on 11 Dec. and met until 20 Dec., ratifying the Constitution on 18 Dec. by a vote of 38 to 0 (*Doc. Hist. Ratif. Const.*, 4:xxi).

Mary Smith Cranch to Abigail Adams

My dear Sister   Braintree December 22ᵈ 1787

I last week heard from all your sons they were well. After this you may read on calmly— We are all well excepting great colds & coughs. I think in this Letter I shall not have to mention the death of any new Friend many very many of my Letters have convey'd the sorrowful tydings of some dear Friend departed, & if you should live to return to us you will find vacancys which will draw Tears from your Eyes—

I have been waiting with anxious expectation for these many months to hear from you not one line since your excursion into the west. By mrs Wilcox I heard of you there she does not mention your being out of health so hope your ride was of service to you cap Cushing has been a long time expected, by him I hope I shall hear of your welfair—

Mr Smith has remov'd into his Fathers House I have been there but every thing is so alter'd that I did not know how to bear the place cousin Betsy is with them & Nabby also nothing else looks as it us'd to—all the Pictures are remov'd & the Parlour is new painted

Mrs Welsh has a son whom they call Henry, & Mrs Otis a Daughter—both Mothers & children were well a few days since

The publick Prints will inform you of the Persons chosen for this State to meet in convention—¹ our Parson will not go, Lucy says because he never went before.² he cannot bear to be put out of the course he has been in for so many years. He will not change his Lodgings because he has not done it before nor marry for the same reason & I know no other why we do not have a new sermon. I am not sure that I have heard one from him since you went away

This Federal constitution makes a great part of the conversation of our Politicians—but as I am not one of them I can say nothing about it— It appears to me necessary to be a great Politician to judge of so large a Plan. Heaven direct them to such determinations as shall tend to make us a happy People— Mr cranch had sat himself down very quietly to watch-work in his little shop—but this Town have call'd him off once more to act for them in this convention. When it is over he will return to his favourite employment again

Such a time for ordinations in our Neighbourhood you never Saw—ten or a dozen at least within these three months & a number of sensible gentlemen they are I hear—but we live the wrong Sind of the Hill for preaching at present— There is a Mr Dawes settled at Situate who is a sensible man & a very good Preacher Doctor Tufts says—

I have not heard from sister Shaw since she returnd in october at least I have not had a Letter— Polly Smith is still with us miss Paine has been with me upon a visit for about three weeks—is in better health than in years past but will never be other than a cripple. She sends her Love & many thanks for her stockings— Mr Palmers Family are to remove to Boston next week they have been greatly distress'd for Bread to eat o my Sister! What a reverse of fortune it falls hard upon us for we cannot see them suffer while our seller can supply them—after all what we can do is but small

Dec. 26th

I have written thus far & disign'd to have added more but I have a chance to send this to Town, & I am so affraid that the vessel will sail without a line from me that I shall send it along short as it is—& will write more if I should have time— I hope I shall not have to write much more to you in so distant a country.— yours affectionately

Mary Cranch

Mrs Hall was well yesterday

RC (NAII:Cranch-Greenleaf Papers); docketed by William Cranch: "Mother to Aunt Adams."

[1] Various Massachusetts newspapers gave considerable coverage to the elections, printing both commentary on potential candidates and the results themselves. See, for instance, Boston *Independent Chronicle*, 6, 13, and 20 December.

[2] Lucy Cranch was unduly pessimistic. Anthony Wibird did attend the ratifying convention and ultimately voted in favor of the Constitution though there is no record of his speaking at the convention (*Doc. Hist. Ratif. Const.*, 6:1463, 1479).

John Quincy Adams to Abigail Adams

Dear Madam.   Newbury-Port December 23[d] 1787.

It is a long time since I wrote you last, but I am perfectly weary of making apologies. I have no doubt but my friends will forgive me, when they recollect the causes which have prevented me from informing them frequently of those trivial events, which the partiality of friendship alone can render interesting. When I was last in Boston, which was about two months ago, I wrote a few hasty lines to my father, intending to write more largely soon after my return to this place.[1] I have delay'd fulfilling my intentions from time to time, either from the want of an opportunity, or from the multiplicity of my employments, and even now, I know not whether this letter will go within these three months.— In the beginning of September I came to this Town, and began the study of the law with M^r: Parsons. I could not possibly have an instructor, more agreeable than this gentleman. His talents are great: his application has been indefatigable, and his professional knowlege is surpassed by no gentleman in the Commonwealth. The study itself, is far from being so destitute of entertainment, as I had been led to expect. I have read three or four authors with pleasure as well as improvement; and the imaginary terrors of tediousness and disgust, have disappeared, upon the first approach. But in their stead other fears have arisen, which create more anxiety in my mind, and which will increase rather than subside. The popular odium which has been excited against the practitioners in this Commonwealth prevails to so great a degree, that the most innocent and irreproachable life cannot guard a lawyer against the hatred of his fellow citizens:— The very despicable writings of Honestus, were just calculated to kindle a flame, which will subsist long after they are forgotten. The author after being hoisted by this weak instrument into the Senate has already return'd to his native insignificancy, and under the new adopted signature of Candidus, defends a good cause without ability and without success.[2] But the poison has been so extensively communicated, that its infection will not easily be stopped: a thousand lies in addition to those published in the papers have been spread all over the Country; to prejudice the people against the "*order*" as it has invidiously been called; and as a free people will not descend to disguise their sentiments, the gentlemen of the profession, have been treated with contemptuous neglect, and with insulting abuse.— Yet notwithstanding all this the profession is increasing rapidly in numbers, and the little business to be done is divided into so many shares, that they are in danger of starving one another.— When I consider these disadvantages, which are in a degree peculiar to the present time, and those which at all times subsist; when I reflect that with good abilities, great application, and a favourable Fortune are requisite to acquire that eminence in the profession which can ensure a decent subsistence, I confess I am sometimes almost discouraged, and ready to wish I had engaged in some other line of life. But I am determined not to despond. With industry and frugality, with Patience and perseverance it will be very hard if I cannot go through the world with honour.— I am most resolutely determined, not to spend my days in a dull tenor of insipidity. I never shall be enough of a stoic, to raise myself beyond the reach of Fortune. But I hope I shall have so much resolution, as shall enable me to receive Prosperity without growing giddy & extravagant, or Adversity without falling into Despair.

I board at a M^rs: Leathers's—a good old woman;[3] who even an hundred years ago, would have stood in no danger of being hang'd for witchcraft: she is however civil and obliging, and what is very much in her favour, uncommonly silent so that if I am deprived of the charms, I am also free from the impertinence of Conversation. There is one boarder beside myself. A D^r: Kilham, (I hope the name will not scare you) one of the representatives from this town, a very worthy man; and a man of sense and learning.[4] was it not for him, I should be at my lodgings as solitary as an hermit: there is a very agreeable society in the town; though I seldom go into Company.

I pass'd two or three days at Haverhill, about a month ago, and had the pleasure of finding M^r: Thaxter; From the severest censurer of every trifling attentions between lovers, he became as fond a shepherd as ever was celebrated in the annals of Arcadia. he expects some peculiar animadversions from you, for his desertion of principles, which he formerly boasted were so deeply rooted in his mind. But it is the old story of Benedick. The absurity, is not in abandoning a vain, ineffectual resolution; but it is in pretending to adopt a resolution, which every day may be rendered futile.

I have frequently been prevented from expatiating in my letters, upon political topics, by the sterility of the subject, an uncommon fertility now produces the same effect. I can only say in general terms that parties run very high, and that we are most probably at the eve of a revolution: Whether it will be effected, in silence, and without a struggle, or whether it will be carried at the point of the sword is yet a question.— The Newspapers, will show you how much the public is engaged in the discussion of the new continental form of government, which I fear will be adopted.

From the remainder of the family, you will probably hear, by the same opportunity, that is to convey this. when I last heard from my brothers they were well.

your ever affectionate Son.   J.QAdams.

RC (Adams Papers); endorsed: "Dec 23 '87 / J Q A."

¹ Not found.
² By this date, two of three articles by Candidus had appeared in the Boston *Independent Chronicle*, 6 and 20 December. A third would appear on 3 Jan. 1788. The belief that Candidus was a pseudonym for Benjamin Austin Jr., who also wrote as Honestus, was widely held (*Doc. Hist. Ratif. Const.*, 4:392–399; 5:493–500, 609–610).

³ JQA lived in Newburyport with Martha Leathers, the widow of a shipwright, until September (JQA, *Diary*, 2:276).
⁴ Dr. Daniel Kilham, Harvard 1777, an apothecary, represented Newburyport in the General Court from 1787 to 1788 (*Doc. Hist. Ratif. Const.*, 4:141, note 2). See also JQA, *Diary*, 2:288 and *passim*.

Abigail Adams to Cotton Tufts

My dear sir   London Jan^ry 1. 1788—

I wrote you by the November packet which Letter I hope you have received before now, in that I mentiond what I wished to have done to the House, particularly the painting & papering. Since that date we have received your favour by Captain Barnard desiring to know how mr Adams would have the land improved, but neither he or I are well enough acquainted with the Land to give any other directions, than, if any requires to be laid down, that it may be done with Grass Seed. he does not propose to have any corn planted, but to improve it wholy to Grass. the Garden we would wish to have put in order, & such seeds sown as may be necessary before we arrive but we hope to be with you the latter end of April, or begining of May. we have concluded to come with Captain Callihan who has the best accommodations for passenger of any merchantman in the Trade. he wishes to sail in March, but I hope it will not be untill April. mr & mrs Smith go in the April packet for New York. We propose leaving London the first of March, & talk of going to Falmouth to embark, but shall be governd by circumstances— as we shall take out some of our furniture, I should be glad the House might be ready for it as soon as we arrive I have one other request to add, which is that you would order a chaise for us, neat & well made. I inclose the Arms which are to be painted upon it.¹ the Time draws very near, and we are begining to make preparation for our departure—

Alass, my dear Sir, How many valuable Friends have I lost since I left you? Should it please Heaven to return me safe to my Native Land—what a Chasm shall I find—the dear hospitable mansion of my uncle bereft of its chief supporters. with what Sensations Shall I enter those doors again. Nor are my thoughts less intent upon an other Vacancy, too painfull to describe—cannot you fill the place to your Satisfaction?[2]

An other Relative too, has left the world, who tho long lost to the World & his Friends, yet whilst living hope remained. unhappy Man. reflections upon this event are too painfull to me. the ties of Nature are powerfull bonds, I feel even the bitteness of them—

our Family, thanks to Heaven are in general, in Good Health; mr Smith has been ill repeatedly Since his return from Portugal, the remains of a Billious fever which he took in the Hot climate of spain, & which nearly cost him his Life. my little Boy too has been very sick cutting Teeth. my own Health is much mended by my last falls excursion—but I fear I shall have a very melancholy event upon my voyage; if it does not take place sooner. Esther seems going fast after her sisters, not in a consumption but for five months labouring under other complaints which if not soon removed must prove fatal, as yet no application has had the desired Effect, dropsy & parilitick complaints are comeing fast upon her, the latter has been kept of for some time by Elictrisity. I mention her Situation by this opportunity, that her Friends may be apprizd of my apprehensions I have the satisfaction to say that she has been a Good Girl untainted by the vile manners of the servants of this Country I have been able always to treat her with the tenderness of a parent, without her ever forgetting her own place & situation. I shall feel her loss most severely.—

I shall write to my Friends by Captain Barnard who is to sail in Febry. in the mean time permit me to offer to yourself and the rest of my Friends, more than the mere compliments of the Season, my sincerest wishes for your mutual happiness, Health of Body & peace of mind not only this, but every succeeding year of your Lives, and Heaven grant that a few months more may make us happy together in our own Native Land—

Believe me dear sir most / affectionately Yours.   A Adams

P S as I do not know of any method of making a chaise go without a Horse Should be glad if you would be looking out one for us—

RC (Adams Papers); endorsed: "M^rs. Adams Lett^r Jan^ry 1. 88 / rec^d. Feb^ry 28—"

[1] AA's drawing has not been found but was probably a copy of the Boylston family's coat of arms, which JA used on passports he issued from The Hague following Dutch recognition of the United States in 1782. For more on these arms, see vol. 4:xv–xvi.

[2] AA and her sisters had discussed among themselves encouraging Tufts to remarry since the death of his wife, Lucy Quincy Tufts, in Oct. 1785 (vol. 7:6–7, 432, 433, 463, 473).

Lucy Paradise Barziza to Abigail Adams

Dear Madam.   Venice, 12th Jan^{ry.} 1788.

If I have failed in my duty untill now, I will differe no longer from emploring my pardon for my neglegence, and to shew you at the same time the sentiments of my perfect remembrance of the many politeness you and your good family have always shown me; and of the perfect esteem, with which I profess myself. I cannot however differe any longer having heard that your husband and family quits England for America very soon. I recieved also the news that my father, and mother thank God are safely arrived in Virginia which has greatly comforted me and sofetened the sorrow which there departure caused me being under continual fears and happrehentions for them. I am sure you will continue us your friendship recommending to you my parents to whom your, and your husbands influence may be of infinite use to and which I shall ever remember with gratitude. I flatter myself that it would not be disagreable If I should give you a short detail of my present situation. I was surprised on arriving at my husbands house, the manner in which I was recieved by all his relations and friends the number of which are very great so that my house was a whole month in a continual bustle from the visits which I did nothing else but recieve morning and evening.[1] His palace is magnaficent and furnished expensively, servants in proportion and horses to the number of 6 for common use. besides that an oppen table so that with that respect I cannot be more contented I have only to reproach myself of my not deserving such a fortune. But what is still better is my husband is of the very first Nobility, he bares also great for the qualities of his understanding and the goodness of his heart. His attachment to me is always the same, and you cannot imagin but that my affection for him is very great. I am just on point of lying in and by the time you recieve this to be safely broght-abed.[2] I thank God have passed my pregency perfectly well. I took the libirty to give you an account of my situation being sure that your goodness would interess yourself in my wellfare. and haveing perhaps an occation of seeing my parents you may comfort them by giving them an account of my happy situation. My Husband joins with me in best compliments to Mr. Adams, and M^{r.} and Mrs. Smith, preserving me your friendship and disposing of me in all occations—

I am. / dear Madam. / Your obliged and / humble servant

Lucy Barziza

RC (Adams Papers).

[1] Lucy Paradise (1771–1800) married Count Antonio Barziza of Venice in March 1787 in London. John Paradise had strongly opposed the match—Lucy Paradise was only sixteen and Barziza was of dubious character and a fortune-hunter—but Lucy Ludwell Paradise supported it and aided the couple in elop- ing against her husband's wishes (Archibald Bolling Shepperson, *John Paradise and Lucy Ludwell of London and Williamsburg*, Richmond, Va., 1942, p. 251–270, 456).

[2] The Barzizas' first child, Giovanni, was born in 1788 at Venice (same, p. 311, 456).

John Adams to John Quincy Adams

My dear John   Grosvenor Square Jan. 23. 1788

I am much pleased with your Oration and much obliged to you for it. it seems to me, making allowance for a fathers Partiality, to be full of manly Sense and Spirit. By the Sentiments and Principles in that oration, I hope you will live and die, and if you do I dont care a farthing how many are preferred to you, for Style Elegance and Mellifluence.

To Vattel and Burlamaqui, whom you Say you have read you must Add, Grotius and Puffendorf and Heineccius, and besides this you should have some Volume of Ethicks constantly on your Table.[1] Morals, my Boy, Morals should be as they are eternal in their nature, the everlasting object of your Pursuit. Socrates and Plato, Cicero and Seneca, Butler and Hutchinson, as well as the Prophets Evangelists and Apostles should be your continual Teachers.[2]

But let me advise you, in another Art, I mean oratory, not to content yourself with Blair and Sherridan, but to read Cicero and Quintilian.—and to read them with a Dictionary Grammar and Pen and Ink, for Juvenal is very right

Studium Sine Calamo Somnium.[3]

Preserve your Latin and Greek like the Apple of your Eye.

When you Attend the Superiour Court, carry always your Pen and Ink & Paper and take Notes of every Dictum, every Point and every Authority. But remember to show the same respect to the Judges and Lawyers who are established in Practice before you, as you resolved to show the President Tutors Professors, and Masters and Batchelors at Colledge.

Mr Parsons your Master is a great Lawyer and should be your oracle.

But you have now an intercourse with his Clients, whom it is your Duty to treat with Kindness, Modesty and Civility, and to whose Rights and Interests you ought to have an inviolable Attachment. Mr Parsons's honour, reputation and Interest Should be as dear to you, as your own.

I hope to see you in May; Meantime I am / with the tenderest affection your Father   John Adams

RC (Adams Papers); internal address: "Mr John Quincy Adams."; endorsed: "My Father 23. Jan^y: 1788." and "M^r: Adams. Jan^ry: 23. 1788." Tr (Adams Papers).

[1] JQA indicated in his Diary that he read Jean Jacques Burlamaqui's *The Principles of Natural and Political Law* in Oct. 1786 and Emmerich de Vattel's *Le droit des gens* in Sept. 1787 (2:109, 118, 287, 292). The other works JA recommended were Hugo Grotius, *The Rights of War and Peace*, London, 1738; Samuel Pufendorf, *Of the Law of Nature and Nations*, 4th edn., London, 1729; and Johann Gottlieb Heineccius, *A Methodical System of Universal Law*, 2 vols., London, 1741, all three of which are in JA's library at MB (*Catalogue of JA's Library*).

[2] JA had previously made similar reading recommendations to JQA; see JA to JQA, 19 May 1783, vol. 5:162–163.

[3] To study without a pen is to dream.

John Adams to Cotton Tufts

Dear Sir   Grosvenor Square Jan. 23. 1788

So many Things appear to be done, when one is making Preparations for a Voyage, especially with a Family, that you must put up with a short Letter in answer to yours.[1]

We shall embark in March on board of the ship Lucretia Captn Calahan, and arrive in Boston as soon as We can: till which time I must suspend all Requests respecting, my little affairs. Your Bills shall be honoured as they appear.

You are pleased to ask my poor opinion of the new Constitution, and I have no hesitation to give it. I am much Mortified at the Mixture of Legislative and Executive Powers in the Senate, and wish for Some other Amendments.— But I am clear for accepting the present Plan as it is and trying the Experiment. at a future Time Amendments may be made, but a new Convention at present, would not be likely to amend it.

You will receive, perhaps with this, a third Volume of my Defence, in which I have Spoken of the new Constitution, in a few Words.[2] This closes the Work, and I believe you will think I have been very busy. I have rescued from everlasting Oblivion, a number of Constitutions and Histories, which, if I had not Submitted to the Drudgery, would never have appeared in the English Language. They are the best Models for Americans to study, in order to Show them the horrid Precipice that lies before them in order to enable and Stimulate them to avoid it.

I am afraid, from what I See in the Papers that Mr Adams is against the new Plan. if he is, he will draw many good Men after him, and I Suppose place himself at the head of an Opposition. This may do no harm in the End: but I should be Sorry to see him, worried in his old Age.

Of Mr Gerrys Abilities, Integrity and Firmness I have ever entertained A very good opinion and on very solid Grounds.— I have seen him and Served with him, in dangerous times and intricate Conjunctures. But on this Occasion, tho his Integrity must be respected by all Men, I think him out in his Judgment.— Be so kind as to send him in my name a Set of my three Volumes.

My Duty, Love and Compliments / where due. Yours most respectfully / and affectionately   John Adams

RC (NN:Manuscripts and Archives Division, John Adams Papers); addressed by AA2: "Honble: Cotton Tufts Esqr / Member of the Senate / Boston / Massachusetts."; internal address: "The Hon. Cotton Tufts."; endorsed: "J. Adams Esq / Jany 22. 1788."

¹Cotton Tufts to JA, 28 Nov. 1787, in which Tufts provided JA with a lengthy report on the activities of the Mass. General Court. Tufts also wrote, "It would give me great Pleasure to have your Sentiments (for my own private Use if not otherways permitted) upon this proposed Constitution—and I

flatter myself that you will not withhold from Your Friend that Light, wch. your extensive Knowledge of Governments & long Experience enables You to afford me" (*Doc. Hist. Ratif. Const.*, 4:326–327).
²See JA, *Defence of the Const.*, 3:505–506.

John Callahan to Abigail Adams

Madam   Hatton Garden Jan^{y:} 31th. 1788—

I had the honor to Receive a few lines from you yesterday, relitive to your passage to America, agreeable to your request, I here Send you the times in writing which will vary little or Nothing From your owne; I apprehend you, missunderstood me the other day, I do Assure you Madam, I had No Such intentions as to increace my Demands. I Only wished to have Convinced you how much pleasure it Would give me, to make my time of Sailing agreeable to your wishes, & Acquainted you of my Resolution of braking my engagements with Mr. Potten, & Others of my friends, who ware disposed to Serve me— Mr. Potten, in particular—who had given me the Refusal of all his freight—Which would have at least loaded half my Ship, upon Conditions—That I would engage to Sail as Early as Others (indeed he gave Me all the Month of Feb^{y.}) but finding you was not willing to Depart from Falmouth till the latter end of

221

march, I was feerfull That My detention in the Channel might proove a great ingery To My freinds, not haveing his or their goods to market as Soon as others I mentioned this Circumstance, the last time. I had the pleasure Conversing with you, for No Other Reasion then to Convince you; how Desireous I was to make everything Conformable to your wishes, and not With Any intentions to en-creese my Demands— I am perfectly Contented With the terms. proposed in your letter of yesterday[1]—you Say you will Agree to give me two hundred pounds, my takeing the furniture from The house, & providing every Necessary provisions for the voyage Stoping For you at Falmouth; Not Exceeding the first of April. provided the weather Will permit. I Could wish you to be there by the 20 or 23[d] of March as Freequently the Easterly winds Sets in about that time, but if It Should Not be Convenient; to be at falmouth then, I will waite till The last of March, or begining of April, &, you may Rest assured Madam—that I will not engage to take any passanger—in the Cabin till I have your approbation & Shall make you acquainted Who the are, before I engage with them; as it is my determina-tion to Render the voyage to you & M[r.] Adams, as agreeable as pos-sib[le] & in Case there Should be only two Servents I do agree to dedu[ct] his or her. passage from the £200— I dont Recolect that anyt[hing] Was mentioned in my being at any Charge: in geting fur-nitur fr[om] the house, but if you think it Reasionable, I will pay the Carting & further more if you M[r.] Adam[s.] or any other persons Judges in those Cases, think me unreasonable—I am perfectly will-ing to make any allowance[s.] that you or they may See fit—& if I can be of any Servis to you, or his Excellency—in buying or Collecting any matter for your voyage or in any other way I beg you or his Ex-cellency will Command me: as it would give me infinite pleasure to Render you Or him Every Servis in my power: M[rs.] Callahan Joinis in Respect. to you & family—[2]

I am— / Madam / your most Obliged humb[e] Serv[t]

John Callahan

PS. I heard yesterday that Madam Belcher: is Dead. if you wish me to write to prudey Spears Sister who lived with M[rs.] Belcher— please to Send me word:[3] I will write her—agreeable to your Direc-tions—

RC (Adams Papers); internal address: "To M[rs.] Adams—" and "M[rs:] Adam[s.]" Some loss of text where the seal was removed.

¹ Not found.

² Lucretia Greene (b. 1748) married Capt. John Callahan in 1774. He named his ship *Lucretia* for her (JA, *D&A*, 3:215; Thwing Catalogue, MHi).

³ Madam Belcher was probably Lydia Brackett Belcher (1734–1787), widow of Na-

thaniel Belcher (1732–1786). Prudence Spear (b. 1763) was Lydia's much younger second cousin, and Prudence's sisters were her twin Mehitable, Thankful (b. 1765), and Abigail (b. 1772) (Sprague, *Braintree Families*, p. 560R, 785R, 4356R, 4365R).

Thomas Jefferson to Abigail Adams

Dear Madam   Paris Feb. 2. 1788

The silk you desired was delivered to m͠r Parker a month ago, on the eve of his departure for England, as he supposed. he went however to Holland. m͠r Valnay is so kind as to take charge of that now, as also of the silk stockings. I doubt whether you may like the stockings on first appearance: but I will answer for their goodness, being woven expressly for me by the Hermits of Mont Calvaire with whom I go & stay sometimes, and am favoured by them.¹ they have the reputation of doing the best work which comes to the Paris market. I inclose you their little note of the weight & price, for they sell by weight.² I inclose also a state of our accounts subsequent to the paiment of the small sum by Col͠o. Smith which balanced our former transactions. you will make such additions & amendments to it as you shall find right. I have not yet been able to find M. de la Blancherie at home so as to settle m͠r Adams's affair with him: but I will do it in time, & render you an account.³ there being no news here to communicate to you, be pleased to accept my thanks for the many kind services you have been so good as to render me & your friendly attentions on every occasion. I have considered you while in London as my neighbor, and look forward to the moment of your departure from thence as to an epoch of much regret & concern for me. insulated & friendless on this side the globe, with such an ocean between me and every thing to which I am attached the days will seem long which are to be counted over before I too am to rejoin my native country. young poets complain often that life is fleeting & transient. we find in it seasons & situations however which move heavily enough. it will lighten them to me if you will continue to honour me with your correspondence. you will have much to communicate to me, I little which can interest you. perhaps you can make me useful in the execution of your European commissions. be assured they will afford me sincere pleasure in the execution. my daughters join me in affectionate Adieus to you: Polly does not cease to speak of you with warmth & gratitude. heaven send you, madam, a pleasant & safe passage, and a happy meeting with all your friends. but do not let them so entirely engross you as to forget that you have one here who is with the most sincere esteem & attachment Dear Madam / your most obedient / & most humble servant

Th: Jefferson

ENCLOSURE

Mrs. Adams in acct with Th: J.

		Dr.		Cr.
1787. Oct. 3.	To paid for 5. aunes cambrick sent by Dr. Cutting	60.ₜₜ	£ 2–10	
				£ s
	By cash to Colo. Smith			2–10
Dec. 19.	By cash by mr̃ Trumbull 120ₜₜ			5–
1788. Jan. 9.	To pd̃ hermits of M. Calvaire 12. pr̃ silk stockings	168ₜₜ		
	To pd̃ for 10. aunes double Florence @ 4ₜₜ–15	47–10		
23.	To pd̃ Ct. Sarsfeld for books for mr̃ Adams	79		
		294–10	12–5–5	
	Balance in favor of Th: J.			7–5–5
			14–15–5.	14–15–5

RC and enclosure (Adams Papers); internal address: "Mrs. Adams"; endorsed: "Mr Jefferson / Febry 2.d 1788"; notation on enclosure: "sent this Balance due to / mr Jefferson by Mrs parker / Febry 22. 1788 / Abigail Adams."

[1] The hermits of Mont Calvaire (also known as Mont Valérian), located near the village of Suresnes, France, were a community of lay brothers. Besides making wine and silk stockings, they also offered accommodations to paying guests. Jefferson visited them often while living in Paris (Jefferson, *Papers*, 12:xxxv–xxxvi).

[2] Not found.

[3] On 6 Sept. 1787, JA wrote to Pahin Champlain de La Blancherie (1752–1811), the publisher of the *Nouvelles de la république des lettres et des arts*, to cancel his subscription. He enclosed that letter with one of the same date to Jefferson, whom he asked to settle his account with La Blancherie. Jefferson indicated that he had taken care of the matter in a letter to JA of 20 Feb. 1788 (JA, *Papers*, 7:360–361; Jefferson, *Papers*, 12:98–99, 317–318, 611).

Abigail Adams to Mary Smith Cranch

London Febry 10th 1788

Since I have had any opportunity of conveyence to my dear Sister, I have received from her Letters of the following dates August 19

Sep^br 23. & 30th october 21 & Nov^br 14th· the contents of which have variously affected me—[1] The Scripture tells us that it is better to go to the House of mourning than the House of Feasting.[2] to that I think I have oftener been calld through the progress of your several Letters, and I may say with dr young

"my dyeing Friend's come o'er me like a cloud"[3]

our Second parents House is become desolate, disconsolate & mourns, but the dear inhabitants have exchanged it for a more permanant inheritance, yet we have reason to bewail their loss, for they were ornaments to Society, and their exemplary Lives adornd the Religion they profess'd. very few persons have closed the last Scenes of Life with So pure and unblemishd Characters as the worthy pair whose memory's deserve these tributary Tears. long may their virtues Survive in our memories and be transplanted into the lives of all their connections. They do Survive them we see in their amiable Children the Fruits of seeds sown by their parents, Nursd with uncommon care, and matured by long & undeviating Labour. I rejoice most sincerely that mr Smith so happily connected himself during the Life of his worthy Father, as it must have afforded him consolation in the close of Life to leave a Friend and companion to his orphan Daughter— my dear Friend mrs otis, I have often thought of her with the tenderest Sympathy. how many Severe trials has She been calld to encounter in the Space of a few years? ["]God suits the wind to the shorne Lamb, Says yorick"[4] and she is blessd with a happy equinimity of temper Supported by those Sentiments of Religion which teach a patient Submission to the dispensations of providence

"Why should we grieve, when grieving we must bear?
And take with Guilt, what Guiltless we might share"

When I reflect upon the Death of an other Relative, I can only say, the judge of all will do right. I cannot however upon a Retrospect of His Education refrain from thinking that some very capital mistakes were very undesignedly made. the experience which you and I have since had with regard to the different dispositions & tempers of children would lead us to a very different conduct. I say this to you who will not consider it, as any reflection upon the memory of our dear parents, but only as a proof how much the best & worthyest may err, & as some mitigation for the conduct of our deceast Relative.

And now my dear sister the period is very near when I am to quit this country. I wrote Dr Tufts that we had taken our passage in Captain Callihans Ship, and that he would sail the latter end of march, or begining of April, so that I hope God willing, to see you & the rest of my dear Friends in May. I have much to do as you will naturally suppose by way of arrangment, and my Health, not what I wish it was. There is a natural tendency in our family to one particular Disorder, Father Aunts & uncle have more or less shared it, and I am not without Similar complants, which like the centinal at the door of King philip, warn me of what frail materials I am compose'd.[5] that was a part of my complant last year and has afflicted me still more greviously this. at present I am relieved & hope that I shall have no return of it through the fatigue which I have to pass through in packing & getting ready for my voyage. I almost wish I had nothing to remove but myself & Baggage, but to part with our furniture would be such a loss, & to take it is such a trouble that I am almost like the *Animal* between the two Bundles *of* Hay

I want to write to you all, yet feel as if I had not a moments time. mr & mrs Smith take private Lodgings next week. in the course of which we have to go to Court & take Leave, to visit all the Foreign ministers & their Ladies & to take leave of all our acquaintance, pack all our Furniture Give up our House discharge all our Bills make and all other arrangments for our departure.

added to all this, I have the greatest anxiety upon Esthers account, if I bring her Home alive I bring her Home a marri'd woman & perhaps a Mother which I fear will take place at sea.[6] this as yet is known only to myself & mrs Smith. Brisler as good a servant as ever Bore the Name, and for whom I have the greatest regard is married to her, but Sitting asside her Situation, which I did not know untill a few days ago, her general state of Health is very bad. I have not made it worse, I hope by what has been done for her, but her Life has been put in Jeopardy, as many others have before her, ignorantly done, for however foolish it may appear to us, I must believe that she had no Idea of being with child, untill the day before she came in the utmost distress to beg me to forgive her, and tho I knew that it was their intention to marry when they should return to America Yet so totally blinded was I, & my physician too, that we never once suspected her any more than she did herself, but this was oweing to her former ill state of Health.

I have related this to you in confidence that you may send for her Mother & let her know her situation. as in a former Letter to dr

Tufts, I expressd my apprehensions with regard to her, & tho the chief difficulty is now accounted for I look upon her situation as a very dangerous one. I have engaged an Elderly woman to go out with me, who formerly belonged to Boston,[7] and I hear there is an other woman going as a stearige passenger, and I shall hurry Callihan to get away as soon as possible, for I think I dread a norester on Board ship, more than an Equinox we have but about ten days longer before we shall leave London—and in addition to every thing else, I have to prepare for her what is necessary for her situation, but tis in vain to complain, & then poor Brisler looks so humble and is so attentive, so faithfull & so trust worthy, that I am willing to do all I can for them. do not let any thing of what I have written be known to any body but her mother. I hope captain Folger arrived Safe with my Letters. adieu my dear sister, do not let my Friends think unkindly of me if I do not write to them. I would had I time my Love / to them all from your ever affectionate / sister AA

RC (MWA:Abigail Adams Letters).

[1] The letter of 14 Nov. 1787 has not been found.

[2] Ecclesiastes, 7:2.

[3] Young, *Night Thoughts*, Night III, line 278.

[4] Laurence Sterne, *A Sentimental Journey through France and Italy*, ch. 65, "Maria."

[5] A number of family members, including AA, TBA, Norton Quincy, and Mary Smith Cranch, suffered from rheumatism (vol. 3:42; 5:267; 6:2, 231).

[6] Esther Field and John Briesler married on 15 Feb. 1788 at St. Mary le Bone church in London. Their daughter Elizabeth was born at sea in May (W. Bruce Bannerman and R. R. Bruce Bannerman, *The Registers of Marriages of St. Mary le Bone, Middlesex*, 9 vols., London, 1917–1927, 4:80; Sprague, *Braintree Families*, p. 829; AA to AA2, 29 May, below). Interestingly, in later years, the family apparently "revised" the Brieslers' marriage date back to Sept. 1787; see JQA's Diary entry for 14 Aug. 1838, D/JQA/33, APM Reel 36.

[7] AA later refers to this woman, who is not further identified, as "old nurse Comis" (to AA2, 29 May 1788, below).

Abigail Adams Smith to John Quincy Adams

London Feby 10th 1788

I have now before me your Letter of the 3d of August[1]—which I intend to answer fully—and then 2dly to proceed to some points of information—and 3dly to some observations and reflection of my own—

in the 1st place I must acknowledge that your complaints against me for not writing are justly founded— I must Confess myself in fault—& this you know is the surest and most effectual way to disarm you of resentment—but who is the American Pope!—

your hopes respecting our Parents returning to America are I think in a fair way to be accomplished— preparations are daily making—for this Event, they have engaged to have their furniture all on Board Callihams Ship—in the Month of Febuary— they Intend Leaving London—after the 24th. and to go to Falmouth there they are to be on the 20th of March— Callihan is to take them on Board at Falmouth after the Equinoxial Storm has blown over and from thence they proceed in a line direct, to the Harbour of Boston

Congress *not* resolving to keep any Person in a Public Character at this Court—and as *usual* have not taken any resolutions respecting the destination of my friend—it is Concluded that they mean he should return also—at the expiration of his Commission—for which Event we are likewise prepareing and with a very Sincere desire that no impediment may intervene to frustrate our present intention of embarking for America in the April Packett which sails from Falmouth to New York—from which Place I hope my next Letter to you will be dated—and where I Shall Hope to see you—at some Leisure period—perhaps during the next Winter vacation—when our Brothers will accompany you but this is looking a great way forward— we will defer further particulars till the period approaches—

respecting your desire that your father Should determine to Spend the remainder of his days in retirement— I cannot agree with you in this wish— it is in his Power to do His Country Essential Service—by assisting in Her Councills—by His opinions, advice, & recommendations,—he has it *I beleive* in his Power to do as much perhaps *the most* towards establishing her Character as a respectable Nation—of any Man in America—and Shall he retire from the World and bury himself amongst his Books—and Live only for himself!— No—I wish it not— I have no desire that he should be chosen Governor of the State—let those Possess that station who are ambitiously grasping—at a Shadow—which I Consider the Honour attendant upon that office to be— but I do hope—upon the establishment of a New Constitution—to see Him in some respectable and usefull Office under it— the Americans in Europe—say he will be Elected Vice President— besides my Brother independant of other important Considerations—he would not I am well Convinced be Happy in Private Life— you will before he arrives in America—have seen two other Vollumes of His Book—and perhaps you will hear from him a system of Government which you may not expect— he is of opinion that some *new* form of Government for our Country is neccasary— he does not wholly approve of the one which has been offered—but

228

he thinks that the People had better adopt it as it is—and then appoint a new Convention to make such alterations as may prove necessary— He wishes they Had Entitled the Chief Magistrate to a greater degree of independance, that they had given him the *Sole* appointment of all Offices—that they had made provision for a Privy Councill—either of His own appointment or chosen by the Senate— and some others which you will hear from himself— if the system at present under Consideration is not addopted I am of opinion that he will assist at a future Convention and have a principle Hand in the framing One which may be adopted— most of the Americans now in Europe are in favour of it—being well Convinced that a Change is absolutely necessary to the respectable Establishment of our Country in the Eyes of Europe—and her importance as a Nation—

I am Sorry to find by your Letter that your spirits are so low—the return of our Parrents will I hope restore them— I do not think you have any reason to be discouraged—by the time you shall have finished your studies of the Law—that Profession will have risen again into reputation amongst the People—I hope— Learning Abilities and industry will ever meet a good reward—and I dare say you will not repent the Profession you have Chosen nor think the time you have spent in the acquirement misplaced— be not discouraged—your Path through Life will not I hope be planted with thorns— you must not however expect to find the assent perfectly easy—but you will often find a Sattisfaction in haveing encountered difficulties— when the dangers are passed away—bear this beleif in Mind—that you were designed for some high and important Station upon the stage,— qualify yourself to fill your part with reputation—and then aspire to that Station which you esteem desireable—and that you may succeed in the Possession is my earnest wish—and if in my *Power* to offer you assistance—my pittance shall be at your Command—

I think I have now answered your Letter—and Shall in the next place proceed to give you some information upon General Subjects which brings me to the 2^d Head of my discource—

we have had rumours of War—which have passed away—but I cannot add—it is as tho they had not been—for it is yet suspected that this Country is two well Sattisfied in their own strength and importance to keep Peace in Europe—for *many succeeding years* to at present there appears no oustensible reason for War— they have Lately proved triumphant in the Subjugation of Liberty in Holland— the Patriotick Party in that Country are quite unplaced—if not unpensioned— many have fled to France and others talk of going to

America— the Baron de Lynden is recalled from this Court— there has been a motion made in the States General—for recalling Mʳ Van Berckel from America. it has not yet been carried but it is expected to take Place as soon as My father takes his Leave—² no Person can travell through the Country (to so great an heighth has the Spirit of Party been extended). without wearing some Badge of Orange, it has also become a favourite colour in this Country,—thus small means are sometimes made Subservient to important purposes—

the French Cabinet seem to be in a State of Petrifaction, whilst the People are looking around them and claiming their rights as Men,—the Royal Authority is disregarded and treated with Contempt. Parliaments return from Exile whom the King has Banished,—*some Persons*. talk of the Nations being better represented than this Nation is at Present,— it is said that the King has given himself up to intoxication and the Queen is Branded with every approbious epithet which Can dishonour Woman,— but I suppose this information and more you have received through the Channel of the News Papers

Monsieur de Callonge who fled from France has been presented Publickly at this Court by the Duke of Queensborougher an Event that has caused much Surprize to Foreigners—³ the Marquis de la Luzern—has arrived here as Ambassador from France, he has lain down the Order of Malta—taken a Wife,—and his own title of Marquis—⁴

I hear of a Ship to Sail this week—and as I would not omit the opportunity of forwarding this Letter—I must omit many things that I designed to have written— we are now very Busy in Packing up and prepareing for our departure if I can find time I will write again by My Mother to you—

Several Ships have arrived without a line from you— I hope you have received my letter of july Last—⁵

remember me to all Friends and beleive me / your affectionate Sister and friend—

A Smith—

RC (Adams Papers).

¹ Not found, but see JQA, *Diary*, 2:269, where JQA states that he wrote to AA2 on 31 July 1787.

² Pieter Johan van Berckel, who had been the Dutch minister to the United States since 1783, was recalled by the States General on 8 May 1788 for "Various Reasons conducive to our Interest" (*Repertorium*,

3:271; *The Emerging Nation: A Documentary History of the Foreign Relations of the United States under the Articles of Confederation, 1780–1789*, ed. Mary A. Giunta, 3 vols., Washington, D.C., 1996, 3:773-774).

³ William Douglas, 4th Duke of Queensberry (1724-1810), was best known for his love of horses and betting. He served as a

lord of the bedchamber to George III from 1760 to 1789 (*DNB*).

[4] Anne César, Chevalier de La Luzerne, had previously served as the French minister to the United States and had known JA and JQA since they sailed from Lorient on the *Sensible* together in 1779. La Luzerne was named minister to Great Britain in fall 1787 and arrived in London in Jan. 1788. At around the same time, he made public his secret marriage to Angran d'Alleray and gave up his rank of chevalier in the Order of Malta. Shortly thereafter, Louis XVI granted him the title of Marquis. La Luzerne would continue as minister to Great Britain until his death in 1791 (vol. 6:129; JA, *Papers*, 8:18–19; William Emmett O'Donnell, *The Chevalier de La Luzerne: French Minister to the United States 1779–1784*, Bruges, 1938, p. 249–250).

[5] AA2 to JQA, 10 June 1787, above, which has a final dateline of 16 July.

John Quincy Adams to Cotton Tufts

Dear Sir.   Newbury-Port Feb[y:] 16[th:] 1788.

I desired my brother Charles when he went from Haverhill, to mention, that I was again in need of a supply of money, and since that time I have been obliged to stop my payments: I am apprehensive he forgot to deliver my message, and take this opportunity to request some money, as soon as may be convenient.

The riotous ungovernable spirit, which appeared among the students at the university in the course of the last quarter gave me great anxiety; particularly as I understood, that one of my brothers, was suspected of having been active in exciting disturbances; but from his own declarations and from the opinion I have of his disposition, I hope those suspicions, were without foundation—[1] I conversed with him largely upon the subject, and hope, his conduct in future, will be such as to remove, every unfavourable impression.

I intended to have paid a visit to my friends beyond Boston, before this, but I find I creep along so slow in my professional studies, that I could not think of being absent from them for a week together: perhaps however in a month or six weeks I may take some opportunity to indulge, for a few days.

I am, dear Sir, respectfully yours   J. Q. Adams.

RC (Adams Papers); addressed: "The Hon[ble:] Cotton Tufts Esq[r:] / Weymouth."; internal address: "Hon. C. Tufts Esq[r.]"

[1] For the Thanksgiving disturbance at Harvard and CA's role therein, see JQA, *Diary*, 2:355–356, and note 1.

Elizabeth Smith Shaw to Mary Smith Cranch

My Dear Sister—   Haverhill February 17th 1788

I hear Judge Seargant is to go to Boston tomorrow, & I will not defer writing a few Lines to my Sister, & most heartily thanking her, for her two kind remembrances of me— When I read that my young Friends designed me a Visit, I felt execeding sorry that they were prevented by the weather— They need not have been frighted, for there is seldom a Time from November, to March but what persons may travel from here to Boston with ease—

The publishment of our Cousin Tufts, & Brooks gives us the greatest pleasure—[1] 'Tis a Consumation devoutly to be wished for— At least, I view it at present, as attended with every circumstance of Felicity, that can give pleasure to near Relatives How would my dear Aunt have rejoiced, had she lived to see them happily connected. I think our Cousin is much improved of late, & will make him an exceellent Wife— Mr Tufts will visit his Friends, be more companionable, & feel tenfold more important than ever he did before—

Yes! as you observe, Weymouth may shine yet—& I may again love to visit the place of my Nativity. But the Sight of it now, excites such a Crowd of Ideas as language cannot describe, & quite overwhelms my Soul with Grief—

> "Sweet little Cottage of my Sire,
> Where when a Child I played—
> *Each Object lives within my Mind,*
> That there the Eye runs o'er;
> The Hamlet, & the Hill behind,
> The apple Tree before—"[2]

At such a Window, I have viewed with perfect tranquility the softened azure, & the variegated Cloud— With such a Friend, seated upon that verdant Bank we talked down the Summers Sun— In *this* cool retreat I tasted the sweets of virtuous Friendship, enjoyed the Feast of reason, & the flow of Soul— Under *that* lofty Oak, I viewed the vast Expanse of Nature—held converse with the Stars—beheld the Moon walking in brightness, & almost paid my homage to the Queen of heaven—

Here lived, & *here* smiled the fond Parents, heightening every Joy—here they poured the fresh Instruction over our Minds—here they gave the wise precept—& there they marked the cautious Line— Let not then, my dear Eliza *ever* wonder if she should again see her Aunt wholly unnerved, & choaked with a train of Ideas, which a sight of this place ever calls up to her view— For Now she must behold the dear Objects of her affections, put far away—& her nearest kindred mouldering in the Grave—

Well might the apostle say, that we [. . . .][3] City—

My Children stood by me when I received your last Letters, anxious to know their Contents— As it happened, there was what would please them both— I told Billy that his Opinion was founded on principles of nature— I asked little Miss, what she would do now— her hopes were all blasted— She had a powerful Rival in her Cousin— She indeed at first looked quite mortified— But she soon collected herself, & with a pride natural to her Sex, said "she did not love, she should not break her heart about it— There were enough other, Gentlemen—though she must say, she thought him very pretty—but she could love him full as well if he were her Cousin—"[4]

I long to hear from Charles & Thomas I charged them to write to me— I do not know that Mr Shaw & I could have given them better advice if they had been our own Sons— I hope they will conduct agreeable to it—& be wiser than they have been, & more cautious of abusing Government, for what they from choice suffer—the Ten shillings penalty, I mean—[5] It was very late when I took my pen in hand, I shall not say half I wish to— my Love to the young Folks— may you all sleep sweetly to night encircled by the watchman of Israel,[6] so may your

E. Shaw

RC (DLC:Shaw Family Papers); addressed: "Mrs Mary Cranch / Braintree"; docketed: "from Mrs Shaw" and "Mrs ~~Peabody~~ Shaw / (15) / feb. 17. 1788."

[1] Cotton Tufts Jr. married Mercy Brooks of Medford on 6 March (*Vital Records of Medford, Massachusetts, to the Year 1850*, Boston, 1907, p. 194).

[2] "Sweet little cottage of my sire, / Where when a child I play'd; / In foreign realms, my whole desire / Pants to enjoy thy shade. / Each object lives within my mind, / That there the eye runs o'er; / The hamlet and the hill behind, / The linden tree before" (Arnaud Berquin, "The Mountain Pipe," *The Children's Friend*, 4 vols., London, 1787, 4:91).

[3] Four or five illegible words.

[4] Betsy Quincy Shaw evidently had a crush on Rev. Jacob Norton of Weymouth, who was engaged to marry her cousin, Elizabeth Cranch.

[5] Both CA and TBA, as penalty for their role in the Thanksgiving disturbances at Harvard, were required to pay for the repairs to the dining hall (MH-Ar:Faculty Records, 5:249–250, 278–279).

[6] Ezekiel, 3:17.

Abigail Adams to Cotton Tufts

Dear sir   Febry 20th [1788] Grosvenour Square

I have written twice to you by way of New York, but do not find by yours that either of them had reachd you, nor have I learnt that Captain Folger was arrived who had all my Letters, except one to mrs Cranch by Captain Cushing.[1] in those Letters you will find what I wisht to have done to the House, as well as other matters respecting our Farm

I believe this will be the last Letter I shall write you previous to my embarking, which I hope will be in March, but is now uncertain on account of the difficulty mr Adams meets with in taking leave in Holland it is high time that we had a Goverment who know how to conduct our affairs with steadiness judgment, &, equity that they may not make themselves contemptable in the Eyes of all Europe. Congress accreditted mr Adams to their High mightynesses and to the Prince of orange, and in a Letter written to Congress more than a year ago, requesting permission to return at the expiration of his commission, he desires that Letters of Recall may accompany his permission, agreeable to the custom & useages of Nations. this he has several times since repeated instead of which they pass only a vote of approbation of his conduct with leave to return, but no Letter, either for this court or Holland. Mr Adams Sent a Letter to the Prince & a memorial to their High mightynessess, through mr Secretary Fagall, but all tho they express their Satisfaction personally as it respects mr Adams, they return the Letters saying they cannot receive his Resignation, but by a Letter from his Sovereign of recall, but shall continue to consider him as minister to them.[2] if this Court do not make any difficulty, it will be from circumstances too humiliating to our Country to be prided in. mr Adams is very apprehensive that he shall be obliged to go over himself to Holland, which at this time will put us to great difficulty as we had begun to pack up & get ready for our departure.

With this Letter I send you the third vol^m of the defence. you will not permit it to go out of your hands untill the others arrive. as mr Adams had been at the whole expence of publishing this work, he could wish that they might not be reprinted untill what are gone out, are disposed of, for tho he never had an Idea of making money of them, he cannot afford to lose so much by them as he must, if they are reprinted. in the last Letter you will find his Sentiments respecting our New plan of Government. Some of his sentiments I presume will be very unpopular in our Country, but time and experience will bring them into fashion. every day must convince our Country men more & more, of the necessity of a well balanced Government and that a Head to it, is quite as necessary as a body & Limbs the Name by which that Head is called is of very little concequence but they will find many Heads a Monster.— I most sincerely wish you my dear Sir every direction & success which honest intentions & upright endeavours after the publick Honour, & welfare deserve. I know you have no sinister motives, no narrow selfish purposes to serve eitheir by the acceptation or rejection of the New system. I wish every one who opposes it, or commends it, acted from motives as pure, and then whatever its fate might be, we should not be involved in anarchy but tares will spring up amongst the wheat, and thistles & Thorns.[3] we must take care that we are not goaded & pricked to death by either— There is at present sitting here one of the most august Assemblies that this country can convene. The House of commons the House of Lord's the Bishops the judges &C all convened in westmister Hall for the Trial of Warren Hastings.[4] about Two thousand persons half of whom are Ladies, attend this trial every day. it is opened with the utmost order & continued with the greatest regularity, & no person admitted to it, but with Tickets which are not very easily procured. as a Foreign ministers Lady I have had a Seat in the Box appropriated for them, and have had the pleasure of hearing mr Burk speak 3 hours. I have been so much engaged in prepairing for my voyage that I have not been able to attend daily, but I propose going again tomorrow to hear mr Fox. The dukes & Lords & Bishops are all Robed, are preceeded by the Herald at Arms, are calld over according to their rank and take their Seats accordingly. The Prince of Wales duke of York Gloster & Cumberland are obliged to a constant attendance mr Hastings appears at present; as Burk call'd him, the Captain Generall of Iniquity,[5] whatever he may have to say in justification of himself, it seems impossible to wash the Ethiope white.[6] my paper warns me to close but not untill I have assured you of the Sincere & affectionate / Regard of Yours   A Adams

PS your last Bill is paid in favour mr Elworthy

RC (Adams Papers); endorsed: "M^rs. Abig^l. Adams / Feby 20. 1788—"

[1] AA to Tufts, 6 Nov. 1787, and 1 Jan. 1788, and AA to Mary Smith Cranch, 8 Oct. 1787 (2d letter), all above.

[2] On 25 Jan. 1788, JA wrote to Hendrik Fagel, secretary of the States General of the Netherlands (JA, *Works*, 8:470), requesting that he forward memorials to William V and to the High Mightinesses of the States General indicating JA's intent to take leave of his post as U.S. minister plenipotentiary to the Netherlands (both dated 25 Jan., *Dipl. Corr., 1783–1789*, 2:829–831). Fagel replied on 12 Feb. that while the memorials were acceptable, they could not substitute for a formal letter of recall from Congress to the Dutch government (*Dipl. Corr., 1783–1789*, 2:828–

829).

[3] AA conflates two biblical references here: Job, 31:40 ("Let thistles grow instead of wheat, and cockle instead of barley") and Matthew, 13:25 ("But while men slept, his enemy came and sowed tares among the wheat, and went his way").

[4] For the Warren Hastings trial, see Descriptive List of Illustrations, No. 6, above.

[5] In Edmund Burke's opening statement at the impeachment trial on 15 Feb., he described Hastings as "a captain-general of iniquity, under whom all the fraud, all the peculation, all the tyranny in India are embodied, disciplined, arrayed, and paid. This is the person, my Lords, that we bring before

you. We have brought before you such a person, that, if you strike at him with the firm and decided arm of justice, you will not have need of a great many more examples. You strike at the whole corps, if you strike at the head" (*The Works of the Right Honorable*

Edmund Burke, rev. edn., 12 vols., Boston, 1866–1867, 9:339).

[6] A common expression, a variation on Jeremiah, 13:23: "Can the Ethiopian change his skin, or the leopard his spots?"

Abigail Adams to Thomas Jefferson

My dear sir   London Feb^ry 21 1788.

in the midst of the Bustle and fatigue of packing, The parade & ceremony of taking leave at Court, and else where, I am informd that mr Appleton and mrs Parker, are to set out for Paris tomorrow morning. I Cannot permit them to go without a few lines to my much Esteemed Friend, to thank him for all his kindness and Friendship towards myself and Family, from the commencment of our acquaintance, and to assure him that the offer he has made of his correspondence, is much too flattering, not to be gratefully accepted.

The florence and stockings were prefectly to my mind, and I am greatly obliged to you sir, for your care and attention about them. I have sent by Mrs Parker the balance due to you, agreeable to your statement, which I believe quite right

Be so good as to present my Regards to the marquiss de la Fayett, and his Lady, and to the Abbés—assure them that I entertain a gratefull rememberance of all their civilities and politeness during my residence in Paris. To mr Short and the young Ladies your Daughters Say every thing that is affectionate for me, and be assured my dear Sir, that I am / with the Greatest Respect Esteem & Regard / Your Friend and Humble Servant   Abigail Adams

RC (DLC:Jefferson Papers).

Abigail Adams to Thomas Jefferson

Dear sir   London Feb^ry 26 1788

Mr Adams being absent I replie to your Letter this day received, that mr Adams has written to you upon the Subject you refer to.[1] our time here is short and pressing, yet short as it is mr Adams is obliged to Set out on fryday for the Hague in order to take leave there, owing wholly to the neglect of Congress in omitting to send

6. "A VIEW OF THE TRYAL OF WARREN HASTINGS ESQR.," BY ROBERT POLLARD AND FRANCIS JUKES, 1789

See page xii

him a Letter of Recall, tho he particuliarly requested it of them, when he desired permission to return, & has several times since repeated the Same request. a memorial would then have answerd, but now it cannot be received, and he finds at this late hour that he must cross that most horrid passage twice, & make a rapid journey there & back again as it would be greatly injurious to our credit & affairs to give any reasonable cause of offence. he would be delighted to meet you there, but time is so pressing that he cannot flatter himself with that hope, nor be able to stay a day after he has compleated his buisness yet as this Letter may reach you about the day he will leave London, you will consider whether there is a possibility of seeing each other at the Hague

I had sent my arrears to you before mr Trumble thought of informing me that it was to be paid to him. the Eight Louis you have since been so kind as to pay for mr Adams, shall be paid mr Trumble—[2]

I thank you my dear Sir for all your kind wishes & prayers, heaven only knows how we are to be disposed of. you have resided long enough abroad to feel & experience how inadaquate our allowence is, to our decent expences, and that it is wholy impossible for any thing to be saved from it this our Countryman in general will neither know or feel. I have lived long enough, & seen enough of the world, to check expectations, & to bring my mind to my circumstances, and retiring to our own little Farm feeding my poultry & improveing my Garden has more charms for my fancy, than residing at the court of Saint Jame's where I seldom meet with Characters So innofensive as my Hens & chickings, or minds so well improved as my Garden.— Heaven forgive me if I think too hardly of them— I wish they had deserved better at my Hands—

adieu my dear Sir and believe me at all times / and in all Situations Your / Friend & Humble Servant   A A

RC (DLC:Jefferson Papers).

[1] Jefferson wrote to JA on 6 Feb. regarding difficulties filling the latest Dutch loan— which had resulted from the suspension of interest payments on the previous loan until the establishment of a new American government under the Constitution—and a possible scheme to deal with the situation.

JA replied on 12 Feb. strongly disapproving of the suggested plan (Jefferson, *Papers*, 12:566–567, 581–582).

[2] On 28 March, John Trumbull gave AA a receipt for eight pounds (equal to eight Louis d'Or), which he took for Jefferson in Paris (Adams Papers).

Cotton Tufts to John Adams

Dear S^{ir}   Boston Feby. 28. 1788

I rec^{d.} Mrs. Adams's Lett^{r.} of Nov. 6. and had wrote a long Epistle of the 21^{t.} Ins^{t.} and put it into the Post Office to go by a Cap. Brown who is to sail from Portsmouth, had also drawn a Bill on you for £150 Sterl^g which I found necessary— But on receiving this Day Mrs. Adams's Favour of Jany 1. and finding that they were not forwarded & that the Vessell would not sail for some Days I thought it probable they would not reach you before you would embark for Boston, therefore withdrew the Letter and got the Bill returned to me— Should this reach you, I would suggest, If you should have more Money than you should judge necessary for immediate Use here, whether it would not be best to lodge it in England to be drawn for after your Return—

In a former Letter, I manifested a Disinclination to purchase Vesey's Place, being satisfied that I could not then strike a Bargain with Him to your Advantage[1] His Ideas of its Value, being far beyond what I conceived you would have judged it worth were you on the Spot or what He could have obtaind for it even on the longest Credit. I did not therefore chuse even to make Him an offer Time has given Him that Conviction, which I was pretty sure it would and has furnished me with an Opportunity of complying with your Wishes and on Terms, that I presume will be agreable to you— a few Days since I purchased it for £200 and have received a Deed—[2] Two Thirds I paid him in Hand and for the other Third he has my Note on your Behalf— I shall be obliged to transact some Part of your Business on Credit, till you Return, having faild of the Benefit of a Draught on you as designed— The several Matters mentioned in Mrs. Adams's Letter shall attend to with as much Dispatch as the State of my Affairs will permit but I must beg you to prepare for some Degree of Mortification on seeing your Farms— The War & Taxes crushed all Improvements— We are but just rising— With your Care & Inspection they will I trust wear a better Appearance— Although a larger Share of my Time & Attention has been devoted to the Affairs of my Friend than to my own private concerns yet all has not been done that I could have wished for—or would have been done, had not a Variety of Embarrassments public & private, prevented—

Allens Farm has been sold, Saml. Quincys also, the Latter I had determined to have secured for you, but was foreclosed—

Our State Convention after a Months sitting closed the 6th. Inst. and ratified the proposed Plan of National Government—[3] I have no doubt but that it will generally obtain and I flatter myself under the Smiles of Heaven that the Establishment of it will sweep away a Number of the Plagues with which this Country is cursed— Accept My Dear S^ir of my ardent Prayers & Wishes for a prosperous Voyage you & your Familys safe Return to your Friends and believe to be— / your Affectionate Friend   Cotton Tufts

P. S. L^t. Governor Cushing died this Morning[4]

RC (Adams Papers); internal address: "His Excellency / John Adams Esq."

[1] See Tufts to AA, 21 May 1787, above.
[2] On 12 Feb. 1788, Cotton Tufts, on behalf of JA, purchased 46 acres "partly upland and partly fresh meadow" and the house thereon, from William and Sarah Veasey for £200 (Adams Papers, Adams Office Manuscripts, Box 2, folder 13).
[3] The Massachusetts ratifying convention sat from 9 Jan. to 7 Feb., approving the Constitution on 6 Feb. by a vote of 187 to 168 with proposed amendments (*Doc. Hist. Ratif. Const.*, 4:xxi).
[4] Thomas Cushing, who had served as lieutenant governor of Massachusetts since 1780, died on 28 Feb. (*DAB*).

John Adams to Abigail Adams

My dearest Friend   The Hague March 4. 1788

After a Passage of two days, against contrary Winds, and a terrible Jolt through the Mud, from Helvoet, I arrived here this day, in good health and not bad Spirits. The Princes Birth day is on Saturday: so that I shall not be able to take Leave before Monday, and if I go to Amsterdam afterwards, I shall not be able to leave that City before Wednesday or Thursday: so that I fear you cannot expect me, till the Week after next.— Mr Dumas prays me to Send you his respects.

My Cockade is Splendid enough for a Lt. General.— Mr Dumas is large enough for a Colonel, or for what I know for a Major General. I have not seen one Person without an orange Ribbon. great Preparations are making for celebrating the Birth day: and all is quiet. Tomorrow I make my first Visits.— Give my Love to Mr and Mrs Smith and to my dear Boy.— and my Respects and Compliments to all Freinds.
yours forever   John Adams

RC (Adams Papers); addressed: "England / For / Mrs Adams / at the American Ambassdors / Grosvenor Square / corner of Duke Street / Westminster / London"; internal address: "Mrs Adams."

Cotton Tufts to John Quincy Adams

Dear S^r   Boston March 5. 1788

I rec^{d.} Your Favour, previous to which I sent you by Post in a Letter to my Brother a Bank Bill of 20 Doll^{rs.}, it would have been sent soon after your Brother mentioned to me your Want of a Supply, had I not heard that you proposed to be at Boston in a few Days— I am exceedingly gratified that your fraternal Advice was given to Mr Charles and I flatter myself that it will with that of his other Friends have a very salutary Effect— The Disorders at our University gave me much Pain and more especially on finding that my young Friend was suspected to me deeply concerned in them, indeed I had never felt so much Anxiety with Respect to Him, as some Imprudencies (at least) had given Countenance to Suspicion, that if well grounded would have deprived Him of that Reputation which He enjoyed before and which had given me a Pleasure, that I had often announced to his Dear Parents and from which they had derived no small Satisfaction—

I rec^{d.} by New York a Letter from your Mother of Nov. 6. and one other of Jany. 1. In the last She informs me of their Design to embark for Boston in Capt. Callihan the latter End of this Month or the Beginning of April, this will make their Return a Month sooner than proposed in the former Letter— I shall find myself much hurried to get Borland's House in order to receive them, as there are still considerable Repairs necessary— Col Smith & Wife go to New York in the April Packet.

A few Days since I purchased Veseys Farm adjoyning that on which Pratt Lives, your Father had discovered a peculiar Fondness for it and had instructed me to give £300 for it, If not to be obtained at less Price, I had declined purchasing it but an opportunity presenting of meeting his Wishes & on Terms that I thought would be highly agreable to him, I struck the Bargain at £200—

A Bank Bill of Ten Dollarss is enclosed And / I am Dear S^{r.} / Your Affectionate Friend   Cotton Tufts

RC (Adams Papers); internal address: "Mr J. Q. Adams."

Abigail Adams to John Adams

my dear Friend   London March 7th 1788

   Not a word have I heard of, or from you Since you left me this
day week. I am anxious to know how you got over & how you do. I
am so unfortunate as to be confined for several days past with an
inflamation in my Throat attended with canker, & some fever. it is
rather abated to day, and I hope is going of. we go on packing, but it
is a much more labourious peice of buisness than I imagind and
takes much more time, I hope we shall finish in a few day's The
New dutch minister was presented at court this week & makes a
splendid appearence with his footmen in scarelet & silver, & a gay
page or Running footman was vastly well Received at Court &c &c[1]
   Nothing from America since you left us.
   Master Billy is sitting upon the table whilst I write and send his
duty to Grandpappa. the Weather is such that I cannot but rejoice
we are not at sea. Scott has been beating in the Channel these ten
days, but every day brings us a prospect of better weather. adieu I
shall be very uneasy if I do not hear from you by this Days post. I
know not where to direct to you so shall cover to Willinks. ever
yours   A Adams.

   RC (Adams Papers); addressed by WSS: "To— / His Excellency / John Adams /
Minister Plenipotentiary / &c. &c. &c / Hague."

   [1] Anne Willem Carel, Baron van Nagell van Ampsen (1756–1851), was named the new Dutch
ambassador to Great Britain in February and served until 1795 (*Nieuw Ned. Biog. Woordenboek*, 2:977–978; *Repertorium*, 3:264).

Abigail Adams to John Adams

My dearest Friend   Grosvenour Square March 11th 1788

   The Mail is this day arrived, but not a Line have I got from you,
nor have I heard a word from you since you left me. I hope you are
well. I am anxious to learn when you expect to get back. I find by
Letters received yesterday from France[1] that mr Jefferson is gone to
meet, you, which will render your visit in Holland much pleasenter
to you. Callihan does not appear in any great Hurry, and I am full in
the Mind that he had rather make it the middle of April before he
sails than go sooner. he will not however have to wait for our things,
as I hope they will all be on Board this week. I shall stay in the

House as long as I possibly can, but if you do not get back before the 20th imagine I shall be in some Hotell.

We have had more Winter since you left London than the whole season before, and Terible Soar throats have been the concequence of the harsh March winds I have had my share of it I hope, which proved very obstinate for several days, & yesterday was the first of my getting out. Mr & Mrs Smith will leave London the 20th

I wrote you by last frydays Mail under cover to messiurs Willinks. my most Respectfull compliments to mr Jefferson. I rejoice in the Idea of your having met again before you leave Europe. the papers give us a magnificent account of preperations in Holland for celebrating the Birth day of the Stadtholder[2]

Nothing from America Since you left me; I find it very lonesome here & Should be more so if I was not so buisily employd in preperations for our departure—

adieu most affectionately / yours   A Adams

after closing my Letter, yours of March the fourth is just brought me. I rejoice to hear you are well. compliments to mr d. & family if you had named the Hotell you were at, I Should not be obliged to Send my Letters to Amsterdam   A Adams[3]

RC (Adams Papers); addressed by AA2: "To / His Excellency John Adam's / &c &c &c / att the Hague / Bath Hotel / Piccadilly"; endorsed: "My dearest Friend / March 11 1788."

[1] Thomas Jefferson to JA, 2 March (Jefferson, *Papers*, 12:637–638).

[2] The *Morning Chronicle and London Advertiser*, 11 March, reprinted a letter from The Hague, dated 6 March, that stated, "The preparations making here for celebrating the anniversary of the birth of the Stadtholder surpasses every thing seen in this Republick on a like occasion; not only the greatest part of the houses, but all the principal streets, will be illuminated in a new taste, and the latter with pyramids and other ornaments." The city also planned to build 100 arches, all "magnificently illuminated," and a 100-foot obelisk facing the stadholder's palace. The celebration itself, with "eleven pieces of superb fireworks," would take place on 8 March.

[3] AA wrote the postscript on a separate sheet of paper.

John Adams to Abigail Adams

My dearest Friend   Amsterdam March 11. 1788.

I have past through the Ceremonies of taking Leave of the States General, the Prince and Princess &c to the Satisfaction of all Parties—and have been feasted at Court, and all that.— made my Compliments to the Prince on the 8. of March his Birth Day, and to the Princess at her Drawing Room &c &c &c. and should have been in

London at this hour if you had not have laid a Plott, which has brought me to this Town.— Mr Jefferson at the Receipt of your Letter, came post to meet me, and he cutts out So Much Business for me, to put the Money Matters of the United States upon a Sure footing, that I certainly Shall not be able to get into the Packet at Helvoet before Saturday; and I much fear not before Wednesday the Nineteenth. This delay is very painful to me, and you must blame your self for it, altogether.

I thought myself dead, and that it most well with me, as a Public Man: but I think I shall be forced, after my decease, to open an additional Loan. at least this is Mr Jeffersons opinion and that of Mr Vanstaphorst.

I hope you will have every Thing ready that by the twenty first or second of March We may sett off together for falmouth from London.

My Love to M^r & Mrs Smith, and kiss my dear Boy.— Compliments to all Friends.— I am very impatient under this unforeseen delay, but our Bankers as well as Mr Jefferson think it absolutely necessary for the Public. I must therefore submit, but, if in Consequence of it you should meet South Westers on the Coast of America, and have your Voyage prolonged three Weeks by it, remember it is all your own Intrigue, which has forced me to open this Loan. I suppose you will boast of it, as a great Public Service.

Yours forever   John Adams.

RC (Adams Papers); internal address: "Mrs Adams."; docketed by JA: "J A to A A / March 11 1788."

John Adams to Abigail Adams

My dear   Amsterdam March 14. 1788. Fryday

I have rec^d yours of the 7.th— I have written you on every Post day.

Mr Jefferson is so anxious to obtain Money here to enable him to discharge some of the Most urgent demands upon the United States and preserve their Credit from Bankruptcy for two Years longer after which he thinks the new Gov't will have Money in their Treasury from Taxes; that he has prevailed upon me to open a new Loan, by Virtue of my old Power.— I was very much averse to this but he would take no denial. I shall therefore be detained here till Monday. But if my Health continues I shall cross over in the Packett of next

Wednesday.— I hope every Thing will be ready for Us to take Post for Falmouth.

The Rich complain, at present in Holland that the Poor are set over them in the Regencies and the old Families that they are set aside by new ones.— Discontent rankles deep in Some Places, and among some Sorts of Men: but the Common People appear to be much pleased.

The Patriots in this Country, were little read in History less in Government: know little of the human heart and still less of the World. They have therefore been the Dupes of foreign Politicks, and their own indigested systems.

Changes may happen and disorders may break out, tho at present there is no apparent Probability, of either.— But as there is no sense of the Necessity of uniting and combining the great divisions of society in one system, no Changes can happen for the better.

My Love to the Children, and believe me very anxious to see you.

John Adams

RC (Adams Papers); docketed by JA: "J. A to J Q. A."

Abigail Adams to Lewis D. Ward

Sir   [*ante* 17 March 1788]

Mr Adams being absent upon publick Buisness in Holland when your Letter came to Hand I take the Liberty of replying to it, as I know he will be so much hurried for time when he returns as to be unable to attend to private matters, but I can answer for him, and am sure that he harbours no resentment against mrs Ward but wishes both of you success in Life & will rejoice to find that you are in Buisness. as to any intelligence respecting Mrs Wards Mother or family we are totally Ignorant about them not having heard a word respecting them Since we came to Europe, but as we expect Soon to return, if Mrs Ward wishes to write to them & will forward a Letter in the course of 8 Days it shall be carefully conveyd to them

I am sorry to hear that mrs Ward has been so ill & sincerly wish her a restoration to Health[1]

Dft (Adams Papers); docketed by JA: "A. A. / 1788." Drafted on the same sheet of paper as AA to John Bowring, [*ante* 30 *March*], below, and filmed at [*March* 1788].

[1] Lewis Ward first wrote to JA on 11 July 1785 requesting assistance in setting himself up in business as a bookbinder. His wife was probably Ann Veasey Ward (b. 1752), the

daughter of Jerusha Boylston Veasey (1719–1797), JA's maternal aunt (Sprague, *Braintree Families*, p. 5207R). Ward wrote again on 29 Feb. 1788, at that point a printer in Birmingham, seeking information about his mother-in-law and reporting news of his

wife's illness. On 18 March, the Wards replied to AA's letter, which they had received on the 17th, thanking her for her favor and wishing the family a safe voyage (all Adams Papers).

Abigail Adams to Margaret Smith

Madam

London Grosvenour Square
April [*March?*] 22 178[8][1]

Altho I have heithertoo felt a diffidence in addressing a Lady with whom I have not the pleasure of a personal acquaintance, I cannot upon this occasion permit my only Daughter to present herself to you in her new Relation, without requesting your kind and parental Reception of her.[2] I have the greatest reason to hope, that she will prove to you, what she has ever been to me, a dutifull and affectionate Daughter.

I have frequently been call'd in the course of my Life to very painfull seperations from some of my nearest and dear connections, but this is the first time that I have Sufferd a seperation from her, and it is the more painfull, as she has always been my companion and associate and I have no other Daughter to supply her place— but I have the Satisfaction and pleasure of knowing that she has one of the kindest and tenderest of Husbands, and every reason to believe that she will find in you Madam an affectionate Friend, and parent, and in the Ladies your Daughters, kind and indulgent Sisters. She has my dear Madam a natural reserve in her manners which I hope will not make an unfavorable impression upon her Friends. the Relationship of sister, is a character She has no remembrance of, and must in some measure plead for her Native reserve, for she is a very Silent Character, and in that respect very unlike her mamma.

For my Lovely Grandson I need ask no favour he has the claim of nature upon you, and will make his own way into your Heart, by his innocent Smiles and winning attractions.

I cannot however close this Letter without requesting you to enjoin upon your Son a particular care and attention to his Health. I am apprehensive that the Heat of our American Summers will, will renew and increase those complaints under which he has so severely Sufferd. I am the more urgent upon this subject, because I do not think he is himself sensible, in how critical a situation an attack of this disorder in a Hot Season, may prove to him. The utmost caution both in diet and exercise are absolutely necessary for him

I beg leave Madam to present my Regards to every branch of your Family. with some of them I feel a degree of acquaintance from a perusal of their Letters, particularly with the lively Sprightly Bell[3] and I anticipate with pleasure the day—Heaven Grant it may not be far distant, when we shall arrive in our Native Country, and I shall one day have the happiness of personally assureing you, with how much Esteem / I am Madam your / Humble Servant

Abigail Adams

FC (Adams Papers); internal address: "wining Mrs Margaret Smith N York"; notation: "Mrs Adams / Coppy of a Letter to / Mrs Margeret Smith / New York."

[1] AA relocated from Grosvenor Square to the Bath Hotel on 17 March. She most likely sent the letter with AA2 upon the Smiths' departure from London sometime around 20 March. The dateline may have been added to the letter at a later time.

[2] This is the only extant letter exchanged between AA and Margaret Smith, WSS's mother. For Margaret Smith, see vol. 7:240.

[3] Perhaps a reference to WSS's sister Belinda, for whom see AA to Mary Smith Cranch, 15 Dec., and note 2, below.

Abigail Adams to John Adams

my dearest Friend   Bath Hotell March 23 1788

I received yours of the 14th and ever Since thursday have been in Hourly expectation of seeing you I hope it is oweing to all the packets being detaind upon this Side, as is reported, and not to any indisposition that your return is delayed, that unpleasing detention is sufficiently mortifying particularly as we wish to proceed to Falmouth as soon as possible, tho I shall fear to go from hence untill the ship is gone, for from the best information I can get callihan has as yet scarcly any thing but our Bagage &c on Board, and even that has been several days delay'd by him. I came last monday Evening to this Hotell, that the Beds & remaining furniture might be sent on Board and the House given up. this will be wholy accomplish'd on the morrow if the weather permits, & has been oweing to that, for several days that all has not been accomplished

The packet arrived this week from Newyork and brings an account that seven states had accepted the Constitution. the Massachusetts convention consisted of 300 & 40 members. it was carried by a Majority of Nineteen Georgia & South Carolina are the two other states of which we had not before any certain accounts. New Hamshire was sitting. Newyork are becomeing more National and mr Duer writes mr Smith, that he may consider the constitution as accepted, & begining to operate at the Commencment of an other Year.[1] Newyork had agreed to call a convention—thus my dear Friend I think we shall return to our Country at a very important period and with more pleasing prospects opening before her than the turbulent Scenes which massachusetts not long since presented. May wisdom Govern her counsels and justice direct her opperations.

mr & Mrs Smith set off this week for Falmouth. she is now confined with a Soar throat, similar to the complaint which afficted me ten days ago. I write in hopes the Baron de Lynden will meet you on your return.

I shall be exceedingly anxious if I do not see, or hear from you soon

adieu & believe me ever yours   A Adams

RC (Adams Papers); docketed by JA: "A A to J. A / 23 March 1788."

[1] William Duer (1747–1799) migrated from England to New York in the late 1760s. He represented New York in the Continental Congress alongside JA and later served briefly as assistant secretary of the treasury department (*DAB*).

Susanna Clarke Copley to Abigail Adams

George Street March 28th: 1788

Mrs: Copley presents Compliments to Mrs: Adams: would have called uppon her this Morning, but that she thinks it must at this time be inconvenient to Mrs: Adams: will be very happy if it is consistant with Mrs: Adams's engagements to have the pleasure of her company at Tea in George street before she leaves London: (but least she should not have that pleasure) takes leave to say that her best wishes ever attend Mrs: Adams: that her Voyage may be prosperous, and that it may be succeeded by the very great pleasure of Meeting her Family, and Friends in health, that all happiness may long attend Mrs: Adams and her Family, and that it will be a great gatifycation to Mrs: C: to hear of the welfare of those for whom she shall retain the highest esteem; and to whom she feels herself much obliged for their Friendship and politeness—

Mr: & Miss C: desire to untite in respectful compliments to Mr: & Mrs: Adams— Miss C: wishes that the Artificial Roses where more worthy Mrs: Adams's acceptance: she delayed doing them hopeing to have had some natural ones to have copyed which would have Made them more perfect—

M^rs: Copley has taken the liberty to send with this a Letter for her Friend M^rs: Rogers, and a parcel from M^r: Bromfield—

RC (Adams Papers).

Abigail Adams to John Bowring

Sir   [*ante 30 March 1788*]

your obliging favour of Feb^ry 27 was brought me in the absence of mr Adams, who is gone to Holland upon publick buisness, and who upon his return will be so much hurried & occupied that I fear he will not be able to attend at all to the demands of private Frindship accept from me sir as his Representitive our mutual acknowledgments for the obliging civilities we received at Exeter & every other place where your family connexions extended, and I assure you sir with great Sincerity that we look back upon the Six weeks we spent in visiting Devonshire & its environs as the most agreeable journey we have made in this Country—[1]

The death of my Brother in Laws two Brothers will be an afflictive intelligence to him & his family, yet one of them has been long lost to his Family and Friends and the other had arrived at a period of Life beyond which few can expect to pass.[2] their amiable and virtuous Characters will always afford a pleasing satisfaction to their surviving Relatives to whom I wish every consolation under their present Bereavement, to yourself and Family, every success in Life, which your Integrity of Character, your industry merit & virtue so justly intitle you to

I am sir with / Sincere Esteem / your Humble Servant

A Adams

Dft (Adams Papers); docketed by JA: "A. A. / 1788." Drafted on the same sheet of paper as AA to Lewis D. Ward, [*ante 17 March*], above, and filmed at [*March 1788*].

[1] On 27 Feb. John Bowring wrote to JA to thank the Adamses for their visit to Exeter the previous year and to wish them a good voyage home to America (Adams Papers). Bowring's letter arrived in London after JA had left for the Netherlands on 29 February. AA likely replied before JA returned, probably on 24 or 25 March, and certainly before the couple left London for Portsmouth on 30 March.

[2] Richard Cranch was born in Devonshire, England, and continued to correspond with his many relatives there long after he emigrated to America in 1746. His two brothers, Andrew and William Cranch, died, respectively, in Dec. 1787 and Feb. 1788. JA and AA had met both men in July 1787 (JA, *D&A*, 3:207–210; MHi:Cranch-Bond Papers, Extract from a Register of the Bond and Cranch Families, 1852).

Abigail Adams' Diary of Her Return Voyage
to America, 30 March – 1 May 1788

MS (M/AA/1, APM Reel 197). PRINTED: JA, *D&A*, 3:212–217. AA began
her Diary in London on 30 March on the eve of the Adamses' departure
first for Portsmouth and then for Cowes, where they were to meet their
ship, the *Lucretia*. AA related the sightseeing they did while waiting two
weeks to board the ship—including visits to Carisbrooke Castle and the
town of Yarmouth—and also the boredom: "Haveing staid at Portsmouth
untill I had read all our Books and done all the Work I had left out, I never
before experienced to such a degree what the French term enui." Finally at
sea, AA found her health better than expected, suffering only from "Want
of Sleep," though her maid, Esther Field Briesler, "is very near her Time,
in poor Health and distressingly Sea sick." AA deemed noteworthy a religious service conducted by Rev. John Murray, but otherwise skipped over
most of the voyage. Instead, she chose to focus on a summation of her
years in Europe: "I do not think the four years I have past abroad the
pleasentest part of my Life. Tis Domestick happiness and Rural felicity in
the Bosom of my Native Land, that has charms for me. Yet I do not regreet
that I made this excursion since it has only more attached me to America."

Abigail Adams to Abigail Adams Smith

Dear Child   Portsmouth Fountain 2ᵈ: April 1788

April the 2ᵈ: and the anniversary of the birth of my dear Grandson
whom I am half distracted to see again, with all his pretty, winning
pranks. God bless and preserve the dear boy and grant us all, a
happy meeting on the other side the great water.

We left London on Sunday about two o clock, and arrived here on
Monday evening, having made a very good exchange of the Bath
Hotel for the Fountain. The Bath Hotel is totally changed from
what it was when we were there three years ago, even in price, for I
think with worse things, it is still more extravagant, but Adieu to
that. Just before we set out Col Trumbull brought Mr Smith's letter
written at Bath and the two letters of recall. The day after the fair,
be sure, they who past and sent them must think so at the time, but
this is the way they always have done business. Your papa wrote a
letter to Lord C. and enclosed it, and another to the Baron de Na-
gal.[1] I do not think it wholly improbable that by the time Mr Smith
gets half way home, he may be appointed to Lisbon. Yet I own this is
a circumstance I should not rejoice in, it would distress me to have
you so far from me, and then the terrors of the climate would still

add to my anxiety. But these are mere conjectural evils, of which you Know, I am not very fond, my maxim is rather to enjoy the present, prudently guarding for the future, and thinking with Pope

> "What blessings thy free, bounty gives
> Let me not cast away."[2]

We propose going to the Isle of Wight as soon as the wind changes, while it holds as it is at present, the Ship cannot get down, if Callihan was otherwise ready, which I do not believe he is. Sunday next is the day on which the packet is to sail, I think. I wish to hear from you before I leave this place. There are but two days in the week, that the Post goes, from this place to Falmouth, Tuesdays, and Friday's. I shall leave orders, here that the letters may be sent to us, should any come after we have past over. I fear we shall not get away this week, if we do in the next, on my own account I should not care, but every day makes it worse for others.

I hope your throat is quite well, as Mr Smith does not mention it, and my little boys teeth quite through. I dont like the idea that he will quite forget me. We want him here very much to enliven the scene, for it is, you may well suppose solitary enough. Your papa reads Mr Necker's last publication upon the importance of Religious opinions, which he likes very much, and I amuse myself in perusing a book Mr Dilly sent me as a present, called Mentoria, written by a Mrs Murry who is preceptress, to the Princess Amelia.[3] The Newspapers tell us, that her majesty is like to add another branch to the Royal line.[4]

Remember me affectionately to Mr Smith and to my dear Billy. Your papa sends you his blessing.

I am my dear child most affectionately / Yours   A. Adams

Tr in ABA's hand (Adams Papers); notation by CFA: "AA to her daughter Mrs W. S. Smith."

[1] On 28 March, WSS wrote to JA from Bath, sending him a letter from Henry Remsen Jr. dated 20 Feb., which in turn enclosed a letter from John Jay to JA, 14 Feb., that contained JA's letters of recall from Congress (all Adams Papers). JA in turn sent them to Francis Godolphin Osborne, Lord Carmarthen, British secretary of state for foreign affairs, and Baron van Nagell, the Dutch ambassador. See JA, *D&A*, 3:210–212, note 2.

[2] Pope, *Universal Prayer*, lines 17–18.

[3] Jacques Necker, *De l'importance des opinions religieuses*, London, 1788, is in JA's library at MB (*Catalogue of JA's Library*). AA was reading Ann Murry, *Mentoria; or, The Young Ladies Instructor, in Familiar Conversations on Moral and Entertaining Subjects*, London, 1787.

[4] This rumor was mistaken. Queen Charlotte gave birth to her last child, Amelia, in 1783.

Abigail Adams to Thomas Brand Hollis

Dear Sir,   Portsmouth, Fountain Inn, April 5, 1788.

There is something so disagreeable to one's feelings in taking a final leave of our friends, and thinking that it is the last time we shall ever meet, that I avoided placing myself in that situation as much as possible. On this account I neither bid my worthy friends Dr. Price or Mr. Hollis adieu; for those two gentlemen I have the greatest esteem and regard, and regret the necessity which deprives me of their personal acquaintence. I will, however, flatter myself that their friendship will extend beyond the spot where it was first contracted, and its kind effusions follow me to a distant land.

May I hope, sir, to hear of your welfare and happiness, in which I shall always rejoice, whenever an opportunity offers, after my arrival in America. The Hyde will ever be remembered by me; and the friendship and hospitality of its owner, as the most agreeable scene in my recollection. I designed to have requested a few of the flower seeds from the garden, that I might have planted them with my own hand, and nurtured them with my own care, whenever I arrive in America.

As you have been pleased to give a station to some of my family round your habitation, there can be no harm in my wishing to transplant some of yours to a soil and climate equally salubrious, and perhaps more productive than their own native clime. We have been waiting here nearly a week for a change of wind, and as we have no acquaintance here, the time is rather heavy. Most of our books we sent on board the ship; and those we have with us, we have read. Good Dr. Wren! I always mourned his death, but never so sensibly felt his loss as now.[1]

Pray remember me affectionately to our friend Mrs. Jebb. Mr. Adams is taking his daily walk. Was he here, I am sure he would bid me present his affectionate regards to you, and join me in every sentiment of esteem, with which I am, / dear sir, / your obliged friend / and humble servant,

                                                              A. Adams.

MS not found. Printed from John Disney, ed., *Memoirs of Thomas Brand-Hollis*, London, 1808, p. 39; addressed: "Thomas Brand-Hollis, esq. / Chesterfield-street, London."

[1] A reference to Rev. Dr. Thomas Wren of Portsmouth, who had died the fall of the previous year. AA had possibly met Wren on the Adamses' trip to Portsmouth in the summer of 1786, and JA had met with Wren when he visited Portsmouth in April 1787 (John Brown Cutting to AA, 25 April, above; vol. 4:201, note 2; 7:221).

Thomas Brand Hollis to Abigail Adams

Dear Madam   Chesterfeild Street 7 April 1788.

It is an ill wind blows no body any good owing to that I received your favor with the greatest sense of gratitude & love for the distinguishd regard you have always showed me which is returned & cherished with increasing interest I was sensible how much you avoided an explanation as to your departure & I was equally unwilling to enquire. I shall always rejoice to hear from you & esteem it among my choicest entertainments & if in any way I can be of service to you in this country command & you will give me pleasure

I wish the seeds had been thought of in time the Poppies much succeed admirably with you & indeed all others only that they are no trouble. you shall be supplied with them & others

I have sent the conquest of Canaan & Cyrus, which I had by me having no time to lose; to take their chance if they meet you they will amuse.[1]

prosperous gales attend you home and may you be happy in the bosom of your family and live to see them follow the distinguished example you have marked out for them is the affectionate wish of / Dear Madam / him who with the greatest regard & esteem / your obliged & sincere friend   T. Brand Hollis

RC (DSI:Hull Coll., on loan); addressed: "Mrs Adams"; docketed: "Brand Hollis / 1st April / 1788."

[1] Timothy Dwight, *The Conquest of Canäan*, and probably Andrew Michael, Chevalier Ramsay, *The Travels of Cyrus: To Which Is Annexed, a Discourse upon the Theology and Mythology of the Pagans*, London, 1727.

John Callahan to Abigail Adams

Madam—   London April: 8th. 1788

I had the Honor of Receiving a letter from you yesterday— we have had such—Boysterous weather Since your Departur from here that for 6 days. I had the Pilot on board, & he Would not ventur to moove the Ship: but She is Now in the Downes & will be at Portsmouth the first fair wind: I Shall proceed from here so as to get to Portsmouth before the Ship so that my Departure from here will in some Measure depend upon the winds— I will wate on Mr. Vassel this Evening with your Commands: Mrs. Callahan returns you her most respectfull thanks For your, kind attention, in remembering here— please To present our Respects to, his Excellency—& am very Respectfully— / Madam / your most humbl servt.

John Callahan

Mr. Ward Boylstons: with whom I had the honor dineing with to-day Desires his most Respectful Compliments to you & his Excellency

RC (Adams Papers); internal address: "Mrs: Adams" and "To Mrs. Adams—"

Abigail Adams to Abigail Adams Smith

My Dear Child: Isle of Wight, April 9th, 1788.

It is now ten days since we left London, and have been waiting at Portsmouth and here for the ship, but cannot yet learn that she has passed Gravesend. The weather is fine, but this waiting is very tedious, in a place where we have no acquaintance, and very little to interest or amuse us.

We took a ride, yesterday, to Newport, the principal town in the island, and visited Carisbrook Castle. This place is famous not only for its antiquity, but for having been used as a prison for Charles the First, who retired to it from Hampton Court as a place of safety, but was afterwards confined there as a prisoner.[1] This castle is now in ruins, and no person can give any account of its origin. The first mention of it which history gives, is about the year 530. It was then said to be a place of some strength; its situation is upon a very high eminence, and the mount which supports the citadel must have been an immense labour, as it appears to have been the work of art. The ascent to it is by a flight of four score steps; but then one is amply repaid for the fatigue, as it gives you an extensive view of the town and river of Newport, the harbour of Cowes, Portsmouth, Southampton, and many other adjacent parts.

One of the most curious things in this castle is a well, three hundred feet deep, and so well stoned that the lapse of ages does not seem in the least to have injured it. It is within the castle, under cover, and the woman who conducted us carried a lantern, by which she lighted a large paper and threw into the well, that we might see its depth. She also threw a pin in, the sound of which resounded like a large stone. The water is drawn up by an ass, which walks in a wheel like a turn-spit dog. The whole place is delightful, though in ruins. This island is a beautiful spot, taken all together, very fertile, and highly cultivated; but water, and not land, is the object we have now in view, and knowing that we must pass it, renders every delay painful.

I wrote you from London and from Portsmouth, but have not received a single line from you since you left me.[2] From Mr. Smith we received letters, whilst he was at Bath, which is the last I heard from you.[3] As the wind is so contrary, I shall venture to send this, in expectation that you have not yet sailed, and requesting you to write and direct your letter to the Fountain Inn, Cowes, at Mrs. Symes'.[4] Send it by the crossroad post to Southampton, by which means it will reach us. How is my dear sweet boy? I think of him by day, and dream of him by night. O, what a relief would his sportive little pranks have been to me, in the tedious hours of waiting,—waiting for winds, for captain, for vessel. I fear all my patience will be exhausted.

I took only a few books, and a little sewing, all of which were exhausted in one week. We got some little recruit, yesterday, at Newport; but that will soon be out. Let me hear from you, my dear child—how you are like to be accommodated, and the name of the packet and captain. We have written to Callihan, but I know he will take his own time, and at the same time assure you it shall be yours. I think he might get to the Downs, if he would exert himself.

My love to Mr. Smith, and my little charmer. Your father sends his love to you all.

I am, my dear child, most affectionately, / Yours,

Abigail Adams

MS not found. Printed from AA2, *Jour. and Corr.*, 2:67–69.

[1] Carisbrooke Castle, a medieval structure built on the remains of a Roman site, was the seat of government on the Isle of Wight when Charles I fled there in 1647. Probably hoping he could escape from there to France if it became necessary, Charles I was instead held as a prisoner at the castle for nearly a year prior to his execution at Whitehall in Jan. 1649 (Karl Baedeker, *Great Britain: Handbook for Travellers*, 8th edn., Leipzig, 1927, p. 67; *DNB*).

[2] The London letter has not been found.

For the Portsmouth letter, see AA to AA2, 2 April, above.

[3] WSS to JA, 28 March (Adams Papers), for which see AA to AA2, 2 April, note 1, above.

[4] AA and JA stayed at the Fountain Inn in Cowes from 6 to 20 April, taking trips from there to see other sites on the Isle of Wight. AA described the building in greater detail in the Diary of her return voyage to America, 30 March – 1 May (JA, *D&A*, 3:212–213).

John Cranch to Abigail Adams

Madam;   London, 11. April, 1788:

Understanding by my sister Elworthy, that your Excellency complains of having read yourself out of books, I am tempted to send you down the latest publication that I can find promises amusement enough to justify me; and accordingly I have to intreat your excellency's acceptance of "Costigan's view of society and manners in Portugal."[1] I was just now in hopes to have gratified your excellency another way—with some letters addressed to you by a Ship arrived at the isle of Wight from Portsmouth in America, which we were informed lay at the General post office; but finding, upon enquiry, that these letters have been forwarded to Grosvenor square, I confide that they will be sent to you by some other hand.

My brother here would run away with all the honor of serving your Excellencies, but that I contrive, now and then, to push myself into some employment subordinate to him, in order to engross as much of that honor as I reasonably can, and with the utmost avidity catch every occasion of shewing that I am; most truly, your excellency's gratefull humble servant   J. Cranch.

RC (Adams Papers).

[1] Arthur William Costigan, *Sketches of Society and Manners in Portugal*, 2 vols., London, 1787, which is in JA's library at MB (*Catalogue of JA's Library*).

John Quincy Adams to Thomas Boylston Adams

My dear Brother.   Newbury-Port May 3d: 1788.

We have mutually been deficient in those attentions, which absent connections ought always to preserve towards one another: the fault has been the greatest on my side, as I was under the additional obligation of setting a good example; but I feel myself at this time peculiarly bound to write to you, to apologize for the rough expressions which upon several occasions I used while I was with you, and which perhaps you may reasonably think, were incompatible with that fraternal tenderness which ought always to accompany fraternal affection— Such expressions were dictated by the imprudence of a momentary impulse; but believe me, my brother, when upon the calmest reflection, and uninfluenced, by any temporary feelings, I assure you, that the warmest wishes of my heart, are for your, honour, your interest, and welfare. These were the motives by which I was influenced, even when my observation bore the appearance of unkindness, and I am still actuated by them while I venture to give you such advice, as I think will tend to promote your best interests.

The Situation in which you are now placed, while it affords you such advantages as may be highly beneficial to you if properly improved, is not without its dangers, which it is your duty to perceive and to avoid. You are young, and if you examine the springs of your own conduct you will find yourself prone to imitate examples which your own reason will condemn. You have therefore need of great judgment, and of great resolution, in order to persevere in that line of conduct which will insure you the applause of the world, and, what is of infinitely more importance the approbation of your own conscience. This indeed is the greatest end to which we can wish to attain.

> "Above all, to thine own self be true,
> And it must follow as the night the day,
> Thou canst not then be false to any man."[1]

If your own heart, can testify that your conduct has always been reconcileable with the immutable rules of justice and truth, you will always enjoy one inexhaustible source of happiness, of which neither the frowns of adverse fortune, nor the utmost efforts of human malice can ever deprive you:— If you will only reflect upon this subject I am perswaded it will be wholly unnecessary for me to say more— You yourself will perceive that nothing can be more pernicious than to adapt your conduct to the wishes of a classmate, in opposition to your own principles. This practice which I have often heard advocated at College, is not only vicious and immoral, but argues great weakness of mind and want of spirit, in not daring to exert that freedom and independence in resisting an equal, which they all think so requisite in withstanding the proper authority of a superior.

But, my friend, in order to secure this same self-approbation; it will not be sufficient to possess the mere negative virtue of doing no harm. You must consider that as a social being it is your duty to increase as much as in you lies, the enjoyments of your fellow creatures.— And as your own inclination has destined you to one of the learned professions, it will appear Evident, that you will answer the end of your existence, only in proportion to the learning and knowlege which you may acquire. And therefore do not think I exaggerate if I say that every hour which you spend in idleness, is an injury which you do to your fellow-men. . . . But this is not all: The same

257

means which tend to increase your usefulness in the world, are also the means by which you will rise to reputation and respectability. I know you are not destitute of that ambition which excites a noble generosity, and you are fully sensible how disgraceful it is to be excelled by a person of inferior talents, and advantages for improvement The world will, and they have a right to say in the language of scripture, "To whom much is given, from him shall much be required."[2] We ought all to recollect that the time which is given to us for the sole acquisition of Science, our Parent was obliged to lose by keeping a school for a subsistence.[3] In short we have every possible reason, to be indefatigably industrious in the pursuit of learning; and to resist them all would argue, the extreme of weakness or of folly.— These cautions are not, I hope necessary for you: I am perswaded you will be attentive to all the college duties, and if you perform them fully, your time will be sufficiently employ'd.

There is one particular which I would recommend to your attention. You will soon arrive at that period of College Life, when a degree of manliness and of dignity will be expected in your behaviour: you must remember, that as you advance, you will be look'd up to, for examples by your fellow students of a more recent standing; and you have had opportunities to observe that the influence of a Senior Class may almost give a tone to the manners of the whole College. Avoid too great familiarities with anyone. There is a certain decorum, and respect which is due, even to our nearest intimates; and be particularly cautious to preserve yourself from a merited charge of trifling or puerility.

And suffer me again to urge you, upon a point which I have repeatedly recommended, a particular attention to composition: I wish you to overcome entirely the aversion you have to writing: an elegant epistolary style, is one of the most useful accomplishments which a gentleman can possess; and it must be acquired if ever, at an early period of life. In your exercices of this kind, you will have the double advantage of affording amusement and satisfaction to your friends, at the same time that you are improving your own faculties and understanding.

If upon reading what I have here written, you should be disposed to think my speculative opinions of little weight, because my practical conduct may not be conformable to them, I only wish you, to ask yourself whether they are not such as must tend to increase your own happiness and usefulness: and if they are, any deficiency in the person who proposes them ought not to diminish their influence in your breast.— recollect the lines of Horace

> —fungar vice cotis, acutum
> Reddere quae ferrum valet, exsors ipsa secandi:[4]

and be perswaded that I should never recommend any acquisition, of which I myself am destitute, unless I regret the want of it.

Give my love to Charles; I hope he is well: he almost told me when I left Braintree that he would not write to me; perhaps he thinks me impertinent in assuming *Mentorial* airs, and dislikes the correspondence; he does not love to be censured; but he has a great deal of generosity at heart, and his disposition is really amiable. He always treated me with the kindness and affection of a brother; &c I am perswaded he will ever conduct in the same manner towards you.

Your affectionate friend & brother   J. Q. Adams.

RC (Adams Papers); endorsed: "May 3ᵈ 1788—"

[1] Shakespeare, *Hamlet*, Act I, scene iii, lines 78–80.

[2] Luke, 12:48.

[3] JA, in order to pay for his education beyond Harvard, kept a grammar school at Worcester for two years after graduation while he studied law at night. As he wrote in his Autobiography in 1804: "A Lawyer must have a Fee, for taking me into his Office. I must be boarded and cloathed for several Years: I had no Money; and my Father having three Sons, had done as much for me, in the Expences of my Education as his Estate and Circumstances could justify and as my Reason or my honor would allow me to ask. I therefore gave out that I would take a School. . . . In this Situation I remained, for about two Years Reading Law in the night and keeping School in the day" (*D&A*, 3:263–264).

[4] I play the whetstone; useless, and unfit / To cut myself, I sharpen others' wit (Horace, *Ars Poetica*, lines 304–305).

Elizabeth Smith Shaw to Mary Smith Cranch

My Dear Sister—   Haverhill May 8 1788—

You cannot think how anxious I have been to hear from my Sister Adams, & you. Two Vessels I saw by the Papers had arrived from London, & I could not but think we had Letters—[1] The intelligence you give me of her Health, makes me feel solemn indeed— It is 18 Months since she has been in a very poor way— I know she is mortal, & must die— But the very Idea of her being separated from us, I cannot think of without a gushing Tear— It is not possible for a Sister to be kinder, than she has been to us— Yes! I must indulge the feelings of human-nature, & pray, that the period may be far distant, when she shall be clothed with immortality, & receive the rewards of her Virtue, & extensive Benevolence—

You have not said one word to me about her Daughter— Is Col. Smith & Family to come with them, or to go to New-york?

I am very sorry Ester has mortified, & grieved Sister by her foolish Conduct— Why did not the silly Girl read her Bible, & be married before?— I think if there is a family Sin, every Branch thereoff ought to be upon the watch, & place a double gaurd on that Vice—² I pity Sister—for instead of Esters of being any help, she will require herself the kindest assistance. If she should be sick aboard Ship, it must be dreary— I have heard nothing from you till last Tuesday, Leonard White came from newbury & brought me your kind Letter favored by Mr Adams, since I received one by Mr Osgood— I wanted to hear from you exceedingly on the account of Cousin Billy, Leonard told me he was at the Office, but he was gone home sick—³ I live at such a distance from many dear Friends that I am obliged to exercise patience, & call forth all the magnimity I can find in my heart, that I may enjoy any kind of Ease—

I cannot think why my dear Betsy Smith is not come yet, By what Mr Bliss said, I concluded she would have been here before now—⁴

I am sorry for Miss Nancy Quincy, it was a sad mistake of her Mothers— Why is the Connection broke of with Mr G——t?— She is a very fine amiable young Lady— She will do good in any Station I dare say— How does Mr N. & my Eliza— I have been looking for them till my Eyes ake— You must all come & see me now in Sammon time, & before Sister Adams arrives, for I shall not then get one of you to look this way for a twelve month, I fear—

Are you not too hard upon father Wibird—perhaps you do not hear aright— Mr Shaw was very happy a Fast Day I assure you, in pleasing every-side— They were both *new Sermons*—& had *that* at least to recommend them— Many of his people wished to have them printed— Mr Thaxter says nothing but the scarcity of Cash has prevented application being made for them— It is very pleasing when our Services are acceptable—

adieu my dear Sister, ever yours in / the warmth of Love & affection

E Shaw—

P S my Sister Adams before she went away gave me Louisas gown which was made out of hers, for my Betsy Quincy— I thought I would not make it for her till she was larger— I attempted to make it this week, but was obliged to lay it aside for I had not one peice of it to help it out— I suppose my sister has some which she would give me if I could ask her— If you think it not be dissagreeable to her, I would thank you to send me some as soon as you can—

RC (DLC:Shaw Family Papers); addressed: "Mrs Mary Cranch / Braintree"; docketed: "M^rs. Shaw. / May 8. 1788."; notation: "To be left at / Mr Dawes office / or house—"

[1] The Boston *Independent Chronicle*, 24 April, reported on the arrival into Boston harbor of the ships *Mary*, Capt. Barnard, and *Neptune*, Capt. Scott, as well as the brig *Nancy*, Capt. York, all from London.

[2] Esther's parents, Abigail Newcomb and Joseph Field, were married in April 1744; their first child, Susanna, was born in June of the same year (Sprague, *Braintree Families*, p. 829, 1661R).

[3] JQA reported on 16 April that William Cranch "has been very unwell, but is recov-

ering" (*Diary*, 2:392).

[4] Possibly Capt. Joseph Bliss (1757–1819) of Concord, who resided near the Lincoln, Mass., home of AA's niece Elizabeth (Betsy) Smith. Bliss served under Gen. Henry Knox during the Revolution and likely had ties to Haverhill, Mass., as he moved in 1790 to its sister town of Haverhill, N.H. (U.S. Census, 1790, Mass., p. 139; William F. Whitcher, *History of the Town of Haverhill, New Hampshire*, Concord, N.H., 1919, p. 3, 482).

Abigail Adams Smith to Abigail Adams

My Dear Mamma: On board ship, May 18th, 1788.

I rose this morning with a fair prospect of landing before night, but alas, we are immersed in fogs and darkness. We have been within a few hours sail of New-York, for several days; but fogs, calms, and contrary winds, have deprived us of the happiness of see-ing our native land; it is a most mortifying situation.[1] I hope you have not known from experience to what a degree it is teasing; but that you are now safely landed and happily enjoying the sweet soci-ety of children, relations, and friends.

We arrived in Halifax, the fourth week after our sailing from Fal-mouth, on the 5th of April. We were at Halifax three days. Colonel Smith received a card from, and dined with the Governor, who was very civil.[2] The town is larger than I expected to find it; it is situated like Haverhill, upon the side of a hill, and is I believe, about as large; the buildings are all of wood, and painted white, which gives them the appearance of stone, and looks very neat. The inhabitants are supplied with provisions, plenty and cheap, from Boston and New-York; and they have fish from the ocean.

Here are two or three regiments, and several frigates. Admiral Sawyer has the command upon this station.[3] The people are trem-bling, lest the port should be shut against the American supplies; and they are in fear of starving, if they should be strictly prohibited.

The country around is a perfect heath; there was not the least verdure to be seen; they speak much in favour of the climate.

* * * * * * * * *

We were in all six cabin passengers. I wrote you from Falmouth of a Mr. and Mrs. T——; he is a native of Maryland, sent early to England for his education; but it is not easy to discover that this was the motive of his visit, unless to be thoroughly knowing in the career of New-Market, Brooks, and every species of gambling, extravagance, and dissipation, was the education intended for him; he is a Lieutenant of the British Navy, was on board the Somerset, and a prisoner in Boston during the war. Three years since he ran off with, and married the daughter of the Admiral, a step which I believe every person but herself, thinks she has much cause to repent of. It is said he has run through his own fortune, and a fortune of five thousand pounds, which his brother, who died in the East Indies, left him; and is now much in advance. They are now upon a visit to his father, who is a man of property in Maryland; and strange as it may appear, although Mrs. T—— is of a most amiable disposition, pleasing in her person and manners, she appears greatly attached to him, and to be happy. I never saw two persons, who excited in my mind so much surprise.[4]

Lord Mountmorris was another singular character;[5] his going to America was the decision of half an hour; he wished us a pleasant passage when we went on board the packet, at three o'clock, and before four o'clock, came himself with his luggage, for America. It was his intention to have gone to New-York; but an invitation from the Governor, to spend a few months with him at Halifax, detained him there. Mr. Lyle, an Irishman, and a civil decent young man, was the sixth. The master of the ship was very young, unacquainted with the coast of America, obstinate and positive in his opinions, without judgment, and having but little experience. The surgeon, as ignorant a young man, as perhaps, ever practised in his profession; coarse and rough in his manners. From this description you may easily imagine, that we could not be much pleased with our situation. All that was left for us, was to make the best of it; we neither complained, fretted, scolded, or used any ungentle terms of discontent, but were silent upon most occasions, as we could not join in the conversation, which was engrossed by some of the gentlemen, upon such topics as we were happy not to have been acquainted with; we should have been happy, could we have retired, but that was impossible. It is, I hope, almost at an end. I shall rejoice when we are landed safely in New-York.

New-York, May 20th [28], 1788.

This day, my dear mamma, completes a week since we arrived in this city. Colonel Smith's friend, Mr. McCormick, came on board and conducted us to his house, where I have been treated with great kindness and attention. My mamma and Miss M. Smith came to town on Friday,[6] and on Sunday I went over to Long Island, to visit the other part of the family; it is a family where affection and harmony prevail; you would be charmed to see us all together; our meeting was joyful and happy.

> "Twas such a sober scene of joy, as angels well might keep,
> A joy prepared to weep."[7]

My time, since my arrival, has been wholly occupied in receiving visits and accepting invitations. I have dined at General Knox's; Mrs. K. has improved much in her appearance. The General is not half so fat as he was.[8] Yesterday we dined at Mr. —— in company with the whole *corps diplomatique*; Mr. —— is a most pleasing man, plain in his dress and manners, but kind, affectionate, and attentive; benevolence is portrayed in every feature. Mrs. —— dresses gay and showy, but very pleasing upon a slight acquaintance.[9] The dinner was *à la mode Française*, and exhibited more of European taste that I expected to have found. Mr. Guardoque was as chatty and sociable as his countryman Del Campo;[10] Lady Temple, civil; Sir J——, more of the gentleman than I ever saw him.[11] The French minister is a handsome and apparently polite man; the Marchioness his sister, the oddest figure eyes ever beheld; in short, there is so much said of and about her, and so little of truth can be known, that I cannot pretend to form any kind of judgment in what manner or form, my attention would be properly directed to her; she speaks English a little, is very much out of health, and was taken ill at Mr. ——, before we went to dinner, and obliged to go home.

Congress are sitting; but one hears little more of them, than if they were inhabitants of the new discovered planet.[12] The President is said to be a worthy man; his lady is a Scotch woman, with the title of Lady Christina Griffin; she is out of health, but appears to be a friendly disposed woman; we are engaged to dine there next Tuesday; Mr. Franks is first aid-de-camp.[13]

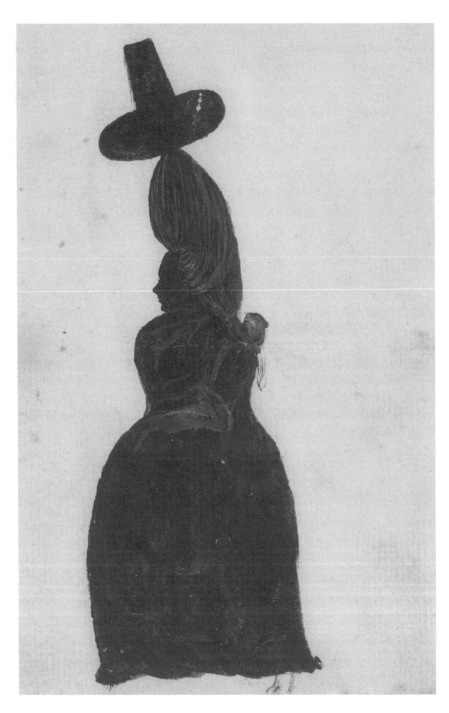

7. MRS. HENRY KNOX, CA. 1790
See page xiii

Every one is kind and civil in their inquiries, respecting my father. Some persons expected he would have taken New-York in his way home; others expect he will make them a visit in the course of the summer; every body inquires if he is not coming; and it seems to be a very general idea that he will come; he will judge for himself of the propriety of a visit to this place. I need not say, that to see both my parents here, would contribute greatly to my happiness. Be pleased to present me, affectionately, to my dear papa.

Mr. and Mrs. P——, embarked in the last French packet, for France, both of them as much insane as ever; they had heard of the death of their daughter, and pretended that this was the cause of their return to Europe. I am told that they found their estate much more productive than they had ever expected, and are going to bring an action against Mr. L——, for the produce, which has been regularly deposited in his hands.[14]

We have taken a house upon Long Island, twelve miles from the city; it is pleasantly situated, and has a good garden, with about fifty acres of land.[15]

* * * * * * * * *

I thought I had no local attachments, but I find a strong *penchant* towards your city; but I do not give a preference, lest I might be disappointed, were I to visit Boston at this time: our minds are strangely but happily flexible, and very soon are we assimilated to the situation in which we are placed, either by design or accident.

I was much grieved to hear of the death of Mr. Lincoln; sincerely do I sympathize with my friend in her affliction.[16] Be so good as to remember me kindly to her, and present my kindest remembrance to all my friends who inquire after me.

We are impatiently expecting to hear of your safe arrival. I have written at my leisure, intending to forward my letter, by the first opportunity, that you may, upon your arrival, hear of our safety. Colonel Smith joins me in his affectionate congratulations to my father and you, upon your return to your native land. We hope to hear from you both very soon.

Your affectionate daughter,   A. Smith.

MS not found. Printed from AA2, *Jour. and Corr.*, 2:70–76.

[1] The Smiths left England from Falmouth on the British packet *Thyne*, Capt. Wolf. They arrived in Halifax, Nova Scotia, on 7 May and finally reached New York on 21 May (JA, *D&A*, 3:216, note 6; *Massachusetts Gazette*, 27, 30 May 1788).

[2] John Parr (1725–1791) was born in Dublin and joined the British Army at age 19, resigning as a lieutenant colonel in 1776. He was appointed governor of Nova Scotia in

1782 but became lieutenant governor in 1786 when Guy Carleton was named governor general of British North America. Parr continued in that position until his death in 1791 (*Dictionary of Canadian Biography*, 14 vols. to date, Toronto, 1966– , 4:603–605).

³ Adm. Herbert Sawyer Sr. served as commander of the Royal Navy's Halifax squadron from 1785 to Aug. 1788, when he left Nova Scotia for England (Julian Gwyn, *Frigates and Foremasts: The North American Squadron in Nova Scotia Waters 1745–1815*, Vancouver, 2003, p. 83–88).

⁴ Philemon Tilghman, the son of wealthy Maryland landowner James Tilghman (1716–1793), was a lieutenant in the British Navy when he eloped with Harriet Milbanke, the daughter of Adm. Mark Milbanke, in 1785. One of Philemon's elder brothers, Richard Tilghman, had worked with the East India Company but died en route from Bengal to London in 1786; prior to that time, he had occasionally assisted Philemon financially (Jennifer Anne Bryan, The Tilghmans of Maryland's Eastern Shore, 1660–1793, Univ. of Maryland, College Park, Ph.D. diss., 1999, p. 8–12, 374–377, 379; New York *Impartial Gazetteer*, 24 May 1788). AA2's letter to AA from Falmouth has not been found.

⁵ Hervey Redmond Morres, 2d Viscount Mountmorres (1746?–1797), an Irishman and author of various books and essays defending the rights of the Irish House of Lords (*DNB*).

⁶ That is, AA2's mother-in-law and sister-in-law, both Margaret Smith.

⁷ "'Twas such a sober sense of joy / As Angels well might keep; / A joy chastis'd by piety, / A joy prepar'd to weep" (Hannah More, *Sir Eldred of the Bower*, Dublin, 1776, Part II, lines 213–216).

⁸ For Lucy Flucker Knox, wife of Gen. Henry Knox, see Descriptive List of Illustrations, No. 7, above. Both were notoriously heavy, sometimes described in New York as "the largest couple in the city" (*DAB*).

⁹ The hosts of the party were John and Sarah Jay (Rufus Wilmot Griswold, *The Republican Court*, rev. edn., N.Y., 1856, p. 91–92).

¹⁰ Don Diego de Gardoqui (1735–1798) served as Spanish minister to the United States from 1785 to 1789 (*Doc. Hist. Ratif. Const.*, 13:223).

¹¹ For Lady Elizabeth Bowdoin Temple and Sir John Temple, see vol. 5:272, 6:81.

¹² That is, Uranus, discovered by William Herschel in 1781.

¹³ Cyrus Griffin (1748–1810), a lawyer from Virginia trained at the University of Edinburgh and the Middle Temple, served as the last president of the Continental Congress. He had married Lady Christina Stuart, the daughter of a Scottish lord, in 1770 in Edinburgh (*DAB*).

For David S. Franks, who had known the Adamses in Europe, see vol. 6:312.

¹⁴ Philippa Paradise (b. 1774), the younger daughter of Lucy Ludwell and John Paradise, died on 4 Nov. 1787 in London, where she had remained at school when her parents returned to Virginia. William Lee, the husband of Lucy Paradise's older sister, Hannah Philippa Ludwell, had long managed the estates inherited by the Ludwell sisters (Archibald Bolling Shepperson, *John Paradise and Lucy Ludwell of London and Williamsburg*, Richmond, Va., 1942, p. 36–38, 293–297, 456).

¹⁵ Their new home, named Beaver Hall, was located in the town of Jamaica in the southwestern portion of Queens County, twelve miles from New York City (Benjamin Thompson, *The History of Long Island, from Its Discovery to the Present Time*, 2d edn., 2 vols., N.Y., 1843, 2:96).

¹⁶ Benjamin Lincoln Jr., husband of Mary (Polly) Otis Lincoln, died on 18 Jan. (vol. 7:205; Benjamin Lincoln Sr. to George Washington, 20 Jan., Washington, *Papers, Confederation Series*, 6:50–51).

Abigail Adams to Abigail Adams Smith

My Dear Daughter: Ship Lucretia, May 29th, 1788.

I hope you are safe landed at Jamaica, before this time, with Mr. Smith and my sweet boy; how often have I thought of him, amidst the turbulent waves, which have so frequently encompassed us upon our passage, and prayed that you might have met with more prosperous gales, and a shorter passage than has fallen to our share. On the 20th of April we embarked from Cowes, from whence I wrote you; we had the wind fair only until we past the Needles,[1] when it came directly ahead, but the tide assisted us, and we strove to work out of the channel until Monday night, when it blew so hard as to oblige us to put into Portland; here we remained a whole week, the same wind prevailing. This place is just by Weymouth, so that our gentlemen went twice on shore during the week; I did not venture, as the wind blew very high. After a week lying here, the wind changed, and we sailed with a northeaster; this lasted us just long enough to carry us out of the channel, when the west wind set in, and alternately we have had a violent blow, squalls, and then calms, from that day to the present; sometimes we have been obliged to lie to, and once to put in our dead-lights; fortunately our ship is much easier than Hyde's, or as the weather has been much worse, I know not what I should have done.[2] 'Tis agreed by all the hands, that they never knew so blustering a May. We have met with several ships, with which we have spoken; and one morning after a very heavy wind we espied a ship in distress, having lost her masts; we steered immediately for her, and found her to be an American ship, captain M——, called the Thomas and Sally, bound to Baltimore.[3] We lay to, and sent hands on board of her, to assist in getting up another mast. We sent our old doctor on board to bleed two men, much hurt by the fall of their masts; and Mr. Boyd, one of our passengers, said he would go on board and see if there were any passengers; as the sea ran high I thought it was rather dangerous, but he was young and enterprising;[4] our mate, carpenter, doctor, and four sailors, accompanied him. It was late in the afternoon before they could get back, and really at the hazard of their lives, for the wind had increased to a storm and the sea ran mountain high; we were all very anxious for them, but happily they all returned safe; Mr. Boyd bringing us an account, that there were four passengers on board, amongst whom was poor Hindman, almost terrified to death;[5] but as the ship was a very good one, and they had got up a new mast, we left them, we hope, safe. We spoke the same day with a brig from London to Virginia, and an American ship from Bordeaux to Boston. For these four days past we have had finer weather, but alas no good winds, and no prospect of reaching Boston until the middle of June, if then.

8. THE NEEDLES, ISLE OF WIGHT, BY WILLIAM WESTALL, CA. 1835

See page xiv

You will be anxious to know how we have done: really better than my fears. With respect to myself, I have been less seasick than when I crossed before: want of sleep I have suffered more from. Your papa has been very well. But Esther you say, what have you done with her? Yesterday at five, she had a daughter, a poor little starvling, but with special lungs, old nurse Comis is just the thing, never sick, can eat and sleep, at all times, as well as any sailor on board. We got through this business much better than I feared we should. I had for the first time in my life, to dress the little animal, who was buried in its clothes. At present, we seem to want only a good wind. I am almost exhausted, and my patience wearied out; if we had been favoured with a fair wind, we should have got home before this matter took place. Brisler has been much the sickest person on board ship. I expected him to have been half nurse, instead of which, he has wanted constant nursing. I hope and pray, I may never again be left to go to sea: of all places, it is the most disagreeable, such a sameness, and such a tossing to and fro. Our passengers are agreeable; our captain is very clever; our ship very clean. We have many things to be thankful for. Adieu!

Yours,   A. A.

MS not found. Printed from AA2, *Jour. and Corr.*, 2:76–79.

[1] For the Needles, see Descriptive List of Illustrations, No. 8, above.

[2] Presumably a reference to Capt. Nathaniel Byfield Lyde's ship, *Active*, on which AA and AA2 sailed to Europe in 1784. For AA's description of that ship, which she found uncomfortable and unclean, see JA, *D&A*, 3:157–158; vol. 5:359, 361.

[3] The *Thomas and Sally*, Capt. F. Dorset (Dorsett), left London on 15 April and arrived safely in Baltimore by 24 June. She lost her foremast and topmast in a gale on 18 May (*Maryland Journal and Baltimore Advertiser*, 24, 27 June; *Pennsylvania Mercury*, 26 June).

[4] The *Massachusetts Centinel*, 18 June, identified him as "William Boyd of Portsmouth." In her Diary account of the voyage, AA indicated that Boyd was "a young Gentleman who received His Education in this Country" (JA, *D&A*, 3:214).

[5] Possibly William Hindman (1743–1822), a lawyer who had studied at the Inns of Court in London. He represented Maryland in the Continental Congress from 1784 to 1786 and later served in both the U.S. House of Representatives and Senate (Edward C. Papenfuse and others, *A Biographical Dictionary of the Maryland Legislature, 1635–1789*, 2 vols., Baltimore, 1979).

Abigail Adams Smith to John Quincy Adams

New York june 8th 1788—

to your Candour my Dear Brother—I must appeal for Pardon that I have thus long delayed to inform you of our safe arrival in this City— I have *presumed* that *we* were *People* of such importance that the news of such an event must have reached you through the

Chanell of the news Papers as soon as it would have done, had I have written you immediately upon Landing—[1] and realy my time has been so wholy occupied in receiving and returning visits—that I have not been able to find one half Hour unoccupied—

I heard this morning by M^r W^m. Knox—who left Boston on Wedensday last,[2] that a Ship was comeing up the Harbour on Tuesday Evening which was supposed to have been Callihan— with all my heart I wish it may so prove for I begin to be anxous for our Parrents—and Shall now be very impatient untill I hear of their arrival, and health if they Sailed when they expected the begining of April they must have had a long and I fear a tedious Passage—

I will hope that ere this you have seen them and that you are all mutually happy— I shall expect to hear from you very soon and very often— the tedious distance we have so long been at—is now lessened—and in four days if you please you may gratify yourself and make me very happy by making me a visit. I do not ask it at present—but when we get settled upon Long Island, where we have taken a House—I shall think you very deficient if you do not make us a visit— it will be advantageous to your health—& I see no injury that so *Steady* and *experienced* a *youth* can receive from a relaxation of a week, or two from hard, and unintermiting studies, we are in daily expectation of the arrival of the Ship which has on Board our Baggage— as soon as it arrives—and we can collect together a little furniture—we shall take up our residence upon Long Island—and in a few weeks I shall inform you that I am ready to receive you—and expect you to set off Post Haste upon receipt of my Summons. if my other Brothers could accompany you at this season I should be very happy—but if they cannot at present I shall request the pleasure and favour of a visit from them the first moment they can find a release from their studies— you must give my Love to them and desire them to write to me soon and often I shall write them very soon—but Mr Gore I am informed Leaves this City tomorrow—and I have only time to finish this Letter—[3]

I have been reading over the letters which you wrote me from this Place[4] many Persons mentioned in them I have become acquainted with—and in general find your observations just— Lady Wheat has lately married Capt Cochrane and goes soon with him to Scotland,[5] Miss Becca sears preserves her Beauty and is very handsome— Mrs Jarvis and Miss Broom arrived in town on Wedensday—and were very well last Evening at Eleven—[6] I supped in Company with them— General Knox has fallen away—and M^rs —— is not *more* than one yard and an half round her waist— they have been very friendly and polite to us since our arrival— Mr Rucker is very ill there is no hopes of his recovery,—[7] *Miss R—— fatter than Miss Adams*,—[8] I have received visits from *Sixty* Ladies so that you, knowing how punctilious *we* Ladies of N York are must easily imagine that I have my hands full (as the saying is)[9] in returning the visits—and accepting invitations to dinner, Tea, and Supper, parties— I am quite impatient to get out of Town—for the weather for two days past has been almost insupportably Warm—

Franks is here and first Aid de Camp to the President of Congress— M^r B—— is here and passingly civil—. M^rs B——m would be wretched if she had not some distant hopes of seeing Europe again—. but has no curiossity nor desire to travell through her own Country— New York does not afford an House—that She could possibly accommodate her family in—[10]

you must write me all the news, and anecdotes that you can hear of— tell me if the report is true that Elisa Cranch is going to enter the Holy Bands of Matrimony and if so—with whom—and offer her my Congratulation upon the Event,— I have seen the American Magazines for this year—and have picked up some news from them— such as an account of Marriages and Deaths— *Cousin Cotton*—is I find Married at last—and Poor Mr Lincoln is Dead— I was greived for my friend M^rs: Lincoln— many many are the ups and downs of Life— were I to visit Boston—I should find a Great chasm in the Circle of my acquaintance—and mourn the Loss of many Kind and good friends—

Federalist, or Ante federalist, is the question—and pray upon which side of the important question do you Stand I could almost answer for you three months forward—for you will find your Father a great Advocate for Federalism— there has been great rejoiceing amongst the Former—at the late accession of Carolina—to the Union—but the friends of the new Constitution are very doubtfull of its Success in this State— the Convention are to meet upon the Seventeenth of this month— Mr Jay is a Member and many other very strenuous advocates in its favour[11]—but the Governor of the State— is said to be opposed to it—and *Some* say he has taken all means to prejudice the Country People—against its adoption—[12] the party against it are silent—and seem to be ashaimed of being known— how it will prove eventually is uncertain— it ever has been and ever will be the Case that upon every Subject there is a diversity of opinion— and it is a very rare instance that People who disagree in Sentiment should be friendly and benevolently disposed towards each other— thus we must ever expect to see—One Party rejoice at the ill success of its opponent—and Useing all the means in its Power to render the opposite disregarded disrespected and—all their measures frustrated—and untill the milenium in Politicks arrives we can not expect any alteration of System— so much for Politicks— I must close my Letter—and request you to remember me to all friends—and beleive me / your affectionate Sister   A Smith—

Coll[n] Smith desires his Love to you—

RC (Adams Papers); endorsed: "My Sister—8. June 1788." and "My Sister. June 8. 1788."

[1] Several Boston newspapers reported AA2 and WSS's arrival in Halifax, beginning with the *Massachusetts Centinel*, 24 May; their arrival in New York was listed in the *Massachusetts Gazette*, 30 May. In Newburyport, where JQA was living, the *Essex Journal* printed the Halifax information on 28 May.

[2] William Knox, the brother of Henry Knox, was a clerk in the war department and later U.S. consul in Dublin (Washington, *Papers, Presidential Series*, 1:196, 5:474).

[3] For Christopher Gore, see vol. 6:377; JQA, *Diary*, 1:330.

[4] JQA wrote three long letters to AA2 when he passed through New York City on his way back to Braintree from Europe; see JQA to AA2, 17 July, and 1, 9 Aug. 1785 (vol. 6:225–231, 242–248, 251–256).

[5] Lady Maria Waite, the widow of Sir Jacob Waite, married Alexander Forrester Inglis Cochrane in April 1788 (*DNB*; John Marshall, *Royal Naval Biography*, 4 vols. in 8, London, 1823–1835, 1:266).

[6] Amelia Broome Jarvis (1765–1788), wife of James Jarvis of New York, and Elizabeth Broome were sisters. Amelia would die on 1 December. Elizabeth later married Col. Joseph Fay of Bennington, Vt. (Donald Lines Jacobus, comp., *Families of Ancient New Haven*, 9 vols. in 3, Baltimore, 1974, 2:344–345).

[7] John Rucker died on 15 June (New York *Independent Journal*, 21 June).

[8] Probably Betsey Ramsay.

[9] Closing parenthesis editorially supplied.

[10] Probably Anne and William Bingham, whom the Adamses had known in Europe. William Bingham represented Pennsylvania in the Continental Congress from 1786 to 1789 (*DAB*).

[11] South Carolina ratified the Constitution by a vote of 149 to 73 on 23 May 1788; the news was widely reported in the New York newspapers in the first week of June. The New York state convention began meeting on 17 June. Although several noted Federalists—including John Jay, Alexander Hamilton, and Robert R. Livingston—were elected delegates, the convention opened with a decidedly Antifederalist majority (*Doc. Hist. Ratif. Const.*, 20:xxiv, 1132–1133; John P. Kaminski, "New York: The Reluctant Pillar," in Stephen L. Schechter, ed., *The Reluctant Pillar: New York and the Adoption of the Federal Constitution*, Troy, N.Y., 1985, p. 79).

[12] George Clinton (1739–1812), a lawyer and former major general in the Continental Army, served as governor of New York from 1777 to 1795 and again from 1801 to 1804. He subsequently served as vice president of the United States from 1805 until his death. An outspoken critic of the U.S. Constitution, he led the Antifederalists in the New York state ratifying convention, where he also served as president (*Doc. Hist. Ratif. Const.*, 19:495; *DAB*).

Abigail Adams Smith to Abigail Adams

New-York, June 15th, 1788.

We are anxiously expecting, by the arrival of every post, to hear of your safety and health. I begin to be very impatient to hear of an event in which I am so much interested. I fear that you have been detained in England longer than you expected, perhaps, by the receipt of the letters Col. Smith forwarded from Bath to my father. Mr. Jay was very much surprised that the gentlemen to whom he entrusted them, should have been so very deficient in punctuality as to keep them so long after his arrival.   *   *   *

We are treated, here, with great politeness, civility, and friendship. We were invited to dine with the Governor, which was a *very particular* favour. He nor his family either visit, or are visited by, any families, either in public or private life, of this place. He sees no company, and is not much beloved or respected. His conduct in *many respects* is censured, perhaps unjustly; he is particular, perhaps, in others. That he is a man of no decided character, no one who sees him will say. To me he appears one whose conduct and motives of action are not to be seen through upon a slight examination. The part he has taken upon the subject of the new Constitution is much condemned. What are his motives, I do not pretend to judge; but I do not believe that he acts or thinks without some *important* motives. Mrs. Clinton is not a showy, but a kind, friendly woman. She has five daughters, and one son; the second daughter is about fourteen years old, and as smart and sensible a girl as I ever knew—a zealous politician, and a high anti-Federalist.[1] The Governor does not conceal his sentiments, but I have not heard that he has given any reasons for them. His family are all politicians. He set off, yesterday, for the Convention.

General and Mrs. Knox have been very polite and attentive to us. Mrs. Knox is much altered from the character she used to have. She is neat in her dress, attentive to her family, and very fond of her children. But her size is enormous; I am frightened when I look at her; I verily believe that her waist is as large as three of yours, at least.

Sir John Temple has taken upon himself very singular airs respecting us. It has been his constant custom to visit every stranger who came to town, upon his arrival. Lady Temple called upon me, at a very late day after we arrived; but Sir J. has not visited Col.

Smith, and says to others, that he does not know in what manner to behave to Col. Smith, because he does not know how he took leave—whether it was a gracious reception that he met with.[2]

I returned Lady Temple's visit by a card, without asking for her, which she complains of. I respect Lady Temple, and as it is probable we shall often meet at a third place, I wished to be upon civil terms with her—particularly as she has often expressed a regard for me since she has been here.   *   *   *   *   Nor will I exchange visits with any lady, where my husband is not received with equal attention.

I hear that my father is chosen a delegate for Congress the next year.[3] I hope he will accept, for, independent of my wish that he should not retire from public business, I think his presence in Congress would do a great deal towards reforming the wrong sentiments and opinions that many are biased by. Both precept and example are wanting here; and his sentiments in politics are more respected than many other persons. It is said he must come and be President the next year. It is, in some degree, his duty to attend the calls of his State, when he will be so serviceable to the cause of the whole.

Every body is looking forward to the establishment of the new Constitution, with great expectations of receiving advantage from it. To me, I confess, the consequences are problematical; and should any one or more States continue to oppose it, and refuse to adopt it, melancholy will be the scenes which ensue, I fear.

The more one sees of the world, and of the business of life, of the less importance do we think them. There are very few who have not personal aggrandizement in view; and there are so many little causes intermingled with the really important, that I begin to think that disinterestedness is a word not to be found in the modern vocabulary.

June 22.

This morning I was made very happy by the receipt of a letter from Mr. Smith, informing us of your safe arrival.[4] I hope, by the next post, to hear particularly, from either my father or yourself. Mr. Smith mentions that you have a lame hand; I hope it is not a serious matter. I am impatient to know more particularly respecting your and my father's health, and minutely respecting your passage. I fear your patience was almost exhausted by Capt. Callihan's delays.

We flatter ourselves with the hope of seeing my father and yourself here in the autumn; be so good as to inform me whether you propose coming.

Bunyan arrived last week, and we expect to get settled in our house at Jamaica next week.[5] I was upon a visit to Col. Smith's family the last week, and returned to town last night. I left your grandson in the care of his grandmamma. He has grown surprisingly, but does not yet go alone; he has not courage enough, and is too wild to venture himself. I endeavour to make him recollect his grandpapa and mamma, and he seems to remember your goodness to him.

Col. Smith desires me to present his duty, and affectionate congratulation upon your safe arrival. He will write soon himself.

I am, with sincere affection, / Your dutiful daughter,

A. Smith.

MS not found. Printed from AA2, *Jour. and Corr.*, 2:80–84.

[1] Cornelia Tappen (1744–1800) married George Clinton in early 1770. Their six children included Catharine (b. 1770), Cornelia (b. 1774), George Washington (b. 1778), Elizabeth (b. 1780), Martha Washington (b. 1783), and Maria (b. 1785). The younger Cornelia eventually married the deposed French minister "Citizen" Edmond Genêt in 1794 (E. Wilder Spaulding, *His Excellency George Clinton: Critic of the Constitution*, N.Y., 1938, p. 30–32, 100–101; John P. Kaminski, *George Clinton: Yeoman Politician of the New Republic*, Madison, Wis., 1993, p. 240, 251).

[2] When JA submitted his resignation as minister plenipotentiary to Britain in a letter to John Jay on 24 Jan. 1787, he recommended WSS for the position of chargé d'affaires in London. Jay's response of 16 Oct. (Adams Papers), however, indicated that Congress had not yet made a decision regarding a replacement minister or chargé. JA replied on 16 Dec. that "Mr. Smith and his family will embark for New York. As Congress have not transmitted him any orders relative to another Minister, or to a Chargé d'Affaires at this Court, the presumption is, that it is either the intention of Congress to have no diplomatic character here, or that other persons are destined to fill it; in either case, Mr. Smith's road is as clear as mine—to return home" (*Dipl. Corr., 1783–1789*, 2:691–693, 796–798, 824–826). No formal letter of resignation from WSS to Congress has been found. See also AA2 to JQA, 10 Feb. 1788, above.

[3] The Mass. General Court elected JA as a delegate to the final session of the Continental Congress on 6 June, but he never attended. The news of his election was reported in the *New York Journal*, 14 June.

[4] Not found, but see AA2 to William Smith, 22 June, below.

[5] Captain Bunyan of the ship *Montgomery*, presumably carrying the Smiths' household goods, arrived in New York from London on 19 June (Philadelphia *Independent Gazetteer*, 24 June).

Elizabeth Smith Shaw to Abigail Adams

Haverhill June 22[d] 1788

Thanks be to an ever watchful & kind Providence that has conducted my dear Brother, & Sister safely to their native Shore— With all the tender affections that ever warmed a Sisters Heart, I bid you welcome—welcome once more to America—welcome my dear Brother to a Land for which you have for many years toil'd & laboured—

I have my dear Sister been exceedingly axious for these three weeks about you— The joyful tidings of your arrival reached me last Friday, & eased my heart of a burden, with which it has been long oppressed—

The dangers Mr Adams has encounterd, & the eminent Services he has rendered his country, cannot be fully known [bu]t to his nearest Connections—& though a grateful people may yield him a tribute of praise yet all the applause, & glory he justly merits may not be given him till some future age—when certain distinctions are lost—when Envy & malice cannot operate—& All the Causes of them are removed—

I hope to have the pleasure of seeing you this week—but unfortunately, am taken to day with an inflamation in my Eyes— My ill humours are always operating some where or other— I think you once told me it was a favour to my friends it was in my blood & not in my temper—

I have been anticipating & participating of the pleasure with which your Children have been presented to their Parents— How precious is a good name, & how pleasing to behold them walking in the paths of Secence, & of Virtue—

My Children present their Duty & partake largely of the pleasure which has overspread the Countenance of Your ever / affectionate Sister   Eliza Shaw

Excuse the writing

RC (Adams Papers); addressed: "Mrs Abigail Adams / Braintree"; endorsed: "Mrs Shaw / June 22nd 1788." Some loss of text where the seal was removed.

Abigail Adams Smith to William Smith

Dear Sir—   New York June 22d 1788

we were made very happy this morning by the receipt of your Letter, informing us of the arrival of my Parents—[1] be pleased to accept our sincere thanks for this early Proof of your attention— I am anxious to hear particularly respecting their Healths— I hope the Lameness of my Mammas Hand which you mention, is not to be of long continueance—

I hope you will excuse the Liberty I have taken of directing Packages to your Care—and will permit me to Continue the same freedom—as it is the most certain method of Conveyance—

permit me to request you, to present my Compliments to your amiable Lady—altho I was not particularly acquainted with her— I am happy to Congratulate you tho at a late Period—upon your Connection and to wish you every possible felicity— Should you visit this Place, Colln Smith and myself shall esteem ourselves very happy to welcome you to our habbitation upon Long Island,—

be so good as to present my Compliments to Dr Welsh and Mrs Welsh—Mrs Otis and family / and beleive me Sir with respect and / Esteem your Hum^ble servt   A Smith

RC (MHi:Smith-Carter Papers); internal address: "M^r W^m. Smith"; endorsed: "A. Smith / NYK 1788."

[1] Not found.

Abigail Adams to Abigail Adams Smith

My Dear Child: Braintree, July 7th, 1788.

It has been no small mortification to me since my arrival here, that I have not been able to hold a pen, or use my hand in writing, until this day. I came on shore with three whitloes upon the thumb and two fingers of my right, and two upon the left hand, so that I could not do the least thing for myself. I begged my friends to write, and let you know of our arrival, after a very tedious passage of eight weeks and two days. My first inquiry was of Mr. Knox, who came on board as soon as we made the light-house, after my dear son and daughter; and by him I had the happiness to learn of your safe arrival. When I came up to town, I received your kind letter with the greatest pleasure; it afforded me much entertainment. I wrote you one letter at sea, which contained a statement of occurrences until a fortnight before our arrival, when my fingers began to torment me.

The newspapers have no doubt informed you of our gracious reception, and of our residence at the Governor's; from whom, and his lady, we received the most pointed civility and attention, as well as from the ladies and gentlemen of Boston.[1] The Governor was for escorting us to Braintree in his coach and four, attended by his light horse; and even Braintree was for coming out to Milton bridge to meet us, but this we could by no means assent to. Accordingly we quitted town privately; your papa one day, and I the next. We went to our worthy brother's, where we remained until the next week, when our furniture came up. But we have come into a house not

277

half repaired, and I own myself most sadly disappointed. In height and breadth, it feels like a wren's house. Ever since I came, we have had such a swarm of carpenters, masons, farmers, as have almost distracted me—every thing all at once, with miserable assistance. In short, I have been ready to wish I had left all my furniture behind. The length of the voyage and heat of the ship greatly injured it; some we cannot get up, and the shocking state of the house has obliged me to open it in the garret. But I will not tire you with a recital of all my troubles.

*   *   *   *   *   *   *

I hope soon to embrace you, my dear children, in Braintree; but be sure you wear no feathers, and let Col. Smith come without heels to his shoes, or he will not be able to walk upright. But we shall be more arranged by that time, and, I hope, the chief of our business done. We have for my comfort, six cows, without a single convenience for a dairy. But you know there is no saying nay.

Sweetly do the birds sing. I will not tell you your brother is here, because he has not written to you. But I must leave off, or you will think me as bad as Esther; indeed, I feel almost bewildered.

Affectionately yours,   A. Adams.

MS not found. Printed from AA2, *Jour. and Corr.*, 2:84–86.

[1] When the Adamses arrived in Boston on 17 June, Gov. John Hancock "having previously ordered, that every mark of respect be paid his Excellency on his arrival, the approach of the ship in which he arrived, was announced by a signal from the Light and a discharge of cannon from the Castle—when off the Castle he was saluted with a federal discharge of cannon from that fortress, and when the ship had arrived at her moorings, the Secretary of the State, by order of his Excellency the Governor repaired in his Excellency's carriage to the end of the pier, from whence, in the State barge, the Secretary waited on the Ambassadour on board, and in his Excellency the Governour's name, congratulated him on his arrival, and invited him and family to his Excellency's seat.... the Pier was crowded—and his Excellency welcomed on shore by three huzzas from several thousand persons." On the following day, the General Court issued a formal statement of congratulations on JA's "many successful labours in the service of your country" (*Massachusetts Centinel*, 18, 21 June).

John Adams to Abigail Adams Smith

My Dear Child: Braintree, July 16, 1788.

Your mamma's hand has been wholly unable to hold a pen, without exquisite pain, from the time of our arrival; and I am afraid your brothers have not done their duty in writing to you. Indeed, I scarcely know what apology to make for myself. Would you believe this is the first day that I have taken a pen into my hand since I came ashore?

I am happy to hear from all quarters a good character of all your brothers. The oldest has given decided proofs of great talents, and there is not a youth of his age whose reputation is higher for abilities, or whose character is fairer in point of morals or conduct. The youngest is as fine a youth as either of the three, if a spice of fun in his composition should not lead him astray. Charles wins the heart, as usual, and is the most of a gentleman of them all.

You, my dear daughter, are in new scenes, which require new duties. Mr. Smith's mother has a right to all the dutiful filial respect, affection, and attention, that you can show her; and his brothers and sisters you ought to consider as your own. When I say this, I say no more than what I know must long ago have occurred to a lady of your reflection, discretion, and sensibility.

I wish to be informed, as fully as may be with propriety, of Mr. Smith's views. My desire would be to hear of him at the bar, which, in my opinion, is the most independent place on earth. A seeker of public employments is, in my idea, one of the most unhappy of all men. This may be pride; but if it is, I cannot condemn it. I had rather dig my subsistence out of the earth with my own hands, than be dependent on any favour, public or private; and this has been the invariable maxim of my whole life. Mr. Smith's merit and services entitle him to expect employment under the public; and I know him to be a man of too much spirit as well as honour, to solicit with the smallest degree of meanness for any thing. But I would not be dependent; I would have a resource. There can be none better than the bar. I hope my anxiety for his and your welfare, has not betrayed me into any improper expressions, or unbecoming curiosity.

You may be anxious, too, to know what is to become of me. At my age, this ought not to be a question; but it is. I will tell you, my dear child, in strict confidence, that it appears to me that your father does not stand very high in the esteem, admiration, or respect of his country, or any part of it. In the course of a long absence his character has been lost, and he has got quite out of circulation. The public judgment, the public heart, and the public voice, seem to have decreed to others every public office that he can accept of with consistency, or honour, or reputation; and no other alternative is left for him, but private life at home, or to go again abroad. The latter is the worst of the two; but you may depend upon it, you will hear of him on a trading voyage to the East Indies, or to Surrinam, or Essequibo, before you will hear of his descending as a public man beneath himself.

Write me as often as you can, and believe me / Your ever affectionate father,   John Adams.

MS not found. Printed from AA2, *Jour. and Corr.*, 2:87–89.

Elizabeth Smith Shaw to Abigail Adams

My Dear Sister—   Haverhill July 26th. 1788

I got home the Friday-noon after I left you, & had the great satisfaction of finding all well—my little Daughters humour much abated, & was going of without a sore forming under her chin, as the Dr feared— But I soon had a bitter ingredient thrown into my lap, by hearing the complaints of my faithful Servant Lidia, who had every Symtom of a voilent fever coming upon her—[1] The Dr thinks her fever is come to the height, but she cannot set up more than ten minutes at a time now—

We ought to prize a good Girl, for we miss & feel the want of them, when taken from business most terribly— Your Family has been sick, as well as mine, & we know how to pity each other, for one we are used to, is worth ten new Servants—

I was fearful Ester would give you trouble when I left you— Her Step, & motions were much too quick for Stability,— I think it was very lucky for Cornish that she was taken sick just as she was— though I presume you do not think it so for yourself— I am sorry you have so much trouble, for Sickness throws everything into confusion—& brings ten thousand wants & cares with it—

I rejoice to hear of your increasing health—may it still keep on, in a happy progression— Cares if not too great, I have often thought were pleasures— Exercise of Body is absolutely necessary to our health— But few (my Sister) like you, can figure in the higher walks of Life, & with so much ease descend to the every concern, & business of your Family— It is happy when Americans can so do—

Peter was taken sick yesterday, but I hope it is nothing more than eating too much green fruit— Betsy Smith came home to me, with her Uncle from Commencement— Dear good Girl she is I am sure I do not know what I should do now without her—

Mr J Q A— went to Newbury a Thursday My Nephews have been rather unfortunate in this visit, on account of our Sickness—[2] But I tell them they never found us so before, & they must take us for better, & for worse—

They do not know half the pleasure, & satisfaction they give their uncle, & Aunt when they make us those visits— They would never fail of coming if they did— I am glad to hear of the health & welfare of Mr & Mrs Smith— I hope to have a Letter from her myself soon—

I hope our Family will soon be well, & yours too—that we may have the pleasure of seeing, & welcoming to our habitation my Dear Brother & Sister—

adieu most affectionately Your / Sister   E Shaw—

RC (Adams Papers); addressed: "Mrs A Adams. / Braintree"; endorsed: "Mrs Shaw / july 26th 1788."

[1] Lydia Springer (b. 1762) of Haverhill was Elizabeth Smith Shaw's long-time servant, first in Haverhill and later in Atkinson, N.H. (*Vital Records of Haverhill Massachusetts to the End of the Year 1849*, 2 vols., Topsfield, Mass., 1910–1911, 1:283; Paul C. Nagel, *The Adams Women: Abigail and Louisa Adams, Their Sisters and Daughters*, N.Y., 1987, p. 65, 69–70).

[2] JQA and TBA rode together from Braintree to Haverhill on Monday, 21 July, and stayed with the Shaws until 23 July, when JQA returned to Newburyport (JQA, *Diary*, 2:433–434).

Abigail Adams Smith to John Adams

Jamaica, Long Island, July 27th, 1788.

Last Thursday I had the pleasure of receiving my dear papa's kind letter of July 16th. I was very impatient to hear of your welfare. My mamma's letter, received a few days before, was the first particular account I had heard of the situation of the health of my dear parents since your arrival. My brothers have been very inattentive to me; I fear they have forgot the duties they owe to an elder and only sister.

It gives me great pleasure, my dear sir, to hear from you that they sustain good and amiable characters. Young men who pass through college without any imputation of misconduct, have laid a very good foundation, and are less liable to fall into errors afterwards. The habit of well doing is not easily overcome, and when it is the result of principle and judgment, the impression is so strong upon the mind as to influence their conduct through life. May you, my dear sir, never have occasion to regret the conduct of any of your children; but that you may have cause to rejoice in the character which they may support through life, is my most ardent wish.

I thank you, sir, for your solicitude respecting my friend and his future pursuits. As yet, I believe, he has formed no determination respecting his future career. At the bar there are so many persons already established by a course of practice, who are known in the

State by common report, that there is but little encouragement for *one* who by long absence has been lost in public view. There is a strong propensity (perhaps it is a natural consequence,) in the people of this country, to misplace the absent by those who are present. A few combining accidental circumstances may bring a man into notice; he will, without any extraordinary exertions on his own part, rise in the opinion of the people; the enthusiasm catches like wildfire, and he is in the popular voice more than mortal.

I think I can, in *our* own State, recollect a *few* instances of this kind, and I believe it is the case throughout the continent, both in public life and in particular professions.

For myself, I confess my attachment to the profession of the law. I think the study of it the most conducive to the expansion of the mind of any of the learned professions; and I think we see throughout the continent, the men of the most eminence educated to it.

*   *   *   *

With respect to yourself, my dear sir, I do not quite agree with you in opinion. It is true that a very long absence may have erased from the minds of many your services; but it will not take a long time to renew the remembrances of them, and you will, my dear sir, soon find them not obliterated.

You have, in a *late* pretended friend, a real rival.[1] The attention *lately* shown you was the highest proof of policy, grounded upon *fear*, that could have been given; it was intended to blind the popular eye, (perhaps it may for a time,) but every person of any discernment saw through the veil.

It is my opinion that you will either be elected to the second place upon the continent, or first in your own State. The general voice has assigned the presidentship to General Washington, and it has been the opinion of many persons whom I have heard mention the subject, that the vice-presidentship would be at your option. I confess I wish it, and that you may accept it. But of the propriety of this, you must judge best.

This State has adopted the Constitution by a majority of three only.[2] It has given great joy to many, that at any events they are admitted to the Union. There have been great exertions made by the opposers of it, to prejudice the minds of the populace against its adoption, by such arguments as would have most weight with them—the addition of taxes, the rise of provisions, and some of the most improbable, though affecting to the lower class of people, that could be invented. The motives of some persons in power in the State, in opposing it, have been attributed to selfish views; whether just or unjust, I know not.

It is now a great question in debate, whether Congress shall remove from New-York, and great exertions are making by some of the southern members, to get them to return to Philadelphia. Upon this question, I presume that selfish views actuate all who are *violent* upon either side, for I do not see that any material advantage can arise to the country from the local situation of Congress, except such as contribute to the convenience of their residence.   *

Believe me your affectionate daughter,   A. Smith.

MS not found. Printed from AA2, *Jour. and Corr.*, 2:89–93.

[1] John Hancock.
[2] The New York Convention ratified the Constitution by a vote of 30 to 27 on 26 July (*Doc. Hist. Ratif. Const.*, 19:lxxxvi).

Mercy Otis Warren to Abigail Adams

My dear Madam   Plimouth July 30th 1788.

one line by my son inquires after the health of my Friend, at Braintree. do you begin to feel at home. & will you not after becoming a little Domesticateed in your native town think of an excursion to plimouth where you will find the same Friend, the same hospitality & undissembleed affection which in my opinion Gives the truest Zest to human life.

you have seen all the Varietiy. & perhaps have tasted as much real felicity in the little social parties as in the pallace of the prince. but you must again go to Court.— but flatter myself you will improve the interem & let us see you again at the unadorned board which satisfies the wishes of circumscribed ambition when blessed with the intercourse of those they Esteem & love.

Hope Mr Adams received a line of Congratulation from Mr Warren sometime since:[1] he means to do himself the Honour & Pleasure of making a Visit to his *Friend* as soon as he is able which I hope is a circumstance not far distant. as he has withing the week past been able to put on his shew which he has not done before for several months.

You will make my most respectful Compliments acceptable to a Gentleman who I hear is employing the short respite from the field of politics & the intrigues of statmen: to the momentary delights of rural peace and the Cultivation of his own Grounds.—

I am my dear Madam as ever / Your affectionate Friend

M Warren

RC (Adams Papers); internal address: "Mrs Adams."

¹ James Warren to JA, 7 July (Adams Papers).

Abigail Adams to Abigail Adams Smith

My dear Child   [6 August 1788]¹

It grieves me to think how little I have been able to write to you since my arrival here. I have set apart many hours which I have determined to devote to you, but family cares company sickness have prevented

I have received all your kind Letters and thank you for the intelligence containd in them I rejoice at your agreeable situation & wish that I could visit you more than in Idea, but at present I do not see any prospect of the kind. Should your Father go on to congress in November of which he is yet doubtfull I do not See that I can by any means leave home. we have come upon a place—wanting but every thing pertaining to Farming & find ourselves destitute of every utensal which we once possess'd so that like Regulas of old we want the most necessary articles for Husbandry.² added to that the Garden was a wilderness & the House a mere Barrack this naturally encumbed us with work people of all kinds &, your Pappa is as he used to say he would, employd in Building Stone wall and Diging ditches. and as he always loves to do things expeditiously, tis not unusual to have ten laboring men in a day. I have get more reconciled to the spot than I was at first, but we must build in the Spring an other kitchen a dairy room & a Libriary of the two last we are quite destitute, and distresst for want of. untill this week I have never been over the Hill since I first came & only once to weymouth, nor have I made a single visit but to my old Friend mrs Quincy Your Brothers have been at Home ever Since I came & I have had much to do for them. Esther is Better tho feeble as usual. but I have had the misfortune of having Cornice the old woman who came out with me taken Sick the very week she was to have left me, with the inflamitory Rhumatisim totally deprived of the use of every Limb as helpless as a baby attended with a voilent fever & for

a month back we have had her to attend She is now better & recoverd the use of them again tho terribly emaciated & weak. She
want very much to go & live with mrs knox but whether mrs knox
would take her is a question. She would be very good to attend
Children is Honest & a hand in Sickness and scarcly ever had a
days Sickness before if you should see mrs Knox I wish you would
mention the old womans desire. I never saw a better creature at sea
than she was. and now my dear Girl you must tell me whether you
cannot come this fall & make us a visit, I long to see you & my dear
Billy. You are the Subject of our daily conversation & I visit the picture as the only substitute, & look at Charles with double pleasure
because he so nearly resembles his Sister. your Friends here all wish
most ardently to see you. I do not find their regard or affection in
any way diminishd towards you. You must come to your cousins Betsys wedding which I presume will be in November— I am not
enough acquainted with the Young Gentleman to judge of him, he
bears a good Character and I hope will make her happy She is a
very deserving Girl, and so is our tranquill Lucy who has been a
good deal with me and assisted me much. but I see no person who
seems so much alterd in the course of four years as your worthy uncle Cranch he is very thin & look more than ten years older. Nancy
Quincy is the same warm Sprightly animated Girl she was when we
left her and mrs Guile as amiable as ever. she came & with mr Guile
& drank Tea with me one afternoon her Eldest son is now at mr
Cranchs and is a sweet little Boy,[3] mrs Storer is with mrs Quiny
with her three daughters who are all ill with the hooping Cough.[4]
mr Isaac Smith Spent the last week with us & preachd here on Sunday. mr wibird like most old Batchelors is become nearly useless,
and fears his own Shadow mr Weld has again met with a most severe stroke & lost his wife a few days after my arrival here, she got
to bed & was seaz'd with the child Bed fever and died the third day
after.[5] miss B Palmer was with her & continues there with Polly
Greenleaf[6] mr Able Allen is married to Nancy Chace & live upon
mrs Apthorps place.[7] Hannah clark married mr Boice of Milton &
lives very well.[8] mrs Allen saild for England a few days before I arrived here & the place is Sold to a mr Black who appears a civil
obliging Neighbour & has a very agreeable woman for his wife.[9]
thus I have given you a Breif account of Some of our old acquaintance. as to our Boston Friends I know not much of them as I only
tarried two days in Town & have never been there since; Mrs Smith

is very pleasing woman & has got an amaizing great Boy for his age & a very fine child he is, cousin William is an attentive Husband & fond Father;[10]

Dft (Adams Papers); docketed: "1788." Filmed at [*ca. Aug. 1788*].

[1] The dating is based on AA2's response to this letter of 13 Aug., below.

[2] Marcus Atilius Regulus, twice Roman consul, served in the Punic Wars and was captured by Carthage in 255 B.C.; he died in captivity. In an explanatory note to Cicero's *Cato Major*, Regulus asks the Roman senate to relieve him of command of the army and navy so that he can return to his farm. He fears that his farm will be ruined if he does not go home, as one manager had died and another had run off with all of the farm implements (*Oxford Classical Dicy.*; Cicero, *Cato Major; or, A Treatise on Old Age*, ch. 20, note 97).

[3] Benjamin Guild Jr. (1785–1858). At this time, Elizabeth and Benjamin Guild Sr. also had a younger son, Josiah Quincy Guild (1787–1861).

[4] Hannah and Ebenezer Storer had three daughters: Hannah (b. 1779), Anna (b. 1780), and Susan (b. 1783).

[5] Abigail Greenleaf Weld, wife of Rev. Ezra Weld, died on 3 July; the child did not survive (*Braintree Town Records*, p. 865; Greenleaf, *Greenleaf Family*, p. 196).

[6] Probably Mary Greenleaf (1757–1804), who married Nathaniel Thwing in 1791. She was the younger sister of Abigail Greenleaf Weld (Greenleaf, *Greenleaf Family*, p. 196).

[7] Abel Alleyne of Braintree married Anna Chase of Bolton on 22 Nov. 1787 (*Vital Records of Bolton, Massachusetts, to the End of the Year 1849*, Worcester, 1910, p. 118). For Grizzell Apthorp, see vol. 7:111.

[8] Jeremiah Smith Boies of Milton announced his intention to marry Sarah Hanson [Hannah?] Clark of Braintree in Sept. 1785 (*Braintree Town Records*, p. 887).

[9] Moses and Esther Black purchased the former Edmund Quincy house (also known as the "Dorothy Q." house, named for Dorothy Quincy Hancock who grew up there) in Braintree sometime before 1790. Black, an Irishman, later served as Quincy's town moderator and represented it in the Mass. General Court (JA, *D&A*, 3:246; Pattee, *Old Braintree*, p. 92, 95, 235, 279–280; U.S. Census, 1790, Mass., p. 196).

"Mrs Allen" was probably Dorothy Harbin Alleyne, the widow of Thomas Alleyne of Braintree. She returned to Braintree the following year. See Cotton Tufts to AA, 20 Sept. 1787, note 7, above, and Mary Smith Cranch to AA, 2 Aug. 1789, below.

[10] William Smith Jr., the first child of William and Hannah Carter Smith, was born on 20 April (MHi:Smith-Townsend Family Papers, Elizabeth H. Smith Scrapbook).

William Stephens Smith to John Adams

Dear Sir.   Long-Island— Beaver Hall August 10th, 1788—

I have been honoured by the receipt of your friendly Letter of July the 16th.[1] I supposed, that on your arrival, various matters would necessarily engage your attention; we sensibly feel for the indisposition of our good Mama, and wish she was near us, that we might each take care of a finger,— previous to our being informed of these reasons of silence, we concluded, that there was some sufficient cause for it, & flattered ourselves daily, that it would be removed— we now, with great satisfaction congratulate you, on the perfect arrangement of domestick affairs, & hope soon to hear of the whole family being restored to their usual health & tranquility— I find my

native City as you do yours—much improved, with respect to Buildings and streets, but I have not yet observed, or been informed of,
any establishments being made, to promote the industry of our
Countrymen, nor any system in our rulers, to check that amaizing
thirst for foreign productions & foreign follies; too many of them,
appear to me rather disposed to loose sight of the American Character, & to be pleased with nothing, but what borders on British or
French, either of which, in my humble opinion will rather injure
than benefit, but I hope (for my Country) that new times & new
seasons are fast approaching, new York has adopted the Constitution, tho with a bad grace, and Congress are now endeavouring,
to put it in train for operation I doubt not but our representatives
under it, will, early attend to the formation of dignified political
systems, and pursue them (as they may begin—*ab ovo*)—*usque ad
mala*—² at present, we have none, & what may appear very extraordinary to you, it was not their intention to be totally unrepresented
at the Court of London— you were permitted to return home in
Complyance with your request, & I was expected, in consequence
of the expiration of my Commission, but the question was never
put, whether the vacancy's should be filled up, or whether, any new
appointments of a less important nature should be made, thus it
rests for the deliberation & decussion of (I may say) the *rising Generation*—³ the present, feel themselves on the decline & are disposed
to leave important points to be settled by those who are to come
after them— we have been received here, with all the attention &
respect we could wish for, and after residing a sufficient time in new
York, to return the civilities offered, we have retired to this place,
where we live in peace & happiness, mutually pleased with each
other & delighted with our Boy, we are all in high health & envy not
the govt—

I have received a very polite & friendly Letter from General
Washington, congratulating me on my arrival & marrige in a manner too flattering—for me to send you a Copy of it—⁴ I have it in contemplation to visit him—nothing prevents my deciding on it, but a
doubt whether M^rs· Smith (*considering Circumstances*) could stand
the Journey,⁵ now sir, If a jaunt here would be agreable to you &
M^rs· Adams & you would wish to visit our Country & friends, as far
as the Potowmack, I have good horses & a Carriage to convey you,
M^rs· A can stay with M^rs· S. while we make the excursion, many of
your friends wish to see you, & I think you may do a great deal of
good— two or three day's will convey you from Boston to new York

by the way of Rhode Island, & one hour & an half after your landing you may Kiss your Daughter & Grandson at Beaver Hall— tell me what you think of the project & whether the whole or any part of it, will be agreable to you— M^rs: Smith joins me with our best affections & wishes to you & Mama & I remain D^r· Sir— / Your most Obed^t· / Humble serv^t·

W: S: Smith

RC (Adams Papers); addressed: "To / The Honourable / John Adams / &c. &c. &c / Braintree / near Boston"; internal address: "To / The Honble· / Jno· Ad[ams]"; notation: "2 14." Some loss of text where the seal was removed.

¹ To AA2, above.
² From beginning to end (literally, from the egg to the apples).
³ The United States did not send a new minister to Great Britain until the appointment of Thomas Pinckney in Jan. 1792.

⁴ Of 1 May 1788 (Washington, *Papers, Confederation Series*, 6:251).
⁵ This is the first reference to AA2's second pregnancy. She gave birth to another son, John Adams Smith, on 9 Nov.; see WSS to AA, 10 Nov., below.

Abigail Adams Smith to Abigail Adams

My Dear Mamma: New-York, August 13th, 1788.

We came to town last evening to dine (by invitation) this day, with the President of Congress, and this morning I had the pleasure of receiving your letter of the 6th.   *   *   *   *

I am very sorry to hear that you have had so much sickness and so many other perplexities to encounter, since your return; it increases my desire to be with you, to assist you all in my power. I hope you will escape sickness yourself, and I wish you would not permit your mind to be anxious. I can see, through your letters, that your spirits are hurried, and your mind in a continual agitation. You must overcome this, or you will certainly be sick.

Your request, my dear mamma, for me to make you a visit in November, I am sorry I cannot comply with it. If I undertake the journey at all this season, it must be much sooner. I most ardently wish to see you, and sometimes think I cannot permit this season to pass, without gratifying myself; but the inconveniences of travelling are so great in this country, that I am not quite determined about the matter. Col. Smith wishes to visit General Washington; but if I were to express a strong desire to go eastward, he would not hesitate to undertake the journey as soon as I wished. But we must sometimes sacrifice our wishes to convenience and prudence. If my father should come on in November, I hope you will accompany him, for I shall be very solicitous to have a visit from you at that time.

What to say, or what to expect, respecting the future *governors* of this our country, I know not. When eleven States have adopted the Constitution, and in reality the Congress ought to have no existence, they are delaying to pass the ordinance for the organization of the new Government, by party cabals and intrigues, by disputing where the new Government shall meet. It has now become a matter of party, *totally*. Every man consults his own views, and endeavours to bring as many others to his side of the question as he can have any influence over. A. B. has built a fine house, and wants to remove to Philadelphia, that he may outshine brilliancy itself.[1] Others have different views; few, I believe, consider the advantage that is to arise to the whole country, or consult convenience at all. The question has now been many weeks in debate, and is not yet decided.

We have dined to-day at the President's—a company of twenty-two persons, many members of Congress, Mr. . . ., &c. Had you been present, you would have trembled for your country, to have *seen*, and *heard*, and *observed*, the men who compose its rulers. Very different, I believe, they were in times past. All were high upon the question now before them; some were for it, and others against it. Mr. . . . was the only silent man at table, and there were very few whose behaviour bore *many* marks of wisdom. To what a state this country is approaching, I don't know; time only can determine.

It is reported that North Carolina has rejected the Constitution by a majority of a hundred.[2] But—to have done with politics.

Col. Smith has received a vote of thanks from Congress, for the manner in which he has conducted the business in Portugal.[3] I do not hear that any new appointments are likely to be made to any foreign power. A General Armstrong, a delegate from Pennsylvania, is the man looking forward to the appointment to England.[4]

Mrs. Knox has gone out of town for some weeks; but when I see her I will mention Cornish to her. I told her that such a person was coming out with you, and she said she remembered her, and should be glad to see her again. General Knox is in Boston; perhaps she had better see him.

Mr. G. . . . called upon me this morning;[5] he tells me that he saw my father and yourself in Boston. He is just the same precise, formal being as he used to be, and speaks so *prettily* that I could not understand him.   *   *   *

Your affectionate daughter,   A. Smith.

MS not found. Printed from AA2, *Jour. and Corr.*, 2:93–96.

[1] Abraham Baldwin (1754–1807), a delegate from Georgia, was originally from Connecticut. He had served in the Continental Congress since 1785, and would serve in the U.S. House of Representatives from 1789 to 1799 and in the Senate from 1799 to 1807. While Baldwin never owned a home in Philadelphia, he did vote in favor of that city over New York as the site for the new government, though he ultimately preferred a more southern location (*Doc. Hist. Ratif. Const.*, 3:308; E. Merton Coulter, *Abraham Baldwin: Patriot, Educator, and Founding Father*, Arlington, Va., 1987, p. viii, 113–114).

[2] The first North Carolina Convention met from 21 July to 4 Aug. 1788 but by a vote of 183 to 83 refused to ratify the Constitution without amendments and a second constitutional convention. The state did not hold a second ratifying convention until Nov. 1789, when North Carolina finally approved the Constitution by a vote of 194 to 77 (*Doc. Hist. Ratif. Const.*, 13:xlii; *The Debate on the Constitution: Federalist and Antifederalist Speeches, Articles, and Letters during the Struggle over Ratification*, 2 vols., N.Y., 1993, 2:1068–1069). The New York *Daily Advertiser* reported this news on 14 Aug. 1788.

[3] On 28 July, Congress acknowledged WSS's work in Portugal and ordered John Jay as secretary for foreign affairs to write to WSS that Congress was "pleased with the manner in which you appear to have treated the affairs" (*JCC*, 34:361–362).

[4] Maj. Gen. John Armstrong (1717–1795), born in Ireland, represented Pennsylvania in Congress in 1779–1780 and 1787–1788. He was best known for his military service during the Seven Years' War (*DAB*).

[5] Probably Elbridge Gerry.

Abigail Adams Smith to John Quincy Adams

Jamaica August 20th 1788—

It was with real pleasure my Dear Brother that I received a few days since your letter of july 20th—[1] It was a scource of double Sattisfaction as it releived me from an anxiety I had felt least you were less disposed to be attentive to your Sister than formerly, and as it informd me of your wellfare, I had sometimes been grieved at others half offended at not hearing from you, but the date of yours and hearing from Mamma that it had been delayed some weeks, by mistake; has releived my mind from every anxiety respecting the decrease of affection or attention—on your part—

it gives me uneasiness my Dear Brother to observe from the tenor of your letter that you permit the Cross accidents of Life to affect your spirits too much, true Philosophy does not Consist in being insensible to them, but in supporting ourselvs above them with becomeing dignity, and in acquiessing with chearfullness to those events which are irremiable, and by striving to attain such a Station in Life as we may not be subjected to their influence

I am going to give you a little advice and to tell you in what respects I think you amiss in your judgement, if you should disagree with me in opinion—I shall expect you to offer your reasons in vindication of yourself—

"you say that a young Man at your time of Life aught to support himself" and regret that it is not in your power to do it— it is not often the Case that young Men of your age let them have been ever so fortunate in acquiring their professions at an early period do it independant of their Parents it is most fortunate for themselvs and their friends if they possess the disposition, which will in time ensure them the ability

your absence in Europe at that period when you would have been pursueing a Profession had you been at home, was not a fault, you was necessitated to it and it will not eventually prove a disadvantage—but I hope may be advantageous to you in future, I think you were right in returning at the time you did and that you discovered a judgement above your years in the path you have pursued since your return— I dont mean to flatter you—

you are now pursueing a profession which is undoubtedly the first of all the Learned Professions—and by which a Man may acquire eminence and independance if he pleases, but you must not be impatient, nor discouraged— for a few years you must acquiesse in the Humble Station of a Student,—as you term it,—and be Content to rise by degrees,—but I see no reason why you should exclude yourself from society,— it is not Policy for you to do it, you should when an opportunity offers visit, and pay any little attention that civility may dictate, to those persons with whom you may have been formerly acquainted and keep yourself up in the minds of People, who are not obliged to remember you unless you are sometimes to be seen

your station even at this period is as respectable for your own Country as the more exalted one in which you have been known in Europe by many of your fellow Citizens excuse the freedom with which I write, and beleive me that it arrises from the interest I feel in every thing which respects your proggress and Situation in Life—

it would contribute greatly to my happiness to receive you here and it will not I flatter myself be a long time before you will find it Convenient to make us a visit— Coll^n Smith will I am sure be very happy to become personally acquainted with you—

I hope my Father will determine to Come on to Congress in November, if a new Election for President should take place I have no doubt but he will be chosen and if there should not—I think it will be of service to himself and to the Country if he accepts of the choise made—

I will indeavour to forward to you the debates in Congress— respecting the place at which the new Government should meet—² you will there see—party interest interfereing and even rejecting arrangements which in duty to their Country ought to have been early decided— tis time indeed that there was a change—

Coll^n Lee from Virginia a nephew of the Mr Lee's[3]—and a Member of Congress told me the other day that it was his opinion, and the opinion of others, and, he spoke as a Southern Man;—that the offices of Vice President and Chief justice, would lay between my Father and Mr Jay,—that he wished my Father might be appointed to the latter and accept of it—for he esteemed it next to the Presidentship—the most respectable under the new Government and that it was esteemed of more importance than the Vice Presidents. I wish our Dear Father to Consider well—as he no doubt will, before he decided against accepting it,

I hope he will not be inclined to going abroad again, his Chrildren are comeing forward into Life and it will be much in his Power to assist them forward by his Precept advice and judgment— a Situation abroad however respectable it may be made—is an exclusion from his friends, and by a Long absence every one is last in the remembrance of his Countrymen—and his family neglected—(at least under our Governments) our Country is not able if they were disposed to make such provision for those Persons who have been long in their service as to render them independant at the decline of Life— nor are they disposed to make any provission for their decendants— every one must move independantly—by the force of his own respectability—in this Country—to be sure Interest and intrigue are not excluded—but this is the Principle— of such service as you can be in promoting my views and designs—so far I will give you my support—provided there is no fear of your *clashing* with my pursuits— I see its operation on many—and I dispise it—but I fear I shall tire your patience with my Politicks both public and private—

I Shall not dispute the subject of Federal or antefederal with you, I think that the Constitution is now too generally adopted by the States to be receded from by any one with good intentions, but of the affect I Confess myself doubtfull— there is a great deal to be done to Sattisfy the Sanguine—and perhaps there may be found more perplexity in doing than is yet suspected by any one— it is a most important and critical era in the fate of our Country— may She be so Conducted as to insure peace tranquility and happiness to her Subjects is my wish, and in this I dare say you will not dissent from your affectionate Sister

A Smith—

RC (Adams Papers); endorsed: "My Sister— 20. Aug^t: 1788." and "My Sister Aug^t: 20. 1788."

[1] Not found, but see JQA, *Diary*, 2:433.

[2] For the debates over the location of the new government, see *JCC*, 34:358–360, 367–368, 383–388, 392–402. They also appeared in the New York *Daily Advertiser*, 21 August.

[3] Col. Henry "Light-Horse Harry" Lee (1756–1818), of the extended Lee family of Virginia, represented that state in Congress from 1785 to 1788. The "Mr Lee's" included Arthur, Richard Henry, and William Lee, all of whom were cousins of Henry's father, Henry Lee Sr. (*DAB*).

Abigail Adams to William Cranch

Braintree August 23 1788

Will you be so kind as to wait upon the Govenour early on monday morning with the inclosed cards and take an answer from him; which Brisler will call for on Monday at mr Fosters. if he has any objection to thursday, let it be fryday only I would wish for a decisive answer. if he agrees to the day proposed, then I would request the favour of you to go with the card to mr Brecks,[1] but if the Govenours engagements are such as to prevent him & his Ladys comeing out on either day, omit carrying the card to mr Brecks— if any thing should prevent Brisler from comeing to town on monday he will be in on tuesday mor͞g. I hope your goodness will excuse my troubling you with this buisness, and believe me your truly & / affectionate / Aunt ⟨right⟩ A Adams

Sunday morg mrs Sewall is at the Govenours[2]

RC (private owner, 1957); addressed: "To / Mr William Cranch / Boston"; and by William Cranch: "His Excellency / John Hancok Esqr / Boston"; endorsed: "Mrs Adams Braintree / August 23^d 1788"; docketed: "Mrs A Adams. / Augt 23. 1788."

[1] For Samuel Breck Sr., see vol. 6:325; JQA, *Diary*, 1:312–313.
[2] Possibly Esther Quincy Sewall, John Hancock's sister-in-law and the wife of Jonathan Sewall (vol. 1:30, 136; *Sibley's Harvard Graduates*, 12:310).

Abigail Adams Smith to Abigail Adams

My Dear Mamma: ⟨right⟩ Jamaica, September 7th, 1788.

I received, on Wednesday last, from the hands of Mr. T——, your letter, No. 4, of August 25th.[1] He was so obliging as to call with it himself, in company with Mr. King.   *   *   *

Mr. George Storer came out last evening to pass Sunday with us, and by him I propose to forward my letter. He is very civil in forwarding letters for me, and is disposed to be sociable; I am glad that he is pleased with his visits to us. There is a satisfaction in renewing our acquaintance with persons to whom we have been formerly known; and particularly so to one who is not disposed to acquire new friendships, or contract new acquaintances. Unless there are some very apparently attractive traits of character to induce me to cherish the friendship of persons with whom I become acquainted, I do not find much satisfaction from them.

When we arrived in this country, I found myself in a land of strangers. There were but two or three persons that I had any knowledge of, and not one that I had any friendship for. I was visited in New-York by fifty or sixty ladies; I returned their visits, and here the acquaintance ceases. There are a few families that I have been invited to; some I have visited frequently, but with no one have I, or shall I, ever become intimate. By retiring to the country we have avoided the society of those with whom I might have (by habit) become familiarly acquainted, without finding any thing in them of much value or importance.

I have been several times to New-York, and have been treated, upon every visit, with as much civility as I had any reason to expect, or wished; but there is no family where I can make a home, and go when inclination would induce, or business necessitate me, with freedom and unreserve; so that I believe I shall pass most of my time at home, to which I find myself daily more and more attached. I have as much society as I wish in our own family, and to me it is more agreeable than any other I could find.

I cannot but *wish* that you could make us a visit with my father, but I think your reasons against it are very forcible. I do not at all wonder that my brothers dissuade you from it. Your presence must fill up a great vacancy in their minds.

Although I wish you to come with my father, to be here in November, yet I see the force of your objections against it. You would not be pleasantly situated in New-York, unless my father were President of Congress; but if you will come and spend a few months with us in the country, and papa go to New-York at such times as he must attend Congress, it would make us very happy. But for you to live at lodgings in New-York would not do at all. You would not be much pleased with the society. They are quite enough dissipated. Public dinners, public days, and private parties, may take up a person's whole attention, if they attend to them all. The President of Congress gives a dinner one or two or more days every week, to twenty persons, gentlemen and ladies. Mr. Jay, I believe, gives a dinner almost every week: besides the *corps diplomatique* on Tuesday evenings, Miss Van Berkell and Lady Temple see company;[2] on

Thursdays, Mrs. Jay and Mrs. Laforey, the wife of the French Consul, on Fridays;[3] Lady Christiana, the *Presidentess*; and on Saturdays, Mrs. Secretary ——. Papa knows her, and to be sure, she is a curiosity.[4]

I begin to doubt whether the States will generally appoint new members to Congress, as their time of continuance will be so short; and I suppose the members who now hold their seats, will be too fond of retaining them as long as they can, to leave their States long unrepresented. A short time will determine the event. I think the present appearances are, that this Congress will continue together until March; or that there will be a dissolution of all government for several months. For these two months past, these *wise counsellors* have been disputing and debating about the place where the new Government shall meet. The question has been brought on every day for the last month, and is not yet decided. New-York and Philadelphia are the points in contest, and neither party can get strong enough to make a majority in favour of either.

I am pleased to find that my politics meet with my father's approbation. I hear from many persons, the place of Vice President, or Chief Justice, assigned to him. Many persons consider the latter as the most respectable situation, and wish my father in it, as better calculated for it than any other man. Mr. Jay has also been mentioned for both, and I suppose every State have assigned every office that is to be created, to persons belonging to themselves; as the people of Philadelphia have already found men within the city, to whom they have assigned every place that is to be at the disposal of the people. There was such a list given out not long since; and so I presume it will be in most of the States.

Mr. —— is injuring his interests, I am informed, by his conduct towards the Lieutenant G. I wonder how he comes to be so mistaken in his politics, for in general he has discovered some knowledge of the human mind, by the manner in which he enforces himself upon the opinions of the people. I see by the papers that he is now putting himself into the observation of the people, in all parts of the State. To me his motives are obvious; but to appear opposed to him would, in my opinion, be the surest means of establishing his wishes.[5] But to have done with politics.

There are eccentric characters in all stations. You were not personally acquainted with Mrs. ——, but you knew her by reputation. She returned to New-York in a late ship, with her son, who is married to a daughter of Mr. ——. He is seventeen years of age, and the lady fifteen; but possessed of an income of £500 per year, and a fortune in reversion. He will be entitled to a fortune of £30,000 when he comes of age.

Mr. B— came out the other day, and dined with us. What an old fop! I was sorry to hear by him that Volnay had failed in business, since we left England, and that Mrs. O— was in great distress there.

Col. Smith had a letter from Mr. Short by the last packet, which mentioned the arrival of Mr. and Mrs. Paradise in Paris.

Cutting writes volumes of speculation to Col. Smith, upon the politics of Europe, and I fear will speculate with himself until he is ruined for any station in his own country.

Your affectionate daughter,   A. Smith.

MS not found. Printed from AA2, *Jour. and Corr.*, 2:96–101.

[1] Not found.

[2] The daughter of Pieter Johan van Berckel, the first Dutch minister to the United States, Miss Van Berckel later married Col. John Christian Senf from South Carolina in New York in 1792 (Charleston *City Gazette*, 4 July 1792; Rev. William Hall, "Pieter Johan Van Berckel, First Minister Plenipotentiary to the United States from Holland," *NYGBR*, 14:112 [July 1883]).

[3] Antoine René Charles Mathurin, Comte de La Forest (1756–1846), served as the French vice consul to the United States from 1785 to 1793. He married Catherine Marie Le Cuillier de Beaumanoir on 27 June 1787 in New York (Hoefer, *Nouv. biog. générale*; *JCC*, 30:13–15; Jacques Henri-Robert, *Dictionnaire des diplomates de Napoléon*, Paris, 1990, p. 223).

[4] Hannah Harrison Thomson (d. 1807)

was the second wife of Charles Thomson, secretary of the Continental Congress, and the daughter of Richard Harrison of Maryland. JA had met her while serving in Congress (*DAB*; JA, *D&A*, 2:133, 136, 264).

[5] Gov. John Hancock had recently insulted his political opponent Lt. Gov. Benjamin Lincoln by denying Lincoln a sinecure post as Captain of the Castle, a position traditionally given to the lieutenant governor to augment an otherwise small salary. Around the same time, in Aug. 1788, Hancock traveled to New Hampshire and back, stopping in towns along the Massachusetts coast; his positive reception throughout the state led to some speculation that he might become the first U.S. vice president (Fowler, *Baron of Beacon Hill*, p. 273–274; *New York Packet*, 29 Aug.).

Elizabeth Smith Shaw to Abigail Adams

My Dear Sister—   Haverhill September 21st 1788

Mr Lincoln has been here for several Days past—[1] Tomorrow he intends to return to Hingham, & has offered to carry a Letter to either of my Sisters— I would not let so good an Opportunity pass, since I have often experienced how good, & how pleasant it was to receive a few Lines from a dear Friend, informing me of particular

Circumstances which are interesting to them, whether it be of Joy, or Grief. I can enter into their different feelings, & find that this sympathy in nature is a source of much pleasure—

Mr Lincoln perhaps may tell you that Mr Adams came here a Saturday, to experience a little of my maternal Care— That he is unwell &cc—

But least you should hear of it, & be too anxious I will tell you that I hope he will be better in a few Days— Mamma will say, "why did he not come home to Braintree—" Because it was too far—& if he can get what he wants, (a little kind attention) nearer, it would not be worth his while

He has not been well since he left Braintree— What did you do to him? did you give him too strong Coffee, & Green Tea— Or did you re[ad] to him some *woeful Story?*—

He cannot sleep a night, & his nervous system seems much affected— Dr sweet has given him the Bark to take, & I went & made him a mug of valerian Tea as soon as he came—[2] He slept quietly last night, & seemed much refreshed, If I can coax him to sleep to night I shall feel quite grateful— For he has not rested two nights together for some time— He is the best man to take his medicine that I ever saw— He hardly makes a wry mouth— As his reward, I shall take him for a Gallant to his Aunt, & Cousin this week, & amuse his Mind by riding, & visiting—&cc &cc I am affraid he has applied himself too closely to his Studies— He is so avaritious in coveting the best Gifts that I fear such intense application will injure his Health, more than he is aware of.

Do not worry yourself by think[ing] that he will make trouble for us— I feel cleverly myself, & Lydia is as well as could be expected—& Cousin Betsy Smith is with me, & is one of the best good Girls in the world— He will have good care taken of him & I feel happy to think I can do no more for your Son, than you would do for mine—

22^d

I have had my wish— Mr Adams slept comfortably last night— Mr Lincoln, & he dined at Mr Thaxters to day— He thinks he is half Curred because he has got somebody to care for him—

I wish you could come to see us soon, because Mr Shaw wishes to go to Bridgwater the first week in October— My best regards to Dr Adams, & love to my Sister Cranch—& believe me to be your / affectionate Sister   E Shaw—

23ᵈ.

Mr Adams has slept these 3 nights very well— I tell Him there is more of an anidoine in *my bed*—than in all the Dr Drugs.

RC (Adams Papers); addressed: "Mrs Abigail Adams / Braintree"; notation: "Honoured by / Mr Lincoln." Some loss of text where the seal was removed.

¹ Rev. Henry Lincoln (1765–1857), Harvard 1786, who would become minister at Falmouth, Mass. (JQA, *Diary*, 2:443, 454–455; *History of Hingham*, 2:467).

² Dr. John Barnard Swett (1752–1796), Harvard 1771, studied medicine in Edinburgh before returning to the United States to practice in Newburyport (*Sibley's Harvard Graduates*, 17:635–638). See also JQA, *Diary*, 2:327–328, 454.

John Quincy Adams to Abigail Adams

Dear Madam.   Haverhill Septʳ: 22ᵈ: 1788.

Mʳ: Lincoln, the bearer, is a young preacher, who belongs to Hingham; he is going home, and I cannot suffer the opportunity to pass unimproved; though I have little to say: except that I have been unwell: my nerves have been disordered, and the words of Henry have [. . .] obtruded themselves upon my mind, at the midnight hour.

> Oh gentle sleep
> Nature's soft Nurse, how have I frighted thee
> That thou no more wilt weigh mine eye-lids down
> And steep my senses in forgetfulness.¹

I came here last Saturday, and have such excellent care taken of me, that I hope to be perfectly recovered in two or three days.

Mʳ Thaxter wishes very much to see the pamphlet containing the correspondence between Mʳ Jay & Littlepage.² I promised him two months ago to procure one of them; and am ashamed of my negligence in forgetting it. Will you be so kind as to send it here by the first conveyance you can find?

I hope to write more fully in a few days; meantime, I remain your dutiful Son.   J. Q. Adams.

RC (Adams Papers); addressed: "Mʳˢ: A. Adams. / Braintree."; docketed by JA: "J. Q. Adams 1788 / 22. Septʳ Haverhill"; notation: "Mʳ: Lincoln." Some loss of text due to placement of the seal.

¹ Shakespeare, *Henry IV, Part 2*, Act III, scene i, lines 5–8.

² This is probably a request for *Answer to a Pamphlet, Containing the Correspondence between the Honorable John Jay, Secretary for Foreign Affairs; and Lewis Littlepage, Esquire, of Virginia*, N.Y., 1787, which itself was a response to an earlier pamphlet of Jay's entitled *Letters, Being the Whole of the Correspondence between the Hon. John Jay, Es-*

quire, *and Mr. Lewis Littlepage, N.Y., 1786.* These two pamphlets outline a disagreement between Jay and Littlepage over a debt Lit-

tlepage owed to Jay ("Littlepage *versus* Jay," Virginia Historical Society, *An Occasional Bulletin,* 40:1–4 [June 1980]).

Abigail Adams Smith to John Quincy Adams

N3

Jamaica September 28th 1788—

this morning my Dear Brother—Mr Storer Came out from New York—to spend the day with us and was the Bearer from thence of your kind letter dated Septr 11th from Braintree,[1] I am very much surprized that you had not at that time received a letter from me, I wrote you in August and Mr Dane took my letter to Frank—and I had expected that you had received it long ere this,— Several of my friends—to whom I was very punctual in writing, I hear complain of my inattention— I fear my letters have miscarried—through the inattention of some Person,— I dont know to whom to attribute it— I shall in future be particularly attentive to whom I entrust them

I am however my Dear Brother the more obliged for your Letter as you had not heard from me—and from the appearance of things had reason I acknowledge; to tax me with negligence—towards you— so well do I know, and experience the Sattisfaction arrising from the receipt of letters from my Best Friends, that I can easily judge of the Chagrine and disappointment that must result from any circumstance which can interfere with their attention towards us—

this seperation of families which prevents us from paying to each other those attentions which our affection would dictate is to me the most painfull circumstance in Life— at times it affects my spirits—but I indeavour to dissipate the present anxiety by anticipating a future situation—when we shall meet together—and enjoy with double pleasure—the mutual interchange of affection and attention which—a Personal interview will render Possible—

the Happiness of our family seems ever to have been so interwoven with the Politicks of our Country as to be in a great degree dependant upon them— I almost hope that my Father may again be called to act upon the Public Theatre— such Men are much wanted altho I do Confess that self interest does not lie dormant in this wish— at Present you and my other Brothers are so much from necessity from home—that I cannot but hope that Mamma will accompany my Father this way at least for a few weeks—. I have made this proposal to her that She should come with my Father the last of next month and spend a few weeks with me—and if She wished to return it would be a fine opportunity for you to Come for her—and would give you an opportunity which I very much wish for—to make me a visit— indeed I begin to be quite impatient to see all my Dear Brothers—. and half wish that we had set out soon after our arrival for the purpose of visitting my friends Eastward—but there were reasons which prevented at the time—and it is not, now in my Power this season—

I Shall be very happy to receive from you an account of your Situation—. and of your acquaintances—for I am greatly interested in your wellfare and Sollicitous for your prosperity and Happiness

do you hear from your friend Murry! you doubtless know that he returnd to Mary Land—more than twelve months since—and has since been making some figure there, as I have heard—.[2] he like most others could not withstand that Vortex of dissipation which Europe presents and which like a Whirlpool draws in almost Every youth who—inadvertently steps into the stream

Poor Cutting will I fear fall a Sacrifise,—Possessed of tallents that might make a figure—had He Steadiness enough to pursue any fixd plan—with decission. he is now wasteing his time to the utter astonishment of all his friends and I beleeive dependant upon the Fortune of the night for the Subsistance of the day—

the Tragical Story you relate has made much talk here as well as with you— that family seem to be devoted to misfortunes of every kind,— if there are any innocent—one cannot but regret that they should be doomed to suffer with those whose atrocity of Guilt is almost unparalleled—

I hope our Countrymen will be Wise enough to take warning from those instances they have recently had of the pernicious affects of Such extravegance, dissipation, and folly;—as have been exhibited to view of late years;— the fatal Consequences which thousands of Innocent Persons experience from the downfall of thease airry fabricks—and visonary Castles of splendor—aught alone to deter others from pursueing So fallacious a Plan of Life—

your friend Munroe—inquired after you the other day—and wished that you would make me a visit which might give him an opportunity of seeing you in New York—[3]

I have sent Mr Storer to meeting with Bellinda that I might write to you— it is I beleive near time for them to return— Coll^n Smith desires to be kindly remembered to you—

write me often and beleive me your affectionate Sister

A.— Smith

RC (Adams Papers); endorsed: "My Sister. 28. Sept^r: 1788." and "My Sister. September 28. 1788."

¹ Not found, but see JQA, *Diary*, 2:453.

² William Vans Murray returned to Cambridge, Md., from London in late 1787 and began his law career; shortly thereafter, he was elected to the Maryland House of Delegates (Peter P. Hill, *William Vans Murray Federalist Diplomat: The Shaping of Peace with France, 1797–1801*, Syracuse, 1971, p. 7–

8). See also vol. 5:344–345; JA, *D&A*, 3:188, note 1.

³ Peter Jay Munro (1767–1833) had accompanied his uncle John Jay to Europe in 1779. While there, Munro corresponded with JQA in 1783 and 1784. He returned in 1784 to New York, where he studied law with Aaron Burr (*Appletons' Cyclo. Amer. Biog.*).

Elizabeth Smith Shaw to Abigail Adams

My Dear Sister—   Haverhill October 3^d 1788—

I am almost affraid you do not love me so well as I hoped you did— If you had have known how much you dissappointed me, & my Friends here, in not making us a visit, your benevolence would have induced my Brother, & you, to have surmountd every Obstacle—

If I had not felt too great a tenderness for the *Parent*, I would have told you that your Son was here very Sick, & had alarming Complaints— And indeed I could have told you so with truth— But I did not want to decoy you here in this way, & make you travel the road with an akeing heart, I know too well the distress of it—

I suppose Mr Adams is with you before this time— He *would* go to Newbury a Tuesday contrary to my advice—& I have been very uneasy about him ever since— I think it is highly necessary for him to be exceeding careful as to Diet, Exercise, &cc— As to Study that must certainly be laid aside for the present— We wished him to have tarried longer here, He knows that I felt a pleasure in attending upon One, who I thought so worthy of our Love, & esteem— I hope he is with you now & much better— My Love to him I will not say to him that I hope Morpheus nightly sheds his Poppies o'er his head, but in a more Christian stile, pray that the good Shepherd of Isreal, who himself never slumbers nor sleeps, would encircle him in the arms of his Love, & remove every disorder,—that his Blood may flow on in a regular & healthful Course, & he perfectly restored—that the rose may again return to his Cheek, & the glow of health smile & brighten in his Face—

I hope to see you next week, if our chaise wheels are done, & nothing happens we expect to come— Mr Allen has been sick with weak Eyes ever since he returned— They were here a Lecture day this week, & gave some account of the dreadful trial she had with her child—¹ I believe she does not want to go another Journey with one—

Please to give my love to my Sister Cranch & Cousins— cousin Betsy Smith begs to be remembered by her Aunts, as well my Son & Daughter.

Ever, & unalterably your affectionate sister   E Shaw[2]

RC (Adams Papers); docketed: "1788 E Shaw."

[1] The Allens' only child, Betsey, who had been born in Aug. 1787, survived to adulthood, marrying Rev. Thomas A. Merrill of Middlebury, Vt., in 1812 (*Sibley's Harvard Graduates*, 18:364, note 17).

[2] The final line and signature were written sideways in the margin.

Abigail Adams Smith to Abigail Adams

My Dear Mamma: Jamaica, October 5th, 1788.

I wrote you a hasty letter from New-York, just to acknowledge the receipt of yours, No. 5, the week before last;[1] since which I have not heard from you, nor have I had an opportunity to write.

*   *   *   *   *   *   *

Pennsylvania has already appointed her Senators, who are Mr. Morris and a Mr. McLain.[2] Poor —— is, then, disappointed; for he went home to make interest for himself, as it was said.

There are two gentlemen,—the one I mentioned in a former letter from the southward, and the other from your State, who is now in Congress,—who are looking for foreign appointments.[3] We are all content that they should receive what they desire, for no one who has been abroad could, I think, wish to go again, knowing how matters must be situated.

Professions are much easier made than fulfilled, especially in these days when *barter* is the fashion. The maxim of the present time is, "if you can be of service to me in promoting my views, I will give you my assistance in yours." Fear oftener actuates to friendly offices, than love. But I am not surprised at these things, for I am vain enough to think I can see as far into persons' characters, sentiments, and the motives which direct their conduct, as most *ladies* of my *age* and *experience*.

I may, sometimes from delicacy, at others from pride, suppress my opinions; but I flatter myself that in many cases I think right.

My father's idea of returning to the bar, (unless he is placed, as he ought to be, in a situation agreeable to himself,) is what I should expect from him, knowing his sentiments as I do; and unless the idea militates with his feelings, I can see no more respectable situation in private life, and no one so independent either in public or private, as he would establish himself in; for I presume the smaller parts of the practice would be wholly excluded by him, and left to young practitioners. It is a profession which I do venerate, and hope one day to see all my brothers, if it is their choice, to pursue this profession, making respectable figures in it. And, if it is not looking too far forward, I would hope that my son might yet become a pupil of his grandfather's. Ever since I have thought at all upon the subject, it has been my opinion that the study of law tends more to mature the judgment, and establish the right character of the man, (provided there are proper principles for the foundation,) than any other profession. There are men without principles in every profession. I do not think that the ill conduct of individuals ought to lessen the respectability of the profession they have made their study, although it may in the minds of some persons have this tendency.

The recent instance of perfidy and unheard of atrocity, which you mention in your letter, and which has made much talk this way, ought to brand with infamy the name and character of the author. Yet it seems hard that innocent persons, if there are any such connected with him, should suffer in their characters and reputations, by their affinity to this fiend of wickedness. This family seems devoted to misfortune of every kind, but I think that this instance must be the criterion of them.

My friends must have thought me very inattentive to them, if they have not yet received my letters. I have answered very punctually almost every letter I have received. It is a great amusement to me, writing to my friends at this distance. I do not find that time lessens the painfulness of a separation from our friends; it is only alleviated by this intercourse by letters. You have been very good in writing me, and yet when I do not get a letter for several weeks, I begin to grow impatient. You must not omit any opportunity of affording me this source of satisfaction.

I am much obliged by your request to have my dear boy with you this winter; but this is a separation I cannot think of. He is a great amusement to me, and becomes daily more engaging.

*   *   *   *   *   *   *

Your affectionate daughter,   A. Smith.

MS not found. Printed from AA2, *Jour. and Corr.*, 2:101–104.

[1] Neither AA's letter to AA2 nor AA2's reply has been found.

[2] William Maclay (1737–1804), a lawyer and judge of the court of common pleas in Pennsylvania, served in the U.S. Senate from 1789 to 1791. Robert Morris (1734–1806) served un-

til 1795 then declined renomination (*Biog. Dir. Cong.*).

³ The representative "from the southward" is possibly Abraham Baldwin, for whom see AA2 to AA, 13 Aug. 1788, and note 1, above. The Massachusetts representative is likely Samuel A. Otis, who wrote to JA on 18 Dec. seeking a position: "The Clerk of the Senate or of the House would give me subsistence for 'I want but little.' . . . If I fail in both these, I think I could discharge the office of Collector of excise Naval officer, or the active offices at home or abroad, for I am a 'Citizen of the world' litterally" (Adams Papers; see also Smith, *Letters of Delegates*, 25:445–446, 470, 474). Otis became secretary of the Senate and served from 1789 to 1814 (*Sibley's Harvard Graduates*, 14:478–480).

William Stephens Smith to Abigail Adams

My dear Madam—

Jamaica Long-Island
Novr. 10th, 1788.

It is with particular pleasure I communicate to you the joyfull news of Mrs: Smiths safe delivery of a Son, which took place between seven & eight the last Evening, she was not the least indisposed untill six o'Clock & by 1/2 past seven all was well & tranquil, both continue composed and easy, but Nabby desires me to tell you that she is much disappointed, she had made the things, to adorn a female & a male has taken possession of them; but she seems to take some comfort in contemplating the beauty of the infant, which (setting asside the partiallity which my mind may very naturally be supposed charged with) is in reallity very striking, I must amongst other favours which I feel gratefull for, particularise one, viz, the Boy has a fine promising Nose & an honest forehead, which I think will be some recommendation to a Lady of his Grandmama's taste & penetration, why will you not come and visit this happy family? but the fault is not in you but in your Stars, we have almost entirely given up the Idea of seeing any of the family, unless the sound advice contained in Mrs: S's last letter relative to her Brother John should put him in motion, which we both seriously wish may be the case—¹ Mrs: Smith joins me in affectionate regards to Sir² & yourself—to Brothers, Aunts, Uncles & the whole interesting train of Relations & friends & Individually, I am with great affection Dear Madam / Yours sincerely—

W: S: Smith

RC (Adams Papers); internal address: "To / Mrs: Adams—"

¹ Not found.
² WSS originally wrote "her Pappa" but crossed out the word "Pappa" and altered "her" to read "Sir."

John Adams to Abigail Adams Smith

My Dear Child: Braintree, November 11, 1788.

Our anxiety for you, in your present circumstances and situation among strangers, (though we doubt not you have many friends,) has prevailed upon me to make a great sacrifice, in consenting to your mother's journey to Long Island.

       *   *   *   *   *   *   *

I am kindly obliged to Col. Smith and to you, for your many invitations, and I have a great desire to see you, your friends, and even your situation. But, as long as this political squall shall last, I can scarcely lie asleep, or sit still, without censure, much less ride journeys on visits to my friends.

If my future employment in public depends on a journey to New-York, or on the feather of being for a week or a day President of Congress, I will never have any other than private employments while I live. I am willing to serve the public on manly conditions, but not on childish ones; on honourable principles, not mean ones.

It is the opinion of good judges, in which I fully concur with them, that there will be no Congress till February; nor then, but merely to declare the old Government dissolved, and the new one in exercise; so that there will be no occasion for me to go.[1]

I find men and manners, principles and opinions, much altered in this country, since I left it. Gen. Knox will tell you, when you see him, how completely I am initiated in the order of Cincinnatus, without any vote of the Society. He has obliged me by two short visits, and is the same sensible and agreeable man as when I formerly knew him.

I am, my dear daughter, with much affection, / Yours,

John Adams.

MS not found. Printed from AA2, *Jour. and Corr.*, 2:105–106.

[1] While various members of Congress did attend between Nov. 1788 and March 1789, no business was transacted (*JCC*, 34:604–605).

John Adams to William Stephens Smith

Dear Sir: Braintree, Nov. 11th, 1788.

I was much obliged to you for a letter by Mr. Nesbit of Philadelphia, and am very sorry I could not have more of his company.[1] He was much esteemed, I find, in Boston.

I wished for you, when he was here, because you could never have a better opportunity of seeing your old military friends. We had a review of the militia, upon my farm; and a battle that threw down all my fences. I wish, however, that Governor Hancock and General Lincoln would not erect their military reputations upon the ruins of my stone walls. Methinks I hear you whisper, it won't be long ere they erect their civil and political characters upon some other of your ruins. If they do, I shall acquiesce, for the public good: Lincoln I esteem very much: the other, I respect as my governor.

$$* \quad * \quad * \quad * \quad * \quad * \quad *$$

You have many friends here, who constantly inquire after your health and happiness. They all would be glad to see you, but none of them so sincerely rejoiced, as your affectionate,

John Adams.

MS not found. Printed from AA2, *Jour. and Corr.*, 2:106–107.

[1] The letter has not been found. Mr. Nesbit is probably John Maxwell Nesbitt (ca. 1730–1802), a prominent Philadelphia merchant and director of the Bank of North America (*DAB*).

Abigail Adams to John Adams

my dearest Friend   Hartford Sunday 16 Nov[br] 1788

We Reachd this place last evening and put up at a mr Avery's private Lodgings, where we are very well accommodated.[1] I am delighted with the veiw I have had of this state, the River is in full sight from the House & the fields yet retain their verdure, Lands I am told are valued here at a hundred pounds pr acre, and it is not unusuall to let the Farms upon this River at four pounds pr Annum pr acre. Manure is generally carried out in the fall. So much for Farming which is in your own way, besides I have learnt a New method of preserving pumpkins which is in my own way. I hope to make the journey usefull to me by further observations. I followd your injunctions stricktly kept open the windows, walkt some times &c but still no remedy against evening air. the day's being short & the evenings fine we wisht to improve the good weather & get on our journey as fast as possible, so rode late in the Evenings by which means I got a sad cold, or rather added to that which I had when I left Home. it is however going of to day. I hope you are relieved from yours, and that without the assistance of Bridgham prescription, I think of you very often and how I shall get back to you. I find the weather full cold enough now for travelling with comfort.

we have a very easy carriage good carefull driver and able Horses, yet find thirty miles as much as we can accomplish in one day. Some of the Road Rough enough as you well remember. our Land-lord who is an intellegent man fell into politicks to day, inquired who were talkd of for Senators in our state, &c but finding no poli-ticians in company few observation were made. he was high in praise of Dr Johnson & judge Elsworth, hope'd the rest of the states would send as good men & then he did not believe that the House of Lords in England could equal them, did not like pensilvana's chusing a Man who had never been heard of before, he might be a good man, but he wanted those men in office whose Fame had re-sounded throughout all the states. I ventured to ask him who were talkd of for Representitives. he said col wardsworth would be one, but that much had not been said upon the Subject yet. our Friend Trumble lives within a few doors of this House.[2] I have sent my compliments to him to come and take a dish of Tea with us, the Messenger is not yet returnd. we propose persueing our journey early in the morning and hope to reach Newyork by thursday Night.

I hope to hear from you by Gen[ll] Knox or mr Jarvis, pray see that our son excercises daily. I shall want to know a little of politicks, but with them I suppose you will tell me I have no Buisness—I design to be vastly prudent I assure you hear all, & say little— I hope you will be in good spirits all the Time I am gone, remembring Solomans advise that a merry Heart does good like a medicine— Love to all my Friends—

Have had a charming visit from Trumble we were so happy & so-ciable—I wish't you had been here to have shared it, we talkd of Books a *little* politicks, &c &c and so long that, the post is just go-ing, and I have only time to Say a good Night and that I am yours most tenderly   A Adams

dont leave my Letters upon the table

RC (Adams Papers); addressed by WSS: "The Hon[ble]: John Adams Esq[r:] / Brain-tree / Massachusetts."; docketed: "[A A] to J A / 1788." Some loss of text where the seal was removed.

[1] John Avery opened a lodging house on Main Street in Hartford, not far from the State House, in Dec. 1787. He advertised "Genteel Boarding & Lodging" and promised that "Breakfasts, Dinners, and Suppers, are provided on the shortest notice, and neat Beds are furnished. He has also the best of Stabling for Horses" (Hartford *American Mercury*, 25 Aug. 1788). See also AA to JA, 22 April 1789, below.

[2] For John Trumbull, JA's former law clerk and lifelong friend, see JA, *Legal Papers*, 1:cxii.

Abigail Adams to Mary Smith Cranch

my dear sister   Jamaica Nov^br 24 1788

I know you will rejoice with me that all was happily over & mrs
Smith safely abed before I reachd her She thought she should do as
she did before, so told no one that she was unwell, untill mr Smiths
mamma & sister could scarcly reach her, and a Negro Woman
whom she has was obliged to officiate for her. happily she had on
some former occasions assisted some of her own coulour, but all
were teribly frightned, however no one sufferd, but mrs Smith & my
young Grandson are as well as usual at this period. Master William
is the very Image of his Mamma at the same age, except that he has
a great share of vivacity & sprightlyness, the merest little Trunchion
that you ever saw, very pleasent & good humourd

I find this place a very retired one Rural & delightfull in the
summer. mr Smith has a large connection of sisters & Brothers, who
as well as his mamma appear very fond of their Sister & her daughter & Grandsons Belinda who keeps chiefly here, is very pleasing &
soft in her manners, much like my Friend Mrs Rogers. I was so
short a Time at Newyork that I saw nothing of it, and I feel as if I
ought to return to my Family again, as soon as mrs Smith gets
about, but it is a long journey & the Stages I find are very inconvenient for a Lady & wholy improper on many accounts for me. they are
not hung upon springs & they drive very Rapidly over very bad road.
I hope you will write me and give me some account of my Family,
about which I am anxious you will learn from Esther how she makes
out I wish to know whether she is able to take the care which is
upon her— I also want to know how mr J Q As health is, I know you
will feel a care for all of them in my absence.— mr Adams will Frank
your Letters which please to direct under cover to Col Smith

my Love to my dear Neices and tell Betsy I design to be at Home
to wedding mrs Smith joins me in affectionate Regard to you &
Family.

I am my dear sister affectionately / Yours   A Adams

I wish my dear sister if it will not dissapoint cousin Betsy that you
would write a line to the chair maker at milton to Send the half
dozen to mr Smiths store in Boston put up so as to send safely on
Board the first vessel which shall sail for Newyork, & let him know
that I will pay him on my return, pray mr Smith to address them to
mr daniel macormick Newyork

RC (MWA:Abigail Adams Letters); addressed: "To / Mrs Mary Cranch / Braintree"; notation by AA2: "M^c· Cormick."

Elizabeth Smith Shaw to Mary Smith Cranch

My Dear Sister—   Haverhill Nov. 26th· 1788

I do not know whether you have heard a word from me since I left you, if you have not, I presume it will afford you some pleasure to be assured that I got home well, though we had an uncommon cold time— We found our own Family in good Health— But Miss Lydia Marsh was very sick with the scarlet fever, & good Mrs Marsh was taken the day we got home with a very voilent fever, which threatened speedy dissolution— But to the great comfort of her Friends, & Relations she is again recovered, & her useful Life is a little longer lengthened out to us—[1]

I heard by Judge Seargant that Sister Adam's was going to New-york, but I doubted whether it were true— But I have since heard that she is gone— Seems to me it was very sudden indeed, for she did not intimate anything of it to me I fear she will always be moving from us— She is so connected in publick Life, & must have so large a Sphere to act in, that it is not likely we shall ever have that sweet enjoyment, in still domestic Life, which we used to experience in the private Circle of dear Friends—

I am glad to hear Mr Adams is better, I should not have thought his Mother would have left him— A journey mig[ht] perhaps, been of eminent service to him—

I am grieved to tell you that our dear Mr Thaxter has had another dreadful fit— It did not last but a few minutes—& he was not so sick afterwards— I really think Mrs. Thaxter suffers more from apprehension than he does in reality— How often does unforeseen Calamity cast a shade over the brightest prospects— The tender affection which subsists between this worthy pair, serves only to sharpen the edge of their affliction— I really fear the distress, & agitation of her Mind, will occasion Mr Thaxter *a third dissappointment*—[2]

Next week Mr Adrews is to be ordained at Newbury—[3] This I presume will afford me the pleasure of seeing many of my Friends this way— among them may I not hope to see Mr Norton, & my dear Cousin— I look earnestly in the news paper, but have not as yet seen his nutials announced to the publick— Whenever that may be, may my young Friends be blessed, & happy— I have got some fine Turkeys I wish you were here to eat them— Mr White, Mr Osgood, &

Mr Bartlet presented us with one—so we have seven for you my friends if you will make haste & come to your ever affectionate

Elizabeth Shaw

PS Love in abundance

RC (DLC:Shaw Family Papers); addressed: "Mrs Mary Cranch / Braintree"; docketed: "M^rs. Shaw / Nov. 26. 1788." Some loss of text where the seal was removed.

¹ Mary Moody Marsh, the wife of Deacon David Marsh, lived until 1794. Lydia (1745–1828) was their daughter (JQA, *Diary*, 1:397; *Vital Records of Haverhill Massachusetts to the End of the Year 1849*, 2 vols., Topsfield, Mass., 1910–1911, 1:213; 2:213, 441).

² Elizabeth Thaxter gave birth to a son, John Adams Thaxter, on 7 July 1789, after two miscarriages (John Thaxter Jr. to Celia Thaxter, 14 Feb. 1789, MHi:Thaxter Family Papers; JQA, *Diary*, 2:388).

³ John Andrews of Hingham, Harvard 1786, was ordained associate pastor of the First Church of Newburyport (formerly the Third Parish of Newbury) on 10 December. Andrews was a friend of JQA's at Harvard (Minnie Atkinson, *A History of the First Religious Society in Newburyport, Massachusetts*, Newburyport, 1933, p. 7, 37; JQA, *Diary*, 1 and 2:*passim*).

Mary Smith Cranch to Abigail Adams

My dear sister   Braintree November 30th 1788

I have been waiting above a week hoping to have a Letter from my dear sister informing me of her safe arrival at newyork Before I can write said I—I think I must have a Letter— you left us so unwell that I have been anxious about you ever since— I have a thousand times wish'd you back again your Letter to Mr Adams dated at Hartford has in some measure reliev'd me— I hope before this that you are rejoicing with your children in the safety of my dear Niece & that you are fondling over this new addition to your Family my sincere congratulations attend you all whenever it shall happen— As soon as mrs smith can be left I am sure you will return— mr Adams looks quite a solatary Being has not been from home excepting when he is upon his Farms since you left him. He calls upon us once or twice a day—but these are only flying visits— I have not yet been able to get him to dine with me altho I have ask'd him repeatedly— I thought surely to have had him & my Nephews at thanksgiving—but his reasons were so amiable that I could not but approve of his refusal— "He wish'd once more to meet his Mother & Brother at his own house upon such an anniversary. He felt assur'd it would be the last that his kind Parent would ever keep with him." she has had a bad fall sin[ce] you left us— she caught her foot in a wheelband as she was crossing the Room & fell— It has givin her a sad shock. she

310

is so feeble that she can scarcly walk your son charles din'd with me to day & says that things go on very peacably at home. I have heard no complaints— As to cousin John—when we turn to Books he will visit us. He has not been in the house since you went away— He says he is well—

I ask'd Mr Adams the other day if he had written to you He said "no—" it was to tender a subject as Dr ——— said "it always made him melancholy—" very well said I— then I know what I have to do or somebody else will be melancholy for want of inteligence— & so my sister you see my scribling Pen is once more set to work—

cousin Tom went last week to Haverhill— mr Andrews is to be or-dain'd at Newbury Port the week after next—which will give your eld-est son & mine a little Journey which will I hope be for the health of both of them The Brother & sisterly affection subsisting between our children gives me the highest pleasure— may nothing ever hap-pen to lessen it—

you will see by the Papers what a contest there has been between the House & senate—The *stuborn* senate—but such ploting & cabal-ing in doors & out is a scandle to our state[1] I foresee that some of our late popular characters will sink into disgrace. The man who dares to pluck the mask from the Face of the dissembling vilain will be feard but must not expect to be belov'd but by the virtuous few— He who acts honestly will not be so much hurt by the ingratitude of those whos interests he has greatly serv'd as one whos motive was mearly the applause of the multitude—because he acted from a bet-ter principle He will like the Being he has imitated rejoice in the good he has accation'd to others altho they may not see the hand from which it came—

December 2'd

I am this day to be favour'd with Mr Adams & your sons company to dine— I should feel an additional happiness if you could all join us I long to clasp the little strangers to my Bosom. Mrs Hall is much better Mr Cranch & I spent the last sunday evening with our solatary Brother & had a choise dish of Politicks for our entertain-ment

william is at home— I had like to have said but I should have said is at your office. His cousin was so desirous of having him for his companion both in his office & in his excurtions on horse back that he has left his master for a little time— our weymouth Freinds are well Mr Tufts is gone to housekeeping—

I inquir'd of mrs Brisler how she did with her kitchen Family— she told me *pritty* well— If there is any thing you wish me or the children to take the care of you know we are bound by every tye of gratitude & affection to afford you every assistance in our power—

we all wish ardently for your return but none with more / sinceritty than your affectionate sister   Mary Cranch

Accept the Duty & Love of your Nephew & Neices's

RC (Adams Papers); addressed: "Mrs Adams / Jamaica. / Long Island"; docketed by JA: "M C to A A"; notations: "Free / John Adams."; "Not"; and "2.16 / 1/4." Some loss of text where the seal was removed.

¹ The *Massachusetts Centinel*, 22 and 26 Nov., printed the debates in the Mass. General Court over the election of senators to Congress from 21 to 24 November. The House initially favored the election of Caleb Strong and Charles Jarvis, but the Senate refused to concur. After several rounds of debate, the two houses ultimately agreed on Caleb Strong and Tristram Dalton (*First Fed. Elections*, 1:514–521).

John Adams to Abigail Adams

My dearest Friend   Braintree Dec.ʳ 2. 1788

Before this time I hope you have the Happiness to See your Daughter out of all Danger and your Son in Law and your two grand children in perfect health. I have no Letter from you, Since that you wrote at Hartford, and I cannot find fault because this is the first I have written to you. We are all very well, and go on very well. Charles came home and Thomas went to Haverhill, last Week.—

We are all in a Lurry with Politicks. Mʳ Dalton and Mʳ Strong are Senators¹ and Mʳ Lowell will be Rep. for the District of Suffolk, as is generally Supposed.— Mʳ Varnum, Mʳ Partridge Cᵒˡˡ Leonard, *Mʳ Grout* Mʳ Sedgwick or Mʳ Lyman Mʳ Jackson or Mʳ Dane or Mʳ Goodhue, Mʳ Thatcher or Col Sewell, are named for other Districts.²

My Love to our Children and Respects and Regards wherever you please.

Dont be uneasy, on Account of your Family here, nor in haste to come home before a good opportunity presents.

I dont enter into any political Details. My Mind has ballanced all Circumstances. and all are reducible to two Articles Vanity and comfort.— I have the ~~Whip-Row~~ Alternative in my own Power. if they mortify my Vanity they give me Comfort.— They cannot deprive me of Comfort without gratifying my Vanity. I am my dearest / Friend your forever   John Adams

RC (Adams Papers); addressed by JQA: "M$^{rs:}$ A. Adams. / Jamaica. / Long Island."; internal address: "Mrs Adams."; notations: "Free / John Adams."; "Not"; and "2.16 / 1/4."

[1] Caleb Strong (1745–1819), Harvard 1764, a Northampton lawyer, served in the Senate until 1796 (*First Fed. Elections*, 1:759–760).

[2] For a full discussion of the elections of U.S. representatives in Massachusetts, including the multiple balloting in some districts, see same, 1:543–742.

Suffolk County elected Fisher Ames over John Lowell (same, 1:743).

Gen. Joseph Bradley Varnum (1750/51–1821), from Dracut, was not elected at this time but would serve in Congress as a representative from 1795 to 1811 and as a senator from 1811 to 1817; Middlesex County elected Elbridge Gerry in his place (same, 1:749, 760–761).

Plymouth and Barnstable Counties elected George Partridge (1740–1828), a Duxbury native, who served from 1789 to 1790 (same, 1:756).

George Leonard (1729–1819), Harvard 1748, from Norton, represented Bristol, Dukes, and Nantucket Counties from 1789 to 1791 and again from 1795 to 1797 (same, 1:753–754).

Jonathan Grout (1737–1807) was elected from Worcester County and served until 1791 (same, 1:751).

Berkshire and Hampshire Counties elected Theodore Sedgwick over Samuel Lyman, among others. Sedgwick (1746–1813), Yale 1765, practiced law and served in the Mass. General Court nearly continuously from 1780 to 1788. He had been a delegate to the Continental Congress from 1785 to 1786 and in 1788, and would serve in the U.S. Congress from 1789 to 1801. Lyman (1749–1802), Yale 1770, was also a lawyer and a member of the General Court from 1786 to 1793. He was later elected to Congress and served as a representative from 1795 to 1801 (same, 1:603, 754, 757).

Benjamin Goodhue was elected to represent Essex County over Nathan Dane and Jonathan Jackson. Goodhue (1748–1814), Harvard 1766, served as a Massachusetts congressman from 1789 to 1796, and then as a senator from 1796 to 1800. Jackson (1743–1810), Harvard 1761, was a Newburyport merchant (same, 1:586, 750, 752).

The three Maine counties—York, Cumberland, and Lincoln—selected George Thacher over Colonel Sewall, probably Dummer Sewall (1737–1832), a lieutenant colonel in the Massachusetts militia who represented Bath in the state ratifying convention. Thacher (1754–1824), Harvard 1776, was a lawyer from Biddeford; he served in Congress from 1789 to 1801 (same, 1:611–613, 760; *Doc. Hist. Ratif. Const.*, 7:1517).

Abigail Adams to John Adams

my dearest Friend   Jamaica December 3^{d} 1788–

This day three weeks I left Home, since which I have not heard a word from thence. I wrote you from Hartford and once from this place since my arrival.[1] I cannot give you any account eitheir of Newyork or Jamaica as I got into the first at seven in the Evening & left it at Nine the next morning, and in this place my only excursion has been in the garden. the weather has been bad cloudy & rainy ever since I came untill within these two days, and now it is very cold & Blustering. when I think of the distance I am from Home, the Idea of winter & Snow has double terrors for me. I think every Seperation more painfull as I increase in Years. I hope you have found in the Learned & venerable Company you proposed keeping, an ample compensation for my absence. I imagine however if these cold Nights last a little vital Heat must be wanting. I would recommend to you the Green Baize Gown, and if that will not answer, you recollect the Bear skin. I hope you will gaurd with all possible precaution against the Riggors of winter. I wish to hear how mr John Q A stands this cold. I hope he rest well, and duly excercises. I learn nothing further in politicks for except when col Smith goes to Town which is but seldom, we hear no News & see nobody but the Family. Mrs Smith remains very well for the Time and young master grows, but he and William should change Names, as William bears not the least likness to His Father or Family & the Young one is very like. for myself I am tolerably a little Homeish, however, the more so perhaps through the fear of not being able to reach it, just when I wish. if our out of Door Family should increase in my absence, I hope proper attention will be paid to the preservation of the Young family. if it should be numerous it will be rather expensive, and I would offer to your consideration whether two of the young Females had not better be put in a condition for disposal, viz fatted. The Beaf I Suppose is by this time in the cellar. I wish you would mention to Brisler & to Esther, a constant attention to every thing about House to Gaurd against the incroachment of Rats & mice. the cider should be drawn off, and my pears and Apples picked over & repack'd. if I should not reach Home by christmass—would it not be best to purchase a pork for winter, & to secure a few legs of pork to Bacon? I wish amongst other things you would frequently caution them about the fires a Nights. I should be loth to trust any one in this Matter but Brisler.—

pray write me by the next post and tell me how you all do.

mr & mrs Smith present their duty pray do not forget to present mine to our venerable parent little William says Grandpa ha ha. I should certainly bring him home if it was not winter and such a distance

Love to mrs Cranch & my Neices:—

Yours most tenderly   A Adams

my Trunk has not yet arrived so that I could not go abroad if I would— Barnard was to sail the Sunday after I left Town

RC (Adams Papers); addressed by WSS: "To / The Honble: John Adams / Member of Congress from / Massachusetts at / Braintree near / Boston."; docketed by JQA: "A. A. / Decr 3^d 1788."; notation: "2.16" and "A. A."

¹ The Hartford letter is dated 16 Nov., above; the second letter has not been found.

Abigail Adams to John Adams

my dear Friend   December 13th 1788

I hope every post to hear from you, but every post has hithertoo dissapointed me. a month is a long time to be absent from Home without learning any thing from you. you have often left me and always was very punctual in writing to me. this is but the second time I have left you, and the first that I have been so long without hearing from you. I have written three times before, but have very little to entertain you with. Politicks are confined much to Newyork the papers of which give us but little information and winter leaves us very little scope for Farming or Husbandry. Col Smith has a fine poultry yard consisting of Turkys Geese fowls ducks in abundance, a pair of very good Horses & two cows, two pointers & two water dog's. the Island abounds with game Quails partridges ducks plovers &c

Having tarried till mrs Smith has got well and about House, I am anxious to return Home again I think I could be more usefull there than here. I should have like'd to have spent one week in Nyork, but shall not tarry a day for that purpose after an opportunity offers for my return. I beg you would write me by the post. mrs Smith desires me to present her duty to you & Love to all her friends. most affectionately / yours   A A—

RC (Adams Papers).

Abigail Adams to John Quincy Adams

my dear son   december 13th 1788 Jamaica

I begin to think I am not of that concequence at Home which I supposed myself, or that you think me less solicitious about my Family than I really am, since a whole month has elapsed since I left you, in all which time I have neither received a single line or heard a word from one member of it. three times I have written to your Pappa once to your Aunt Cranch, and now I try you to see if I can be favour'd with a few Lines at least. The subjects I wish you to write upon, is first How your Father does, yourself and Brothers come Next, your Grandmamma uncles & Aunt & cousins next to them our domesticks. The Family here are well, and Since Barnard chuses to keep the Trunk which was committed to him, or rather we cannot learn anything of him, I am incapacitated from making any visits in Newyork, but shall embrace the first fall of snow to return to massachu. again

I have only seen one Newspaper from our state since I came here, and that mr George Storer sent me last week. it containd the choice of Senators.[1] I was glad to see our Senate act with proper spirit and dignity. Virgina you will see by the papers, is lighting up a fire the G——r and assembly of N york tis said will blew the coals.[2] Col duer dined here last week, it was his opinion that there would not be any congress this winter. a few members only were come.

This place is much more retired than Braintree. most of the Families who reside here were Tories during the war. Some of them are so still. Col Smith has not a single acquaintance upon the Island whom he visits, he belongs to a club in Newyork of which mr Jay Benson Hammilton duer King and a Number of other Gentlemen are members, they usually meet once a week and dine together.

I am very desirious of getting Home before the Jan'ry vacancy. Col Smith will bring me, and your Sister seems very much inclined to make us a winter visit as she thinks she could accomplish it with more ease to herself and little ones than any other way. She is extreemly desirious to see her Father Brothers & Friend's. I fear to encourage her as the accommodations upon the Road are very indifferent for a winters excursion with young children, but if the Sleying should be fine I think she will try it. if the Snow Should keep of, why I do not know how I shall return. I wish I could be assured of getting back with half the convenience I came, aya Say you, I told you so mamma. So you did, but I thought I was doing what duty and maternal tenderness demanded of me, and I shall not regreet it tho I should encounter many difficulties in concequence of it.

pray accommodate your Father with writing materials and tell him I am very Solicitious to have under his own Hand that he has not sufferd with the cold and from yours that you Rest well, and are better than when I left you.

Yours most affectionately

A Adams

RC (Adams Papers).

[1] Probably the *Massachusetts Centinel* whose 26 Nov. issue contained the conclusion of the debates in the Mass. General Court regarding the election of senators.

[2] The Virginia legislature approved a resolution on 20 Nov. calling for a second convention to consider amendments to the new Constitution (rather than having the new Congress consider amendments). The resolution included a draft letter to Gov. George

Clinton of New York asking that he present
the resolution to the New York legislature for

concurrence (*First Fed. Elections*, 2:273–279;
Massachusetts Centinel, 3 Dec.).

Mary Smith Cranch to Abigail Adams

My dear sister   Braintree Dec.ʳ 14 1788

I do indeed rejoice with you all upon the happy event which took
place in mr smiths Family before your arrival I hope my Neices
health is perfectly restor'd that the young gentlemen are both very
well—& that you may soon return accompany'd by Coll.ⁿ smith
whom I wish much to see— you must not think of comeing in the
stage. It would be highly improper upon every account— we receiv'd
your letters last week & were impatient enough till we had—

I call'd upon mr Adams yesterday & found him looking with great
pleasure upon 15 head of young Heifers which he had just purchas'd—¹ He is determin'd to have stock enough I think you must
build a dairy room next spring I am sure if they should all have
calves. mr Adams will cover his Farms with living creatures if he
does not have some other imployment soon—but by what I can hear
it is probable he will—

The chairs you mention have been here these three weeks—but
you shall have them— I sent yesterday to have some more made &
suppose I can have them— Betsy says if she does not have them till
the spring she does not care she has some which she can put into
the chamber. she wishes you to be here when she is married—but I
believe you must come soon if you are— It has become such a serious matter with her that I really wish it was over— she will have no
health till it is she wants you to say a few cheafull incouraging
things to her— her Cousin too must spair an hour from her Nursery
to inliven her Ideas.

Mrs Brisler has retain'd her health bejond my expectaton— I hear
no complaints of any kind from any one your son is not returnd
from ordination mine did not go— mr cranhs was taken very ill the
morning he was to have gone. & I feard he would have had a settled
fever but it is gone off; I believe it was a cold & too great attention
to watch work, your sons at college I hear are will,— I have told mrs
Brisler to acquaint me if there is any thing to be done for them she
has sent some of mr adams linnen to be repair'd & Lucy has done it

mr cranch & william are gone to spend this evening with your
lonely Friend— He has his easy chair before the fire & the Tables
cover'd with books & papers just as he told you he would

317

mr Brisler will take the chairs to mr smiths store tomorrow & I hope they will reach you safe

I wish to look in upon you all— I cannot bear this separation—& must I hope it will be continu'd?— can I be so publick spirited? If I am I shall sacrifice a very great part of my private happiness— remember me most affectionately to mrs smith & till her that neither time nor distance has or ever will lesson my love for her— I long to squeese the little Boys & make them love me

I am my dear sister with the most ardent affection ever yours—

Mary Cranch

The whole Family Join me presenting congratulations & Love oh! for a good pair of eyes & a good pen!

RC (Adams Papers).

¹ A receipt in JA's hand shows that he purchased fifteen yearlings from his cousin Ebenezer Adams on 15 Dec. for a price of £16.9.1 (NN:Presidents' Papers).

Abigail Adams to John Adams

My dearest Friend   Jamaica december 15ᵗʰ 1788

It was not untill yesterday that I received your Letter & mrs Cranchs. mr mccomick came up & brought them both to my no small satisfaction, and this was the first that I had heard from Home since I left it, except by the News papers which I have engaged George Storer to forward to me. I have written to you every week since I left you, and Subjected you to more postage than my Letters are worth, which I did not know untill Saturday when mr Jay offerd to Frank my Letters & requested me to have mine sent to him. Members of congress it seems have not that privilege but when they are upon duty. mr Jay came out on Saturday to visit me. he had been waiting some Time for mrs Jay, but the children were sick with the measles and prevented her. Col smith was gone to Town, so we had all the Talk to ourselves, and very social we were, just as if we had been acquainted Seven years. He expresst a great desire to see you, and thought you might have come on without subjecting yourself to any observations, tho he knew your Reasons were those of Delicacy. I replied to him that your wish to see him was mutual that a visit from him to you would have made you very happy, but that you was become quite a Farmer and had such a fondness for old Professions that you talk'd of returning to the Bar again. he replied with some warmth, that if your Countrymen permitted it, they

318

would deserve to be brought to the Bar—that you must not think of
retireing from publick Life. you had received your portion of the
bitter things in politicks it was time you should have some of the
sweets. I askt him where he thought the sweets in the new Government were to grow. he smild and said that he hoped for good things
under it. I askd him whether the oppositition in virginia was not
likely to become troublesome, particularly when joind by this state.
he said it was his opinion that they might be quieted, by the New
Governments assureing them that a convention should be called to
consider of amendments at a certain period. Col Smith dinned at
club on Saturday. col Hammilton shew him a Letter from madison
in which he "Says, we consider your Reasons conclusive. the Gentleman you have named will certainly have all our votes & interest
for vice President," but there is interest making amongst the anti-
feds for Clinton both in Newyork and virginia, and if the Electers
should be of that class tis Said General washington will not have
the vote of his own State for President.[1] Col Wadsworth says he is
sure of connecticut with respect to a vice president— I am rather at
a loss to know how to act. I find there is much inquiry made for me
in Newyork. one Lady is sending to know when I am comeing to
Town & an other where I shall keep and Tickets for the assembly
have been sent up to me. mr Jay requested me to make his House
my Home, but I have no maid with me and should experience many
difficulties in concequence of it if I went where I should be exposed
to so much company and I was previously engaged to mrs Atkinson,
but my Trunk with all my Cloaths is not yet arrived, & I am Sadly
of, even here having only one gown with me. and I must be obliged
to return home without even Seeing Newyork should Barnard be
driven off to the west Indies, if a good snow comes I shall not wait.
the Ladies must stay their curiosity till my Leve day, and if that
never comes, they will have no further curiosity about seeing A A—
who it seems was of so much concequence or somebody connected
with her, that at every Inn upon the Road it was made known that I
was comeing. I find the peice called a Tribute justly paid &c is in
the Nyork & conneticut papers—[2] I see several political maneuvers
in our Boston papers particularly the Letter which places ~~you~~ a certain Gentleman in the chair dividing the state into two parties one
for the Late & the other for the present Governour, & supposing
they mean both to unite in mr A.[3] an other peice dated at Braintree,
which I am persuaded was never written there I dare say I shall tell
you News out of your own papers[4]

319

Mrs Smith desires me to present her duty to you. she is very weak yet, but otherways well. mr Jay upon seeing william cry'd out well here is Grandpappa over again. he is a fine red cheekd chubby Boy, as good temperd as I ever saw a child. Mrs Cranch says you are very solitary and that she cannot get you to see her. they tell me here that the Great Folks in Newyork are never solitary, if the wife is absent why they supply her place, now rather than my Husband should do so, I would stick to him, cleave I believe is the proper word all the days of my Life. I hope the Lads are all well and that Esther takes good care of them & of their things. Mrs Smith says I am in better spirits since I got my Letters. I believe it is true I know I was near home sick before. I think of a thousand things which I ought to be doing, and here I am near 300 miles distant. my duty to your good mother, I hope she has recoverd from her Fall & is able to visit you sometimes. pray write me all about the Family and cover your Letters to mr Jay— adieu most affectionately yours—

A Adams

RC (Adams Papers); docketed by JQA: "A. A. / December 15ᵗ 1788."

[1] Probably James Madison to Alexander Hamilton, 20 Nov., not found, for which see Hamilton's letter to Madison of 23 Nov. (Hamilton, *Papers*, 5:234–237).

[2] This article first appeared under a London dateline in the *New York Packet*, 21 Nov., and was subsequently reprinted in the *Connecticut Journal*, 10 December. When the *Massachusetts Centinel* printed it on 3 Dec., it used the headline "A Tribute—Justly Paid—to *Mr. Adams*." It celebrated JA's public career to date, noting in particular his work negotiating treaties with the European powers and securing a loan from the Netherlands, as well as his publication of the *Defence of the Const.*

[3] In the twentieth letter in a series, "Francois de la E——" commented on the politicking in Massachusetts, arguing that the state was divided into two parties, "Hancockonians" and "Bowdoinites." He believed that the Bowdoinites planned "to exert the whole of their influence in favour of the Hon. John Adams, Esq; in order to place him in the chair of government the next year; and I am induced to believe they will effect it; for Mr. Adams is generally beloved by both parties, his great talents acknowledged by every one, and his persevering friendship to the American cause, has got him a name and character which will be lasting as the pages of time" (Boston *Herald of Freedom*, 8 Dec.).

[4] Another piece in the same issue entitled "Unbiassed and Impartial" and signed at Braintree, 5 Dec., by "Suffolk" disparaged "the peculiar method lately taken with respect to Representatives for our Federal Government." He critiqued the newspapers for writing as if the question had already been decided and was not up to the people of the state (same).

Abigail Adams to Mary Smith Cranch

my dear sister   Jamaica December 15 1788

I thank you for your kind Letter of Novᵇʳ 30th Decᵇʳ 2d you judg'd rightly I was almost melancholy to be a month from Home, and not to hear once from Home in all that Time, but the post is long in comeing I am Eleven miles from York with a great Ferry between, and you are ten from Boston so that we do not always get our Letters ready for post day. I wrote you the day after I arrived here & trust you have long ago got the Letter. your Neice is very well, except weak, & very free with her mamma as I can instance to you, for having written a Letter to her pappa & seald it, she comes in & says o, mamma what is the Letter seald, why I must see it, and very cordially opens it to read. the little Boy grows finely, but I dont feel so fond of him yet as I do of william. whether it is because he was Born in our own House, or the first or the best temperd child I cannot determine.

Dec'br 18th.

Mrs Smith has had several of her Neighbours to visit her since I have been here they appear to be geenteel people, but all the acquaintance she has upon the Island are of the ceremonious kind. In their own Family are four young Ladies all of them agreeable sensible well behaved woman Peggy the Eldest is tall, agreeable rather than handsome, and the most particularly attentive to her manners without discovering any affectation of any Lady I have met with.[1] Belinda the second daughter has less of person to boast of than her Elder Sister, but she has that Interesting countanance & openness of manners that Interests you at first sight, nor are you dissapointed upon a further acquaintance. her temper and disposition appear perfectly amiable accommodating and kind. I have more acquaintance with her than with either of the others. I found here when I came taking charge of mrs Smiths Family during her confinement. this she performd with much ease and tender sisterly affection.[2] at Home their mamma has used them to the care of her Family by Turns each takes it a week at a Time. Charity is the third daughter, and if it was not for the loss of one Eye which she was deprived of at two years old I think she would be the Bel of the Family. she has been absent till last sunday ever since I came. I have seen her but once. she is more social has, Read more and appears to have the greatest turn for literature of either, she has a taste for drawing for musick &c the fine arts seem to be the objects of her attention, and as she has a most inquisitive mind she would shine with brightness if she had Books to direct her and masters to instruct her. she dresses with neatness but great simplicity rather in the Quaker stile, avoids all publick company assemblies &c but is strongly attachd to her Friends. I take from mrs Smith part of her History for as I ob-

321

servd before I have seen her but once[3] Sally is the fourth daughter about 17. tall as mrs Guile a fine figure & a pretty Face unaffected and artless in her manners, modest & composed. she wants only a little more animation to render her truly Interesting she has dignity, & that you know is inconsistant with a gay, playfull, humour,[4] this Belinda has. They are four fine women and well educated for wives as well as daughters. there are two young ones Betsy & Nancy one of ten and the other seven years old.[5] Daughters so agreeable must have a worthy mother, and this is universally her character. Mrs Smith is a Large tall woman, not unlike mrs Gray She is about 50 years old and has been a very Handsome woman, tenderly attachd to all her children. she has I tell her been too indulgent to her sons of whom she has four, but of them an other Time.[6] she is really a Charming woman as far as I have been able to form an acquaintance with her, and she has been here a good deal & I have visited her. we have had company several Times from Nyork and I have & many and repeated requests to go there, but my Trunk is, I know not where. I have only one morning gown & a Green Sattin which I very fortunatly had in my small Trunk or I should not have been able to have seen any body I have no shoes but the pr I wear no Bonnet, very little Linnen & only my calimanco skirt, and there are very few things of mrs smiths that I can wear, I am sadly of. we had yesterday a cold snow storm, hardly enough to cover the ground, but it has cleard up very cold, I think of my poor dear & pitty him. I long to get back to my Family, but must wait for snow as the roads are too bad to Travel without I regreet daily the distance, but mrs Smith comforts herself with thinking that I shall very soon be nearer to her, but I fear I shall not have much comfort if that should happen tis only on plain ground that one walks easily, up hill or down is painfull. I am affraid J Q will turn Hermit, if buisness does not soon call him into the world, but how much better is this, than having no given object no persuit— I had rather a son of mine should follow any mechanical trade whatever than be a Gentleman at large without any occupation

I am sorry to hear my good Mother has met with such an accident. it is one source of my anxiety to get home, that I have thought for some months that she would not Live through the winter. pray present my duty to her and tell her that her Grandchildren & great Grandchildren talk of comeing to see her. my Love to my two daughters, tell Betsy she must not steal a march upon me. if she waits an other month mrs Smith will come & be Bride maid. present me kindly to Brother cranch & go as often as you can & see my good Gentleman. tell Esther she must write to me & let me know how she makes out. my fingers are so cold I can Scarcly hold a pen. adieu my dear sister write as often as you can, mrs Smith desires me to present her duty & Love. she will write soon. Yours most tenderly

A Adams

RC (MWA:Abigail Adams Letters); docketed: "Letter from M^rs / A: Adams, (Pha.) / Jamaica, Decr 15th / 1788."

¹ For Margaret Smith, WSS's eldest sister, see vol. 7:441. For further genealogical material on the Smith family, see Marcius D. Raymond, "Colonel William Stephens Smith," *NYGBR*, 25:153–161 (Oct. 1894).

² Belinda Smith (b. 1765) married Matthew M. Clarkson of New York (Sarah Johnson Lynch to ECA, 26 Aug. [1893?], Adams Papers, Genealogical Materials, folder 9).

³ Charity Smith married first Benjamin Shaw (1758–1807), then Capt. Abraham W. Long. She settled in Boston and ran a ladies' academy (same; JA, *D&A*, 3:237; *NYGBR*, 15:136 [July 1884]).

⁴ Sarah (Sally) Smith (1769–1828), designated as SSA in *The Adams Papers*, married CA on 29 Aug. 1795 in a double wedding with

her elder sister, Margaret. SSA and CA had two daughters, Susanna Boylston Adams (1796–1884) and Abigail Louisa Smith Adams (1798–1836). After CA's death in 1800, SSA and her two children lived with AA and JA for a time in Quincy.

⁵ Elizabeth Smith (b. 1778) married John Smith Jr., a merchant from Baltimore. Ann (Nancy) Smith married Josiah Masters (Sarah Johnson Lynch to ECA, 26 Aug. [1893?] and 31 Aug. 1893, Adams Papers, Genealogical Materials, folder 9).

⁶ The Smith sons, besides WSS, included Col. John Smith; Justus Bosch Smith (1761–1816); and James Smith (b. 1773), who married Ann Ross (same).

John Adams to Abigail Adams

My dearest Friend   Braintree Decr 28. 1788

I have rec^d your favours of the 3 and 13th and have opened that to our Son, who has been absent from me these 3 Weeks at Newbury, where I Suppose he is very well.— I am as anxious as you are about your coming home. There are but two Ways. 1. if Coll Smith can bring you and his Family with you, will be the more obliging and agreable. 2. if he cannot, I must send your eldest son, with a Coach from Boston, to wait on you. as soon as I can receive a Letter from you, informing me, of the Necessity of it, I will Send him off.— I expect him every day from Newbury Port.— All has gone very well at home, and all your Friends are in health. Your sisters Family are in affliction by the Death of Gen. Palmer.¹ You will not expect from me, much upon Public affairs. I shall only Say that the federal or more properly national Spirit runs high and bids fair to defeat every insidious as well as open Attempt of its Adversaries. This gives us a comfortable Prospect of a good Government, which is all that will be necessary to our Happiness. Yet I fear that confused and ill digested Efforts at Amendments will perplex for sometime.

I am very Sensible of that Affection which has given the Name to my Grandson, but although I have twice sett the Example of it, I do not approve of the Practice of intermixing the Names of Families. I wish the Child every Blessing from other Motives, besides its name. My Love to Mr & Mrs Smith; the sight of them and their two Sons with you, will give me high Pleasure. I am with the tenderest Affection / your

John Adams

RC (Adams Papers); addressed: "To / Mrs Adams / at Col. Smiths at / Jamaica, Long Island. / to the Care of Mr McCormic / New York"; internal address: "Mrs Adams."; notation: "2.16"; "~~Not~~"; and "Free: / John Adams."

[1] Gen. Joseph Palmer died on 25 Dec., probably due to exposure (*DAB*; *Grandmother Tyler's Book*, p. 89–93).

Abigail Adams to John Adams

my dearest Friend   New york Jan^ry 12th 1788 [1789]

I last wednesday received yours of Dec^br 28 and should have answerd by the post of thursday but that the mail for thursday closes on wednesday Evening and does not give time for any replie to Letters which come by that post. I wrote you from this place on sunday last.[1] at that time I was in hopes I should have been on my journey home before this, as we have every thing in readiness to set out the day that we can get a sufficient quantity of snow. Col Smith will bring me home at all events, even tho I should finally be obliged to come in a carriage which we should be glad to avoid at this Season as the Roads are bad, and the Ferries worse for crossing the stages change at the Ferries, & do not cross at this season

Mrs Smith would even now venture to providance by water rather than be dissapointed of her visit but with a young Baby and at this dangerous Season of the year Her Friends all disswade her. tho I am sometimes more than half a mind to try it, the expence of taking a coach & sending for me at this uncertain period when it might be detain'd by Snow before it reach'd half way, would be really too great and I had rather suffer many inconveniencies than you should attempt it. half a foot of snow or less would answer very well, & we have daily reason to look for it. we have however concluded not to bring william with us, as we imagine he will be much more troublesome than the Baby. this is the Time that I hoped to have been at Home. I know you must be Lonesome—and my Boys want looking after or rather their things.

I am glad to find that Massachusetts behave so well. in this state the Legislature & senate are at such varience that it is not expected that there will be any choice at all, and should that be the case, they have little hopes of keeping Congress here.[2] you judged right with respect to the sitting of Congress. there is not the least probability of there meeting, nor is there any occasion for it, on account of ushering in the New one. for when the New Senate & House come together they chuse a pressident to receive and count the votes from the different States, & declare the choice this is said to be the mode pointed out by the constitution. the next post will bring us the choice of conneticut.[3]

Since my arrival in Town I have received every mark of politeness and attention from this people which I could have desired. Sir John & Lady Temple were among the first to visit me. I have been to Count montier to a Ball given by him;[4] and to the Assembly. I have dinned at one place & supped at an. or nether Sat at table (for suppers I discard), untill I am fully satisfied with dissipating. we have however kept very good Hours, as mrs Jay is like to have an addition to her Family she is obliged to be circumspect.[5] my own Heaeth is much better this winter than it has been for several years. I attribute it much to my Journey. I want to know how you bear the cold. last Evening we had a light fall of snow just sufficient to cover the Grund but it will all run to day. the clouds are however gathering for more. I hope I shall not have occasion to write again before I see you. my Love to the children & to Brother & Sister Cranch with whom I sympathize under their late affliction. I would write to sister—but hope soon to see her. be so good as to tell Brisler that he must keep some of the pears untill we come mr & mrs Jay desire their affectionate Regards to you. he is a plain as a Quaker, and as mild as New milk, but under all this, an abundance of Rogury in his Eye's. I need to say to you who so well know him, that he possesse' an excellent Heart. mrs Jay has all the vivacity of a French woman blended with the modesty & Softness of an American Lady.

adieu visiters call upon me. I have received & returnd more than forty visits already—

Yours affectionatly

Abigail Adams

RC (Adams Papers); addressed by John Jay: "The Hon'ble / John Adams Esqr / Boston"; docketed by JQA: "A. A. / Jany 12th 1789."; notation: "John Jay."

¹ Not found.

² The New York legislature was sharply divided between an Antifederalist-controlled assembly and a Federalist-controlled Senate; consequently, the state failed to choose any presidential electors and had no vote in the first presidential election under the new Constitution. The legislature likewise did not select any representatives until April nor any senators until July (*First Fed. Elections*, 3:197).

³ On 7 Jan., the Connecticut legislature chose seven men to serve as presidential electors: Thaddeus Burr, Matthew Griswold, Jedidiah Huntington, Samuel Huntington, Richard Law, Erastus Wolcott, and Oliver Wolcott Sr. The day before, the legislature had elected five Federalists to represent the state in Congress (*First Fed. Elections*, 2:5, 7).

⁴ For the Comte de Moustier, see Thomas Jefferson to AA, 30 Aug. 1787, note 2, above.

⁵ Sarah Jay gave birth to a son, William Jay, on 16 June 1789 (*DAB*).

Mercy Otis Warren to Abigail Adams

Plimouth feb 3ᵈ 1789

How dos my dear Mʳˢ Adams like the City of New york: its manners & amusements as it may probably be her future residence I hope she found every thing prefectly agreable— shall I hope before you fix in that distant abode that you will make us an Visit at Plimouth: to such a traveler the journey can be nothing. and since that Mʳˢ Adams, friendship is unimpaired: I should think (judging from my own feelings) that no stimulous would be necessary but the recollection of former mutual Confidence & affection. such a Visit would give particular pleasure to me not apt to change her attachments either from time place absence or other accidents—

I hope you left Mʳˢ smith & her little ones well & happy I should be pleased to see the Attention of the young Mother at the head of her Family where I dare say she acquits herself to the approbation of her Friends. her maternal tenderness she has from instinct. her domestic avocations she has been taught by early Example, & her own Good sense will ever make her respectable. you know my partiallity towards her. I loved her from a Child nor has absence made any abatement. therefore you will mention me with affection when you Write again.—

Is my Friend Mʳˢ Montgomery yet sailed for Ireland.—¹ I will not ask any more questions least the number of your replys should preclude some sentiment of your own when I am again Gratifiied with a letter.

My pen has lain Comparitively still this winter, I have been sick: very sick and very long, nor have yet been out since the middle of october. but hope as the spring approaches to revive with the summer insect: & if able to take wing shall probably alight among those whose converse both improves & enlivens the social hour.

If the Coll & M^rs smith should Visit the Massachusets in the spring: before you leave it: I hope they will extend their Journey to Plimouth. & I am sure they have no friends who will recieve them with more sincere Cordiallity than this & your affectionate Friend

M Warren

RC (Adams Papers); addressed: "Mrs Adams / Braintree."

¹ Janet Livingston Montgomery (1743–1828) was the widow of Gen. Richard Montgomery and the eldest child of Margaret Beekman and Robert Livingston. The general had been born in Ireland, and in the summer of 1789, Janet Montgomery went there to visit his family (Katherine M. Babbitt, *Janet Montgomery: Hudson River Squire*, Monroe, N.Y., 1975, p. 3, 14, 20–22; *DAB*).

Elizabeth Smith Shaw to Abigail Adams

My Dear Sister—   Haverhill February 14th. 1789

You cannot think how mortified & grieved I was, by being so *unexpectedly* disappointed, of seeing my dear, long absent Friends last night— Mrs Smith had kindly given me information of the intended Visit—& as the Weather was uncommonly fine, though it had injured the smoothness of the road in some measure, yet *here* it was no impediment to any ones business—

In the full assurance of seeing you here, We had made all the preparation in our Power,— Perhaps you may say, "that should not be much—" However true the remark, yet I hope my friends will never measure my Love & Affection, by the ability I have to express it— Respect, Love, & Esteem on this occasion, would in a particular manner have induced me to exert myself to accommodate my beloved Friends—& We made three Beds, & laid our Table for you— The Clock struck three, four, five, six,—the table still waiting, for we thought if you did not dine, you might sup here— Judge Seargant & Lady, Mr Thaxter & Lady were to drink Tea with us,— So you may fancy to yourself, what a curious figure we made to our Neigbours— Judge Seargant, Mr White, & Mr Thaxter had all sent written Invitations to his Excellency &ccc to dine with him upon such, & such a Day— Four Families of us, were I assure you, most *unmercifully* dissappointed—

Is it not actionable?— What if we should sue for damage?— I fear now you will not be able to make us the Compensation we wish,— that is a Visit— Judge Seargant is obliged to leave the Town next monday, upon his judicial department, & to him he said, "the dissappointment was irreparable"— It might be years before he could have an Opportunity of seeing his old *Friend*— We all mett to Day at his House, looking very sorrowful, heartify sympathizing with each other— Mrs Seargant has been peculiarly unfortunate— Last Fall she shortened her visit to her Friends at Salem, & hastened home, fearing you would come to Town in her absence.

And now the People *say*, they believe, you do not care much for your Haverhill Friends, or you would have tried Wheels, if runners would not answer—for the Snow is so level, that you might have travelled with either—

I did indeed hope that my Brother Adams would have visited in the Town where his three Sons had lived so agreeably (as I suppose they did) in his absence, where they were kindly noticed not only for their own worth, but had respect shewed them, on account of their Fathers Character—

I could not help contrasting the dissapointment we had met with, with the punctuality which our dear Father always observed towards his friends, & say, that if you had one drop of his Blood stiring in your veins, you would have pushed forward, & not have failed coming— Mr Shaw went to Lincoln last week & carried Cousin Betsy, & returned by the way of Medford last Thursday, 38 mile with only one horse, & Mr & Mrs Allen got home from Boston before night last Friday—

Mr Adams must have been very lonely without you this winter,— I have often thought of him, & wondered how he could be willing to let you leave him— I am sure his Daughter is laid under great Obligations by the Sacrifice— Permit me to congratulate you both upon the birth of your second grand son— May he be as great a Patriot—as wise, & good as his grand sire— I have not room to say more than that I am your Sister   E Shaw

RC (Adams Papers).

Abigail Adams to Sarah Livingston Jay

my dear madam   Braintree Febry 20th 1789

When I left your Hospitable mansion, I did not design so many days should have elapsed, before I had express'd to you the pleasing sense I entertaind of your kindness and Friendship. they have left a durable impression upon my mind, and an ardent desire to cultivate them in future.

I reachd Home Ten days after I left Newyork. we had an agreeable journey, good Roads fine weather and tolerable accommodations. our Musk and Lemon Brandy were of great service to us, and we never faild to Toast the donor, Whilst our Hearts were warmed by the Recollection. I hope my dear madam that your Health is better than when I left you, and this not for your own sake only, but for that of your worthy partner, who I am sure sympathized so much with you, that he never really Breakfasted the whole time I was with you; my best Regards attend him. I hope both he and you will one day do me the Honour of visiting Braintree, where I would do all within my power to Render the fireside as social and as pleasing as I found Broad Way.

If Miss Levingston is still with you pray present my Regards to her.[1] my Love to Master Peter, the Grave Maria & the sprightly little French Girl.[2] Compliments to Mrs Knox to Lady Kitty, and to all the other Ladies from whom I received particular attentions whilst at Newyork,[3] and do me the Favour to let me hear from you by the first opportunity— This Letter will be deliverd to you by mr Ames, the Suffolk Representitive, a Young Gentlemen of an amiable Character and very good abilities,[4] he was so good as to offer to take Charge of any letters I might have for Newyork. I have embraced this opportunity to present my little Friend Maria with a Book which I hope may be pleasing & usefull to her

mr Adams joins me in affectionate Regards to mr Jay, & best wishes for your Health and happiness— be assured I am my dear Madam with sentiments / of Esteem and Regard Your / Friend & Humble Servant   Abigail Adams

RC (NNC:John Jay Papers); addressed: "To / Mrs Sarah jay— / Newyork"; endorsed: "Mrs: Adams / 20 Feby: 1789."

[1] Probably Susan Livingston (1748–1840), Sarah Jay's sister, who married John Cleves Symmes in 1794 (*Selected Letters of John Jay and Sarah Livingston Jay: Correspondence by or to the First Chief Justice of the United States and His Wife*, ed. Landa M. Freeman and others, Jefferson, N.C., 2005, p. 8).

[2] The three surviving Jay children: Peter Augustus (1776–1843), Maria (1782–1856), and Ann (Nancy, 1783–1856), who was born in Paris during the peace negotiations (same, p. 12, 22).

[3] Probably Catherine Alexander Duer, for whom see vol. 6:230, note 13.

[4] Fisher Ames (1758–1808), Harvard 1774, a lawyer from Dedham, Mass., served in Congress from 1789 to 1797 (*DAB*).

William Stephens Smith to John Adams

Dear Sir—   Newyork april 6[th.] 1789—

M[r:] Bourne has this moment waited upon me and informs, that he has been honoured by the senate with the appointment of being the Bearer of their Dispatches to you, relative to your election as Vice President of the Western Empire, upon which please to accept of my affectionate congratulations and of my sincere prayers that Heaven may guide and protect you in this great Career—[1] The Virtuous members of this Government are very anxious to see you here, they promise themselves great aid in their pursuits from your Council and influence, and I am sure you will not fail in being here as soon as possible, your Country expects that your motions will be rapid after you recieve the official information, and when you consider that during the interregnum, the United states loose one thousand *p[r.] Diem*, I am sure you will haste to shelter them all in your power from greater loss—

My Calculation is that if this Gentleman travels by Land this will be presented to you on saturday next but If with a fair Wind he attempts the Water Communication, it may possibly reach you before— but Calculating on the former, I take the liberty of supposing that you will finish the Governors Ceremony on monday and rest, tranquilly at Watertown the same Evening, so that agreable to Contract you will arrive here on the Monday following, in which case I will meet you 15 or 20 miles out of town and inform you of the opinions at present Circulating here—[2] I think it will be of service that M[rs:] Adams should accompany you, for various reasons, both public & private, which it may be as well not to commit to paper— should you not leave Braintree before Monday, will you be so good as to write me by sunday's post informing me of your arrangements, and intentions,[3] this Letter will reach me the saturday night before you, and give me some hours to arrange my movements and to meet you prepared to relieve M[rs:] Adams from the hurry and Ceremony which will accompany your reception

for further particulars I refer you to the Letter from M[rs:] Smith to her Mama[4] and am / D[r.] Sir, Yours affectionately   W: S: Smith

RC (Adams Papers).

[1] While the new federal government was scheduled to begin meeting on 4 March, the Senate did not have a quorum until 6 April (the House achieved a quorum on 1 April). Accordingly, on that day, Congress counted the ballots from the first electoral college.

George Washington was elected president unanimously. JA was elected vice president with 34 electoral votes (out of a total possible 69 votes); the remaining votes were split among several other candidates (*First Fed. Cong.*, 1:7–9; 3:7).

The Senate appointed Sylvanus Bourne to notify JA of the election results. Bourne (1761–1817), Harvard 1779, was from Boston originally; he would later serve as the American consul at Amsterdam from 1794 to 1817 and have an extensive correspondence with JQA (*First Fed. Cong.*, 1:9; *Harvard Quinquennial Cat.*; Cornelis A. van Minnen, *American Diplomats in the Netherlands, 1815–50*, N.Y., 1993, p. 21).

[2] Bourne arrived in Boston with the news of JA's election on Thursday, 9 April, and JA set off for New York on the following Monday, 13 April. Much fanfare marked the event: "On this happy occasion, his Excellency our worthy Governour and Com-

mander in Chief exhibited every possible mark of attention and respect for the Vice-President of our great American Republick, by ordering a military escort of Horse to attend him through the counties of Suffolk, Middlesex and Worcester, by giving an elegant colation at his house to a numerous collection of gentlemen who assembled there to take leave of the Vice-President, and by various honourary notices, both civil and military, which the Governour most opportunely displayed, and which our patriotick countryman richly merited." For a complete description of the festivities accompanying JA's departure, see *Massachusetts Centinel*, 15 April, and Boston *Independent Chronicle*, 16 April.

[3] JA's reply has not been found but based on WSS to JA, 19 April (Adams Papers), it was dated 10 April.

[4] Not found.

James Lovell to Abigail Adams

April 12th. 89.

M[r]. Du*err*, as you pronounce it, and my Wife seem to think alike as to the Powers of an Ambassadress when placed as an Helpmate to the Ambassador. M[r] D. had an Idea of an handsome Face M[rs]. L thought only of the Good Sense of the Lady. If this is *ambiguous*, y[r]. best Friend can make it plain so far as relates to Du*err*.[1]

As to M[rs]. L I will show her to you in a Minute, just as She appeared the first Instant her Eyes were opened this Morning "Well M[r]: Lovell I think as others do, you are too confident about your office;— you ought to go to New York;— One of your main Expectations has failed you already;— your Friend Portia is *not* going on to Congress." Good Morning Ma'am, replied I, "I am *sorry for that*."—a Pause—

Indeed, Portia, there was not so much Compliment in my Reply as a Stranger would guess there was. "I am sorry," because I could say twenty Things to you which I would not *dare* to trouble your Husband with. I could talk to *you* about Insurgents, and the Tools of the Tools of Insurgents, down to *the Successor* of the Successor of your humble Servant late a Naval officer, for the Port of Boston. But really I should not have thought of this Subject if I had not heard it said Yesterday by one of the veriest of that Tribe "*my* Friends have spooken to M[r]. Adams about *me*." Curses on their Impudence! it makes no Odds to them whether Virtue or Vice is in Rule; they *hope* with good Grounds under the latter and they *dare* to ask Patronage of the former. In this Commonwealth, I have seen them have every Advantage. Vice triumphant, they have turned out of Place whom they would; and upon a Change in Government they held their Offices because the virtuous would not take the *vicious* Mode of turning any Man out who *did his Duty* let him have gotten into office how he might. By being the accidental but *Kidney,*— Deputy of Nat. Barber for 3 *Months* only, the present Naval Officer was preferred before John Rice who had served 3 *years*, with me faithfully scientifically & amiably. But I would only be understood here as remarking who ought *not* to have the Naval office of this Port. leaving it totally with my Betters to say who shall have it.[2] The present Incumbent *may* have *one* advocate at Head Quarters if M[r.] O should be chosen Clerk of the Senate.

"Scratch *now* for me and I will *always* scratch for you," has been the perpetual Rule of that *republican Electioneering Set*, to which the Two in Question belonged— A caucasing-Town-Meeting Bulldog like Barber or one of a more sly least like his Successor, must have had many Promises of *future* Friendship from would-be Representatives Senators & Governors in this Town, who thought that the Road of Promises was the broad one to Preferment.

I am Madam, yours respectfully   J L

RC (Adams Papers).

[1] James Lovell and AA briefly revived their correspondence for three letters after a five-year hiatus. He also wrote to JA on this same date seeking an office in the new government (Adams Papers). For more on Lovell's unusual letter-writing style, and his correspondence with AA, see vol. 3:xxxiv–xxxv.

[2] Lovell had been appointed naval officer for the port of Boston in July 1784, succeed-

ing Nathaniel Barber, with John Rice serving as his deputy. Lovell remained in that position until 1787 when he was replaced by Barber. The state again named Lovell to the post later in 1789 (vol. 5:355, 357–358; *Fleet's Pocket Almanack*, 1785, p. 26; 1786, p. 20; 1787, p. 39; 1788, p.55; *Sibley's Harvard Graduates*, 14:45).

John Adams to Abigail Adams

My dear   Havilands at Rye. April 19. 1789

I have been so diligent on the Road and so much interrupted by Company at the Taverns that this is the first time I have been able to get an opportunity to write to you. We arrived at this house last night (Saturday) Shall rest here to day and go into N. York tomorrow.—[1] at Hartford, the Manufacturers presented me with a Piece of

Broadcloth, for a Suit of Cloaths. at N. Haven the Corporation presented me with the Freedom of their City.— at both these Towns the Gentlemen came out to meet us, and went out with us.—[2] at Horseneck, we were met by Major Pintard, & Captain Mandeville with a Party of Horse from the State of New York, and there is to be much Parade on Monday.—[3] Before this I presume, the Printers in Boston, have inserted in their Gazettes, the Debates of the House of Representatives, which are conducted with open Galleries.[4]

This Measure, by making the Debates public will establish the national Government, or break the Confederation. I can conceive of no medium between these Extremes.— By the Specimens that I have seen, they go on with great Spirit, in preparing the Impost, which is a favourable omen.— My Love to the Children and Duty to my Mother, &c.   John Adams.

RC (Adams Papers); addressed: "Mrs Adams / at Mr John Adams's / Braintree."

[1] First run by Dr. Ebenezer Haviland and later by his widow, Tamar, Haviland's Tavern (also known as the Square House) had been a popular stopping point on the Post Road in Rye, N.Y., since about 1770. JA had previously visited the tavern at least twice, riding to and from the Continental Congress in 1774 (Charles W. Baird, *Chronicle of a Border Town: History of Rye, Westchester County, New York, 1660–1870*, N.Y., 1871, p. 145–147; *D&A*, 2:102, 158).

[2] On 16 April, JA passed through Hartford where "an escort of the principle gentlemen in town, the ringing of Bells, and the attention of the Mayor and Aldermen of the Corporation, marked the Federalism of the Citizens, and their high respect for that distinguished patriot and statesman" (Hartford *American Mercury*, 20 April).

That same day, the city of New Haven voted to give JA "all the rights Privileges and immunities of a free Citizen of the said City of New Haven" (Adams Papers). Ezra Stiles noted in his literary diary that on 17 April JA

"was escorted into T^o^ by 35 or 40 Horse & phps 60 Chaises. . . . He rested in the City an Hour, when the Diploma of the Freedom of it was presented to him" (*The Literary Diary of Ezra Stiles, D.D., LL.D.*, ed. Franklin Bowditch Dexter, 3 vols., N.Y., 1901, 3:351).

[3] The *Norwich Packet* reported that "the light horse of West Chester county" escorted JA's entourage from the Connecticut line to Kingsbridge. Major Pintard was probably Lewis Pintard (1732–1818) of New Rochelle, a merchant who had assisted American prisoners in New York during the Revolution. John Mandeville was named captain of the Westchester Light Horse in 1786 and served until 1790 (*Norwich Packet*, 8 May; *DAB*; Hugh Hastings, comp. and ed., *Military Minutes of the Council of Appointment of the State of New York, 1783–1821*, 4 vols., Albany, 1901, 1:80, 178).

[4] The Boston *Herald of Freedom* began printing the debates on 14 April; various other Boston newspapers soon followed suit.

Abigail Adams to John Adams

my dearest Friend   Braintree April 22^d^ 1789

I received mr Bourn's Letter to day, dated this day week, and I was very happy to Learn by it that you had made so Rapid a progress.[1] I hope you stoped at my old acquaintance Avery's, and that you met with as good entertainment as I had led you to expect. all your Friends rejoiced in the fine weather which attended you, and conceive it, a propitious omen. I enjoyed, the Triumph tho I did not partake the 'Gale, and perhaps my mind might have been a little Elated upon the Late occasion if I had not have lived Long enough in the world to have seen the fickleness of it, yet to give it, its due, it blew from the right point on that day.

Mr Allen was so polite as to come out to Braintree to day to know if I had any Letters or package that I wish'd to send forward to you, & that he would take them. I pomis'd to forward a Letter & News papers. mr A. I presume has *buisness* of *importance* by his return so soon. I hope it is not an office that a Friend of yours now hold's, and who is in some little anxiety about his own Fate. I received a Letter from him this Evening. I will inclose it by *an other* opportunity, yet I promisd to mention to you what I conceived almost, or quite needless, because I knew your sentiments with respect to him so well, that I was sure you would interest yourself for his continuance in office whatever the *System* might be. if I have written a little ambiguously you may the more easily guess at the person meant.[2]

The Children are now at home. Charles tells me that the Class which take their degree leave colledge the 21 of June and that if you have occasion for him he can come on as soon after that day as you wish, that he can have his degree as well as if he was present. he seems to be fond of the thought of getting rid of the parade of commencment. if it would be no injury to him, I should be equally fond of getting rid of a trouble in which there is very little Satisfaction, a good deal of expence & generally many affronts given by omissions

I mentiond it to the dr & he approves it. I wrote thus early that I might know your mind upon the subject. you will give me the earliest information respecting prospects I hope you will be carefull of your Health, and be enabled to go through the arduous task in which you are engaged. I wish to hear from you as often as possible. my Love to mrs Smith & childr[en.] Let Brisler know that his wife & child are very cleverly, that she is able to Nurse it, & much better than she was before she was confin'd[3] mr Bass moves tomorrow into our House.[4] I have reserved a part of it for Esther if Brisler should continue at Newyork, and that will obviate the difficuly of being alone in a House. I had the misfortune of loosing one of the Young creatures a day or two after you left me by the Horn sickness it faild of eating in the morning & before I could get any body to it, it was dead— the Horns were hollow upon inspection but I suppose your Farm is quite out of your head by this Time & you will only think of it as a departed Friend, & without the consolation of thinking its situation better'd, the 20 Trees are all set out, & came in good order.

I am my dearearst Friend / most affectionatly yours

A Adams—

RC (Adams Papers); addressed: "To / His Excellency John Adams / vice President of the united states / Newyork"; endorsed: "Portia / 22[d.] Ap. 1789. / ans[d.] 1. May. by Brisler." Some loss of text where the seal was removed.

[1] Not found.

[2] See James Lovell to AA, 12 April, above, and AA to Lovell, 22 April, below.

[3] The Brieslers had a second daughter, named Abigail, early in 1789 (Sprague, *Braintree Families*, p. 829).

[4] Possibly Joseph Bass (1723–1800) and his wife Hannah Banks Bass (Sprague, *Braintree Families*, p. 376; AA to JA, 14 March 1794, Adams Papers). See also Cotton Tufts to AA, 20 July, below.

Abigail Adams to James Lovell

My Dear Sir   Braintree April 22. 1789

I this evening received your letter of April 12[th.] tho' you love a labyrinth you always give a clue. M[r] & M[rs] L may be assured that an old friend so well qualified for the office he holds will not be forgotten, and that it would be of little consequence whether P: is at Braintree or N York.[1] M[r] L is surely sufficiently acquainted with my friend to know that he may be sure of his interest. I presume the enquiry will be in the appointment of offices, Who now holds them? Are they qualified? Have they discharged the office with fidelity? Why displace a man worthy of his trust? I know M[r] A is sufficiently sensible of the importance of having the naval office filled by a gentleman of firmness and integrity, and I can scarcely think there can be any occasion of calling to his mind the man who in former times has fought by his side and of whose indefatigable industry and perseverance in the cause of his country he is so perfectly acquainted, and whose sufferings he has felt! Yet that P——a may have the merit of a mite She has this evening in a letter to her best friend reminded him that there are persons upon the spot and going there who think to carry their point by solicitation and unwearied application the method by which the Clerkship to the Senate was carried

My best regards attend M[rs] Lovell who has really flattered me by hinting that it was in my power to serve her or her family, of this I am sure I cannot fail if my power be half equal to my inclination

I am &c &c &c &c   A A

Tr in MCHA's hand (Adams Papers).

[1] That is, Portia, AA herself.

John Adams to Abigail Adams

My dearest Friend   New York. April 22. 1789

This is the first Moment I have been able to Seize, in order to acquaint you of my Arrival and Situation. Governor Clinton The
Mayor of New York,[1] all the old officers of the Continental Government, and the Clergy, Magistrates and People, have Seemed to emu-
late the two houses of Congress, in shewing every respect to me and
to my office.— For Particulars I must refer you to the public Papers.[2]
Yesterday for the first time I attended the Senate. Tomorrow or next
day, The President is expected.— M[r] Jay with his usual Friendship,
has insisted on my taking Apartments in his noble house. No Provision No Arrangement, has been made for the President or Vice P.—
and I See, clearly enough, that Minds are not conformed to the
Constitution, enough, as yet, to do any Thing, which will Support
the Government in the Eyes of the People or of Foreigners. our
Country mens Idea of the "L'Air imposant" is yet confined to volun-
teer Escorts, verbal Compliments &c.

You and I however, are the two People in the World the best
qualified for this Situation. We can conform to our Circumstances.— And if They determine that We must live on little, We will
not Spend much.— every Body enquires respectfully / for M[rs] A. of
her affectionate   J. A.

RC (Adams Papers).

[1] James Duane.
[2] The *Massachusetts Centinel* reported on
29 April that "the Cavalcade which escorted
his Excellency into the city, was numerous,
and truly respectable." Among those meeting
JA was a military escort, members of Congress, and "a large number of citizens, in
carriages and on horseback. On passing the
fort, a federal salute was fired. His Excellency alighted at the house of the Hon. John
Jay, Esq."

Abigail Adams to John Adams

my dearest Friend   Braintree April 26. 1789

Major Gibbs Captain Beals & mr Woodard all are going to New-
york, and all have desired Letters, but as they all go at the same Time
one Letter must answer.[1] I wrote you this week by mr Allen, since
which nothing has transpired in our little village worth communicating. the Newspapers I inclose to you all that I get in the course of a
week, but the printers or the persons to whom they are committed,
think as you are absent, it is of little concequence whether I get

them or not. the Torrent has subsided & a calm has ensued. Laco I see has advertized his *Works* to be sold in a pamphlet[2]

I wish to know where & How you are accommodated, and what ever else you may think proper to communicate. I have heard only once from you at Hartford & fear I must wait a week longer, before any intelligence reaches me. pray is it prudent discreet or wise, that the debates of the House should be publish'd in the crude indigisted manner in which they appear to be given to the publick?—

Have you seen your little Grandsons yet? how is mrs Smith I hope she will write me I shall be very lonesome when our sons are gone to colledg Next week, only I am buissy about the Garden, tho I have had Time to get very little done. I have been obliged to have all the wall of the great pasture poled the sheep became so troublesome & wandered every where, & to day have been building the wall against Mr Bass—

The Family are well. Esther is tolerable the Baby has a bad soar mouth— pray burn all these Scribles for fear you should leave or drop any of them—any where

Let me know how you do— I cannot Say I am very well, tho better for this fortnight than I was before you went away. I hope your journey will be of service to you but I fear too much perplexity in Buisness for you.

adieu & believe me most affectionatly / Yours—

Abigail Adams

RC (Adams Papers); addressed by TBA: "His Excellency John Adams / Vice President of the United States, / New York—"; endorsed: "Portia. Apr 6. / 1789"; notation: "Favored by / Mʳ Woodward."

[1] Major Caleb Gibbs (ca. 1750–1818) had commanded Washington's bodyguards from 1776 to 1779. He later served as the civilian superintendent of the Charlestown Navy Yard (James Archer O'Reilly III, *Memorials of the Massachusetts Society of the Cincinnati*, Boston, 2004, p. 142–143).

[2] Stephen Higginson, writing under the pseudonym Laco, published a series of articles attacking John Hancock in the *Massachusetts Centinel*. These pieces were gathered together and printed as *The Writings of Laco, as Published in the Massachusetts Centinel, in the Months of February and March, 1789*, Boston, 1789 (Boston *Independent Chronicle*, 23 April).

John Quincy Adams to Abigail Adams

Newbury-Port April 27ᵗʰ: 1789.

I expected to have received ere this some Letters either from Braintree or Boston; But excepting what I have collected from the Newspapers I have heard neither directly nor indirectly from either. Had any good opportunity for sending, presented itself I should have written, although the only topic of information, would have been concerning myself.— The sum total of my news is that since I return'd to this place, my health has been better than at any time since last September; and that scarcely any thing of my complaints remains, except the spasms, which are not frequent, nor very troublesome.

I hope you have not given up the thoughts of making a tour to Haverhill, and shall be ready to meet you there, upon the shortest notice.— I should wish to know, when you expect to set out for New-York, and whether you depend upon my attendance.— It is possible that circumstances may be so situated, as to render it inconvenient for me to leave this place, in the course of the ensuing summer.— If you should not go, till the latter end of June, and my Father should be willing that Charles should be absent from Commencement, I imagine there would be no great difficulty in obtaining leave from the College government, and he might attend you.— However; if Circumstances should not be very untoward, I shall be able to go; and my own inclinations, induce me to wish much to go; as it will probably be the only opportunity I shall have to see my Sister, and perhaps my other friends, for several years to come.

M^rs: Hay is going away this morning, and I fear I shall lose the opportunity unless I come speedily close.

Your dutiful Son—   J. Q. Adams.

P. S. There are in a draw of one of the desks or tables in the chamber where I lodg'd a pair of old silver buckles. I wish to have them sent to me. If you will please to give them to W. Cranch, he will transmit them—

RC (Adams Papers); addressed: "M^rs: A. Adams. / Braintree."; docketed: "J Q Adams / April 27th 1789"; notation: "Hon^d: by / M^rs: Hay."

Abigail Adams to John Adams

my dearest Friend   Braintree May 1. 1789

I received your kind favours of the 19 & 22 of April. the printers were very obliging in taking particular care to supply me daily with the paper's by which I learnt the arrival and Reception of the Pressident, & vice Pressident. if I thought I could compliment in so courtly and masterly a stile, I would say that the address to the Senate was exactly what it ought to be, neither giving too little, or too much, it has been much admired, yet every one do not see the force of the first part of it;[1] when I read the debates of the House, I could not but be surprized at their permitting them to be open, and thought it would have been a happy circustance if they could have found a dr Johnson for the Editor of them. I think there is much of the old leaven in the New Loaf "I dare not lay a duty upon salt, the people will not bear it, I dread the concequences to the people" is a language to teach the people to rise up in opposition to Government, the people would bear a 5 pr ct duty upon every article imported, & expect as much, but will grumble perhaps at the duty upon molasses. be sure it is a little hard for *us Yankees* who Love it so well & make such liberal use of it, it has already raised the price of it here. I hope the Senate will never consent to draw backs. it will be a constant source of knavery, will not small duties operate best, be most productive and least atroxious? Johnson, whom you know I have lately been reading with great attention, and have become his great admirer, more fully convinc'd than ever, that he was a very accurate observer of Human Life & manners. Johnson in one of his papers proves that there is no such thing as domestick Greatness—[2] such is the constitution of the world that much of Life must be spent in the same manner by the wise & the Ignorant the exalted and the low. Men However distinguish'd by external accidents or intrinsick qualities, have all the same wants, the same pains, and as far as the senses are consulted the same pleasures. the petty cares and petty duties are the same in every station to every understanding, and every hour brings us some occasion on which we all sink to the Common level. we are all naked till we are dressed, and hungry till we are fed. the Generals Triumph and Sage's disputation, end like the Humble Labours of the smith or plowman in a dinner or a sleep— Let this plead my excuse when I frequently call of your attention from weighty National objects to the petty concerns of domestick Life. I have been trying to dispose of the stock on Hand, but no purchaser appears—immediate profit is what all seek, or credit, where little is to be given. the weather is cold the spring backward, and the stock expensive. you will not wonder that I am puzzeld what to do, because I am in a situation which I never was before. yours I presume cannot be much better the Bill is setled with 48£· 18s damages— vacancy is up and the children have returnd to Cambridge.

my best Respects attend mr Jay and his Lady whose health I hope is mended. you do not mention mrs Smith or the little Boys—nor have I heard from them since mr Bourn came. by the way I heard a

Report yesterday that Marble Head & Salem had voted you an anual present of ten Quintals of fish.—³ how well founded the Report is I can not presume to say, time must determine it. I want to hear how you do & how you can bear the application & confinement of your office. I say nothing about comeing. you will know when it will be proper & give me timely notice. the Children desired me to present their duty. I am my dearest Friend with the tenderest affection ever yours—   Abigail Adams

Esther is very impatient to hear from her Husband the child is better & she comfortable put your Frank upon your Letters if you please

RC (Adams Papers); docketed: "Mrs Adams 1st May."

¹ JA was introduced to the Senate on 21 April, at which time he addressed the members, praising them as "celebrated defenders of the liberties of this country" and George Washington as "one, whose commanding talents and virtues, whose over-ruling good fortune have so completedly united all hearts and voices in his favor." He went on—anticipating some of his later difficulties as president of the Senate—to offer an apology: "Not wholly without experience in public assemblies, I have been more accustomed to take a share in their debates, than to preside in their deliberations. It shall be my constant endeavor to behave towards every member of this MOST HONORABLE body with all that consideration, delicacy, and decorum which becomes the dignity of his station and charcter: But, if from inexperience, or inadvertency, any thing should ever escape me, inconsistent with propriety, I must entreat you, by imputing it to its true cause, and not to any want of respect, to pardon and excuse it." For the full text of JA's address, see *First Fed. Cong.*, 1:21–23. It was first published in full in Boston in the *Massachusetts Centinel*, 29 April. No MS copy of the speech is extant in the Adams Papers.

² In *The Idler*, No. 51, Samuel Johnson wrote, "It has been commonly remarked, that eminent men are least eminent at home, that bright characters lose much of their splendor at a nearer view, and many who fill the world with their fame, excite very little reverence among those that surround them in their domestick privacies." James Boswell entitled this essay "Domestick Greatness Unattainable" in his *Life of Samuel Johnson, LL.D.*, 2 vols., London, 1791.

³ On 16 March, the inhabitants of Marblehead voted to address to JA their thanks "for your faithful and unshaken patronage of the Fisheries. . . . We therefore being now legally assembled in Town Meeting pray your Excellency to accept this our Unanimous Address as expressing Our Sence of those essential benefits which now we enjoy in the preservation of the Fishery, for which we believe Ourselves more Especially indebted to your Excellency. while we are enjoying the fulness of those, benefits we pray your Excellency will indulge us to furnish your Table with a Small Share of the fruits of your good Services" (Adams Papers). See also AA to JA, 25 Oct., note 3, below.

John Adams to Abigail Adams

My dearest Friend   New York May 1. 1789

It has been impossible to get time to write you.— Morning, Noon, and Night, has been taken up with Business, or Visits.— Yesterday the President was Sworn, amidst the Acclamations of the People.—

But I must refer you to Gazettes & Spectators.—[1] I write this abed.—
M[r] Allen del[d.] me, Yesterday your Letter.— I like very much your
Plan of coming on, with Charles and Thomas, before Commencement. But as yet I have no House, nor Furniture.— When you come
you must bring, Table & Chamber Linnen and the Plate, and I expect, some beds.— But all is uncertain as yet.— You may send by a
Stage, or a Cart to Providence and there embark, many necessary
Things in the Packett.— The House of Representatives will I hope,
soon determine some thing.— But my Expectations are not raised.—
I fear We shall be Straightened, and put to difficulty to live decently.— We must however live in Proportion to our means.

The President has received me with great Cordiality, of affection
and Confidence, and eve[ry] Thing has gone very agreably. His Lady
is expected this Month.

My Duty to my Mother, Love to Brothers Adams Cranch &c &
sisters and every friendly, grateful sentiment to our Honourable D[r.]
our Guardian Protector & Friend, and to M[r] Quincy, whom I had
not opportunity to see, before I came away, and to all other friends
& Acquaintance &c.

I ought to thank Capt[n.] Beal, Mr Allen Mr Black &c for their
obliging Attention in accompanying me, on my Journey.

You will receive by Barnard, some more fruit Trees. The Ladies
universally enquire very respectfully after M[rs] Adams, when she will
arrive &c.

The last Sunday, I Spent very agreably at Col Smiths.— Nabby
and the Children very well. William, had no Knowledge of me, but
John knew me at first glance.

I long to take a Glance at my [farm?] but this cannot be.— write
me as often as you can.— Yours with the tenderest Affection.

John Adams.

I have Sent the Horse. You may sell him or give him to my worthy
son John, for his Health, if you think it possible to pay for his Keeping.

RC (Adams Papers); addressed: "M[rs] Adams / Braintree." Some loss of text
where the seal was removed.

[1] For the 30 April inauguration of George Washington and JA, see Descriptive List of Illustrations, No. 9, above. The *Massachusetts Centinel*, 6 May, was the first Boston newspaper to
report on the occasion.

9. "FEDERAL HALL, THE SEAT OF CONGRESS,"
BY AMOS DOOLITTLE, 1790
See page xv

Elizabeth Smith Shaw to Abigail Adams

My Dear Sister—   Haverhill May 2ᵈ 1789

By the News Papers, I find you have met with a temporary Loss—
The United suffrages of my countrymen have once more taken my
Brother Adams from *you*—from rural retirement—& the sweets of
domestic Life, & again placed him in the political Hemisphere,
where his merit—his knowledge—his patriotism—his virtue, will (I
presume) shine with conspicuous Lustre, though surrounded by a
multitude of bright Luminaries—

It is indeed a new & untried Scene which he is now called to act
in, & I do not wonder that your considerate, & reflecting mind feels
a degree of solicitude, & anxiety— Great heights we know are always
dangerous, but more espicially, (as[1] you have most strikingly represented it) "When glazed with Ice—" & surrounded by those, who
from base, & mercenary motives, may wish their ruin— The best
Hearts, the wisest, & the coolest Heads we know are requisite— And
those who are entrusted with the Care of national Government,
need in a peculiar manner to make the prayer of the King of Israel,
that they may know how to give Laws to this great People—[2] Yet after all, the operation of the wisest, & most equitable Laws (says Dr
Gibbons)[3] is uncertain— It depends upon the temper, the genius, &
even the Climate—[4]

But I quit this subject, & beg to know when I am to be favoured
with the promised visit— I hope you will not come without letting
me know of it beforehand, because this is a very busy Season, for
those of us, who depend cheifly upon homespun for their cloathing—& I would wish to sweep the flax, & the Tow from the Hearth at
lest— Industry is the Basis of Independance, & can the Daughters of
America look more lovely, than when they "seek wool, & flax, &
work digligently with their hands"?—[5]

Your eldest Son has made us one short visit the other Day— He
could stay but one night, because he came on buisiness He was well
the last week, but complains that he has not heard from any of you,
since he went to Newbury— My other Nephews I suppose have been
with you— I can find their visits to their Uncle, & Aunt have been
much less frequent, since their Mamma's return,—& I cannot wonder at it— But they must not forget how much we love their Company—

343

Judge Seargants Family being so near to us—is a most agreeable Circumstance. We are really very happy in a mutual desire, to render kind Offices to each other—

Mr & Mrs Thaxter are in better health than they were some-time past— Mr Thaxter is one of the most benevolent Men in the world— The People bless him—& wish him length of Days—which I think is something remarkable considering his Profession—[6] I often think his Character answers in some measure to that of the Man of Ross—[7]

Do not let it be long, before I have the pleasure of seeing you here—

You have an Nephew, & two Neices who wish most ardently for the pleasure—

But I hope your visit will not be, when the Judge & his Lady are out of Town—

Adieu my Dear Sister, & / believe me most affectionately Yours

Elizabeth Shaw—

RC (Adams Papers).

[1] Opening parenthesis supplied.

[2] In 1 Kings, 3:7–12, Solomon asks the Lord to grant him the understanding he needs to become a wise king of Israel and "to judge this thy so great a people."

[3] Closing parenthesis supplied.

[4] Thomas Gibbons, *Sympathy with Our Suffering Brethren, and an Improvement of Their Distresses Shewn to Be Our Duty*, Lon- don, 1755.

[5] Proverbs, 31:13.

[6] John Thaxter practiced law in Haverhill.

[7] The Man of Ross, described in Pope's *Moral Essays*, "Epistle III. Of the Use of Riches," was John Kyrle of Ross, Hereford- shire, who was known for his public spirit- edness (Brewer, *Reader's Handbook*).

John Adams to Abigail Adams

My dear Portia   New York May 3. 1789

I must finally conclude to request of you to come on to New York as soon as possible and bring Charles and Thomas both with you if you can— if they cannot come at present let them follow as soon as they can be permitted.— I design they shall both Spend the Vacation here at least.— I want your Advice about furniture and House. bring Polly Taylor with you.— You had better land on Long Island and go directly to Jamaica to Mrs Smiths. The Journey to Providence is not much and the Passage from thence pleasant, at this season. My Love to all   John Adams.

RC (Adams Papers).

Abigail Adams to John Adams

My dearest Friend   Braintree May 5th 1789

Mr Dawes sent me word that he was going to Newyork this week. I would not omit any opportunity of writing to you, tho I know I must sometimes perplex you with domestick matters I would not do it, but that I wish your advise and direction.

I wrote you in my last that the wall was compleated between mr Bass & you, and Barley has been sown. the Hill before the window, your Brother has had cleard of stones, & gatherd up the overpluss manure and laid where directed. I requested him to dispose of the young stock if he could, but he has not been able to. I procured a load of Salt Hay for the stock since you went away pay'd Thayer 6[£.] 12[s] 11[d] for the Hay I had of him, & this day am obliged to purchase more English Hay. the wall upon the Hill was poled agreeable to your direction & the sheep put there & Hay given them, but the season is so backward & the flock so large that they are pinch'd. the dr has agreed to take off this week 3 Heffers & the 10 weathers[1] & pay the childrens Quarter Bills which amounts to Sixteen pounds. thus two anxieties I am relieved from But your Brother upon clearing this Hill insists upon it, that it is trod down so hard by the cattle that it will produce no grass this year and the best thing which can be done with it, is to plow it up. to this I could give no consent, knowing how averse you were to any such thing, but yesterday hearing that a Tax Bill was comeing out this month, he got quite discouraged & came to tell me that he would not have any thing to do with the place for that he should never get suffcent of from it, to pay the Taxes— I offered him a part of the sheep, that he should take 20 & leave half the profits of them, Lambs & wool this year, or I would do any thing reasonable that he should desire. as I had not been abl to part with the oxen, French should help cart out the manure but he was sure that you would think he might make so much more than it was possible for him to, that you certainly set him down for Knave or fool—& he would hade no further concern with it, unless it was to render me any assistance— I hope however he will consider further about it, in the mean Time I wish you would write to him, or me; the manner in which Glover has Beals's place is I suppose a reason with him for thinking that he cannot make this answer. I have got Finil to work with French & must get the manure upon the Grass as soon as possible— I will exert myself to the best of my ability, but it really worried me so much that I could not sleep last Night— the Cows have not calf'd yet, & really every thing seem's to have gone wrong, veal has got to two pence pr pound. Spear brought me a Parish Rate this week of three pounds 16 shilling & Eleven pence[2] and yesterday col Thayer sent a deed of the woodland.[3]

As you were always Remarkable at a difficult case, I wish you would direct me what to do with those which at present surround me

pray burn all my Letters I suppose you are perplexd with National difficulties which will puzzel you as much as my domestick affairs do me. it is hard to have both I have not heard from you since the 22ᵈ of April— we are well as usual. yours affectionately

Abigail Adams

RC (Adams Papers).

[1] Wethers are male sheep, usually castrated (*OED*).

[2] Probably Lt. Seth Spear who served as assessor for the North Precinct of Braintree until March 1789 (*Braintree Town Records*, p. 579, 585).

[3] The Adamses purchased a six-acre lot of woodland from Ebenezer Thayer Jr. on 16 Feb. (Adams Papers, Wills and Deeds, Deacon John Adams and JA, 1736–1822).

Abigail Adams to John Quincy Adams

my dear son   Braintree May 5ᵗʰ 1789

Mrs Hay call'd, and left me your Letter. tho I have not written to you before I have had you constantly upon my mind, and have been anxious for your Health. I have heard of you several times. I think you would mind an advantage in drinking valerian & camomile Tea, for those spasm's you complain of. I am not able to say to you as yet, when I shall go to Newyork. I have received only one Letter from your Father since he arrived there, & that was written two days after he got there. he was then at mr Jays, who would not permit him to go to Lodgings, & no arrangment had then been made. The News papers give you all their movements, and more than in prudence ought to be made publick— I was much surprizd to find there debates open. I cannot think any National advantage will arrise from this measure

Pray how did you like the address to the Senate? it has been much admired this way. I think with you respecting Charles's going to Newyork, and I had written to your Father upon the Subject. I have many reasons for wishing to avoid comencment, some of them you can Guess at. I am now in a greater puzzel than I have been yet. when your Father went away he thought he left the care of his place to his brother, but last Evening, he came & told me that he was discouraged and would not undertake it, that he should not be able to make enough off, of it to pay the Rates.

The Bills I mentiond to you were finally returnd protessted with 48. 18 shilling damage and interest upon them The first set went with the Letters in a vessel of mr Boylestones loaded with oil, but which vessel never arrived—so that the Bill was protested as it says, for want of advise—a most unfortunate affair this. I know you will feel anxious, as well as I, but I think some arrangment will and must take place at New york soon. I will write to you as soon as I know— I wish to meet you at Haverhill and was in hopes of doing it soon, but if all the Farming buissness is Thrown upon me just at the period when I was pleasing myself with being Free from it, I do not see how I can leave home. I shall however get Dr Tufts to talk with mr A. and see if nothing can be done to make him easy—he think your Father has so much higher notions about his Farm than he can possibly answer, that he shall come under Blame. I know I shall let me conduct how I will, but I will do, to the best of my judgment & abide the concequence

Your Father wrote me from Hartford that the Manufactores waited upon him & presented him a piece of cloth for a suit of Clothes. the story in the News paper sometime since was without foundation.[1] the Morning your Father sat out, we had an increase in our Family. Luckily it was all over before the Light Horsemen got here to Breakfast. I was glad on Brislers account as he went away easier— W. C went to Boston on saturday. mr daws goes to N york on thursday—all the world are flocking there, how many must return dissapointed—

I shall write you next by the post & let you know what I can Learn from N york I have had two Letters from your sister,[2] in both of which she expresses her anxiety for your Health & her wish to see you there. adieu write to me by mr smith who I hear is going to Newbury port— yours / affectionately   Abigail Adams—

May 6th 1789

Brisler returnd last Evening from Newyork by him I Received Letters from your Father & sister.[3] no arrangments yet. your Father was at mr Jays. he writes me that he hoped there would be in a few days. he approves of Charles comeing to him provided we should get to

Housekeeping, ~~Nine~~ 18 dollars per month for keeping two Horses 20 shillings a week for servants Board is pretty handsome— Your Father writes me that the pressident Received him with great affection & cordiality, that he treated & conversed with him in great confidence— you will see by the papers the whole of the ceremony of the administration of the oath to the Pressident, but least you should not get it soon I send you my paper I will not go away untill I see you again at Haverhill or Braintree. your sister sends her Love [to] you

    yours affectionatly   A Adams

RC (Adams Papers); addressed: "To / Mr John Quincy Adams / Newburry Port"; endorsed: "My Mother— May 5 & 6. 1789." and "Mrs: Adams, May 5. 1789." Some loss of text where the seal was removed.

[1] Newspaper reports in late March had quoted a letter from Braintree, dated 24 March, stating that "his Excellency JOHN ADAMS (the glory of our town, and I believe I may add, one of the ornaments of the age) has lately received an elegant suit of AMERICAN BROADCLOTH, manufactured at Hartford, in which he will make his appearance as VICE-PRESIDENT of the United States" (*Massachusetts Centinel*, 28 March).

[2] Not found.

[3] AA had received JA's letter of 1 May, above; the letter from AA2 has not been found.

Abigail Adams to John Adams

May 6th 1789

Brisler arrived last Evening and brought yours of May the 1st I have not time to notice all I want to in it, I wish to know whether you would like that I should engage Daniel as coachman who drove you to Newyork when you get to House keeping, and what are the wages given. Tom we can never keep if we wish fer peace— would not the House out of Town be most agreeable to you and most for your Health?

you mistook me if you thought I meant to bring ~~Charles~~ Tommy. he will [stay?] at colledge till the middle of july, tis only the class who [take?] their degree that can leave college in june, & the President must be written to for the purpose. you did not write me as if you had thought maturely upon it, I would not wish to do any thing without your free consent and advise

    my Letter is waited for.

    yours   A Adams

compliments to mr Jay who with your permission is a great favorite of mine to Mrs Levinstong[1]

RC (Adams Papers); addressed: "To / His Excellency John Adams / Vice President of the united / States / New York." Some loss of text where the seal was removed.

[1] Probably Susannah French Livingston (1723–1789), wife of William Livingston and Jay's mother-in-law (*Selected Letters of John Jay and Sarah Livingston Jay: Correspondence by or to the First Chief Justice of the United States and His Wife*, ed. Landa M. Freeman and others, Jefferson, N.C., 2005, p. 8).

Abigail Adams to John Adams

my dearest Friend   Braintree May 7th Fast day [1789]

our parson has been praying for you to day that you may be enabled to discharge the high and important Trust committed to you with equal integrity and abilitis as you have heretofore excercised in Negotiations at Foreign courts & embassies abroad, and with equal Benifit & satisfaction to your Country. I have been reading with attention the various addresses to the Pressident & his replies. they are all pathetick but none more so than that to the citizens of Alexandera.[1] throughout all of them he appears to be most sensibly affected with the supreme and over Ruling providence which has calld him to Rule over this great people rather to feel Humble than Elated, & to be overpowerd with the weight & Magnitude of his Trust, who that reflected, who that weigh'd & considerd but must lay his Hand upon his Breast, & say what am I? that this great Trust is committed to me? your Legislature are promulgating a perfectly New doctrine. I had always supposed that in point of Rank the Senate were superiour to the Representitives. this perfect equality brought to my mind a story told of Johnson, that dining one day with mrs Macauley She was conversing upon her favorite topick of the Natural equality of Man— Johnson heard her very gravely, after some time he rose from table & bowing very respectfully to the servant who waited behind his chair, pray mr John, take my place & let me wait in my Turn. you hear what your mistress Says; that we are all equal—[2] there debates as given to the publick do not prove them all solomans, forgive me if I am too sausy—tis only to you that I think thus freely.

I shall not forward the papers of this week they contain nothing more than what you have already had— I hope it will not be long before you will be able to take a House. living upon a Friend cannot be long agreeable to you I know and now John is away I fear you will suffer some inconvenience I cannot prepare my things for Removal untill I hear further from you, but I should suppose it would be best to get mr Tufts vessel to take them either here or at weymouth. If there are any Number of Books that you would wish for I will have them pack'd & ready if you can point them out; with regard to the Horse I should be very glad that our son might have him, but upon maxims of prudence will it do at this time? I need not give my reasons for the Question. French must be paid before I leave home. there are six months wages due to Brisler on the first of May, which he will have occasion to leave with his wife, & to purchase some articles of furniture. I shall be obliged to pay for what work has been done by your Brothers hands upon the place—an expence I would not have incured if I had supposed he would not have kept the place— you wish to give a look at your Farm, the Hills begin to look Green, but the season is so backward that scarcly a Tree has leaved Lilack excepted. 3 hands with a Team were all yesterday employ'd in picking up the stones, thrown out of the ditches & carried upon Quincy medow in the manure. I could have wished more manure might have been put there, attempted it but found it would cut the ground to pieces— tomorrow will be employd in carrying on the manure behind the House, & clearing the Ground of stones— the sheep have gone very quiet since the wall was poled the Weathers excepted whom no fence would hold but they are parted with.— shall I do all the work necessary upon the place for the present, and at my leaving it request your Brother to take it, he paying one third of the taxes upon it, or shall I leave it to him to say upon what terms he will look after it. mr Baxter very kindly sent me word yesterday that he would hire it for four years but I asked no Questions, presuming you had rather it should lie unimproved. Your son Tom says if he was out of colledge he would come & live with Pheby & Abdee & improve it himself before it should go a beging thus— one of your Townsmen told me the other day that he was very sorry you was gone away, for there was nobody left in Town to buy Land. all your Friends desire to be affectionatly rememberd to you, but none more tenderly than your ever / affectionate   A Adams

compliment to miss Levingstone, and all the Ladies who so kindly inquire after your Friend

RC (Adams Papers); addressed: "To / His Excellency John Adams / vice President of the united / States / Newyork."

[1] A number of Boston newspapers printed the addresses made to George Washington by a variety of groups, including the city of Philadelphia, the commonwealth of Pennsylvania, the Pennsylvania Society of the Cincinnati, and the University of Pennsylvania,

among others. The Address of the Citizens of Alexandria begins, "Again your Country demands your care. Obedient to its wishes—unmindful of your own ease—we see you again relinquishing the bliss of retirement, and this too, at a period of life, when nature itself seems to authorise a preference of respose!" It goes on to describe Washington as a model for youth, an improver of agriculture, a friend of commerce, and a benefactor of the poor, concluding, "To that Being, who maketh and unmaketh at his will, we commend you—and, after the accomplishment of the arduous business to which you are called, may he restore to us again the best of men, and the most beloved fellow-citizen."

Washington replied that "those who know me best, (and you, my fellow-citizens, are, from your situation, in that number) know better than any others, my love of retirement is so great, that no earthly consideration, short of a conviction of duty, could have prevailed upon me to depart from my resolution 'never more to take any share in transac-

tions of a publick nature.' For, at my age, and in my circumstances, what possible advantage could I propose to myself, from embarking again in the tempestuous and uncertain ocean of publick life? . . . All that now remains for me, is, to commit myself and you to the protection of that *beneficent Being*, who, on a former occasion, hath happily brought us together, after a long and distressing separation.—Perhaps the same gracious PROVIDENCE will again indulge us with the same heart-felt felicity. But words, my fellow-citizens, fail me. Unutterable sensations must then be left to more expressive silence: While, from an aching heart, I bid you all, my affectionate friends and kind neighbours, farewel!" (*Massachusetts Centinel*, 2, 6 May).

[2] This story first appeared in *The Beauties of Samuel Johnson, LL.D. . . . to Which Are Now Added, Biographical Anecdotes of the Doctor*, 7th edn., London, 1787. James Boswell also included it in his *Life of Samuel Johnson, LL.D.*

John Adams to Abigail Adams

My dearest Friend   New York May. 13. 1789

I have taken an House, and now wish you to come on, as soon as possible.— It will be necessary to send by Water all the Carpets that are not in Use, and several Beds, Bedsteads, Bedding Bed and Table Linnen,—Plate, China &c if you can convey it to Providence would come better that Way. The House is on the North River about a mile out of the City, in a fine situation, a good Stable, Coach House, Garden, about 30 Acres of Land. it goes by the name of M[r] Montiers House.—[1] We may keep, two Cows, on the Pasture. The Rent is 50 or an 100£ less, than for a poorer House in the City.

Charles and Thomas had better come on with you, at least the former.— Brisler and Polly Taylor, at least must come.— I inclose a Letter to President Willard[2] & am / yours most tenderly

John Adams

RC (Adams Papers); internal address: "M[rs] Adams."

[1] For Richmond Hill, the Adamses' home while JA served as vice president in New York City, see Descriptive List of Illustrations, No. 10, above. The house originally belonged to Maj. Abraham Mortier, a British officer, who built it around 1767 (Stokes, *Iconography of Manhattan*, 1:416–417).

[2] Not found.

10. RICHMOND HILL, BY CORNELIUS TIEBOUT, 1790
See page xv

John Adams to Abigail Adams

My dearest Friend   New York May 14. 1789

I have rec^d yours of the 5th.— If you think it best, leave Thomas at Colledge: but I pray you to come on with Charles, as soon as possible.— as to the Place let my Brother plough and plant if he will, as much as he will. He may Send me, my half of the Butter Cheese &c here.— As to Money to bear your Expences you must if you can borrow of some Friend enough to bring you here. if you cannot borrow enough, you must Sell Horses Oxen Sheep Cowes, any Thing at any Rate rather than not come on.— if, no one will take the Place leave it to the Birds of the Air and Beasts of the Field: but at all Events break up that Establishment and that Household.— A great Part of the Furniture must be shipped for this Place. as to Daniel, he has a Wife and cannot leave her: besides he makes great wages where he is:[1] but if you have a Mind to bring Daniel you may. We can do without him.

I have as many difficulties here, as you can have; public and private. but my Life from my Cradle has been a Series of difficulties and that Series will continue to the Grave,.— I hope Brisler will come; but if he cannot We can do without him.— I have taken Montiers House, on the North River, a mile out of Town. There is room enough and Accommodations of all sorts.—but no furniture.

I am &c, tenderly   John Adams

RC (Adams Papers); addressed: "Mrs Adams / Braintree / near Boston"; notation: "free / John Adams."

[1] The remainder of this paragraph was interlined.

William Stephens Smith to Abigail Adams

My dear Madam   Newyork May 14th. 1789.

I have the happiness of informing you that M^rs: Smith and the Boys are in high health and that your presence here as soon as you can possibly make it convenient will be very agreable and is in a great degree necessary— M^r. A has taken a House about one mile from the City as he has informed you, and in his Letters has said something about the removal of furniture— on this subject permit me to say that you cannot bring too much—for if the future arrangement of Congress should extend to the furnishing of your

House the articles which you have, at a first estimate will me more advantageously employed than if you were to permit them to remain unused during the period which you will be absent from Braintee and if no provision of that kind should be made, you will save at least 2 or 300£ by bringing on what furniture you have for at present it is a very expensive article in this place— therefore I would advise that you should hire a good Sloop, let her be brought to the nearest landing place and well packed, and after she is loaded and ready to sail let D^r. Tufts insure her Cargo to this port valued sufficiently to cover the property & let her be ordered to proceed about one mile up the north river where we being informed of her arrival will pay the necessary attention to what she convey's— she can then proceed to within 100 yards of the House & the expence & risk of land Carriage be avoided— in this way if Briessler Comes he can with convenience bring his family &c— you will notice I am in haste & remain / Sincerely yours &c.
                                                                        W: S. Smith

RC (Adams Papers).

Abigail Adams to John Adams

My dearest Friend   Braintree May 16 1789

I yesterday received yours of May the 3^d by Captain Beal's in which you request that I would come on imediatly Yours of May the first mentions several articles which you suppose it will be necessary for me to send forward, but add all is as yet uncertain, so that I am in doubt what to do, particularly as I have laid before you Since, a state of my difficulties to which I could have wish't some replie, that I might have known how to proceed agreeable to your wishes; I cannot get your Brother to say upon what Terms he will take the place. he insists upon it that all that can be got from it this year will not more than pay the Taxes, and as a proof he brought me this afternoon a Tax for the high way of Two pounds Nine shillings this added to the parish Tax makes five pounds Eighteen shillings, this added to the Tax we have already paid makes Sixty dollors, but I know very well that if he improved it, they would not tax it so high & then a part of this is for woodland mr Black complains most bitterly, his Taxes are just double. I have not contracted any debts to the amount of a dollor since you left me, two articles only I have been able to part with (, excepting what the Dr took,) a Hog & a Calf, the proceeds of which I was obliged to lay out in Hay for the stock & to send to a distant part of Weymouth for it. they ask 3 shillings pr Hundred Captain Beals is obliged to go to Boston to Buy Hay. there has not been such a Demand for these Several years. mr Black is obliged to Buy, the pastures are quite Bare, & the vegetation very slow & the weather very cold. I do not think I shall be able to get to you in less than three weeks from this Time, & how I shall then be able to leave our affairs is uncertain, no offer of any sort has been made for the oxen. your Brother thinks they had better be sent upon an Island to fat, the scow[1] must lie where it is, for I cannot get any Sale for it. the Horse, I have put upon sale at 80 dollors, but your Brother says I may think myself very well of, to get 70. if I understood Brisler right, you said he should be given to J Q A rather then parted with at less— Barnard arrived this week, and I sent Brisler to Town immediatly for the Trees, they are much smaller than the Rhoad Island Greenings, all of which appear to have taken & are very fine Trees. I have got them all set & properly Guarded so that I hope we shall have an additional quantity of good Fruit I have yet got some Russets as fair as when they came from the Trees. Your Mother is as well as usual & yesterday with our Horse & chaise undertook a ride to Abington where she proposes to spend a fortnight. I have not been from Home but one half day since you left me. Esther was confined & I have had nobody but Polly with me, and I have had my Hands full of spring work for my children, untill Louissa came about a week ago to make me a visit I find her so helpfull to me that I shall keep her till, I come on. I do not like to sleep alone I am so subject to those Nervious affections, that I am some times allarmed with them. with respect to a House, I rather wish you to take one before I come on. Mrs Smith can judge as well as I can, but whether you do or no, I will endeavour to be with you in the course of three weeks from this Time. if you can possibly get time I wish you would say whether I must bring Linnen China Glass kitchen furniture Plate, looking glasses I would not remove and Beds if I leave any in the House I can take only three, or rather I should have said, if I left enough to accommodate us when we come home to see how our Trees grow &c the Hill begins to look finely and & Garden much better for New setting what Box I have had taken up, but it is like diging up so many Trees with large Roots, & I believe to speak within moderate Bounds, it would take a Gardner a Month to do it properly— Thayer is chosen Rep, again. the Shaiseites were very low. Vinton had only one vote,[2] General Lincoln is chosen for Hingham.

judge Sergant & Lady kept sabbeth with me on their way to Barnstable Court, and desired to be affectionally rememberd to you. judge Cushing has visited me twice. Your Book is his Travelling Companion he says, but he could not possibly part with it yet. I have requested him to deliver it to mr Cranch if I should be absent when he comes again. is mrs Washington arrived yet? I wish she would get there before me— I dont very well like all I see in the papers—. pray write to me by the next post after you receive this Letter. the Printers have sent the papers to you they say, so that I have lost sight of several of them this week all Friends desire to be rememberd to you— most affectionatly / yours   A A

RC (Adams Papers); addressed: "To / His Excellency John Adams / vice President of the united States / Newyork."

¹ A large, flat-bottomed boat (*OED*).

² Gen. Ebenezer Thayer was elected representative from Braintree by a majority of 34 votes (*Braintree Town Records*, p. 589-590). For Capt. John Vinton's earlier opposition to Thayer, see Mary Smith Cranch to AA, 27 May 1787, and note 4, above.

John Adams to Abigail Adams

My dearest Friend   May 18 1789

I am in such a situation that I cannot see the way clear for you to come on, till some resolution is passed in the House.— You will be as ready as you can, and I will write you the Moment ~~to come on.~~ any Thing is done.— I will resign my office rather than bring you here to be miserable.

Yours eternally   John Adams.

RC (Adams Papers); addressed: "Mʳˢ Adams / Braintree."

John Adams to Abigail Adams

My dearest Friend   New York. 19. May. 1789

inclosed is a Letter from Captⁿ· Brown who commands the best Packet between Providence and this Place.—¹ He called very politely and respectfully to offer his service in bringing you to New York.— if you can let him know the time when you can come, he will be ready.

I have taken an House: but have nothing to put in it, [no]r to live on.— nothing is yet determined, I never felt so [ir]resolute and undetermined what to do.— I approve of the Idea of Sending the Furniture by Tirrell, and some of the Books—not many.² But I think it is

best to wait till Something is determined by the House.— I have
written another Letter to President Willard, asking leave for Charles
to come with you.—[3] I must give up the pleasing Idea of Seeing Thomas, for the present.— Mr & Mrs Smith were in Town to day, and I
dined with them at Mr Mc·Cormicks. They and their Children are
well.— I have this moment recd a delightful Letter from Dr Price, in
which he remembers you with the kindest affection.[4] I will write
you, the Moment any Thing is settled.

My Sincere Thanks to Mr Wibird for his Remembrance of me in
his Prayers. It is to me, a most affecting Thing to hear myself prayed
for in particular as I do every day in the Week, and disposes me to
bear, with more Composure, Some disagreable Circumstances, that
attend my Situation.— My Duty to my Mother and Love to all.— I
hope my Brother will take the Place, and plant the Hill— You must
take the best Advice you can, and do as well as you can. I have it
not in my Power to assist you, but with [the] / best Wishes of yours
most tenderly   John Adams

RC (Adams Papers); addressed: "Mrs Adams / Braintree / near Boston"; notation: "Free / John Adams." Some loss of text where the seal was removed.

[1] Capt. James N. Brown, who sailed the sloop *Hancock* between Providence and New York, wrote to JA on 18 May (Adams Papers): "Hearing that your Good Lady is to Come On from providince to york by Water & Concious of haveing the best accomedated packet in That Line Induces me to Solicit the honour of Bringing Mrs Addams on & be Assured good Sir that It Shall be my Whole Study to accomedate her Ladyship." Brown also recommended Mr. Daggett's Inn, where AA eventually stayed in Providence (see AA to Mary Smith Cranch, 19 June, and note 3, below).

[2] Capt. Joseph Tirrell (1752–1825) of Weymouth carried freight between Boston and New York in the schooner *Weymouth* (*New York Journal*, 4 Dec. 1787; *History of Weymouth*, 3:361, 4:660).

[3] Not found.

[4] Richard Price wrote to JA on 5 March (Adams Papers). He commented that "my best complimts wait on Mrs Adams. My congregation can never forget that She and you once made a part of it. May Heaven grant you both whatever can make you most happy."

John Adams to Abigail Adams

My dearest Friend   New York. May. 24. 1789

I have received your Letter of the 16th.— I have taken a large and
handsome house, in a beautiful Situation, about two miles out of
the City, upon the North River. The Rent is less, than I must have
given for a much meaner house in Town, without any such accommodations of Stable Garden, Pasture &c

I now desire you to come on, as soon as possible, and to Send by
Tirrell, or some other Vessel, Beds, & Bedding—all the Linnen for

Beds & Table, Knives & Forks, China, Glass, Kitchen Furniture—in short all the [fur]niture of the House in a manner. Some of the smaller looking Glasses—but the large ones, not yet.— Yet I dont know but it would be best to bring even them.— Furniture here is monstrously dear. Ask the D[r.] if it is adviseable to insure? My Books some of them may come too— The Books I wish for, are hume, Johnson Priestley, Ainsworths Dictionary,[1] and Such other Books as may be most amusing and useful— The great Works and Collections I would not bring on. But Blackstone and De Lolme on the English Constitution and the Collection of American Constitutions I would have Sent on.—[2] I am encouraged to expect that the House will do something that will enable Us to live, tho perhaps not very affluently.

The Place must be left, as you can.— I can form no Judgment about it.— Charles must come with you.— And Polly—and Elijah, if his Parents are willing.

M[rs] Washington, will be here before you, without doubt—she is expected daily.— My Garden is preparing for your Reception, and I wish you were here.

my dearest friend Adieu   J. A.

Livy and Tacitus & Cicero I would have sent, and a Plutarch in french or English &c.

RC (Adams Papers); addressed: "M[rs] Adams / Braintree near / Boston"; notation: "Free / John Adams." Some loss of text where the seal was removed.

[1] Robert Ainsworth, *Dictionary, English and Latin: A New Edition, with Great Additions*, ed. Thomas Morell, London, 1773 (*Catalogue of JA's Library*).

[2] Jean Louis de Lolme, *The Constitution of England; or, An Account of the English Government*, London, 1775. For *The Constitutions of the Several Independent States of America*, see JA, *Papers*, 11:477, note 1.

Abigail Adams to John Adams

my dearest Friend   Braintree May 26 1789

I hope Barnard has arrived with the things which I sent by him. if there is any person in the House they had better be sent immediatly to it there to lie untill I arrive on the Recept of your Letter May 3'd I sent directly to Town and finding Barnard almost ready to sail I got him to take as many things as I could get ready, they are carpets linnen &c. after I had done this I sat out to visit my sister at Haverhill, leaving word that I would have any letter which should come in my absence sent to me. two days after I left Home I received yours of may 13 & 14th. if I had been at Home I should immediatly have gone about packing some part of my furniture, but to day mr Ward deliverd me your Letter of May 18th I am glad you have determined to proceed no further then taking a House, untill you know upon what terms we are to put our selves in motion. tho I was only absent one week from home I was so uneasy after I received your Letters in which you desired me to come on (directly, least you should think I made an unnecessary delay) that the pleasure of my visit was much diminished. yet I knew mr Tufts vessel was not returnd and that I must wait the return of Barnard before I a could possibly send any thing further. it is a very unpleasent Idea to me, to be obliged to pull down & pack furniture which has already sufferd so much by Re-moval just as I have got it well arranged. it is no trifling affair & will require no very short time to accomplish. if you please & it must be done; I will only take such things as will enable us to keep House for the present. if our Masters will please to furnish us two Rooms in a proper manner I can put up sufficient for the remainder of the House, but as I know not how to take any steps at present I shall let every thing remain in quiet. but for me to come to N York with Charles and one or two domesticks, before I can go to House keep-ing would only tend to embarrass us all, & tho I know your situation must be painfull & dissagreable to you, I fear I should only increase rather then lessen your difficulties. I would wish to know if I do not ask an improper thing, whether you would be willing I should bring Louissa with me. I find her so usefull with her needle, at any House work at the Ironing Board, that I think she would be to me a very great assistance, but at the same time if you are not intirely willing, or have the least objection, I shall not repeat my request— she has two qualities which you value—silence & modesty

Mr Allen brought your Letter of May 19th. I found it this Evening upon my return. Captain Brown is the Captain with whom Brisler came home, & with him he has desired me to go, as he has a great opinion of his civility. Daniel I found was married and in a pretty way of Buisness, so I have not said any thing to him. I shall be obliged to send the Horse to J Q: A. I cannot get any offer for him, tho I have sent to Ballard[1] & to Bracket, several Gentleman have lookd at him, but he is known in Town to have broken a chaise for woodard all to peices, a circumstance I never knew untill I offerd him for sale.[2] I could have disposed of him but for that circumstance & his being too Headstrong for Ladies to manage our son says it will cost him this summer as much to hire Horses to attend court as the keeping that horse will amount to, but I tell him he must sell him if he can. The president has received both your Letters and will ask consent of the Corperation for charles.[3] he has a French oration given him for his part at commencement. The president & Lady have sent me word that they design to visit me on Saturday next & dine with me. our good Friends judge Dana & Lady kept Sabbeth with me on their way to Plimouth court. it grieved me to see him in such ill Health I found him better on my return from Haverhill. I lodged at his House. I came through Town & dined at Dr Welchs, where I met with mr Pearson, who was very full with his remarks upon the answer of the House to the President.[4] he was much disgusted with the manner & stile of it. "This is what we have Thought fit to address to you" was the Language of superiours to an inferiour. Stiling him fellow citizen, was in his opinion very improper, he was no more their fellow citizen whilst he was President of the united states, than the King of G. B was fellow Subject to his people— I read the debates of the House and I have watch'd a certain character much celebrated, & from the whole I have drawn up this conclusion, that he either does not possess so great talants as he has been said too, or he is aiming at Popularity, at the expence of his judgment & understanding Honestus, pronounces mr Madison the wisest & best man in the House, but time will unvail Characters. I do not like his Politicks, nor the Narrow jealousy he has discoverd.

I have an opportunity of sending this Letter written in great haste as you will perceive—

Yours most tenderly and / affectionatly   A Adams

inclosed is Barnards Receit[5]

RC (Adams Papers).

[1] John Ballard operated a livery stable at Bromfield's Lane in Boston (*NEHGR*, 140:36 [Jan. 1986]; Boston *Independent Chronicle*, 9 Apr. 1789, 17 June 1790).

[2] Probably Joseph Woodward of Braintree, who had served as a surveyor of highways for the town in 1788 (*Braintree Town Records*, p. 579). He wrote to JA on 15 and 30 May 1789 (both Adams Papers) seeking positions in the new federal government and also mentioned on the 30th having seen AA recently.

[3] Not found.

[4] For the House's address to George Washington, see *First Fed. Cong.*, 3:45–46.

[5] Not found.

John Quincy Adams to William Cranch

Newbury-Port. May 27^{th:} 1789.

I should have answered your last favour,¹ ere this [but in?] [con-se]quence of the information you gave me, I went to Haverhill [last?] Thursday and returned but the day before yesterday. Regularly the Sunday is my scribbling day, but as there are several opportunities for sending at present, I [can]not suffer the week to pass over without noticing you, and must there fore [steal?] an hour or two from—from whom?—why first negatively not from my Lord Coke: no nor from any other Lord or gentleman that has any connection with laws, except the eternal and immutable laws of nature. But from the divine Shakespear whom I read with more fervent admiration than any thing—but enough of this.

[With respect?] to Charles the tender solicitude, which you feel in regard to his conduct is only an additional evidence of a disposition, which I have long known to be peculiarly yours. it adds to the number of obligations for which I feel myself indebted to you, but it cannot add any thing to the settled opinion which I have of the excellency of your heart.— I wrote him a very serious Letter three weeks ago and conversed with him at Haverhill upon the subject in such a manner as must I think lead him to be more cautious.² However I depend much more upon the alteration which is soon to take place in his situation, than upon any advice or counsel, that I can ever give him. I am well convinced that if any thing can keep him within the limits of regularity, it will be his knowlege of my fathers being [near him and the?] fear of being discovered by him.—

If you have an opportunity to send to Braintree I wish you would inform my Mother, that by sending the articles [which?] I [men]-tioned to her, immediately to Boston, I shall probably soon get them here. But 17? Cave, Cave, Cave!³

You say nothing concerning the Letter which I [enclosed in my?] last for Thomas & C^{o:} I should be glad to hear if it was transmitted to them.—⁴ I believe I shall not soon attempt to mount my Pegasus again Some of the *characters* contained in a certain *Vision* which [you] have seen have been handed about in this Town. All of them have been applied to as particular persons, and reports have been spread, that I avow'd myself to be the author, and named the said persons for whom they were written— Not a word of truth in all this, and yet it has made me enemies—⁵ And the circumstance has been

employ'd as an argument to prove me to be the author of a scurrilous enigmatical list which I have mentioned to you heretofore.[6]
"He abuses people in rhyme, and therefore, he doubtless abuses
people also in prose." Such is the reasoning; and so little capacity or
inclination is there to distinguish between a Satire and a lampoon.—
If you wish to thrive in the world and to pass for an amiable, clever,
discreet good man, let your invariable maxim be NEVER TO DIS-
APPROVE.

Adieu.   J. Q. Adams.

RC (MHi:Adams Papers, All Generations); addressed: "Mr: W[m] Cranch. /
Boston."; endorsed: "J. Q. A. / May 27. 1789."; notation: "Favd. by Mr: Smith." Some
loss of text where the seal was removed and the paper damaged by water.

[1] Not found.

[2] Not found, but JQA mentioned in his
Diary that he wrote to CA on 2 May. The
brothers may also have had a conversation on 25 May, when JQA was at Haverhill
(D/JQA/14, APM Reel 17).

[3] This sentence was written sideways in
the margin beside this and the following paragraph.

[4] Neither JQA's letter to William Cranch
nor one to Isaiah Thomas & Company has
been found, but one of JQA's poems appeared in the next issue of Thomas' *Massachusetts Magazine* under the pseudonym Al-
cander (May 1789, p. 321).

[5] For JQA's satirical poem, "A Vision,"
about several young women in Newburyport,
see *Diary*, 2:154, 381. On 10 June 1790, William Cranch wrote to JQA of an encounter
Cranch had with a mutual acquaintance,
Betsy Foster. Cranch reported that Foster
said "she did not know any person she
should be so afraid of, as you. I demanded
the grounds upon which she had formed
such an opinion. She said she was not much

acquainted with you, but that she had in her
pocketbook a little piece of satirical Poetry
which she thought would justify her fears.
She then produced a Copy of *the Vision*. She
was charmed with it, but she could not help
being afraid of the Author." Foster went on
to describe parts of the poem as "illiberal"
and "very unjust." Cranch assured Foster
that "if there is anything illiberal in the *Vision* I was certain you could not be the Author" (Adams Papers).

[6] This "enigmatical list" appeared in the
29 April 1789 issue of the Newburyport *Essex
Journal*, which is apparently no longer extant. An article in the *Essex Journal*, 6 May,
signed Eugenio claimed in regard to the list
that "I must confess I never was witness to
so much scurrillity and baseness— Who but a
ruffian—a villain—an enemy to the loveliest
work of God—a base traducer of merit, would
lurk behind the Printing Press, and throw
promiscuously arrows poisoned with obscen-
ity and defamation, to wound the bosom of
the defenceless fair."

Abigail Adams to John Quincy Adams

my dear son   Braintree May 30th 1789

I have sent you the Cloth the coat & Boots. the Glass I have not
yet been able to find. inclosed is an other article the amount of
what I engaged to you. The Horse I had engaged to keep for a Gentleman till Monday next, so that I could not without forfeiting my
word let him go till twesday provided I should not sell him to him. I
am sorry, for if I should not part with him then: I should not make

any further trial and should be glad to get him to you as soon as possible— when I got home on twesday Evening, I received a Letter from your Father in which he says after many deliberations he has concluded that I shall not come on, untill the House pass some resolution respecting him. this I think the most prudent desicion, for to be there with a thousand wants & demands & no resources is much worse than being here at any rate. it has given me a little farther respit. I must request you in my absence to attend to your Brother Tom, to watch over his conduct & prevent by your advice & kind admonitions, his falling a prey to vicious Company. at present he seems desirious of persueing his studies preserving a character and avoiding dissipation, but no youth is secure whilst temptations surround him, and no age of Life but is influenced by habits & example, even when they think their Characters formed. I have many anxious hours for Charles, and not the fewer, for the new scene of life into which he is going, tho I think it will be of great service to have him with his Father, & more to take him intirely away from his acquaintance. I have written to him upon some late reports which have been circulated concerning him.[1] I hope they are without foundation, but such is the company in which he is seen that he cannot fail to bear a part of the reproach even if he is innocent. if you should be able to send again, next week let me know one day before hand, & the Name of the person by whom you send, for if I had sent the Horse to Brackets I should not have known whom to have inquired for— I have not heard from your uncle since we left him, I hope he is better—

The Bundle I shall send this day to mr Smiths— pray write me and let me know how you do from time to Time. Yours most affectionatly

A Adams

PS I received a line from W C. that the Gentleman by whom you sent for the Horse was gone to Pownalborough[2] it was well I did not send him to Town. I do not know how you will get him unless you come to Boston for him in the course of the week. Brislers Note is inclosed[3]

RC (Adams Papers).

[1] Not found.
[2] Not found.
[3] Not found.

John Adams to Abigail Adams

My dearest Friend   New York May 30. 1789

Your old Acquaintance M[r] Harrison of Cadiz will deliver you this, if you should not, as I hope you will, be Sett off for this place before he can reach Braintree.—

I expect you, here indeed in a Week or ten days at farthest, from this date. Mrs Washington is arrived. My House and Garden want us very much. We Shall be obliged to bring all our Furniture and most of our Books, except the Law books and the great Collections, such as the Byzantine History, Muratory, the Encyclopædia &c[1] But I hope you will come on, and send Beds and necessaries as soon as possible. Barnard has delivered here, some Trunks & Cases but no Keys nor Letter informing what is in them.— We must make this place our home, and think no more of Braintree, for four years, not forgetting however our Friends there. and what is the most disagreable of all: We must live, as I apprehend, in a Style much below our Rank and station.— I Said four Years, upon the supposition that the Government should support itself so long: but it must be supported by Providence if at all, against the usual Course of Things, if the human Means of supporting it, should not be soon better understood. You and I can live however as plainly as any of them,

    yours most tenderly   J. A.

RC (Adams Papers); internal address: "M[rs] Adams."

[1] Edward Gibbon, *The History of the Decline and Fall of the Roman Empire*, 6 vols., London, 1777–1788; Lodovico Antonio Muratori, *Annali d'Italia dal principio dell' era volgare, sino all' anno 1750*, 12 vols. in 6, Naples, 1773; and Denis Diderot and Jean le Rond d'Alembert, eds., *Encyclopédie*, 3d edn., 38 vols., Geneva, 1778, are all in JA's library at MB (*Catalogue of JA's Library*).

Abigail Adams to John Adams

my dearest Friend   Sunday May 31. 1789

I received yesterday your Letter of May the 24th and shall begin tomorrow to get such things in readiness as will enable us to keep House. I feel a reluctance at striping this wholy at present, because I am well persuaded that we shall in some future period if our lives are prolonged return to it, and even supposing a summer recess, we might wish to come & spend a few months here. an other reason is, that I do not wish to bring all our own furniture, because congress are not, or do not possess sufficient stability to be sure of continuing long in any one state,— I am fully satisfied with the House you have taken & glad that it is a little removed from the city. the advantages will overbalance the inconvenience I doubt not. I suppose Barnard has arrived before this. would it not be best to let him know that he will have a full freight ready, returns as soon as he will, and that I must look out for some other vessel if he delay's, tho I have not the least prospect of getting one, for mr Tufts's is yet at Newyork Barnard's is calculated for the Buisness, & I could get a small vessel to come here to mr Blacks & take in my things & carry them along side of Barnard, which will be less expence, & damage than carting them to Boston. in the mean time I will get the Dr to look out, & see if any other vessel can be hired for the purpose provided Barnard should delay at Newyork. this you can advise me of by the next post. with the greatest expedition I do not think I can get them ready under a week— I must leave Brisler to come by water with them, if you think it best for me to come before my furniture is ship'd, but I do not see what advantage I can be of, to you situated as you are. an additional incunberence to mr Jays family would be still more indelicet than imposing the vice Pressident upon him for several months, and rendering his situation so delicate that he could neither leave him with decency, or stay with decorum, and to be at Jamaica I could do no more than if I was at Braintree to assist in any thing the Trunks which I sent contain Bed & table Linnen some Cloths & the cases contain carpets. I will however be directed wholy by your wishes & come next week if you think it best, and you have any place to put me. you must be sensible from the tenor of Your Letters that I have not known hitherto what to do, any more than you have from your situation, What to direct. you will be as patient as possible & rest assured that I will do my utmost with the means I have, to expidite every thing. as to insurence there will be no occasion for it by Barnard who is so well acquainted with the coast, & at this season of the Year

The Pressident & Lady dinned with me yesterday.[1] he has got permission for Charles's absence— Polly Tailor would cry a week if I did not bring her, for a House maid I know not where I could get her equal. Elijahs mother thinks it is too far for her son to go, but if they consent mr Brisler can take him on Board Barnard when he comes, but I shall not press it. Poor daniel has been sick with a soar which gatherd in his Throat & which nearly proved fatal to him. he expected from you some gratuity for himself, oweing to the multiplicity of cares which on all sides surrounded you, at that time, it was omitted. as it was Customary & daniels expectations were dissapointed, he mentiond it to one or two persons, amongst whom woodard was one, who having just returnd from Newyork, clapt his hands into his pocket & taking out two crowns, gave them to him, telling him that you was so much engaged at the time, that it had slipt your mind but that he saw you at Newyork & that he had brought them for him. this came to my knowledge by the way of mr Wibird who insisted upon letting me know it. I immediatly repaid mr woodard & thank'd him for his kindness—

your Brother I believe will take care of the place when I leave it. the leave for Breaking up the Hill came too late for this season, the weather is remarkably cold & Backward, the pastures bare & vegetation very slow there is a fine blow upon the place, & if the frost last week which killd Beans, has not injured the Blossom, we shall have a large crop of fruit. I had yesterday a fine plate of fair Russets upon the table, sound as when they were taken from the Trees my Garden looks charmingly, but it wants warmth— I have got some Large asparagrass Beds made, & my little grass plots before the door, pay well for the manure which I had put on in short I regreet leaving it. your Mother is well as usual. her Eyes are very troublesome to her. you will let me hear from you by the next post. I hope to be able to relieve you soon from [all?] domestick, cares & anxieties. at least my best endeavours sh[all] not be wanting. I know you want your own Bed & pillows, your Hot coffe & your full portion of kian where habit has become Natural.[2] how many of these little matters, make up a large portion of our happiness & content, and the more of publick cares & perplexities that you are surrounded with, the more necessary these alleviations our blessings are sometimes enhanced to us, by feeling the want of them. as one of that Number it is my highest ambition to be estimated, & shall be my constant endeavour to / prove in all situations & circumstances / affectionatly yours

A Adams

RC (Adams Papers); addressed: "To / His Excellency John Adams / vice president of the united States / Newyork." Some loss of text where the seal was removed.

[1] That is, Joseph Willard, president of Harvard, and his wife, Mary.
[2] Cayenne pepper, which was used medicinally as a stimulant (*OED*).

Lucy Ludwell Paradise to Abigail Adams

My Dear Madam—   Wednesday June the 3ᵈ· 1789

Since my return to England, I have been told of the great Civilities you were pleased to Shew to My Dear Deceased Child. I return you a thousand thanks for it and I wish it may ever be in my power to shew you what I feel upon the occasion. As it was not the fault of any Person, but the Will of God, I endeavour to receive it with all the resignation I am able— I hope that you, and all your amiable family, enjoy the Blessings of health, happiness, and prosperity, in as high a degree, as I know they Merit. I beg you will have the goodness to present my best Compliments to them.

I have the honour to Congratulate you and your Family upon the appointment of Mr· Adams to be our Vice President to our Newly Established Federal Constitution. God Grant that it may be productive of every good to our Country: and I make not be least doubt of it, since we are happy to have the Wisest and best of Gentlemen to Govern Us. We are a Great Nation and with good Laws to make People Industrious and oblige them to pay their debts; We shall be the First Country in the World. Our Friend Mr· Jefferson talks of returning to America soon, pray My Dear Madam send him back to Paris as soon as you can. He is a Most excellent Man. I am under the Greatest of obligations to him, and My Dear Friend Dr· Bancroft. Indeed, I do not know what I should have done in my afflictions since My return to Europe, had not Providence been graciously pleased to raise up these two excellent Gentlemen to assist Me.

Mr· Trumbulle has just finished a Picture that does him great Credit.[1] I always rejoice when our Country Men excels the Europeans. Mr· Freine often talks to me about the Civilities he received from his Excellency Mr· Adams[2] he desired Me to present his Compliments to you Mr· Adams and all your amiable family. He is a most excellent good Man, and I wish if his Court sent a Minister to America they would send him, you know him so well, I need to say No more about him. Be pleased to make my best Compliments to his Excellency General and Mrs· Washington to General and Mrs· Knox—and family, to Sr· John and Lady Temple, to Mr and Mrs· Jay, Mr and Mrs Kemble[3] Cyrus Griffin, and the Foreign Ministers and their Families, and to My Dear and old Friend Dr Franklin and his truly good Daughter and all her family.[4] I hope to be honoured by the return of the packet with a Letter from you—

Dear Madam / I have the Honour to be / Your Most Obliged / Humble Serv[t.]   Lucy Paradise

P. S It is reported the Dauphen *of Frençe is* Dead[5]

I am fixed in London until May Next In Margaret Street N[o.] 45 Cavendish Square London

RC (Adams Papers); addressed: "To / Her Excellency M[rs.] John— / Adam New York / North America"; internal address: "M[rs.] Adams"; docketed: "Lucy Paradise."

[1] John Trumbull completed the third and largest rendition of his *Sortie Made by the Garrison of Gibraltar* during the spring of 1789 in London, where it was exhibited in a public hall from April to July (Trumbull, *Autobiography*, p. 148–150).

[2] Ciprião Ribeiro, Chevalier de Freire, the Portuguese chargé d'affaires in London, whom the Adamses had met at the home of the Paradises. He served as Portugal's minister in the United States from 1793 to 1801 (vol. 6:209; *Repertorium*, 3:321).

[3] Peter Kemble (1739–1823), of the New York commercial house of Gouverneur & Kemble, was married to Gertrude Gouverneur, the sister of his partners (New-York Historical Society, *Colls.*, 17:xv [1884]).

[4] Franklin's only daughter, Sarah (Sally, 1743–1808), had married Richard Bache (1737–1811) in 1767. Together, they had seven children, including Benjamin Franklin Bache, who had been a schoolmate of JQA's in Passy, France (*Notable Amer. Women*; vol. 3:15, 5:459).

[5] Louis Joseph Xavier François, the French dauphin, died on 4 June 1789 of tuberculosis (Schama, *Citizens*, p. 356–357).

John Adams to Abigail Adams

My dearest Friend   New York June 6. 1789

I must now most Seriously request you to come on to me as soon as conveniently you can. never did I want your assistance more than at present, as my Physician and my Nurse. my disorder of Eight years standing has encreased to such a degree as to be very troublesome and not a little alarming.—[1]

I have agreed to take Col Smith and his Family and Furniture into the House with us and they will be removed into it by next Wednesday.— If Charles has a Mind to stay and deliver his French oration at Commencement, I am willing, and I think it will be greatly for his Reputation and Advantage. in that Case Charles and Tommy may both come to gether to New York after Commencement by the Way of Rhode Island, or by the Stage.

As to Louisa, our Family will be very great, and vastly expensive and House very full. if you think however you can find room and Beds &c I will not say any Thing against your bringing her.

You must leave the Furniture to be packed by others and sent after you— We must have it all removed and Sent here, as well as all the Liquers in the Cellar, and many of the Books, for here We must live, and I am determined not to be running backward and forward, till the 4 years are out, unless my Health should oblige me to resign my office of which at present there is some danger.

It has been a great dammage that you did not come on with me yours affectionately   John Adams.[2]

RC (Adams Papers); addressed: "Mrs Adams / Braintree / near / Boston"; internal address: "Mrs Adams."; notation: "Free / John Adams."

[1] For JA's illness dating back to his time in Amsterdam, possibly malaria or typhus, see JA, *Papers*, 11:469–470, note 1.

[2] On 7 June, JA wrote another brief letter to AA (Adams Papers) largely reiterating his comments here and again urging her to come as quickly as possible. He did add that if CA decided to stay for commencement, John Briesler should accompany her to New York.

Abigail Adams to John Adams

my dearest Friend   Braintree June 7th 1789

I this day received the Federal Gazzet, tho I got no Letter from you, I was in hopes to have heard this week in replie to what I wrote on Sunday last. Since that time mr Smith has been in Treaty for me, with two conneticut sloops one of which demanded 50 pounds freight for 2 thirds of his vessel. the other 40, each of them were about 70 Tuns he then applied to Blagett, Barnards owner[1] & has agreed with him for 33 pounds for the whole of the hole of the vessel, and if I do not fill her a deduction to be made it has already taken me a thousand of Boards besides the Boxes which were not broken up, to case what furniture I propose bringing. Brisler has done it all heitherto, I shall be ready for Barnard by the middle of the week, and his owner has engaged that he shall sail as soon as he is ready tho I shall not pretend to bring some of my best furniture What I have put up will be fully adequate to the provision voted, which I think is a thousand dollors less than has been given to Secretaries which have been sent abroad, but perhaps I see only in part.[2] I enclose you a mem. of expences to which I am in part knowing.[3] many others you must already have incurred, & can fill up the Blanks better than I presume they do not mean that house rent is to be included in this estimate. not one single step do that House take without discovering the greatest jealousy of the Senate who before ever heard of putting the two Houses upon a par?

I think Sir I have never petitioned for any office, for any Relation of mine. mr Sam^ll Tufts of Newburry port was formerly in an office which he discharged with fidelity to the publick. mr Dalton can inform you whether, it was Naval officer or collector of impost & excise; I am not certain which, but his character as an honest industrous capable man will not be disputed, and perhaps it may not be thought amiss to bring him forward again.[4]

our season is very dry & thee prospect of a good crop very doubtfull.

you have not once told me how your Health is, our Friends are all well as usual— I shall write you again as soon as I hear from you— Love to mrs Smith & her Boys

believe me / most affectionatly / Yours   A Adams

RC (Adams Papers); addressed: "His Excellency John Adams / Vice President of the United states. / New York—"; docketed: "A A to J A / 1789."

[1] Possibly Samuel Blodget, owner of the *Boston Packet* (*Ship Registers and Enrollments of Boston and Charlestown*, Boston, 1942, p. 27; vol. 7:393).

[2] At this time, Congress was just beginning to consider compensation for the president, vice president, senators, and representatives. Congress ultimately resolved to give $25,000 per annum for the president and $5,000 per annum for the vice president (*U.S. Statutes at Large*, 1:72; *Massachusetts Centinel*, 10 June 1789).

[3] Not found.

[4] Cotton Tufts apparently also approached JA regarding a job for Samuel Tufts, Cotton's brother, a Newburyport merchant who had previously served as collector of duties and excise for Essex County (*Fleet's Pocket Almanack*, 1786, p. 22; vol. 7:273). JA replied to Cotton on 28 June indicating that Samuel would need to contact George Washington directly about any positions (NN:Harkness Coll.).

Abigail Adams to John Adams

my dearest Friend   Sunday Braintree june 14. 1789

I last Evening received your Letter of june 7th I will set of on Wednesday for Providence and embark in the first packet for Newyork. pray get an oz of glober salts and half oz manna & take immediately, an oz of antimonial wine & take 30 drops three time a day.[1] I will be with you however as soon as possible. Barnard got in on fryday. we had two days of voilent and incessant Rain, which tho much wanted, prevented him from unloading his Grain. he has promised me that he will be ready to take my things on Board by wednesday. they are now nearly all ready, and I shall leave Brisler to finish and get them on Board. I and my Neice have gone through the package of every Brittle article, and I think have made them secure I presume there will be more than an hundred packages

When I think of the expence we have formerly been at in casing & packing these same articles I find it now a very triffel in comparison, tho be sure I have not taken near all my things, and a small part only of the Books, but we have gone through it all with our own hands. we have orderd it thus. we have launchd the Scow, & mean to put all the things into it at different Time's & Barnard is to come up to the mouth of the creek by mr Blacks & take them on Board. I have done the best in my power with every thing here, but that best is not so much to my satisfaction as I could wish.

we will endeavour to do every thing that falls to our share with as much calmness & composure as possible, & where they do not go according to our minds, we will bring our minds to go according to them if possible. let sail over the Rocks & Shoals with as much safety as we can, happy if we split neither upon the one, or founder upon the other. Charles has been at home with me for a week and I think it best as he has taken leave, to bring him on. if he stays a̶ c̶o̶m̶m̶e̶n̶c̶e̶m̶e̶n̶t̶ some entertainment will be expected, and I shall not be here to attend at all to it. I thank you for your permission to bring Louissa. she will save me very soon the hire of one person. she has been leaning to dress Hair of Mrs Brisler and she will take a great deal of care of, of me buy her needle work, and indeed every kind of attention that she can pay either to you or to me. her temper is perfectly mild, and I think her every Way a good child— adieu my dearest Friend pray take care of your Health. I shall consult dr Tufts & take his advice— my Head and Hands are so full of Buisness that I Scarcly know what I have written— Love to mrs smith & Regards to mr & Mrs Jay— from your ever / affectionate   A Adams

RC (Adams Papers); addressed by CA: "His Excellency John Adams.— / Vice President of the united States / New York"; endorsed: "Mrs Adams. / June 14. 1789."

[1] Glauber's salt, sulphate of sodium, named for Johann Rudolf Glauber, who first produced it artificially, had purgative qualities. Similarly, manna, the dried gum of various plants, was used as a laxative, and antimonial wine—sherry mixed with antimony—was used as an emetic (*OED*).

Abigail Adams to Cotton Tufts

Sir   Braintree june 17. 1789

Not being able to dispose of my oxen as I expected, & to have taken half the money for them, I do not find myself able to pay French without taking less than 50 Dollors with me, 46 of which it will take for my conveyence to Providence & passage on Board the packet.

I must therefore request the favour of you sir to pay him for seven months wages at 50 dollers pr year. you will see by the papers that I have settled an account with my Brother & pay'd Spear a Parish Rate I have an account with vezey, it cannot be large as he was pay'd last fall, a small accompt with mr Marsh & something to be setled with deacon Webb. I do not recollect any thing Else. I have left the Horse with my Brother for sale out of which he is to pay 20 dollors to col Thayer for the wood Land. my oxen I wish to have sold as soon as possible, by note if a responsible person can be found who wants them. Thomas spoke to me for a Hat a round one is all he wants. I fear sir that we shall fall in your debt, and wish you would let me have given you a Note for the thirty pounds I had of you I have paid Brisler half a years wages 10.£ 6.ˢ ᵈ out of the Thirty & sent my son 20 dollors, Boards Nails and other expences attendant upon getting my furniture on Board, and some small articles of cloathing for Tom & Charles, has taken away all that I sold my stears & wool for. at present I fear we shall not be able to remitt any thing to you, but when I get to House keeping I shall be better able to judge– I cannot but repeat my sincere acknowledgments to you for all your kind and Friendly attentions, and believe me Dear Sir your / ever affectionate   Abigail Adams

P S I have given French an order which he will present to you with my papers you will find an account vs John Newcombs[1] he has one against me which will nearly balance, not quite I believe because I cannot get him to settle I inclose you a Note for the money due to French–

RC (NHi:Misc. Mss. Adams, Abigail); endorsed: "Mʳˢ· A. Adams June 17. 1789."

[1] Probably John Newcomb (1761–1823), a member of a Braintree family of stoneworkers. The bill in question was likely for the construction of a wall just completed between the Adams and Bass properties (Sprague, *Braintree Families*, p. 3431R, 3434, 3435, 3449, 3450, 3454; U.S. Census, 1790, Mass., p. 196; AA to JA, 26 April and 5 May, both above).

Abigail Adams' Directions Concerning Their Massachusetts Houses and Farms

[*ca. 17 June 1789*]

Mr Bass is to pay 20 Dollors pr Year and the Taxes for one half the House and the whole, of the small garden this Rent is to be paid this Year in work to me or my order Pheby is to pay four dollors a year the year to commence from July 1.ˢᵗ 1789 Seven months she has lived in the House to be given to her— Mrs Palmer is to pay 15 dollors pr year She is to have what is now upon the Garden, the fruit excepted which is Leased to Brother Adams. Mrs Palmer is to have the potatoes planted behind the House. she is to have what wood remains in the Yard after mrs Brisler moves: during her stay the wood to be in common, 2 small plumb Trees near the House to go with the house The Horse Cart sadle Bridle—Farming utensals sledge to be deliverd to the dr

memorandum

Deacon Webb had two ox hides one cow one stear & two calf skins[.] of Him received one Side of Leather[.] mr marsh may have taken some uncertain[1]

MS (Adams Papers, Adams Office Manuscripts, Box 1, folder 1); endorsed by Cotton Tufts: "M$^{rs.}$ Adams / [Directions?]."

[1] Cotton Tufts wrote beneath this line that "Mr Marsh has had one Side 25$^{W.}$" costing £1.1.8. According to Tufts, Marsh also had taken "one ox hide & Cow hide" at the same price for a cost of £0.2.4.

Abigail Adams to Mary Smith Cranch

my Dear sister   providence june 19. 1789

This day is the Aniversary of my Landing in Boston and Tomorrow that of my departure from it. many are the mercies I have to be thankfull for through all my Perigranations, all the painfull scenes I have past through, has been the temporary seperation from my Friends, fatigue either of Body or Mind I scarcly name amongst them for I have my pleasures and gratifications which I set down as a balance to them. cousin Lucy has told you that I left Home about 8 oclock we proceeded to Man's Inn in Wrentham before we stop'd 27 miles where we dinned upon Roast veal roast chickings sallad &c, west India sweet meats I ought not to forget in the desert, it is really a very good Inn.[1] we sat off at three oclock and reachd Attlebouroug about five where we Bated & Met with mr & mrs Mason & miss Powel going to Newport.[2] we past an agreeable Hour to gether at Six we renewed, our journey and reach'd Providence at half after Seven. we put up at daggets Inn just at the entrance of the Town Situated upon a Hill opposite the State House commanding a fine view of the River & the whole Town. we are tolerably well accommodated, but should have been much better if the Governour had not taken the best Chamber before I came, (the court being now in

Session) and he has not had the politeness either to offer to give it up or to make me a visit, tho he has had much conversation with Polly and now & then takes a Peap at me from entry.[3] my first inquiry was after a packet. I found only Browns here, he came & I like him he has a very good packet & Bears a good character himself, but Says he cannot be ready to Sail till saturday morning, the wind to day is directly against us.

In about an hour after my arrival I received the visits of the following persons— mr & mrs Arnold,[4] the Gentleman was one of the Committe who came to mr Adams—from the Towns of Newport & Providence mr & mrs Francis. this Lady is the daughter of mr John Brown of this Town, so celebrated for his Wealth[5]—miss Bowen the sister to the late Governour,[6] Col Peck, mr Robins Tuter to the Colledge & mr Shrimpton Hutchinson and Mrs Nightingale,[7] all of whom in the Name of many other gentlemen & Ladies regreeted that I had dissapointed them in not letting it be known when I should be here as they had agreed to meet me several miles out of Town. mr & mrs Francis invited me to take up my abode with them. I excused myself, but have promised to take Tea & spend the Evening if I do not go out of Town. this morning I am to take a ride with them to see the Town & to return my visits, if I am not prevented by company but my wish is not to be detained a moment. pray write me & let me know by the next post whether my furniture is all on Board Barnard & when he will Sail— I should be glad to hear how mrs Brisler is. I left her in great affliction.

I feel the want of mrs Brisler as a Hair dresser, on other accounts Polly does very well Matilda is well, & her finger much better. let mrs Storer know if you please— my best Regards to all my dear Friends. it grieved me to see you so dull, you used to keep up your Spirits better do not let them flagg. a merry Heart does good like a medicine we shall hear often from one an other, and the Seperation be renderd less painfull by that means—

This moment a Card is brought me from mr Brown & Lady with an invitation to dine with them to day & that they will visit me at ten—I accept it, as Brown cannot go till tomorrow. adieu my dear sister most / affectionatly Yours.   Abigail Adams—

RC (MWA:Abigail Adams Letters); addressed: "To / Mrs Mary Cranch / Braintree"; endorsed by Richard Cranch: "Letter from M[rs] A / Adams, Providence, / June 19[th.] 1789."

[1] This Wrentham, Mass., inn was originally run by Pelatiah Man (b. 1689) and

then by his son David (b. 1724) (George S. Mann, *Genealogy of the Descendants of Rich-*

ard Man of Scituate, Mass., Boston, 1884, p. 22; *Boston Evening Post*, 19 May 1755).

[2] Jonathan Mason Jr. (1756–1831), Princeton 1774, was a former law clerk of JA's who married Susan Powell (1760–1841) in 1779. From 1786 to 1796, he represented Boston in the Mass. General Court, and he later served as a U.S. senator. Miss Powell was probably Susan's sister, Anna Dummer Powell (1770–1848), who married Thomas Perkins in 1800 (vol. 4:337; *DAB*; Boston, *24th Report*, p. 299; *NEHGR*, 26:143 [April 1872]).

[3] John Collins (1717–1795) served as the third governor of the state of Rhode Island from 1786 to 1790; he had previously represented Rhode Island in the Continental Congress from 1778 to 1781 (*DAB*).

Daggett's Inn, which had been recommended to AA by Capt. James Brown, was probably run by the same Daggett family who operated the ferry across the Seekonk River along the main route between Boston and New York (JA to AA, 19 May, note 1, above; Edward Field, *State of Rhode Island and Providence Plantations at the End of the Century: A History*, 3 vols., Boston, 1902, 2:535–537).

[4] Probably Providence merchant Welcome Arnold (1745–1798) and his wife, Patience Greene Arnold (1754–1809). Arnold was a business associate of John Brown and Joseph Nightingale (Franklin Stuart Coyle, *Welcome Arnold (1745–1798), Providence Merchant: The Founding of an Enterprise*, Brown Univ., Ph.D. diss., 1972, p. 6–7, 12).

[5] Abby Brown (1766–1821), the daughter of Sarah Smith (1738–1825) and John Brown (1736–1803), of the wealthy Providence merchant family, was married to John Francis (1763–1796) of Philadelphia. Together, John Brown and John Francis formed the company of Brown & Francis, which was the first Providence house to engage in the China trade (James B. Hedges, *The Browns of Providence Plantations: The Colonial Years*,

Providence, 1968, p. xx, 19; *DAB*).

[6] Jabez Bowen (1739–1815), Yale 1757, served as deputy governor of Rhode Island for most of William Greene's administration from 1778 to 1786, at which time he was appointed a delegate to the Annapolis Convention. He married Sarah Brown (1742–1800) in 1762. Bowen had several sisters, at least three of whom—Nancy (1762–1801), Betsey (b. 1765), and Frances (b. 1768)—were still unmarried (Dexter, *Yale Graduates*, 2:452–454; *Representative Men and Old Families of Rhode Island*, 3 vols., Chicago, 1908, 1:1009–1011; James N. Arnold, *Vital Record of Rhode Island, 1636–1850*, 21 vols., Providence, 1891–1912, 14:112, 527).

[7] Probably Col. William Peck of Providence who had served as the adjutant-general of the Rhode Island militia during the Revolution (*JCC*, 8:561; Rhode Island, *Acts and Resolves of the General Assembly, 1783*, Providence, 1785, Evans, No. 18150, p. 11).

Asher Robbins (1757–1845) was appointed tutor at Rhode Island College (later Brown University) in 1782 and remained in the position until 1790. He subsequently studied law and became a U.S. district attorney, state assemblyman, and later U.S. senator serving from 1825 to 1839 (*Biog. Dir. Cong.*).

Shrimpton Hutchinson (ca. 1718–1811) had previously been a Boston merchant, running a store called the Three Sugar Loaves and Cannister on King Street (*Boston Evening Post*, 18 Dec. 1749; Arnold, *Vital Record of Rhode Island*, 13:516).

Probably Abigail Belcher Nightingale (1720–1794), widow of Samuel Nightingale (1715–1786) and mother of Providence merchants Samuel (1741–1814) and Joseph Nightingale (1748–1797) (William Richard Cutter, *New England Families Genealogical and Memorial*, 3d ser., 4 vols., N.Y., 1915, 2:928–929; *NEHGR*, 109:4 [Jan. 1955]).

Mary Smith Cranch to Abigail Adams

My dear Sister   Braintree June 21[d] 1789

I last evening receiv'd your kind Letter from Providence but shall not be able to get one to you by tomorrows Post—but shall write by the next I have not seen mr Brisler since you went away but heard that your Goods were puting on Board the vessel yesterday

This day Twelves months I accompany'd my dear Brother & Sister to the House of God to offer with grateful hearts I hope our acknowledgments ffor the favours we had receiv'd during our long Separation from each other Providence has again call'd you from me & tho it is what I ought to have wish'd as a Lover of my country, I must mourn as an affectionate Sister, I do not know why I have found it so much harder parting now than before, but it really is so. I have more difficultis to incounter now than then. & my prospects are gloomy. this is one reason I believe— I feel as if I should want the kind Soothings of my Sisters I wish & try to be chearful I know it is my duty to be so. but I cannot always succeed— Patience & resignation are the great dutys I have to exerccesse Hope & Trust must be their attendants or the Heart would faint my wishes are not large. there is therefore the greater probability that they may be gratified— Honour without profit we have had enough of— To pay our debts, to live decently & to see our Friends in the way we have been use'd to is not an unreasonable wish? is it my Sister?— but however providence may See fit to dispose of us I hope to be resign'd— I will rejoice in the prosperity of my Friends & endeavour to find my Happinss in doing what I can to make others so—

Before this reaches you I hope you will have arriv'd safe & made your Friends happy by your presence, I will rejoice in their joy. I will think of you as a happy circle, & place myself among you. I will repair to the nursery & play with the sweet little Boys, William do not break your little Horse & go tell mama who sent it to you—

Pray tell me what kind of a Being they have fore a Governor in Rhode Island— I hope Polly told him whose Grandaughter she was— I was once in company with the Browns at major Fullers. There were a number of the Family din'd there Louisia must be much gratified by the new Scene which has open'd upon her— Her modest mild manners will gain her many admires. She will be flutter'd round. your watchful eye will ever be upon her I know— my dear charles will I hope guard against every temptation to evil— tell him that I love him with an affection little short of what I feel for my own son— tell him also if you please that as he has his companions now to chuse anew that I conjure him by all that is sacred as he values his reputation among the virtuous & worthy of mankind— as he would not imbitter the declining years of his Parents & wound the hearts of his Friends to be careful who he admits to call him thier Friend & associate He will write to his cousins I hope I wanted to say a great deal to him before he went away but I could not—

I thank you my dear Sister for every expression of your affection in whatever way discover'd— The suit of velvet will be very useful the contents of the Bottles will be kept to ristore the languid spirit—

I shall expect to hear as much Politick from you as you can with safety convey. I shall feel importan then among your Friends— I am so pleas'd with Judge Dana & Lady that if I should go to cambridge I shall make them another visit, & must have a little politicks to talk of you know if I should—

remember me affectionately to mr Adams to mr & mrs Smith & all my Friends & accept / the warmest affection of your / grateful Sister   Mary Cranch

you cannot think how I am worried with my Girl She is not worth a copper I am in chase of another [. . .] could not come

RC (Adams Papers).

Abigail Adams to Mary Smith Cranch

My dear sister   Richmond Hill june 28th 1789

I wrote you from Providence some account of my polite reception there & closed my Letter just as I had accepted an invitation to dine with mr Brown & Lady. the forenoon was pass't in receiving visits from all the principal gentlemen and Ladies of the Town, who seemed to vie with each other, to convince me that tho they were inhabitants of an Antifederal state. they were themselves totally against the measures persued by it, and that they entertaind the highest Regard and Respect for the Character with which I was so intimately connected, altho to their great mortification they had been prevented the Honour of having any share in placing him in his respected station[1]

Mr Brown sent his Carriage & Son to conduct me his House which is one of the Grandest I have seen in this Country. every thing in and about it, wore the marks of magnificence & taste.[2] mrs Brown met me at the door & with the most obliging Smile accosted me with—["]Friend I am glad to see the here" the simplicity of her manners & dress with the openness of her countanance & the friendlyness of her behaviour charmed me beyond all the studied politeness of European manners— they had colleted between 22 persons to dine with me tho the notice was so short, & gave an Elegant entertainment upon a service of Plate. towards Evening I made a Tour round the Town, & drank Tea & spent the Evening with mr & Mrs Francis whom I mentiond to you before. here the company was much enlarged, & many persons introduced to me who had no opportunity before of visiting me, amongst those Ladies, with whom I was most pleased was the Lady & two sisters of Governour Bowen.[3] about Eleven I returnd To my lodgings and the next morning went on Board the Handcock packet we had contrary wind all Day, by which means we did not reach Newport untill Seven oclock. I had been only a few moments arrived when mr Merchant came on Board and insisted that I with my whole Family should go on shore & Lodge at his House. he would take no refusal. he sent his daughter down to receive & accompany my Neice, & came himself in a few moments with a carriage to attend me. at his House I was kindly & Hospitably Treated by his Lady & daughters.[4] we slept there & the next morning were early summond on Board the packet. Captain Brown had very civily taken his wife to attend upon me, & accomodate me during my passage[5] I found her a very well Bred Geenteel woman, but neither civility attention or politeness could remedy the sea sickness or give me a fair wind or dispell the Thunder Gusts which attended us both night & day. in short I resolved upon what I have frequently before, that I would never again embark upon the water, but this resolution I presume will be kept as my former ones have been. we were five days upon the water. Heat want of rest, sea sickness & terror for I had my share of that, all contributed to fatigue me and I felt upon my arrival quite tame & spiritless Louissa was very sick, but behaved like a Heroine Matilda had her share but when she was a little recoverd she was the life of us all Polly was half dead all the Passage & sufferd more from sea sickness than any of us. Charls eat & slept without any inconvenience. when we came to the wharff, I desired the Captain to go to our Friend mr MacCormick and inform him of my arrival, if he was not to be found to go to the Senate Chamber & inform mr A. who from the hour of the day I knew must be there. mr otis the secretary came to me with a Carriage & I reach'd Richmond Hill on Thursday one oclock to my no small joy I found mr Adams in better Health than I feard mr & mrs Smith quite well & every thing so well arranged that Beds & a few other articles seem only necessary towards keeping House with comfort, and I begin to think, that my furniture will be troublesome to me, some part of it I mean whilst mrs Smith remains with me. master John was grown out of my knowledge, wil-

378

liam is still at Jamaica. our House has been a mere Levee ever since I arrived morning & Evening. I took the earliest opportunity (the morning after my arrival) to go & pay my respects to mrs Washington mrs Smith accompanied me. She received me with great ease & politeness, she is plain in her dress, but that plainness is the best of every article. she is in mourning, her Hair is white, her Teeth Beautifull, her person rather short than otherways, hardly so large as my Ladyship, and if I was to speak sincerly, I think she is a much better figure, her manners are modest and unassuming, dignified and femenine, not the Tincture of ha'ture about her.[6] *his majesty* was ill & confined to his Room.[7] I had not the pleasure of a presentation to him, but the satisfaction of hearing that he regreeted it equally with myself. col Humphries who had paid his compliments to me in the morning & Breakfasted with me, attended mrs washington & mr Lear the Private Secretary, was the introducer—[8] thus you have an account of my first appearence— the Principal Ladies who have visited me are the Lady & daughter of the Governour Lady Temple the Countess de Brehim, Mrs Knox & 25 other Ladies many of the Senators, all their Ladies all the Foreign ministers & some of the Reps.

We are most delightfully situated, the prospect all around is Beautifull in the highest degree, it is a mixture of the sublime & Beautifull— amidst it all I sigh for many of my dear Friends and connections. I can make no domestick arrangment till Brisler arrives— remember me affectionatly to all my Friends particularly my aged parent, to my children to whom I cannot write as yet to my dear Lucy & worthy dr Tufts in short to all whom I love yours most tenderly   A Adams

RC (MWA:Abigail Adams Letters); addressed: "To / Mrs Mary Cranch / Braintree."

[1] The state of Rhode Island had declined to send delegates to the 1787 Constitutional Convention, to hold a ratifying convention, or to select electors to choose a president and vice president. Under increasing commercial pressure and in order to participate in the debates over the Bill of Rights, Rhode Island finally called a convention and ratified the Constitution in May 1790 by a vote of 34 to 32 (Florence Parker Simister, *The Fire's Center: Rhode Island in the Revolutionary Era, 1763–1790*, Providence, 1979, p. 233–240).

[2] John Brown's house, located at the corner of Power and Benefit Streets in Provi-dence, was considered at the time one of the finest homes in America. Today it houses the Rhode Island Historical Society. John and Sarah Brown's only surviving son, James (1761–1834), chose not to enter the family mercantile business (James B. Hedges, *The Browns of Providence Plantations: The Colonial Years*, Providence, 1968, p. xx, 19, 199).

[3] For the Bowen family, see AA to Mary Smith Cranch, 19 June, note 6, above.

[4] Henry Marchant (1741–1796) had known JA in the Continental Congress, where Marchant served from 1777 to 1779. He repre-sented Newport in the Rhode Island General

Assembly from 1784 to 1790 and was a staunch advocate of ratification. He and his wife, Rebecca Cooke, had two daughters, Sarah and Elizabeth, as well as a son, William (*DAB*; James N. Arnold, *Vital Record of Rhode Island, 1636–1850*, 21 vols., Providence, 1891–1912, 4:104).

⁵ Capt. James Brown was married to Free-love Brown (ca. 1765–1819), the daughter of Col. William Brown of Providence (Arnold, *Vital Record of Rhode Island*, 13:221, 14:541).

⁶ For Martha Washington and her family, see Descriptive List of Illustrations, No. 11, above.

⁷ George Washington's illness was more serious than most people realized, with a fever stemming from an infection connected to a tumor in his leg. He had the tumor removed on 17 June 1789. By early July, he was able to conduct government business though he remained weak for some time thereafter (Washington, *Papers, Presidential Series*, 3:76–77).

⁸ Tobias Lear (1762–1816), Harvard 1783, originally from New Hampshire, served as Washington's private secretary from 1786 to 1793 (*Harvard Quinquennial Cat.*; Washington, *Papers, Presidential Series*, 1:98).

John Quincy Adams to John Adams

Dear Sir. — Newbury-Port June 28th: 1789

It has not been altogether from a neglect of my duties that I have hitherto omitted writing you; from situation as well as from inclination, I have been in a great measure secluded from such political information, as might afford you any entertainment, and from a proper modesty, I thought it best to forbear transmitting, any insignificant details concerning my own person.— Even now the same motives which have hitherto deterred me from writing, are not without their influence: but perhaps a moment's relaxation from the affairs of a Nation, to attend to those of a private and domestic nature, may not be disagreeable; and if my Letter should be impertinent, I shall at least solace myself with the reflection that it can probably only add one, more to an innumerable quantity of a similar nature.

Three months have elapsed, since my return to this Town. My Health has been restored beyond my expectations, and I have been able without injuring it, to devote a larger portion of my Time to study, than I hoped to when I left Braintree.— Lord Coke, Saunders, Hale and Blackstone have contributed to add to my small stock of professional knowledge; and I have made some researches into the doctrine of pleading.¹ My greatest apprehensions at present, are with respect to the practical part of the profession. The skill to apply general knowledge to particular cases, is no less important than the knowledge itself; and a new piece of mechanism, will often perform its operations with great irregularity, however well it may be constructed. I remain still in a state of irresolution and suspense with respect to the place of my future residence. I have consulted Mr: Parsons upon the Subject: he said he could not advise me so

11. "THE WASHINGTON FAMILY," BY EDWARD SAVAGE, 1789–1796
See page xvi

well at present, as he might after the federal judiciary System shall be established; because he knew not what vacancies might be created by that circumstance. He however hinted that if either himself or M^r: Bradbury should be removed he should recommend this place to me.—² I know not what his own expectations are; but I have some reason to suppose he has his eye upon two offices; those of the district Judge, and Attorney general; either of which I believe would suit him well.—³ And by his putting the supposition of his being taken off from the practice I have conjectured that there was in his own mind, an idea of the probability of his appointment.— As I believe his talents are much better calculated to administer laws than to make them, I wish he may succeed. Perhaps even an involuntary consideration of my own interest, has some effect to give a bias to my opinion. I am the more free to make this confession, because I suppose the appointments are all adjusted ere this, and I shall not therefore appear in the humiliating light of a solicitor; which I wish ever to avoid; and in which I am well perswaded I should be unsuccessful were I now to assume it.

As our Newspapers are probably transmitted to you with regularity, I can give you very little news in the public Line. The very great majority of votes by which M^r: H. was reelected, and the influence which was successfully exerted for M^r: A. appeared somewhat singular, after the event of all the contests relating to the federal elections; There have been a variety of subordinate political manoeuvres in the choice of representatives of the different towns. Those in Boston, you have undoubtedly been informed of. There was in this town a faint struggle for a change in the representation; but the old members came in with a respectable majority.

Our general Court, after sitting, about a month, and busying themselves upon the subject of Finance just sufficient to refer it over to the next Session, have adjourned to some time in January; when it will be too late in the political year, to adopt any decisive measures.⁴ There has been a scheme on foot for sinking our State debt by means of a Lottery. From M^r: Parsons's conversation I have supposed that the plan originated with him; and in his speculative principles he thinks it would reconcile the claims of public Justice, with the interests of an impotent debtor. The proposal was to redeem £40,000 of the debt, by refunding only £10,000 in Specie to the adventurers.— Besides the impropriety of encouraging a gambling disposition among the people, I confess the plan appears to me equally inconsistent with the dignity of a sovereignstate and with the integrity of an honest debtor. For whatever expedients may be used to conceal or disguise the iniquity of the transaction, nothing can be more clear than that where a debt of £40,000, is paid with 10,000 the creditor must be defrauded. The bill pass'd in the House by a majority of 73 to 52, but was non-concurred by the Senate.

The High Sheriff of this County, M. Farley, died about a week since. The place has been offered to M^{r:} Jackson, who has declined accepting it: and M^{r:} B. Bartlet of Haverhill is named as the person who will probably be appointed.[5] My Mother and Brother I suppose have arrived at New York before this. They left Boston ten days ago. If it should be convenient and agreeable, I shall ask permission to pay you a visit about the beginning of October. I mentioned September to my Mamma; but I did not then recollect that our Court of Common Pleas sits in this town in that Month; when my attendance at the office will probably be required.

Col^{l:} Smith and My Sister, with their children I hope are well. I know not what apology I shall make to them for not having written to them; I intend however soon in some measure to repair my fault.— I shall hope at least to hear often from my brother Charles; he is still more averse than I am to epistolary exertions; but it is an aversion which I hope he will make a point of overcoming.

The proceedings of Congress have almost entirely superseded all other subjects of political speculation. The revenue bill has hitherto chiefly engaged the public attention. The original duty upon molasses, exceedingly alarmed many of our West India merchants, and whatever may be said of discarding all local & personal considerations, they have not I believe, been so much pleased with any Act of the President of the Senate, as his turning the vote for reducing the duty to 3 cents. This observation however only applies to a few; for I do not know that the circumstance is generally known.—[6] The Judiciary bill has not yet been published here: I had a transient sight of a copy, which I believe M^{r:} Dalton sent. M^{r:} Parsons thinks 6 Judges will not be enough; and objects to the joining the district Judge to the other two in the circuits. Because it gives him a casting voice in affirming his own decisions.[7]

I am, Dear Sir, your dutiful Son.   J. Q. Adams.

RC (Adams Papers); endorsed: "J. Q. A. June 28. / ans^d July 9. 1789."

[1] JQA was likely reading Sir Matthew Hale, *The History and Analysis of the Common Law of England*, London, 1731, and Sir Edmund Saunders, *Les reports du tres erudite Edmund Saunders . . . des divers pleadings et cases en le Court del bank le Roy* (*The Reports of the Most Learned Sir Edmund Saunders . . . of Several Pleadings and Cases in the*

Court of King's Bench), 2 vols., London, 1686. For JQA's comments on William Blackstone's *Commentaries* and Sir Edward Coke's *Institutes*, see *Diary*, 2:372–373.

[2] Theophilus Bradbury (1739–1803), Harvard 1757, initially practiced law in Falmouth, Mass. (now Maine), where his law students included Theophilus Parsons. He moved to Newburyport in the late 1770s. He served in Congress from 1795 to 1797 and as a judge on the Mass. Supreme Judicial Court from 1797 until his death (*Sibley's Harvard Graduates*, 14:143–146).

[3] Parsons never held any federal positions, nor did he leave Newburyport until 1800, though he was named chief justice of the Mass. Supreme Judicial Court in 1806 (*DAB*).

[4] The General Court met from 27 May to 26 June, after which it adjourned until 13 Jan. 1790 (Mass., *Acts and Laws*, 1788–1789, p. 604, 611).

[5] Gen. Michael Farley of Ipswich, a former member of the Mass. General Court and Executive Council, died on 20 June. He was succeeded by Bailey Bartlett of Haverhill, whom Gov. John Hancock appointed to the position on 1 July. Bartlett continued in that position, with one brief interval, until his death in 1830 (D. Hamilton Hurd, comp.,

History of Essex County, Massachusetts, 2 vols., Phila., 1888, 1:619, 2:2009–2010).

[6] For the records of the debates in the Senate over the duty on molasses, see *First Fed. Cong.*, 9:55, 57–58, 66–68. "An Act for Laying a Duty on Goods, Wares, and Merchandises Imported into the United States" ultimately set the rate at 2 1/2 cents per gallon (1st Congress, Sess. I, ch. 2, sect. 1). While the Senate debates were secret, the Massachusetts newspapers did report what they could learn on the subject, focusing particularly on the duties on molasses and rum; see, for example, *Massachusetts Centinel*, 6, 17 June 1789.

[7] The judiciary bill, "An Act to Establish the Judicial Courts of the United States," was signed into law on 24 September. It provided for six Supreme Court justices (one chief justice and five associates). It also established a structure in which the circuit courts, which reviewed district court decisions, would include a district court judge and two Supreme Court justices. In the final version of the law, however, a district court judge was specifically forbidden from voting on any appeal of his own decision (1st Congress, Sess. I, ch. 20, sects. 1, 4).

Mary Smith Cranch to Abigail Adams

My dear Sister   Braintree July 5th 1789

I promiss'd to write you by the Post when your Furniture Sail'd but Doctor Tufts Said he had done it—[1] I hope you have it safe & that it has been more fortunate than in its last voyage— I heard you did not leave Providence till the monday after you left us. I want to hear of your arrival reception &c—how you found mr Adams mrs Smith & her little ones—whether she will continue in the House with you & whether you have not all been made Sick with the continue'd heat of the last fortnight. we have not had such for several years. it has fallen hard upon me because I have had such poor help. Ester Baxter has been with me for the last week or I believe I should have been quite sick.[2] I have now got a Girl from milton who appears as if she would do after I have taught her to cook & do twenty other things which she knows nothing of at present— It is very unreasonable that such an one should demand the same wages that a Girl, has who does not want such teaching but so it is—

mrs Palmer has mov'd into your house[3] I have been their but a few moments since They appear to be much gratified with their situation mrs Brisler has been very well for her has been threaten'd once or twice with one of her ill turns but they went of. her eldest child will soon run alone she leads about prittily

I heard last week from both your sons they were well— uncle Quincy was at meeting last Sabbath— what a life he leads without a creature about him in whos Society he can take any pleasure— I could not live so

I saw your mother Hall today she was as well as usual. every thing in Braintree remains as when you left it excepting that old Benjamin cleaverly dy'd last week & that Becca Field made young—Ben—pay her four dollars for attempting to get into her Lodging room window in the night[4] she came with a complant to mr Cranch & he write him a Letter which frightned him heartlly

Mr Guild I hear is gone to New york by him I hope you will write me. you are in the midst of the busy world I almost out of it. I have very little variety in my circle & what I tell you in one Letter I must repeat in another. I should write oftener if my stock of inteligence was greater or more important.—

July 6th

I have just been gratified with a Letter from my dear sister, mr woodward took it out of the Post office this morning I am indeed rejoic'd to hear of your safe arrival after so painful & dangerous a voyage. Hear I was pleasing my self that you had fine weather & a good wind for such we had hear— I should have been distress'd indeed if I had known your situation— I have an oppertunity to send this immediately

adieu yours most affectionatly   Mary Cranch

RC (Adams Papers); addressed by Richard Cranch: "To / M^rs. Adams / Lady of the Vice / President. / N: York"; docketed: "Mrs Mary Cranch / to Mrs A Adams / July 5th 1789."

[1] Not found.

[2] Esther Baxter was probably the daughter of Daniel Baxter and Prudence Spear, born prior to 1774. She married Eben Newcomb Jr. in 1794 (Joseph Nickerson Baxter, *Memorial of the Baxter Family*, Boston, 1879, p. 22–23, 27).

[3] Mary Cranch Palmer, the widow of Gen. Joseph Palmer, moved into the Old House with her two daughters, Mary (Polly) and Elizabeth Palmer. Mary Cranch Palmer remained there until her death in Feb. 1790; the two sisters stayed until Elizabeth's marriage to Joseph Cranch in the summer of 1790, when all three moved to West Point, N.Y. (Mary Smith Cranch to AA, 28 Feb. 1790, Adams Papers; *Grandmother Tyler's Book*, p. 109–110).

[4] Benjamin Cleverly (1710–1789) was a life-long Braintree resident and had served

as constable and surveyor of highways for the town. A loyalist, he was declared "Inimical to the United States" in 1777 but continued to live in Braintree until his death on 3 July 1789. His eldest son Benjamin (b.

1731/32) was a cordwainer (*Braintree Town Records*, p. 297, 312, 481–482, 690; Pattee, *Old Braintree*, p. 144; Sprague, *Braintree Families*, p. 1085, 1085R).

John Adams to John Quincy Adams

Richmond Hill New York July 9. 1789

I thank you my dear Son, for your dutiful Letter of the 28th. of June, and rejoice, with exceeding Joy, in the recovery of your health

My Advice is, to give yourself very little Thought about the Place of your future Residence. a few Months will produce changes that will easily Settle that Question for you. Mr Parsons's great Law Abilities make me wish that the Public may be availed of them, in one of the most respectable Situations, and I doubt not that he will be promoted either on the State Bench or an higher.

I Shall be very happy, my Son, to See you here, whenever the Journey may be most convenient to you and to Mr Parsons: but I should wish you to be here when the House is Sitting, that you may hear the Debates, and know the Members. Charles has been very industrious and useful to me, Since his Arrival. He is gone with his Brother and Sister, on a visit to Jamaica. I will enjoin upon him a constant Correspondence with you.

I am of Mr Parsons's opinion that Six Judges are not enough. his objection to joining the district Judge to the other two in the Circuits, has been obviated, by excluding him from a Voice in any Cause, which he may have adjudged before.

Your Letter my Son is full of matter, and has given me great pleasure. I wish you to write me, once a Week.– I am at a loss to guess, how you came by the Anecdote, that I turned the Vote for 3 Cents on Molasses. one Penny a gallon, would go so far towards paying my Salary that I think the Molasses Eaters ought not to be so stingy as they are to me. but neither Molasses, nor fish nor millions upon millions of Acres of Land, will ever be of any Service to you, or even make me comfortable. I must be pinched and Streightened till I die, and you must have to toil and drudge as I have done. do it, my dear son with out murmuring. This is entre nous.– Independence, my Boy and freedom from humiliating obligations, are greater Sources of happiness, than Riches.

My office requires, rather Severe duty, and it is a kind of Duty, which if I do not flatter myself too much, is not quite adapted to my Character.— I mean it is too inactive, and mechanical.— The Chancellor sometimes wishes to leave the Woolsack,[1] and engage in debate. but as it cannot be done, I am content, tho it sometimes happens that I am much enclined to think I could throw a little light upon a subject.— if my health and Patience should hold out my four Years, I can retire and make Way for some of you younger folk, for one Vacancy makes many Promotions.

if you have turned Quaker, with our H. of Reps, as from the outside of your Letter one would suspect, I think you ought to have Thee'd and Thou'd your Correspondent in the Inside.—[2] if not, you ought to have given him the Title of Goodman, or Something, according to the Doctrine in Shenestones School Mistress.

> Albeit ne flatt'ry did corrupt her Truth
> Ne pompous Title did debauch her Ear
> Goody, Goodwoman, Gossip, N'aunt, forsooth,
> or Dame, the Sole Additions, She did hear;
> Yet these She challeng'd; these She held right dear;
> Ne would esteem him Act, as mought behove
> Who Should not honour'd eld, with these revere;
> For never Title yet so mean could prove,
> But there was eke a mind, which did that title love.[3]

I am my dear Child, with the tenderest / Affection your Father
John Adams.

P. S. There was a public Character among the Romans, who was called Prince of the Senate, Princeps Senatus, I believe.[4] as you may have leisure I wish you would look in Livy, Tacitus Cicero and all the rest, and write me what you find concerning him.

RC (Adams Papers); internal address: "Mr John Quincy Adams."; endorsed: "My Father. 9. July 1789." and "M^r: Adams. July 9. 1789." Tr (Adams Papers).

[1] A reference to the seat of the Lord Chancellor in the British House of Lords, made of a square parcel of wool (*OED*).

[2] The cover to this letter, with the address, has not been found.

[3] William Shenstone, *The School-Mistress, a Poem. In Imitation of Spenser*, London, 1742, lines 73–81.

[4] In the Roman senate, the *princeps senatus* was the first name on the senate list as compiled by the censors. Once granted this position, he retained it for the rest of his life. As *princeps senatus*, the senator had the right to speak first on any motion and consequently could be extremely influential in debates (*Oxford Classical Dicy.*).

Abigail Adams to Mary Smith Cranch

my dear sister   Richmond Hill july 12th 1789

I received your kind Letter by mr Brisler who reachd here on the 4th of july, Since which you will easily suppose I have been very buisily engaged in arraneging my Family affairs. this added to the intence heat of the season Some company (tho for three days I was *fashionably* not at Home,) and some visiting which was indispensable, having more than fifty upon my list, my Time has been so wholy occupied that I have not taken a pen, yet my Thoughts have not been so occupied, but that they have frequently visited you, and my other Friends in the Neighbourhood, and tho I have here, as to situation one of the most delightfull spots I have seen in this Country, yet I find the want of some of my particular connection's but an all wise Providence has seen fit to curtail our wishes and to limit our enjoyments, that we may not be unmindfull of our dependance or forget the Hand from whence they flow. I have a favour to request of all my near and intimate Friend's it is to desire them to watch over my conduct and if at any time they perceive any alteration in me with respect to them, arising as they may suppose from my situation in Life, I beg they would with the utmost freedom acquaint me with it. I do not feel within myself the least disposition of the kind, but I know Mankind are prone to deceive themselves, and Some are disposed to misconstrue the conduct of those whom they conceive placed above them.

our August Presiddent is a singular example of modesty and diffidence. he has a dignity which forbids Familiarity mixed with an easy affibility which creates Love and Reverence. the Fever which he had terminated in an absess, so that he cannot sit up. upon my second visit to mrs Washington he sent for me into his Chamber. he was laying upon a settee and half raising himself up, beggd me to excuse his receiving me in that posture, congratulated me upon my arrival in New york and askd me how I could realish the simple manners of America after having been accustomed to those of Europe. I replied to him that where I fund simple manners I esteemed them, but that I thought we approachd much nearer to the Luxury and manners of Europe according to our ability, than most persons were sensible of, and that we had our full share of taste and fondness for them. The Presiddent has a Bed put into his Carriage and rides out in that way, allways with six Horses in his Carriage & four attendants mrs Washington accompanies him. I requested him to make Richmond Hill his resting place, and the next day he did so, but he found walking up stairs so difficult, that he has done it but once. Mrs Washington is one of those unassuming Characters which Creat Love & Esteem, a most becomeing plasentness sits upon her countanance, & an un-affected deportment which renders her the object of veneration and Respect, with all these feelings and Sensations I found myself much more deeply impressd than I ever did before their Majesties of Brit-ain.

You ask me concerning politicks, upon my word I hear less of them here, than I did in Massa'ts the two Houses are very buisy upon very important Bill's the judiciary, and the Collecting Bills.[1] the Senate is composed of many men of great abilities, who appear to be liberal in their sentiments and candid towards each other. the House is composed of some men of equal talants, others—the de-bates will give you the best Idea of them, but there is not a member whose sentiment clash more with my Ideas of things than mr. G——y he certainly does not comprehend the Great National System which must render us Respectable abroad & energetick at Home and will assuredly find himself lost amidst Rocks & Sands—

My dear sister some parts of your Letter made me melancholy. are you in any difficulties unknown to me I know very well that a small Farm must afford you a scanty support and that you are a sufferer from being obliged to receive pay in paper but I know your Pru-dence & oeconomy has carried you along, tho not in affluence, yet with decency & comfort, and I hope you will still be able to live so. you have one daughter comfortably situated, your son will from his merit & abilities soon get into some buisness your other daughter, you have every reason to be satisfied with do not look upon the gloomy side only. how easily might your situation be changed for the worse. even if you were in possession of Riches yet there is a com-petancy which is so desirable that one cannot avoid an anxiety for it. I have a request to make you, desire mr Cranch to make out his ac-count which he has against mr A. I gave cousin Lucy a memmoran-dum—let the balance be drawn and inclose to me, and I will send you a Receit in full This I consider myself at full liberty to do, be-cause the little sum Lent you was my own pocket money. put the Letter under cover to mrs Smith, it will then fall into no hands but my own but cover the whole for a frank to mr A.— do not talk of oblagations. reverse the matter & then ask yourself, if you would not do as much for me?

I wish it was in mr A's power to help mr Cranch to some office at Home which would assist him. mr A exprest the same wish to me, but at present he does not see any, tho a certain Lady in the full assurence of hope, wrote him that he now had it in his power to establish his own Family & Successfully help his Friends and that she is sure of his Patronage—for certain purposes—to which mr A. replied, ["]that he has no patronage but if he had, neither her children or his own could be sure of it beyond his own clear conviction of the publick good, that he should bely the whole course of his publick and private conduct, and all the maxims of his Life, if he should ever consider publick Authority entrusted to him, to be made subservient to his private views, or those of his Family and Friends." you cannot mistake who the Lady was, I know no other equally ambitious, but I presume her pretentions & those of her Family will fail, as I think they ought to if one Quarter part is true which has been reported of them.[2] I fancy a constant correspondence is kept up between mr W——n & mr G——y and like enough with several other jealous Partizans, but I hope they will never have sufficient interest to disturb the Government. I really believe mr G——y to be an honest man. the other has been grosely misled, and I do soberly think by the unbridled ambition of one She told me upon her last visit, that she did not perceive any alteration in *mr A's* conduct towards them. I am sure she must have told what was not true if she had said there was none in mine, for I feel it, and I cannot deceive. with regard to mr A he has dealt by them like a sincere Friend, and an honest Man and their own Hearts must approve his conduct, however grateing to their feelings. I am most sincerely sorry for the cause. they were my old and dear Friend's for whom I once entertaind the highest respect

Col mrs Smith Charles & little Jack are gone this week to Jamaica to get out of the Bustle at home and are not yet returnd. C. will not go into any company but such as his Father or col Smith introduces him to. he appears steady and sedate & I hope will continue so— Time and example will prevail over youthfull folly I trust. my Love to mrs Norten, how does she do? Louissa appears very happy, but I am obliged to keep her a mere prisoner on account of the small Pox of which there is always danger in N York as soon as the weather will permit shall have her innoculated. I find as many servants necessary here as in England, but not half as well calculated for their buisness. the distance from Town requires one or two extra as they are obliged to go & come always four, & frequently six times a day.

we have to send constantly to market in addition, but not withstanding all this I would not change this situation for any I know of in Town. Richmond Hill is situated upon the North River which communicates with Albany. Pauls hook as it is calld is in full sight, & the Jersy shore.[3] vessels are constantly passing up & down. the House is situated upon a high Hill which commands a most extensive prospect, on one side we have a view of the city & of Long Island, the River in Front, Jersy and the adjasant Country on the other side, you Turn a litle from the Road and enter a Gate a winding Road with trees in clumps leads you to the House, and all round the House, it looks wild and Rural as uncultivated Nature. the House is convenient for one family, but much too small for more, you enter under a Piazza into a Hall & turning to the right Hand assend a stair case which lands you in an other of equal dimensions of which I make a drawing Room. it has a Glass door which opens into a gallery the whole Front of the house which is exceeding pleasant. the Chambers are on each side. the House is not in good repair, wants much done to it, and if we continue here I hope it will be done. there is upon the back of the House a Garden of much greater extent than our Braintree Garden, but it is wholy for a walk & flowers. it has a Hawthorn hedge & Rows of Trees with a Broad Gravel Walk.

how happy would it make me to see here my dears Brothers Sister Nephew Neices, and to delight them with the prospect. mr Guile & dr Craigy dinned with us yesterday.[4] I find I have local attachments, and am more rejoiced to see a citizen of my own state than any other. Remember me affectionatly to my worthy Mother & Family to mrs Palmer & family who I hope are comfortably situated, to mrs Brisler too. I hope she will be able to come this way before long

my Letter is written in haste the weather very hot and I too laizy to Coppy

most affectionatly yours   A Adams

Tell Lucy she must write to me

RC (MWA:Abigail Adams Letters).

[1] The collection bill, which became "An Act to Regulate the Collection of the Duties Imposed by Law on the Tonnage of Ships or Vessels, and on Goods, Wares and Merchandizes Imported into the United States," was first considered by the House on 29 June and debated there until 14 July, when it was approved and sent to the Senate for concurrence. The Senate approved it with amendments, and it was signed into law on 31 July (*First Fed. Cong.*, 1:83–102; 3:100–111, 125).

[2] Mercy Otis Warren wrote to JA on 7 May that he had "reached the acme of applause: & are placed in a situation to do eminent service to your Country to Establish your family & to assist most *Esentially* your

Friends. . . . and though none of my Family are soliciting at Court I am perswaded you will not forget them at a time when you have it so much in your power to oblige—without injury to yourself, your Family or your Country." JA replied on 29 May much as AA quotes him above (*Warren-Adams Let-*

ters, 2:310, 313–314).
[3] Paulus Hook later became Jersey City, N.J.
[4] Andrew Craigie (1743–1819) of Boston had served as apothecary general of the Continental Army during the Revolution (*DAB*).

Cotton Tufts to Abigail Adams

Dear Cous[n]   Weymouth July. 20. 1789—

I am much pleased to hear that you have a commodious Seat, its Scituation delightful & Prospect pleasant—

We have had a fine Commencement & the Performances of the Day were spoken of with much Applause— Most excellent Things were said of the President & Vice President of the United States— their Characters were displayed in the brightest & strongest Colours

It is a satisfaction to the great & good, that their virtuous Deeds meet with the approbation of the wise & sober, it helps to sweeten some of the bitter Potions that they must partake off in their noble Pursuits & Progress through Life—.

Since You left us We have had a Plenty of Rain the Earth has assumed a new Appearance and Vegetation has been as sudden & great as I have ever known— Prospects of Grain & Hay are very good

Your oxen I could not get pastured for fatñing— After some Time I sold them on short Credit for 48 Doll[rs.]— The Farming Tools I took to my House, have sold part of them & shall sell the Remainder as opportunity presents— The ox Cart & Mud Boat remain at Braintree— I believe I shall get them to Weymouth in a Day or two, that they may be under my Eye & at Hand for Sale— I think it was Your Intention to have both sold, I fear they will not fetch near the first Cost especially the Mud Boat— Badcock whose Note you left with me, died some time past, I am informed that his Estate will not pay 10[s]/ p[r] £.[1]

M[rs.] Bass wishes to have Your half of the Corn, planted in the Garden by Jos. Field. At present Field reaps the Benefit of the whole Garden—

Pheebe not long since applied for Permission to let a Black Family into her Chamber— this I utterly refused—

M[r.] George Storer appeared solicitous to know wheth[r.] the Place purchased of Borland, would be let another Year—& what would be the Rent in Case of its being let— With respect to the first. I told him that it was probable that it would be leased, but what the Rent would be I could not tell— He wished me to give my Opinion upon the Matter to h[is] Father— I referred Him to you— it appeared [to me?] that it was some sudden Start and not well digested—as Farming he said was his Object— Be it let to whomsoever it may, I hope it will be to some one who will render You a Profit—

Your Two Sons were here on Sunday are both well, Thomas has a good Chum assigned him—[2] He sat off for Haverhill Yesterday with his Brother— Be pleased to remember me to M[r] Adams & your Children—

I am with Affection / Yours   Cotton Tufts

I wish you to let me know, which of our News Papers are forwarded to you by the Printers at Boston and whether you would have them all continued—

RC (Adams Papers); addressed: "M[rs.] Abigail Adams"; internal address: "M[rs.] Abigail Adams—"; docketed: "D[r:] Tufts to / J Adams / 1789." Some loss of text where the seal was removed.

[1] For the financial transaction between JA and Moses and Huldah Babcock, see vol. 5:154–155. Moses Babcock died on 16 May (*Milton Records: Births, Marriages and Deaths, 1662–1843*, Boston, 1900, p. 205).
[2] Possibly Thomas Gray (1772–1847), Harvard 1790, one of seven Harvard students and recent graduates who may have lived together in Cambridge. Gray would go on to serve a long pastorate at the Third Parish of Jamaica Plain (U.S. Census, 1790, Mass., p. 137; *Harvard Quinquennial Cat.*; Harriet Manning Whitcomb, *Annals and Reminiscences of Jamaica Plain*, Cambridge, 1897, p. 33–34).

Mary Smith Cranch to Abigail Adams

My dear Sister   Braintree July 30th 1789

I can never Sufficiently express my thanks or my gratitude for your last kind & affectionate Letter & you must not laugh at me nor chide me when I tell you that I sat & weept over it as if it had brought me some evil tydings I felt the full force of that maxim of Solomons "It is more blessed to give than to receive" But my dear Sister you must forgive me if I tell you I cannot accept your generous proposal—for tho I have not been able to return the Loan so soon as I expected I shall be in a capasity to do it some time or other— I hope soon—but I have met with so many dissapointments that I am affrai'd to promise any thing. I depended upon my dairy to discharge some small debts I was oblig'd to make in order to furnish Betsy we have lost four of our best cows in about a year & we are now oblig'd to turn off the best in our yard for a strange swelling she has under her throat which will kill her if it cannot be remov'd

& so my prospect of a good dairy this summer is again blasted—but this is from the hand of a good providence & I must not complain I am sorry I have ever let any thing slip from my pen to give my Sister pain but my spirits are at times so low that I cannot always mantain that fortitude of mind which enables its posseser to behave with propriety under the various trials they may be call'd to sustain

I often feel myself surrounded with difficulties which I cannot remove— The necessary wants of a Family & of children are more known & more felt by the mistress than any one else & they are not a burthen where they can be easily supply'd— our Farm is too small to give us a living & pay the Labour & the Taxes notwithstanding mr Cranch Labours very hard upon it himself His Watch business which is very small here & the courts is all the ways he has to raise cash— The education of a Son & the Settleing of a Daughter are heavey matters where the income is so small. We have purchas'd nothing for cloathing but bare necessarys for several years I have exerted all my strength & all my abilities to manage with prudence & [economy?] whatever came under my department but what is this towards the support of a Family— I am mortified I am greiv'd that I cannot do more to assist my Friend. His not receiving his money for his publick Services oblig'd him to borrow While our son was at college & there has never yet been a time that he could get his debt but at such a loss as we could not think of but this we should not mind if he could get into any business I say any for there is nothing which is lawful that he would not do—which would inable him to work himself out of his difficulties— His abilities & his integrity may yet procure him a living not too labourous for his health & age this is the height of his wishes & of his ambition & I will hope that something may yet turn up to his advantage we do not look up to mr A as the Lady did you mention If he should ever be able to help him to any thing It will not be because he is his Brother or his Friend only we are greatly oblig'd to him for his good wishes

I have now my Sister laid before you some of the causes of my anxeitys—& if you can place yourself for one moment in my situation you will not say that I have no reason for my dejection—but I hope it does not arise to a sinful anxiety & discontent this is what I am constantly striving against I am naturally very chearful & having open'd my heart to you—I know I shall feel better— I have been oblig'd to wear a countiance which badly indicated the feelings of this heart least I should give pain to my Family—

394

The weather has been so very hot that I have been almost wore out with that & having so much work to do I have only a little girl of sixteen years old with me She is sprightly but ignorant—

I shall finish this sheet that it may have no connection with another which I shall write, but not to night for tis Twelve a clock now. & I cannot see streight—

so good night my dear dear Sister

RC (Adams Papers); endorsed: "Mrs Cranch / july 30th / 1790."

Mary Smith Cranch to Abigail Adams

My dear Sister   Braintree August 2ᵈ 1789

I have been several times to your new house but I do feel such a want of my dear sisters smiling countinance that I do not know how to bear the house I go into the best Parlour & set my self down & view mrs Smith & the coll— this gives me some pleasure but I want to put little Jack in her arms I do wish to see & hug the little creature again that sweet archness in his countinance I shall never forget[1]

I have a pretty little Boy of my own a son of mr Hunts from the wist Indias mr Durant brought him for his health & to be educated he is five years old— he is a well behave'd amiable Cchild very sprightly & playful—but easely manag'd you know how dearly I love to have little Folks about me mr Durant wish'd me to take him & I have done it— He is as fond of us all as if we were his own Family— but I find I feel more anxious least any thing should befall him than if he was my own Son— He is not only the only Son of his Parents but all the child they have left having lost four they sent this away to save him. He told me last night that "God had been pleas'd to take from him all his Brothers & sisters but he had mark'd him for no dye"

Mrs Durant is just gone[2] she has had a most painful consumtion— Sally Austen liv'd but a little while after you went away[3] mrs Austen is intitled to all our pity. She behaves with great propreity— these my sister are trying Scenes indeed

Mrs Smith very unexpectedly got to bed with a Daughter about a fortnight since she wak'd with a cat of Mrs Greens upon her stomack—& it frighten'd the poor little girl six weeks too soon into the world[4] it is a weak thing but we hope it will live mrs Smith was so frightend that she sprung out of Bed & ran into Nabbys chamber & lay upon her bed & cry'd an hour she thought it was a rat not having a cat in the house

your mother Hall I believe is well but I have been so confin'd by having such poor help that I have not been to see her

Mrs Pallmer & Daughters are well they look very nice & comfortable sister is with mrs Norton. she is—*so so*—but heaves many a sigh for aunt adams— Lucy has been in Boston for these ten days visiting about a thing she has not done for these seven years—

Cousin John spent a week with us at commencment— Thomas returnd with him & went to haveral & is *not* yet come home they were both well

Lucy wants much to know if you found your china safe— you met with better luck I hope than when you came from England

Mrs Alleyn is return'd she could not be contented from her son—

Mrs Brisler has her health remarkably well— her last Baby is a Picture the other is much better & stronger than it was

Mr Cranch has been at court these ten days & had it not been for my little Boy I should have been very dull

I went the other day to make Mrs Bass a visit at your old house I have never before sat down in it, but such a variety of thoughts arose in my mind as gave me both pleasure & pain— I am determin'd not to indulge these lonely feelings—having injoy'd a good for so long a time— shall the loss of it make me overlook all my present injoyments? It shall not I will add the past to the present & anticipate good things to come: this is much more rational & more Philosophical is it not?

I did design to have added more but I have an oppertunety to send this now

RC (Adams Papers); endorsed: "Mrs Cranch / August 1789."

[1] Possibly a reference to Mather Brown's portraits of AA2 and WSS, which later hung in the parlor of the Old House; see vol. 6:xiii–xiv, 217; 7:xii–xiii, 219. Cranch had had the opportunity to meet John Adams Smith when AA2 and WSS visited Braintree earlier that year between 25 Jan. and 20 March (D/JQA/14, APM Reel 17).

[2] Cornelius Durant (1732–1812) was a merchant of Boston and St. Croix. His second wife, Maria Fenno Durant, died on 5 Aug. in Little Cambridge (now Brighton). Durant's first wife, Mary Tothill Durant (b. 1729), had previously married and divorced Richard Hunt (d. 1765) of Boston and Quincy. The five-year-old child was probably a son of one of Mary's three sons from her first marriage, Richard Tothill Hunt (b. 1751), John Salmon Hunt (b. 1752), or George Shoars Hunt (b. 1754) (Waldo Lincoln, *Genealogy of the Waldo Family: A Record of the Descendants of Cornelius Waldo of Ipswich, Mass., from 1647 to 1900*, Worcester, 1902, p. 79; Joseph Palmer, *Necrology of Alumni of Harvard College, 1851–52 to 1862–63*, Boston, 1864, p. 454; W. L. G. Hunt, *Genealogy of the Name and Family of Hunt*, Boston, 1862–1863, p. 348).

[3] Sarah (Sally) Austin (b. 1765), daughter

of Nathaniel and Anna Austin, died on 7 July (Boston *Independent Chronicle*, 9 July; Roger D. Joslyn, comp. and ed., *Vital Records of Charlestown Massachusetts to the Year 1850*, 3 vols., Boston, 1984, 1:413).

[4] Hannah Carter Smith gave birth to a daughter, Elizabeth Storer Smith, on 19 July.

See also AA to William Smith, 10 Aug., below. Mrs. Green was the Smiths' neighbor Hannah Storer Green (1738–1811), wife of Joshua Green (1731–1806) and longtime friend of AA (U.S. Census, 1790, Mass., p. 183; vol. 5:306).

Abigail Adams to Mary Smith Cranch

my dear sister   Richmond Hill August 9th 1789

If I should ask why I have not heard from my sister or Friends, for several weeks past, would she not answer me by retorting the question? in replie I could only say that I had designd writing every day for a long time, but we have had such a lassitude of weather, and such a long continuence of it, that I have really felt unfit for every thing which I was not necessitated to perform, & for many of those which I have been obligated to, from my situation, such as dressing receiving & paying visits, giving dinners &c I have never before been in a situation in which morning noon & afternoon I have been half as much exposed to company. I have laid down one rule which is, not to make any morning visits myself, and in an afternoon after six oclock I can return 15 or 20 & very seldom find any Lady to receive me, but at Richmond Hill, it is expected that I am at Home both to Gentlemen & Ladies when ever they come out, which is almost every day since I have been here, besides it is a sweet morning ride to Breakfast I propose to fix a Levey day soon. I have waited for mrs washington to begin and she has fix'd on every fryday 8 oclock. I attended upon the last, mrs smith & charles. I found it quite a crowded Room. the form of Reception is this, the servants announce—& col Humphries or mr Lear—receives every Lady at the door, & Hands her up to mrs washington to whom she makes a most Respectfull curtzey and then is seated without noticeing any of the rest of the company. the President then comes up and speaks to the Lady, which he does with a grace dignity & ease, that leaves Royal George far behind him. the company are entertaind with Ice creems & Lemonade, and retire at their pleasure performing the same ceremony when they quit the Room.[1] I cannot help smiling when I read the Boston puffs, that the President is unmoved amidst all the dissipations of the city of New york.[2] now I am wholy at a loss to determine the meaning of the writer. not a Single publick amusement is their in the whole city, no not even a publick walk, and as to Dinners, I believe their are six made in Boston to

12. "THE REPUBLICAN COURT (LADY WASHINGTON'S RECEPTION DAY)," BY DANIEL HUNTINGTON, 1861–1865
See page xvii

one here, unless it is for some particular person to whom a Number of families wish to pay attention. there are Six Senators who have their Ladies and families with them, but they are in Lodgings the chief of them, & not in a situation to give dinners— as to the mode of visiting, less time is expended in this way, than in sending word to each person & passing an afternoon with them, tho I own on the score of pleasure that would be to me the most agreeable. I have returnd more than Sixty visits all of them in 3 or 4 afternoons & excepting at the Pressidents, have drank tea only at two other places and dined but once out, since I arrived

Indeed I have been fully employd in entertaining company, in the first place all the Senators who had Ladies & families, then the remaining Senators, and this week we have begun with the House, and tho we have a room in which we dine 24 persons at a Time, I shall not get through them all, together with the publick Ministers for a month to come the help I find here is so very indifferent to what I had in England, the weather so warm that we can give only one dinner a week. I cannot find a cook in the whole city but what will get drunk, and as to the Negroes—I am most sincerely sick of them, and I can no more do without mr Brisler, than a coach could go without wheels or Horses to draw it. I can get Hands, but what are hands without a Head, and their chief object is to be as expensive as possible. this week I shall not be able to see any company unless it is to Tea—for my Family are all sick mrs smiths two Children with the Hooping cough Charles with the dysentary, Louissa & Polly with a complaint Similar. To Charles I gave a puke last night & his complaints have abated. Louissa & Polly are to take one to night. if we had not been so fortunate in our situation I do not know how we could have lived. it is very sickly in the City.

As to politicks, I presume many of the dissapointed Candidates will complain. some will quarrel with men & some with measures. I believe the Presideent Strove to get the best information he could, but there are some men who will get much said in their favour when they do not merit it.— the News papers will give you the Debates of the house to the President their system is as liberal as I could expect I leave the world to judge how it is with respect to their vice President from whom they expect more entertainment the House was New furnishd for the President & cost ten thousand Dollors as the Board of Treasury say.[3] the use & improvement of this they have granted him, which is but just & right. He never rides out without six Horses to his Carriage, four Servants, & two Gentlemen before him, this is no more state than is perfectly consistant with his station, but then I do not Love to see the News writers fib so. He is Perfectly averse to all marks of distinction say they, yet on the 4th of july when the cincinnati committee waited upon him he received them in a Regimental uniform with the Eagal most richly set with diamonds at his Button, yet the News writers will fib—to answer particular purposes—[4] I think he ought to have still more state, & time will convince our Country of the necessity, of it. here I say not any thing upon the subject. it would be asscribed to a cause I dispise if I should speak my mind. I hear that the vote which mr A gave in the Senate, respecting the Removal of officers by the President independant of the senate, has been by some of his own state construed, as voting power into his own Hands—or having that in view, but his Rule through life has been to vote and act, independant of Party agreeable to the dictates of his conscience and tho on that occasion he could have wisht on account of the delicacy of his situation not to have been obliged to have determind the Question, yet falling to him, he shrunk not,[5] not a word did any of our state say when his vote reduced the duty upon molasses, all was silence then they could not possibly asscribe it to any Sinister motive but uneasy wrestless Spirits are to be found in all quarters of the world.

And now my dear sister I wish to know how you do. mrs Norten Lucy not a line from either, nor a word from sister shaw.

Mr Bond will tell you that he saw us all, he was out two or three times. I wish you could come with our dear Brother Cranch & spend the Evening with us. We do not have company on Sundays. we go to meeting, but alass I do not find a dr Price. I hope I shall visit Braintree next summer. I wonder sister Smith has never written a word to Louissa. I am glad to find Tommy has got a good Chum. I hope he will continue steady. Charles studies with mr Hamilton goes to the office when his Father goes to senate & returns with him at 4 oclock.[6] he has not discoverd the least inclination for getting into company and has no acquaintance but George Storer— pray make my best Regards to all my Friends, to my Mother present my duty. Remember me to mrs Palmer & family. the Beautifull prospect here from every quarter makes me regreet less than I otherways should do the spot I quitted. the rooms are lofty and was the House in good repair I should find it, very convenient for my own Family. at present we are crowded for want of Chamber Room. my family consists of 18— How does the place look. I must get my Butter all put up & sent me from Braintree. I have Breakfasted constantly upon milk, I cannot eat the Butter here— I must write the dr upon several subjects by twesdays post. I shall not get ready by this.

pray let me hear from you. the season is plentifull. Let us rejoice & be glad Cheer up my good sister, a merry Heart does good like a medicine— we all send abundance of Love— I must go to look after my invalids

ever yours   A Adams

RC (MWA:Abigail Adams Letters).

[1] For Martha Washington's levees, see Descriptive List of Illustrations, No. 12, above.

[2] The *Boston Gazette*, 27 July, printed a letter "From Correspondents" regarding the debate over the appropriate title for the president. The piece stated that "our beloved President stands unmoved in the vortex of folly and dissipation which the city of New-York presents—despising and rejecting titles and pecuniary emoluments with the truly republican spirit with which he has always been distinguished."

[3] A committee of the House of Representatives, which was convened to prepare a report on appropriate compensation for the president and vice president, recommended in mid-July "that it would be proper to allow the President 20,000 dollars per annum, exclusive of the expences of secretaries, clerks, furniture, carriages and horses. To the Vice President 5,000 dollars per annum." This touched off a lengthy debate as to what the government should appropriately provide to a new president and whether or not to enumerate such additional expenses. One representative also noted that $10,000 had already been spent on preparing a house and furnishings for the Washingtons. The House ultimately moved to strike out the exclusion clause.

The debate regarding the vice president's salary focused on whether he should receive a salary or merely a per diem and in what amount. There was no discussion of paying him any additional sum for his expenses (*First Fed. Cong.*, 11:1093, 1098–1099, 1111–1117, 1129–1130, 1131–1136).

[4] On the 4th of July, members of the Society of the Cincinnati called on both Washington and JA in honor of the day, prior to proceeding first to St. Paul's Chapel and after to the City Tavern. Washington was unable to attend the events himself due to ill health. While some newspapers omitted any mention of Washington's dress in their coverage of the day's events, the *New York Packet*, 7 July, did note that following a military parade, the soldiers "passed the house of the President of the United States, who appeared at his door in a suit of regimentals, and was saluted by the troops as they passed."

[5] For JA's own record of the debates on the portion of the foreign affairs bill considering the president's right to remove officers unilaterally from the department of foreign affairs, see *D&A*, 3:217–221.

[6] CA studied law with Alexander Hamilton from July to September, at which time Hamilton was appointed secretary of the treasury. CA then transferred to the law office of John Laurance, where he remained for two years (Hamilton, *Papers*, 5:363–364; JA to John Laurance, 19 Sept., LbC, APM Reel 115).

Abigail Adams to William Smith

my Dear Sir   Richmond Hill 10 August 1789

Give me leave to congratulate you & mrs Smith upon the Birth of a Daughter. I hope both the Mamma and Infant are in good Health, as well as master William my Grandchildren are much afflicted with the Hooping cough we have had a succession of extreem Hot weather, and tho we have one of the most airy situations near the city, I have sufferd much from the Heat. It would make us very happy to see you here, and if mrs Smith should not Nurse her little one, a journey would serve her Health as soon as the weather grows cooler. mr Guild gave us the slip, quit unexpectedly. I expected to have seen him before he left New-York. tho I find many good things here, there are some, which either from local attachment, or real superiority I prefer from my own state, in concequence of which I must trouble you with a commission. it is to procure me a keg of Tongues & 2 doz Hams of mr Baldwin[1] & forward them by Barnard or any other opportunity, together with the account which shall be paid to Barnard. the Hams here are misirable so is the Butter I propose getting mine all from Massachusets as soon as the weather will permitt. present me affectionatly to all my Friends and / be assured of the sincere Regard / of your affectionate Friend   A Adams

RC (MHi:Smith-Townsend Papers); addressed by WSS: "Mr: William Smith. / Merchant / Boston"; endorsed: "New York. Augt 89 / A Adams—"

[1] Enoch Baldwin, a butcher, operated first out of Faneuil Hall and later from Salt Lane in Boston (Boston, *27th Report*, p. 20, 23; *Boston Directory*, 1796, p. 15).

Abigail Adams to Mary Smith Cranch

my dear sister   Sepbr 1 1789 Richmond Hill

I Received your kind Letters and meant sooner to have replied to them, but many avocations have prevented me. I am fully apprizd of all you mention in your Letter respecting your situation and wanted no apoligies for your conduct, but I still insist upon what I first wrote you, & it will pain me to hear you say any thing more upon the subject I never could apply it more to my satisfaction, I shall never I trust feel the want of it, if I should and you are in a situation to render me service, I will then accept it— I regreet that it is not in my power to assist my Friends more than I do, but bringing our minds to our circumstances is a duty encumbent upon us we have lived through dangerous times, and have reason to be thankfull that we are still in possession of our Liberty & so much of our property; yet still there is no reason in our being cheated by our Friends as well as Robbed by our Enemies. I have reason to think that congress will take up the matter and Fund the Debt. I wish they would set about it before they adjournd or rather defered their adjournment, till they had compleated more buisness but they have had arduous work, and want a respit.[1]

I fear they will Remove from this place I am too happy in the situation of it, I fear to have it lasting I am every day more & more pleased with it; should they go to Philadelphia I do not know how I could possibly live through the voilent Heats but sufficient to the day; I am sorry to hear mrs Norten is unwell, but from your Letter suppose her situation will be mended by time and you will e'er long know that a Grandchild is almost as near to your Heart as your own children;[2] my little Boys delight me and I should feel quite melancholy without them William came from his Gandmamma Smiths an almost ruind child, but I have brought him to be a fine Boy now.

my dear Lucy I long to see her I am glad she is gone from home to amuse herself a little. I wish she could come to Richmond Hill and she would say it was the most delightfull spot she ever saw. my Love to her and cousin William. Louissa is worried that her Mother does not write to her—I really am surprizd that she has not written a single line either to me or to her, because I wrote to her before I left home[3] and I cannot suppose that she could take any umbrage at my taking her away; I wish you would write to her and let her know that Louissa is uneasy upon the subject, and has written to her I believe more than once.

I wish you would be so good as see if you can procure me two dozen Bottles of Rose water and send by Barnard who has saild for Boston.

I propose to have Louissa inoculated for the small pox this month. I have now nearly got through all the company that we propose to dine this Session & I have not heard, that any of them were so near being [. . .] as to render it necessary to apply to the Humane Society. the Spirit of Rebellion is not yet quell'd in Massachusets, the coals are blowing again and with a malice truly infernal, what will not dissapointed ambition Stick at?

> "oh what a world is this, when what is comely
>   envenoms him that bears it,
> Be thou as chast as Ice, as pure as snow
> Thou shalt not escape calumny"[4]

pray present my duty to my worthy mother & a kind remembrance to all inquiring Friends and be assured that I am my dear sister most affectionately / Yours   A Adams.

ps I find the Author of the Libel (for such it is,) calld the Dangerous vice, is Ned Church, a dissapointed Seeker but why his malice should thus vent itself against mr A I know not, unless he thought himself neglected by him I remember he wrote a letter to mr A when we were abroad soliciting the place of consul to Lisbon which mr A never answerd. I have past him I recollect two or three times in comeing from Town & I rember now that mrs Smith observed to me that he look'd so surly she hated to see him. It appears now that he offerd this peice to the Printers here who all refused to be concernd with it, he sent it Boston & took himself off to Georgia.[5] he never was the person that either visited or spoke a word to mr A. since he has been in N York mr A says, that one day at the Presidents Levee he was Speaking to the President & Church bowed to him. he could not whilst addressing the President return his bow with Propriety. his intention was to have gone & spoken to him afterwards, but the Room being full he did not see him afterwards. this I suppose Church construed into Pride and contempt, & being dissapointed in obtaining a place from the Pressident, he vented all his malice upon the vice, & conceiving the Topick he took to be a popular one he has discoverd a temper as fit for Rebellion murder Treason as his unfortunate Brother.[6] I could wish that the Author might be fully known to the publick with regard to the subject of a proper title for the Pressident mr A never has or will disguise his opinion, because he thinks that the stability of the Government will in a great measure rest upon it. Yet the subject here is scarcly mentiond, & the Boston News papers have rung more changes upon it, than all the News papers in the united states besides I think in holding up Church to view, it would not be amiss to state his conduct with regard to the spanish vessel[7]

It was a relief to my mind to find the Author Church. I was really apprehensive that a Female pen had been dipt in full in concequence of dissapointed views a Brute to attack me who never in thought word or deed offended him, or have ever been in this Country to Ball's plays or Routes, but malice was his motive & Revenge his object. the vice Pressident ten times to one goes to Senate in a one Horse chaise, and Levee's we have had none. the Pressident only, has his powderd Lackies waiting at the door, so that under a Hipocritical mask he attacks one & hold the other impiously up & stiles him a saviour & God how inconsistant, railing at Titles & giving those which belong to the deity. How must a wretch feel who can harbour Such a temper?—

but adieu my dear sister, thus it is to be seated high. I pray Heaven to give me a conscience void of offence, and then the curse causeless shall not come[8]

Your affectionatly   A A

RC (MWA:Abigail Adams Letters); addressed by WSS: "Mrs Mary Cranch / Braintree."

[1] Congress did not take up the question of funding the debt until its second session in spring 1790 (*First Fed. Cong.*, 3:381, 399).

[2] Jacob and Elizabeth Cranch Norton had their first child, Richard Cranch Norton, on 12 March 1790 (*History of Weymouth*, 4:444).

[3] Not found.

[4] AA is combining her Shakespeare quotations. The first two lines are from *As You Like It*, Act II, scene iii, lines 14–15; the second two are from *Hamlet*, Act III, scene i, lines 140–141.

[5] In Aug. 1789, Edward Church (1740–1816), initially of Boston and later of Georgia, published a satirical poem entitled "The Dangerous Vice ——" in Boston (Evans, No. 21736). It attacked JA as "Ye lucky Fav'rites! dandled—G—d knows why! / In the soft lap of pamper'd luxury; / Who reap the harvest of the lab'rer's toil, / And thankless batten on unlawful spoil; / Who drain your country of her stinted store, / And wasting thousands— *yawn for thousands more*" (lines 4–9).

Three years earlier, on 14 Jan. 1786, Church had written to JA (Adams Papers) requesting to be appointed U.S. consul at Lisbon, a letter JA apparently never answered. Prior to the publication of the poem in 1789, he had also approached George Washington and Henry Knox seeking an office. In June 1790, he was finally appointed consul at Bilbao, although he never served, and in 1792, consul at Lisbon, where he remained until 1796 (*Sibley's Harvard Graduates*, 14:389–393).

[6] For Benjamin Church, Edward Church's brother, who was jailed for treason during the Revolution, see JA, *D&A*, 3:384–385.

[7] In 1782 and 1783, the Continental Congress received complaints from the governors of Cuba and New Orleans regarding the seizure of the Spanish ship *San Antonio* in the Gulf of Mexico by the Massachusetts privateer *Patty*, owned by Edward Church. The Massachusetts courts eventually ruled the seizure illegal and a violation of neutral rights (Smith, *Letters of Delegates*, 20:144–146; *JCC*, 24:227–228).

[8] "As the bird by wandering, as the swallow by flying, so the curse causeless shall not come" (Proverbs, 26:2).

Abigail Adams to Cotton Tufts

Sep^tr. 1. 1789[1]

with regard to politicks the debates of the House will give you an Idea of them, as yet there has been but little Heat upon any Subject, but there is a questions comeing on with regard to the permanant Residence of congress which I fear will create parties, & much vexation. I should think that in the present state of their treasury, an expence so unnecessary ought to be avoided as even removeing to Philadelphia. every person here who have not sufficient funds of their own has been obliged to Borrow of the Bank for to supply their daily necessities and I do not Imagine that the publick could derive any essential Benifit from a Removal, for my own part I dread this continual Roling.

With Regard to my own domestick affairs I scarcly know what to write. I think it would be adviseable to Let our whole place & House together provided any gentleman wanted it, as early in the spring as might be. the Boat & Cart had better remain, particularly the cart than be under sold Such is the uncertainty of all Humane affairs, that we may wish to return to the use of them sooner than is apprehended and not even be in possession of sufficient cash to purchase them. the Butter upon Pratts Farm I should like to have put up for me, & some cheese. we give for every pound of butter here 18 pence Hogs lard is an other article which I propose getting from home. Ham's are as much better with us as can well be conceived; Field was to render to you half the produce of the Garden. I am happy to learn that Thomas has a good Chamber Mate, much depends upon that. Charles is very attentive to the Buisness of the office, but I fear will lose his master, by his becomeing a minister of state. mr Hamilton is talked of for that department. mr Adams is well and will write to you soon. the Senate are so close to Buisness & he frequently has so much reading to do & such constant attention to the debates, that he comes home quite exhausted & unable to take his pen our situation is a very Beautifull one and I feel in that respect quite happy, but I find myself much more exposed to company than in any situation which I have ever before been in. the morning is a time when strangers who come to Nyork expect to find mr Adams at home. this brings us Breakfast company besides it is a sweet morning retreat for fresh air & a cool Breize. I should like to visit my friends during the adjournment but our Finnances will not admit of much travelling.

mr King makes a very Respectable figure as a Senator, and mr Ames does credit to our state. mr Madisson is a very amiable character a man of virtue & probity. mr G— what can I say, you see him always in the minority, you see him very frequently wrong and the poor man looks gastly. I believe he is woried mortified and quite in the Horrors a constant correspondent of W——n–& his wife all of whom see nothing but Ruin & destruction before them, & who will again set our state by the ears if possible—watch them closely. I have only Room to add yours / Sincerely   A Adams

RC (NHi:Misc. Mss. Adams, Abigail); endorsed: "Mrs. A. Adams 1790."

[1] The letter is a fragment and missing at least its first page and possibly more. The dateline appears at the bottom of the final page, near the signature.

John Adams to Thomas Boylston Adams

My dear Son   Richmond Hill Septr 2 1789

I have this morning received your manly letter of 25th Ult.—[1] I had long intended to write you but as you observe avocations have always intervened. Public business my son, must always be done by somebody.— it will be done by somebody or other— If wise men decline it others will not: if honest men refuse it, others will not. A young man should well weigh his plans. Integrity should be preserved in all events, as essential to his happiness, thro every stage of his existence. His first maxim then, should be to place his honor out of the reach of all men: In order to this he must make it a rule never to become dependant on public employments for subsistence. Let him have a trade a profession a farm a shop, something where by he can honestly live, and then he may engage in public affairs, if invited, upon independant principles. My advice to my children, is to maintain an independant character, tho' in poverty and obscurity: neither riches nor illustration will console a man under the reflection that he has acted a mean a mercenary part, much less a dishonest one— Your handwriting and your style are in my eye and judgment, beautiful— go on my son pursue your mathematics and your morals. Come with your brother, and be here at the meeting of Congress on the first of December. Then we will converse upon these and other subjects, mean time write me, if it is but a line every week.

Your father   J Adams

LbC in WSS's hand (Adams Papers); internal address: "Mr Thomas B Adams / Student Harvard Colledge"; APM Reel 115. Tr (Adams Papers).

[1] Not found.

Mary Smith Cranch to Abigail Adams

My dear Sister   Braintree September 8th 1789

I am quite discourag'd writing by the Post I know not if you have ever receiv'd one Letter Which I have sent by them I have sent two long ones the Last I put into the office a month ago last Saturday.[1] I should have written oftener if I had not suspected that Letters directed to Mr Adams where taken out by somebody who had no right to them— I hope I am mistaken—but I cannot conceive why you have not got many Letters which have been sent you; Doctor Tufts

407

thinks his have met with the same fate as he has receiv'd no answers to many which he has sent you. Mr Cranch wrote to Mr Adams in July & inclos'd a Letter to Mr Bond giving him an account of his sister Ebbits sudden Death.[2] mr Bond wrote a Letter to Mr Foster a fortnight after this & had not then heard of it. I inclos'd a letter in my last to you for Mrs Brisler to her Husband she has just receiv'd a Letter from him dated the 30th of August & she says it does not appear that he had receiv'd it which makes me think mine has not reach'd you. I shall be very sorry indeed if it has not as I had written things which I should be unwitting any body should see but you— I wish you would number your Letters for the future I will mine—& I shall write by private hands as much as I can. Mr Charles Ward Althorp will return to new york soon I sha[ll wr]ite by him—.[3] we are all well I have heard fr[om] Haverhill Newbury & Cambridg our connexions there were also in health

old Deacon Webb has left us. he dy'd last week.[4] Mrs Hall was at meeting a Sabbath day but complain'd much of her Eyes

The last Letter I receiv'd from you was dated the 9th of August & gave me an account of the sick state of your Family I have been waiting impatiently to hear further I hope Mrs Smiths children will not have the cough bad. poor little creatures I feel anxious for them— I do not wonder you were all sick— The weather was so very hot here that I some times thought we should be made sick too but a finer season for every kind of produce I never saw— the air has been remarkably clear tho so very hot—owing I suppose to the thunder so frequent at the south ward

I have seen the Fragment—

> "Her end when, Emulation misses
> She turns to envy—stings & hisses["]⁵

Pray write as often as you can— It is one of the greatest comforts I have—to receive such proofs of the affection of my Sister—

remember me kindly to all my Freinds and accept the warmest affection of your Sister   M C

RC (Adams Papers); addressed by Richard Cranch: "To / Mrs· Abigail Adams / Lady of the Vice President. / Richmond-Hill, near / New York"; docketed: "M Cranch to / A Adams / 1789." Some loss of text where the seal was removed.

¹ 30 July and 2 Aug., both above.

² Richard Cranch's letter to JA has not been found. William Bond's sister-in-law, Ebbett Cranch, a niece of Richard Cranch, died at Falmouth, Mass. (now Maine), in July (MHi:Cranch-Bond Papers, Extract from a Register of the Bond and Cranch Families, 1852).

³ For Charles Ward Apthorp, see vol. 6:411.

⁴ Deacon Jonathan Webb of Braintree

died on 1 Sept. at age 92 (Sprague, *Braintree Families*, p. 5387R).

[5] Jonathan Swift, "Verses on the Death of Dr. Swift," lines 35–36.

Cotton Tufts to Abigail Adams

Dear Madam—   Weymouth Sep[r.] 15. 1789.

Your Favour of the 1[st.] Ins[t.] I rec[d] the 11[st.] and shall give orders to Pratt relative to the Butter &c Not having received an Answer to Mine respecting the Cart &c and finding no Opportunity to dispose of the Cart to Advantage I got L[t.] Bates to apprize it which he sat at £7.10.0 and had concluded to take it to my own Use if you approved of it, but as you think it will not be best to sell—I wish to use it till the Spring & will account with you therefore— The Mud Boat I have got to Weymouth and found that it wanted the Eye of a Master— I do not expect that it will fetch more than £10 or £12. if sold as Gondalos that will serve the same Purpose have been sold at that Rate— I shall not However dispose of it without particular Directions tho I am of opinion it will be best to sell it if any Thing near the Worth can be obtained— Adams informs me that He must leave the House (at Boston) if the Rent is not reduced—[1] I fear I shall not be able any longer to get £40 per ann[l] from any Person, as Rents are exceeding low and but little Money in Circulation As soon as may be I wish to know your Mind on this Subject as well as with Respect to the Mode of adjusting Our Account whether it is agreable that M[rs.] Cranch should audit it as heretofore— You will be so kind as let Cousin John, know that I answerd his Draught on me as soon as I became possessed of it being a Day or two after he left Boston—[2]

I wish to know what Papers are forwarded to you from the Printers at Boston and whether you would have all of them sent on—

The Author of the scurrilous Poem referred to in yours is well known here and it is generally reputed and considered as the Work of a malicious & disappointed Seeker—[3] it appears to me to be a Stab upon the President through the Side of the Vice President and as paving the Way for an Attack upon Him, whenever a favorable Opportunity shall present— Too many there are to our Sorrow, that can never be contented but in Broils & Contests, Wishing to embroil Government, and to throw our publick Affairs into Confusion, they are seeking every Occasion to gratify their restless Spirits and to wriggle themselves into Places favorable to their Desig[ns] But as they are generally devoid of Principle, they sooner or later fall into the Pit which they have diggd for others—

Be pleased to remember me to Mr Adams & your Children—and accept of the best Wishes / of Your Affectionate Friend & H Ser

Cotton Tufts

RC (Adams Papers); internal address: "M^rs· Abigail Adams—" Some loss of text due to a torn manuscript.

[1] That is, Thomas Adams, editor of the Boston *Independent Chronicle*, who was renting the Adamses' Court Street house in Boston (vol. 7:424, 425–426, note 6).

[2] JQA recorded in his Diary on 7 Sept.: "I found the stage to Providence will go tomorrow morning at 4 o'clock. being destitute of cash, I obtained of my friend J. Phillips the loan of a sum sufficient for my journey, for which I drew an order upon D^r· Tufts" (D/JQA/12, APM Reel 15).

[3] See AA to Mary Smith Cranch, 1 Sept., note 5, above.

Abigail Adams to Elizabeth Smith Shaw

Richmond Hill Sep^br 27. 1789

I write to you my dear sister, not from the disputed Banks of the Potowmac, the Susquehanna or the deleware, but from the peacefull Borders of the Hudson, a situation where the Hand of Nature has so lavishly display'd her Beauties, that she has left scarcly any thing, for her Handmaid Art, to perform.

The House in which we reside is situated upon a Hill, the Avenue to which is intersperced with Forest Trees under which a shubery rather too Luxurient and wild, has taken Shelter, owing to its having been deprived by death some years Since, of its original proprieter who kept it in perfect order. in Front of the House the Noble Hudson rools his Majestick waves bearing upon his Bosom innumerable small vessels which are constantly [. . .]ing the rich product of the Neighbouring soil to the buisy hand of a more extensive Commerce. Beyond the Hudson rises to our view the fertile country of the Jersies, coverd with a golden Harvest, & pouring forth plenty like the cornicapia of Ceres. on the right Hand an extensive plain presents us with a view of Fields coverd with verdure and pastures full of cattle, on the left, the city opens upon us, intercepted only by clumps of Trees, & some rising ground, which serves to heighten the Beauty of the scene, by appearing to conceal a part on the back Ground is a large flower garden inclosed with a Hedge and some very handsome Trees. on one side is a Grove of pines & oaks fit for contemplation—

> "in this path
> how long soe'er the wanderer Roves each step
> shall wake fresh beauties; each short point present
> A different picture, New and yet the Same"[1]

410

if my days of Fancy and Romance were not past, I could find here an ample field for indulgence, yet amidst these delightfull scenes of Nature, my Heart pants for the society of my dear Relatives and Friends who are too far removed from me. I wish most Sincerely to return & pass the Recess of Congress at my Habitation at Braintree, but the season of the year to which they have adjourned renders the attempt impractacable, tho I am not the only person who question there making a congress again till April, but the punctuality of mr Adams to all publick Buisness would oblige him strickly to adhere to the day of adjournment, however inconvenient it might prove to him.² he has never been absent from his Daily duty in Senate a single hour from their first meeting, and the last months Buisness has press'd so hard that his Health appears to require a recess.

Shall I ask my Sister why she has not writen me a line since I came to this place. with regard to myself I own I have been cautious of writing. I know that I stand in a delicate situation. I am fearfull of touching upon political subjects yet perhaps there is no person who feels more interested in them, and upon this occasion I may congratulate my country upon the late judicial appointments, in which an assemblage of the greatest talants and abilities are united, which any Country can Boast of, Gentlemen in whom the publick have great confidence & who will prove durable pillars in support of our Government³

Mr Jefferson is nominated for Secretary of state in the room of mr Jay who is made chief Justice thus have we the fairest prospect of setting down under our own vine's in peace, provided the wrestless spirit of certain characters who foam & frett, are permitted only their hour upon the Stage and then shall no more be heard, off, or permitted to sow the seeds of discord amongst the real defenders of the Faith

Mrs Smith has written to you.⁴ she is now at Jamiaca with her youngest son. Louissa is well, & soon to be inoculated for the small pox. present me kindly to mr & mrs Thaxter, and to the little Namesake⁵ God Bless him for his Parents sake & long preserve them to each other. your Nephew J Q Adams hurries me so least he should miss sending his Letters by this post, that I am obligd to break of more abruptly than I designd and subscribe my self most affectionately / yours   A Adams

Love to mr Shaw & to master & miss Shaw— Remember me to my Neice E Smith and to all other Friends

RC (DLC:Shaw Family Papers); addressed by AA2: "M^rs: E. Shaw. / Haverhill.";
notation: "Octr. 2. Favor^d. by M^r. W Smith." Some loss of text where the seal was
removed.

¹William Mason, *The English Garden: A Poem. In Four Books*, Book 1, lines 212–215.
²On 26 Sept., the Senate agreed to adjourn on 29 September. The body reconvened on 4 Jan. 1790 though it did not achieve a quorum until 6 Jan. (*First Fed. Cong.*, 1:207, 213).
³On 24 Sept. 1789, George Washington nominated John Jay to become the first chief justice of the U.S. Supreme Court. At the same time, he nominated John Rutledge, James Wilson, William Cushing, Robert H. Harrison, and John Blair as associate justices. All but Harrison, who was unable to take his seat due to ill health, eventually served in some capacity (*Doc. Hist. Supreme Court*, 1:1–2, 9).
⁴Not found.
⁵For the birth of John Adams Thaxter, see Shaw to Mary Smith Cranch, 26 Nov. 1788, and note 2, above.

William Cranch to John Quincy Adams

My Good friend—   Boston Oct. 1. 1789. thursday.

Altho I have written you before, I know you have no objection to recieving another letter before you answer my last—¹ My greatest motive for writing now is to know the truth of a Report which has been industriously spread here within this week past, "that there is so great a Coolness between the P——t & V-P——t that they do not speak to each other." I know that there are some people, (I hope but few) who wish to cherish a jealously in the minds of the good people of Massachusetts, towards the Vice President— I have some reason to think that D^r. Demigog is one—² And I doubt a little whether your father's quondam pupil, (with a flat nose) may not be another.³ He seems to be crazy after the phantom popularity. The aforesaid D^r. and he are very intimate, of late— It is said too that the Vice President's influence is much diminished. And as a proof, it is said that judge Tudor has lost the Office of Attorney to this district in the federal Court—⁴ All these things are said by a certain set of people in this town, with a view to detract from the Character of a man who has done more for his Country than any other man, now in it— I have attended but very little to politics lately—but this has caught my Ear as I passed— I know not but that the distinction of *Southern* & *Northern* may have an Influence even upon the greatest Man, But I cannot believe it. The people of the new England States are crazy. They are divided among themselves. They can not see their own Interest—blind as Beetles—

I was at Exhibition Tuesday last— Your Brother was well— Dr Tufts was in town to day—[. . .] [. . .]erting—

I wish you would give the [enclosed?] letter, to Charles— He will be so kind as to deliver it— [. . .] you have rec^d your Coat— Our friends at Braintree were well this Morning—

Your sincere friend   W^m· Cranch

RC (Adams Papers); addressed: "Mr John Quincy Adams / New York"; docketed: "Wm Cranch / October 1st 1789." Some loss of text where the seal was removed.

¹ Not found.
² Perhaps Dr. Charles Jarvis (1748–1807), Harvard 1766, who had a long history of service to the city of Boston and had recently been elected to the Mass. General Court. In his Autobiography, JA wrote of Jarvis' "virulence against me," possibly connected to the animosity between JA and Edward Church, who was Jarvis' cousin (*Sibley's Harvard Graduates*, 16:376–383; JA, *D&A*, 3:384–385; AA to Mary Smith Cranch, 1 Sept., and note 5, above).
³ Probably Jonathan Mason Jr.
⁴ Judge William Tudor, JA's former law student, wrote to JA on 27 July (Adams Papers) about the maneuvering for judicial appointments going on in Massachusetts. Tudor noted to JA that "to no Person but to yourself . . . have I ever hinted a Wish to be noticed in the Places that must soon be disposed of. But you will now give me leave to say that I should be pleased with an appointment to some Office (the advocateship is now out of the Question) which my Education might enable me to discharge the Duties of." JA replied on 18 Sept. (MHi: Tudor-Adams Papers) counseling patience: "how the President will decide, on the judiciary Appointments I know not.— There is no System nor Harmony among the Men from Massachusetts—one recommends one, and another another. Dont you be chagrin'd, mortified humiliated nor vexed let it go as it will." Tudor did not receive any appointment but was eventually admitted to practice law before the district and circuit courts in 1796 (*Sibley's Harvard Graduates*, 17:261).

Abigail Adams to Mary Smith Cranch

my dear sister   Richmond Hill october 4th 1789

I wrote you a Letter last week, but as it did not get to the Post office, I have detaind it with an intention of sending you one of a later date. I believe I have received all your Letters. your last was dated Sep^br 8th I have not written to any of my Friends so often as I ought to. you know very well that when a person is fixed to any particular spot, that very few subjects worth communicating can occur. as I have not been to any publick amusement, I cannot say any thing upon that score, but I can tell you something which may well excite your surprize. it is that I have cause every Sunday to regreet the loss of Parson Wibird, and that I should realy think it an entertainment to hear a discourse from him. do not however tell him so, but except three sermons which three NewEngland Clergymen have preachd to us, I have been most misirably off. Dr Rogers where we usually attend, has been unable to preach ever since I have been here¹ and the pulpit has been supplied as they could procure *Labourers*—by

Gentlemen who preach without Notes, all of whom are predesti-
narians and whose Noise & vehemence is to compensate for every
other difficency to go to meeting & set an hours & half to hear a
discourse the principals of which are so totally different from my
own sentiments, that I cannot possibly believe them, is really doing
penance. I have sometimes gone to St Pauls.² there I find much
more liberal discourses, but bred a desenter and approveing that
mode of worship, I feel a reluctance at changing tho I would always
go to church, if I resided where there was no other mode of worship.
the Clergymen here I am told are so Rigid that their company is very
little sought after. they never mix with their people as they do with
us, and there is in there Air and countanances that solemn Phiz and
gate which looks so like mummery that instead of Reverence they
create disgust, and they address their Audience with so much self
importance, and Priestly despotisim, that I am really surprizd at
their having any men of sense and abilities for their hearers; I have
seen but one exception to this character & that in a dr Lynd who is
really the best & most liberal of the whole sett.³ we have in Massachusetts a sett of clergy that are an honour to Religion, to Learning,
& to our country, and for whom I feel an increased esteem & veneration since my Residence in Newyork. I do not however mean by
my remarks that they are not Religious moral men here. I never
heard a Syllable to their injury, but they certainly are men of very
mean capacities when compared to those of our state. there is no
man of esteemed eminence amongst them even as a divine

The adjournment of Congress leaves me a leisure which I most
sincrely wish I could improve in visiting Braintree. if they had honestly adjournd to April, I say honestly for many of the southern
members will not get here till then, I should not have hesitated in
comeing on immediatly & spending the winter with my dear Friends
in B. but it has been my Lot to be fetterd one way or an other. the
liberality of Congress obliged me to remove most of my furniture so
as to make it quite inconvenient for us to pass a part of our Time at
our own Home, without being at a Considerable expence, and the
prospect of a return in december very much discourages me in my
progect. mr Adams's close & unremitting attention to Buisness during Six months, has made a journey quite necessary for him, yet he
will not go unless it is to his own Home. my son J Q A proposes returning this week to Boston & Brisler leaves me tomorrow.⁴ How
the machine will get on without him I know not. I have offerd him
what I esteem very liberal wages, & double what I can get others for,

13. PARK ROW AND ST. PAUL'S CHAPEL, NEW YORK, BY CHARLES MILBOURNE, 1798
See page xviii

who would perform the mechanical part of Buisness as well perhaps as he but I know not where to find Honour Honesty integrity & attachment. he pleads the state of his family which I know it would be difficult to remove, but 200 dollars pr year are not so easily earned in massachusetts, and are really more than we can afford. he has it at his option to return if he cannot succeed at home. I do not wish my offer to be known, and I think he will find it difficult to support his Family when he once comes to stand upon his own legs for them; which he has never yet done. From six years trial of him I can give him the best of characters, and I never expect to find an other so particularly calculated for me and my Family his Errors are those of Judgment or rather the want of judgment and upon that Rock I am fearfull he will Split, when he comes to act for himself.— the Letter you mention for mr Bond was Sent directly to his Lodgings upon our receiving it.

I hope the appointments in the judicial Line will give Satisfaction, notwithstanding some dissapointments. if I may judge by the News papers, there is no state in the union where there are so many grumblers as in our own. it has been my Lot in Life to spend a large portion of it in publick Life, but I can truly say the pleasentest part of it was spent at the foot of pens Hill in that Humble cottage when my good Gentleman was a practitioner at the Bar, earnt his money, during the week, & at the end of it poured it all into my Lap to use or what could be Spaired to lay by. nobody then grudgd us our living, & 25 years such practise would have given us a very different Property from what we now possess. it might not have given us the 2^d Rank in the united states, nor the satisfaction of reflecting by what means & whose exertions these states have arrived at that degree of Liberty Safety & independance which they now enjoy. if the united states had chosen to the vice P.s Chair a man wavering in his opinions, or one who sought the popular applause of the multitude, this very constitution would have had its death wound during this first six months of its existance. on several of the most trying occasions it has fallen to this dangerous *vice*, to give the casting vote for its Life—there are several members of the House & some of the S——e who are to say no worse wild as—Bedlammites but hush—I am speaking treason. do not you betray me

Remember me kindly to all inquiring Friends—and believe me my dear sister / Yours most / affectionatly   A Adams

RC (MWA:Abigail Adams Letters).

[1] Rev. John Rodgers (1727–1811) was the pastor of the Presbyterian church of New York, which was divided between two churches, one at Wall Street near Broadway and the other at the corner of Beekman and Nassau streets. Rodgers, who had trained for the ministry under Gilbert Tennent, served the New York parish from 1765 until his death, though he was forced to vacate his post during the British occupation of the city (Jonathan Greenleaf, *A History of the Churches, of All Denominations, in the City of New York*, N.Y., 1846, p. 126–133; Sprague, *Annals Amer. Pulpit*, 3:154–165).

[2] St. Paul's Chapel, an extension of Trinity Episcopal Church, opened in 1766 between Fulton and Vesey streets. George Washington attended services there, and it is today the oldest public building in continuous use in New York City (Greenleaf, *History of the*

Churches, p. 61–62; www.saintpaulschapel .org, 26 Jan. 2006). See also Descriptive List of Illustrations, No. 13, above.

[3] Rev. William Linn (1752–1808), Princeton 1772, was a Presbyterian and Dutch Reformed minister and schoolteacher originally from Pennsylvania. In 1786 he was called to become associate pastor of the Collegiate Dutch Reformed Church in New York. During his tenure there, his reputation was such that he was also invited to become the first chaplain to the House of Representatives, beating out John Rodgers for the position (*Princetonians*, 2:231–235).

[4] JQA recorded in his Diary that he left New York on 5 Oct. aboard the *Rambler*, arriving in Newport on 6 October. He continued by stage, arriving at Boston on 8 Oct. and Braintree on 9 Oct. (D/JQA/14, APM Reel 17).

Abigail Adams to Cotton Tufts

Dear sir   october 5 1789

Your favour of 15 sep[br] I have not yet replied to. with regard to the House, I wish it was as moveable an article as a Carriage I would then get you to send it by Barnard to Newyork where I should meet with no difficulty in getting four hundred Dollors rent. now I should be glad to get as much for the 5 Houses we own in Braintree together with the Farms belonging to them.[1] the expence of living here is Double I believe in all most every article, in wood & Hay including the carting three times as much; for Instance, the carts here are very small drawn buy two Horses. they carry only 100 foot of wood at a time so that it costs four shillings to convey a Cord of wood about the distance from your House to mr Nortens. to this you must add four shillings more for sawing it, and your wood costs 5 dollors pr cord, and this is the lowest rate trust the Dutch to make their penny worths out of you.—

the House being in Boston we must take what we can get, say 36 or 34, but let them go out rather than let it for less than 30. the cart you may use when you please. the Scow mr Adams thinks had better lye by than be sold so low provided any shelter can be found. the tools that remain you will let them lye for the present. we have been very near determining to come home & spend the winter, & nothing prevents us but the foolish adjournment of congress to a period when they know the Southern members will not come, so that a part of the Body only will be here a useless expence to the states. had they set one month more & then adjournd to April, it would have been much more convenient. by the way I see the Boston Newspapers report that congress agreed to Borrow 50 thousand dollors of the Banks of Newyork & Phyladelphia as the Bill past the Senate the united states were to be at no expence at all. Pensilvania was to erect the Buildings & make every accommodation at their own expence, but the whole is happily posponed.[2] it was unwise to bring on a subject which must necessaryly involve them in dispute, before any means was devised for the payment of publick creditors, or any way markd out for discharging the publick debt—

my good sir when do you give me an Aunt? or am I now to congratulate you upon that event.[3] be it when it will, I most sincerely rejoice in any circumstance which may tend to augment your happiness. my best Respects to the Lady of your choice. I doubt not that she has great personal merit, and is certainly entitled to my esteem & Regard on that account, but the Relation in which you are about to place her shall be followd by all that respect & Reverence which my Heart pays to worth like that to which she is to be united, and may God Bless you together is the very sincere wish of dear / Sir your affectionate / Neice   A Adams

PS Remember me kindly to mr & mrs Tufts to mr & mrs Norten & cousin Lucy Jones

mr Adams wishes you to send by dr Craigy or any private Hand a Box of such pills as I brought for him when I came

RC (NHi:Misc. Mss. Adams, Abigail); addressed by AA2: "Hon^{ble:} Cotton Tufts / Boston"; endorsed: "Mrs. Abig^{l.} Adams's / Lett—Octo. 5. 1789."

[1] Besides the Old House, the Adamses owned four additional homes in Braintree, along with considerable additional acreage: JA's childhood home (the John Adams Birthplace), which JA purchased from his brother, Peter Boylston Adams; the home where JA and AA lived prior to their time in Europe (the John Quincy Adams Birthplace), which JA inherited from his father; a house purchased from Joseph Palmer in 1771; and another house purchased from William and Sarah Veasey in 1788 (vol. 1:23, 2:252; "An Account of the Real Estate of Hon^r. Jno. Adams Esq. lying in Braintree & Milton," [*post* Sept. 1787], Adams Papers, Wills and Deeds; Adams Papers, Adams Office Manu-scripts, Box 2, folder 13).

[2] The "Act to Establish the Seat of Government"—to determine a permanent home for the new federal government in Pennsylvania—was first introduced in the House of Representatives on 14 Sept., where it was eventually approved. But the Senate, after considerable debate, decided on 28 Sept. to postpone action on it until the next session. Prior to the formal introduction of the bill, early discussion of the residence issue included the suggestion of borrowing money for the purpose, with the figure of $100,000 the most frequently cited in the Boston newspapers (*First Fed. Cong.*, 1:203; 3:206, 222; 11:1457–1459; *Massachusetts Centinel*, 12 Sept.).

³ Cotton Tufts married his second wife,   on 22 Oct. (*Sibley's Harvard Graduates,*
Susanna Warner (1754–1832) of Gloucester,   12:499).

Susanna Clarke Copley to Abigail Adams

Dear Madam   London Oᵒcʳ: 6.ᵗʰ 1789

Your Favor of July 14ᵗʰ: I duely received,¹ and feel myself not a
little flattered by your kind remembrance, and shall be ever highly
gratified in retaining the friendship which flows from so good and
benvolent an heart as you possess: as in this state we have *very* often
occation to lament the seperation from those we esteem: so we have
had much reason to regret the loss of yourself, and worthy Family
from our society: but shall all ways take great delight in hearing of
yours, and their prosperity

Indeed my dear Madam shining abilities: (as well as virtues) are
so necessary for the Public Welfare; that they will be drawn forth
from the private shade of domestic Felicity, and happy is it for the
world when they are; as they cannot fail of stimulateing to Virtue,
and all will admire, even where they may fail of invitation— The
Friends of America here, are felicitateing them selves uppon the
wisdom which their Country have shone in choice of their Senators,
and which we sincerely hope, will be productive of its prosperity: as
well as of that, of those individuals who are acting for them. Mʳ:
Copley desires to join me in respectful Compliments to your self,
Mʳ: Adams, Colonel, and Mʳˢ· Smith; it gives me pleasure to hear of
the increase of Mʳˢ: Smiths happiness; (as I look uppon every addition to her Family in that light) and most sincerely hope that they
will be renderd lasting comforts to her, and hers.—

By Captain Scoot I had the pleasure to send the Silk according to
your direction, and hope I have not exceeded the price that might
have been expected, I found it difficult to get a lutestring with any
kind of Figure as that kind of Silk is too thin to admit of it, and the
Stripes for Mourning are of so little variety and rather common; so
that I have sent a gray Silk of a little better quality with a Spot,
which is suitable, either for Spring, or Autumn, as well as for winter, and Shall be very happy if it Should prove to be what might be
Wished for. the silk was 6ˢ· 6ᵈ pʳ: Yʳᵈ: and as it was not quit so wide
as a lutestring have sent 20 Yʳᵈ· instead of 18

I should have done myself the pleasure of writing sooner had not
my absence from Town prevented my knowing when the Vessels
have sailed for New York: My dear Betsys health has required my

spending the chief of the summer with her in the Country, and I am very sensible that you my dear Madam; will rejoice with me in the present prospect which I have of her perfect resotration. I left her a short time since with my Father at Tunbridge Wells, as I wish her have all the benefit she can from the country before the winter takes place—[2]

Prehaps this may find the Doc[r]., and M[rs] Jefferies in New York as they where uncertain in what part of America they should fix when they left us, but I hope where ever it may be that Success may accompany them,[3] we are now about parting with another Friend, this is indeed not plasant; I had much rather this pleaseing commodity Should be brought to us— by M[r] Trumbull you will be informed of every particular with regard to this place as well as of your Friends in it, and therefore I will not intrude farther uppon you at this time, than to beg your acceptance of my best wishes for your / health and happiness / and beleive me to be / Madam, with great estee / Your Friend, / and, Humble Servant   S: Copley

RC (Adams Papers); endorsed: "Mrs Copley october / 6th 1790."

[1] Not found.

[2] Richard Clarke (1711–1795), Harvard 1729, lived in London with his daughter and son-in-law. The Copleys' daughter, Elizabeth Clarke (1770–1866), eventually married Gardiner Greene in 1800 (*Sibley's Harvard Graduates*, 8:550, 561; Martha Babcock Amory,

The Domestic and Artistic Life of John Singleton Copley, repr. edn., N.Y., 1969, p. 108, 440).

[3] Dr. John Jeffries and his second wife, Hannah Hunt Jeffries, arrived in Boston in November, welcomed by JA among others (*Sibley's Harvard Graduates*, 15:425–426).

Abigail Adams to Mary Smith Cranch

my dear sister   Richmond Hill october 11 1789

Mr Adams Sets of tomorrow morning on a visit to Braintree. I would gladly have accompanied him, but so many difficulties arose in the way, that I gave up the Idea. if I had come we must have gone to housekeeping, & by that time I had got things any way convenient, I must have returnd, & that at a season of the year when it would have been cold & unpleasent travelling. I find myself attackd with my Rhumatick complaints upon the Setting in of cold weather, and am obliged to be very circumspect.

The constant application to buisness for six months has made it necessary to mr Adams to take a jouney and he promises me that he will go to Haverhill and visit his Friends, but [you] are like to have an other visiter, the Pressident Sets out this week for a like excursion. He proposes to go as far as Portsmouth he would have had mr Adams accept a seat in his in coach but he excused himself from motives of delicacy. we yesterday had a very pleasent Party together. the whole family of us dinned with the President on thursday, and he then proposed an excursion to long Island by water to visit Princes Gardens, but as mrs Washington does not Love the water we agreed that the Gentlemen should go by water and the Ladies should meet them at a half way House and dine together, and yesterday we had a most Beautifull day for the purpose the President V P. col S. major Jackson mr Izard &c went on Board the Barge at 8 oclock.[1] at Eleven the Ladies namely Mrs. washington mrs Adams mrs smith miss custos Set out in mrs Washingtons coach & six & met the Gentlemen at Harlem where we all dinned together & returnd in the same manner. we live upon terms of much Friendship & visit each other often whilst the Gentlemen are absent we propose seeing one an other on terms of much sociability. mrs Washington is a most frindly good Lady, always pleasent and easy doatingly fond of her Grandchildren to whom she is quite the Grandmamma.[2]

Louissa & John A. S are both innoculated for the small pox on fryday last. I hope my son J Q A arrived safe (as well as Brisler). I suppose he led you to think that I should visit you as he was very urgent for me to come. I think it not unlikly that there will be a summer recess next year & then I hope to see you all. I wish you would be so good as to get some Brown thread for me of mrs Field three Skains of different Sizes. mr A will pay you for her, & for the Rose water, which you have procured. Ruthe Ludden who lives with mrs Field promised me that she would come and live with me when ever she was out of her Time.[3] if she holds of the same mind I will Send for her in the spring either by Barnard or the stage. I wish you had polly Tailer. to live alone she is a very excellent Girl but she was never made for society and power was never worse used than in her Hands. I tell her sometimes that if I had taken mrs Brislers advice I never should have brought her. of all things I hate to hear people for ever complaining of servants but I never had so much occasion as since I came here one good servant attached to you is invaluable. the one who attends mr Adams is good for nothing that I know of but to look after his Horses. he has servd us as a coachman ever since I have been here. I hope Brisler will return, but I would not urge it too much, as the best people may take advantage of their own concequence and importance.

How is mrs Norten does she begin to look stately? I shall want to see her. Lucy I hope is well I pleasd my self for a week with the Idea of spending three months with you, but it cannot be

I will thank you to look over mr Adams things for him & see that they agree with the list which I will send as soon as I know what he takes— Love to mr Cranch Remember me kindly to my Mother & all other Friends. yours most affectionatly   A Adams—

RC (MWA:Abigail Adams Letters); addressed by AA2: "Mrs Mary Cranch / Braintree."

¹ Major William Jackson, who had previously escorted CA home from Europe in 1781, was serving as one of Washington's secretaries (vol. 4:170–171; *DAB*).

² For Martha Washington's grandchildren, see Descriptive List of Illustrations, No. 11, above.

³ Ruth Ludden (b. 1772) was the daughter of Benjamin and Ruth Ludden of Braintree. She was not available to work for AA until she turned eighteen, still more than a year away (*Braintree Town Records*, p. 837).

John Adams to Abigail Adams

My dearest Friend   [Fai]rfield Oct: 14. 1789

Mr Dalton, Mr Jenkes and myself are at Penfields in good health and Spirits.— My Horses perform very well and my Servant tolerably.

We have met with nothing but Rocks in the Road to molest us. These have jolted us very rudely but Salubriously. I shall keep Mr Dalton company to Boston at least to Cambridge.

according to present Conjectures We shall Spend the Sabbath at Springfield. My Love to my Young Lawyer, and all the rest

yours   J. A.

RC (Adams Papers); addressed: "Mrs Adams / Richmond Hill / New York"; internal address: "Portia"; endorsed: "Mr A october / 14 1790"; notation: "free / John Adams." Some loss of text where the seal was removed.

Mary Smith Cranch to Abigail Adams

My dear Sister   Braintree october 1[5?]th 1789

I have at last receiv'd your Letter but never was poor creature more dissapointed I thought to be sure that it contain'd orders for me to get your house in order for your reception cousin John had not a doubt but you would come. Lucy was going to spend a week at Lincoln but as aunt adams was so soon to be here she desir'd to be sent for home Sister Shaw was comeing in expectation of seeing our dear Freinds & in short we were all on Tip-Toe with expectation & I can not yet give up the fond Idea my dear Sister come— every body knows that you have remov'd almost all your Furniture— we will assist you with any thing we have— Mrs Palmers Family are ready to relive to any part of the house. I wish you would accept of such an entertainment as I could give you I have a room & chamber at your service but this I know would not be so convineent or comfortable as your own— Mr Brisler says that the expence of coming will not be equal of your staying at home— I hope you will come—but whether you do or not—you will want a number of things sent round— Mr Brisler thinks he had better Send your small wines & that your Porter had better be sold here to keep it in that cellar this winter would be runing a great risk of having it Froze. I wish you would write immideatly & let us know what you would have done would you have the winter Fruit & the Butter from your Brother adams's—

Mr Brisler has I believe very wisely conclu'ded to return to you— Mrs Brisler is very desirous that he should. but what will you do with your house maid you will never have any harmony in you Family while you keep her, I certainly would send her home she would do tolarably well alone, but nobody could ever live with her at Mr Apthorps—

25th

I had written thus far disigning to send it away immediately—but before I could finish my Letter I had news of the Vice Presidents leaving new york, & concluded you was with him & was not undeceiv'd till Mr Adams arriv'd without you. & now only think how we were dissapointed & yet I cannot say but your reasons for not comeing are good— I wish Mr Adams would accept of a room & chamber with us I do not know what he will do when Mr Brisler & his wife leave him— I think he would be more comfortable with us some body must take care of his things & him too you best know whether you can trust the new servant with the key of your cellar & other matters, here will be nobody to oversee him— Mr Brisler says he will not leave Mr Adams till you say what shall be done— he thinks it will not do to stay till the cold weather sets in before he removes his Family. he means they shall go by land— I have been in Boston till yesterday ever since I reciev'd your last Letter but will see after your Thread & Ruth Ludden this week— I am now fixing cousin Tom for winter & for a Journey eastward with his Papa— I expect Sister Shaw tomorrow— how she will be dissapointed not finding you here!— Lucy wint yesterday with her uncle & cousin to see the triumphal entrance of the President into Boston—& is not yet return'd the arches were erecting when I left the Town but as we could not all be present I stay'd at home to take care of the House you will see a pompous account of it in the prints depend upon it.[1] The poor governor was taken with a violent fit of the Gout which render'd him unfit to grace the Ceremony with his Presence & will it is suppos'd prevent him from making the first Visit—

Doctor Tufts was married I suppose last thursday he went for that purpose when I am more acquainted with our new aunt I will give you my opinion of her— I rejoice for cousin Lucys sake—but I think there will be no *heart* felt harmony between the son & new mother

Mrs Norton increases in size very fast & wishes you could be with her in march. she would be very well if she did not have so much of the Teeth ache but she is sadly afflicted with it. Do you think Polly Tailor would do for me if you should not be able to keep her I am affraid she has been so long use'd to high living that she would not know how to accomodate her self to such strick rules of eoconimy as she must submit too here. In many things I know her to be vastly superior to the girl I have with me. this girl can spin Polly cannot, tis true Nabby does not get much time to spin she does not know how to do house work half so well as polly does nor will she turn it of so fast—but then I give her but 1/6 a week you may if you please talk to her as supposing I might take her if she should be very desirous of it. if you should wish to part with her— she will never bear to be made of any importance

I wish if you should have any chance to make an inquiery of Doctor Rush about that magnificent Funeral in Philadelphia which our neighbors have heard of & nobody else knows any thing about. I should be glad— They continue to send & receive Letters from the Family I understand they did not all founder at sea as we expected they would—[2]

I am very glad that the vice President & President are upon such friendly terms I never suppos'd it otherways notwithstanding those who wish'd it might not be true have been so busy in spreading reports of the animosety subsisting between the Familys— I have taken care to read such parts of your Letters as would contradict such Idle storys— As to the Fragment it was not even a nine days wonder here— it was despis'd by every body of any sentiment or goodness. The Authors revengful temper is well known & he has really hurt nobody but himself.

I think those who are admitted to spend a social hour with Mrs Washington must be much pleas'd with her, from your discription of her I think her Levee days are not the pleasantest she spends. I hope I shall see the President before he returns

By this time I suppose Louisia & the dear little Boy are begining to feel the effects of their dessorder I hope they will not be bad I shall feel anxious till I hear again

How happy I should feel to spend a few Days with you in this recess fall from the shackels of ceremony— The sweet Little Boy I have with me makes our house chearful— he is a fine Child full of chat & very sensible— If it was not for him I should sometimes be very melancholy.—

Mr Cranch desires me to present his Love to you & tell you he was as much dissapointed as any of us by your not comeing he is as thin as he was last fall the heat & hard work of the summer has carried away all the Flesh he had peck'd us in the winter

I am sorry for your attacks of the Rhumatism— I am sadly worry'd with it myself & am now scarcly able to sit in my chair I am in so much pain with it—

You will write me soon I hope as I wish to know what you would have sent to you by Barnard— give my Love to all my Cousins & accept the affectionate Love of your / grateful Sister

Mary Cranch

RC (Adams Papers); endorsed: "Mrs Cranch / octr 1– 1789."

[1] Washington's visit to Boston—and to the rest of New England—was a major event in the fall of 1789 and received extensive newspaper coverage throughout the country. Besides holding a procession featuring military units, merchants, tradesmen, and public officials, the city of Boston also built a colonnade and "triumphal arch" inscribed "To the Man who unites all hearts" to honor Washington and held various dinners in his honor. The Boston *Independent Chronicle*, 29 Oct., noted: "When an occasion presents itself, in which the People of the United States can testify to distinguished merit, their respect and esteem—they have never been known to let it pass unimproved.— What then were to be expected from them, when an opportunity offered of personally paying these tributes to a Man, in whose character, whatever is Great and Good— whatever dignifies and adorns human nature, are so happily united?" AA probably first read newspaper reports of the event in the New York *Daily Advertiser*, 31 Oct.; see AA to JA, 3 Nov., note 2, below.

For a full discussion of Washington's tour, see Washington, *Papers, Presidential Series*, 4:163, note 3.

[2] Mary Smith Cranch again questioned AA about this family in a letter of 20 Feb. 1791 (Adams Papers). At that time, she identified them as William Henry and Sarah Price Brown of Philadelphia, and indicated that Sarah Brown's death in Jan. or Feb. 1789 had precipitated a massive funeral led by Dr. Benjamin Rush.

Abigail Adams to John Adams

My dearest Friend   Richmond Hill october 20. 1789

I yesterday received your kind favour dated at Fairfield and am happy to find that you had advanced thus far with no greater inconvenience than Rocky Roads & a Blundering Servant I will take better care of his Horses than he appears to have done of his master, for the old Proverb was never more verified, what is every bodys buisness, is nobodys buisness, than in Roberts going of without your Bagage, but he was still more culpable, to leave a part of it at Kings Bridge when it was sent on to him. your shoes & Night cap were brought back by col Smith when he returnd Home. I presume the President will overtake you on the Road [as?] he sat of on Thursday. he went in his chariot alone, & his two [sec]retaries on horse back. you recollect what past the saturday Evening when you took leave of him. on Sunday he exprest himself anxious to mr Lear least he had not been sufficiently urgent with you to accompany him, & desired him to come out to you. mr Lear in replie observed that if he came out, it was probable that you would think yourself not at liberty to refuse, & that it might break in upon your own arrangments. he will I fancy send you an invitation to accompany him to portsmouth which I hope you will find it convenient to accept. I went in to Town on saturday & brought out miss custos, & in the afternoon mrs Washington & mr Nelson & Lewis came out and drank Tea with me.[1] this morning mrs W sent out her Servant to request that the Family would come in and dine with her to day & this being the last concert, that we should go together to it this we comply with as you will readily suppose— col smith Major Butler mr King Webb, Platt, Lawrence &c are all gone to long Island on a grousing Party.[2]

our Family are better than for a week past. two days after you went away, George the footman was Seaized with a Plurisy Fever and that to so high a degree that I was obliged to have his bled Blisterd &c in the course of a few hours, but taking it immediatly, he is on the Recovery, but every person in the Family have had the Epidemick disorder which has so generally prevaild in a greater or lesser degree. as to small pox neither Louissa or John have had it, the dr says oweing to their being sick with this disorder, & that two disorders will not opperate at the Same time, but I fancy much more owing to the matters not being good.

the last Post brought you a Letter from our Friend mr Hollis dated in june.[3] he makes many complaints and is much Grieved at not having heard oftner from you, Sa[ys he], but on 2d thought I will inclose you the Letter that you may write to him. there is also a Letter from the dr in which he request to know what Quantity of cheese we shall want.[4] perhaps you would like that made under your mothers care best. all the butter that can be procured from either place some of the Russet Apples the Pears—N york cannot shew the like—Hams &c

Charls is very steady to the office in the day and to his own Room in the Evening— my duty to mother Love to Brothers & sisters Nephews and Neices— Let me hear from you as often as you possibly can. I rejoice in the fine weather you have & hope Your journey will prove highly benificial to your Health. I wish that a visit from the President may tend to conciliate the minds of our Nothern countrymen & that they will lay asside all sedition & evil speaking. a peice signed a centinal in Edds paper of last week dated Philadelphia, but I believe written in Boston is worthy Notice,[5] might be call'd Treason against the Government it is very seditious.

adieu yours most affectionatly   A Adams

william says duty to Ganpa. want him to come home & go see the cows—

RC (Adams Papers); docketed: "Mrs Adams to / John Adams / October 20th 1789." Some loss of text where the seal was removed.

[1] Both Robert Lewis (1769–1829) and Thomas Nelson Jr., son of the late Gov. Thomas Nelson of Virginia, served as Washington's secretaries (Washington, *Papers, Presidential Series*, 1:397–398, 3:202).

[2] Pierce Butler (1744–1822) was a U.S. senator from South Carolina. An Irishman, he had served as a major in the British Army before marrying the daughter of a South Carolina planter and settling there in 1771. He also represented the state in the Constitutional Convention (*DAB*).

Samuel B. Webb (1753–1807) served in the Continental Army as a secretary to George Washington among other posts, rising to the rank of brigadier general. After the war, he became a mercantile agent in New York City (*Doc. Hist. Ratif. Const.*, 5:876).

Richard Platt (1755–1830), Princeton 1773, worked as a broker in New York City and as

treasurer of the Ohio Company (*Colonial Collegians*).

John Laurance (1750–1810) was a representative from New York. He had formerly served as judge advocate-general of the Continental Army from 1777 to 1782 and was a well-respected lawyer (*DAB*). See also AA to Mary Smith Cranch, 9 Aug., note 6, above.

[3] Thomas Brand Hollis to JA, 6 June (Adams Papers).

[4] Not found.

[5] This article, "Centinel, Revived. No. XXX. To the People of the United States," appeared in Benjamin Edes' *Boston Gazette*, 12 Oct.; it was originally published in the Philadelphia *Independent Gazetteer*, 10 September. The piece argued that "the establishment of a consolidated or national government, in a country of such immense extent as this . . . would necessarily be de-

structive in so superlative a degree of that happy equality and diffusive ease with which the people of these United States have been hitherto so remarkably blessed." It went on to suggest that the solution was not to dissolve the federal government but rather to amend "the new constitution in such manner as to make the general government of the United States a confederation of *efficient* republics—preserving to each every essential power of government, except what may be absolutely necessary to transfer to Congress, for the general regulation, and common defence of the whole union."

Lucy Cranch to Abigail Adams

My dear Aunt—   Braintree October 23. [1789]

Though we were all happy to see my honoured and revered Uncle again in his favorite Braintree, yet we were disapointed, greatly in not seeing you with him— we had indulged ourselves in the pleasing hope of meeting the sister the Aunt the Friend we all so greatly love and esteem. your presence would have enlivened our circle—and made many of the winter hours pass more cheerelly— we should have regreted the disapointment more if the season had not been too far advanced to make your return to New-York agreable. and we would not purchase pleasure at the price of your health and comfort—

There are great preparations makeing in Boston for the reception of the President— one plan was to erect a Colossal statue which should represent Genl Washington—and all the people were to walk under it.

Was there ever any people who acted so inconsistently as some of ours do, to clamour and rave if there is a shaddow of power given their rulers and at the same time pay them homage in a manner that would disgrace the subjects of the Grand Turk—

Mr Brisler desired I would let you know, that he was determined to return to you—and would beg of you to secure him a room and bed room in French-Peters house which is in the road just below your house, the Coach man says they were not ingaged when he came away— he would be glad to have five or six cord of wood laid in for him—as he thinks it can be procured cheaper now than when he returns— he means to send his things round by Bearnad now, and go on with his wife as soon as possible— he wishes much to hear from you again before he goes—

Mama has been in Boston since Tuesday— Cousin Thomas has gone to town for her to day— Uncle, and Mr Wibird dined with my Father and me to day— they are now below feasting upon politics— The good Dr Tufts—I suppose was married yesterday—

remember me kindly to all my Cousins—and be assured my dear Aunt that I am at all times your gratefully / affectionate and dutiful Neice   Lucy Cranch

RC (Adams Papers); addressed: "Mrs Abigail Adams / New-York"; endorsed: "Lucy Cranch / october 23 1790"; notation: "Free / John Adams."

Abigail Adams to John Adams

my dearest Friend   Richmond Hill october 25 1789

I presume you have reachd Braintree before this day I hope the sight of your Friends and of your Farm has restored your Health and spirits. you did well to flee before the very sickly period Mr Maddison lies very ill at Philadelphia, & it is reported that the Speaker of the House died last week by the Bursting a Blood vessel in this Epidemick cold, which scarcly one escapes. I hope however the report may not be true, as I have not seen any mention of it in the papers.[1] Count Moutier & family saild last week as silently as possible. no mention of them in the papers, or other notice taken every thing appears perfectly quiet & easy.[2] Boston papers only are seditious I think from the complexion of some peices which I read in them the massachusetts is brewing mischief.

inclosed is a letter which I wish you to answer immediatly. I have received the fish in four Boxes & tried some of it, which proves very fine.[3] one Box I have sent to mr Jay as a present from you. our Family is better than when I wrote you last, little John excepted who is very sick cutting his Eye teeth.

If Brisler is at Braintree would not you wish him to Bottle the sherry wine which we used part of, & pack it for this place. the other cask I would not remove.

I wish to hear from you and from the children. mrs Cranch wrote me that John was very unwell with his cold. it was taken here I believe, and he ought to be attentive to it. my affectionate Regards to all Friends from / Your ever affectionate   A Adams

RC (Adams Papers).

[1] This rumor was false. Frederick Augustus Muhlenberg, the Speaker of the House, lived until 1801 (*DAB*).

[2] The Comte de Moustier was unpopular as the French minister to the United States.

James Madison wrote to Thomas Jefferson on 8 Dec. 1788 that "Moustier proves a most unlucky appointment. He is unsocial, proud and niggardly and betrays a sort of fastidiousness toward this country. He suffers also from his illicit connection with Madame de Brehan which is universally known and offensive to American manners." In France, Jefferson pressed for a change in ministers, which led to Moustier's departure in Oct. 1789 (Jefferson, *Papers*, 14:340–341, 520–522). Contrary to AA's comments, several of the New York newspapers included short pieces on his formal leave-taking; see, for example, *Gazette of the United States*, 14 Oct.; *New York Journal*, 15 Oct.; and *New York Daily Gazette*, 15 October.

³On 30 Sept. Marston Watson of Marblehead wrote to JA on behalf of a "Fish Club of Gentlemen in this Town bearing Strong Sentiments of Esteem & respect for your private Character, and with all others of your Coun-

trymen cannot but admire the lustre of your public Negociations while in Europe, & the more, as they feel Indebted for your good Service to their branch of business;—therefore hope that they may be Indulg'd to offer with Propriety, attendant on their Sincere Expressions of Gratitude, a few Quintals of their best Table fish" (Adams Papers). JA replied on 7 Nov., thanking Watson for the fish and reiterating his belief that "the Fisheries, are so essential to the Commerce and naval Power of this Nation, that it is astonishing that any one Citizen should ever have been found, indifferent about them" (Dft, Adams Papers). See also AA to JA, 1 May, note 3, above.

Abigail Adams to Mary Smith Cranch

my dear sister   Richmond Hill Nov^br 1 1789

A strange phenomanan has happend in our Family. I believe I wrote you that Louissa and John were both innoculated for the small pox but neither of their arms shew'd any proofs after the 2d Day. Louissa was soon seizd with the cold & Fever which has so universally prevaild here. upon the 10 day John was very sick apparantly the symptoms of the small pox, but they lasted only one day on the 17 day the child had an inflamation in his Eyes a fever in his Head was sick and oppressd at his stomack, but not the least redness upon the arm. we had no apprehension that it was the small pox. on the 19 day he began to have a small Eruption upon his face, his symptoms went of & he has had the small pox finely about a hundred which have fill'd. Louissa has been innoculated from him, and from the appearance of the arm we think it has taken. I hope she will have it as favourable as the child. he could not have taken it in any other way as he was not out of the House, but why he should take it, & Louissa not, cannot be accounted for in any other way, than that two disorders would not operate at the same time.

I yesterday received a Letter from cousin Lucy of oc^br 25 one from Tommy & one from Sister Shaw—and Last week yours october 12 came to hand.¹ I put into mr Adams's Trunk the cushion I promisd you. I should have sent it sooner, but hoped to have brought it. all the things on the Top belong to J Q A, as you will see. I wish you would send them to him, or let him know that you have them. when Brisler leaves the House I should be glad to have the things left inventoried, not that I fear loosing by the Family who are now there, but for my own satisfaction. there was one thing which I forgot to mention. I have papers in the Escritore which I lent Mrs Bass. the key is on the Bunch with mrs Brisler I wish cousin Lucy to go & take them a way, put them in a draw or Trunk at the other House. I hope to come to Braintree in the course of an other year, and see all my dear Friends. I wish the dr much happiness with his *Young wife*, is she not young for him?— mrs Norten must have much satisfaction in the event, if she proves as I hope & doubt not she will a kind Aunt and an agreeable companion. I hope my dear sister has re-coverd her spirits. none of us live without our anxieties, tho some are of a much more painfull kind than others.

How is our worthy uncle Quincy. mr Adams I dare say will visit him as often as he can I hope you will see our worthy President. he is much a favorite of mine I do assure you. tell mr Adams that mrs Washington Says she has a present for him when he returns. it is true she says it is of no great value, but she will not tell me what it is, nor let me see it till he returns. I told her I would be jealous but it did not provoke her to shew it me. we are at present all very well. Louissa innoculated the 2 time on thursday last I hope mr Adams will not put of his return so late as he talkd of when he sat out. the weather will be soon very cold and uncomfortable. remember me kindly to all my Friends. I am very bad about writing; not half as good as when I was in England. the reason is I have few subjects, few new objects, the men & women here are like the men & women else where, & if I was to meet a curious Character I should not venture to be free with it.

I wish to have our winter Apples pears Butter some cheese Bacon Tongus &c all from our own state & what I cannot get from the Farm I would get put up in Boston, such as Hams & Tongues I mentiond all these things to mr Adams but do not know that he will be attentive about them. any Letters which may be taken out of the post office addrest to the Vice Pressident of the united states, you may venture to open the covers of whether mr Adams, is with you or not for you may be sure that they come from Richmond Hill.

adieu my dear sister and believe me most affectionatly yours—

A Adams

mrs smith & master william magpye as I call him send duty—

RC (MWA:Abigail Adams Letters); addressed: "To / Mrs Mary Cranch / Braintree."

[1] Lucy Cranch to AA, 23 Oct., is above. The letters from TBA, Elizabeth Smith Shaw, and Mary Smith Cranch have not been found.

John Adams to Abigail Adams

My dearest Friend   Braintree Nov. [*1*] Sunday 1789

I thank you for your kind Letter inclosing that from our Friend Hollis.[1] The Influenza is here as general as it was at N. York.— Your youngest Son has been laid up with it at Mr Cranche's; but is better. Mr Wibird is confined with it, so that We had no Meeting. I have been to visit him: He is not very bad: but not fit to go out. My great Horse, had a Misfortune last night in the Stable, that he will not get over this fortnight. I am thankful that he is alive.

Mr Brisler is preparing his Goods to go by Bernard, who Sails on Wednesday, and will go with his Family next Week in the Stage.

I have Spent a Week in Boston which I have not done before these fifteen years. General Washington between Sam. Adams and John, The Fratrum dulce Par, mounted up to View in the Stone Chapell and in Concert Hall to be sure was a Spectacle for the Town of Boston. The Remarks were very Shrewd— Behold three Men, Said one, who can make a Revolution when they please. There, Said another are the three genuine Pivots of the Revolution. The first of these Observations is not I hope, so true as I fear the last is. of all the Pictures that ever were or ever will be taken this ought to be done with the greatest Care, and preserved in the best Place. But H.'s Creatures will cast a Damper upon that.

The Presidents Behaviour was in Character, and consequently charming to all. I write no Particulars, because the News papers will give you the details.— His Reception has been cordial and Splendid. His Journey will do much public good.

I Shall return, in the first Week in December, if not sooner, and bring Thomas with me.— You must be very prudent and cautious, of my Letters. Let them be seen by none, but the Family: for altho I shall write no harm there are Chemists who are very skilful in extracting evil out of Good.— I have Seen the new Mrs Tufts, and admire the Drs Taste. She is in appearance, a fine Woman.

RC (Adams Papers); endorsed: "Mr A Nov^{br} / 1789 1"; docketed: "Copy M^r· J. Adams / 1789. 1."

[1] AA to JA, 20 Oct., above.

Mary Smith Cranch to Abigail Adams

Dear Sister   Braintree November 1ᵈ 1789

The dull weather of Last week has prevented sister Shaw from making her visit or she would have been here mourning with me the absence of our dear sister. I hope she will be here on Teusday if she is not I fear she will not come this fall— She has already put it of too long—the fine weather is all over. Doctor Tufts has taken the advantage of it & brought home his wife as snug as can be— Mrs Quincy & Miss Nancy are going with us to make the wedding Visit this week. Mr Wibird is too unwell to preach to day has got I suppose the Washington cold— every body who was at the parade the Day the President enter'd Boston took a cold. People stood at the windows some of them Six hours, waiting for his arrival— Having got a good situation they were affraid to leave it least they should not be able to recover it again; The day was dreadful raw & uncomfortable Lucy & Miss Hazen are gone to weymouth to meeting & to see the Bride. Lucy has not yet seen her aunt but both of them have such colds they were not fit to go out— Here is your son Tom confin'd with it he has been threaten'd with the Rhumatism but I hope he will not be bad—

Mr Adams was here last evening & was well, I wish'd him to stay here but he was so busy picking out Books to send by Barnard that he could not. When Mr Brisler leaves him he will come— I am sorry too hear that cousin Louisia & the little Boy did not take the Small Pox it is a pity to have so much anxiety for nothing: but I hope the will do well yet

I have seen Ruth Ludden she says she shall not be eighteen till next fall— she will then come if you are not supply'd Mrs Feild is spining your thread

What is become of Betsy Crosby Miss Soper desir'd me to ask you to give me the true situation She is in if you had seen or known any thing of her[1]

The dull circle in which I move furnishes me with so little to intertain you with—that I find it difficult sometimes to muster up matter for a Letter—

Mr Brisler has felt a little diffident about returning without your further orders— he hopes he has not do[ne] wrong— I assur'd him you would be glad to recc[ommend] him if he was convinc'd that he could not do so [well?] in any other way

433

I hope I shall receive a Letter from you before I close this. if I should I may add more than that.

I am with Love to all my Freinds your / affectionate Sister

Mary Cranch

Mr Cranch desires his Love may be presented

Nov^b. 4th

no Letters from you— We are all indisposed with colds but nobody quite sick— old mrs Thayer is here upon her mendicant visit She is in her ninety second year & can walk a mile or two yet. & has knit 5 pair of stockings with in five weeks three pair of which were for men!

RC (Adams Papers). Some loss of text where the seal was removed.

[1] For Elizabeth Anne Crosby, see vol. 5:187–188. Miss Soper was probably one of her maternal aunts (Pattee, *Old Braintree*, p. 156).

Abigail Adams to John Adams

my dearest Friend   Newyork Nov^br 3. 1789

I did not write to you by the last post. I was in hopes to have received a Letter from your and to have known from under your own Hand how your Health was. Tommy wrote me by your direction;[1] and I heard by other Hands of your safe arrival and the News papers inform us that by desire of his Honour the Leiu^t Govenour you was in the procession to accompany the President to his Residence.[2] there is a vile mischevious junto in Boston, but I shall lose the whole chain. the Printers have not sent on the papers Sinc you left here; pray order them continued. But now with regard to our own affairs Brisler sends me word that he proposes to return & bring on his Family, & I have engaged two Rooms for him in the House at the End of our Land, adjoing to the corn Feild which will be very near and convenient for him. I am not at all satisfied with the Hand I have with me and with Regard to the coachman, you will not confide in him further than you can see, him Brisler will tell you that with Liquors he cannot be trusted. I mention this least Brisler should be obliged to come away before you. the Porter which is in the cellar you will either have sent on, or dispose of as it will freeze, the red wine & any other you chuse you will direct Brisler to put on Board Barnard, 200 weight of cheese & all the Butter which can be procured. I hope you will conclude to return sooner than you talkd of. the Trunk of cloaths which you had sent by Barnard you can leave without any inconvenience till Spring.

we have no News here except the expected return of the commissoners from Georgia who it seems have been very unsuccessfull, & concequently must expect many unfavourable reports with respect to them, some of which are already in circulation;[3] the district court meet this day the Marshal is qualified and attends. the Rank & presidence was yesterday setled & the Marshal is to take Rank of the district Attorney.

our little John has had the small pox finely & is quite recoverd of it Louissa is innoculated from him— pray present my duty to your good mother Love affection where due. congratulation to our New married Friends, for me, and accept the affectionat Regard / of Your

A Adams

Suppose the horse cart Horse sled & one sadle which the dr has in his care & the Saw should be put on Board Barnard we shall find them very usefull

RC (Adams Papers); addressed: "To / The vice President of the / united states / Braintree"; docketed: "Mrs Adams to / John Adams. / November 3rd 1789."

¹ Not found.
² The New York *Daily Advertiser*, 31 Oct., reported, "a Correspondent observed with great pleasure the Vice-President in the Procession from the State House; who at the request of the Lieut. Governor proceeded with the Procession to the Residence of the President."
³ In the fall of 1789, in an attempt to resolve land disputes between residents of the state of Georgia and the Creek Nation, George Washington sent commissioners to

Rock Landing, Georgia, to open negotiations with the Creeks. The Creeks, however, pulled out of the discussions because of the commissioners' support for Georgian land claims, and the commissioners came back to New York without an agreement (Francis Paul Prucha, *The Great Father: The United States Government and the American Indians*, 2 vols., Lincoln, Neb., 1984, 1:54–55). A report of the commissioners' return appeared in the New York *Daily Advertiser*, 29 October.

Abigail Adams to Mary Smith Cranch

my dear sister   Nov^br 3. 1789 Richmond Hill

I did not receive your Letter dated 25 untill sunday Evening which made it too late to write by the last post in replie to it.[1] I do not know any thing that I wisht more for than to have past the winter at my own House for a summer situation this place is delightfull & the House convenient, and except its being Bleak and perhaps difficult of access in some parts of a severe winter, it is more to my mind than any place I ever lived in. in point of oeconomy it would be very advantageous to be able to live at Home part of the year and the winter in particular. wood being the most expensive article here, Nut wood, What we call walnut is 7 dollors pr cord and oak cost me five brought to our door between 40 & 50 Cords of which we shall consume in a year, as we are obliged to keep six fires constantly, & occasionally more the hire of servants is an other very heavy article part of which we might spair at Braintree. our House we must keep & pay for—but I should wish if a recess of any length should take place again to spend it with my Friends at Braintree. my constant family is 18, ten of which make my own Family. both mrs Smith & I am disposed to accommodate as much as possible, but difficulties will arise with the best servants sometimes, & we can neither of us boast that all ours are of the best kind

I have a pretty good Housekeeper a tolerable footman a midling cook, an indifferent steward and a vixen of a House maid, but she has done much better laterly, since she finds that the housekeeper will be mistress below stairs. I wish Polly was in Braintree, and meant to have taken her with me if I had come, but I do not know what to say with regard to her suiting you. she is very far from being a Girl that will turn off work quick, her constitution has been ruined by former hardships, and she is very often laid up. she has not method or regularity with her buisness, all her buisness here is to make 4 or 5 beds, & clean round Rooms which are almost coverd with carpets, all the Brass is cleand by the footman she helps wash & Iron, but I have been obliged to hire when I have wanted more cleaning than that done in a day, and Every days work to pay 3 shilling a day for. I suppose I must keep her till spring, unless she should become more than usually quarelsome. with regard to drink I meet with no difficulty with her on that account, and she has an attention to my interest more than any servant I have besides, when mr Brisler is absent. she keeps no company, and is fond of the children, so that she has her good Qualities, for which I am ready to credit her.

I have written to mr Adams respecting the coachman who certainly is not to be trusted with keys of a cellar—[2] he always slept in the stable and was never in the House but at meal times, or as a porter at the door when we had company to dine. he is a good coachman and that I believe is all— I hope mr Adams will return Sooner than he talks of, for I am sure when Brisler goes he cannot be well accommodated in his own House, and the Roads will every day be proving worse. 200^{wt} cheese all the Butter from mothers my half from pratts is what I should like sent I should like a good Hog or two, but pratts pork is not worth having, and I shall have some of my own here.

I think Brisler much in the right, both for me and himself. he will be better of than his master & may lay up more money, but what could he do at home to earn 200 Hard dollors. I think his Family may live very well upon one hundred. I have engaged 2 good Rooms for him for 32 dollors & a half his Wood I suppose will cost him 25 dollors, but suppose he only lays by 50 a year, tis more than he could do & mantain himself & family where he is.

I wrote to him by the last post,[3] let him know if his Family can come on without him & mr Adams wishes him to stay with him, that they shall come here till he & his Things arrive— but he must be here by the Time that Barnard is to look after his things—

I wish mr Adams would return with the President, as I know he will be invited to, & let Tommy take his sulky & come on with that

my Love to mrs Norten, to cousin Lucy and all inquiring Friends. my most affectionate Regards to mr Cranch remember me to Mrs Palmers Family—

Yours most affectionatly   A Adams

RC (MWA:Abigail Adams Letters); addressed: "To / Mrs Mary Cranch / Braintree."

[1] See Mary Smith Cranch to AA, 1[5?] Oct., above, for which the final dateline is 25 October.
[2] 3 Nov., above.
[3] Not found.

Martha Washington to Abigail Adams

My dear Madam   Wednesday Morn 4 November [1789]

I should have been very happy to have seen you yesterday.— and am truly sorry the bad day disapointd me of the plasure, your servant brought you kind favor yesterday while I was at dinner.[1] he could not stay and the evening was so bad,— I have the plasure to ask you, how your self M[rs] Smith Miss Smith and the little ones are to day, I intended yesterday after the sermon to bring the children out with me on a visit to you, but the weather prevented me—

I will my dear Madam—doe myself the pleasure to dine with you on satterday with my famly and shall be very happy with Geneal Knox—and the Laides,—mentioned or any others you plase

I am dear Madam with esteem your / affectionate Friend / and Hble Sr   M Washington

Our best wishes to M[rs] Smith &ca

RC (MHi:Waterston Autograph Coll.); addressed: "Mrs Adams"; endorsed: "Mrs Washington / Nov^br 4 1789."

¹ Not found.

Abigail Adams to John Adams

my dearest Friend   Nov^br 10th 1789

Tis more than a month since you left Home, and except the few lines from Fairfield, I have not received a single Letter from you. I have written to you every week, and should have been very happy to have learnt from your own Hand that you was benefitted by your journey and that you was conveniently accommodated. I get only one Boston paper, so that I am in the dark with regard to the politicks of massa, save what is retaild here

mr Jay received Letters from mr Jefferson yesterday dated 5 August. he had not then received his Letters of recall.¹ he writes very cautious with regard to the state of France, says that the disturbances had subsided in a great measure

The marshal is gone to serve a writt this morning upon a captain of a vessel who has defrawded the customs. it is the first which has been issued & it runs in the Name of *the People*— he thinks that there is a difficulty arising with respect to the prisons. a marshal is obliged to give Bonds and committ his prisoner to the Jails of the state & into the custody of officers over whom the Federal court has no controul who will bear him harmless if the Prisoner excapes?

The weather is remarkably fine I have got the chief of our winter wood, but at a most terible price the oak cost 32 6 pr cord, and walnut 50 it shall be the last time that I will be so taken in by dependance upon others. the Carman found he could not make money enough by getting it, and so would not stand to his agreement. if Barnard is not saild pray tell Brisler to Buy me 30 or 40 dozen of Eggs & put on Board. they have got them up to 1/6 pr dozen. Butter a shilling pr pound by the firkin. it really would have been worth while to have bought our vegetables in Boston, potatos particularly for they are at 3 shilling a Bushel by the Quantity Turnips at 1/6. malt is an other article, that I should have been glad to have had 6 Bushel of, but I fear I am too late for Barnard.

we are all well. mrs washington and Family dined with me last saturday together with General & mrs Knox and mrs Green.²

Duty and Love where due pray write by the Next post to your ever / affectionate   A Adams

438

RC (Adams Papers); addressed by AA2: "The Vice President / of the United States / ~~Braintree~~ / New York"; docketed: "Mrs Adams / to John Adams / Nov 10th 1789"; notation: "5: 8 / 5 8 / returned 10: 16." This letter was originally mailed to Braintree then redirected back to New York.

[1] For Thomas Jefferson's letter of 5 Aug. to John Jay, see Jefferson, *Papers*, 15:333–334. Jefferson first requested to be allowed to take a leave of absence from France to return to the United States in Nov. 1788. Jay sent him permission on 19 June 1789, which he received on 23 Aug. (Jefferson, *Papers*, 15:202–203).

[2] Catharine Littlefield Greene (1753–1814), the widow of Gen. Nathanael Greene, had moved to New York City in the summer of 1789 to attempt to persuade Congress to settle her husband's war accounts (Washington, *Papers, Presidential Series*, 3:390–391).

Abigail Adams to John Adams

my Dearest Friend   Nov[br] 14 1789

I received yours of Nov[br] 4. on thursday last.[1] Brisler and his Family got here the same Day & are waiting the arrival of Barnard to go into their House. the President got home on fryday last, looks much fatigued with his jouney, and has beat out all his Horses. Brisler says the Roads are getting very bad, and that you will find it very tedious travelling in a few weeks pray take care that your little vehicle does not overset. I wrote you respecting Several articles which I supposed might come with Barnard, but my letters will be too late unless we venture them when he comes on again. Charls wants to have some cider sent, and I think half a dozen Barrels would not be amiss— I wish Brother would get me 20 or 30 dozen of Eggs put into Brand & send me when Barnard returns. we are all well cold excepted. I believe Louissa has the small pox. she has had Some symptoms, but no Eruption worth mentioning & not one that has fill'd. mrs Izard has lost her Baby with it.[2] Richmond Hill has lost much of its Beauty Since you left us. the Trees are all stripd & look dreary but the prospect is Beautifull tho in Ruins.

Remember me affectionatly to all inquiring Friends and believe me most tenderly / and affectionatly / your   A Adams—

RC (Adams Papers); addressed by AA2: "The Vice President / Of the United States / ~~Braintree~~ / New York"; docketed: "Mrs Adams / to John Adams / November 14th 1789"; notation: "~~10~~ / 8 / returned 8 / 16." This letter was originally mailed to Braintree then redirected back to New York.

[1] JA to AA, [1] Nov., above.
[2] William Izard, the son of Ralph and Alice DeLancey Izard, was born on 1 June and died in Nov. (*SCHGM*, 2:216 [July 1901]).

439

John Adams to Abigail Adams

My dearest Friend   Braintree Saturday Nov. 14 1789

I am impatient to return but partly on Account of my Son who wishes to Stay at Colledge as long as he can, and partly, on Account of my Books and other Things which I wish to get ready before I go, to be sent to N. Y. I fear I shall not see you these three Weeks. I should however break away if I were not necessitated to wait for my horse, whose Lameness is not wholly cured.

Excepting the Influenza which is universal our Relations and Friends are all very well.

The Accident to my horse, has been a vexatious Thing and has deprived me of half the Pleasure and half the Exercise I intended.— This Horse I am told here got cast in the Same stable last year.

My Farm I found as I expected—poor enough.

I live with my Mother and Brother. and We live like Princes, in great Luxury.— You knew my Mother. She has the Influenza, severely: but is very active.

The President is at Home eer now, no doubt.

Mr Brisler is arrived I hope without any Accident with his Family. This will be some Relief to Us, as it will take off, much care from your mind. I wish I could send Boys and Girls from hence, to supply all the Places in the House that you want filled.

There is a Calm a Silence and a Tranquility that is very remarkable in this Part of the Continent. May it be equal at the southward and long continue in both! i. e. may We be enabled to give Satisfaction to the Multitude of our Brethren[1]

RC (Adams Papers).

[1] This is the last letter exchanged between AA and JA until 24 Nov. 1792 (Adams Papers).

Abigail Adams Smith to Elizabeth Cranch Norton

Richmond Hill Novr 15th 1789—

almost twelve months have elapsed since the date of your last letter,[1] I am conscious that this chasm in our Correspondence my Dear Eliza has been my own fault and very often have I reprimanded myself for my inattention—in not having noticed your last kind Letter,—but many casualties have intervened to prevent me from writing, which I hope will gain me your favourable indulgence for past ommisions when I promise future amendment,— perhas when your family has enlarged as much as mine you may be less surprized at my want of punctuallity, I have thought of you often since I had the pleasure of seeing you, and have frequently heard of your health with much pleasure

I am again blessed with the society of my own family and I consider it as amongst the happiest Events of my Life; early after my Father arrived here, he requested with earnestness that we would take up our abode with him,— the affection which has ever dictated all his actions towards me, was too deeply impressed upon my heart to permit me to hesitate to Comply with a request which would in any degree accommodate himself and family;— we therefore accepted his profered kindness, and have resided with his family ever since;— my youngest Son has just recovered from the small Pox, & Louisa has had it very favourably and is now recovering—

I Congratulate you upon the acquisition your family Circle has lately made—(in a small society the addition of one who is disposed to promote sociability; quallified to perform the Duties of friendship; and capable of contributing their part of those attentions which render Life valuable; and upon the agreeable performance of which, much of our happiness depends,) is almost inestimable, be pleased to present me respectfully to this new relation, and offer my Congratulations to the good D^r if you please upon his Marriage.

I wish I could bring you acquainted with my friends—in this part of the World—that you would be pleased with them I am very sure— for they possess more of the qualifications essential in the Characters of amiable Women and agreeable Companions—and as few of the defects as any Ladies—I have been acquainted with; they are very different and yet variously pleasing— the grave and the gay are very happily blended in their minds which they have Cultivated,— and well furnished, their dispositions are lively, but tempered with judgment,—and they are well quallified, to fill the various Stations of Life,—with dignity;— their early expectations were very flattering; but they were soon Initiated into the School of adversity,— they have not sunk under the presure of misfortunes,—but have risen superior—to its influence,—and have quallifed their minds to their present situation, which tho not so affluent as they *once* had a right to expect, is, yet very eligable— by the ravages of War, their Habitation was utterly destroyed, and their Lands laid desolate;—

I hope my Dear Cousin that you enjoy your health and preserve your spirits you must not permit them to be depressed, for I beleive

441

that in almost every Situation which our imaginations have pictured as dangerous and distressing the reality falls short of our expectations, I cannot wish you more favour than I have received, that you may enjoy an equal degree is my earnest desire—

Colln Smith joins me in Compliments to Mr Norton, and all friends who may inquire after your / sincere well wisher, and friend—   A Smith—

RC (MHi:Christopher P. Cranch Papers); docketed: "Mrs· A Smith to ~~Miss E Cranch~~ / Mrs· Norton 1789."

¹ No letters from Elizabeth Cranch Norton to AA2 have been located.

Abigail Adams to John Quincy Adams

my dear son   Newyork 22 Novbr 1789

one would suppose that the waters between N york and Road Island had produced the same effect upon you, that the Poets feign of the River Lethe, not a Line, not a word from you since you quitted Richmond Hill. are you so wholy absorpd in the study of the Law of Nations as to forget those of Nature?

I have been very sorry since you left us that your visit was made just at the period it was. a few untoward circumstances combined to render it less agreeable to you than it would have proved since. I should not have consented to your leaving us, if I had thought I should not have follow'd in a few days but the season of the year in which I must have returnd, & the arrangments I must have made to have tarried only two months quite discouraged me. at the next adjournment I hope to come on and pass several Months at Braintree.

Since I saw you, you have had an illusterous visiter. I hope you was one of the Choir who so aptly Serenaded him, with "the Hero comes." he was much gratified with the attention shewn him: I have it from his own Mouth. is it in Humane Nature to be otherways? he ought to be immortal, for who can ever fill his place— I ought to inform you that the day after you left us, you had an invitation to dine there.¹ we live in a most friendly intercourse, & madam makes very few visits but those of ceremony when she does not request my Ladyship to accompany her and I have several appointments of that kind now on Hand Let not the Busy fiend envy propogate reports so basely false as that there is any coldness Subsisting between the Families— Massachusetts alone could be guilty of such baseness. I hope the presence of the Late visiter has banishd antifederialism

I hope you have visited your Father since the misfortune of his Horse has prevented him from the excursion he intended.

Your Friends here desire to be rememberd to you and chide you for not writing. believe me most affectionatly / your &c

Abigail Adams

RC (Adams Papers).

¹ Two days later, on 24 Nov., George Washington invited AA to join him in his box at the theater. AA accepted the invitation and attended a production of *The Toy; or, A Trip to Hampton Court*, along with a number of other government officials and their wives (Washington, *Papers, Presidential Series*, 4:321–322).

Abigail Adams to Cotton Tufts

My dear sir Newyork Nov^br 22 1789

I congratulate you and the Lady to whom you are united upon your Nuptials, and most sincerely wish you a renewall of all your former happiness, with corresponding dispositions, and inclinations. the domestick circle is alone capable of yealding satisfactions, which an intercourse with the word and all its amusements never can afford. in Buisness or in pleasure the participation of a dear Friend, makes more than half the enjoyment. there is a period of Life too, when neither buisness or pleasure can be persued with the ardour of Youth. then it is that we feel more sensibly the want of domestick tranquility and retirement. may your declining years my dear sir be as repleat with happiness as the visisitudes of Humane Life will permit, and when this transitory scene ends, may you meet the Reward of a good and Faithfull Servant

I wrote to you by my son sine which I have not heard from you.¹ I have now to request you to procure for me 400 wt of Butter and to send it by Barnard. I have been dissapointed here, and it is so scarce and dear that I am sure I cannot now procure it. Barnard has orders to bring several hundred firkins, & I wish you to secure mine as soon as you receive this Letter, I also wish to have a Barrel of Beaf put up by Baldwin & a couple of dozen of Hams. mr W Smith will tell you who I mean if you are at any loss. there is also a sley to be sold for 8 dollors by packard who Lives with mr Black² Mears has an other with harness for 11.³ I will thank you to see them both & to Buy one or the other & send by Barnard I must give ten pounds currency for one here, and we must have one, for to go to market in winter, living two miles from it, and never being able to Buy at our door the marketting all being carried into the city by water. if you will be so good as to procure these things and send me the Bill by Barnard with an order for him to receive the money I will pay it to him the Horse cart & sled if not sold will amply repay us if we can get it here, as we cannot get a carman to come out of Town to bring any thing under four shillings.

Barnard is to sail this Day & will tarry not more than ten days after he arrives if he should be full the sley will be of more importance to us this winter than the cart. if one must be left I wish it may be that. the fruit which I have received this year was gatherd a month too soon, badly packd and is half ruind but, as I expected nothing better I am not so much dissapointed—

I hope I may be able to come home at the next adjournment of congress—

Present me affectionatly to my New Aunt to your son daughter and Neice to mr & mrs Norten and believe me my dear sir most affectionatly / your Neice   A Adams

RC (NHi:Misc. Mss. Adams, Abigail); addressed by AA2: "Honble Cotton Tufts / Weymouth"; endorsed: "M^rs. Abig^l. Adams / Lett^r. Nov. 2^d. 1789 / rec^d. the 29th."; notation: "Hon^d by / Genl Lincoln."

[1] Possibly 5 Oct., above.
[2] Probably Joshua Packard, who may have lived in the household of Moses Black (d. 1810) (*Braintree Town Records*, p. 621; Sprague, *Braintree Families*, p. 693).

[3] Probably George Mears (Mearsh), a member of one of the original German families to move to Braintree in 1752 (Pattee, *Old Braintree*, p. 59, 478).

John Quincy Adams to Abigail Adams

Newbury-Port December 5th: 1789.

No, my dear Madam, I have not tasted of the waters of Lethe, nor have the Laws of Nature, been obliterated from my heart, by too close an attention to those of Nations. The reasons which have hitherto prevented me from writing since I left you, are various; but would not be very interesting in the detail, for which reason I shall, omit the unnecessary tediousness of a justification, and offer you a reparation instead of an apology.

I flattered myself long with the expectation of seeing my father in this Town; and until your Letter arrived, but two days ago; I never knew that his Horse had met with a misfortune; I am still ignorant of its nature; and did not abandon the hopes of seeing him, untill I was informed he had been gone a week on his return to New-York. My friends in this quarter are not even so liberal in their communications as I am to you; my brothers both seem to make it a point to receive my letters with silent pleasure; and upon enquiring at thanks-giving time how Tom did, of one of his classmates; he answered that he then supposed him to be in New-York.

Two and twenty hours after I left you at Richmond-Hill, I landed at Newport, and the Thursday following arrived in Boston. I pass'd two or three days at Braintree; quite sick of what I then thought only a severe cold. I have since been induced to suppose it was the *influenza*. This disorder has since then been almost universal in this State; and I have been upbraided for singularity in enjoying good health, while all the world were more or less diseased. It has not however been fatal in any instance that has come to my knowledge in this neighbourhood.— When I say I have enjoyed good health, it must be understood as they say, with a grain of salt. The ancient quarrel between the powers of drowsiness and me has threatened to break out again; and a few nervous twitches have hinted to me the propriety of suffering no intermission in the article of exercise. I have scarcely been out of Newbury-Port, since my return from New-York; but I intend next week to spend a day or two at Haverhill. I was not one of the choir who *welcomed* the President *to New-Englands shore,* upon his arrival here by land. I was however in the procession, which was formed here to receive him, in humble imita-tion of the Capital. And when he left us, I was one of the *respectable citizens* (as our news-papers term them) who escorted him on horse-back to the lines of New-Hampshire.[1]

You, my dear madam, have abundant reason to know that your eldest son is not by any means destitute of that bubbling Passion called Vanity; and therefore you will excuse him, and allow a little parental indulgence, when he informs you of the petty honours which accrued to him in consequence of this same visit of the President; and you will make all the necessary allowances if he states facts, which are really true, in such a manner as shall exhibit him in the most advantageous light—and thus I begin.

I had the honour of paying my respects to the President, upon his arrival in this town, and he did me the honour to recollect that he had seen me a short time before, at New-York. I had the honour of spending part of the evening in his presence at Mr. Jackson's. I had the honour of breakfasting in the same room with him, the next morning at Mr. Dalton's. I had the honour of writing the billet which the major general of the County, sent him to inform him of the military arrangements he had made for his reception. And I had the honour of draughting an address, which with many alterations and additions (commonly called amendments) was presented to him by the Town of Newbury-Port.² So you see

"I bear my *blushing* honours thick upon me."³

But as half the truth is often times a great falsehood I am constrained to account for these distinctions, in a manner, which I must honestly confess, defalcates considerably from the quantum of my importance. To the peculiar civility of Mʳ⁻ Jackson and Mʳ⁻ Dalton, I am indebted for having been thus admitted into the Company of the President. One of the major general's aid de camps, is my fellow student; he was then much hurried, with other business relating to the same occasion; and at his request I wrote the billet. Mʳ⁻ Parsons was chosen by the Town to draught the address; and his indolence, was accommodated in shifting a part of the burthen upon his clerk: so that all my dignities have not been sufficient to elevate me above the insignificant station of a school-boy; in which character I still remain, your dutiful Son. But to turn from trifling, to a subject to me very serious, I must observe, that my own reflections upon the subject of the place of my future residence, are daily becoming more and more perplexing. You well know the objections which I have against Braintree, and I may safely appeal to your Judgment for their validity. my father's determined predilection, is the only circumstance that could give that place any claim to fixing me, under the present relative situation of my cousin Cranch and me.— Boston is strongly recommended to me by several of my friends, whose opinions in favour of the capital, are much more favourable than my own. Greater necessary expence, more necessary dissipation; and a more numerous competition for the favours of employment, are not circumstances, calculated to decide my preference. This town, while inhabited by the two most eminent barristers in the County, and an attorney, who though young is much respected, does not offer me a prospect in any manner alluring; though I should here enjoy the advantage of being more extensively known, than in any other part of the Commonwealth.— However I will postpone the full discussion of this matter till the appointment of our two Judges shall take place; after which I shall state my case fully to my father, and found my determination, upon his final opinion.⁴

I shall certainly write before long to my Sister; whose absence during so great a part of the Time, that I spent with you, is still a subject of much regret to me. My affection for her, and for all my friends at Richmond-Hill, I trust is not of that kind, which is weakened by absence; and I hope they will all do me the justice to believe that my sins of omission, are not the result of insensibility. My Father and Col.: Smith, will please to accept of my dutiful and affectionate remembrance. Louisa will accept an apology, for what she has before this probably forgotten: that in the hurry with which I left Richmond-Hill, I forgot even to take my leave of her. Charles and Tom, I hope will devote a few leisure moments to fraternal correspondence; to which they may depend upon receiving punctual returns. William has doubtless forgotten his uncle Jack; who wishes very much to have a little more *fun* with him. John I suppose from your not mentioning him in your Letter has got well through the small-pox.— Your affectionate Son.   J. Q. Adams.

RC (Adams Papers); addressed: "Mrs: A. Adams. / New-York."; docketed: "JQ Adams / Dec 5th 1789."

[1] Washington passed through Newbury-port on 30 Oct., greeted by a parade and fireworks. He remained in town overnight and left for Portsmouth, N.H., the following morning "under the same escort which conducted him to this town, to which were added, a large number of military and other gentlemen of Newbury-port" (Newburyport *Essex Journal*, 4 Nov.).

[2] JQA's draft "Address from Newbury-Port, To President Washington" welcomed Washington to Newburyport and expressed "sentiments of joy, resulting from principals perhaps less elevated but equally dear to their hearts; from the gratification of their affection in beholding personally among

them, the friend, the benefactor, the father of his Country" (M/JQA/46, APM Reel 241). The final version, as printed in the Newburyport *Essex Journal*, 4 Nov., included several additional paragraphs. For Washington's reply, see Washington, *Papers, Presidential Series*, 4:259–260.

[3] Shakespeare, *Henry the Eighth*, Act III, scene ii, line 354.

[4] JQA wrote to JA on 19 March 1790 outlining his various professional options and ultimately indicating his decision to move to Boston. He set up a law office there in August at the Adamses' Court Street house (Adams Papers).

Martha Washington to Abigail Adams

Tuesday Eening December 8th. 1789

Mrs. Washington presents her best compliments to Mrs. Adams, and will thank her to say at what hour it will be agreeable to visit Mrs. Graham's School tomorrow morning.—[1] Mrs. Washington encloses Mrs. Graham's note,[2] by which Mrs. Adams may see the time that will be most convenient for Mrs. Graham.— Mrs. Washington will be happy to hear that Mrs. Adams and her family are in good health.—

RC (Adams Papers); addressed: "Mrs. Adams— / Richmond Hill—"

[1] In fall 1789, a Mrs. Graham began advertising "Boarding and Education for Young Ladies" at a school at 59 Maiden Lane, New York (New York *Daily Advertiser*, 26 Sept.). Martha Washington may have been seeking a school for her granddaughter, Eleanor Custis.

[2] Not found.

Hannah Quincy Lincoln Storer to Abigail Adams

Boston Dec^m ^th12 1789

Will My good and worthy friend M^rs. Adams, give Me leave to request her acceptance of a Small Tub of Butter? Such as we think very good, and I hope it will not come a miss, as we hear it is a Scarce Article in Newyork—

What think you dear Madam of the Match going on in Our family? do you think My Sister Nancy calculated for a *Ministers Wife?* a M^r. *Packard* of *Marlborough* is the selected *PARSON*.[1]

After offering My best regards to your fireside, I leave you My friend with the Same Sentiments of esteem I ever entertained for you when our intercourse was freer than it can be Now, Your at Such a remove from Me— I Now often wish you was Near enough for me to injoy in your Company what Gives Me delight, to think of— And what I again hope to injoy Tho' when our friends are Separated from us, it is Never Certain that they will Meet again—as the late Accounts from abroad of My only Brothers Death Convinces Me—[2] the particulars of which have Not yet come to hand—

I fear I have tresspas'd upon your patiance & Shall only add that I am Sincerly your / Affectionate   H Storer

N— B— the Butter was put a board Barnard & directed to Gorge's care

RC (Adams Papers).

[1] Rev. Asa Packard (1758–1843), Harvard 1783, was called to the ministry at Marlborough and ordained there on 23 March 1785. He married Nancy Quincy in July 1790 (Charles Hudson, *History of the Town of Marlborough, Middlesex County, Massachu*setts, Boston, 1862, p. 200–202, 208).

[2] Samuel Quincy, Hannah Storer's only surviving brother, died on 9 Aug. 1789 en route from the West Indies to Bristol, England (*Sibley's Harvard Graduates*, 13:488).

Cotton Tufts to Abigail Adams

Dear Cousin   Boston Decr. 20 1789

Yours of the 22^d. I rec^d. on Sunday last, by Gen Lincoln— the several Articles You requested me to procure I shall collect as soon as possible— I have made Enquiry for Butter but have not met with any that is good a considerable Quantity has been sent to New York by a Vessel that saild a day or two past— It is somewhat doubtful whether I shall be able to buy the Hams already prepared, if not shall engage them so as to send them in Season for Your use— Barnard is expected every moment

It was hinted to me by a Friend, that Governor. H——k considered himself as somewhat neglected by Mr. Adams; having invited Mr. A—— to dine with him (at a Time when He invited the President—) Mr. A. accepted the Invitation, but did not attend—& tho Mr. H. saw him afterwards, He made no Excuse nor did He send any Billet of Excuse—& it was further added that Mr. A. did not call on Him when He left the State— I have just mentiond this—not that I suppose it a Matter of the highest Consequence—but imagine that it must be a matter which if explaind, would remove all Suspicion, as well an Imputation of Neglect— I shall write further a few Days hence, have now only Time to say that I am with great Sincerity Yr. affect Friend   Cotton Tufts

Beg the Favour of You to forward the Letter to Mrs. Rutgers—who is the Executr. of Dr. Crosbys Will—[1]

RC (Adams Papers); endorsed: "Dr Tufts / December 20 / 1789."

[1] Dr. Ebenezer Crosby, Harvard 1777, was born in Braintree in 1753. A professor at and trustee of Columbia College, he died on 16 July 1788. Crosby had been married to Catharine Bedlow, daughter of Catharine Rutgers and William Bedlow; Mrs. Rutgers was probably a relative of Catharine Crosby's (*Appletons' Cyclo. Amer. Biog.*; Ernest H. Crosby, *The Rutgers Family of New York*, N.Y., 1886, p. 11).

The postscript was written sideways in the margin.

Abigail Adams Smith to John Quincy Adams

Richmond Hill December 27th 1789—

I have lived long in expectation of the pleasure of receiving a letter from my Dear Brother but at length I am reduced to despair; and am led to inquire what has prevented the fullfillment of a promise which you made at your departure upon my requesting you to write;— I hope you did not suppose that my absence during your visit arrose from any inattention towards yourself;— most certainly if I had had the least Idea of your leaving us so soon I should not have taken that time for my visit, it has been a scource of Chagrine to me eversince

Mamma received a letter from you last week which is the first line that any one of this family have received from you since you left us; we heard of your safe arrival through my Aunt Cranch, and we have since heard of you both from the President and Mr Dalton.

upon the receipt of your Letter your Father said that he had Conversed with Mr Dana when he was at Cambridge upon the subject of your setting down in Boston, and that M^r D—— had advised to it, that he himself had Considered the subject and that he had no objection to your going to Boston, Mamma desired that he would write to you upon the subject and I suppose he will ere long,—but as it was a subject in which I knew you were much interested I thought I would mention it; as the earliest information is sometimes of some importance—, I am happy that your wishes upon this subject are answered, as I should think it a preferable situation, for Business to any Country Town, some might offer as an objection the Number who are pursueing the same objects, but a young Man of your abilities persevereance and industry need not fear of being placed in the Back Ground; most sincerely do I wish you success in your undertakeings; and pursuits, both Honourable, and profitable;— Charles is very attentive to his Office—and begins to like New York—, Thomas has been with us some time, but thinks he prefers Cambridge to New York,— as to News I donot hear of any except a Confirmation of the Account that North Carolina has adopted the Constitution,[1] the Members of the Government are assembling daily and tomorrow night is the day they are to meet,

it is reported that Miss Thomson Mrs Gerrys Sister is soon to be Married to Mr Coles one of the Virginia representatives—a Widower with two Chrildren—[2] Mr Jefferson has arrived in Virginia but not yet come to New York,— I suppose you have heard of the arrival of Mr Trumble, he has come to take a Number of portraits which may enable him to pursue his American peices but intends returning soon to England,—[3] this is not the Country for him to paint for emolument, and we must acquire taste before his merits can be fully known

I hope I shall have the pleasure of receiving some testimony of your remembrance soon— if you have *one favourite* do not let that one Possess the whole of your Social Affection it will not diminish for one object by being extend to others— the President told Mamma that he was informed that her Son was more attentive to his Books than to the Ladies, perhaps you may think it the greatest Compliment that could have been paid you but I hope you will not rank inattention to your friends amongst the first of your good qualities

Coll^n Smith desires to be remembered to you and William sends his Duty—
remember me to those who / inquire after your Sister

A Smith—

RC (Adams Papers); internal address: "Mr John Quincy Adams—"; endorsed: "My Sister. 27. Dec^r: 1789." and "My Sister Dec^r: 27. 1789."

[1] On 21 Nov., the second North Carolina convention ratified the Constitution by a vote of 194 to 77 (*Doc. Hist. Ratif. Const.*, 13:xlii).

[2] Catherine Thompson (1769–1848), sister of Ann Thompson Gerry, married Isaac Coles (1747–1813) of Virginia on 2 Jan. 1790. Coles represented Virginia in Congress from 1789 to 1791 and again from 1793 to 1797. With his first wife, Eliza Lightfoot (d. 1781), he had two sons, as well as a daughter who died in infancy (vol. 7:141, 142; *VMHB*, 21:203 [April 1913]; *Biog. Dir. Cong.*).

[3] John Trumbull remained in the United States until 1794; during that time, he painted numerous portraits and miniatures, including several for his historical series and three of JA (Theodore Sizer, *The Works of Colonel John Trumbull: Artist of the American Revolution*, rev. edn., New Haven, 1967, p. 7, 18).

Appendix

Appendix

LIST OF OMITTED DOCUMENTS

The following list includes 65 documents that have been omitted from volume 8 of the *Adams Family Correspondence*. Each entry consists of the date, correspondents, form in which the letter exists (Dft, LbC, RC, etc.), location, and publication, if known. All copies that exist in some form in the Adams Papers are noted.

1787

14 March	Abigail Adams to John Quincy Adams, RC (Adams Papers).
16 March	Abigail Adams to Mary Smith Cranch, RC (MWA: Abigail Adams Letters).
27 April	William Stephens Smith to Abigail Adams Smith, PRINTED: AA2, *Jour. and Corr.*, 1:126–127.
27 April	William Stephens Smith to Abigail Adams Smith, PRINTED: AA2, *Jour. and Corr.*, 1:128–130.
28 April	William Stephens Smith to Abigail Adams Smith, PRINTED: AA2, *Jour. and Corr.*, 1:131.
5 May	William Stephens Smith to Abigail Adams Smith, PRINTED: AA2, *Jour. and Corr.*, 1:132–136.
10 May	William Stephens Smith to Abigail Adams Smith, PRINTED: AA2, *Jour. and Corr.*, 1:136–139.
14 May	William Stephens Smith to Abigail Adams Smith, PRINTED: AA2, *Jour. and Corr.*, 1:139–142.
19 May	William Stephens Smith to Abigail Adams Smith, PRINTED: AA2, *Jour. and Corr.*, 1:142–150.
20 May	William Stephens Smith to Abigail Adams Smith, PRINTED: AA2, *Jour. and Corr.*, 1:150–152.
[25 May]	John Brown Cutting to Abigail Adams, RC (Adams Papers).

455

25 May	William Stephens Smith to Abigail Adams Smith, PRINTED: AA2, *Jour. and Corr.*, 1:152–153.
26 May	Cotton Tufts to Abigail Adams, RC (Adams Papers).
31 May	William Stephens Smith to Abigail Adams Smith, PRINTED: AA2, *Jour. and Corr.*, 1:153–164.
10 June	William Stephens Smith to Abigail Adams Smith, PRINTED: AA2, *Jour. and Corr.*, 1:166–169.
18 June	William Stephens Smith to Abigail Adams, RC (Adams Papers).
18 June	William Stephens Smith to Abigail Adams Smith, PRINTED: AA2, *Jour. and Corr.*, 1:170–172.
[25] June	William Stephens Smith to Abigail Adams Smith, PRINTED: AA2, *Jour. and Corr.*, 1:173–176.
30 June	William Stephens Smith to Abigail Adams Smith, PRINTED: AA2, *Jour. and Corr.*, 1:177–183.
3 July	William Stephens Smith to Abigail Adams Smith, PRINTED: AA2, *Jour. and Corr.*, 1:183–184.
4 July	Abigail Adams to Cotton Tufts, RC (Adams Papers).
9 July	William Stephens Smith to Abigail Adams Smith, PRINTED: AA2, *Jour. and Corr.*, 1:184–188.
11 July	Abigail Adams Smith to Thomas Jefferson, RC (MHi:Jefferson Papers); PRINTED: Jefferson, *Papers*, 11:580–581.
16 July	William Stephens Smith to Abigail Adams Smith, PRINTED: AA2, *Jour. and Corr.*, 1:188–197.
17 July	John Cranch to Abigail Adams, RC (Adams Papers).
[19] July	Abigail Adams to Cotton Tufts, RC (NHi:Misc. Manuscripts, A).
19 July	Cotton Tufts to John Adams, RC (Adams Papers).
23 July	Thomas Jefferson to Abigail Adams Smith, FC (MHi:Jefferson Papers); PRINTED: Jefferson, *Papers*, 11:618.
31 July	William Stephens Smith to Abigail Adams Smith, PRINTED: AA2, *Jour. and Corr.*, 1:197–199.
13 Aug.	Mary Wentworth to Abigail Adams, RC (Adams Papers).
20 Aug.	William Stephens Smith to Abigail Adams Smith, PRINTED: AA2, *Jour. and Corr.*, 1:199–200.

27 Aug.	William Stephens Smith to Abigail Adams Smith, PRINTED: AA2, *Jour. and Corr.*, 1:201–202.
18 Sept.	Cotton Tufts to John Adams, RC (Adams Papers).
29 Sept.	Anna Quincy to Abigail Adams, RC (Adams Papers).
18 Oct.	Cotton Tufts to John Adams, RC (Adams Papers).
4 Nov.	Thomas Brand Hollis to Abigail Adams, RC (DSI: Hull Coll., on loan).
19 Nov.	M. E. Milles to Abigail Adams, RC (Adams Papers).
22 Nov.	Lucy Ludwell Paradise to Abigail Adams, RC (Adams Papers).
12 Dec.	Abigail Adams to Thomas Jefferson, RC (DLC:Jefferson Papers); PRINTED: Jefferson, *Papers*, 12:417.
[1787–1788]	Abigail Adams to Mrs. Byag, RC (DSI:Hull Coll., on loan).

1788

7 Jan.	Thomas Brand Hollis to Abigail Adams, RC (Adams Papers).
24 Jan.	Thomas Brand Hollis to Abigail Adams, RC (Adams Papers).
[17? Feb.]	Clement Cotterell Dormer to Abigail Adams, RC (Adams Papers).
22 Feb.	Mary Smith Cranch to Abigail Adams, RC (Adams Papers).
[Feb.?]	Clement Cotterell Dormer to Abigail Adams, RC (Adams Papers).
18 March	Lewis D. and Ann Veasey Ward to Abigail Adams, RC (Adams Papers).
28 March	Abigail Adams, Receipt of John Trumbull, MS (Adams Papers).
28 March	John Jeffries to Abigail Adams, RC (Adams Papers).
14 April	John Cranch to Abigail Adams, RC (Adams Papers).
28 Nov.	George Storer to Abigail Adams, RC (Adams Papers).
15 Dec.	Ebenezer Adams, Receipt of John Adams, MS (NN: Presidents' Papers).

1789

4 April	John Brown Cutting to Abigail Adams, RC (Adams Papers).
27 April	James Lovell to Abigail Adams, RC (Adams Papers).
1 May	Abigail Bromfield Rogers to Abigail Adams, RC (Adams Papers).
6 May	Mercy Otis Warren to Abigail Adams, RC (Adams Papers).
7 June	John Adams to Abigail Adams, RC (Adams Papers).
19 July	Abigail Adams Smith to Hannah Carter Smith, RC (MHi:Smith-Carter Papers).
20 July	John Jeffries to Abigail Adams, RC (Adams Papers).
20 July	Hannah Fayerweather Tolman Winthrop to Abigail Adams, RC (Adams Papers).
20 Sept.	Abigail Adams to Rebecca Leppington, Dft (Adams Papers).
7 Oct.	Lucy Ludwell Paradise to Abigail Adams, RC (Adams Papers).
17 Nov.	Hannah Storer Green to Abigail Adams, RC (Adams Papers).
24 Nov.	George Washington to Abigail Adams, RC (DSI: Hull Coll., on loan); PRINTED: Washington, *Papers, Presidential Series*, 4:321–322.
[1789?]	Martha Washington to Abigail Adams, RC (Adams Papers).
[1789–1790?]	Martha Washington to Abigail Adams, Dft (ViMtvL).

Chronology

Chronology

THE ADAMS FAMILY, 1787–1789

1787

2 April: William Steuben Smith, AA2 and WSS's first child, is born in London.

24 April: JA departs for Portsmouth with John Brown Cutting to attend a hearing for a man accused of counterfeiting American currency. JA returns to Grosvenor Square by 30 April.

24 April – 30 Aug.: Congress sends WSS on a diplomatic mission to Portugal. He travels by way of France and Spain and writes AA2 at least 23 letters over the course of the trip.

25 May: The Constitutional Convention convenes in Philadelphia with a quorum of seven states.

25 May – 9 June: JA travels to the Netherlands with John Brown Cutting to salvage American credit there.

26 June – 11 July: Mary (Polly) Jefferson, accompanied by her family's slave Sally Hemings, arrives in London from Virginia. She remains under AA's care until she is escorted to Paris to join her father.

18 July: JQA and William Cranch graduate from Harvard College.

20 July – ca. 20 Aug.: AA, JA, and AA2, with her three-month-old son, William Steuben Smith, tour the county of Devonshire by way of Plymouth. Along the way, they visit Richard Cranch's family in Exeter.

21 July: CA and TBA arrive in Braintree to visit the Cranches.

25 July: CA leaves Braintree to visit the Shaws in Haverhill. TBA joins him on 1 August.

mid-Aug.: CA and TBA leave Haverhill to begin their junior and sophomore years, respectively, at Harvard.

27 Aug.: William Cranch begins his legal studies with Thomas Dawes in Boston.

3 or 10 Sept.: William Smith Jr., AA's brother, dies of "black jaundice."

8 Sept.: JQA begins his legal studies with Theophilus Parsons in Newburyport.

17 Sept.: The Constitutional Convention in Philadelphia adopts a new constitution and sends it to Congress for debate.

20–28 Sept.: Congress reads and debates the Constitution, then transmits it to the states for ratification.

26 Sept: Cotton Tufts purchases the Vassall-Borland estate on behalf of the Adamses. The farm, eventually known as the Old House, becomes JA and AA's permanent residence in Braintree (later Quincy).

Sept.: JA publishes the second volume of his *A Defence of the Constitutions*.

16 Oct.: Isaac Smith Sr., AA's uncle, dies.

ante 20 Oct.: JA, AA, and AA2 visit Thomas Brand Hollis at the Hyde for a week.

13 Nov.: John Thaxter Jr. marries Elizabeth Duncan of Haverhill.

29 Nov.: Following Thanksgiving dinner, a disturbance breaks out in the dining hall at Harvard, with students breaking windows and furniture. CA, a waiter in the hall, is punished for refusing to give evidence against his classmates and is dismissed from his job; TBA is also fined for participating.

18 Dec.: Jacob Norton is ordained at Weymouth, the first permanent minister there since the death of William Smith, AA's father.

1788

9 Jan.: The Massachusetts state ratifying convention begins meeting in Boston; John Hancock is chosen president.

28 Jan. – 4 Feb.: CA and TBA visit JQA in Newburyport during part of their winter vacation.

6 Feb.: Massachusetts ratifies the Constitution by a vote of 187 to 168.

15 Feb.: Long-time Adams servants Esther Field and John Briesler marry in London.

20 Feb.: JA is granted a final audience with George III and formally takes his leave.

29 Feb. – 24/25 March: JA travels to the Netherlands to take leave of the stadholder and the States General. While there, at the request of Thomas Jefferson, he negotiates a fourth loan for the United States.

Feb.: JA publishes the third volume of his *A Defence of the Constitutions*.

ca. 20 March: AA2 and WSS leave London for Falmouth to sail to the United States on the ship *Thyne*. They embark for America on 5 April, sailing to New York via Halifax.

30 March: AA and JA depart from London first to Portsmouth then to the Isle of Wight to board the *Lucretia*. The vessel finally sails for Boston on 20 April.

21 May: AA2 and WSS arrive in New York City and establish their residence at Beaver Hall, Jamaica, Long Island.

6 June: The General Court elects JA to represent Massachusetts at the last sitting of the Continental Congress, but he does not serve.

17 June: JA and AA arrive in Boston where they are greeted by Gov. John Hancock and other Massachusetts dignitaries.

20 June: JQA is reunited with his parents at Boston and Braintree. John and Elizabeth Smith Shaw join the family at Braintree on 25 June, and CA comes down from Cambridge the following day.

mid-Aug.: CA begins his senior year at Harvard. TBA begins his junior year.

20–30 Sept.: JQA goes to Haverhill to be nursed by his aunt Elizabeth Smith Shaw for an illness related to recurring insomnia.

9 Nov.: John Adams Smith, AA2 and WSS's second child, is born on Long Island.

12 Nov. – late Jan. 1789: AA visits New York to assist AA2 after the birth of John Adams Smith.

1789

25 Jan. – 20 March: AA2 and WSS return with AA to Braintree for an extended visit with family and friends.

11 Feb.: Elizabeth Cranch marries Rev. Jacob Norton of Weymouth.

4 March: The First Federal Congress convenes in New York City.

6 April: The Senate attains a quorum. It proceeds to open and count the votes of the electoral college. George Washington is unanimously elected president; JA is elected vice president, receiving 34 out of 69 votes.

13 April: JA departs from Braintree to assume his new office in New York. He stops along the way for celebrations at Hartford and New Haven, among other towns, and reaches New York on 20 April.

30 April: George Washington takes the oath of office as the first president under the new Constitution; JA is sworn in as vice president.

ca. 13 May: JA rents Richmond Hill, an estate on the Hudson River about two miles outside of the city, to serve as the Adamses' home in New York.

10 June: AA2, WSS, and their children move into Richmond Hill with JA.

17 June: AA leaves Braintree en route to New York, traveling via Rhode Island. She is accompanied by CA; her niece, Louisa Smith; and two servants. They arrive at New York on 25 June.

14 July: The storming of the Bastille marks the beginning of the French Revolution.

15 July: CA graduates from Harvard. He does not attend the commencement ceremony, however, as he has already moved to New York.

July–Sept.: CA studies law with Alexander Hamilton. After Hamilton is named secretary of the treasury, CA joins the law firm of John Laurance to complete his legal education; he remains there for two years.

7 Sept. – 14 Oct.: JQA leaves Newburyport and travels to New York to visit his family, arriving on 16 September. While in the city, he meets the president and attends sessions of Congress and the Supreme Court. JQA departs on 5 Oct., arriving back in Boston on the 8th and in Newburyport on the 14th.

26 Sept.: The Senate confirms Thomas Jefferson as secretary of state.

29 Sept.: The first session of Congress adjourns.

12 Oct. – late Nov.: JA visits Braintree.

15 Oct. – 13 Nov.: George Washington tours the New England states; on 24 Oct. he passes through Boston, where a procession is held in his honor. JA, TBA, and Lucy Cranch attend the festivities.

22 Oct.: Cotton Tufts Sr. marries Susanna Warner of Gloucester.

30 Oct.: JQA is part of the contingent welcoming Washington at Newburyport; the next day, he helps to escort Washington to the New Hampshire border.

12 Nov.: Esther and John Briesler and their children arrive in New York to work for the Adamses.

late Nov.: TBA visits his parents in New York; he stays until Jan. 1790.

Index

NOTE ON THE INDEX

The index for volume 8 of the *Adams Family Correspondence* is designed to supplement the annotation, when possible, by furnishing the correct spellings of names, supplying forenames when they are lacking in the text, and indicating dates, occupations, and places of residence when they will aid in identification. Markedly variant spellings of proper names have been cross-referenced to what are believed to be their most nearly standard forms, and the variant forms found in the manuscripts are parenthetically recorded following the standard spellings. Cross references under maiden names are used for women who were single when first mentioned in the text and were married subsequently but before December 1789.

Branches, departments, and positions within the U.S. federal government are indexed individually under the name of the entity, with subdivisions as appropriate. For example, the Supreme Court is found as a subentry under "Judiciary, U.S." while "Presidency, U.S." stands as a main entry.

Subentries appear in alphabetical order by the primary word of the subentry. Abbreviations are alphabetized as if they were spelled out, thus "JQA" is alphabetized under "Adams."

The Chronology, "The Adams Family, 1787–1789," has not been included in the index.

The index was compiled in the Adams Papers office.

Index

AA. *See* ADAMS, ABIGAIL SMITH (1744–1818, wife of John Adams)

AA2. *See* ADAMS, ABIGAIL, 2D (1765–1813, wife of William Stephens Smith)

ABA. *See* Adams, Abigail Brown Brooks (1808–1889, wife of Charles Francis Adams)

Abbot, Benjamin (Harvard classmate of JQA), 91; identified, 92

Abdee, Phoebe (Adams family servant): TBA wants to live with, 350; assists with Harvard commencement celebration, 132; housing of black family and, 392; manages Adams dairy, xxv, 185, 186, 193; rents Old House, 372–73; Elizabeth Shaw on, 136; mentioned, 315

Abdee, William (Adams family servant), 136, 350

Abington, Mass., 165, 355

Active (merchant ship), 267, 269

ADAMS, ABIGAIL, 2D (Nabby, Amelia, 1765–1813, daughter of AA and JA, wife of William Stephens Smith, designated as AA2 in *The Adams Papers*)

BOOKS AND READING

American Magazine, 271; Bible, 82; Hannah More, 263

CHARACTER, APPEARANCE, HABITS

AA on, 119, 246; clothing of, 278, 322; compared to CA, 285; Mary Cranch on, 19, 147, 318; health of, xxii, 76, 80, 81, 128, 131, 133, 142, 248, 251, 281, 304, 308, 314, 315, 317, 320, 321, 341, 353, 378, 399; health of after birth of William Steuben Smith, 24, 28, 37, 39, 40, 44; insight of, 302; letter-writing of, xxi–xxii, 440–41; nicknames of, 75; portraits of, 100, 101, 395, 396; William Steuben Smith compared to, 194, 308; Mercy Warren on, 326

DOMESTIC LIFE

AA buys fabric for, 44; AA sends furniture to, 308; concern for CA, 84; birth of John Adams Smith, xxxii, 304, 308, 310, 312, 317, 321, 328; birth of William Steuben Smith, xxii, xxiii, xxxi, 5, 6, 12, 13, 19, 53, 81, 95, 122, 133, 141, 142, 419; as bridesmaid, 323; John Cranch requests news of Cranch family in U.S. from, 88; family of, 32, 275, 408; lives at Richmond Hill with Adamses, xvi, xxxi, 368, 378, 384, 436, 441; marriage of, 2; as mother, xxi, xxii–xxiii, 169, 326, 441; moves to Long Island, xxvi, 134, 169, 230, 260, 265, 266, 270, 275, 277, 294; moves to private lodgings, 226; nurses children, 37, 114, 119, 191; pregnancy of, 5, 6, 12, 19, 53, 271, 287, 288, 294, 300, 305; prepares mourning outfit, 70, 72; riding, 6, 39; separation from family, xxxi, 32, 299; sewing, 5; William Smith carries packages for, 276; WSS's family and, 279; Royall Tyler and, x, xxv, 19, 22; Vt. land and, 34; visits Jamaica, Long Island, 411

LETTERS

Letters: To AA (1788), 261, 273, 288, 293, 302; To JA (1788), 281; To JQA (1787), 81; (1788), 227, 269, 290, 299; (1789), 449; To Elizabeth Cranch (1787), 127; (1789), 440; To Lucy Cranch (1787), 115; To William Smith (1788), 276

Letters: From AA (1788), 250, 254, 266, 277, 284; From JA (1788), 278, 305; From WSS (1787), 27, 77, 148

Letters to, from, omitted: to Thomas Jefferson listed (1787), 456; to Hannah Carter Smith listed (1789), 458; from Thomas Jefferson listed (1787), 456; from WSS listed (1787), 455 (8), 456 (11), 457

MENTIONED

23, 60, 68, 73, 91, 105, 107, 108, 137, 170,

ADAMS, ABIGAIL, 2D (*continued*)
200, 208, 218, 240, 244, 245, 334, 339, 370, 371,
376, 377, 393, 410, 429, 431, 437

OPINIONS AND BELIEFS

CA, 450; Adams brothers, 281; artists in
U.S., 450; Mary Barclay, 86; Thomas Barclay,
86; Boston, 265; Marquise de Bréhan, 263;
Bernardo del Campo, 263; Edward Church,
404; George Clinton family, 273; compares
Brit. and U.S. weather, 128; U.S. Constitution, 271–72, 274, 282–83, 289, 292, 295; Continental Congress, 82; John Brown Cutting,
300; Europe, 84, 229–30, 291; Europe as "Vortex of dissipation," 300; extravagance, 300;
fame and reputation, 282; foreign service,
302; friendships, 115, 127–28; Don Diego de
Gardoqui, 263; Elbridge Gerry, 289; Moses
Gill, 86; Christina Griffin, 263; Cyrus Griffin, 263; Halifax, 261–62; John Hancock, 295;
John Jay, 263; Sarah Jay, 263; Jefferson's
daughters, 86; Henry Knox, 263, 273; Lucy
Knox, xiv, 263, 273; legal profession, 282, 302–
303; letter-writing, 303; marriage, 441; moral
development of college students, 281; Comte
de Moustier, 263; William Vans Murray, 84,
300; John Paradise, 265; Lucy Paradise, 265;
passengers on trip to U.S., 262; political debates, 271–72; pregnancy, 441–42; John and
Jane Rucker, 85; satire, 82; Rebecca Sears,
270; self-interest in politics, 274, 302; ship-
board conversation, 262–63; WSS, 115, 128–
29, 274; WSS's career prospects, 281–82;
WSS's family, 115, 263, 441; William Steuben
Smith, 81, 115, 128; George Staunton, 86;
Deborah Stewart, 85; Elizabeth Temple, 263,
273–74; John Temple, 263, 273–74; Hannah
Thomson, 295; transatlantic crossings, 262–
63; U.S. government location, 291–92; U.S.
government members, 289; U.S. government's provisions for its ministers, 292

RELATIONSHIP WITH JQA

on JQA's career prospects, 16, 85, 229,
290–91, 450; on JQA's health, xxviii, 84; on
JQA's romantic interests, 82, 450; JQA visits
in New York, 270, 291, 300, 338, 446, 449;
correspondence with, xxii, 11, 12, 39, 84, 86,
125, 141, 228, 229, 230, 270, 271, 272, 278, 281,
304, 383, 446, 447, 450

RELATIONSHIP WITH PARENTS

on AA, 320; AA and JA's move to New York
and, 322, 355; as AA's secy., 2, 12, 69, 111, 126,
127, 151, 195, 309, 412, 418, 422, 439, 444; on
JA's advice, 292; on JA's possible influence on

Congress, 274, 291; as JA's secy., 221; on JA's
service to U.S. and possible retirement, xxxiv,
84, 228, 282, 292, 302–303; carries letters for
AA, 247, 389; concern for arrival of AA and JA
in Boston, 270; correspondence with AA, ix,
xiv, 251, 262, 265, 281, 286, 290, 303, 330, 337,
347, 348; correspondence with AA and JA,
255, 274; correspondence with JA, 286; dockets AA's correspondence, 21, 54, 65, 96, 124,
134; on possible positions for JA, 274, 282,
291, 292, 294, 295, 299; reads AA's mail, 321;
separation from, xxxii, 246, 250–51, 265; visits
with, 274, 285, 288, 294, 299–300, 305, 344

SOCIAL LIFE

at Bath, 81; possible family visits, 228,
270, 284, 327; on Long Island, 263, 275, 321;
socializes with Washingtons, 379, 397, 421;
visits and dinners in New York City, xxxii,
263, 270–71, 273–74, 288, 289, 293, 294, 357;
visits Cranch family in England, 158, 160,
249; visits Jamaica, Long Island, 386, 390;
visits with Martha Jefferson in France, 93;
Mercy Warren invites to visit, 327

TRAVELS

arrives in New York, 263, 269–70, 272, 277;
to England (1784), 269; limited by pregnancy, 287; plans to return to U.S., 115, 216,
228, 241, 243; to U.S. (1788), xxv, xxxii, 247,
248, 250, 261–63, 265, 266, 275, 296; visits
Bath (1787), 81; visits Braintree (1789), 316,
396; visits English countryside (1787), x, 25,
71, 76, 84–85, 87, 115–16, 118, 126, 127, 128,
129, 130–31, 175–76, 177–82, 249; visits Halifax, 261–62, 272; visits the Hyde (1787), 195;
possible visit to Mass., 288, 322, 323, 324, 327

WRITINGS

Journal and Correspondence, 28, 72, 78,
87, 129, 148, 265, 269, 275, 278, 280, 283, 289,
296, 303, 305, 306; uses cipher in letter to
WSS, 78

Adams, Abigail Brown Brooks (1808–1889,
wife of Charles Francis, designated as
ABA in *The Adams Papers*), 251
Adams, Abigail Louisa Smith (1798–1836,
daughter of CA and SSA): identified, 323

ADAMS, ABIGAIL SMITH (1744–1818, wife
of John, designated as AA in *The Adams
Papers*)

BOOKS AND READING

Aesop, 226; Bible, 4, 25–26, 27, 118, 155,
175, 191, 225, 235, 307, 339, 349, 403, 405, 411;

ADAMS, ABIGAIL SMITH (*continued*)
affairs in New York, 325; political circumstances in, 38, 44, 105; origins of political parties, 405; trappings of office for president, 399–400, 404; publication of debates in House of Representatives, 337, 339, 346; life in public service, xxii, 25, 416; future rebellions, 1, 2, 40; relationship among France, Britain, and, 1; relationship between Britain and, 2, 33, 36; desire to return to, 4; St. Paul's Chapel, 414; salary provided to U.S. ministers in Europe, 238; Shays' Rebellion, 1, 2, 4, 8, 38, 113–14, 152, 248; site for U.S. government, 403, 405, 418; stability of new government, 364–65; tariffs, 339; taxation as "price of their freedom," 8; Vt. statehood, 34; vice presidency, 340; Washington's New England tour, 427

Miscellaneous: Active, 269; clothing as "the Female sphere," 26; convent education, 108, 119, 151; dangers of bad examples, 10; dangers of arrogance, 187–88; dangers of excessive study, 188; dangers of luxury, 45–46, 47, 203; debt, 7; diet, 125, 247; treatments for diphtheria, 126; domestic happiness, 339, 366, 443; domestic work as "province of the Female Character," 25, 26; equality, 349; evil in the world, 4; exercise, 12, 188, 247, 307; exercise as "the kind goddess of Health," 26; family, 113, 313; female education, xxiii, 25–26, 27; female education as "like going into a Beautifull Country, which I never saw before," 25; friendships, 293–94; the future, 6; gardens, 355, 366; God and creation, 4; handwriting, 11; Harvard commencement celebrations, 334, 371; hotels, 333, 373–74; land, 7, 203; life as lawyer's wife, 416; *Lucretia*, 269; marriage, 8, 30; "an unprincipald mob is the worst of all Tyrannies," 38; moral precariousness of youth, 363; repeated moving, 359; newborns, 269; Old House, ix, x, xxvi, 277–78; paper currency, 2, 7, 34–35, 36; Richmond Hill, xvi, xxxv, 365, 379, 388, 391, 392, 400, 401–402, 403, 406, 410, 411, 435, 439; "I can ride in a one horse chaise the rest of my Life without being at all mortified," 44–45; servants, 32, 217, 348, 390–91, 399, 421, 434, 436; slavery, xxiii; social life in New York City, xxxv, 325; swimming, xi; travel, 31, 192, 227, 266–67, 269, 308, 316, 378; Veasey property, 105; war, 11; Warrens' office seeking, 390; distinguished women, 30–31; older women as mothers, 192

RELATIONSHIP WITH JA
JA as secy. to, 108; JA dockets correspondence of, 245, 248, 249, 312; on JA's address to Senate, 338–39; on JA's *Defence of the Const.*, xxiv., 12, 38, 40–41, 79; on JA's departure for New York, 334; on JA's forgetfulness, 431; on JA's political philosophy, 12, 400; JA's public service and, xxxiv, 2, 6, 187, 203, 234, 411, 416; on JA's vote on removal of foreign officers, 400; chides JA, 243; concern for JA's health and well-being, 323, 366, 368, 370; correspondence with, xliii, 72, 80, 307, 310, 311, 314, 316, 320, 321, 325, 334, 335, 337, 341, 346, 347, 359, 360, 363, 365, 366, 427, 436, 437; difficulties faced by, 117; difficulties of separation from JA, 32, 310, 322, 328; dockets JA's correspondence, 89; instructs JA on household issues, 434; limitations on as JA's wife, 411; organizes meeting between Jefferson and, 244; patronage appeals to JA, 331–32, 334, 335, 370; purchase of Veasey property and, 104–105; quotes JA, 390, 392; requests assistance from JA in farm management, 345, 346; WSS encourages to accompany JA to New York, 330

RELATIONSHIP WITH CHILDREN
AA2: on AA2, 119, 246; AA2 as good nurse, 191; AA2 as secy. to, 2, 12, 69, 111, 126, 127, 151, 195, 309, 412, 418, 422, 439, 444; AA2 dockets correspondence of, 21, 54, 65, 96, 124, 134; AA2 reads mail of, 321; buys fabric for AA2, 44; names for AA2, 75; sends letter of introduction to Margaret Smith, 246, 247; separation from AA2, 246, 250–51; possible visits with AA2 and WSS, 284, 285, 288, 294, 299–300, 304

CA: SSA lives with after CA's death, 323; approves plan for CA to move to New York, 346; concern over CA's behavior, xxviii, xxix, 363, 390, 400, 427; sends clothing for CA, 192–93

JQA: on JQA, 32, 116–17, 184; JQA concerned about economic independence from, 290–91; JQA dockets correspondence of, 200, 314; on JQA's future, 117; JQA's graduation from Harvard, 184; advises JQA, 16; concern for JQA's health, 12, 125, 188, 308, 314, 316, 346; concern for JQA's single-mindedness, xxvii, 322; gives horse to JQA, 355, 359–60, 362–63; sends books to JQA, 11, 40, 42, 125, 140; sends clothing for JQA, 125, 189, 192, 193, 195, 362, 363; sends goods to JQA, 361, 430; sends money to JQA, 372

TBA: TBA as secy. to, 337; advises on TBA's studies, 10; concern for TBA's moral development, xxix–xxx, 363; recommends TBA join military company, xxx, 11; sends clothing for TBA, 32, 192–93

363, 429; correspondence with JQA, xxviii, xxx, 361, 362, 383, 386, 444–45, 447; Elizabeth Cranch on, 169; Mary Cranch and, xxx, 3, 132, 171, 310, 311, 317, 376; death of, 323; education of, 270; on expulsion of friend from Harvard, 171; forwards letter for William Cranch, 413; on Anna Frazer, 144; friendship with George Storer, 400; graduates from Harvard, xxviii, 334; handwriting of, 11; skips Harvard commencement, 334, 338, 346–47, 348, 357, 360, 365, 368, 369, 371; health of, 212, 378, 399; William Jackson escorts to U.S., 422; legal training of, xxviii–xxix, 400, 401, 406, 427; letter-writing of, xxxvi, 383; lives with Shaws, 328; marriage of, 323; moves to New York, xvi, xxviii, 334, 338, 341, 344, 346, 347–48, 351, 353, 358, 359, 361, 368, 371, 383; performs at Harvard exhibition, 89, 165, 170, 171, 174; pocket money for, 163, 172, 202; relationship with JQA, 17, 241, 259; requests cider from Braintree, 439; returns to Harvard, 17, 144, 337, 339; romantic interests of, xxx, xxxi, 144, 169; Elizabeth Shaw and, xxx, 276; Thanksgiving disturbance at Harvard and, xxviii, 231, 233, 241; Cotton Tufts and, 241, 345; Vt. land and, 34; visits Boston, 142; visits Braintree, 94, 284, 299, 312, 371; visits Cranches, 15, 197; visits Jamaica, Long Island, 386, 390; visits Shaws, 138, 144, 343; mentioned, 10, 20, 41, 44, 116, 177, 189, 198, 201, 210, 215, 294, 304, 315, 316, 325, 333, 340, 393, 410

Adams, Charles Francis (1807–1886, son of JQA and LCA, designated as CFA in *The Adams Papers*), xxix, 251

Adams, Deacon Ebenezer (1737–1791, cousin of JA), 318; receipt for JA listed (1788), 457

Adams, Elihu (1741–1775, brother of JA), 259

Adams, George Washington (1801–1829, son of JQA and LCA, designated as GWA in *The Adams Papers*), xxix

Adams, Deacon John (1691–1761, father of JA), 259, 418

ADAMS, JOHN (1735–1826, designated as JA in *The Adams Papers*)

BOOKS, READING, AND EDUCATION
AA2 believes he should not "bury himself amongst his Books," 228; in AA's absence, 317; JQA's Harvard commencement oration,

219; Robert Ainsworth, 358; Jean le Rond d'Alembert, 364; attends Harvard, 259; Bible, 219; William Blackstone, 358; Hugh Blair, 219; Jean Jacques Burlamaqui, 219, 220; Joseph Butler, 219; Cicero, 219, 358, 387; *Constitutions of the Several Independent States of America*, 358; William Cranch's use of law library, 16, 119; Denis Diderot, 364; Edward Gibbon, 364; Hugo Grotius, 219, 220; Johann Gottlieb Heineccius, 219, 220; David Hume, 358; Francis Hutcheson, 219; Samuel Johnson, 358; Juvenal, 219; lack of on trip to U.S., 252, 255, 256; library at MB, xli, 43, 251, 256, 364; library at Old House, 105, 170–71, 202; library at Richmond Hill, 350, 356, 358, 433, 440; Livy, 358, 387; Jean Louis de Lolme, 358; Muratori, 364; Jacques Necker, 251; Plato, 219; Plutarch, 358; Joseph Priestley, 358; Samuel Pufendorf, 219, 220; purchase and use of for *Defence of the Const.*, 42, 43, 60, 105; purchase of books and newspapers, 42, 59, 224, 382; Quintilian, 219; receives books from individuals, 253, 256; seeks precedent for vice presidency in Roman history, 387; sends books to individuals, 206, 221; Seneca, 219; William Shenstone, 387; Richard Sheridan, 219; Socrates, 219; study of government, 211; Tacitus, 358, 387; teaches school to pay for legal training, 258, 259; Emmerich de Vattel, 219, 220

CHARACTER, APPEARANCE, HABITS, DOMESTIC LIFE
advises WSS on career prospects, xxxii, 281; character of, 279, 336, 404, 406; clothing of, 240, 317, 426; Mary Cranch and, 95, 422, 423, 430; domestic needs of, 366; exercise of, 252, 440; as farmer, 318, 334–35; as grandfather, 242, 275, 314, 341, 427; health of, 12, 105, 187, 244, 247, 269, 281, 306, 316, 334, 337, 368, 369, 370, 378, 411, 414, 418, 420, 427, 429, 434, 438; Jefferson sends Mirabeau's letter to, 112; letter-writing of, xxi–xxii, 315, 432; *Monthly Review* on, 79; names Peacefield, x; political influence of, 41, 84, 319, 400; portraits of, xviii, 110, 111, 451; punctuation of, xxxviii; reads French and Italian, 105; relationship with Thomas Brand Hollis, 252, 253; relationship with Jay, 318, 329, 336; relationship with Jefferson, 106, 110, 223; relationship with Washington, 348, 424; religion of, 357; seasickness of, 66–67, 69; servants for, 421, 426, 437; Elizabeth Shaw on, 328; WSS as secy. to, 149, 407; William Steuben Smith

Index

Index

Index

479

Index

Art. *See* Paintings; Sculpture

Articles of Confederation, xxxii. *See also* Continental Congress

Artisans. *See* Tradespeople and artisans

Artois, Charles Philippe, Comte d' (later Charles X of France), 84, 87

Arundel (U.S. ship), 93

Asia Minor, 194

Astor, John Jacob (fur trader), xv–xvi

Astronomy, 62, 65, 182, 263, 266

Athens, Greece, 47

Atkinson, Elizabeth Storer (wife of John), 199, 319

Atkinson, John (Brit. merchant), 199

Atkinson, N.H., 281

Atlantic Ocean: AA on crossing, 227, 266–67, 269; crossing of, xiv, xxv, 107, 131, 216, 221–22, 226, 242–43, 250, 261, 265, 270, 274, 278; weather on, 13, 222, 251, 261, 266–67

Atlee, William (father of William Augustus), 8

Atlee, William Augustus (Penn. Supreme Court justice): identified, 8

Attleboro, Mass., 373

Austin, Anna Kent (cousin of AA), 148, 205, 395, 397

Austin, Benjamin, Jr. (Honestus, Boston merchant): AA on, 7, 8, 38; attacks lawyers, 214; as Candidus, 214, 216; elected to Mass. state senate, 8, 214; as Honestus, 7, 8, 38, 214, 360; on Madison, 360; *Observations on the Pernicious Practice of the Law*, 7, 8; Shays' Rebellion and, 7, 38

Austin, Hannah (daughter of Anna), 147, 148, 205

Austin, Nathaniel (husband of Anna), 148, 397

Austin, Sarah (Sally, daughter of Anna), 395, 396–97

Australia, xv

Auteuil, France, xxvi, 93

Avery, John (Conn. innkeeper), 306, 307, 333

Avery, John (Mass. secy. of state), 278

Axminster, England, xxiii, 88, 131, 156, 158

Babcock, Huldah (wife of Moses), 393

Babcock, Moses (of Milton), 392, 393

Bache, Benjamin Franklin (son of Sarah), 368

Bache, Richard (husband of Sarah): identified, 368

Bache, Sarah Franklin (daughter of Benjamin Franklin): identified, 368

Baker, Samuel (of Bolton), 59; identified, 61

Baldwin, Abraham (of Ga.), 289, 302, 304; identified, 290

Baldwin, Enoch (Boston butcher), 443; identified, 402

Ballard, John (Boston stable owner), 359; identified, 360

Baltimore, Md., 267, 269, 323

Bancroft, Dr. Edward (Amer. speculator), 367

Bank of New York, 405, 418

Bank of North America, 306, 418

Barbary States, 13, 31, 78, 86

Barber, Nathaniel (of Boston), 332

Barclay, Mary (wife of Thomas), 86

Barclay, Thomas (former U.S. consul to France): AA2 on, 86; JA on, 74; imprisonment of for debt, 69, 70, 71, 75, 76, 78, 80, 86; mentioned, 72

Barclay, Moilon & Co., 86

Barlow, Joel: *The Anarchiad*, 140, 141

Barnard, Capt. Thomas (of the *New York Packet*): AA on, 365; arrives in Boston, 355, 370, 449; arrives in New York, 365; carries goods for Adamses from Braintree to New York, 315–16, 319, 341, 358, 359, 364, 365, 369, 370, 371, 374, 402, 425, 433, 434, 435, 437, 438, 439, 443, 444, 448; carries goods for Brieslers from Braintree to New York, 428, 432; receipt from, 360; sails to Boston, 403, 444; sails from Boston, 314; mentioned, 417, 421

Barnard, Capt. Tristram (of the *Mary*): arrives in Boston, 198, 261; arrives in Britain, 105, 116; carries goods and letters from Adamses to U.S., 2, 4, 6, 11, 19, 56, 118, 125, 127, 173, 177, 193, 196, 217; carries goods and letters to Adamses from U.S., 21, 61, 216; sails to Britain, 200; sails to U.S., 85, 116, 129; mentioned, 84, 104

Barnard, Dr., 197

Barnstable, Mass., 21

Barnstable County, Mass., 59, 313, 356

Barrell, William (Phila. merchant), 57; identified, 59

Barrett, Margaret Hunt (wife of Nathaniel), 85

Barrett, Nathaniel (Amer. merchant), 85

Barron, Oliver, Sr. (father of Oliver), 92

Barron, Oliver, Jr. (of Chelmsford), 91; identified, 92

Bartlett, Bailey (of Haverhill), 206, 309–10, 383, 384

Barziza, Count Antonio (of Venice), 218, 219

Barziza, Giovanni (son of Antonio), 219

Barziza, Lucy Paradise (wife of Antonio): identified, 219

    Letter: To AA (1788), 218

Bass, Deacon Benjamin (of Braintree), 104, 162, 337, 345, 372; identified, 106

Index

tution and, 271, 272, 273, 316–17; contends for vice presidency, 319; greets JA in New York, 336; invites AA2 and WSS to dine, 273; marriage of, 275

Clinton, George Washington (son of George), 273; identified, 275

Clinton, Maria (daughter of George), 273; identified, 275

Clinton, Martha Washington (daughter of George), 273; identified, 275

Clothing: AA leaves at Braintree, 435; AA on as "the Female sphere," 26; AA on popularity of plaid, 38–39; for Adams brothers, xxx, 16, 62, 164, 372; aprons, 5, 109, 111; bear skin, 314; breeches, 125; for children, 112; christening suit, 5, 38, 54; coats and jackets, 15, 20, 26, 39, 44, 53, 55, 109, 110, 111, 125, 133, 136, 192–93, 195, 362, 413; combs and brushes, 111; costs of, 65, 110–11; for Cranches, 394; dresses, ix, xi, 19, 64, 66, 95, 110, 111, 135–36, 143, 147, 319, 322; of Dutch minister to Britain, 242; in Europe, 5; face makeup, 66; footwear, xxvi, 26, 66, 133, 143, 175, 176, 192, 278, 283, 322, 362, 426; gloves, 110, 111, 150, 151; hair pieces, xiv, xxvii, 136; hair rings, xxxi, 144; handkerchiefs, 5, 111; for Harvard commencement, 52, 60; headwear, xi, xvii, 5, 26, 32, 39, 66, 70, 72, 110, 186, 194–95, 322, 372; of John and Sarah Jay, 263; leather, 373; mourning outfits, 70, 72, 419; for newborn, 269; nightwear, 111, 314, 426; ornamentation for, xxvi, 5–6, 54, 110, 240, 278, 338; patterns, 195; prohibition on importation of silk, 5; Quaker style, 321; regimental uniform, 400, 401; ribbon, 5, 26, 39, 66, 111, 143; sashes, 26, 38; seasonal attire, 419; second hand, 195; for servants, 136, 242; sewing of, 5, 20; shirts, 62, 125, 134; skirts, 5, 39, 53, 110, 322; in Spain, 78; for stadholder's birthday, 240; stockings, xi, 3, 64–65, 66, 68, 95, 109, 111, 189, 192, 213, 223, 224, 236, 434; suits, 332–33, 347, 348; for swimming, xi, 155; thread, 421, 423, 433; toothbrushes, 111; undergarments, 5, 39, 44, 171, 317, 322; uniforms for Harvard students, 195; in U.S., 150; of Martha Washington, 379; wearing of for political reasons, 230, 240

Fabric: broadcloth, 192, 332–33, 347, 348, 362; calico, 38, 111; cambric, 62, 183, 224; chintz, 43–44, 133, 143, 147; diaper, 111; dimity, 44, 110; flannel, xi, 110; flax, 343; florence (silk), 208, 224, 236; gauze, xiv, 5, 186, 195; homespun, 343; Irish Holland, 110, 112; Irish linen, 111; lace, ix, 5,

110, 111, 150, 151; linens, 3, 32, 62, 64, 109, 118, 133; lustring (silk), 3, 419; manufacture of, 88; muslin, 5, 39, 110; sale of, 372; satin, ix, 125, 322; Scotch plaid, 26; silk, 5, 6, 19, 38, 39, 52, 53, 95, 133, 175, 192, 223, 419; velvet, 377; wool, 343, 345

Cobham, England, 23, 24

Cochrane, Capt. Alexander Forrester Inglis (Brit. naval officer), 270, 272

Cochrane, Lady Maria Waite (wife of Alexander), 270, 272

Codes and ciphers, 72, 78

Coke, Sir Edward: *Institutes*, 361, 380, 384

Coles, Eliza Lightfoot (1st wife of Isaac): identified, 451

Coles, Isaac (of Va.), 450; identified, 451

College of Physicians of Philadelphia Medical Society, 33

Colleges and universities, 25, 33. *See also names of individual schools*

Collins, John (gov. of R.I.), 373–74, 376; identified, 375

Collins, Stephen (Phila. merchant), 57, 59

Columbia College, 101, 449

Comis (Cornice, Cornish), Mrs. (nurse), 227, 269, 280, 284–85, 289

Concord, Battle of. *See* Lexington and Concord, Battles of

Concord, Mass., 97, 99, 261

Congress, U.S.: AA entertains members of, xxxv, 379, 399; AA on, 364–65, 369; JA encourages JQA and TBA to observe, 407; JA's salary, 341, 353–54, 356–57, 363, 369, 414; adjournment of, 402, 414, 417–18, 444; competition between branches, 349, 369; debates and approves collection bill, 333, 339, 383, 384, 389, 391; debates and approves judiciary bill, 383, 384, 389; debates compensation for federal officials, 370, 399, 401; debates site of, xxxv, 283, 289, 325, 403, 405, 410, 418; elections to, 295; funding of national debt and, 59, 402, 405; powers of, 428; difficulty of achieving quorum, 417–18; recess of, 411; seat of, xv, 342 (illus.); settlement of war accounts by, 439

House of Representatives: AA on, 346, 389, 416; chaplain of, 417; debates of, 360, 386, 405; election of representatives to, 312, 313, 320, 326; members of greet JA in New York, 336; Samuel Otis seeks to become clerk to, 304; public nature of debates of, 333, 337, 339, 349; achieves quorum, 330; remarks to Washington, 360; resolutions of, 356; service in, 269, 290, 329, 384, 427, 450, 451; speaker of, 429

Index

Delft, Netherlands, 193

Denmark, 120

Devonshire, England: Adamses plan to visit, 84–85, 88, 109, 115–16, 118, 127, 128, 130–31; Adamses visit, 87, 156, 158, 177, 190, 249; John Cranch on, 88; as Richard Cranch's birthplace, 249; mentioned, 162

Diana (brig), 12

Diderot, Denis: *Encyclopédie*, 364

Dilly, Charles (London bookseller), 251

Disney, Rev. John (Brit. clergyman), 207–208; *Memoirs of Thomas Brand-Hollis*, 252; *The Works . . . of John Jebb*, 125, 126

Divorce, 396

Doane, Elisha (of Cape Cod), 100

Doane, Isaiah (son of Elisha), 100

Dogs, 129, 190, 254, 315

Domestic work: Adamses need new kitchen for Old House, 284; airing beds, 207–208; beer-making, 57; brass polishing, 436; butter-making, 436; cheese-making, 57, 145, 172, 427, 436; childcare, xxii–xxiii, 28, 83–84, 87, 92, 93, 94, 114, 118, 269, 285; cleaning, 118, 126, 436; cooking, 28, 93, 121, 132–33, 312, 384, 399; dishwashing, 132, 136; food preparation, 66, 306; hairdressing, 371, 374; housework, 424; ironing, 359, 436; knitting, 434; laundry, 171, 436; maid duties, 28; nursing, xxii–xxiii, 119, 285, 297, 334, 402; wet nursing, 65; artificial rose making, 248; sewing, xxx, 44, 64, 65, 70, 95, 110, 133–34, 147, 164, 186, 195, 197, 255, 260–61, 317, 343, 355, 359, 371; spinning, 424, 433; setting and clearing tables, 132, 142; tea making, 127; washing, 111, 126; drawing water, 254; as women's work, 25, 26, 27

Dominica, West Indies, 69, 71, 72

Doolittle, Amos (engraver), 342 (illus.); identified, xv

Dorchester, Guy Carleton, 1st Baron, 29, 30, 33, 34, 36, 266

Dorchester, Mass., 20, 166

Dormer, Clement Cotterell (Brit. master of ceremonies at court): letters to AA listed (1788), 457 (2)

Dorset (Dorsett), Capt. F. (of the *Thomas and Sally*), 267, 269

Dover, England, 28, 112

Downs, The, England, 253, 255

Dracut, Mass., 313

Drayton, William (S.C. lawyer), 111, 152; identified, 124

Drury, Luke (of Grafton), 22, 97, 99

Duane, James (mayor of New York), 336

Dublin, Ireland, 265, 272

Duer, Catherine Alexander (wife of William), 329

Duer, William (N.Y. merchant), 316, 331; identified, 248

Dukes County, Mass., 313

Dumas, Anna (Nancy). *See* Veerman, Anna Jacoba Dumas

Dumas, Charles William Frederic (U.S. agent at The Hague): as JQA's tutor, 51; appeals to JA for protection during Dutch revolution, 188, 189; lacks formal commission from U.S., 188; correspondence with JA, 188, 189; dines with JA, 68; dress of for stadholder's birthday, 240; salary for, 189; mentioned, 55, 243

Dumas, Marie (wife of Charles), 188, 243

Duncan, Elizabeth. *See* Thaxter, Elizabeth Duncan

Durant, Cornelius (Boston merchant), 395; identified, 396

Durant, Maria Fenno (2d wife of Cornelius), 395, 396

Durant, Mary Tothill (1st wife of Cornelius): identified, 396

Durant family, 22

Durfee, Thomas (of Freetown), 59; identified, 61

Dutch Reformed Church, 417

Duxbury, Mass., 313

Dwight, Thomas (of Springfield), 3

Dwight, Rev. Timothy (of Conn.): *The Conquest of Canäan*, 253

Dyck, Anthony van (Flemish artist), 182

East India Company, 266

East Indies, 262, 266, 279

Eaton, Peter (Harvard classmate of JQA), 91, 92

Eden, William (Brit. envoy to France), 183

Edes, Benjamin (Boston printer), 427

Edgcumbe, Sir Richard (of Devon, England): identified, 162

Edinburgh, University of, 266

Edinburgh, Scotland, 266, 298

Edmund of Woodstock (son of Edward I), 180, 183

Education: AA2 on, 169; AA and Martha Washington visit school, 447; AA attends scientific lectures, xxiii, 25; AA on, xxiii, 3, 8, 10, 27; AA on for women as "like going into a Beautifull Country, which I never saw before," 25; JA on, 130, 219, 220; JA teaches grammar school, 259; TBA on dangers of college, 17; for Adams children, 202; in Britain, ix, 262, 266, 269; convent, 93, 108, 119, 151, 183; cost of, 60,

493

258; of Mass. clergymen, 414; Isaac Smith Jr. as tutor at Harvard, 200; of William Smith Jr., 225, 232; in U.S. versus France, 150–51; for child from West Indies, 395; for women, 25–26, 137, 145, 321, 323, 447. *See also* JQA–Education; Harvard College

Edward I, King of England, 180, 183

Edward III, King of England, 183

Edward ("the Black Prince," son of Edward III), 180, 183

Edwards, Abigail Fowle Smith (1679–1760, grandmother of AA), 192

Effingham, Catherine Howard, Countess of, 120, 121

Ehrensvärd, Carl August, Baron von (Swedish minister to Spain), 76; identified, 77

Elections: AA on, 117; Brit. Parliament, 45; U.S. Congress, 295; Continental Congress, 274, 275; president of Continental Congress, 274, 291, 294; Md. House of Delegates, 301; Mass. General Court, xxxiii, 8, 17, 18, 19–20, 22, 53, 54, 58, 59, 61, 62–63, 65, 89, 97, 99, 102, 104, 105, 214, 355, 356, 382, 413; Mass. governor, 17, 22, 38, 39, 53, 59, 61, 97, 282, 382; Mass. lieutenant governor, 98, 99; Mass. ratifying convention, 201, 206, 209, 212–13; U.S. president, xxxiv, 282, 319, 325, 326, 330–31, 379; presidential electors, 319, 325, 326, 379; protested, 62–63, 65; U.S. representatives, 312, 313, 320, 326; U.S. senators, 307, 311, 312, 313, 316, 326; Elizabeth Shaw on, 53; U.S. vice president, xxxiv, 282, 292, 295, 319, 320, 330, 331, 343, 367, 377, 379; voter turnout in, 22

Electoral College: selection of electors, 319, 325, 326, 379; Senate counts votes of, xxxiv, 330–31

Elijah (Adams family servant), 358, 365

Elizabeth I, Queen of England, 180, 183

Ellsworth, Oliver (of Conn.), 307

Elworthy, Elizabeth Cranch (niece of Richard Cranch), 31, 65, 256

Elworthy, James (husband of Elizabeth, London merchant): John Cranch on, 256; financial transactions with Adamses, 7, 103, 211, 235; visits Adamses, 33–34; mentioned, 31, 65

Emerson, Ralph Waldo, 173

Emerson, William (of Concord, Mass.), 171; identified, 172–73

English Channel: Adamses travel through en route to U.S., xxv, 267; delays in crossing, 222, 242, 247; crossing of, 68, 112, 242; mentioned, 106, 182

English language and literature: JQA gives oration in at Harvard commencement, 19,

52, 60, 85, 96–97, 135; of Marquise de Bréhan, 263; dictionary of, 358; conference in at Harvard commencement, 60; use of for Harvard commencement exercises, 135, 138; presentations in at Harvard exhibition, 19, 91, 143, 219; study of in Harvard private societies, 140, 141; translation of European constitutions into, 220

Epictetus: *The Enchiridion*, 32, 34

Episcopal Church of America, xviii, 414, 417

Eppes, Elizabeth Wayles (sister-in-law of Thomas Jefferson), 107, 118; identified, 108

Eppes, Francis (husband of Elizabeth), 108

Eppes, John Wayles (son of Elizabeth), 108

Erasmus, 68

Essequibo (Dutch colony), 279

Essex County, Mass.: appoints high sheriff, 383, 384; bar association of, 130; collection of duties and excise for, 370; elections in, 209, 313; mentioned, 59

Essex Journal (Newburyport, Mass.), 272, 362, 447

Europe: AA2 on as "Vortex of dissipation," 300; AA compares U.S. to, 3, 9, 113, 250, 388; AA on, xxii; AA on need for U.S. to avoid involvement in, 185; AA on U.S. failure to follow etiquette of, 234; Adamses' time in, xxix, 291, 292; Amer. fondness for goods of, 287; Americans' desire to live in, 84, 271; clothing styles in, 5; debates over U.S. Constitution in, xxi, 229; Paradises return to, 265, 367; political situation in, 106, 125, 164, 166, 183–84, 189, 296; religious observation in, 197; Cotton Tufts requests information on, 211; mentioned, 49, 228, 272, 301, 418, 422. *See also names of individual countries*

Evans, Huldah Kent (wife of Israel), 137, 187

Evans, Rev. Israel (of Concord, N.H.), 137, 187

Exercise: AA on, 12, 26, 39, 40, 247, 307, 314; JA's limited by lame horse, 440; JQA neglects, 15–16, 84; horseback riding, 16, 17, 23; promotes good health, xxx, 78, 94, 102, 122, 188, 202, 280, 301, 306; riding, 6, 24–25, 32, 39, 94, 297; Elizabeth Shaw on, 301; walking, 12, 252

Exeter, England: Adamses plan to visit, 128, 131; Adamses visit, xxiii, 129, 158, 249; manufacturing in, 88; mentioned, 148, 159

Exeter, N.H., 137

Fagel, Hendrik (secy. of the States General), 234, 235

Fairfield, Conn., 422, 426, 438

Falmouth, England: AA2 and WSS travel to

Index

194, 217, 243, 246–47, 250–51, 384, 395, 408, 420; weight gain, 20; weight loss, 15, 94, 121–22, 125, 425; whitlows, 277, 374; whooping cough, 285, 399, 401, 408
Remedies: air purification, 126; antimonial wine, 370, 371; blistering, 426; bloodletting, 79, 83, 267, 426; camomile tea, 346; catnip, 186; cayenne pepper, 366; cleanliness, 28; cold baths, 28, 94; cold medicine, 123; country setting, 25, 26, 29, 114, 118, 125, 126–27, 130, 348; diet, 15, 16, 125, 247, 301; electricity, 217; evacuation from area of outbreak, 126; fresh air and exercise, xxx, 12, 39, 40, 78, 84, 94, 102, 122, 188, 202, 247, 280, 301, 306, 307, 314; Glauber's salt, 370, 371; guaiacum, 17, 22; hyssop, 186; inoculation, 194, 203, 390, 403, 411, 421, 425, 426, 430, 431, 433, 435, 439, 441, 447; lime water (recipe), 125; manna, 370, 371; mineral waters, 93; mint, 186; pennyroyal, 186; pills, 418; prescription medicines, 69, 75, 83–84, 87, 306; quinine, 118, 126, 297; riding, 140, 341; sassafras tea, 17; sleep, 297, 298, 314, 316; smoking articles to purify, 126; surgery, 380; swimming, 155, 161; travel, xxiii, 105, 113, 114, 126–27, 155, 168, 173, 194, 198, 206, 212, 217, 270, 309, 325, 337, 419–20, 427, 438; valerian tea, 297, 346; vomiting, 399; warmer weather and climates, 126, 205
Heath, Gen. William (of Roxbury), 98; identified, 99
Hebrew language, 91
Heineccius, Johann Gottlieb: *A Methodical System of Universal Law*, 219, 220
Hellevoetsluis, Netherlands, 73, 74, 240, 244
Helme, Elizabeth: *Louisa; or, The Cottage on the Moor*, 26, 27
Hemings, James (Jefferson family slave), 92, 93
Hemings, Sally (Jefferson family slave): AA on, xxiii, 94, 108, 109; AA purchases items for, 106, 108–11; escorts Mary Jefferson to Europe, 92, 93; stays with Adamses in London, xxiii, 118
Henry I, King of England, 180, 183
Henry II, King of England, 180, 183
Henry Frederick, Duke of Cumberland and Strathearn, 235
Herald of Freedom (Boston), 320, 333
Herefordshire, England, 344
Herschel, Sir William (Brit. astronomer), 182, 266
Heyward, James (of S.C.), 110, 114, 124, 152
Higginson, Stephen (Laco): *The Writings of Laco*, 337

Hill, Alexander (Boston merchant), 105; identified, 106
Hill, Edward (son of Alexander), 106, 175; identified, 176
Hill, William (Harvard classmate of JQA), 91; identified, 92
Hilliard, Mary (daughter of Timothy), 94; identified, 96
Hilliard, Mary Foster (wife of Timothy), 15, 21, 94, 96
Hilliard, Rev. Timothy (of Braintree), 15, 96; identified, 21
Hindman, William (of Md.), 267; identified, 269
Hingham, Mass.: churches of, 55, 175; elects Benjamin Lincoln to Mass. General Court, 355; ordains Henry Ware, 174, 175, 205, 210; mentioned, 20, 22, 200, 296, 298, 310
History, xi, 245
Hodgdon, Alexander (Mass. politician), 17; identified, 22
Holbein, Hans (German artist), 182
Holidays: Christmas, 314; fast day, 260; Fourth of July, 400, 401; Thanksgiving, xxviii, 206, 231, 233, 241, 310, 445
Holland and West Friesland (province of the Netherlands), 40
Hollis, Thomas Brand (Brit. antiquarian): AA sends oration to, 195; Adamses visit, 195; advises AA on health issues, 69, 75; correspondence with AA, 195, 208; correspondence with JA, 427, 432; dines with Adamses, 71, 125; friendship with Adamses, 252, 253; on situation in Netherlands, 207; receives Harvard honorary degree, 195; sends books and prints to Adamses, 207, 208, 253; sends books to Harvard, 125; plans to visit London, 207, 208; letters to AA listed (1787), 457; (1788), 457 (2)
Letters: To AA (1787), 207; (1788), 253
Letter: From AA (1788), 252
Holton, Samuel (of Danvers), 59; identified, 61
Homer: *The Odyssey*, 114, 190–91, 192
Honestus. *See* Austin, Benjamin, Jr.
Hopkins, Lemuel: *The Anarchiad*, 140, 141
Horace, 65; *Ars Poetica*, 259
Horne Tooke, John (Brit. politician): identified, 87; *Letter on the Reported Marriage of . . . the Prince of Wales*, 83, 87
Horsecombe Vale, Bath, England, 162
Horseneck, N.Y., 333
Horses: accident to JA's, 432, 440, 443, 444; JA on, 422; for JA's chaise, 404; disposal of Adamses', 341, 350, 353, 355, 359–60, 362–

63, 372, 373; Adamses wish to purchase, 217; baiting of, 67; of Barzizas, 218; care for, 421, 426; for drawing carts, 417; George, Prince of Wales, sells, 73; price of, 355; racing of, 230, 262; rocking, 376; for sea-bathing machines, xi, 157 (illus.); of WSS, 315; stabling of, 307, 348; for Washington's carriage, 388, 399, 401, 439; safe for women, 360

Horsham, England, 159, 175–76

Hoskins, William (debt collector), 99

Hotels: AA on, 190, 316, 329; AA's reception at in New England, 319; John Avery's (Hartford, Conn.), 306, 307, 333; Bath Hotel (London), 243, 247, 250; John Cranch on in Devonshire, 88; Crown Inn (Portsmouth, England), 23; Daggett's Inn (Providence, R.I.), 357, 373, 375; Fountain Hotel (Portsmouth, England), 250; Fountain Inn (Cowes), 255; at Harwich, England, 66; Haviland's Tavern (Square House, Rye, N.Y.), 332, 333; in Kingsbridge, England, 160; Man's Inn (Wrentham, Mass.), 373, 374; Mareschall de Turenne (Rotterdam), 67; hermitage of Mont Calvaire, 224; Penfield's (Fairfield, Conn.), 422; "Inn near Mr Rigby's Farm," 66, 68; at resorts for sea-bathing, xi

Houses: JA Birthplace, 418; JQA Birthplace, xxiv, 3, 20, 47, 95, 131, 174, 416, 418; of Adamses in Europe, xxvi, 226; of Adamses in Mass., 56, 200–201, 369; of Adamses in New York, 336, 341, 344; of Barzizas, 218; Beaver Hall, 265, 266, 275, 277; of Moses Belcher, 56, 58–59, 163; of Brieslers in New York, 434, 437, 439; in Britain, 129, 155, 156, 176, 190; of John Brown, 377, 379; building and maintenance of, 20, 21, 56, 57, 100, 104, 118, 189, 200, 201, 314; destruction of in Amer. Revolution, 441; destruction of in Dutch revolution, 185, 193; of Elworthys, 31; in Halifax, 261; of John Jay, 319; in New York City, 271, 287; ornamentation of in Netherlands, 243; of Palmers of Horsham, England, 176; for U.S. president, 399, 401; of Shaws, 39; of Isaac Smith Sr., 204, 212, 216, 225; of William and Hannah Smith, 143. *See also* Old House; Richmond Hill

Hudson River: AA on, 410; Adamses' furniture transported on, 354; Richmond Hill situated on, 353, 357, 391; mentioned, xv, xvi, 351

Hull, Nancey (daughter of William), 133, 134

Hull, Sarah Fuller (wife of William), 133, 134

Hull, Col. William (Newton lawyer), 133, 134

Humane Society, N.Y., 403

Hume, David, 358

Humphreys, Col. David (U.S. diplomat), 133, 379, 397; *The Anarchiad*, 140, 141

Hunt, George Shoars (son of Richard): identified, 396

Hunt, John Salmon (son of Richard): identified, 396

Hunt, Richard (of Boston), 396

Hunt, Richard or John or George, 395

Hunt, Richard Tothill (son of Richard): identified, 396

Hunting, 315, 426

Huntington, Daniel (Amer. artist), 398 (illus.); identified, xvii–xviii

Huntington, Jedidiah (of Conn.), 326

Huntington, Samuel (of Conn.), 326

Hutcheson, Francis (Scottish philosopher), 219

Hutchinson, Shrimpton (Boston merchant), 374; identified, 375

Hyde, The (Brit. estate), 125, 195, 252, 253

Independent Chronicle (Boston), 8, 216, 261, 331, 410, 425

Independent Gazetteer (Phila.), 37, 427–28

Independent Journal (N.Y.), 10, 121

India: AA on Brit. rule of, 9; Warren Hastings and, xii–xiii, 235; mentioned, xv, 86, 119

Ipswich, Mass., 384

Ireland: AA on, 120; House of Lords, 266; linen manufacturing, 112; Janet Montgomery visits, 327; mentioned, 85, 86, 119, 262, 286, 290, 326, 427

Isabel (Jefferson family slave), 92, 93

Italian language, 105

Italy: JA collects books on history of, 43, 105; JA's *Defence of the Const.* analyzes republics of, 42, 48, 193, 194; mentioned, 93

Ivers, Thomas (Mass. politician), 17; identified, 22

Ivybridge, England, 159

Izard, Alice DeLancey (wife of Ralph), 439

Izard, Ralph (S.C. politician), 421, 439

Izard, William (son of Ralph), 439

JA. *See* ADAMS, JOHN (1735–1826)

JA2. *See* Adams, John, 2d (1803–1834)

Jackson, Jonathan (Newburyport merchant), 312, 383, 445, 446; identified, 313

Jackson, Maj. William (secy. to Washington), 421, 422, 426

Jamaica, 69, 71

The *Adams Family Correspondence* was composed in the Adams Papers office using Microsoft Office Professional with style sheets and programs created by Technologies 'N Typography of Merrimac, Massachusetts. The text is set in eleven on twelve and one half point using the Linotype-Hell Postscript revival of *Fairfield Medium*, a design by Rudolph Ruzicka that includes swash characters especially designed for *The Adams Papers*. The printing and binding are by Edwards Brothers of Ann Arbor, Michigan. The paper, made by Finch, Pruyn & Company and distributed by Lindenmeyr Munroe, is a grade named *Finch Fine Vanilla*. The books were originally designed by P. J. Conkwright and Burton L. Stratton.